ALSO BY RICHARD BEN CRAMER

What It Takes: The Way to the White House

JOE DIMAGGIO

THE HERO'S LIFE

✦

RICHARD BEN CRAMER

SIMON & SCHUSTER

New York   London   Toronto   Sydney   Singapore

This Large Print Book carries the
Seal of Approval of N.A.V.H.

SIMON & SCHUSTER
Rockefeller Center
1230 Avenue of the Americas
New York, NY 10020

Book design by Ellen R. Sasahara

Manufactured in the United States of America

1   3   5   7   9   10   8   6   4   2

Library of Congress Cataloging-in-Publication Data is
available.

ISBN 0-7432-0638-X

Permissions appear on page 957.
Picture credits appear on pages 959–960.

FOR MY OWN HEROES OF THE AGE,
BRUD AND BLOSSOM CRAMER

JOE DIMAGGIO

THE HERO'S LIFE

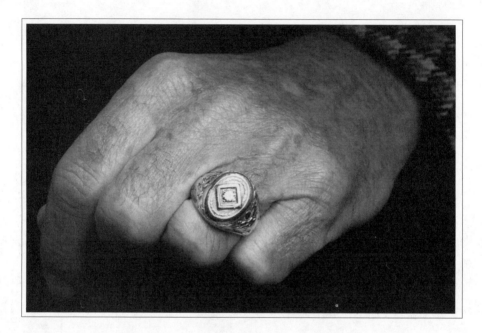

Joe's World Series ring from his rookie year, 1936.

PROLOGUE

✦

I REMEMBER THE LAST PUBLIC DAY of Joe's life, the last day of that splendid Yankee season, a sunny Sunday in the Bronx, September 27, 1998—Joe DiMaggio Day, the mayor had proclaimed it. The Clipper was coming back to Yankee Stadium to receive nine replica World Series rings—a gift from the Kaiser, George Steinbrenner. The story was DiMaggio had left his original rings in his suite at the Hotel Lexington (back in the 1960s, when DiMag kept a place in New York for business), and someone stole them all, except the '36 ring, from Joe's rookie year, which was the only one he ever wore—he wore that ring for sixty-one years straight.

He had the ring on that Sunday as he rode around the warning track in a 1956 Thunderbird convertible. He wore a jacket and tie, of course, and held both hands above his head—half a wave, half a blessing, like the Pope does. He'd part his hands, throw them open toward the crowd, both at once, so his thanks, his acknowledgment—and more, a whiff of his chrism, some glint of his godhood—would fly from him back to the crowd, to all those thousands standing on the steep tiers, in their shorts, with their beer cups, cheering his name in the midday glare. Joe would say he was touched by their welcome. But they were the ones who'd feel touched by the hero.

That was the last distant view he permitted. I didn't go anywhere near him that day—didn't try to intrude, try to ask questions. We'd been through all that. Joe didn't want to help with biography. He didn't want to help anybody know his life. It was a smart move by a smart man—canny, anyway. In latter years he cultivated the distance that set him apart from every other person of fame. He was revered for his mystery. We cheered him for never giving himself entirely to us.

Still, even in that Sunday's wash of reverence, DiMaggio seemed a sad figure. It wasn't just the effects of age—the way he'd shrunk—that bent old man who took his rings behind home plate and tottered off the field. (There was no working microphone. Maybe the hero had nothing more to say.) More to the point, it was his cloak of myth that had shrunk. The lies around him were growing cheap. This tale of the stolen rings, for example. Joe didn't lose those rings to theft. More likely he traded them for free lodging, food, transportation, services of every kind. That whole Joe DiMaggio Day wasn't about rings, but about history and Joe's need to win; about Mickey Mantle and the way Joe resented him; and money, mostly money, as it mostly was with Joe.

The real story went back to 1995 and the day the Yankees dedicated to Mickey Mantle the fourth monument in the history of the Stadium. That was a big day at the ballpark, an emotional day—the Mick had just died—and of course DiMaggio had to show up. Joe resented that. When had Mantle ever showed up for him? . . . But what really griped him wasn't Mickey's monument in left center field. He'd been offered a monument, but turned it down. (He complained: *Were they trying to bury him already?*) No, what set Joe to seething was the special ball they used in that day's game. It was a regulation Rawlings game-ready Mickey Mantle Commemorative Ball, authorized by Major League Baseball. Right away the collectors and dealers in memorabilia bid those balls up to three hundred per. That was twice as much as Joe was getting for his balls—which were autographed! That burned up the Clipper good. From that day forward, DiMaggio (to be precise, Yankee Clipper Enterprises) had angled for a DiMaggio Day and a special DiMaggio ball—also by Rawlings, also regulation-made, game-ready, American League— except, *except* . . . these could be signed by the Clipper himself. That would be a four-hundred-dollar ball, *at least!* And for starters Joe would autograph the fifteen thousand balls that he was demanding, free, from the Rawlings Company (you know, for use of his name). Fifteen thousand free balls, a few months to sign 'em . . . and (even at wholesale) that would be a cool three million, cash (in hundreds, please: Joe's favorite).

Of course, no one was going to tell that story on

Joe DiMaggio Day—or write it in the papers. So they wrote about remembered autumns of glory, about the love affair of the hero and the Yankee fans. For sixty years writers had to make up what Joe cared about. As Joe himself once explained: "They used to write stories about me like they were interviewing me, and never even talked to me." But now, most of the guys who knew him—who could cobble up a good DiMaggio quote—were gone.

So Mike Lupica, from the *Daily News* (Joe's favorite among the new generation), would settle that day for the wistful "So many memories. So many seasons." . . . And for the *New York Times,* Dave Anderson (one of the last guys who knew Joe when) would write: "After the ceremony, he returned to that shadowy corridor behind the dugout, sat down, opened the box with the World Series rings and stared at them. 'Aren't they beautiful?' he said."

The fact was, DiMaggio was never wistful. (At that moment, he was furious.) And he never spent an instant in his life to marvel at the beauty of anything. Except maybe a broad. Which wasn't marveling— that was wanting. Wanting he did. That was why he'd hauled himself out of bed at four in the morning, coughing up blood from the cancer he wouldn't speak about . . . to get to the airport, to fly to New York in time for his day. That was want. That was DiMaggio. If you lost track of that hunger, that toughness, you lost his core.

There wasn't another eighty-three-year-old in the

country who could have held up that day, looking good—not with Joe's irritated eye (something like chronic conjunctivitis), the old arthritis, the scoliosis that hunched his back into a painful curve, the pacemaker that kept his heart beating, the Lasix (a horse diuretic) that kept the fluid away from the pacemaker (and made Joe pee, seemed like every ten minutes). And now, the cancer that he would only call pneumonia—maybe he had pneumonia, too. That wouldn't have mattered: Joe was going to make it through. Nobody else had his grit—he always played hurt. Or his focus—Joe would bring those balls home.

Nothing stopped him. Nothing turned his head. You could admire him for that. He was one of a kind. I also remember the day, five years back, when I was starting this book, first asking about DiMaggio. I had a long, rambling interview with an old baseball man named Frank Slocum. He'd spent his whole life in the game. He'd known DiMaggio for sixty years—saw him when he came up, he'd met Joe's brothers, parents, wives—saw him every which way. We talked for two hours, then three. Finally, I put away my notebook.

"I'll tell you one more thing," Slocum offered, after I'd stood up to leave. "You go out there and ask around. If you meet any guy who says, 'Oh, I know someone just like that DiMaggio,' I'll tell you this: That guy's a liar."

BOOK I

DESTINY

1930–1935

◆

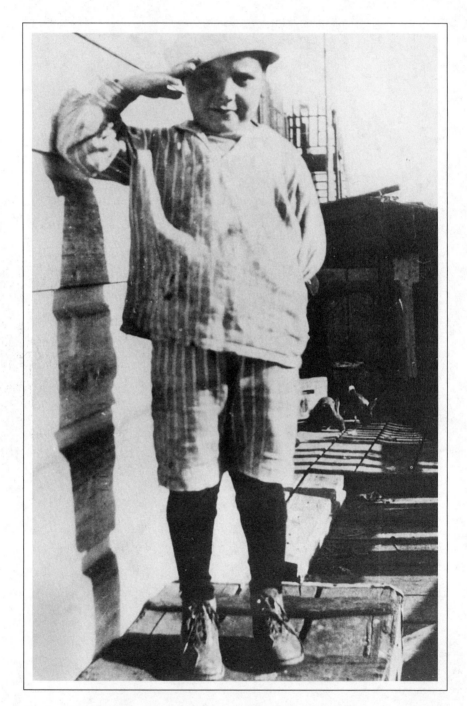

Joe DiMaggio, 1920, Taylor Street, San Francisco.

The North Beach Playground, San Francisco.

North Beach in the 1920s.

CHAPTER 1

✦

JOE DIMAGGIO SAT ON THE TAR OF
the playground, with his back against the wall on
the Powell Street side, his legs cocked in front of
him like a couple of pickets. At fifteen, Joe was
mostly legs—leg-bones, more like it—and a head
taller than his friends. It was Niggy Fo who gave
him his nickname, *Coscilunghi*—that meant
"Long-legs" in Sicilian.

All the boys on the North Beach playground had
names—that meant you were in, you belonged
there. There was Shabby Minafo and his brother,
Bat (he only wanted to bat), and Hungry Geraldi
(he could really eat); Friggles Tomei had those
fancy feet at second base; Lodigiani they called
Dempsey, because he once decked a guy in a fight;
and Niggy, of course, got his name for his dark
skin. They were always on the playground or on the
street. Who had room at home? On this spring afternoon, in 1930, they were playing Piggy on a
Bounce—one guy with a bat, everyone else in the
field, and one guy would hit till someone caught
the ball, or caught it on one bounce, and then the
batter had to take the field.

4

Joe was at the playground most days, too . . . but like today—not exactly with them. He'd come out of his house, down the hill from Taylor Street—but he'd sit apart, watching in silence, arms draped across his knees in a pose of solitary sufficiency. Or maybe it wasn't all pose. Joe was different from the other guys. They always wanted to play ball. They were desperate to play ball—even if they could barely play. Joe could play. But you had to *get* him to play.

Bat Minafo and Frank Venezia always picked the teams. They were little guys, but pretty good players. They'd flip a coin, and whoever won would pick Joe. Guys would actually say, "Oh, you got Joe, you're gonna win." It wasn't just the way Joe could hit. (Even those mushy city-issue softballs, Joe could hammer them the length of the playground, a block and a half, into the swimming pool.) . . . But more than that, it was the way he was in a game. He had to win. That was the reason he'd play—he wanted to win something. Sometimes, Bat and Frank would make everybody throw in a nickel or a dime, and they'd play winner-take-all. Then Joe would play, for sure. But playing just to play . . . well, mostly he'd sit.

In the long fingers of his right hand, he'd dangle a smoke in front of his shins—if no one was looking. There were rules about smoking, but not for Joe. The playground assistant was a guy named Rizzo. He only had one arm, but he played a mean game of tennis. He'd throw that ball up, whip his racket around with the same hand, and *bang*—the guy could murder the ball. No one but Joe could return his serve. So Rizzo let Joe smoke—sort of a tip of the cap. Still, Joe was furtive, so no one would mooch. If he had a pack, he'd keep it in his sock. If anybody saw it, that pack was a goner. Mostly he'd roll his own. A pouch of Bull Durham cost the same five cents, but he could roll a hundred smokes. A nickel was something to hold on to in Joe's world.

At that Powell Street playground wall, he was at the center of everything he knew. There, arrayed in front of him, chasing that city softball, laughing at each other, tearing up their shoes on the tar, were the boys who were personages in his life—apart from his family, it was almost everybody who mattered. That day, it was Niggy Fo, Shabby, Bat; there was Nig Marino watching from the side (Niggy was a fighter, not a ballplayer); big George Solari in the outfield; Hungry, Friggles, and Banchero in the infield; Ciccio LaRocca on the mound. And the batter was Frank Venezia, who was slapping line drives all over the lot (and laughing at Ciccio, who usually got him out with five pitches) . . . that was one reason Frank would remember the day—he never thought he was that good with the bat.

They all lived within ten tight blocks. Joe knew their little brothers, who tagged along and tried to play. He knew their sisters, who played rotation basketball at the hoop past left center field. (Well, he knew the sisters by sight: Joe never said five words in a row to anybody's sister.) He knew all their houses, and who slept where. He knew their mothers, and where they shopped. He knew what their fathers fished.

On the left, past third base, was the boys' bathroom. Joe spent a lot of time in there, playing cards. Joe was good at cards. But that was like baseball: he wasn't just playing. Joe and Niggy Marino used to box the cards—fix the deck—or they'd play partners, and kick each other to signal for discards: five kicks meant to throw the five, two for the deuce, etc. By the time they finished, their legs were black-and-blue. But they went home with a few extra nickels—money from the patsies. Poor Frank Venezia! He played all the time and never caught on they were cheating him. But that was Frank. He just thought he was lousy at cards.

Past the outfield, past the basketball and tennis courts and the open swimming pool, Columbus Avenue cut the playground off at an angle. Nothing was exactly square in North Beach—a neighborhood of odd intersections and acute hillside corners—because Columbus sliced through the street grid diagonally, from the office buildings downtown, north and west to Fisherman's Wharf. Columbus was the hub for Italian San Francisco, and the boys' window on the ways of the world. On Columbus, at the corner of

the playground, they'd catch the F-car downtown—
Stockton Street, all the way to Market. After school,
kids rode two for a nickel.

A block and a half up Columbus lay the expanse of
Washington Square, the *gran piazza,* like a carpet of
green spread in front of the great Sts. Peter and Paul's
Church. The Italian Cathedral of the West was at that
time only five years old—Joe had seen the whole
thing built. But its massive twin spires, the solemn
gleam of the grand marble altar, even the bright modern classrooms for the School of Americanization,
were designed to bear witness eternally to proud *Ital-*
ianità and the achievement of his parents' generation. On the grass in front of the church, the men of
the community gathered every afternoon for coffee
(maybe a little wine) and argument—though Joe's
dad seldom made an appearance. Giuseppe DiMaggio wasn't much for talk.

Near the church on Columbus stood the other
institutions of the grown-up world: there was the
Valente-Marini Funeral Home (you could pass from
your christening at Sts. Peter and Paul's to a coffin—
hopefully not too fast, but all within a couple of
blocks). Up the street, there was the community hall,
Casa Fugazi, named for *Commendatóre* John F.
Fugazi, a banker and one of the early Italian-
American *prominenti.* At Columbus and Stockton
stood the Bank of America, whose founder, A. P. Giannini, was most prominent of all *prominenti.* On
Columbus, too, there was the library—but no one Joe

knew went to the library. The boys were more interested in other cultural sites on Columbus, like
LaRocca's Corner, where the wiseguys played cards
all day over cups of LaRocca's homemade wine.
(Prohibition was an approximate science in North
Beach, and Vince LaRocca, Ciccio's uncle, was "well
connected.") And nearby were the nightclubs, the
Lido Cafe and Bimbo's 365 Club, with their showgirls—tall gorgeous girls, who'd come from all over
. . . though not from North Beach. No Italian family
had showgirls.

From Columbus came food for the neighborhood
tables—from Molinari's big new deli, and Cali-
gari's bakery on Green, just off the Avenue. On
Columbus at Green was the Buon Gusto Market,
and off Columbus, on Powell, there was Celli's,
where they made the best pasta and let you buy on
credit. In Joe's crowd, there were months when
everybody ate on credit—say, before crab season
began. Clothes, same way: without credit, you'd
wear your big brothers' stuff forever. Every family
ran a tab at Tragone's, on Columbus, for clothes
and shoes. You could get the shoes cheaper at Gal-
lenkamp's, on Kearny Street—but that was all the
way downtown. (And it was some kind of Kraut
chain, strictly cash-and-carry.)

Three blocks west of the playground was Joe's
first school, Hancock Elementary, just up the alley
from his house. The school was built into a down-
slope, so the recess yard in front of the school was

a flat pad of concrete below street level. And a pathway, like a little bridge, led from the street to the school's main door. In that recess yard, the boys used to play a kind of baseball—but with no bat: you'd just whack the ball with your hand and run like hell to first base, which was a basement doorway. Joe was the only boy who could smack the ball over the bridge. He had long arms and big hands he could swing like a hammer. That was his main distinction at Hancock. That and penmanship. One of the teachers, Mrs. Lieboldt, made her kids do every exercise in the workbook—perfect round O's, straight lines crossing T's . . . then she gave out fancy certificates: "For acquired excellence in practical BUSINESS WRITING by study and practice from The Zaner Method of Arm Movement Writing. (The Zaner-Bloser Co., Columbus, Ohio)." It was the only school honor Joe ever won. (But everybody got one, even Niggy Marino—and Niggy got thrown out of all his schools. Even the Ethan Allen School for tough kids, they threw him out.)

Joe's second school, two blocks east, was Francisco Junior High. Nobody made him do anything there. Joe and Frank Venezia used to sit in class like a couple of dummies—they never kept up on the reading. The other kids gave all the answers. They just seemed smarter. Actually, Joe wasn't stupid. But he never wanted to open his mouth, say something wrong, and *look* stupid. That came from home. In the flat on Taylor Street, they talked Sicilian. Everybody laughed at Joe's lousy Sicilian. (Even his little brother, Dommie, made fun of him.) And shame was what Joe couldn't stand. He was a blusher. (That embarrassed him, too.) So, he just grew silent. His sisters talked about him behind his back: they thought he was "slow." . . . Anyway, Joe didn't have to talk at school. None of the teachers made him talk. They just moved him on, year after year. It was like no one even knew he was there.

Joe knew well enough to get along in his world. He knew how to strip the copper wire from dilapidated buildings and the lead from around the pipes. He could sell that stuff for four cents a pound any day. Of course, the way Joe was, he wanted six cents. There was a junk dealer who came up Columbus—used to stop at the corner of the open field where the boys played hardball. They called it the Horses' Lot because the Golden State Dairy turned its horses loose there, afternoons and weekends, when they weren't out with the milk wagons. Where Columbus Avenue cut off the Horses' Lot (in left center field), there was a wall of billboards. That's where the junk man stopped to rest his horse. They called him Blue Wagon. "Four cent f'coppa . . ." Blue Wagon would say. Joe would mutter to his friends: "C'mon, Jew 'im down." (Of course, he meant Jew him up—but that didn't sound right.) Sometimes, they could keep

Blue arguing long enough to steal something off the back of his cart. Next day, they'd sell it back to him. Niggy Marino figured out how to wrap all the guys' wire together around a cobblestone—and sell the whole bundle as copper.

Niggy was a leader. He could fight better than anyone—and did: he had a bout almost every day. He'd take care of all the other guys' fights, too. Niggy led the raids when the grape trucks would rumble in. All the papas made wine in their basements, and the grapes arrived in big, rattling farm trucks—tons at a time. When the trucks geared down for the hill in North Beach, Niggy would climb on the back, or he'd get Frank Venezia to run the truck down (Frank could run like a deer), and they'd throw grapes off to everybody else. Niggy had another trick when the pie truck showed up at the grocery. The driver knew the Dago kids would try to steal his pies. So he'd park where he could see his truck's back door while he was in the store. Niggy would saunter over to the truck, pull the back door open, take out a pie, and stand there, cool as an ice chip. Sure enough, here comes the pie man out of the grocery, screamin' bloody murder, and Niggy would take off. When he got around the corner with the pie man in pursuit, all the rest of the boys would step up to the truck and walk away with fifteen pies. They'd eat till they were sick and sell the rest, twenty-five cents apiece.

That sort of money could take them to the movies. Hell, the way they worked it, a dime took them all to the movies. One guy would buy a ticket at the Acme, or the Peni-a-cade—those were the two cheapest theaters—and then the guy who paid would fling open the back doors and everybody else got in free. (How's the usher supposed to catch fifteen guys?) It was movies that brought the roar of the Twenties to North Beach. Romance at the captain's table on some swank ocean liner, champagne socialites dancing in speakeasies—the boys knew all that stuff from picture shows. When pictures started *talking,* in 1927, even North Beach was abuzz. But when *The Jazz Singer* finally arrived, they charged a quarter to see it. So Joe didn't go. Anyway, Joe didn't favor movies with a lot of guys in tuxedos, singing and dancing. He liked that desperate squadron of airmen in *The Dawn Patrol* . . . or tommy guns in the streets of Chicago—Edward G. Robinson in *Little Caesar* . . . or maybe best of all, Gary Cooper, *The Virginian*—or Johnny Mack Brown, the Alabama running back (hero of the Rose Bowl in 1926), who now bestrode the screen as Billy the Kid.

Outside the picture shows, it was like the boom of the Twenties never happened—not in North Beach. In Joe's world, the papas still woke in the middle of the night and walked down the hill to the wharf and their boats. They'd be back in the afternoon, each with a catch to sell, with nets to fold, with maybe a secret paper sack (illegal striped bass, to carry home for supper). In Joe's world, meat was still for Sundays—and Mondays, when the mamma made the leftover scraps into stew or soup.

Maybe Joe's house was poorer than most: nine kids, and a dad whose boat wasn't big enough for crabbing. But everybody had leftovers on Monday—and the same pasta underneath. All the boys on that ballfield could trace their personal histories back to the rocky Sicilian coast—to Sciacca, Porticello, Ísola delle Fémmine—all the parents came from the same poor towns. Even in the present, on this vast new continent, the lives they made (and taught to their sons) had the clammy jumbled intimacy of the village. Take LaRocca's Corner, up on Columbus: the building was owned by an uncle of the pitcher, Ciccio LaRocca. But the apartment upstairs was the home of the batter, Frank Venezia (Vince LaRocca was his uncle, too). And now that Frank's dad had died (eating bad clams), Vince LaRocca was trying to marry Frank's mamma. This was a world folded in on itself.

And the future . . . well, that seemed just as contained—and alarmingly close. With Frank's dad dead, Frank would have to go to work, for good. Niggy Marino's dad was sick: Niggy would have to take over the boat. Joe's older brothers Tom and Mike—they already had to go fishing. No one ever saw them playing ball anymore.

Joe didn't want any part of a boat. He couldn't

stand the sea, the smell of the fish. But even so, he would have bet five to one his future lay somewhere between that wall on Powell Street and the foot of Columbus—Fisherman's Wharf. At that point, he couldn't see how he would ever escape his father's life, much less the world of North Beach. He barely left the neighborhood now. Why would he? Except when his mamma sent him off to buy meat—that was cheaper over the hill, a half-mile away, in Chinatown. And afternoons he made the trip downtown to sell newspapers. That's how he brought money home—and escaped having to help his dad unload and fold the nets on Fisherman's Wharf.

That's why he was waiting at the playground, that afternoon. He and Frank Venezia would always share a nickel tram fare down to Market Street, to pick up their papers. They should have been on their way already. Joe never liked to wait. And if you showed up late, you could get screwed. They'd give half your papers to some other guy.

"Frank! Come on!" he yelled. "Are you comin' or not?"

But Frank was still batting—Piggy on a Bounce. And he told Joe to cool his heels. Just a few minutes more . . . he was on a streak!

JOE SOLD *THE CALL* AT SUTTER AND Sansome, near the Market Street trolleys. It was three cents for the paper and the kid who sold it got to keep a penny. On a good day, you'd come home with a buck and a half—two bucks or more if the World Series was on or Lindbergh was flying. When Dempsey knocked out Firpo, you could sell 'em for a quarter—people wanted the paper that bad. All the North Beach boys sold papers, if they didn't have some other job. Tony Santora worked at Hyde and Union, Shabby Minafo had the Standard Oil Building, Dario Lodigiani sold at Montgomery and Sutter, Frank Venezia was three blocks away at Battery and California. Joe had a good corner, banks on both sides and offices stacked on the floors above. By four P.M. there was a steady stream of businessmen heading home. They wanted papers. He didn't have to say a word. Joe's little brother, Dom, started hawking papers before he was ten (he took the corner right across from Joe)—and even Dommie brought home more than a dollar a day.

The best spot was the safety zone where the Market Street trolleys stopped. That was Niggy's. Who was gonna fight him for it? In the safety zone, a guy would flip you a nickel, you'd hand him his paper and then dig around your pockets, like you had to hunt around for two pennies change. Half the time the guy's streetcar would come, and he'd say, "Forget it," and jump on his tram. Niggy was in tight with the wholesaler, Howie Holmes. One day, Howie told Niggy that some guy was giving his paperboys a hard time. So Niggy went and punched the guy out. After that, Howie would leave Niggy's papers in the safety zone. Nig could pick 'em up any time he wanted. Niggy made a lot of friends with his fists.

One afternoon, Niggy's little brother jumped on a streetcar to sell his last papers, but the conductor smacked him, and shooed him off the car. Joe got the number of the tram and told Niggy. The next time that car came through, Niggy jumped on, walked up to the conductor and hit him in the jaw with a straight right hand. The conductor went down—change was rolling all over the car—and Joe and Niggy took off, laughing. Joe still had papers to sell, but, for once, he didn't mind. "You hit him a pretty good shot," he said. Niggy nodded happily: "He won't hit no little kids anymore."

If Joe ever got in a beef, Niggy was there to take care of business. Not that it happened much: Joe never courted trouble with his mouth. And he wasn't the kind to push his way into someone else's fight. That was one thing the guys liked about Joe: he didn't try to be like anybody else. He didn't have to fight. That was fine for Nig. He didn't have to try to talk to girls. That was Ciccio's specialty. Joe was sufficient to Joe.

That's what Frank Venezia admired, why he liked to hang around with Joe. They were both quiet. But Joe was without *need* to talk. Joe was quiet at the bottom of himself. He had control. That's the way he was with a bat. Never eager, never jumping at the ball.

He'd just stand there, while it came to him. Then he'd hit the tar out of it. That's the way he was about everything. If they had a good day selling papers—they had enough to give to their mammas, and then some—Frank would stop with the other guys at the U.S. Restaurant, on Columbus: fried ham on French bread, a big sandwich for a dime. But it wasn't really about the food. They were young, out at night, with money in their pockets—how could they just go home? . . . But Joe would say, "You guys go on." And he'd be gone, with his dime still in his pocket. Joe always brought his paper money home. His parents were strict about that. But he always had some quarters, if he needed them, for cards. One time, Frank and Joe signed up for the Christmas Club at Bank of America. You'd put in fifty cents a week, and in December, you got a fortune—twenty-five dollars. Frank gave up by summertime, took his money out, blew it that day on a new glove. But Joe kept going and got all the money. And that was *his*. Frank always figured that Joe's family didn't know about that twenty-five. The way Frank saw it, Joe was always a winner. And in his own eyes, Frank was always a loser.

Except today, with that bat in his hands, at Piggy on a Bounce. Frank hit for, musta been, forty-five minutes straight! It was like magic, like he could hit any pitch, any way, anywhere he chose. He could see the ball just sittin' there for him—then he'd cream it. It was like he imagined Joe always felt. . . . *Jesus—Joe!*

Frank had forgotten about Joe sitting there. Frank turned around now. But Joe was gone.

THAT WAS THE YEAR THEY'D GOT-ten so close. Frank and Joe had always been friends, but since that past September, they'd spent just about every day together. What happened was, they got to Galileo High School, and that's where their string ran out.

They were hopeless from the day they walked in the door. They'd sit in class, and it was like the rest of the kids had grown up in some other country. "Who knows this?" the teacher would say, and everybody else would stand up, waving their hands with the answer. Joe would look at Frank, Frank would look back at Joe: *What the hell's going on here?*

They'd never taken a book home. But they'd always got through with passing grades—they made no trouble. The only thing they cared about was sports. But at Galileo, they didn't even get into gym class: they got put into ROTC, the fuckin' army class! As if Joe was gonna march around with a stick on his shoulder, like a *stronzo*. Forget it!

And then, Italian class! The teacher was Mr. Zuberti, a stuck-up Florentine or Genoese—from up North somewhere, where they thought Sicilians were scum. He'd pick 'em out. Conjugate this verb! *(What the hell's a verb?)* . . . One morning, Zuberti threw Joe out of class. Joe didn't say a word. Just stood at his desk and walked out, while everybody stared at him. His face was burning red. Joe heard the giggles behind him, as Zuberti sang a little song, in Italian, to Frank: *"Oh, YOU'LL be the next to go . . ."*

And that was the end. Later that day, in Mrs. Cullen's English class, Joe was sitting next to Tony Santora, and he muttered: "I won't be here this afternoon."

"Why not, Joe?"

"My father comes in with the boat about one. If I don't help clean up, I don't eat tonight."

Of course, that was bullshit. Joe missed most days at Fisherman's Wharf. But this much was true: he didn't come back to school—that day, the next day, or any day thereafter. Frank started playing hooky, too.

They had the same routine. They'd get up in the morning, get ready for school. They'd have some bread, milk with a little coffee, walk out the door and turn down the sidewalk toward Galileo High . . . then they'd wander off to the park.

They'd hang around Marina Park all morning, watching the older guys with their "tops"—a monte game, where the aces and deuces show up, and you bet against the come. The older guys were always trying to take some young sucker for a buck or two. Joe and Frank would take lunch along, or figure out some way to eat. They could never go near the Wharf: someone would see. The playground was out: they'd be spotted for sure. Sometimes, they'd spend a nickel for the ferry and ride all the way across the Bay— mostly in silence. They were just killing time, like a lot of guys. In that winter, the turn of the 1930s, a couple of young men with time on their hands was nothing to draw a stare. One day, outside the Simmons Bedding plant at Bay and Powell, Frank counted fifty men on the corner. Nobody had anywhere to go.

About three o'clock, Joe would have to check in at home. That was the rule in his family, and Joe obeyed rules. He'd bang the door like he was coming home from school, say hello, make sure no one knew anything. Frank had no one to check in with at home. He'd go to the playground, to see if he could get into a game for a while, before they had to go sell papers.

It went on for months—Joe and Frank hanging out all day—until Joe got caught: the school sent a letter home. Joe got a beating from his older brothers. And he was summoned to see the principal, Major Nourse. (No one knew why he was called Major, but the title fit him: he was discipline, first, last, and always.) Tom, the eldest DiMaggio brother, took Joe back to school. But when they got there, Major Nourse wasn't in.

They sat on chairs in the hallway. And they sat.

They sat an hour, an hour and a half. The chairs were hard. They sat.

Finally, Joe said, "Tom. They don't want me."

"Okay," Tom said. They got up and walked out. And that was the last day Joe went to high school.

He promised Tom he'd go to "continuation class"—the school for dropouts. But Joe never went there either.

For a while, he hung around with Frank—who was still on the loose—the school never cared if he came back. But soon, Frank had to go to work. He hooked on—as much as he could—at Simmons Bedding, in the steel mill plant. He tied bed rails into bundles and loaded them onto trucks. That was five bucks a day.

Joe tried his hand as a workin' stiff, too. He worked a week or so for Pacific Box, stacking wooden crates, or bringing slats to the men at the nailing machines. The work was stupid, and the money wasn't great—ten, twelve bucks a week. Joe moved on to the orange juice plant. But that was worse: up to your ass all day in sticky juice, with acid eating into the cuts on your hands. And for what? He didn't even make a full week there.

There wasn't anything that he wanted to do, except to have a few bucks in his pocket—and avoid his father's boat. He went back to selling papers.

Frank thought maybe Joe could hook on at Simmons Bed. They had jobs there, if you knew someone. And they had a ball team. Maybe they could both play. He would have talked to Joe about it.

But they weren't talking.

After Frank made Joe wait for Piggy on a Bounce, Joe had to take the streetcar downtown—on his own nickel. After that, Joe wouldn't talk to Frank for a year.

Rosalie and Giuseppe DiMaggio.

**Fisherman's Wharf, at the foot of
Columbus Avenue.**

Joe with his mamma, sisters, niece, and nephew.

CHAPTER 2

◆

WHEN JOE BOMBED OUT OF SCHOOL, his father was disgusted and affirmed. What's the point of being Sicilian if you're not convinced the world will do you dirt in the end? Giuseppe DiMaggio was a man of the old verities: hard work will maybe earn you a living, if you keep your nose clean and don't say a word. Without hard work, you're a bum, *magabonu.*

He was a small man, but thick through the chest, shoulders, and neck, from hauling up net through the water. He wore a brown fedora, even in shirtsleeves, and, like the other men of the Wharf, a sash to hold his pants up. He had a small, old-country mustache. Sometimes, he clenched in his teeth a short black cigar of the sort the fishermen called *Toscani.* He fished six days a week, made some wine in the basement, raised nine kids, and kept his troubles to himself.

Giuseppe had come to America in 1898, when his in-laws wrote from Collinsville, California, and told him the fishing was good. A young man who'd work could make enough money to buy a small boat and make a living on his own. That pretty well described the limits of Giuseppe DiMaggio's ambition. He had

just married Rosalie Mercurio, a girl from his village—and their first child was on the way. Giuseppe
decided he would go to the New World for a year. In
the worst case, he'd come home with some money. As
it turned out, he would stay for the rest of his life. He
was a Californian for the next fifty years. But an
American he never quite became.

Giuseppe was fully formed in the old and wary
spirit of his native land. Through Sicily's long history—centuries of conquest by Greeks, Romans,
Arabs, Europeans—authority was always imposed
from without. The only institution in which you had a
say was your family. And even there, it was better to
keep quiet. (The island's most famous export, *la
Cosa Nostra,* was created to protect the peasants
from predatory government, nobles, church—authority of any stripe. Small wonder, *la Mafia,* too,
was organized on family, and silence.) In Sicily, a
young man learned early to keep his head down and
follow the ways of his father—all the more in
Giuseppe's poor village, where seamanship and net-
craft, passed from father to son, spelled the difference between survival and extinction. Ísola delle
Fémmine ("Island of the Women") was a tiny outcrop
of rock, a mile off the main island coast. The name
came from Roman times, when this was the island of
exile for wives who could not stay faithful while their
soldier-husbands were at war. In Giuseppe's day, the
islet was formally a part of the province of Palermo,
but, in fact, was cut off from everything save the

Tyrrhenian Sea. Even by the standards of Sicily, it was backward; and its sons—formed, as was their home, by wind, waves, tide, and changeless time— bore its heritage of stillness and isolation.

After four years, when Giuseppe sent for his wife and daughter, and moved them into a house in Martinez, California, they began a life that must have seemed wholly new—not just half a world away from their old village, but centuries distant, too. Martinez was an East Bay hick town to Americans; yet, for the DiMaggios, it was unimaginably modern. There were electric streetlights (eight of them, on Main Street); factories worked day and night; there were great steamboats plying the Carquinez Strait (even some fishing boats had engines!), and just twenty paces from their house, there were the gleaming rails of the Southern Pacific: hundreds of trains rattling through every day.

Still, in most ways, Giuseppe stood apart from all the bustle. He had only a few words of English, and none of the skills of the machine age. He got his little boat (and named it for his bride, the *Rosalie D.*). In time, he even had a motor in it. But his life still ran to the rhythm of the tides, followed the shad, sturgeon, sardines; still, he rose in the silent darkness, spent his day alone with the weather. Home was a cabin on the dirt road of Grainger's Wharf, closer to the fish than those newfangled streetlights. This was the wrong side of the tracks in Martinez. The Anglos called this zone the Portuguese Flats *(Porta-geeze* was the way they said it), which may have meant some Portuguese once had lived there, or may simply have implied that it was filled with greasers. (In those days, such distinctions didn't have to be nice.) In fact, the Flats were filled with Sicilian fishermen, who'd taken over the wharf in Martinez, and now re-created their old-country villages in the twentieth-century U.S.A.

Every afternoon you'd see them with their wine and food, outside on Marrazani's porch, or next to the fish shed of the buyer, Pellegrini. Sundays, the street became a *bocce* court. Saturdays, after the boats came in, a score of kids played in the dirt between the troughs where the nets were tanning in a soup of redwood bark. The mothers were outdoors, too, recrocheting the rips in the nets with new flax and hand-carved wooden needles. Talk was in Sicilian, and about Sicilians—there was so little contact with anyone else. Or they'd talk about the fish: "How's the run?" . . . "When you think we'll see salmon?" . . . like farmers talking weather 'n' wheat in some tiny town in Kansas—everything else was too distant to merit talk.

Giuseppe's house had a living room and a closet-sized bedroom in front, a kitchen and another bedroom behind. The outhouse in back hung over Alhambra Creek, where Giuseppe also tied up his boat. Next door, in an identical tiny wooden house, lived his brother, Salvatore, also a fisherman, who had also married a Mercurio—Rosalie's sister, Frances. It seemed like the DiMaggio-Mercurios were making a pretty good village by themselves. Kids kept coming, more or less every two years. Giuseppe's first child, Nellie, had been born in his absence, in Sicily. In America came Mamie, Tom, Marie, Michael, Frances, Vince, Joe, and finally, Dominic. Papa Giuseppe gave all the boys the middle name Paul—for Paolo, his favorite saint. By the time Joseph Paul was born, in 1914, there wasn't anyplace in the Martinez cabin where there wasn't a DiMaggio asleep or at play.

When Joe was still a toddler, his sister Frances was playing on the railroad tracks and got a hot cinder in her eye. In Martinez, the only doctor who served the Sicilians was the man who'd delivered Joe, Dr. Marrefew—the fishermen called him *il Dottore del Dichu,* the Doctor of the Ditch (the Creek)—and all he could do was bandage the eye. So Rosalie DiMaggio had to take Frances twenty-five miles across the Bay to San Francisco—back and forth, back and forth to the doctors—while Rosalie's sister and Giuseppe watched over the other kids. That couldn't go on for long. Within months, Giuseppe moved the whole brood into the city, to a North Beach apartment just up the hill from Fisherman's Wharf, where he could dock his boat. And there, on Taylor Street, they'd stay for the next twenty years. That's where all his younger kids would come of age, in the city . . . which, as a true Sicilian, Giuseppe considered "just his bad luck."

YOU COULD CALL IT A CASE OF TOO much change or too little. San Francisco was a big town, worldly, even elegant in spots—as distant in tone and tempo from Martinez as that town was from Ísola delle Femmine. But Giuseppe couldn't change that much, that fast. He still couldn't speak English, couldn't read anything, even Italian. For that matter, he couldn't speak Italian—not the pure Northern language of the Genoese and Florentines who ran North Beach. Giuseppe's guttural Sicilian patois marked him from the first syllable as low-class, or none.

The Northerners had come to California generations before, from the Gold Rush days of the mid-nineteenth century. They didn't think of themselves as Italians—Italy wasn't yet united. They were Genoese *(Zinesi),* Piedmontese, Ligurians, or Florentines. They came with their educations, some with money, all with precise and unshakable ideas about class. *Zinesi* wouldn't talk to *Siciliani,* even if they could. In San Francisco, the Genoese were merchants, produce purveyors, and scavengers. (In fact, the garbage trade was their monopoly, a license to print money.) They were landlords. They were truckers and teamsters. They ran the wharves and the fish business. When Sicilian fishermen started to arrive, around the turn of the century, they had to fight their way in.

For some families, that struggle was a spur—even a blessing. The crab fisherman Lorenzo Maniscalco had his boat sunk, his family threatened—but Lorenzo was fearless. He bought a new, bigger boat; he fished the rocks, closer than any other man would dare; he put out to sea in weather that no one else would brave. He became the King of the Crab Fishermen, lived in a mansion in the Marina and, Sunday afternoons, drove his wife and twelve children through the old neighborhood in a Buick touring car. Another crabber, Giuseppe Alioto, fought his way into wholesaling—he became the first Sicilian buyer—and then expanded into the restaurant business. He sent his sons to the church school at Sts. Peter and Paul's, and enrolled them in the ambitious Salesian Boys Club. He encouraged them to study music, poetry, acting, law . . . and his son Joe would become a visionary mayor of San Francisco.

Giuseppe DiMaggio kept his head down and stayed small. He came with his old double-prowed boat: the Monterey hull, sixteen feet long. That was too small for crab or salmon, too small for anything outside the Golden Gate, in the open sea where the rich fishing lay. So Giuseppe stayed inside the Gate, only fished the Bay, where the best he could find was herring, or shad (at three cents a pound—and that, only for females). Most days, he simply hauled up bait fish—nothing worth eating—and sold his catch to more adventurous men. Or he sold to the processors of fish meal and fertilizer, the lowest end of the business. It was the marine equivalent of rag-picking: collecting by weight what others disdained.

No DiMaggio boys were sent to the church school, where Salesian priests groomed the future *prominenti.* For one thing, there was no money for tuition.

But it wasn't just the cost. In Giuseppe's view, the Salesians weren't for "people like us." Those priests (all from the North) preached aspiration, advancement, Americanization. The Salesian Boys Club was known for its acting troupe, musicianship, debaters—and that new American sport, basketball. The director, a dedicated soul named Angelo Fusco, lavished attention on boys who'd "go far," like that *Zinese* boy, John Molinari (who would become a state Supreme Court justice), or that bright *Siciliano,* Joe Alioto.

Giuseppe DiMaggio never talked about his boys "going far." He talked about them going onto his boat, to learn their trade, to work hard, so they could sleep in a house with a roof. He talked about them bringing home money, so they could eat. They were not to waste time—for instance, playing that baseball. That was *buono per niente*—good for nothin'—except wrecking shoes.

And Giuseppe had his way; his lessons took—at least with the first boys, Tom and Mike, who'd mostly grown up in that village on the flats of Martinez. In a good Sicilian home, you didn't question. You had no right to say your father was wrong. And Giuseppe's first boys were good Sicilian kids. Tom, the elder, was small like his papa, and just as quiet. But he had a precocious wisdom about him. You could go to Tom with a problem; he'd listen intently, and then, with just a few words, he'd sort it out for you. Mike was a big, husky, rawboned kid. They used to say he could hit a baseball harder than anyone else in the family. And he had a temper. You didn't want to get on Mike's wrong side. Both boys learned to fish on their father's boat, from the time they were nine or ten years old. Sometimes they'd be out all night, napping on the floor planks, while the tide drifted Giuseppe back to his nets . . . whereupon they'd wake to help haul in the catch, and make for the Wharf in time for school. By eighth grade, both boys had left school, and Tom, confirmed in his father's trade, got his own boat (though he was New Worldly enough to pick one with a big hull for crab and salmon). Mike was supposed to work his father's boat and train Vince, the next in line. (If Giuseppe had a dream in life, it was to own a *big* boat, with all five sons aboard.)

But that's where Giuseppe's bad luck started, with the third son, Vince: a city kid, a playground kid, a thoroughly American boy. Vince was good-looking—he took after the Mercurio side—and forward. He said what he thought. In fact, he talked all the time—sometimes loudly, sometimes profanely—and when he didn't talk, he sang. He had a love of music and a beautiful voice. His dream was to be an operatic tenor, or maybe a singer with a big band. And that was the problem: not the music but the dreaming. Vince had the crazy American idea that he could be whatever he wanted to be.

He'd hang around LaRocca's Corner in the evening, and offer to sing a few songs for the patrons. He thought, if they liked his music, maybe they'd give him a couple of bucks. Or maybe someone would give him a singing job—that could be his big break. Or he'd hang around with his friends, playing baseball (Vince could hit the ball a mile, like Mike), and think, maybe he could be a great ballplayer. That was his second dream: big-time baseball. Where he wouldn't hang around was Fisherman's Wharf, waiting for his papa, to help with the nets. And the real problem was, Vince was never penitent: he wouldn't hang his head and promise to obey. He'd just say: "Papa, I was in a game." In Giuseppe's household, that made Vince a rebel.

Today that seems the mildest noncompliance. Vince still sold papers, and brought the money home. There were some days he did go out to fish with Mike, so Giuseppe could stay home. He didn't hate his dad—or the boat, the sea, the work. But all that was Papa's life, not his.

Even then, at Fisherman's Wharf, there were fathers who spoke proudly of their sons who were learning new trades, making their way in this new country. Maniscalco's boy, Louie, had his own bakery business. And Pat, the firstborn, was enrolled in a *college*. But not Giuseppe DiMaggio: he never talked much about his sons, and never with pride. His sort of Sicilian feared envy like the evil eye. If you didn't show yourself, you could never be judged. (And if you talked too much about your business, someone might come and be your partner.)

The sad truth was, Giuseppe had no idea what to

do with Vince. They fought bitterly. When Vince got an offer to play ball in the Lumber Leagues of Northern California, Giuseppe told the boy he couldn't go. Vince was underage, and Giuseppe refused to sign the contract. Vince appealed to his mother, but she wouldn't make the fight. "I'm going to go," Vince said. "Do you want me to go with your will, or against it?"

So Vince faked his age, signed for himself, and ran away to play ball. That was bad enough. But when word came back that Vince had met a girl up North—he wanted to marry!—Giuseppe hit the roof. It was the son's job to work and bring money home, to support the family—not to run off and make his own family, more mouths to feed. And before he'd even made a dime! And refused to do a man's work—*he played with a ball,* like a boy on the playground! *Magabonu!* Of course, Giuseppe forbade the marriage. When Vince refused to break off with the girl, Giuseppe would talk no more. Vince had disobeyed. He was not welcome at home. Giuseppe had lost a son.

And so the father's wary eye fell upon the fourth son, his namesake, Joe. He was two years younger than Vince and, in his father's view, had at least one foot on the same slippery road to perdition. True, Joe was quiet, he didn't openly disobey. And girls—no worry there. Joe was so shy, he'd run out of the house whenever his sisters had their girlfriends over. But he didn't learn in school. And he couldn't keep a job. So, okay . . . Joe would fish. Giuseppe would *make* the boy fish.

And he might have, too, if it hadn't been for Rosalie, his wife. She'd watched Giuseppe with Vince—and she'd held her tongue. But she wasn't going to lose another son.

"Il é bonu, Lasce sta','" she told Giuseppe, in flat and final intercession.

"He's a good boy. Leave him alone."

THE OTHER ITALIANS USED TO SAY, *"I Siciliani—si voi cambiare la mente, bisogna tagliare la testa."* (The Sicilians—if you want to change their minds, you have to cut off their heads.) But they were mostly talking about the men. As every Sicilian boy knew, if you wanted something, or had a problem to talk over, you went to Mamma. And in the DiMaggio household on Taylor Street, Rosalie, the mamma, wasn't just *consigliere,* but chief.

She was the everyday discipline in the children's lives—although the worst thing she could say was, "Wait till your father comes home." Then you could really be in the soup: you had the wild card to deal with. Mostly, even that was sham. Giuseppe would sit the errant child down in the living room, and he'd order gravely: "Rosalie, you go back to the kitchen." But of course, she'd already told him what to say.

Rosalie was slightly taller than Giuseppe, quicker in her movements, sweet-faced and modest in de-

portment. She was always in the Taylor Street flat, either in the kitchen, or on the service porch behind the
kitchen. On the porch stood the galvanized tubs for
washing, and the *ballataro,* the washboard. She
washed by hand for the family of eleven. She ironed
next to the stove, at first because the iron had to heat
on the fire, and later because there was a light that
hung down there, and she could plug in the heavy
electric iron over the bulb. She cooked three hundred
and sixty-five days a year, baked the family's bread,
scrubbed the wooden floors on her knees, sewed and
darned clothes, and made the down mattresses,
which lay everywhere in the four-room flat. Late at
night her children would hear her, still in the kitchen,
cleaning up. And they'd wake to the scent of chicken-
feet singeing on the gas fire in the morning, as Rosalie began the soup for that day's dinner.

She was source of all tenderness in the household,
and faith. She used to tell the little ones stories at
night, to soothe them into sleep. They were simple
stories, maybe from the Old World, or maybe she
made them up herself. They were often about the
Madonna, and want. There was one wherein the
Madonna visited a family so poor that the children
had no clothes. There was not enough fabric to make
anything—just a scrap of cloth. But the Madonna
began to sew with the scrap, and as she sewed more
cloth appeared. As she finished one shirt, there would
be just a bit more fabric . . . and she began to sew
again—and again—and by miracle, by faith . . .

there were clothes for all. There was another tale of a family that had no water to wash, but the Madonna poured the tiny jug of water they had . . . and by miracle, by Her Grace, there was water for all.

The reality of miracles, of intercession, was a given, a concommitant of Rosalie's faith—like fish on Friday. In cases of special need or trouble, most North Beach women would visit the neighborhood witches, black-garbed crones who'd mix up some oil and water, chant the old words that even Sicilians couldn't understand, and call down blessings, curses, or prophecies *("Beware of the one next door!")* . . . after which, they'd be paid a couple of bucks, and you could go home with your mind at ease. But as with featherbeds or loaves of fresh bread, Rosalie took care of this herself. If one of her kids had woe or sickness, she'd sit the child on a chair in the living room on Taylor Street (it had to be the front room, for this was a formal matter). She'd put a dish on the sufferer's head, pour oil and water onto it, and read the skim of the oil on the water. Then she'd chant the ancient words she knew from her girlhood, and lift from her troubled child the evil eye.

Of course, this wasn't precisely Christian, but it all went together in North Beach. In the grand Church of Sts. Peter and Paul, there were a dozen statues of uncertain provenance that were nevertheless honored by the priests. What happened was, someone would visit the Old Country and come back with a sculptured "saint" (and the seller's tales of miraculous power). The people of North Beach would begin to pray to this statue in some basement, and word would spread and the crowds would grow thicker . . . until the priests figured it was better to bring them all back to church. So, the statue would get a little chapel on the side; the priests would sprinkle Holy Water on it, and everybody would be back in the fold. For her part, Rosalie was a regular at Sts. Peter and Paul's—morning Mass, rain or shine. (Giuseppe wouldn't go, even on Sundays. Confession wasn't for him. He used to say he wouldn't tell his sins to any other man.)

The only other time you'd see Rosalie out in the neighborhood was when she went to shop. She used to go with her sister, Maria (Mamie, they called her), who married the fisherman Joe Clima. They looked like twins, *le Signore Clima e DiMaggio,* even though Mamie was really the elder. If Rosalie went out in the evening (say, on those rare nights when Giuseppe wasn't home), she'd take a daughter or two, and her basket of mending, and she'd sit with Mamie, talking and sewing. These days, they had a lot to talk about.

For when Joe stopped speaking to Frank Venezia, he drifted away from his old crowd. He didn't go to the playground, or play ball at the Horses' Lot. He didn't do much of anything, except hang out with Mamie's son, Joe Clima. The cousins had become best friends. And Joe Clima wasn't doing much either—except running with the fast crowd, scamming here and there for a couple of bucks, and playing cards for money.

What was gonna become of these boys?

You have to understand, in these ladies' minds, the fate of their Joes was linked from the start—because of the name. The way Sicilians did the names, the first boy was named for the father's father (so that was Sal for the Climas, and Tom for the DiMaggios). Then the second boy got the name of the mother's father (so that was Mike for both families). The third son was named for the father's oldest brother (Frank Clima and Vince DiMaggio). And the fourth was named for the mother's oldest brother—that was Joe. And so, these drifting boys bore a name beloved to both these mammas—that of their brother Joe.

In the Climas' flat on Columbus Avenue, Mamie Mercurio Clima voiced the traditional Sicilian view. Rules had to be made. Something had to be done. These boys were going to end up in trouble. It was 1931, jobs were hard to find. How were they ever going to land on their feet?

But Rosalie Mercurio DiMaggio had faith in her Joe. Why? Who could tell? Maybe she'd seen something in the oil and water in a dish on his head. Or maybe she'd beseeched the Madonna, and found answer to her want. But she said—as she spoke in matters of faith—against all comers and, at that moment, all evidence: "Leave him alone," she said. "Joe's gonna do fine."

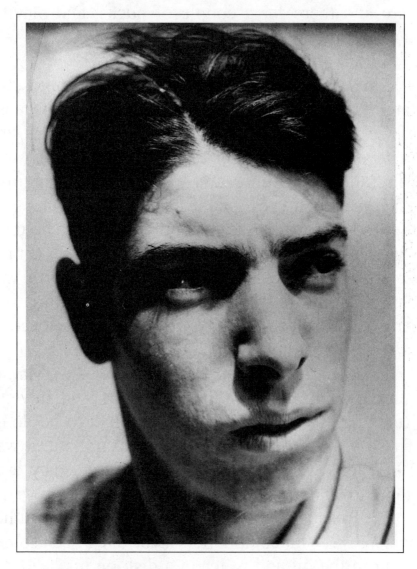

Portrait of a pro: San Francisco, 1932.

**The boy who loved
baseball: Vince DiMaggio.**

A classy outfit: the Rossi Olive Oil squad.

CHAPTER 3

✦

AS IT HAPPENED, THE TURN IN
Joe's life took about thirty seconds and was accompanied by no claps of thunder—no one saw the
Madonna. Frank Venezia and Bat Minafo saw Joe,
walking across the street. As Frank remembers, they
were just hanging out at that Powell Street playground wall. And Joe was out shopping for his folks,
on his way to Chinatown. Bat said, "How 'bout Joe?
Go ask him."

Bat and Frank were choosing up for real, now.
The guys had got together in a club—they called it
the Jolly Knights. They had a clubhouse over a
garage at Columbus and Filbert, where they'd sit
around at night, playing cards. Joe came by a
couple of times. But he wasn't a member. He was
busy with his pal Joe Clima. Once a month, once
every six weeks, they'd hold a dance at the clubhouse, too. But, of course, Joe would never come
to those.

But this was the best part. Now they were going
to have a ball team, an official team, with uniforms
and everything. Bat was always half-mental—

hyper, anyway—and now, with this team, he was jabbering. "Go ahead, ask him. G'wan, Frank. Ask him!"

Frank said, "You call him."

"No, you call him."

"He ain't talkin' to me."

Bat insisted, "Just ask him. Go on! Ask him anyway."

So Frank called to Joe and trotted across the street. He tried to make his voice sound like it was special— that's why he was trying to talk to Joe. "Hey, Joe, we're gonna make a team. A real team—with uniforms and maybe shoes, and, well . . .

"D'you wanna play?"

Joe didn't bat an eye, like he and Frank talked every day. Joe said, "Okay."

THERE'S A GORGEOUS MYTH ABOUT Joe DiMaggio—how he got into baseball—a tale so sweet it was in all the books for fifty years. The basis of the story is that Joe was the boy who only loved baseball. That's why he wouldn't fish. He'd rather play ball with his friends. He just *had* to play ball.

And then his brother Vince got a job on the San Francisco Seals, and Joe went to see him at the ballpark. And he was peering through a hole in the fence (there's always a hole in the fence in these stories . . .) when along came a scout, to ask: "What're you doin', boy?"

In the best version of this tale—the one Joe would put into his own book, *Lucky to Be a Yankee*—the scout, Spike Hennessy, gets off a snappy line: *"Never stand on the outside looking in, unless it's a jail."* . . . Then, Hennessy hauls Joe up to the owner of the Seals, Charley Graham, who not only gives DiMaggio a fistful of passes, but asks him to work out with the team.

And the rest, as they say in these stories, is history: how Vince gets Joe a chance to play, at the end of the '32 season (when the Seals are looking for a fill-in shortstop); and Joe hooks on with the team for the '33 season, and he's a sensation—such a star that the Seals put him in the outfield, and they have to shuck one outfielder, so they get rid of Vince . . . and Joe takes his own brother's job. (Ain't that ironic?)

It's so good, so neat, that it ought to be true—hell, it almost is . . . except for the fundamental basis of the tale: Joe wasn't the boy who loved baseball. Vince was.

In fact, by 1930, Joe had walked away from baseball. If he played anything, it was tennis. Mostly, he just didn't play. His attitude on baseball wasn't too far from his dad's: there was no money in it—so what was it good for?

But it was true he found the game again, in 1931— when Bat and Frank signed him up to play for the Jolly Knights. That sounded okay to Joe: he signed up for the shoes.

THE TRUE IRONY WAS, JOE DIDN'T get real spikes, just the regular old clodhoppers from Tragones. They nailed spikes onto the bottom. Still, things were different.

Now, the boys were playing against good teams, men who played a serious game. There were club teams and company teams all over the city, grouped into leagues and scheduled on diamonds—three or four games in a row on every diamond in every park, every Saturday and Sunday, year-round. It was all organized by a human computer named Al Earl—he'd set up all the games—from a sporting goods store on Mission Street. Mondays, in the paper, there'd be a whole page of box scores: results for every team in town. And there was a column chronicling the semipros. That's where Vince had got his first press notices (while he played for Jack's Haberdashery). And that's when the scouts offered Vince a paying contract. Those were stakes Joe understood.

Joe was different, too. While he was away from baseball, he'd filled out. He was just about six feet now, and not so skinny. He'd always been able to hit some balls hard—but now, everything he hit was a shot. And there was something else new: his delight in his power. "Watch me hit this one out," he'd tell Niggy Marino at the Horses' Lot. Then he'd smash the next pitch toward those billboards in left center field. Even with a mushy tapcd ball, and a bat held together with nails and tape, he'd hit 'em over the billboards, onto Columbus Avenue. One time he hit a car, and that was the end of that game. Everybody ran like hell. The driver caught a couple of kids, but they wouldn't squeal on Joe. He was a leader now: with Joe at third base or shortstop, the Jolly Knights were sweeping their league.

That fall, Frank and Bat found a sponsor, a grocer named Rossi who had his own brand of olive oil— and that raised the pride in their club to near swagger. Al Earl put the Rossi Olive Oil team in the B division, but anyone could see they were a classy outfit: brand-new uniforms, twenty-five dollars a month for shiny new balls and bats (they even got Bat a catcher's mask) . . . and, best of all, they went everywhere in the Rossi Olive Oil truck. They went to San Quentin for a nerve-racking contest with the prisoners. They had guards for umpires, and Rossi played pretty well. But the game was called a tie—four to four—because they almost had a riot. It got to the fourteenth inning, and the cons were throwing anything they could grab out the windows. Everybody had bets on the game. So the warden stopped it: "Okay! Time for dinner!" But the Rossi guys didn't fight the call. You fought up there, you could get killed. Anyway, dinner was welcome: Hungry Geraldi ate four servings of boiled beef. Another time, Vince DiMaggio called from Northern California, and challenged Rossi Olive Oil to play his club, in Fort Bragg. So the North Beach boys rode up there and beat the hell out of them. Those Rossi Olive Oils were good!

With Joe and Shabby Minafo in the middle of the order, they were always going to score. Sometimes, if he wasn't fishing, Mike DiMaggio would come in as a ringer, and then it was a murderers row. If Joe played third, they'd have Frank Venezia at second base, Al Tomei at short (and leading off—Friggles was a sprinter for Commerce High School). Banchero could play infield or outfield, Ciccio or Red Albano would pitch. The lineup was set by the manager, Niggy's brother, Joe. They called him, naturally, Connie Mack Marino. He was the first guy to try Joe D. in the outfield—because the first baseman, Fo Gelardi, used to beef: "Jesus! He's knockin' my hand apart. I can't catch him!" (Joe liked to power his throws, too.)

Joe didn't care where he played—as long as he could knock in those runs. He'd do whatever it took to win. Once, he was at shortstop against Bayview Park, and a guy hit a pop fly to center. Joe turned around and took off. Everybody started yelling, "Let it alone! Joe's after it!" . . . He caught that fly ball in dead center field.

He always did something that made people talk. But if you brought it up to him—how well he played, what people were saying—he'd only shrug: "Well, it's good they think I'm okay." If Rossi won, Joe was all smiles. If they lost, he went silent and sour. If they lost and he had a bad day, you didn't want to get near him. Mostly they won. They climbed straight to the top of the B division. The guys were sure they were going to be an A team. And then, who could tell? Maybe the Valley League, where they'd schedule your game at Funston Park, and there'd be five or six hundred people watching, and you'd pass the hat afterward—you could come home with five or ten bucks, just for playing!

But they were still in their first year when they had the game at Jackson Playground, against a team called American Building. Joe hit a huge home run. The clubhouse was way out past left field, and Joe hit it over the clubhouse. There was a guy in the stands watching the game—Bummy Bumgartner: his team was called Sunset Produce, and they had the next game on that diamond. When Joe hit the home run, Frank Venezia got up off the bench, went over toward the baseline to straighten out the bats on the grass. He looked up—he was going to shake Joe's hand—but Joe was over by the stands. Frank saw Bummy Bumgartner slipping Joe two bucks. The next week, Rossi Olive Oil had to limp along without its cleanup hitter. Joe was playing for Sunset Produce.

IN FACT, HE WOULD PLAY FOR FIVE
or six different clubs in that spring and summer of
1932. Joe became a hitter for hire. He was playing
weekends, and most weekdays, too, into the long
evening light. In his days with the Jolly Knights, even
with Rossi, the other boys had to go to Joe's house,
wake him up, make sure he'd show. But now, for a
couple of bucks, he'd be there early—any diamond in
the city.

For the most part, he was playing shortstop,
where he made his share of mistakes—or more. Joe
had never had any coaching. He hadn't even played
for Francisco Junior High (the teams were lousy).
And with his years away from baseball, he hadn't
even seen as much of the game as the average
sandlot kid his age. But now he was learning, so
fast you couldn't even see it happen—like Mozart
learned piano: altogether, and instantly. Say, on a
Tuesday, Joe saw a guy hook-slide into third base.
Well, that Thursday, Joe would hit a gapper through
left center, and he'd pound around to third and
cap it off with the damnedest hook-slide anybody
ever saw—catch the corner of the bag with the
toe of his trailing foot—as if Ty Cobb had taught
him, and he'd practiced for five years. Or say he
saw some flashy shortstop take the throw on a
double play while he was crossing second base,
and make his own throw to first when momentum
had carried him past the bag, past the runner, two
steps toward right center field. Well, Joe'd try that,

too. Of course, it was anyone's guess where his throw would end up. But, what the hell. No one paid him for fielding. He was the kind of shortstop who might let in a couple of runs. But he'd knock in six.

In eighteen games with Sunset Produce—that was against A-league pitching—Joe hit for an average of .632. The Sunsets were so delighted, they gave him a prize: real spikes—the featherweights, kangaroo skin—the kind he'd wanted since the start. Looking back, that sounds like a small thing. But Joe would remember those shoes forever. Or maybe what he re- membered was the feeling (it hadn't happened so often in his life) when he set out to get something and, with baseball, he got it.

And the Sunsets weren't the only ones who took note. The world of baseball in San Francisco was woven together with a million strands of talk. The semipro players knew each other from school teams, boys clubs, playgrounds. They talked their game nonstop. Semipro managers and sponsors vied with one another to recruit the best talent. A kid who got on base two out of three times was never going to stay a secret. "Bird-dogs" and paid scouts reported to the professional teams, the San Francisco Mission Reds and the San Francisco Seals (not to mention the Oak- land Oaks, across the Bay). The scouts and the teams made a living by finding local talent to develop and sell.

In *Lucky to Be a Yankee,* DiMaggio would profess surprise—oh, he was shocked!—when the scout, Spike Hennessy, retailed his career to the owner of the Seals. *"I hadn't realized how closely Hennessy had been watching our sand-lot games until I heard him tell Graham all about me."* But that was just Joe doing his Gary Cooper thing (Aw, shucks). And it satisfied a 1940s American public that didn't want its heroes to strive too much. (Our icons were good, as were we, and our nation, by grace of God, by the magic of America.)

But the fact was, Joe was the hottest kid on the semipro circuit, and had been for months. One pro team, the Mission Reds, already had invited him for a tryout. Jim Nealon, the *Examiner* columnist on local baseball, started writing Joe up ("looks like a comer . . .") when he hit two home runs for Rossi Oil in the B-league playoff.

Nor could Joe's new career remain any secret at home. But that was all right, now. The reason, once again, was Vince. The Seals had signed Giuseppe's estranged son, and sent him to their "farm"—the Tucson club, in the Arizona State League. Vince got a little money to sign and even less to play. But after three or four months—who said he never learned from his dad?—he'd spent absolutely nothing. When the Arizona league disbanded in midsummer, the Seals called Vince back to San Francisco. And, unannounced, he walked back into the Taylor Street flat.

Decades later, Vince told the story to Professor Jack B. Moore:

"So with all the bonuses and everything that I had coming from the club, when I came home I had $1,500. . . . So I came home and I walked in. My Dad—he didn't say much—but I knew he was waiting for an opportunity. My mother, when she saw me, she put her arms around me. Dad was in the kitchen. He was having a little wine, and he had some peaches cut, and he was dipping peaches in the wine. When I went in and greeted him he looked at me and greeted me more or less saying, what are you doing here?

"So I said, 'Dad, I've come home. If it's all right, I'd like to stay here.' And I said: 'This is what I earned, and this is what I'm bringing home.'

"Right away, before he could say anything—I brought it in cash, I didn't bring no check, I brought it in cash so he could see it was more than a piece of paper: he knows the cash, but he didn't know anything about a check, so I had it all in cash—and the first thing he says when he saw the money was, 'Where'd you steal that money?'

"I said, I earned it. I said, you come with me, I'll introduce you to my boss. So, the next day, sure enough, he went and talked with the owner, Mr. Graham, and they had a little conversation."

Of course, Mr. Graham talked English, and Signore DiMaggio spoke Sicilian. But the old fisherman got the point. The money was real, legal, and his. So Vince got to live at home for a few months. And Joe, he played baseball, whenever he wanted.

AND THE REST REALLY WOULD BE HIS- tory—with a bit of myth on top. At the end of that '32 season, the Seals outfielder, Henry (Prince) Oana was working up a barnstorming trip, starting in his native Hawaii. He asked for permission to miss the Seals' last three games, and take the short- stop, Augie Galan, along with him. "Who's going to play short?" asked the manager, Ike Caveney. And then, as a matter of historical fact, Vince DiMaggio did pipe up: "I got a brother who's a shortstop—and a good one!"

So Joe played those last three games with the Seals, got himself a couple of hits, and an invitation to next year's spring training. And there he would prove that all the talk about him wasn't fiction. He would make the jump, in less than two years, from playground games to the Pacific Coast League—just a notch below the majors. And that would be, in real- ity, miraculous.

But it would never be quite miraculous enough for public consumption—not quite neat enough for one column of newsprint. So, that's where the myth would begin to cover the facts. Because the next year, 1933, Joe wouldn't just stick with the club. He would become a sensation—a huge story. In fact, he would jump from the sports page to the front page before the newspapers could learn to spell his name. (Mostly, they would go with "DeMaggio.") . . . But how would they make a big story with this kid—who would never say more than "Pass the salt"? Well, they would do their best:

The poor Italian boy, who learned to hit with a broken oar for a bat . . .

His papa wanted him to fish, but DeMaggio only loved baseball . . .

His brother got him a job—his own . . .

In other words, they would give him a story— or bits and pieces of old, proven stories—from the tasty American melting pot stuff, to Cain and Abel.

Joe would rankle for years under the legend that he'd come up in '33 to steal his brother's job. (He would always protest: Vince was injured—he couldn't throw. He was going to be cut, no matter for whom.)

But for the rest of the myth, Joe would play along nicely. If the writers were gonna try to make him a hero, what's he supposed to do—stop 'em? If they meant to turn him into the Dago poor boy who loved the Great American Game . . . if they wanted him to face down the old-world papa, and show him, in

America, dreams really do come true . . . if they needed Joe to stand for all the miracles that happen with vision, belief, and good ol' American spunk— well, why not? . . . Joe wouldn't take Vince's job— just his story.

**Charley Graham and his Seals, and Joe, center,
with his bat, 1933.**

**Running his home run all the way back
to the dugout.**

Joe DiMaggio as a rookie with the Seals, 1933.

CHAPTER 4

✦

WHEN JOE GOT THE INVITATION TO the Seals' spring training, all the boys in North Beach knew he would stick. Of course, they talked about his chances, but there wasn't any debate: at least someone from the neighborhood was going to make it. It was strange how the least forthcoming guy in their crowd (Joe was almost invisible!) came to be the one—like money in the bank. But if you knew Joe, it all went together. He had that quiet in the bottom of himself—like an absence more than anything they could name—that made him a zero, and a sure bet. They knew Joe was going to take care of business because that's all Joe did.

Of course, at that moment, no one could see it whole. But that was when the world leaned in on their lives, a time of choices—no choice was how it felt: '33 was a tough year to be chasing dreams. Niggy's glory was boxing; he'd rather fight than eat. He was training at Joe Roche's gym—got a half a dozen fights and won them all, four by knockout. He was fast on his feet, and strong for a lightweight. If he got you in a clinch, you didn't move. He was underage, so he used his father's name: "Joe (Babe) Marino," read the yellow embroidery on the back of his blue robe. The *Oakland Tribune* said he had more color than a Fourth of July parade. But he only got twenty-five or thirty-five bucks a bout. So, next day, he'd be fishing again. Niggy's dad couldn't earn a penny—arthritis in his legs—he couldn't even get out of the house. (They didn't have walkers in those days, so Papa Marino stumped around with a chair for thirty years.) Then, Niggy got a fight on the radio. His brother was listening at home. Niggy's mom kept asking, "Who's this Marino?" The brother said, "It's another guy, different family." But it got to the fourth round—the announcer's screaming, "MARINO CUT IN THE EYE! MARINO'S BLEEDIN' ALL OVER!"—and Niggy's mamma had a heart attack, right there, next to the radio. After that, she told him, "You want me to live, or what?" And Niggy went to fishing full time.

Shabby Minafo almost went Joe's route: he jumped ship from the Rossi Olive Oils, and was making ten bucks a game for Horseshoe Tavern. He was a good outfielder, and could hit a ton. He got a minor league offer from the Cincinnati Reds. But they only paid seventy-five dollars a month (and you had to buy your own equipment and food). Shabby was bringing home a hundred a month from Pacific Box. So his oldest brother said, "You ain't goin'." And Shab stayed at Pacific Box for ten years, till he went in the service.

The rest of the Rossi team finally made it to the Valley League—as high as they could go—but it didn't last. Andy Banchero took the test to become a fireman,

and after that, he was sitting in the firehouse weekends. Friggles Tomei went to work in an office and
gave up on the game. Ciccio was still a hell of a pitcher,
and a switch hitter, but his dad got sick with the dia-
betes so Ciccio had to fish. If he had any spare time, he
did his Don Juan thing with the showgirls—"American girls," as the boys called them. He had one girlfriend, Mickey Nichols, a dancer at the Lido Cafe, who
lived out west in the Avenues. Sometimes, he'd hang
around with the Powder Puff Twins (nice girls—and
they *were* twins, but they had to stuff their bras with
powder puffs to look right on stage). Most of the other
guys had North Beach girlfriends—good Italian girls
whom you had to take out weekend afternoons, and
you couldn't touch 'em or you'd have their brothers to
deal with. If the fellows played any ball now it was
with teams where they worked. Frank and Bat were
both at Simmons Bed—good ball team there—but
after a while they, too, gave up. It wasn't their team. In
the end, that's what baseball was for them: their team,
their friends . . . when that ended, it was over for them.

But not for Joe. Joe was going to take care of business because he could treat the game as business. It
wasn't all tied up in his head with friends and the
neighborhood, playground days and glorious dreams
at night. Joe was living home, on Taylor Street, but no
one from the neighborhood saw him. First, there was
the Seals' winter league squad, and then spring training. He'd come home, eat, sleep, and go train again.
When his name was in the paper, someone at the

playground would bring that up. "D'you see Joe got a write-up?" (Someone else would say, "Yeah. Joe's doin' good.") The papers called him "the shortstop from North Beach." But everything that used to be North Beach for him was left behind.

One time that winter, Frank Venezia was selling papers at his corner, and saw Joe coming back from the big sporting goods store, Hirsch & Price. Joe was getting ready for the winter league, and he had his new spikes—showed 'em to Frank.

"God, Joe, wouldn't it be something if you went all the way?" Frank knew the Seals sold players to the big leagues; and he had pictures in his head from his own night-dreams. "What if you go up to the majors? What if it's the Yankees!"

Joe didn't say anything, or even smile. It wasn't any dreamy gee-whiz to him. It was something harder, more real, from the first day. But that was nothing he would say.

Frank didn't understand that silence. He thought about that for years . . . till he gave up thinking that Joe was like him. Sometimes, people still tell Frank: *If you hadn't signed Joe up, he could've drifted out of baseball for good.* But Frank doesn't buy it anymore.

"Nah," he says. "It's like one of them oyster pearls. Somebody woulda found him."

OF COURSE, IN HARD TIMES, PEOPLE just think life is harder. It wouldn't come clear till after the fact that the Great Depression was working for Joe. Two years after the stock market crashed, Charley Graham, the Seals' boss, had decided that the slump would soon be over. So he built a million-dollar ballpark. By 1933, the new Seals Stadium was still heavily mortgaged, the team still owed rent on the old ballpark, and attendance was down—who had a quarter for a ticket? The Seals had to shuck their best-paid veterans and fill the roster with kids.

A local Italian boy who could hit was a good bet. Graham had done well with "his Latins." A Castilian left-hander with the unlikely name of Vernon Gomez was the Seals' star pitcher till '29, and then fetched a pretty $35,000 from the New York Yankees. The local shortstop, Frankie Crosetti, helped the Seals win a pennant in '31, and then was sold for a fortune— $72,000!—also to the Yanks. And in San Francisco, Italians were no longer at the bottom of the lineup. When the city fathers vowed to fight hard times with a grand new public work—the Golden Gate Bridge—they turned to the banker A. P. Giannini to make the dream real. ("We need that bridge," he said. "We'll take the bonds.") And when the great bridge broke ground (just as Joe was trying out for the Seals), the mayor with the silver shovel was the Honorable Paesano, Angelo Rossi.

Joe knew nothing of the city's demographics or the club's economics. He only knew he didn't have much time—a few games in the winter league and one month of spring training—to show he belonged with the Seals. He knew the shortstop job was held by a rising young pro named Augie Galan (who would later become an All-Star with the Cubs). And Joe had to know, in addition, that he wasn't the best rookie shortstop in camp. The best was another local kid, Tony Gomez.

Gomez had all the moves around the middle infield. He and Eddie Joost (another future big-leaguer) had formed the best double play combination in the city for their championship American Legion club. Gomez had range, quick hands, a sure throw; he could hit, he could run, he was seventeen years old, and he'd work cheap. He was perfect . . . except for one thing. Gomez came from Latin stock—he had handsome high cheekbones, black curly hair, and skin the color of coffee with a little cream. When he got to camp, started taking grounders, the first thing he heard was someone in the stands, asking, "Who's that black bastard?" Later, one of the coaches cleared everyone else off the infield, and started smashing ground balls at Gomez—trying to knock him over. Tony kept picking up everything hit at him (and making throws to Joe DiMaggio at first base) . . . until one of his legs cramped. You brought your own equipment in those days, and Gomez was wearing strips of rubber tire to hold up his stirrup socks. Gomez hobbled off and sat down. DiMaggio sidled into foul ground and muttered to him: "You better get up. Don'cha see who's up in the stands?" Charley Graham was watching from a grandstand seat—

along with his pal, the all-time great (and California retiree), Ty Cobb. But Gomez couldn't get back on the field that day, and didn't get much chance after that. Ten days later, the manager, Jimmy Caveney, took Tony aside. "Gomez," he said, "you better quit playin' ball. You're too black." Tony Gomez was finished with the Seals.

Any misstep, any problem, was grounds for a cut at the Seals' camp. There were a hundred and fifty kids on the winter league teams, sixty by the start of spring training. The impoverished Seals only meant to pay eighteen or nineteen players for the season, and there were twenty trying to come back from the '32 team. In *DiMaggio: An Illustrated Life,* Dick Johnson and Glenn Stout note the sad case of catcher Charley Wallgren, who was cut from the '33 Seals for a bad case of jock itch.

But the grim rules didn't apply to Joe. On the first day of spring training, Abe Kemp, the *Examiner*'s veteran baseball writer, was sitting in the grandstand next to Charley Graham, watching the kids at infield practice. Joe DiMaggio picked up a ball at shortstop and heaved it right past Graham's head. "I'll say one thing about that kid," Graham remarked mildly. "He's got a hell of an arm." In the Seals' last exhibition games, against the local rival Missions, Galan was benched with an injury: Joe got a start at shortstop and committed four errors. Even Abe Kemp, who called himself a Pollyanna ("If you can't write something nice about a ballplayer, don't mention his name") wrote in the *Examiner* that young DeMaggio was "doing the best he can, but appears bewildered."

Still, Joe was bound to make it—for two simple reasons: he was hitting; and no pitcher could stop him from hitting. Anyone who saw him at bat knew instantly, this was a special case. It wasn't one or two shots into the blue beyond—this wasn't a sporadic prowess: it was every time he stood at the plate, cocked his bat once at the pitcher (whatever pitcher), and then stood still and easy, feet spread about a foot apart, bat up behind his right ear, the weight of his body held effortlessly back, until he saw the pitch (whatever pitch)—whereupon he would slash it on a hard line, somewhere. Even Tony Gomez, who was contesting (he thought) for the same job, used to stop whatever he was doing and stand behind the cage to watch Joe hit. "Just a little resin bag in his back pocket . . ." Gomez recalled, more than sixty years later. "One squaring of his bat . . ." And then Gomez searched for that word—the word many people used to describe Young Joe, because it evoked not just stillness, but beauty. "Then, the guy was a *statue.*"

NO SCOUTING REPORT EVER LISTED "beauty" amid the stats on speed, arm strength, or homers. It's not a word that baseball men use. They're more given to mechanical metaphor ("Has all the tools"), or if they're really at a loss, they'll compare a kid to a known major-leaguer ("Has Colavito's arm").

But it was beauty (or something akin—classicism, grace . . .) that made the baseball men talk about Joe. Jack Kofoed, columnist for the *New York Post,* wrote up a conversation between Charley Graham and his manager, Jimmy Caveney, just after Joe DiMaggio had left the room.

"Graham looked after the loosely built six-footer, who packs 190 pounds on his athletic frame, and said:

" 'Give him a couple of years Jim, and Di Maggio is going to be one of the greatest ball players in the country.'

" 'I'm sure of it,' said Caveney.

" 'Did you ever see a better natural stance at the plate or a guy who took a freer cut at the ball?' . . .

" 'Yes, sir, he's as loose a swinger as Joe Jackson was, and that's saying something.' "

Caveney was a good baseball man. In other words, he could barely form a sentence—and seldom tried. But he'd watch the diamond for hours, mute, his eyes in a squint between his graying brows and a steaming teacup. Within the lines of that diamond he knew what to do. So that spring, he made Joe DiMaggio his project.

Caveney had been a shortstop in the early 1920s for the Cincinnati Reds, and he tried to teach Joe how to set his feet, how to snap a throw sidearm. Joe's sidearm throws would break seats behind first base. Caveney thought the kid must be pressing, thinking too much: he tried to talk with Joe, to relax him. But between those two, conversation didn't last a minute.

(Joe said two words: "Yes" and "sir.") On a hunch, Caveney tried the kid at first base. But the footwork at first has to be quick, light, precise, like a dance . . . and the hunch proved wrong: Joe couldn't dance.

Or maybe, to be fair, Caveney was half-right: Joe couldn't dance *and* think. At the plate, his footwork was flawless. (There wasn't much—one quick stride from his stance and his whole body was into the swing.) But it was clear Joe didn't have to think at the plate—or worry. As a hitter, he had total and marvelous confidence. It was the one thing in his life where he'd always been better than anybody else. He didn't have to figure it out, or explain it. He couldn't explain it. Unlike the other phenom from the Coast League, Ted Williams (who would sign with San Diego in 1935), DiMaggio never tried to turn hitting into science. "It has always been a theory of mine," he said in *Lucky to Be a Yankee,* "that hitting is a God-given gift, like being able to run fast, or throw hard." Even near the end of his career, after he'd studied the game for twenty years, Joe's theory remained the same. When the young catcher Larry Berra made bold one day to ask the eminence, Joe, how to approach a certain pitcher, DiMaggio snapped: "Just walk up to the plate and *hit* the ball. There's no talent involved."

That no-talent was Joe's ticket. "Caveney," Abe Kemp reported in the *Examiner,* "has a problem on his hands finding a spot for Joe DeMaggio. As a shortstop this lad has little to commend him, but as a hitter he attracts attention." That was a cautious Kempian understatement: Joe was something more than interesting. But the assessment of Caveney's problem was correct: it wasn't whether to keep Joe, but where.

By the time spring training began, Charley Graham was already negotiating Joe's contract with his oldest brother, Tom. (Unlike brother Vince, Joe was going to be a family business.) In *Lucky to Be a Yankee,* Gary-Cooper DiMaggio said that first contract took him by surprise. They just called him to the office one day, and there it was—two hundred twenty-five dollars a month. (How nice!) *". . . and I put my John Hancock on the dotted line without any hesitation or conversation whatsoever. I don't think I ever since signed a contract in baseball, even my first one with the Yankees, which gave me as big a kick as that original contract with San Francisco."* . . . But in the real world, the bargaining went on for more than a month: offer and counteroffer, back and forth, Tom and Mr. Graham, until the DiMaggios pushed the Seals to double what most rookies made. Then it was Giuseppe, not (the underaged) Joe, who was summoned to the office and that dotted line . . . upon which the old man painstakingly—but happily—signed. That two twenty-five was also twice what Giuseppe had made in the best month of his whole laboring life.

WHEN THE SEALS BROKE CAMP, AT the end of March, Joe's position was listed as "utility"—which was to say, in the field, he was of no utility. But Caveney was still trying. In the third game of the season, eighth inning, Seals behind, the manager sent Joe in to pinch-hit for the right fielder. Joe quietly flied out. But for the ninth, Caveney told him to go play right field. Joe thought he must be joking—unlikely in Caveney's case—or he must have meant Vince, who was still with the club, but riding the bench with his sore arm. Or what about "Prince" Henry Oana, the veteran Hawaiian? He could play. Joe said to Vince: "I never played right field in my life." Vince said: "I know . . . but you're going to start now." So Joe stood in right field for the last inning, luckily untroubled by any fly balls. And after that game, both Vince and Oana were cut from the club.

That spring was wet and cold; the fans were staying away in droves. And the Seals were cutting everyone with serious experience and salary. There were rumors that Seattle was going to fold, and that would have made the Pacific Coast League crumble. In fact, all the PCL owners were talking about shutting down for the year—they'd try to start up again in 1934. (They might have done it, but the baseball commissioner, Kenesaw Mountain Landis, threatened to make all their players free agents.)

So, whether he knew it or not, Joe was going to play, and perform—or he'd be fired, too. What he did know was he was suddenly alone. He'd come into that clubhouse as "Vince's kid brother," but now

Vince was gone. Joe had made the club (he thought) as the fill-in shortstop. But now he would find himself bouncing between right field and center—great expanses in the new Seals Stadium—both equally mysterious to him. He was eighteen years old, he'd never been away from home. He didn't know anybody—or how to get to know them. He didn't have the gift of the glad hand or ready smile, and had not a word for the writers in the clubhouse. He was startled when he read an early description of himself in the paper: "a gawky, awkward kid, all arms and legs like a colt, and inclined to be surly." But that was how he seemed. The other Seals saw him in the corner—silent, smoking, making (as they saw it) no effort to be friendly—so they left him alone. And he floundered.

He went at his outfield job like a Sicilian fisherman—alone out there in the weather, talking to no one, vaguely suspicious, treating anything that came his way as a threat. The outfield played to two of his strengths: he could run—even if he was fooled on a ball, he might make up the ground with pure speed—and he could throw as hard as he wanted. In fact, in his first start in right, two Portland baserunners tried to filch extra bases, and he gunned them both down. That convinced Caveney he could get along with Joe in the field. But through most of April, Joe was stumbling along with a .250 average—anemic by PCL standards—and the Seals were awful. They had marched (largely unwitnessed from the grandstand) straight to the Coast League cellar, with nine wins and eighteen losses.

With any other hitter, it would have been safe to assume that the pitchers had caught on: someone had found a way to get Joe out, and after that, well, word travels fast. But Joe wasn't any other hitter: he could hit any pitch, any pitcher alive, when he was right. Of course, at that point, no one could be sure—least of all Joe. But there were indications that his problems were mostly from the neck up. Near the end of April, the desperate Seals re-signed Vince DiMaggio for two weeks—and for those two weeks, Joe hit over .300.

But then, May 8, Vince was cut from the team again, and Joe sank like a scuttled boat. He wasn't hitting for average (he was *under* .250); he wasn't hitting for power (one extra-base hit in fifty at bats). If the Seals hadn't been in such desperate shape (they even tried a pitcher, Jimmy Zinn, in the outfield), Joe's chance might have been over.

On May 28, last day of a home stand, the Seals played a doubleheader and won both. The first was a laugher, 10–2—though not for Joe: he went oh-for-four. The second game, the Seals won 3–1, Joe hit a double. And suddenly (was Mamma Rosalie at work at home?) the evil eye was gone. The Seals went north for a doubleheader at Seattle: Joe went six-for-ten, his best day yet in professional ball. Five more games against Seattle: Joe hit in all of them—two hits in four of the games, two home runs in the series.

Back home for a full week of games against Oakland: Joe got a hit in every game—.400 for the series.

And just as suddenly, the Seals were winning. At least they won as often as they lost. (They still didn't have any pitching, but if they gave up fewer than ten runs, they had a chance.) Seattle came in for the next week: the scores show what kind of games they were (7–5, 8–5, 12–5, 9–6). But the Seals won half of them, and Joe hit in all of them—for an average of .520 in that series.

No San Francisco writer would call this a streak, yet—not a mere twenty-three straight games. The PCL was a batter's league, and a lot of guys kept hitting for two or three weeks before they cooled off. (When Joe got his first hit in that May 28 double-header, the opposition Portland outfielder, George Blackerby, was at the close of a thirty-six-game spree—still well short of the league-record forty-nine.) If any writer did think of DiMaggio-and-streak, they'd have reckoned, surely someone would stop him soon. In fact, the next day, at the start of a series with the local rival Missions, Johnny Babich almost did.

Babich was only one year older than Joe, and at the start of a career that would carry him to the Dodgers and Braves, and on to a reputation as a "Yankee Killer" with the Philadelphia A's. He'd come from the lumber country up North, and signed with the Seals, but when they wouldn't give him the contract he wanted, he jumped crosstown to the Missions. He was a big right-hander, a power pitcher, and a tough competitor. That year, he would win twenty games with the last-place Missions; and that day, in Seals Stadium, no one could touch him. Babich was out to show the Seals that he'd been worth every dime he asked for.

But for once, the Seals also got good pitching—from the sometimes-outfielder Jimmy Zinn. (That's another reason Babich wanted that game—Zinn was his old Seals roommate.) In the bottom of the eighth, it was still 0–0, and DiMaggio was hitless. But then the Seals' new center fielder, Elias Funk, got on with a double. And Babich tried to throw a fastball past Joe . . . who hit a line drive to left—a white blur through the late, slanting light. By the time the left fielder turned and took two steps, the ball was over his head, and it crashed into the left field wall and rolled away while DiMaggio rolled around to third. That triple knocked in the only run—a run neither Joe nor Babich would forget. Zinn and the Seals won 1–0. And Joe was their new game-breaker.

The next day Joe went two-for-three, and once again, his hit in the ninth knocked home the run that made the difference. The Seals won 6–5, and in the clubhouse they all came to shake his hand. No one could stop him when he was right, and now everything was right in Joe's world. When Vince got a job with the Hollywood team, the Stars, that monkey was off Joe's back: the DiMaggio boys were both playing, at last. It was three DiMaggio boys, in fact: little

Dommie got his name in the paper as the infield star for his Boys Club and Legion teams. (Dommie didn't have Joe's God-given power, but he was smart and he worked hard on his game. And when he got his glasses, and could finally see the ball at the plate . . . well, all of Giuseppe's sons could swing the bat.) Now the flat on Taylor Street was a baseball industry, with Giuseppe as the proud proprietor.

The old man no longer went out to fish, but he still woke by habit in the dark before dawn. Now, he didn't go for his boat, but for the *Chronicle*, the morning paper. Giuseppe still couldn't read a lick, but he knew the Sporting Section was the one on green paper. And he knew the Seals' box score would be on that green front page. His thick index finger would count down the Seals' order—one, two, three—till he got to the only name he could recognize: "J. DeMaggio." He knew the first number after the name was how many times Joe came to bat, the second was how many hits. If Joe got a hit, Giuseppe would put down the paper, satisfied, maybe have a cup of coffee. If it was more than one hit, the coffee could wait: he had to wake Rosalie to tell her.

In those days, there was often more than one. Through the series with the Missions, Joe hit in every game, at a .440 clip. Now, there were plenty of people who'd talk about Young Joe's "streak." Abe Kemp noted in the *Examiner* that "De Maggio" had hit safely in thirty straight games, though the kid ("greatly improved," Kemp conceded) still had a long climb before he'd threaten the mark of old Jack Ness, first-sacker for the Oakland Oaks, who had hit for forty-nine straight in the summer after Joe was born.

The Seals were on their way to L.A., where the Angels' ace, tough Bobo Newsom, almost justified Kemp's caution. Newsom was a bear: six foot three, more than two hundred pounds; he was twenty-six, had appeared three years in the majors already, and still had another twenty years in his arm. He would win thirty games for the Angels that year, and in L.A.'s Wrigley Field, he had DiMaggio handcuffed all day . . . until the ninth, when Joe got his last chance. The kid cocked his dark hickory bat once, then took his statue's stance. *Whack!* A bullet, line drive, base hit. And then, a strange thing happened: though Newsom was their hero and the Angels their team, the Wrigley fans gave an audible cheer.

Wherever the Seals played, the crowds were growing: people wanted to see this kid hit. When the Seals came home, and Joe's streak stood at thirty-seven games, the word was out in San Francisco. More than five thousand fans came to 16th and Bryant, Seals Stadium, for the start of the series with the Hollywood Stars. Of course, it was a big day, the July Fourth doubleheader. But when Joe hit in each of those games, the lead on the sports page wasn't "Seals, Stars Split a Pair." The Seals were nowhere in the pennant race—the only story in San Francisco baseball was "Young Joe." Even the most conservative writer on the beat, the *Chronicle*'s statesman in residence, Ed. R. Hughes, had trouble getting the result of the game into his first paragraph, when the kid's streak turned forty and the record was in sight: "Young Joe De Maggio of the Seals, who is on his way to tie the record for batting in consecutive games set in 1915, had to wait until the eighth inning yesterday to get his hit, but when he got it, [it was] a good one, a line drive to left field good for two bases. He has now hit safely in 40 consecutive games. But that hit did not save the Seals, for Hollywood won the game 4 to 3."

Some of the writers dropped the news of the games completely: their stories were just about Joe. Some took the family angle, asking Vince DiMaggio, "fly-chaser for the Hollywood club," what he would do if his kid brother needed a bingle to keep the streak going, and hit the ball toward him. ("I would stand on my ear to try to get the ball," said the soldierly Vincent.) There were discussions of the rival pitchers' sportsmanship. (In nine games with the Stars in that series—two doubleheaders in a week-long visit—no one would walk Young Joe to keep him from hitting.) There were comments from the avuncular manager, Caveney, and the scout who got credit for finding the kid, Spike Hennessy, about Joe's surprising talent. ("The best natural hitter since Paul Waner . . .") The writers mined comment from the injured third baseman, Leo Ostenberg, who revealed that he gave the kid a "pep talk" before each at bat, and had counseled him (Ostenberg was a dapper professional) that it wasn't good form to wear a bright yellow shirt around a hotel lobby. But "Young Joe De Maggio" still had nothing to say for himself. Abe Kemp ran an interview with Joe in which the whole column was Kemp's questions: Joe's responses were grunts or shrugs. By the close of the series with the Stars, the *Chronicle*'s Hughes started covering gestures—noting, with a touch of asperity, the North Beach boy's lack of drama: "Young Joe is probably scared half to death as he nears the hitting record of Ness, but he does not show it in his actions. [His] face is so expressionless that some one has called him 'Dead Pan Joe.' Even Buster Keaton himself could not show less emotion. The customers are all pulling for Joe, but until last Saturday he showed no sign that he knew it. But that day, after he had walloped two hits in the first game, and got one his first time up in the second game, he touched the rim of his cap in acknowledgement of the applause."

Up in the press box, they all called him Dead Pan, and complained to one another. But what could they do? The Seals needed a hero. San Francisco needed a story. And here was a local kid who'd come from baseball-nowhere to flirt with history—on their beat! So they wrote up his silence as humility, courage, mute concentration in pursuit of his American dream. Uncle Charley Graham was raking in the money at the turnstiles; attendance had doubled, and was climbing still. People would come to the game (it seemed like half the crowd was talking Italian) and after Joe got his hit, they'd leave. What the hell, they still paid their quarters. From the headlines, you couldn't even tell there'd been a game—just Joe. Here's the eight-column screamer from the Sporting Green, after the first game of a series with the L.A. Angels:

DE MAGGIO HITS IN 47TH STRAIGHT
Local Youth
Near Record
Of Jack Ness
Line Drive in Third Fol-
lows Intentional
Walk in First
Inning

The papers, the Seals, and the city were (literally) banking on Joe. Charley Graham started planning and publicizing a celebration for the next night game, which would be the fiftieth of Young Joe's Streak, when he would set the new record. Graham ordered a fancy watch, engraved to mark the occasion. And that was when he finally asked Joe how to spell his name. Graham told the writers Joe's response: "Aw, spell it any way you want to." (But Graham persisted and learned it was "DiMaggio.") . . . It would have been an awful letdown if he'd fallen short at that point—(perhaps) for Joe, (and surely) for the team, the fans, the town. In our age, it would be the kind of thing for which they'd call in therapists—to counsel the grieving victims in the aftermath. But it wasn't just a simpler age back then. It was Joe. What made everyone so cocksure was that quiet his North Beach pals knew—the same thing the writers all complained about—that was his armor. Dead Pan Joe was not going to fall victim to the pressure (what pressure?), the hoopla, or anything else. In the forty-eighth game he hit a double to drive in a run. In the forty-ninth game, to tie the record, he hit a single on the first pitch he saw in the first inning, a home run on the first pitch he saw in the fourth, and a line drive single, for good measure, in the eighth.

The Seals were so certain that Joe would take care of business the next night, they held the ceremony for his new record before the fiftieth game even started. The Honorable Paesano, Mayor Angelo Rossi, presented the gold watch from Charley Graham. The Jolly Knights were in attendance, to present Joe with a fine leather traveling bag. The Seals gave him a check. (And why not: the crowd of ten thousand in the Stadium that night would pay Joe's salary for the year.) Then Giuseppe and Rosalie DiMaggio were invited onto the field—the old man in his fedora—and introduced like ambassadors to the home plate umpire, shaken by the hand by Charley Graham, and kissed (to great huzzahs from the crowd) by Mayor Rossi. Then Joe, with his arms full of flowers, walked Rosalie to the Seals bench, while their fellow San Franciscans rained cheers upon mother and son. . . . Reaction from Joe? There was none. That was for the writers to make up. (Said the *Chronicle,* next morning: "No doubt the youngster was pleased, as who wouldn't be?")

Well, here was his reaction:

In the top of the first, the Angels looked like they would bat forever—five hits, three runs . . . until DiMaggio captured a drive to right field and threw a BB to the plate to double up the L.A. runner trying to score. Side retired, the Seals came in to hit. There was a base hit by the leadoff man, Sever, a walk to Galan, and both men moved up on an infield ground ball: runners on second and third, one out—and Young Joe at bat for the first time. Photographers edged closer and closer to the plate, pans of flashpowder held toward the kid's face. On the mound, big, glowering Bobo Newsom humped up and threw the ball as hard as he could . . . the powder flared in a shock of lurid white . . . the kid swung and missed. The crowd was standing, screaming for Joe, booing the photographers. The Seals were bellowing at Newsom and the ump. ("Get those bastards outa his face!") Charley Graham jumped over the box seat railing, onto the field, and ordered the photographers away from the plate. With a rolled-up program, Graham beat the cameramen back from the foul line. Newsom threw again. Joe swung—*crack!*—and the ball took off on a line, past Newsom's ear, and safely into center field for two Seals runs . . . for history and the record . . . for the triumph of truth, justice, the American Game, and its thousands of new San Francisco fans.

"Joe De Maggio," wrote Ed. R. Hughes (who, in the excitement, hadn't quite caught up with the spelling), "18-year-old batting sensation of the Coast League, either has nerves of steel, or he has no nerves at all."

Reaction from Joe? He just kept going. He hit in every game with the Angels, and then it was off to Sacramento—and the biggest crowds ever seen there—half of 'em screaming for the San Francisco rookie, half for the hometown Senators to stop him. After one game in which Joe's only hit was a ground ball that the shortstop couldn't field cleanly, irate fans stormed the press box. The official scorer, Steve George, sports editor of the *Sacramento Bee,* had to be escorted from the ballpark by police.

Truth be told, a bit of help from the scorer (or the shortstop) wasn't out of the question. They were all, one way or another, in the baseball business. And this mute boy with nerves of steel had saved the season—put the fans back in the seats. But now, it was clear, the kid was tired (though of course he wouldn't say so). In the last week, his hits were bleeders and bloopers—too many balls never got past the infield . . . until at last, against Oakland, in his sixty-second game, Young Joe was stopped. The writers said he must be relieved. DiMaggio didn't say that—or anything else.

He finished the year at .340, with his name misspelled nationwide by the Associated Press, with his picture in *The Sporting News,* with rumors flying that some major league club was offering $40,000 for him (or was it $60,000?) . . . and with the certainty that he'd done what he came to do: he'd made himself a big-time pro player, a kid with a future, a success in his father's house—and in North Beach, where his name would be honored, and where he could spend all the winter months. And he wouldn't have to lift a finger.

OF COURSE, THE OLD NORTH BEACH crowd was excited when Joe came back. He'd been living home (at least half the nights) during the whole season, but somehow they hadn't seen him.

Niggy Marino saw him first. Nig was on his way to the whorehouse, Peggy's, at Columbus and Taylor—Peggy was Niggy's pal. She'd gone to all his fights, bought him his fightin' togs, shoes and everything—and that beautiful blue robe. Even after he quit boxing, Niggy was a good customer.

All of a sudden, Niggy heard Joe's deep voice: "Where you goin'?"

"Hey! I'm goin' to get a piece o' keister. You wanna come?"

"Aw, Nig, I don't have any money." (That much hadn't changed.)

"Awright, you sonofabitch, come on. I'll pay for ya." Niggy knew Joe had more money than all of 'em put together. But, hell—what's a buck and a half? Nig was proud to buy Joe his first girl.

All the rest of the guys would have done anything—everything—for Joe, too. He'd made them proud. He'd mastered the world that they'd only dreamed about. But they couldn't think of a thing they could do for him. They thought, maybe, he'd want a job. Most ballplayers had jobs in the winter. But Joe said, no, he just wanted to rest. They would have bought him food—they were always offering. But Joe said he didn't want to eat extra and put on weight—that could be a problem.

What they wanted was just to spend time with him, to hang around, like before . . . to hear all about his new world, about the Seals, and the pitchers from the other clubs, and Caveney and Charley Graham, and Portland—and Hollywood! But Joe didn't say much.

Tell the truth, he wasn't around much. And when he did come around, he wasn't alone. There was a guy with him, a new guy. They knew who he was: he was older, Tom's age—one of Tom's friends—Shirts De-Marco. (Everybody called him Shirts; no one knew why. His real name was Tony.) And now he went everywhere with Joe, like a shadow.

Joe would come out, and the guys would say hello, and they'd be starting to talk—nothing special, just hanging out—but the minute they got talking, Shirts would break in.

"Joe. You want anything?"

"Joe—you want a sandwich?"

"Joe. You want I bring you a Coke? . . ."

Joe and Lefty O'Doul, 1935.

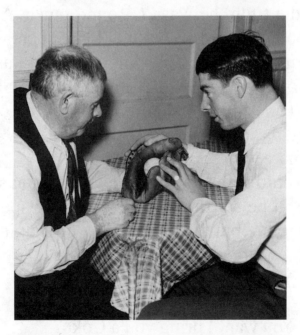

**Baseball, as Giuseppe DiMaggio
learned, was the most excellent game.**

And Joe got stiffed—he's peelin' potatoes.

CHAPTER 5

✦

IT WAS AN ODD WAY TO BECOME A
man—instantly and in the public view—but by the
time Joe DiMaggio turned nineteen and signed for a
second year with the Seals, he was the man on that
club, a big man for the league. The Coast League of
the 1930s wasn't like the minors we think of today—
a bunch of kids packing dreams and acne cream on
the bus for a summer or two. (And, hey, if it doesn't
work out, there's always college.) The National and
American Leagues had not yet pushed west of St.
Louis: in the other half of the nation, the PCL *was* the
big league. There were men on every club who'd
done their years in Chicago, New York, Pittsburgh
. . . and then went west to play out the string—in better weather, often at the same salary. For that matter,
there were men who wouldn't go to the majors: they
wouldn't take a pay cut for Boston, or Philadelphia.
There were players who did ten or fifteen seasons, all
in the PCL—some always waiting for that big year
that would send them back east, but most just working men who made their living from baseball.

And a serious sort of living it was. The guaranteed
contract was fifty years away—if you got hurt, you

lost your job, simple as that. (And oftentimes, the doctor bills were yours, too.) You took what you could get from your club, your owner—and earned it. If you lost your spot in the lineup, your pink slip was probably on its way. (A hundred boys were hungering to take your place.) And while you played, you played to win: postseason money was, for most men, the difference between a good year and just another year older. So, Joe had to make the move, in one year, from a boy among boys to a man among men . . . which he did, on the field; what he didn't know, he covered with his silence.

For nine innings, every afternoon (or in the evenings, Tuesdays and Fridays), he was the best player on the Seals—smarter every day in right field, fast and clever on the basepaths, and the best hitter his teammates had ever seen. But it wasn't just the skills: on the field, he did everything right—seriously, like a veteran. Before the game, he shagged his flies, took ground balls, and loosened his arm properly. He took his turn in the cage and worked on his stroke, with purpose. He learned the pitchers (not just the opposition, but his own pitchers—where to play behind them). He ran out his ground balls and pop-ups. He backed up his center fielder, hit his cutoff men. When the Seals needed runs, and he had a chance to drive them in, he wouldn't pass the buck and work a base on balls. He wanted to win, and he had a winner's instinct. And even more: he was correct in those matters that went beyond that day's game. He didn't beef, and make enemies of umpires. He never riled the other team, and made them play harder. If he hit a home run, he ran it out, all the way to the bench, and didn't make a show that some pitcher would remember.

One time (once in his life) he got in a fight on the field: that was his first year, after his batting streak had made him persona non grata with a lot of pitchers in that league. The game was at Oakland, and the Seals were hammering the Oaks' southpaw, Roy Joiner, early and often that day. In the first inning, on a play at the plate, Joiner had to cover; DiMaggio came streaking down from third, and slid in hard. Joe was out, but Joiner said something (it was about Joe's mamma, or pretty near). So Joe squared off and tried to hit him. But Joe couldn't fight, and Joiner could. He floored the kid with a left, the benches emptied, everybody stormed the plate, pushing and shoving . . . until Joe stood up, and Joiner hit him again. Joe went down with Joiner on top of him; the other players finally pulled Joiner off, and the game resumed. Joiner pitched six scoreless innings after that. But DiMaggio still went two-for-four.

And that was his only problem on the diamond. Apart from his poor fisticuffs, he just got better. For the first two months of his second season, he was hitting .370, knocking in an average of a run every game. But baseball wasn't just a job, it was a life. And off the field, Joe couldn't quite catch up. He'd left most of his old friends behind. New friends—he didn't seem to want to make any . . . or he just didn't know how.

OTHER THAN JOE, THE STAR OF THE club was Sam Gibson, a big right-hander who'd win twenty-one games with the Seals that year. But Gibson was fifteen years older than Joe—he'd already spent five years with the Tigers, Yankees, and Giants back east—a fussy old Southerner who never talked much to the kids he now played with . . . save to pace the dugout, clucking: "Gimme some runs, now. Git some runs, y'all. Ah need 'em."

The other famous Seal, in '34, was Noble Winfield "Old Pard" Ballou, one of the first relief-pitching specialists in organized ball. He had a big overhand curveball—he called it his drop-pitch, or downer— that was murder on anxious late-inning hitters: they'd just beat it into the ground. Pard had also done four years in the majors, with the Senators, Browns, and Dodgers (and with indifferent success). He was thirty-seven, even older than Gibson—who used to reward him, when he saved a win, with a bottle of Old Grand-Dad, the whiskey from Pard's home state of Kentucky. Alas, by the time Joe came along, Grand-Dad was Pard's best friend. You'd see him in the early innings, asleep in the bullpen from last night's exertions; and then around the middle of the game, Pard would disappear. In the late innings, if a pitcher got in trouble, the batboy, little Artie Dikas, would have to jump in a car and race around the left field fence to the Double Play Tavern, where he'd find Ballou, with his head on the bar. "Pard! Come on! You're goin' in!" So Pard would get back to Seals Stadium, take ten or fifteen warm-up throws . . . they'd bring him in—bases loaded, no one out—and after nine or ten of his famous downers, Pard would have them out of the inning.

(The other guy who drank was Frankie Hawkins, third baseman for Oakland, and then for the Seals. If he didn't drink, he would have been great—but he drank ugly. Jigger Statz, the L.A. Angels center fielder, robbed him of hits three times in one day, and after the game, when Frankie's wife came to get him at the locker room, he punched her in the mouth. She left him.)

Most of the younger guys stuck to beer after games, except for special occasions. A lot of them were family men who'd disappear after home games, and you wouldn't see them till BP the next day. On the road, they went to a ton of movies. Guys who'd been around the league a few times would have friends, people to see, dinners to go to in this town or that. Even rookies would get dined around— ballplayers were royalty everywhere they went—by friends, friends of friends, or some ethnic or fraternal group. Steve Barath, a young third baseman who was Joe's roommate on the road for a while, used to get invitations from Hungarians in every city. The Italian groups wanted to feed and fete the second baseman,

Art Garibaldi—and, of course, most of all, they wanted Young Joe. But only Garibaldi would attend. Joe turned down all invitations. There'd be strangers. He wouldn't know what to say.

The veterans (married or not-anymore) would have "special friends" around the circuit—ladies whom they'd visited over the years. But that was strictly a winking matter, seldom talked about and never flaunted. That delicacy wasn't about their wives back home, or morality of any sort—except the baseball sort: with curfew at midnight (or two hours after a night game), you weren't supposed to be partying too hard, or too long. (When Rabbit Maranville, the old Boston shortstop, made manager, he used to tell his players: "If you can't get in her pants in two hours, you call me.") But, tell the truth, women just came—or came and went—with the life.

Most night games at Seals Stadium were Ladies' Nights. Any female got in for fifteen cents (just the price of the tax). In fact, that was one big reason there *was* a new Seals Stadium. Up until 1931, the Seals had played at Recreation Field, the aptly named "Old Rec." One feature of that park was the betting section in the upper stands. (It wasn't exactly legal, but no one bothered the bookies up there; they took wagers on the game, the inning, or the batter.) And then, too, down the first base line, there was the "Booze Cage," a section of seats separated from the field by only ten or twelve feet and a chain link fence, where the price of a ticket also bought a shot or a beer. (In Prohibition, that turned illegal, too, but they'd serve mixers, and you could bring your own bathtub hooch.) Old Rec was a great place to watch a game, but it was a stag affair. With Mr. Graham's new million-dollar "palace," baseball bid to become—had to become—a respectable entertainment for "mixed company."

Since the Great War, and through the 1920s, more and more girls had gone to work outside their homes—at least, until they married. They had money, independence, and free time. Why shouldn't they be fans? It wasn't a feminist matter: there was no parallel interest in a women's league, or girls teams at school. In fact, the ballpark was alluring, especially, as a male place—as smart and stylish for a girl-about-town as smoking (over highballs!) at a table near the dance floor, or showing up in furs at a heavy-weight fight. In fact, for most working girls, the ball-park was even better—cheaper, for one thing (and you could tell your parents you'd been there)—the kind of place you could go with your girlfriends, all dressed up in heels and gloves, or a sundress with a picture hat on weekend afternoons. So there they'd be, laughing together, pointing, or waving at the boys in those caps and flannels—especially at that shy, slender hero, Joe DiMaggio. *"Joe! Joe! Hit a home run!"* . . . *"Yoo hoo! Joe! Hit one for me?"*

Mostly, Joe wouldn't even look up. (What if she talked to him, and he had to talk back?) . . . On the road, his roomie, Steve Barath, used to go to the dime-a-dance joints. But Joe didn't know how to dance, and he wasn't going to pay a dime to learn. "He was just backward," Barath recalled. "He'd just sit in the hotel with *The Sporting News* from St. Louis, checking a lot of guys' averages. I lived with him for weeks and we never even had a conversation."

Still, there was one girl at Seals Stadium, a local girl—and not just local San Francisco, but North Beach. That's how he found out her name: Lucille. He knew the people she was with. And she was gorgeous. And then she started coming to all the games—he knew she was watching him. So for a few weeks, he was on alert about that. He looked up Ciccio LaRocca (Ciccio knew all the girls, Joe figured) and asked about her, actually *talked* about her! But then it got to talking with her, and that was harder. And she was Italian, so that meant parents—you had to meet the family. And she was North Beach, so the parents knew parents who knew parents . . . and it got to the point, someone asked Joe: How was Lucille? And that was the end. Joe shied like a startled horse. He liked girls fine, as far as that went. But he liked it better when no one knew his business.

See, Joe had to have a private life, almost before he had a life. He was, after all, Giuseppe's son; and if the old man wouldn't reveal his sins, even to a priest, well, neither would the son—though in Joe's case, his sins were hardly mortal. Joe had a funny attitude about people watching him. He was sure they always did. That was fine on the ballfield, where he could be perfect, or pretty near. But any other time, anywhere he might show at a disadvantage—well, it made him edgy. From the start, he had to have it both ways: he wanted to be well known at what he was known for— and for the rest, he wouldn't be known at all.

Joe used to let Ciccio see him with girls, because Ciccio knew girls—and he'd known Joe forever. They'd gone to school together, they'd played for Rossi Oil. They used to fight all the time—wouldn't talk for weeks—but they'd still play together. The fact was, Joe now had use for Ciccio's style, the way he talked to girls, the way he'd drive them around. (Ciccio was just a fisherman—thirty-five dollars was a good week for him—but he always could get a car. And he knew how to drive. Joe couldn't drive worth a damn; it made him nervous.) Ciccio used to needle him about being tongue-tied. "You don't know what to say? How 'bout, 'Hello'?" Joe would just smile, shrug, and take it. That's why Ciccio was the only one who knew about Vi Koski. She was the first girl who stuck.

She was about Joe's age—eighteen, nineteen— when Joe saw her at the ballpark. Violet Koski was from Finnish stock (she lived in West Portal, safely out of Joe's neighborhood)—slender, with brown hair and fair skin. She was lovely, and she had spunk. Violet worked at Stein's Drug Store at Stockton and Sutter streets, and on her days off she'd come to Seals Stadium. Joe saw her sitting behind the dugout. "C'MONNN JOE! HIT A HOME RUN!" She talked to him one day, and when he didn't answer, she talked to him again. That's how it was: she kind of asked him out. He made Ciccio go with him to the drugstore to see her. (As Ciccio says, "He wouldn't go no place alone.") And then Joe wanted to double-date: Ciccio would take out Vi's little sister, Toinie.

Ciccio and Toinie would go with Joe and Vi to the Steins' house. They were the drugstore owners, and lived on the far side of the Twin Peaks tunnel. Joe would just sit there, silent, and Violet would talk— she could chatter—or Ciccio and Toinie would talk. Sometimes, the four would go out on the boat, if Ciccio got a trip organized. It was okay for Ciccio to see that, too. He knew how Joe was supposed to hate the sea, didn't like to fish, couldn't stand the smell . . . all that was true, sort of. But Joe didn't mind the smell if he was fishing just to screw around. He liked a boat fine if it was Ciccio's boat, taking Joe and Violet, Toinie and Ciccio, out to Paradise Cove, behind Alcatraz, toward Strawberry Point, with a big pot for pasta, and some Dago bread, and wine. (Joe's father still made wine, just as Ciccio's had before he took sick.) They'd cook the pasta, picnic, swim, and drink. And then the couples would separate, to "explore" some recondite bit of terrain.

After a while, Toinie and Ciccio started fighting. So then Toinie went with Ciccio's brother, Pete. Ciccio would bring along Mickey Nichols, the dancer from the Lido Cafe. Ciccio had to be there, not just for the boat, but so Joe would be easy. Joe had to have one of his guys along, mostly Ciccio or Shirts, or he'd be nervous. When the Seals were in town, and Joe got an off day, Ciccio would stay home from fishing. Joe would get up and get breakfast by ten or eleven, then walk the block and a half to Ciccio's house to pick him up. They'd go straight to LaRocca's Corner and play *Briscola* all day. It was a four-man card game— you made points, taking tricks: the Queen counted two, Jack and King were four, Ace was eleven, and treys were worth ten. It was complicated, but Joe was sharp, a good gambler, a card-counter; he'd win all the time. Every couple of weeks, Joe would have to go for an interview—with Prescott Sullivan, the columnist at the *Examiner,* or the *Ernie Smith Show* on the local radio. (Smith liked to put Joe on at least once a month.) Then Ciccio couldn't go fishing. First of all, he had to drive. And anyway, Joe wouldn't go alone. In the interviews, Joe would answer the questions: "yes," or "no." (Radio or print, it was all the same.) "Well, Joe, you certainly have gotten off to a wonderful start. To what do you attribute your success?" And Joe would say: "Aw, I don't know." . . . But afterward, he'd ask Ciccio two or three times: "How was that?" Ciccio had to tell him, "You were fine." "You sounded great." Joe would ask: "You don't think it was too much?"

In all, it was a neat system, well controlled, the prototype of the DiMaggio life. At home, he had his family to take care of his person and his business. (Tom had worked out a nice raise for Joe's second contract.) He had Ciccio and Shirts as buffers against the predations of society, whenever he left the house. On the road, he was always with the team, among whose members no one knew him well. He had Vi, and no one at home (or on the team) knew anything about her. His tracks were covered—as they would always remain. But then, late May, in his second year with the Seals, Joe's new life almost crumbled.

IT WAS MAY 20, 1934; OR, MORE likely, the wee hours of May 21—the date is in question, like everything else.

The Seals were in town, winding up a series with the Hollywood Stars—led by their slugging outfielder, Vince DiMaggio. During that week, the Seals and the San Francisco sporting press beat the drum repeatedly to promote the rivalry between the two brothers. Feature stories retailed anew how Joe took Vince's job, how their fisherman father had never liked baseball, how the boys had learned to hit with oars . . . all the old chestnuts were roasting that week. Joe and Vince made some joint broadcasts on the local radio, giving baseball tips to the hometown kids—which was also good for attendance . . . and a fine crowd appeared for the big windup, a Sunday doubleheader, Family Day at Seals Stadium.

This much is known: the whole DiMaggio clan was invited to mark the celebration. Both Vince and Joe went two-for-seven. The Seals and Stars split the two games. And when the second game was called on account of darkness, all the families in attendance adjourned, to further celebrate their familyhood.

Here's how Joe told the subsequent events, in *Lucky to Be a Yankee:*

"After a double-header at Seal Park in June, I went to the home of one of my married sisters for dinner. It had been a long day at the ball park and when dinner was over, I decided to take a jitney cab home. I was riding in close quarters, cramped, and my left foot must have fallen asleep from the awkward position in which I was sitting. Getting out of the cab, I put that leg on the pavement first, with all my weight on it. Down I went, as though I had been shot.

"There was no twisting, just four sharp cracks at the knee, and I couldn't straighten out the leg. The pain was terrific, like a whole set of aching teeth in my knee, and I don't know yet why I didn't pass out.

"There was a movie house nearby, the Milane, and a friend of mine, whom I knew only as Frank, was the manager. He drove me to the Emergency Hospital. . . ."

Well, as they said in the movies of the day: that was his story—and he was sticking to it. He told the same tale in 1989, in Volume I of *The DiMaggio Albums* . . . with a couple of new details:

"Before the next game I telephoned the manager of the Seals, Ike Caveney, and told him I was in a lot of pain and couldn't walk. Charley Graham, the club president, sent a physician over to see me. He determined it was a torn cartilage. Later he put my leg in an aluminum splint from ankle to buttock, which I wore for what seemed the longest six weeks of my life. After it was taken off, I tried to come back that season, but couldn't."

The problem is, all the details—old and new—are wrong, or at least they don't mesh with the few known facts. The date, the location, the events, and the aftermath are all a confection—cotton-hero-candy—that were used for the next sixty years to show how the fates threw Joe into peril, but with pluck, faith (and a smile from Above), the Hero's Life proceeded.

The *Examiner* did the honest spadework: the overnight city staff talked to the hospital, and got the police reports. In the next day's *Examiner,* the story said: "Joe DiMaggio, ace slugger and outfielder of the Seals, suffered injury to his knee early this morning when he fell entering his automobile. . . ."

The paper put the incident well after midnight—on Market Street in downtown San Francisco—not outside the Milano Theatre in North Beach (where, incidentally, jitney cabs didn't run).

"DiMaggio, police reported, was getting into his car, parked at Fourth and Market Streets, when he suddenly lost his footing on the running board, grasped desperately to save himself, and fell."

That's an intriguing sentence. If Joe was at Fourth and Market, in the wee hours (after curfew)—where no sister lived, where nothing but bars and nightclubs were open—how loaded was he? If Joe (in point of fact) did not yet have a car of his own, but always had people to drive him around, who was driving? (And whom did Joe protect for sixty years?) If Joe had to grab desperately to save his footing on the running board, and the resulting fall was severe enough to almost ruin him for life—was the car moving? And how fast?

Alas, there were only questions, no answers. Who would supply them?

After the *Examiner*'s overnight police grunts did their honest labor, the story moved back to the sports staff—to Abe Kemp, the self-styled Pollyanna, who was very much a part of the baseball business in San Francisco. (Kemp told Jerome Holtzman, for the oral history *No Cheering in the Press Box:* "Hell, I could have written some of the most scandalous stories of all time. But I didn't.") . . . The *Examiner*'s digging was over.

Charley Graham, the chief of the baseball business, only wanted this story to die a quick death. He was in debt, and Joe DiMaggio was the most valuable asset on his balance sheet. Before the accident, Graham was whispering about offers of a hundred thousand dollars for the Dago boy's contract. If the kid got stinko, fell down, and now he might never be the same—well, Graham wasn't going to advertise that.

The family was (as always) silent. If, in fact, Vince's visit didn't prompt a warm family dinner . . . if, in fact, Vince was cut off from the family fold again (having married that girl after all, and worse still, having sired a daughter whom he did not name for Rosalie, the grandma—a terrible slap!) . . . well, that was private family business. And no one named DiMaggio was going to discuss it.

The confection served everybody's interest because it served Joe's, and he was the meal ticket. If he wanted to say his foot fell asleep in a cab, well, let sleeping dogs lie. If he said he couldn't play for the rest of the year—in fact, he did, but not well or wisely—let him cover his tracks. No matter what he said, he couldn't bury the most momentous fact. Word travels fast in baseball, and word was: DiMaggio was damaged goods.

IN THOSE DAYS, SCOUTING WASN'T science: there was no sheaf of computer printouts with rankings for all the players in the bushes. It was word of mouth and long dirt roads—hard on cars, and harder still on the two or three dozen full-time men who covered the country for the major league clubs. In the sports page argot, they were called "ivory hunters"—which was a cliche by '34, but one that aptly hinted at the vast and viny thickets they explored: thousands of semipro and factory clubs, legion ball, high school teams, and small-town independent leagues . . . players touted by their coaches or managers, written up in local papers, whispered about by commission scouts or bird-dogs (who were paid when they found a kid worth signing)

. . . three million square (and squarely baseball-crazed) miles. In most towns, you couldn't fill a phone booth with the boys who *didn't* play ball.

The scouts made their reputations with the stars they'd signed. For example, one tricky operator with the dee-licious monicker of Cy Slapnicka was the ace of Indians scouts for thirty years, and finally general manager of the Cleveland club. But in baseball he was, forever, "the man who signed Bob Feller." One future Hall of Famer, descried behind a barn somewhere, could make your club a fortune and become your calling card for life.

But the scouts kept their jobs with the boys they didn't sign. Sure, it was good scouting to know about that phenom pitcher in East Jesus, Indiana. But the great scout got to know that kid—and his high school coach, his mom, his minister . . . and was the first to know when that boy threw his arm out, trying to hit a squirrel with a rock. That's how you *saved* your club a fortune—not once in a lifetime, but every year.

And so, in the absence of science, there was art, anecdote, and a dose of idiosyncratic prejudice. Kevin Kerrane's anatomy of the scouting life, *Dollar Sign on the Muscle,* tells of one of the first great scouts, Brooklyn's Larry Sutton, who never appeared (rain or shine) without umbrella, and who preferred to sign light-haired players (because he believed they held up better in the summer heat). That Cleveland ace, Cy Slapnicka, gave up on the Hall of Fame pitcher Lefty Gomez because of a prejudice even more arcane. As Abe Kemp told the story in *No Cheering in the Press Box,* Slapnicka had a ten-day option to buy Gomez from the Seals for fifty thousand dollars and three players. Then he stopped by Charley Graham's office, and asked permission to visit the Seals' locker room.

"About a half hour later," as Kemp recalled, "Slapnicka came back and said, 'Charlie, I'm going to forfeit my option on Gomez.'

"Graham says, 'Tell me something, Cy. Why did you change your mind?' . . .

" 'Well,' he says, 'I'll tell you, Charlie. I saw Gomez undressed in the clubhouse, and anybody who's got a prick as big as he's got can't pitch winning ball in the major leagues.' "

In 1934, Abe Kemp was also scouting, on the side, for the White Sox. Along with Slapnicka, and every other scout in the territory, he had Joe DiMaggio on his A-list—a can't-miss prospect—until Joe's knee blew out. And then, like every other scout, he backed off . . . every scout but one.

After the Family Day doubleheader, Joe had made the trip with the Seals to Los Angeles, where Caveney kept him under wraps through most of the series with the Angels. In the Saturday game, six days after the injury, Joe pinch-hit a home run— made the Seals a winner—but walked around the bases. The next day, he pinch-hit a double, but limped and hopped into second base—and everyone in baseball knew the kid was in trouble. Abe Kemp got a call from Chicago: Harry Grabiner, GM of the White Sox, wanted to know about DiMaggio's knee.

"I don't know anything about his knee, Harry. Outside of that you can go the limit."

"How are we going to find out about his knee?"

Kemp said, "I don't know."

But the local scout for the Yankees, Bill Essick, had lived for a while in North Beach (in fact, across the street from the DiMaggios). He said he could find out about the knee—and quietly, he did. On the say-so of the club's chief West Coast scout, Joe Devine, the Yankees paid for their own orthopedic specialist to examine DiMaggio's knee. There was no reason, the specialist said, that a healthy nineteen-year-old couldn't heal perfectly from that injury. The New York club kept the information under wraps and waited out the season.

Joe Devine had always liked DiMaggio. As the scouts say, he liked the kid seventy-five thousand dollars—before the knee got hurt. Devine was barely forty years old but already a consummate baseball man, and a modern one. He'd started as an outfielder, but never amounted to much as a player. During World War I, he managed a shipyard team in Seattle, and at the close of the war, started scouting for Seattle. Then he managed Calgary, scouted for the Pittsburgh Pirates, managed the San Francisco Missions, coached in Albuquerque (where he watched a young prospect named Vince DiMaggio) . . . and, at last, hooked on with the Yankees as their West Coast chief. By that time, 1932, Devine had four ways to evaluate a player and only two dealt with natural ability. First, Devine would rate a boy's body: looseness, reflexes, strength (and the speed of mental responses). Second, for infielders and outfielders, there was foot-speed. Third, there were mechanical skills: batting, fielding, throwing. Devine held those apart from a player's bodily gifts, because skills could be taught (or at least might improve). But in his fourth criterion, Devine was a pioneer. "The fourth essential," he said, "covers character and disposition, personal habits and diet. I always talk to a prospect, investigate his way of living and find out with whom he associates. How much he eats is important, too. How many fine-looking prospects have you seen hog their way back into the minors? If a player is absolutely dumb I will not consider him unless his tremendous ability counterbalances his mental handicaps. Usually I pass up the moron ballplayer. He is outdated." Joe Devine liked DiMaggio's fluidity, strength, speed, and skills—but he also liked a card-counter.

By '34 the Yankees also liked Italians, especially West Coast Italians, with whom they'd enjoyed two decades' success—starting with Ping Bodie, who was born in San Francisco with the name Francesco Stefano Pezzolo, and became the first "son of Caesar" in the major leagues. Bodie was a strutting, vainglorious "slugger" (before Babe Ruth redefined that term) who was slow of everything but mouth. (When he once attempted a steal and was thrown out by ten yards, the Hearst columnist Bugs Baer wrote: "There was larceny in his heart, but his feet were honest.") Nevertheless, after 1918, when he came to the Yanks, Bodie became a favorite of both writers and fans. In 1925, the Yanks signed a PCL second baseman, Tony Lazzeri, who became a fixture in their Murderers' Row. Not only was he better than Bodie—he was smart, sure afield, averaged almost .300, and was always good for ten to fifteen home runs—but his clearly Italian name made the Yanks the team of choice for half a million new metropolitan fans. When the team followed up six years later and brought in the Seals' Frank Crosetti at shortstop, their Italian-American following was cemented.*

Clearly, the Yanks and DiMaggio would be a marriage heaven-sent (as would the union between Charley Graham's mortgage and the beer-barrel fortune of the Yankee owner, Jacob Ruppert). But it was

---

* Across the Harlem River, the rival Giants were digging for another vein of ore: John McGraw spent the 1920s searching for a terrific Jewish player. McGraw never found a great one, or didn't know it when he saw one *(Oy! On Hank Greenberg this Irish putz passed?)*—but the theory on creating new fans was sound: in '28, when the Giants' new second baseman, Andy Cohen, drove in two runs in the home opener, the crowd surged onto the field and carried him around on their shoulders, like the groom at an Orthodox wedding. The Polo Grounds box office started getting letters from Jewish kids, asking for seats behind second base.

the Seals—and DiMaggio, himself—who almost broke up the wedding. Joe tried the leg again in early June, but the pain drove him out of the lineup. At the end of the month, he was pinch-hitting again, and by July he was playing every day, though the knee still wasn't right. Graham and Caveney wouldn't sit the boy down. That would be admitting the damage. And Joe insisted he was okay, though his average since the injury was only .270.

In the first inning of a game on August 10, DiMaggio came in on a liner to right and fell down in the field. When he batted in the first, he tried to run out a grounder, and then limped back to the bench. When the inning ended, Joe stood up to take the field, but the knee buckled and he collapsed on the dugout floor. Scouts and fans watched DiMaggio struggling vainly to get up . . . and from that moment, Joe's season was over. In the next day's paper, the *Examiner* sports editor, Curly Grieve, wrote the dirge:

"As he hobbled to the dressing room, the muscles of his face were drawn tight, his eyes expressed the fear and grief that weighed down his heart. He seemed to sense that this hour and day was a critical one in his life. Joe was a $50,000 bundle of ivory to the Seals. His sale seemed definitely assured. And leading the pack of bidders was the impressive checkbook of Colonel Jake Ruppert, part-owner of the New York Yankees. . . ."

But as Grieve surmised, even the Yankees took pause from Joe's latest collapse. In 1934, surgical repair of a knee was science fiction, as likely as a man on the moon. Either the knee would heal on its own . . . or Joe would be the most famous rookie in the Crab Fisherman's Association.

ONCE AGAIN, IT WAS HARD TIMES that put the wind back in Joe's sails. Even for the Yankees—the richest club in the big leagues, the first dynasty in American sport—'34 was a tough year, and the future looked grimmer still.

That was the year it came painfully clear, the foundation of that dynasty had crumbled: the mighty Bambino was on his way out. For the last two years, Babe Ruth had been fading—ever slower in the outfield, less productive at the plate, more difficult in the clubhouse (he barely deigned to speak to the new manager, Joe McCarthy). Still, there he was, every day—a threat in the lineup and the sentimental favorite of fans. But the Yanks weren't about sentiment: that September, the Babe would play his last in pinstripes. And for the first time, the Yankees had to dream up a future in the House that Ruth Built—without Ruth.

With the Babe's strength ebbing, the Yanks had finished out of the money for two straight years: in '33 they ran second to the Senators; in '34 it was the Tigers. That wasn't acceptable. For the Yankees' owner, the brewery heir Jacob Ruppert, what mattered wasn't "how you played the game." (In '31, when Joe McCarthy had just come over from the

Cubs, the Yanks played .614 ball—but finished thirteen and a half games back of the Philadelphia A's. Ruppert snapped at his skipper: "I will stand for your finishing second because you are new to the league—but I warn you, McCarthy, *I don't like finishing second.*" "Colonel," said McCarthy, "neither do I.") In the Bronx, second place wasn't just a sporting shame. New Yorkers didn't come out for also-rans: without a pennant, attendance fell, revenue went down. And the hard-eyed, bristle-browed GM, Ed Barrow, had to stop using the lure of World Series money to haggle down his players on salary: without a pennant, costs went up. More than any other club in the country, the Yankees' business wasn't baseball, but winning.

Ruth's demise would leave a hole in the outfield and a chasm in the middle of the order. Gehrig was still a force, but as Gehrig (and the standings) had shown, he couldn't carry the club. The Yanks were built on power, big innings, and runs in bunches. Barrow had to sign a power-hitting outfielder—or gamble on remaking the club from the ground up. Barrow was not a gambling man.

Of course, he didn't much like betting on some Dago boy's knee, either—even with assurances from doctors, even on the say-so of the best scouts in the business. But as the season ended, he had to make a move.

"Don't give up on DiMaggio," Bill Essick told Barrow. "I think you can get him cheap." That was the sort of thing Barrow liked to hear.

And Essick was right on the money. Charley Graham was desperate to realize some value from his wounded star. Attendance was lousy—the Coast League was down almost a quarter-million ticket sales. Graham's mortgage hadn't grown any smaller, and the Bank of America took whatever money he had. So the Yankees constructed a deal tailor-made for Graham's hard times, and their own.

They would buy DiMaggio for $25,000—which was half, or a third of the sum that Graham once hoped for . . . but the Yanks would throw in five players—prospects of middling caliber—so Graham could field a team next year. The Yankees would save a bundle, and Graham got something he could hold on to (instead of cash, which the B of A would have seized). But there was more: Graham could also fill his seats next year—because he got to keep DiMaggio for one more season. And the Yanks got to keep their money until the kid's knee was proven sound.

It was the kind of deal in which nobody gambled—as Barrow later said, "the best deal I ever made." Once the season ended, it went together in a hurry, too. The San Francisco papers got the word November 24, 1934, the day before Joe's twentieth birthday. Joe got the word from the newsmen: they tracked him down at home, by phone. They were coming over. They had to get a comment—and a photo!—right away! . . . But when they got to Taylor Street, there was Joe, in the kitchen, bare-chested, in his best suit pants, trying to iron his white shirt. So they had to wait while he got ready—then they posed him *(No! Not just sittin', do something!)* peeling potatoes.

Of course, the way Abe Kemp wrote it, they'd just found Dead Pan Joe peeling potatoes in a suit and tie. But, what the hell, it was all PR . . . as was the quote they helped him with *("It's a fine birthday present!" said Joe.)* . . . as was the little favor they did at the same time for Uncle Charley Graham—reporting the rosy lie that the Seals got their asking price, $75,000, for their "bundle of ivory."

The unreported part of the story was how disappointed Joe was. Not about the Yanks—that part was fine—but the deal . . . For almost a year, Tom DiMaggio had been cajoling Charley Graham: when the scouts came calling, Joe should get a portion of his purchase price. And Graham had agreed—or, at least, he played along. If he didn't, Tom said, Joe could walk away from baseball, take up fishing, and nobody would make a dime.

So they had a quiet agreement—had to be quiet because organized baseball had made the "reserve clause" an article of religion. That clause meant the club owned the contract and all rights to the player. A player horning in on the deal when he was sold, or traded—well, it looked like extortion, in those days. If anyone found out, Judge Landis might have made Joe a fisherman for good. . . .

So Joe's $6,500 share would have to be paid under the table. But that was before he busted up his knee—

when the price for him was $75,000. With the re-
duced price, Joe got cut out of the deal—stiffed—
he's peelin' potatoes. And no one (least of all he)
could say a word about it.

Still, Joe did receive one fine present that winter,
the best gift any young hitter could get. Charley Graham fired the Seals' manager, Ike Caveney, and replaced him with one of the game's great men—and
one of its greatest batters—Francis Joseph "Lefty"
O'Doul.

IN SAN FRANCISCO (WHERE HE GREW
up, and debuted as a pitching star), O'Doul was celebrated as the Boy from Butchertown. In Philadelphia
(where he played outfield—and hit .398!) he was the
Hero of Baker Bowl. From his years as a dandy (and
Irish icon) in New York, he was famous as the Man in
the Green Suit. In Tokyo (where he traveled off-
season, as ambassador for the Great Game) he was
the Father of Japanese Baseball. Everywhere he was
known, and everywhere beloved: Lefty had the gift
of greeting life with a glad heart.

When Graham wooed O'Doul home as skipper for
the '35 season, he was calling in the biggest name in
San Francisco baseball (the city would hold a parade
whenever Lefty came home for the winter) . . . a
winner on the diamond, and a consummate showman
(he'd keep a big red bandanna in his pocket to wave,
maddeningly, at opposition pitchers) . . . one of the

few baseball men who knew pitching and hitting, both from the inside . . . and withal, a handsome character, who had the generosity to teach.

In years after, O'Doul would insist, the only thing he could do for Joe DiMaggio was "change nothing"—Joe could hit, already. But that was overmodesty. Joe was a great line drive hitter—a gap hitter who battered fences in the PCL. But Lefty had played in Yankee Stadium, where the wall in left center was more than four hundred fifty feet from the plate. Lively Coast League doubles, or even home runs, would quietly expire in a New York center fielder's glove. So Lefty talked to Joe about looking for a pitch he could pull. (The left field corner in the Bronx was only three hundred feet away.)

The wonderful thing was, Lefty only had to say it. Joe would take it from there. He could do anything he wanted with a bat, or anything Lefty told him to do. In O'Doul, Young Joe found a craftsman he could learn from. Lefty was fresh-arrived from the world where Joe was headed, a world of great names from Joe's *Sporting News.* That world came alive when Lefty told his stories of New York. "Mel Ott and I would practice nothing but pulling the ball for hour after hour. Ott could put the ball within *inches* of the foul pole." And so, in that '35 season, Joe had a new request for the BP pitchers: "Pecker-high, middle-in." He wanted a ball he could turn on, to pull it (where else?) inches from the foul pole.

Joe talked more to Lefty in a week than he'd talked

in the prior two years with the Seals. Lefty could make a street lamp talk. Now, the Seals' clubhouse was full of talk—and laughter. Rainy days, O'Doul would give the batboys a dollar and send them off to the Fox Theatre at Market and 10th. They adored him, as did the players, suddenly freed of rules. Lefty didn't care what they did at night—just be ready to play. He'd say: "If you come into a bar and I'm there, don't you dare try to get out without coming over and having one with me." (O'Doul's own drinking was famously major league. When Lefty wanted to open his own bar, Ty Cobb, the shrewd businessman, declined to go partners—for the businesslike reason: "He drinks more than me.") Outside the world of baseball, Lefty showed an even freer hand. Once, at a small-town bar in Calaveras County, Lefty spotted an aged man drinking alone, and told the barkeep: "Give the old-timer a drink." But the bartender said the man came in every day, had one beer, and then left. O'Doul took out his checkbook, wrote a sum, and signed it: "Buy him a beer every day for the rest of the year."

Sometimes Lefty took Joe along on his progress through San Francisco—and Joe would soak it all in: the way Lefty talked, how much he tipped, how much he gave to bums, how he signed autographs for kids while he walked, how many friends he gave a big hello. Lefty had more Italian friends than Joe did. Fridays, before a night game, Lefty would take Joe to the winery in North Beach—the Brucato brothers' cask room—where thirty or forty people (politicians, opera stars, winery workers) would feast on crab *ciop-pino* for lunch, while Lefty regaled them with stories. Or O'Doul would invite Joe to join him for lunch at the home of one of the *prominenti,* Allesandro Baccari. (But Lefty would have to get there early to help Signora Baccari shell peas for the *pasta con piselli.)*

The biggest thing Joe learned from O'Doul was how to live like a hero. Everybody knew Lefty, everybody watched him, said hello to him, loved him. And in the middle of it all, Lefty did just what he wanted. He was handsome, at home anywhere he went, always the best-dressed man in the room. The admiration of males he accepted with offhand grace, and to the adoration of females he extended a courtly and catholic welcome. Kids—there wasn't anything he wouldn't do for them. (Charley Graham, unwisely, made a deal with Lefty—if he'd stop giving away so many baseballs to kids, Graham would hold a Kids Come Free Day. When more than ten thousand little freebies came out, Lefty climbed to the stadium roof, with flour sacks full of free balls to scatter.) . . . For Joe, this brush with the hero's life wasn't quite like hitting—he couldn't just do it himself the next day. But if he was going to be a big-leaguer, a *New York* big-leaguer . . . this was his chance to learn at the master's knee.

From the moment that season started, there was no doubt: Joe was going to New York. His speed was back, the knee had healed—at least it was solid enough—and his outfield play was something better than that. For the first time, he wasn't just making the plays, he was making remarkable plays, and making them look easy. Now, at the plate, he wasn't just a natural, but a polished hitter. Under O'Doul's approving eye, Joe raised his already gaudy average more than fifty points that year. Through the summer and into the fall, he was flirting with .400, racing toward a batting crown. In fact, all the Seals were hitting, and for the first time in years, fighting for a pennant. San Francisco baseball was a grand and glad story that year. And everywhere in the league, the headliner was Young Joe.

"DiMaggio plays ball with a grim intensity," wrote Billy Stepp of the *Portland News-Telegram.*

"You've seldom seen a more accomplished flychaser," Cliff Harrison noted, in the *Seattle Star.*

"DiMaggio never makes a mistake on the bases," said Rudy Hickey of the *Sacramento Bee.*

"DiMaggio," Gene Caughlin wrote, in the *Los Angeles Post-Record,* "is likely to kill an opposing infielder at any time."

But those were just the congregants' murmured devotions compared to the Hallelujah Chorus in San Francisco. Even Abe Kemp dropped all caution and called the case, once and forever: "In passing," he wrote, near the season's close, "just a word about Joe DiMaggio, who has finally convinced me that he is the greatest ballplayer I have ever seen graduate from the Pacific Coast League. And I have seen all of them since 1907."

Joe lost the batting crown on the season's last

day—to Oscar Eckhardt, a slap hitter who could run like crazy. The final league stats read: "DiMaggio .398, Eckhardt .399." But the Seals won their pennant and the championship playoff with the L.A. Angels. After that, the only story in town was whether the Yanks had sent Young Joe his contract. As Kemp remembered, it was hell-on-wheels getting information from the Taylor Street household: "Joe's mother was impossible. You'd phone and ask for Joe, and she'd say, *'No, Joe da' home.'* That's all we ever got. *'No, Joe da' home.'* " Kemp finally got his story from a Post Office pal who looked up the registered mail receipts. There it was—Joe had signed for a letter. So they knew he'd gotten a contract. But for how much? They never could find out.

Actually, Joe had gotten several contracts. The first called for $5,625 in salary, barely more than Joe made with the Seals. Joe consulted Lefty, who brought in an expert—a man who could squeeze a nickel till the buffalo on it was dead from lack of air. "Kid," Ty Cobb said, "get a pen and some paper." Then he dictated for Joe a polite and recalcitrant letter to the New York GM, Ed Barrow. And that worked out fine. Barrow sent back a contract for $6,500. "That's not enough," Cobb said. And he dictated to Joe an even more polite and implacable response. So Barrow sent back a third contract: $8,500!—with a note attached: *This is the limit. Don't waste another three-cent stamp. Just sign it. And tell Cobb to stop writing me letters.*

NOW THE NEW YORK PAPERS GOT into the act in force. When the Pinstripes finished out of the money for the third straight year, it was the winter's business to analyze the "pennant problem"—and its possible solution, viz., "Joe De Maggio." There were stories when the Yankees' owner, Jake Ruppert, made a West Coast visit and met his future star. ("He seems," said the Colonel, "a difficult young man to get acquainted with.") There were stories as the Yankees picked up their option on Young Joe. (The Red Sox counteroffered $65,000, a quick and tidy profit for the Yankees, who declined.) Another round of stories covered DiMaggio dickering on his contract. (Maybe the boy was not so timid, after all.) And in every round, there was lip-smacking rehearsal of his statistics, comments on his excellence, speculation on his impact. The *New York Sun*—which wasn't any more breathless than the competition—announced in one headline:

YANKS PIN HOPES ON ROOKIE
Di Maggio, Sensational Outfielder, May Be
Deciding Factor in Pennant Problem

The New York sports pages exhibited such a flush of Joe-fever that the *Sporting News* weighed in, ostensibly to protect the boy:

Di Maggio Comes Up With Two Strikes
on Him as Innocent Victim
of Lavish Newspaper Ballyhoo

REACHES BIG SHOW WITH BRILLIANT RECORD

Fans Expect Recruit
from Coast to Be Cobb,
Ruth, Jackson in One

Of course, they thought all the hoopla would shake him. They didn't know Joe.

They thought the "big jump" to the Yankees might trip him up. But he'd already climbed, in three years, from nothing and nowhere—a boy without prospects—to become the most heralded young man in the country. The move to New York was a baby step, after that.

First chance he got, the Yankees' Ed Barrow made a fatherly point of talking to Joe. The GM counseled the boy: don't get too worked up about all the good news, don't pay too much attention, don't let it get . . .

"Don't worry, Mr. Barrow," Joe cut in. "I never get excited."

BOOK II

THE GAME

1936–1951

At the All-Star break, July 1936.

Choosing up with Frank Crosetti and Tony Lazzeri.

With the proud owner, Jacob Ruppert.

The big time, in the big Bronx clubhouse.

CHAPTER 6

✦

JOE DIMAGGIO, TWENTY-ONE YEARS
old, tall and slender, hawk-faced and buck-toothed,
slow to smile and reluctant to speak, made his first
trip east of the Rocky Mountains on his way to spring
training in 1936. The Yankees made sure their prize
package wouldn't have to travel unattended: they de-
puted their two veteran Italian stars, Tony Lazzeri
and Frank Crosetti, to fetch Joe from his home
on Taylor Street, and take him cross-country in
Lazzeri's new Ford. That was no mean drive—San
Francisco to St. Petersburg, Florida—more than a
week on two-lane roads that zigzagged from town to
town, and turned to gravel or rutted mud where there
were no towns to be found. Lazzeri drove for hours
the first day, then turned the wheel over to Crosetti.
Crosetti drove through the afternoon, then turned to
the back seat, where Joe was lounging. "Your turn,"
said Crosetti. And DiMaggio, in his longest speech
of the day, said, "I don't drive."

"Let's throw the bum out," said Crosetti. But of
course, they didn't, and Joe gazed out the window for
three thousand miles.

For DiMaggio, this was his first look at the vastness of the country he would thrill with his exploits. In a few years, he would be said to represent this land and exemplify its virtues: aspiration, hard work, native grace, and opportunity for all. But even as a rookie-to-be, yet to face his first big-league pitch, Joe was separated from the common conditions of American life, walled off as surely as he was behind the Ford's plate glass.

As the three Yankees left San Francisco, there were thousands of men who'd moved (some with their families) into shantytowns near the staging piers for the new Golden Gate Bridge. There were men who'd literally sit on those piers all day, watching, waiting, for some poor SOB to fall off the high girders, so they could take his job: bridge work paid fifty-five dollars a week. But Joe would make more than that every time he pulled on his stirrup-socks and played for two hours in the sunshine. As the three Yankees passed, more thousands of desperate families were heading west, with everything they owned piled on their Model T's— fleeing from the parched plains, hoping for a living wage in California. On the roads themselves, there were tens of thousands of laboring men, bent to their shovels or barrows of gravel. The endless national routes had been laid out and numbered in the 1920s, but it was the Depression, FDR, and the PWA that made them into highways for the fortunate motorists. The New Deal's Public Works Administration paid not quite four bucks a day. The new friends Joe would find in New York flipped that sort of money to the hat-check girl.

The strange fact was, Joe was probably closer in his thinking to those rootless Okies, or the sweating shovel men on the road verge. But he never would be among them. He'd passed them, as he passed them now, so fast he never even saw their faces. When next he would meet them, if ever he did, those faces would display awe at his presence, joy at his godlike glory among them, avarice for his autograph or some token of him. For he had been touched (they'd read all about this, heard him on the radio, they'd seen him in *Life* magazine) . . . as if the Hand of God had reached down and made this man great—uncommon, unlike them—and that would wall Joe away forever.

He'd jumped from newsboy to national star without apprenticeship, no stops in between—from the commonest kid to king—and his feet had barely touched ground. That made him an odd mix: majestic and modest at the same time. His attitudes, his tastes, were those of the boy who hawked the *Call* at Sansome and Sutter. He was mindful of rules, compliant to authority; still, he angled for every edge, as the newsboy fumbled in his pocket till the trolley came, so he could walk away with two extra pennies. He didn't need and wouldn't have liked extravagant living of any sort. (He, Lazzeri, and Crosetti each tossed in fifteen dollars for the trip across the nation—and Joe was surprised, in the end, when he had to come up with two or three dollars more.) Fancy people—those with status, importance—made him so nervous he wouldn't say a word. But he showed not a moment's doubt when he told Mr. Barrow and Col. Jacob Ruppert to take their first five-thousand-dollar contract and go shit in their hats.

He was a kid who could say, earnestly, he didn't want a fuss made over him. But there hadn't yet been a day of his life, either at home or on the road with his club, when his needs and wants had not been seen to by others. This he accepted (by now, he expected) with regal entitlement. Truly, he could say he was "just a rookie, nothing special." But when confronted with the names of the game's greatest pitchers—Schoolboy Rowe, Lefty Grove, Dizzy Dean, Carl Hubbell (not one of whom he'd ever seen)—he was as truly convinced that he would hit them all, that there was, in fact, no pitcher alive who could stop him. DiMaggio could believe (and even say) he was just trying to make good and help his team win ballgames. But at the same moment, he was convinced (as who would not be, with his life thus far?) that it was his destiny to be a great star.

Now, what that was, what that meant, he had very little idea. Lazzeri and Crosetti knew more. They timed their trip to make St. Petersburg at night, after newspaper deadlines. At least the kid would get his feet on the ground before the writers were on him like flies.

Still, by the time Joe dressed the next morning, walked to Miller Huggins Field, and put on a uniform

(Number 18), word had spread: the great hope had arrived. And a score of New York writers gathered, all starved for copy, all waiting for him.

"Hey, Joe!" yelled the first one who saw him, as he trotted onto the field. "Give us a quote, will ya? . . ."

"Don't have any," Joe murmured, as he loped by. He didn't know what they meant. He thought, maybe "Quote" was some kind of soft drink.

No matter: they didn't quote him; half of them spelled his name wrong (he was back to "De Maggio" again) . . . but they all knew the story. As the dean of New York baseball writers, Dan Daniel, wrote in the *World-Telegram:* "Here is the replacement for Babe Ruth."

THAT WAS A LEAD THAT PACKED A ton of freight—undue pressure on the kid, of course. But business was business. And the business of those writers was to make heroes, to make Larger-Than-Life, to make the Great National Game a drama to hold readers in thrall.

Dan Daniel, who sometimes signed a piece "Daniel," or sometimes "Daniel M. Daniel," was really Daniel Margowitz, born to a family of doctors who were mystified and dismayed when their boy gave up on medicine, and started writing baseball, in 1909. But young Dan saw great things in the National Pastime, which label (and product) he promoted with zeal for fifty years. Under Daniel's eye, and the spur of his stories, baseball transformed itself from a ragbag collection of unstable and vaguely disreputable clubs to America's premier live entertainment—a crucial national industry, governed only by its own rules, but no less solid (and more popular, always) than the U.S. Treasury.

He wasn't the game's greatest *literateur:* that title had long since passed to Damon Runyon, Ring Lardner, Grantland Rice, and then to those whippersnappers, Jimmy Cannon and Red Smith. Daniel preferred to write fast and badly. (His highest stylistic touch was to turn adjectives into verbs—viz., " 'I'm just in a slump,' he morosed.") At the *Telegram,* he owned the Yankee beat, and as the lead sports writer, covered other big baseball and boxing stories, too. To that he added a daily column, "Daniel's Dope" (which title gave the rest of the writers unending jokes). And every week, he sent some five thousand words by telegraph to St. Louis, where Taylor Spink printed them in his nationwide *Sporting News*.

Withal, Daniel was a statesman of the baseball nation: chairman of the writers' association, counselor and agent to both players and management, shepherd to The Game itself. He dressed for the role of Secretary of State: French-cuffed shirts under vest and suit coat. (August, a hundred and six degrees in the press box in Chicago, there's Daniel in his vest and jacket.) He boasted of personally ending Babe Ruth's holdout of 1930 (when he cowed the Bambino with a lecture on the Great Depression—an event that previously had escaped the Babe's attention). Daniel chided the industry as a whole for missing its chance to promote attendance with radio and film. "I do believe that baseball lags behind the times," he wrote. "It has snubbed most of the up-to-the-minute agencies for spreading the gospel of the game, creating a wider human interest in the players and the drama of the man in the field."

Promotion, drama: these Daniel understood. And when he made DiMaggio the successor to Babe Ruth, Daniel also knew he was reaching for the trump card. (When he'd ended that holdout for Ruth in 1930, he intervened for one compelling reason: "Without the Babe there wasn't an awful lot to write about.")

But if DiMaggio flopped? Well, Daniel would have gone on. Consistency wasn't at issue. One year, when the American League beat the Nationals 12–0 in the All-Star Game, Daniel wrote that the NL was fast becoming a minor league. Three months later, when the Cardinals beat the Red Sox in the World Series, Daniel wrote that the National League had shown anew its clear and dangerous superiority. When some whippersnapper pointed out the contradiction, Daniel shrugged: "I warned them both," he said. "Now they're on their own." And Daniel was hardly alone as he grasped for this rookie's coattails. After Joe's first day of spring training, the gray and eminent *Herald Tribune* informed New York: "Rookie Outfielder Blasts Three Homers in Debut" . . . and only in the body of the story did one learn, that was at batting practice—scrimmage games hadn't even begun.

IN A SENSE, THE WRITERS DIDN'T have any choice. Not if they wanted to keep their jobs. And that was the best job on any newspaper. Baseball writers had status, visibility, more freedom than any other reporter, more travel, more good times, and more money. They had opportunities to moonlight—ghostwriting for magazines or memoirs; one way or another, they dined out on friendships with the heroes of the age. They never had to sit in an office, they took winters off, had a month (with their families) in Florida for spring training . . . and every bit of it on the cuff. And the quickest way to lose it all was to run afoul of the fellows in the business—not the newspaper business, but the baseball business.

Everybody knew stories of writers who annoyed the club management, or players, and that was the last you ever saw of them—unless you happened to have business in the courthouse of Bayonne, New Jersey. Club owners thought nothing of complaining to the editors, and their complaints carried weight. It was the ball clubs, not the papers, that paid for the writers' train fares, their hotel rooms, their food and drink. Why shouldn't the teams have the sort of writers they wanted?

But it wasn't really threat that kept the hero machine humming; the club was a traveling fraternity. The men at spring training—or on those three special railroad cars, heading north—were your buddies, your meal-mates, the first guys you talked with at breakfast about some story in the paper, and the last guys who said good night as you padded, with your toothbrush, in your skivvies, up the Pullman corridor to your bunk. Sure, you were there to cover the club, but when the club did well, you did well. Sure the players were celebrities— good for them! (Good for you!) That didn't mean you could fire away at will. If a player got so stinko he couldn't play the next day's game—he was still puking while they played the anthem . . . well, "stomach flu" was close enough. (It covered the main point: he was out of the lineup.) If two or three writers were drinking in the anteroom of Babe Ruth's suite, while the Sultan of Swat was disporting in the bedroom with a succession of female fans . . . well, of course their feature stories on the great Bambino were bound to mention his vast appetites. But it was always about his eating a dozen hot dogs (no, make that two dozen) before the game.

It was Ruth who set the standard for the press, as he did for so much of the modern game. He was not only the drawing card and brand name for his team and town, but the one-man focus of fan attention, and fount of copy, for the country as a whole. It wasn't just his home runs—they changed the way baseball was played. But his blaring character, his individual, grandiose glory made a collection of local clubs, local attractions, into the National Game—an industry marketing its personalities. In New York, where the cult of Big Names was centered, the tabloid press sprouted and grew up feeding on the new appetite for personalities. In particular, the *New York Daily News,* with the largest circulation in the country, set its first roots in Ruthian soil. Marshall Hunt, the *Daily News*'s man with the Yankees, stayed professionally and personally close to the Bambino. In fact, the Yankees used to send Hunt with Ruth, down to Hot Springs, Arkansas, to boil some winter fat off the Babe in the baths.

"We played golf every morning," Hunt told Jerry Holtzman, in *No Cheering in the Press Box,* "and then we'd get tired of the food in the hotel and I'd hire a car and we'd go out in the country looking for farmhouses that said 'Chicken Dinners.' What Babe really wanted was a good chicken dinner and the daughter combination, and it worked that way more often than you would think. After maybe about a month of that we would join the main team in Florida or New Orleans, wherever it was. We did this every year, all the time he was in New York."

But when the editors of the *Daily News* needed information on a story about a paternity suit against Ruth . . . Hunt stalled, talked it over with the Babe, and finally told New York:

"Listen, we've got along fine with the Babe and he's done a lot of things for us. You try to get somebody else to worm this thing out in New York, and not through the Babe, because we don't want to go on this personal bend."

In the end, they were all in the baseball business together. And so, when Daniel anointed this West Coast rookie as successor to Ruth, and the hero machine kicked into action, it didn't merely send the call, "All Hands on Deck!" It also sent the message, "Handle with Care."

FOR JOE DIMAGGIO, THERE WAS NO choice at all. As the club's chattel, he was at the disposal of management, writers, fans, like any wooden seat in the ballpark. He could be what they required, or go back to Fisherman's Wharf. Anyway, Joe wouldn't kick: as he wrote in *Lucky to Be a Yankee,* he thought all the writers "treated me swell." It was up to him to be as good as they said.

And to their obvious astonishment, he was. In the Yankees' first grapefruit game, against the Cardinals, DiMaggio hit third—the Babe's old spot—and in his first at bat, smashed a line drive triple to left over Muscles Medwick's head. For Joe, that was an omen: his first hit that won him his job with the Seals was a triple, too. So he relaxed, and lined out three more singles. For the writers, this was rapture. Dan Daniel was already elbow-deep into his grab bag of ethno-geographic metaphor: "The San Francisco Italian," Daniel vehemed, "became a veritable Vesuvius of fire and action."

By that time, Daniel couldn't help himself. He was, to put it baldly, in love: "The Italian lad has big strong arms, with tremendous wrists. His back muscles ripple in their sheaths. . . ."

Another game against the Cardinals, and Joe got two more hits, the first another triple that rattled up against the wall in right center, where the numbers 420 had been painted. ("Soon Lou Gehrig walked and the pair put on a double steal in which the fleet Giuseppe scored. . . .") His third game, against the Cincinnati Reds, Joe went four-for-six, and was cheered from the grandstand by a crowd three times larger than the Yankees usually enjoyed. "Never before . . ." announced the Secretary of State, "has a recruit fresh from the minors created the furore which Di Maggio has stirred up, or intrigued the fans so thoroughly with the magic of his bat and his possibilities in the American League."

By the end of that story, Daniel was on to another burning question (and another errand for the Yankee management): Where would Joe play, and whom would he dislodge? Daniel's eye fell (not by happenstance) upon center field, where the Yanks' best outfielder, Ben Chapman, was established. Chapman (or in Danielese, "The Alabama Arrow") was fast and able, a career Yankee, and career .300 hitter. But he was a holdout. The Yanks were trying to make him swallow a cut in salary (from twelve thousand dollars to ten), so Chapman was working out at home, in Birmingham. Daniel's mention of center field was designed to pressure "Chappie" into the fold.

The Chapman story, almost lost in the "furore" over DiMaggio, was a window on the character of the Yankees and their writers. The real story with Chapman was he had a temper, and he showed it. To the Yankees that made him a "loudmouth." The club and the writers had celebrated his talent when he came up; had passed congratulations all around when Chapman was moved from the infield to the outfield, and led the league in assists; they had sung of his speed and daring when he led the league in stolen bases. But he wouldn't shut up and simply act glad to be living his life in pinstripes. When he held out in '36, all at once the songs turned sour. "Chapman should be the best player in baseball," the manager, Joe McCarthy, was quoted in the *New York Post,* "but his temperament is all wrong." Within ten days, Chapman signed for the proffered ten thousand dollars (with a two-thousand-dollar bonus, if he kept his mouth shut and played hard all year), but the writing was on the wall. Two months later, he was dealt off to the Senators. And thus, the Yanks solved their "temperament problem."

There was no evidence, then or now, to suggest

that Joe took heed of Chapman's troubles . . . or noted that his own pinstripes, uniform Number 18, belonged the year before to Johnny Allen—a splendid pitcher, another "temperament problem"—who'd been shuffled off to Cleveland. How could Joe read a warning for himself in the orgiastic praise around his name in the papers? Joe was never going to be a "loudmouth"—that was clear. But a holdout? . . . Well, if he did his job, if he did everything they could ask, if he was perfect, Joe was sure he'd be rewarded.

He was doing more than anyone could ask. In his fourth spring game, against the Boston Bees, he had another two hits. His batting average now stood at .600. . . . But after one of those hits, he was forced at second base, and as he slid in, the Boston fielder, Joe Coscarart, stepped on DiMaggio's left foot. The next day, Joe's foot was swollen. And that was another harbinger of things to come. Joe turned himself over to the trainer . . . who promptly turned that bruised foot into a medical drama.

Earle V. "Doc" Painter, trainer to the Bronx Bombers, considered himself a scientist in a world too long beset by ignorance. Not for him the old-fashioned rubdowns and slatherings of liniment: these he regarded with contempt. The old-time trainer, he insisted, "slapped and pounded and rubbed the patient, until he took all the life out of the player's muscles." Doc Painter, in contrast, had a thoroughly modern regimen of treatments that included cups of sweet tea with lemon before dinners, "gobs and gobs of tepid salt water" as a cure for indigestion, laxatives for players who were "constipated through over-exercise" . . . and for players (especially old-timers) exhausted by "the nervous, physical, exciting life of baseball," the stimulant of "an occasional highball."

Joe would have been better off with a couple of stiff drinks. Instead, the Doc put Joe's foot into a Diathermy Machine, which was a new-age wonder designed to bring heat to internal tissues. High-frequency electrical impulses were supposed to increase drainage, decrease swelling and pain. But Painter cooked Joe's foot until it looked like a broiled red pepper. At that point, Joe had a real medical problem: first-degree burns, and a chance of infection or blood poisoning. Painter said a week to ten days of rest would make Joe as good as new. But DiMaggio wouldn't play for more than a month. He would miss the rest of the spring exhibitions—and the first three weeks of the season, as well.

Members of the fraternity set to putting the best face on this debacle. Carefully, repeatedly, they absolved Doc Painter with a gush of pseudoscience: high blood sugar in the skin of Joe's foot made him extrasensitive to heat . . . no way Painter could have known—he was blameless. And anyway, maybe this was good for the team, allowing the veterans some attention (and ink) now that the Walloping Wop would be absent for a week or two. Poor Lou Gehrig.

He'd spent his career in the shadow of the Babe. And now, when he had a chance to top the marquee, along came this rookie, and once again stolid Lou got buried in the ballyhoo.

The strange thing was, the ballyhoo didn't even pause for a day, just because Joe stopped playing. It was more grandiose, more imaginative, once the scribes didn't have to write what the kid actually did in a game. Here came the stories about the boy who loved baseball; learning to hit with broken oars; taking his brother's job. Right away, Joe started working on his "autobiography"—an eight-part series to run in the *World-Telegram,* under Joe's byline—though the prose (and the story line) was purely Daniel's Dope. "Just imagine how I feel about all this!" it began, with ingenuous exclamation. And there followed a winsome sketch of a boy who'd never been to the big city—wondering if big, tough New York could find a place in its big, tough heart for a scared kid like him.

"With this little introduction, let me start where I should have started—from the beginning. My full name is Joseph Peter Di Maggio, Jr. . . ." (Thus Joe attained his first major league record: youngest player ever to get his own name wrong in his autobiography.)

In fact, Joe was already in New York and doing fine. The Yankees were scheduled to barnstorm north—games in a half-dozen Southern cities, on and off the trains . . . so they sent Young Joe ahead to consult with doctors and to rest his foot in the Hotel New Yorker. There he was visited by more big-league writers, for interviews that showed him to be nothing like a scared boy.

Frank Graham, the influential columnist for the *New York Sun,* came to ask Joe about his impressions of the big city. "Right now, it looks a lot like San Francisco," Joe said. Graham tried another tack:

"How did he like Joe McCarthy and the rest of the Yankees?

" 'Fine.'

"What did Joe [McCarthy] say to him when he reported?

" 'Nothing much.' "

DiMaggio wasn't frightened of New York, of Joe McCarthy or the Yankees—nor of shrugging off an interview with some big-cheese columnist. True, Joe was green, a rookie, just twenty-one; but he'd already seen how these press guys worked. He played, and they wrote about him. He sat out, and they wrote feverishly. He talked, and they wrote what he said. If he said less, they wrote even more.

Joe didn't have much schooling—no education in media, of course. But there were some things he'd learned as a kid. And there was one thing he could spot a mile away—knew it as a birthright, saw it in North Beach every day . . . and saw it now. Whenever he held back, or walked away, he could see it: in the way these writers came after him, in their smiles, their eyes, in their columns of newsprint. Joe DiMaggio knew everything there was to know about guys on the make.

IN THE FIRST THREE WEEKS OF THE season, the Yankee box office got hundreds of letters asking: When would DiMaggio play? The papers covered his medical exams, his every appearance at the ballpark, the new layers of skin on his foot—"The Most Famous Hot-Foot in Yankee History." The *New York Times* ran a lively exchange of letters from readers arguing out the pronunciation of "Dee-Mah-Jee-Oh." The Yanks were playing well, but not well enough: after eighteen games, at eleven and seven, they were just where they'd finished the last three years—second place. Finally, the papers trumpeted the glad news: the kid would play on Sunday, May 3, against the St. Louis Browns.

A crowd of more than twenty-five thousand (by far the largest since opening day) braved cool and showery weather to cheer the debut. "An astonishing portion of the crowd," said the *New York Post,* "was composed of strangers to sport—mostly Italians—who did not even know the stadium subway station." Perhaps it was these new fans who screamed in glee when Young Joe, now wearing Number 9, made his first plate appearance—with Yankee runners on first and third—and bounced a tame ground ball to third base. But all the fans rose to cheer when Crosetti, the runner on third, got into a rundown, the Browns threw the ball away, Crosetti scored, and DiMaggio ended up on second base—whence he later scored on a double from Chapman.

Joe was up again in the second, and looped a single to center field. In the sixth, Joe got ahold of a pitch from "Chief" Elon Hogsett and drove it, as the *Post* remarked, "like a cannon shot between the center and left fielders," and DiMaggio had his first big-league triple. In the eighth, Joe hit another line drive single to right. The game as a whole was never in doubt: the Browns' pitching was awful; but who cared? The *Daily News* ran DiMaggio headlines three inches high, but in the lead tried to keep matters in perspective: "This is the story of Joseph DiMaggio, a kid of 21 from San Francisco, though it might be proper to mention that the Yankees beat St. Louis 14–5, at the Stadium yesterday." The *Post* one-upped the competition, not only with its screamer headline ("DI MAGGIO IS YANK HOPE"), and a lead on DiMaggio ("He clicked."), but a half-page cartoon of Young Joe smashing a baseball into the heart of New York ("It's in the Baggio for Joe Di Maggio . . .") and a three-stanza paean of praise entitled "Calling All Fans!"

Oh, I am Joe Di Maggio,
　　Come, folks, and have a look.
I scintillate, I simply glow,
　　Although I'm just a rook.
I pop the pill a wicked whack

And make opposing pitchers crack—
I'm one for stardom's book! . . .

In fact, Joe was the lead nearly every day, in every paper, as the Yanks reeled off six wins in his first seven games. In the Thursday game (Joe's fourth), the catcher, Bill Dickey, was the hitting star, with two home runs and four of the Yankees' six runs driven in. But Stanley Frank, the *Post*'s Yankee writer, begged his readers' pardon as he made Joe the lead, once more.

"Excuse it please, but that Di Maggio boy is in again today. In again on top of the ballgame and the Yankee story, as he has been every day since Sunday, when he stole the show in his major league debut. Young Joe seems to have a positive genius for dominating situations. . . ."

Frank explained that Dickey got the hits, powered the Yanks to a 6–5 lead. But in the ninth inning, the Tigers put men on first and third, with no one out, and only one run needed to tie. Charley Gehringer drove a high fly almost to the warning track in left field, where DiMaggio caught the ball, and fired it toward the plate . . .

"Pete Fox, who ranks among the first ten fastest men in the league crouched tensely on third and was off when the ball touched Joe's glove.

"It was a 20 to 1 bet that Fox would score standing up, but he was out by five feet despite a desperate slide."

After forty years in baseball, Ed Barrow called it the best peg to the plate he'd ever seen. Frank called it "an incredible throw," a "spectacular heave." He said Joe had a better arm than the Yankees' gold standard, Bob "The Rifle" Meusel. But in the end Frank could make only one comparison:

"Maybe Joe, in whose honor a large Italian flag was unfurled yesterday by an exhuberant customer, has another positive genius. The sort that a big guy who once played right field had for making the right play instinctively. Babe Ruth."

The next Sunday, against the Philadelphia A's, Joe hit his first home run; the Yanks took the contest 7–2, and for the first time moved ahead of Boston, into first place. "Hero No. 1," the *Daily News* called him—under a picture of Joe, trotting his home run home. And in the photo caption: ". . . Nice going, Joe!"

The Sunday after that, on his first western road trip, Joe was honored by the Italians of Cleveland, who presented him with a leather traveling bag and kit before the game. They were apparently ignorant of the jinx such pregame gifts were supposed to bring . . . but so was Joe: he followed up with two doubles to power another Yankees win.

Two days later, it was Joe's teammates who showed what they thought of him. In the ninth inning of a 10–4 Yankee blowout, DiMaggio singled, and then Gehrig hit an infield ground ball. DiMag barreled into second base hard—he never ran any other way—and broke up the double play by wiping out the Indians' shortstop, Billy Knickerbocker . . . who then tried to teach this rookie a lesson, by throwing the ball straight down at Joe's head. Fortunately, he missed. DiMaggio was oblivious—he looked up from his slide, saw the ball on the ground, and didn't know what happened—but Tony Lazzeri led eighteen Yanks in a dash from the dugout to protect Young Joe. Then the Indians poured out of their dugout, and the umpires raced in to stop the fight. No punches were thrown, but the message was clear: *Hands Off Our Boy.*

By late May, Joe was leading the league with a .411 average, and the Yankees were streaking. On the last day of May, they won their fifth straight, to sweep the Red Sox (whom they now led by four and a half games), when DiMaggio singled in the seventh to tie, and tripled in the twelfth to win, the game. Almost forty-two thousand fans (including Mayor Fiorello La Guardia) left Yankee Stadium to tell of the rookie's glory. Young Joe had to leave the ballpark in a phalanx of cops, to protect him from adoring fans.

In June, the New York papers counted and re-counted Joe's streak of hitting in eighteen straight games. Then they raised panicky alarums as Joe stopped hitting (oh-for-twelve!), but the hand-wringing ended when he drove in five runs against the Browns with a homer, triple, and single. "YANKS SCORE, 12–3, AS DIMAGGIO STARS," the *New York Times* reported. Almost lost amid the effusions was the fact that Gehrig also powered the Yanks, with a homer, double, and single of his own. It was seldom mentioned all year that Gehrig was having a banner season, that Dickey was pounding the ball flat; that the whole Yankee offense was producing runs at the rate of the mighty '27 Yanks; or that the champion Tigers had lost two great stars, Hank Greenberg and Mickey Cochrane, to medical woes. The story was painted in bold black and white: the Yanks, resurgent, were racing toward a pennant. And the reason for resurgence was Joe.

Nor were the New York papers alone: the Yanks were the story everywhere in the country, and the Yankee story was Joe. Writers in every AL town used the coming of the rookie wonder to build attendance for their local clubs. In the month before the All-Star Game, the AP feature on the daily star of baseball named the rookie Di Maggio seven times. (Dizzy Dean, with four mentions, ranked a distant second.) Little wonder, in the count of two million ballots from fans in forty-eight states and Canada, Joe led the voting for the AL All-Star outfield. And in case anyone had missed the story, *Time* magazine took the occasion of the All-Star Game to look in on baseball—and on the cover (where portraits of presidents and foreign kings were the staple) there appeared a full-length photo of DiMaggio, pinstriped, at the Yankee Stadium plate, in graceful follow-through after another mighty line drive clout.

True, he had only two months under his belt; but

he'd played the game flawlessly. Not just the baseball game, with nine men on the field, but the larger hero game—the one the writers played, with the management, and all the fans. Joe had made everybody look brilliant: the Yankee scouts, the general manager, Ed Barrow (attendance was up two hundred thousand), and Col. Ruppert, who wrote the check. Joe had proven true all the breathy praise of the writers who called him the Yanks' messiah—and the fans who believed them. What he'd never done was fail; never tasted the gall that the hero machine could heap on a loser. But now his time came, at the worst moment: while the nation looked to Braves Field in Boston, for the fourth year of baseball's All-Star Game.

The American League was three-and-oh in the game Daniel called "The Midsummer Classic." Only once (for three innings) had the NL even held a lead. And never before had a rookie taken part in this showcase of the game's greats. But DiMaggio started in right field—and proved a disaster. In the second inning, with one runner on, the NL catcher, Gabby Hartnett, hit a liner toward Joe in right field. He charged the ball and bent for a shoestring catch, but the ball hit the grass and went right by him, to the wall, for a triple and a lead for the Nationals. In the fifth, with the NL ahead 2–0, Joe's old Seals teammate (now a Cub), Augie Galan, hit a homer to the foul pole in right. Then Billy Herman singled, and DiMaggio kicked the ball around in right field till Herman wound up on second base. From there, Herman would score an unearned run that clinched the game for the Nationals.

At the plate, Joe's day went just as badly. In the first inning, against Dizzy Dean, Joe hit into a double play. In the fourth, he popped up against Carl Hubbell, and hit a weak comebacker to Hubbell in the sixth. In the seventh, Joe had his chance for redemption when he came up against Lon Warneke, with the bases loaded, two outs. Joe hit a liner toward short, where Leo Durocher snared it, and the AL rally was over. Again in the ninth, again with two outs, he had another chance, with Gehringer on second as the tying run. But Joe popped up again to end the game, the first NL win. And DiMaggio was the goat, nation-wide.

That was a day Joe would never forget. More than a decade later, he would make that experience Chapter One of *Lucky to Be a Yankee.* Even fifty years later, Joe would still be complaining that he would have had Hartnett's line drive in the second, if the great AL pitcher Schoolboy Rowe hadn't been warming up near right field—and ordered him to play deep on Hartnett. *("Hey, Rook! I said move back! This guy's going to hit it out!")* . . . Joe would also stew for fifty years about the writers (another All-Star lineup) who covered that game—Granny Rice, Dan Parker, Bill Corum, Damon Runyon. "Runyon," Joe would say, "was the only one who didn't rip me." Of course, he'd remember the others, too—he could recall them by name, and what they wrote. They taught him a lesson, or confirmed a lesson he was already prepared to believe:

They were fans, they were friends . . . as long as he was a winner. But that could all be over in a day.

IT WAS A CHARACTERISTIC TURN OF phrase with which DiMaggio described that game:

"This was the fourth All-Star Game, and the National League had yet to win one," he recalled in his memoir. "I don't even feel that they won this one, even though the scoreboard showed four runs for them and three for us. The Nationals didn't really win it—I lost it."

That was the distillation of DiMaggio's worldview—and the Yankee ethic, expressed in one phrase. That's why DiMaggio and the Yanks were such a perfect match, and why his Yankees were different from every other club.

From our remove, at the end of the century, the Yankee Dynasty might look like a single seamless era of triumph—from the Babe and Murderers' Row in the twenties, through Joe's years in the thirties and forties, to Stengel and Mantle in the fifties and sixties. (Only blind loyalists would try to stretch the run into the years of Kaiser George.) . . . And it's true that the Yanks did dominate for almost fifty years: six pennants in the 1920s, five in the 1930s, five in the

1940s, eight in the 1950s, and five (in the first five years) in the 1960s. But from the inside, those were three distinct eras, and very different clubs.

Ruth's Yankees were all about high-hat and high times, three-run homers and 12–5 wins. The first year the Yankees won the pennant, in '21, they didn't just lead the league in home runs (and scoring), they hit three times as many homers as second-place Cleveland. (The Bambino himself hit twice as many as his nearest competitor—who was his teammate, Bob Meusel.) Of course, they swaggered: those Yankees were playing (they had invented) a different game than any other team could play. They were like the U.S. after World War II—the only country on the planet with the A-bomb.

Joe's Yankees were a cooler edition of the Pinstripes. When hard times hit in the 1930s and the Bambino's Bombers had played out the string, the ethic of the day became "Buckle Down." Along with the pennants, high living was gone. While the Babe was in flower, he'd pushed his own salary to a soaring eighty G's . . . but when Joe came up, the highest wage (Gehrig's) wasn't even half that much. As skipper, the Yanks had installed a demanding taskmaster, Joe McCarthy. Marse Joe didn't like "comfortable ballplayers." He didn't like characters, loudmouths, or oddballs. Swagger he simply wouldn't permit. He wanted players who did the little things right, who took every advantage, who stuck to business at all times. The Yanks still featured a powerful lineup—

but there was power all over the league now. These Yankees couldn't play a different game than other clubs. They just had to play better.

That was the mantra these Yanks heard eight months a year: no mistakes! McCarthy wouldn't harp on physical errors—a ball that dropped, a throw that sailed . . . anybody—everybody—had to contend with that sort of mistake. But a mental mistake— throwing to the wrong base, laggard or stupid baserunning, a lapse in concentration at the plate— that was a failure to pay attention . . . and that was in- excusable. McCarthy would turn to a rookie on the bench and ask, "What's the count?"—just to see if his head was in the game. McCarthy's rules were as square and unyielding as his jaw. On the road, every Yankee had to show up for breakfast, eight-thirty A.M., coat and tie, in the hotel dining room. Mc- Carthy didn't have to run curfew bed checks: he just checked their eyes in the morning. In the Yankee locker room, there was no shaving, no radio, no card games, and no pipe-smoking. "This is a clubhouse," McCarthy said, "not a club room."

Any player who thought about something other than baseball—other than winning baseball—was Joe McCarthy's ex-player. Once, when McCarthy was riding his boys hard (after two losses to Detroit), outfielder Roy Johnson complained, "What does Mc- Carthy want? Does he want us to win every day?" Johnson was unloaded to the Boston Bees. Winning every day was exactly what McCarthy wanted—all he wanted, all he thought about. His long-suffering wife was under instructions to pray for the Yankees every day at early Mass. One day, when her prayers were unavailing and her Joe came home discouraged by another loss, Mrs. McCarthy offered this solace: "Joe, we still have each other."

"Yes, dear," said McCarthy with a wan smile. "But in the ninth inning today, I would have traded you in for a sacrifice fly."

Small wonder, McCarthy and Ruth barely spoke. No rules, no stringency could bind the Bambino's joys—certainly none from "a weak-hittin' busher," which is how the Babe referred to his skipper. (Ruth thought *he* should have got the manager's job.)

And no wonder, Joe DiMaggio became McCarthy's perfect player. Of rules Young Joe was always mindful. Joys, he seemed to have none, save the one that McCarthy courted: winning.

From the start, Joe DiMaggio played ball the new Yankee way—with total attention, with maximum effort, with the certainty every moment that a million eyes were upon him. If DiMaggio talked, it was about baseball. He would never attract McCarthy's ire by laughter or ease after a loss: if the Yankees lost, Young Joe was as sour as the skipper. If the Yankees lost and Joe D. had made a mistake (or even failed to deliver), he was inconsolable—*he'd lost that game.*

In the decade to come, the pressure of winning, the woe of loss, would pile up on McCarthy until it seemed he was (literally) shrinking—he would retreat to remoteness and secret communion with a bottle. But the presence (and growing awe) of Joe DiMaggio in that clubhouse would continue to enforce the ethic of *"not losing."* More and more, that became the Yankees' way—the only way, as long as DiMaggio was there. That was how the Yankees were different—perhaps the biggest reason they were winners—and the reason they were respected, so much feared, and so richly hated.

Even a dozen years later, when McCarthy was long gone, a kid second baseman named Jerry Coleman would come up to the Yanks, sit in Joe D.'s clubhouse, and arrive at a chilling realization.

"Any other team," Coleman remembers, "guys would sit at their locker before the game and think: 'I'm gonna do something great today. I'm gonna hit a home run. I'm gonna win the game!'

"But the Yankees were different. Every day, you'd think: 'I'm not gonna be the one to make a mistake. I'm not gonna be the guy to screw up and lose this game.'

"By the end of two years, I was eating mush for breakfast. That was the only thing I could keep down before a game."

TWO WEEKS AFTER THE ALL-STAR Game, DiMaggio almost screwed up in a mortal way. He was back on track at the plate, playing right field steadily—his embarrassment in Boston was fading into memory—when, in a game against the Tigers, DiMaggio raced into right center, chasing a high drive off the bat of Goose Goslin.

The center fielder that day was Myril Hoag, who also took off after Goslin's liner. DiMaggio and Hoag collided at full speed—head-to-head—and both dropped to the ground like they'd been shot. Goslin scored an inside-the-park home run; after several minutes, DiMaggio and Hoag finally rose, and both men played out the inning. But Hoag was still woozy on the bench and sat out the rest of the game. Clearly, DiMaggio had caused the foul-up: the center fielder has the right of way on any ball he can get to. But no one said anything. The Yankees won the game. And Hoag was still in the lineup the following day.

Two days later, Hoag was found unconscious in his hotel room. At Harper Hospital in Detroit, doctors suspected his collision with DiMaggio had caused a blood clot in Hoag's brain. The Yankees had to move on. Their train was rolling toward Cleveland as surgeons drilled three holes to relieve the pressure in Hoag's skull, and then waited . . . there was nothing more they could do. Brain surgery was an infant science in 1936. Hoag might die, or might live on with brain damage—no one could predict. The Yankees learned by long-distance telephone that Hoag had survived the operation. In time he would recover fully, and play for another eight years in the bigs.

The collision with Hoag could have made Joe one of those sad specters of baseball history—like Carl

Mays, who could never live down his fatal beaning of Ray Chapman in 1920. But as it turned out, Joe was unscathed. Instead of a specter, he became a center fielder. McCarthy said he had that spot in mind from the start.

"Finally I decided he was ready so I moved him into center field," McCarthy told Maury Allen, in *Where Have You Gone, Joe DiMaggio?* ". . . He never would have become the great outfielder he was if I hadn't moved him. He needed that room to roam in Yankee Stadium. That's the toughest center field in baseball and only the real great ones can play out there.

". . . Once he got out there he stayed out there. He did everything so easily. That's why they never appreciated him as much as they should. You never saw him make a great catch. You never saw him fall down or go diving for a ball. He didn't have to. He just knew where the ball was hit and he went and got it. That's what you're supposed to do. The idea is to catch the ball. The idea isn't to make exciting catches."

Last-ditch drama wasn't McCarthy's style. With the rookie DiMaggio in center field, the Yankees clinched the pennant on September 9, the earliest date in the history of major league baseball. And they finished nineteen and a half games ahead of the second-place Tigers. After that season, the baseball writers awarded Lou Gehrig (.354, 49 HRs, 152 RBIs) the title of American League MVP. In those exacting days, no rookie would be considered for that prize. But the difference in the Yanks' performance—in every account that autumn—was credited to Joe. There was no Rookie of the Year ballot (that wasn't invented till 1940), but in '36, they wouldn't have needed a vote. The only question was whether Joe D. (.323, 29 HRs, 125 RBIs) was the best rookie *in history*. . . . But that debate wouldn't begin in earnest until the Yanks met the Giants for the title of titles—World Champs—in the subway Series of 1936.

In New York, the Giants still bore the mantle of class they'd earned through the long reign (1902–1932) of John J. McGraw. Now they held sway in the National League under their player-manager (and future Hall of Famer), first baseman Bill Terry. In the outfield, they were led by another all-time great, the National League home run leader, Mel Ott. And on the mound, they had the stopper of the age (and National League MVP), "King" Carl Hubbell.

It was a measure of the excitement that Young Joe's Yanks had stirred that they were favored eight-to-five by the bookies. But in Game One, the Yanks were mesmerized by Hubbell's screwball—they were beaten soundly, 6–1—and the Giants' outfield didn't have to make a putout all day.

That would be the last time the Yanks could be put to sleep. They came back in Game Two with eighteen runs and won in a laugher. Game Three was squeaky-tight, a 2–1 Yankee win. And the next day, the Yanks got revenge on Hubbell, when Gehrig won the game with a two-run homer.

The Giants were down three games to one—but they wouldn't fold. In Game Five, they eked out a 5–4 win in the tenth inning, to send the Series back to their home park, the Polo Grounds. In Game Six, the Yanks jumped out to a commanding three-run lead, but the Giants chipped away, chipped away—single runs in the fifth, the seventh, and the eighth . . . By the ninth inning, the Yanks were clinging to a one-run lead, and facing the possibility that they'd let the Giants back into the Series—then everything would rest on Game Seven, in the Polo Grounds—perhaps with the hypnotist, Hubbell, on the mound again. . . .

But it never got that far. In the ninth inning of Game Six, DiMaggio led off with a line single into left field. Gehrig singled and DiMaggio raced around to third. The next hitter, Dickey, bounced a sharp one-hopper to first baseman Bill Terry, who made the right play—he grabbed the ball and looked across the diamond, to freeze DiMaggio on third base. . . . But DiMaggio wasn't on third. He'd broken for home as the ball left the bat. Now he stopped in no-man's-land, while the crowd (and the Giants) screamed for Terry to gun him down.

Terry fired the ball to third—but DiMaggio broke again for home. Third baseman Eddie Mayo whipped the ball past Joe to the plate, and the catcher, Harry Danning, blocked the baseline, crouched for collision.

But DiMaggio didn't run into Danning. Joe didn't even slide. Instead, he launched himself into the air—head first, over the tag, completely over Danning . . . and in the air, Joe twisted his body, still falling . . . till he landed back of Danning, in the dirt, with his hand on the Polo Grounds plate.

And that was the end of the Giants. Danning was so flustered he juggled the ball while two remaining Yankee runners each took another base. Then the rest of the Giants came unglued . . . and the Yanks poured seven runs across (the last on Joe's second hit of the inning). The final tally was 13–5. The Yankees were the World Champions—and a new era of their dynasty was launched.

Joe had hit .346 for the Series. In the aftermath, the Giants' manager, Terry, could only pay homage: "I've always heard that one player could make the difference between a losing team and a winner, and I never believed it. Now I know, it's true."

Withal, those words from Terry were not the highest accolade for Joe in that Series. The topper came after the second game, also in the vast oval Polo Grounds—in fact, at the farthest reach of that oval. It was near the end of the Yankee blowout—18–4, the scoreboard read—and as the Giants took their last at bats, many of the 43,543 fans were on their way to the exits. That's when the public address announcer asked all present to stay at their seats, until one special fan, Franklin D. Roosevelt, could get to his open limousine and ride off the field through the center field gates.

It was just moments thereafter that the Giants' slugger, Hank Leiber, swung at a fastball from the weary Lefty Gomez and launched it like a mortar shell toward the fence in center field.

DiMaggio was off before the crack of the bat could be heard in the stands. He turned his back and raced for the deepest curve of the horseshoe. He was 475 feet from the plate when he made the impossible catch—over his shoulder, still running flat out . . . in fact, he just kept running, through the notch in the fence, up the steep stairs that led to the players' club-house, in deepest center field. Then, he remembered—*Roosevelt!*

Near the top of the stairs, Joe stopped, turned and stood with the ball in his glove, while the car came toward him. There he was—the nation's savior—in the back seat, with his hat cocked up, his trademark grin around the cigarette holder. Joe, without think-ing, stiffened to attention as the car rounded the cen-ter field gravel track, with all eyes upon it—save for Roosevelt's eyes. He looked to the stands, then to the stairway, until he found Joe . . . and then FDR lifted a hand in a jaunty wave from the brim of his hat. And from the crowd there was a final, rippling cheer, as the Dago boy from Fisherman's Wharf was saluted by the President of the United States.

Lefty Gomez showing Joe around town, 1937.

Celebrating: Joe McCarthy and his perfect boy.

**At home with the nieces, and a plateful
of Mamma's spaghetti.**

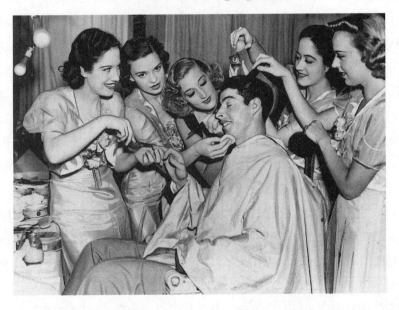

**The showgirls take good care of Joe on the set
of *Manhattan Merry-Go-Round*.**

CHAPTER 7

♦

BY LINGUISTIC HAPPENSTANCE, *FAME*
is the Italian word for hunger. And by '36, the Italian-
Americans were famished for respect.

They were the largest immigrant group in California. They'd helped to build the New World's new
world and, by their labor, they had hauled their families, their colony, into the economic mainstream. In
San Francisco, they had good jobs, businesses, political power; they'd built churches to promote and display their faith, and schools to foster their heritage
for a new generation—nine Italian language schools
in San Francisco alone, and forty-seven in the state as
a whole. But by 1936, those schools were under attack as instruments of fascist propaganda from Mussolini . . . and by the end of that year, all those
schools were closed.

These Italian-Americans were of two worlds, and
alas, at that moment, with honor in neither. Mussolini had been their champion, the modern strongman who would make their old nation a power, a
world model. ("You're the tops: you're Mussolini,"
wrote Cole Porter, in '34.) The matrons of North
Beach proudly sent *Il Duce* their gold wedding

bands. He would melt them down to fund the glory of
La Nuova Italia and send back copies of the rings,
made by Italian craftsmen in steel.

But by '36, to most Americans, Mussolini had become a villain and a running joke: he was the bald-
headed butcher of Ethiopia, a strutting speechifier in
the newsreels, Hitler's Dago stooge. Now the North
Beach ladies kept their steel rings in drawers at
home; the papas put their children into the public
schools; they changed the names of their businesses
and clubs into English . . . after all, weren't they
good Americans?

But whom did they have to show off in America?
Sacco and Vanzetti? Frank Nitti? Capone? Those
were the only Italians in the movies—anarchist
bomb-tossers, or tommy-gun killers—except for
character-cameos: the tricky little organ grinders,
talky fruit peddlers, and hand-waving hankie-
sniffing opera fops.

To be sure, from where the *immigranti* stood, in the
pride of *Italianità,* these North Beach faithful saw
plenty of Italians of distinction, achievement. There
were famous artists, like Joe Stella, and America's
greatest conductor, Toscanini. There were popular
pols like their own Mayor Rossi, Maestri in New Or-
leans, and New York's La Guardia; captains of fi-
nance like A. P. Giannini; inventors and scientists
like Marconi (who'd won a Nobel Prize!) or Fermi
(who'd win just two years thence). But somehow, the
image of Italians in America hadn't caught up.

It didn't seem fair. It was *ingiusto!* Even the *melangian'* (the eggplants) in Harlem had their own champion, their own exemplar of strength, silent courage—one of those quiet American heroes. When Joe Louis won the heavyweight crown, every black man in the U.S.A. walked taller. So whom did the Italians have? Primo Carnera!

Da Preem! . . . The very nickname was an incantation of sorrow—a stain on the honor of their people. Primo Carnera had been a circus strongman back in Italy, before he started boxing, and came to this country as the Great Dago Hope. He was truly a giant—six feet six, and easily an eighth of a ton. He looked indestructible, just exactly what Mussolini claimed he was—a fascist hero, the new Italian, man of steel.

And he was going to be the champ! The papers all said so. They called him "The Ambling Alp." They said there was no one in the ring who could stand up to him—that huge right hand! They said, all his fights, he won them easy! . . . And then he was the champ—for one shining moment. So, they said he won it with a phantom punch—no one could see it. So what? An Italian was the *Champeen of the World!* Coast to coast, in every town, every Italian neighborhood, there were bonfires of celebration, and Italian boys who burned with pride.

There was only one problem: Primo's huge right hand couldn't really dent a sheet of tinfoil. He did win the crown with a phantom punch—arranged in advance by his secret backer, Owney "The Killer" Madden, one of the big New York mobsters, owner of the Cotton Club in Harlem. In fact, the whole thing, start to finish, was a put-up job, a wise-guy fix. Those other fights—Primo *did* win 'em easy . . . there wasn't any fighting going on. And the newspaper stories, well . . . those writers took money from the Madden boys, too. What the hell, Madden would get it all back—and millions more—from the sucker Dagos, who'd put their sucker salaries on Primo Carnera, when Madden put him in the ring against a real fighter. That bout came in 1934, when Max Baer made a monkey of the man of steel. Baer knocked Carnera down twelve times—a record. And before it was over, he'd almost killed him.

The saddest part was, everybody knew the fix was in, all the wiseguys, all the real fight fans—everybody was in on the scam—except poor Carnera, and the sucker Dagos. They only found out too late, when they'd lost their money . . . when it turned out their shining knight was a bum, a puppet, a clown act . . . when Carnera and Mussolini became interchangeable punch lines on the same jokes—those old jokes about fighting Italians. By 1936, Carnera had left the ring. The Italians were still searching for their American hero. And then, like an answered prayer to the saints, there was Joe.

DiMaggio was everything Carnera wasn't: young, slender, quiet, dignified—and home-grown. He wasn't from Mussolini, or for Mussolini. Joe was everything the papers said and more. (Next year, he might break *all* the records!) He played that clean American game, not in nighttime smoke, sweat, and spattered blood, but in God's own sunshine, on pristine grass. He was strong, but shy—a regular Joe—from a big family, working people, who'd made their way by honest labor. He played for the team whose very name stood for America. By his natural grace, he'd made them champions. (And whom did he invite to the World Series—brought across the country for that brilliant event? His mamma!) . . . DiMaggio was their American story. Here was the face they could show in their new world.

So, when Joe came home from his rookie season, there were thousands of *paesani* waiting for his train . . . who shanghaied him off the platform and drove him in an open car, cheering his name through the downtown streets . . . all the way to City Hall, where they bore him on their shoulders to the mayor's office, so the Honorable Angelo Rossi could present him with the key to the city.

THERE WAS NOTHING JOE COULDN'T have in San Francisco—nothing in North Beach, surely. Whatever was in the gift of its citizens was his, if he would deign to take it. And at home, well, whatever he did was fine—wonderful—he was the engine of their progress. In retrospect, these were the best times for the family. So many miracles!

Joe had brought home an extra six thousand four hundred dollars, a winner's World Series share. That made almost fifteen thousand dollars *in one year*. . . . But it wasn't just prosperity, it was promise: vastly more to come. Tom and Joe were already talking about next year—maybe twenty-five thousand dollars in salary alone. And it wasn't just Joe. It was promise all around.

With the money Joe brought, Mike got his own boat—crab in the wintertime, salmon in the summer. Mike was on his own now, with a good wife who became a part of the family. Tom was still living at home, and crabbing—though his quiet good sense had now won him a second job: vice president of the Crab Fisherman's Association. And, still, he was running the family business—much more business than there used to be: Tom and Joe were planning to open a restaurant, were looking for a partner; they'd build a big place right on Fisherman's Wharf—*Joe DiMaggio's Grotto*—how could it miss? . . . Vince was out of the household, married in Southern California, and seldom spoken of—but he wasn't cut off from his mamma's prayers. And now they were answered: Vince's contract was bought by the Boston Bees. Now there'd be two DiMaggios in the big leagues. . . . And that same winter, Dommie got his chance with Mr. Graham and the Seals. He was going to have a contract—and play outfield like his brothers.

It was like some giant, unseen hand had pushed open a door, and behind it lay a wide new world for them. No witch in the neighborhood could ever have foretold that Rosalie DiMaggio would cross the nation in a Pullman parlor car, and spend two weeks without chores of any sort, while she watched the World Series and saw the sights in New York (the great Liberty Statue that she'd glimpsed one fearful dawn, more than thirty years before) . . . while she slept in a Mayflower Hotel suite, while the restaurants of the great city strove to please her, while the newspapers begged for her picture and a few words. Who could have dreamed that up? "I don't know what to do here," said Rosalie DiMaggio. "There is no work. I wish there was some cleaning to do here, or some dishes I could wash and dry."

Who among the thousand poor and wary souls on Ísola delle Fémmine would ever have hoped—would ever have risked the evil eye to dream—that he and his sons would own two splendid boats (with motors!) . . . that he might be shopping for a splendid house—to own it free and clear—with a bed for every child (no, a *room* for every child) . . . that he wouldn't have to fish at all, but would dress every day in a three-piece suit and tour the wharves as a statesman, an elder uncle—*Zio Peppe*—to the workingmen of the fleet. How could Giuseppe (even now) believe that he was invited, with Signor Crosetti, to lunch at the house of Signor Lazzeri *(a Genoese),* where photographers would make a picture for the nation, a picture the proud papa would hand to his daughter, to paste in her scrapbook about the famous family he made. All from playing with a ball!

Now, in the mornings, Giuseppe would unstick the flaps of some envelope that had come to the house, and on that scrap, with an awkward hand, he would write down numbers in a system of his own devising. The grandchildren who played around the house would find these odd papers, and though it wasn't their place to ask, they would wonder: *Papa can't write the words we use, but he's writing numbers just like us* . . . and, of course, no one knew why . . . until one of the grandkids was learning long division at school, and Giuseppe told her he would set her a problem. If a baseball player goes to bat four hundred and twenty-nine times, and he makes one hundred fifty-eight hits, how is he doing? Just as she'd learned at school, the girl worked the problem atop a long stairway of subtractions . . . three, six, eight, two, nine . . . but before she could finish, Giuseppe gleefully took his hand off his envelope: 3 6 8, it said. He'd taught himself how to track Joe's average.

Baseball, Giuseppe maintained, was the most excellent game; and his sons (though he wouldn't say this aloud) played more excellently than anyone else. With each new family triumph, he would gravely receive *auguri*—congratulations from the other papas at the Wharf. With each new tribute he would modestly concur, claiming nothing for himself. *"Figghiu miu ha fattu bravu."* Yes, my son has done well.

Now, if Joe happened to be rising, wanting coffee, just as Giuseppe was anticipating his midday meal . . . well, no longer did the old man think his son a lazy, lag-abed bum. Joe had to get proper rest. Or if Joe happened to be coming home as the sky was growing light (and Giuseppe finished *his* morning coffee) . . . that was not Giuseppe's affair. That was strictly Joe's business. And the old man could have confidence: he'd never hear about that business from others; he'd never have to explain away anything that Joe did. For if his namesake had learned nothing else from Giuseppe, surely, he had taken in Lesson Number One: no one else should ever know your business. Reputation is like currency, to be held in the fist: everybody else wants to take it from you.

JOE DIDN'T SPEND MUCH TIME IN the neighborhood, except at home, except to sleep— or except when photographers had to make his picture. They'd always want a shot of him at Fisherman's Wharf, holding up a crab, or mending his brother's nets—like that's how Joe spent the winter.

But no matter how ridiculous, the pictures were important to Joe—each one a message to the Yankees, about his contentment at home, about his popularity . . . about the hero game. Joe and Tom had sent back the Yankees' contract. That hardnose, Barrow, was offering no more than Joe had made as a rookie. Then, Barrow sent a second contract—a substantial raise, fifteen thousand dollars. But Joe wouldn't sign. He wanted twenty.

So, there were more pictures on the wire—of Joe with his old neighborhood pals . . . singing! They put Joe in the front, holding an accordion that he couldn't play. They got the name of the club wrong; they called it "Jolly Rogers." But it got the message across: Joe was with friends, unconcerned.

In truth, that was about the only time that Joe got together with the Jolly Knights. His friends were older now. Shirts DeMarco was still around wherever Joe went, joined now by a happy fast talker, a some-times fisherman named Reno Barsocchini. They were what the boys called "fast clippers." They didn't hang around North Beach. That was too close, too many eyes, people who knew Joe—it made him nervous. And they didn't spend their time singing.

Niggy Marino ran into Joe one time that winter, downtown—Fourth and Mission—in a whorehouse run by a madam named Flo. The place was famous for young girls—none over twenty-one—and Joe had a bevy around him, like a pasha. He seemed glad to see Niggy, even offered to pay for Niggy's girl. (He owed him one.) But Niggy was Sicilian enough to know, he couldn't take anything from Joe. "Naw, I done it already," Niggy said, and got the hell out of the place. Anyone from home was going to make Joe tense.

Joe was more and more nervous as the winter wore on. It turned out people knew him all over town.

Everybody asked about his contract. And Barrow, in New York, had him listed as a holdout. Wire photos were all very well but no one, least of all Joe, believed that he was going to hang around mending nets. The ace of the pitching staff, Red Ruffing, was holding out—and Gehrig, the Iron Horse, the MVP. Joe figured those guys would get the attention (and any extra money in the budget, too). Joe was a poker player: he knew when to fold a losing hand. He would settle for seventeen thousand dollars, double his rookie pay.

The truth was, Joe knew, just like his dad: everything he had came from playing ball. And he would hold what he'd attained with a white-knuckled fist. He'd let nothing take it away: no mistakes! No bad contracts, no bad seasons; if he could prevent it, not one bad game; no whispers to dull the shine on his name, no bad stories, not one bad photo.

There was another old friend who saw DiMaggio that winter—when Joe and his entourage left town so they could relax in private. Tony Gomez, the shortstop who was too black to play for the Seals, was playing in the lumber leagues in Reno, Nevada, and working that winter for a Reno garage. A newspaper friend tipped Tony off: "You know who's in town? It's your pal, DiMaggio."

Tony and the newsman found Joe in a nightclub, about five P.M., having a couple of belts. Joe remembered Tony, of course.

"Hey, Gomez, how you doin'?"

"Hey, Joe, let's take a couple of pictures—you and me."

Joe was off his stool in a flash. "Not here! Shit! NOT HERE!"

THE STRANGE PART WAS, THE PRES-sure went away when Joe went east again to play ball. At least it was different, easier. No one could control the game, of course, but Joe was in charge of every-thing *he* did. On the field he could do everything right.

He wanted a full spring training, to start the year at the top of his game. But medical woes once again in-tervened. This time, he played but nine exhibitions. Then, he couldn't raise his arm without pain. So the Yanks sent him north alone, once again, to the doc-tors: this time, it was tonsillitis (and the nerve inflam-mation had spread to his arm). So, there was a tonsillectomy—and once again, a drumroll of three weeks, before Joe trotted out to center field.

On May 1, DiMaggio made his first start, and it looked like a replay of last year's heroics: Joe went four-for-four against the Red Sox, the Yankees won 3–2, and DiMaggio figured in every run they scored. Daniel crowed in the *World Telegram:* "DiMaggio is back." But it wasn't the same old Joe.

He was better. It was hard to believe, but he was just twenty-two, a growing boy: now he was almost six feet two, close to two hundred pounds, and every extra pound was bad news for pitchers. Joe widened his stance at the plate, cut down on his stride till he was even more motionless . . . and took off on a home run tear.

In early June, he hit two in one game against the hapless Browns to put his season total at eleven. By July 4, he got to twenty, with a grand slam that broke up a tie game, and gave the Yanks a doubleheader sweep. There were sixty-one thousand fans in the park that day, and as the *New York Times* described the scene, "The stands shook with shouts and stomping, a deafening crescendo of shrieks, cheers, whistling and handclapping. At the plate there began a demonstration of affectionate mobbing that continued on the bench as every player pummeled and thumped the youth."

This was living! Or this was his life now. In the season, every day, he had things to do—and he did them. No one could ask for more. And no one would ask about anything else. In New York, Joe would take a cab—or even better, get a ride—from his Edison Hotel suite (they gave him a break: five bucks a day—he could pay the whole thing from his meal money) . . . to the Stadium, arriving sometimes by eleven A.M. The game wouldn't start until three o'clock, but in the locker room, Joe was safe, at home. This was in accord with the Yankee ethic; Joe McCarthy wanted his boys in their roost, talking baseball. "Guys who rush in and out of the clubhouse," the skipper always said, "rush in and out of the big leagues." After games, DiMaggio would stay later than anyone else: maybe after two or three hours he'd emerge. That way, even the die-hard kids with autograph books would have given up. He wouldn't have to talk to anyone.

On a stool in front of his locker, legs crossed, a smoke in his hand, he had everything he needed: a baseball game to think about, guys to listen to, guys who catered to him. The chief of the clubhouse (Clubhouse Boy, he was called, no matter his age) was Pete Sheehy, who'd come running if Joe even looked his way. "Half-a-cuppa-coffee-Pete," Joe would murmur, like a good-luck mantra, every fifteen minutes or so. Sheehy would appear instantly with the half-a-cup, and some half-baked wisecrack to keep Joe loose. Pete had been around forever— since the days of Ruth, anyway—so he had needling rights. One day, DiMaggio was pulling on his pants, when he stopped, and fingered gingerly at something on his buttock, something that hurt. Joe craned his neck around, trying to see, but that was hopeless. "Hey, Pete!" he called. "Come look at this. I can't see what the hell this is." Pete appeared, bent at Joe's behind and announced, rather louder than was required: "It's a pimple from all the guys kissin' yer ass."

Joe took it from Sheehy; he knew Pete loved him. The sure sign was the number on Joe's pinstripes: Pete handed out the uniforms. The Yankees had invented numbers on the back of the jersey—along with the pinstripes (designed by Col. Ruppert's tailor, to make the Babe look not-so-fat). The first Yankee numbers reflected, simply, the batting order: so, the Bambino was Number 3, Gehrig was Number 4, etc. But after that first generation of Bombers, Sheehy took over, and the numbers became his judgment call. When Joe came up, Pete gave him a respectable Number 18, which had been worn by the pitcher Johnny Allen until McCarthy exiled him to Cleveland. By the time Joe actually played in a major league game, Sheehy had revalued him to Number 9 (i.e., the best number unworn by the Founding Fathers). And now, Joe had received Pete Sheehy's highest tribute: there was the Babe, there was Gehrig . . . and Number 5 was DiMag.

Anyway, Joe liked wiseacres. They made him laugh. They said the things he wouldn't or couldn't say. If some of the jokes were on him, that didn't bother the Daig (as they called him—short for Dago, of course). Actually, the Yankees had a nickname problem. With Lazzeri and Crosetti still anchoring the middle infield, Lazzeri became Big Dago, Crosetti was Little Dago, and Joe was simply Dago, or Daig. One day, the best joker (and star left-hander) on the club, Vernon "Goofy" Gomez, was holding a lead against the woeful Browns—late innings, one man out, and one Browns runner on first. The next batter slapped a comebacker to Gomez, who wheeled around to start the double play . . . but fired the ball way over second base, into center field—straight to DiMaggio, who was charging in to back up the play.

That put Brownies on first and second, and in the Yankee dugout, the skipper was furious. When the inning ended—Gomez pitched out of the jam—Joe McCarthy climbed all over his pitcher.

"We should've had a double play! What the hell are you thinkin' out there?"

"Someone shouted, 'Throw it to the Dago,'" Gomez replied mildly. "Nobody said which Dago."

McCarthy turned to the dugout at large and barked: "From now on you'll specify which Dago, you hear me?"

Then, he noted all his boys laughing into their hands. Gomez was the only one who could needle McCarthy.

Gomez was Joe's road roomie now, and El Goofo took care of the kid, like Joe was his silent little brother. In every town, the Knights of Columbus, the Verdi Association, or some other Italian-American club, wanted Joe to grace their meeting, their dinner. Joe couldn't turn them all down . . . but he wouldn't go without Lefty.

"We would sit through these boring dinners," Gomez recalled to Maury Allen, in *Where Have You Gone, Joe DiMaggio?,* "and finally the guy would get around to introducing all his cousins and uncles and friends in the audience. Joe would get up, the crowd would give him a big hand, and he would say, 'Thank you for inviting me. Now you can hear Lefty tell some funny stories.' Then he would sit down and I would have to entertain them for twenty minutes before we could go home. Then they would load him down with presents and that would be the evening. He'd come home with a dozen shirts or a golf bag or a watch or a toilet set or luggage or something like that.

". . . Everybody who knew Joe in those days knew he didn't talk. I remember a two-week road trip— New York, Chicago, Detroit, Cleveland, and St. Louis. Two weeks, not one word. I'll tell you what he did do. He would take along one of those small radios on the trip and listen to the radio, the big-band music and those old quiz shows. Dr. IQ and things like that. He'd read the sports pages and he'd read—well, he'll probably kill me for this but he loved to read *Superman* comics.

"One day we were walking down the street of some town and he suddenly turns to me and says, 'Lefty, you know what day today is?' I say, 'Yeah, Wednesday.' Then he says, 'No, no, today is the day the new *Superman* comes out.' Every Wednesday there was a new issue. So now he sees this newspaper stand and looks to see if they got comic books. He points to it and wants me to get it for him. He stands off to the side. Hell, he was Joe DiMaggio and if the newsstand guy saw him buy *Superman* comics it would be all over the world. I got one of those faces nobody could ever recognize so he wants me to buy it for him. 'Joe, is this what you want, the *Superman* comics?' He looks around at a couple of people there and he says, 'No, you know I wouldn't buy that.'

Then I walk away and he motions again. I finally buy it for him and he stuffs it into his pocket. He spends the night with Superman."

IN HIS SECOND YEAR, DIMAGGIO WAS threatening to break the greatest record in American sports—Babe Ruth's mark of sixty home runs—and the wires flashed his every at bat to fans across the nation. Joe had twenty-three by mid-July, when sixty thousand Cleveland faithful paid their way into Municipal Stadium, rooting for their own kid phenom, Bob Feller, to shut DiMaggio down. Rapid Robert threw harder than any man in the game. And with an unhittable curveball to match his heater, the eighteen-year-old ace was on his way to four consecutive years as the AL strikeout king. But Feller wasn't too bright. Instead of working Joe with that wicked curve, Feller kept trying to throw the fastball by him. Joe touched him up for a double and a triple, and then in the ninth, two outs, game tied, DiMaggio smashed a grand slam.

BULLETIN:
NY 5, Cle. 1; HR DiMaggio (24);
DiMaggio 5 RBI . . .

At the end of July, DiMaggio hit three in one weekend, two in one game, to raise his total to thirty-one homers.

DiMaggio One Ahead of Ruth Pace in '27 . . .

Two days later, almost sixty-seven thousand fans came to Yankee Stadium—on a *Tuesday*—for Gehrig Appreciation Day, Lou's 1,900th straight game. Lou got a pocket watch presented by the Broadway star George M. Cohan; the Yankees got a doubleheader sweep over the White Sox; and Joe got the cheers for his thirty-second home run.

Poor Larrupin' Lou. For thirteen years, he'd played every game at first base—played through seventeen different fractures of the small bones in his hands and fingers. He'd been friendly to his fellow players, modest with the writers, a sterling model for the city's youth . . . but he never could be the star.

Not that he didn't try. Gehrig (actually his smart wife) hired a publicist and business manager— Christy Walsh, an aggressive tout who'd kept Babe Ruth out of bankruptcy by booking him for exhibition games, shows, promotions, and moving pictures. Walsh said Gehrig should change his public image, and offered him to the movie world as America's next Tarzan. Alas, the Coast producers took one look at Lou in lion skins and decided he looked better in knickers. His legs would never make the grade. Lou did land an endorsement deal for Huskies Cereal, from Quaker Oats. But it only made him famous as a boob. On a nationwide radio show, Lou was asked what he ate of a morning, and in his nervousness blurted out, "a heaping bowlful of Wheaties!"

Walsh finally got Lou into a picture show, a mod-
ern-day western, wherein Lou appeared as Lou (in
pants) and routed the bad guys by hurling billiard
balls at their heads. Reaction was more or less
summed up by Jack Miley, the *New York Daily News*
writer, whose comments were reprinted nationwide:
"As an actor he's a good first baseman. He oughta let
it go at that. . . .

"Lou is a helluva good ballplayer," Miley wrote,
"but he lacks color and you can't smear that stuff on
with a brush. . . . If anybody is going to replace Ruth
and overshadow his teammates as an individual attraction with the Yanks, it will be DiMag and not
Gehrig. . . . When it comes to that personal magne-
tism, you've either got it or you ain't. Like love, you
can't buy it in a store. Roosevelt has it; Hoover
hasn't. Dempsey has it, but not Tunney. DiMaggio,
like Ruth, has; but not Gehrig."

Gehrig acknowledged his deficiencies in the
"color" department. He thought the cause was his
shyness, the lack of a snappy line: "When these writers would ask me questions," he was quoted by his biographer, Ray Robinson, in *The Iron Horse,* "they'd
often think I was rude if I didn't answer right away.
They didn't know I was so scared I was almost shit-
ting in my pants."

But Joe was as shy—and just as silent—as Gehrig.
The difference was that Joe was aware from the first
moment, aware at every moment, of the hero game.
He was alive to the power of the camera: he made

himself available, he could smile, and he knew when to smile. With writers he was as alert, as poised and pent as he was in center field. Positioning was the edge in both games.

Joe didn't have to say much. Any words from him were like a confidence that he bestowed, not to be misused. If Joe talked to a couple of writers, they felt like they were on the inside. "Get a load of that blonde," Joe would say—and they'd never forget it. They'd never forget: *"DiMag said that to me!"* He could bring them in—just enough—so they could play the big game together.

The morning after Gehrig Appreciation Day, Joe was out early, off to the Bronx—not to the ballpark, but farther uptown, to the Biograph Studios on East 175th. He was going into the movies, too, with a cameo as a would-be singer in *Manhattan Merry-Go-Round*. A reporter from the *Telegram* watched Joe sit for makeup, then pose amid a gaggle of show-girls—one of them combing his hair, another giving him a manicure. And Joe leaned over to the newsman (just man-to-man, of course), and whispered: "This is hotter'n a ballpark!" After the manicure, Joe confided: "The smart thing I do is never fall in love. I just talk a good game with women."

Joe only had three lines in the movie, but he screwed them up enough to require twelve retakes. Plenty of fun could have been made of that. But in the paper, next day, there was no mocking "analysis" of

Joe DiMaggio, thespian. The writer mentioned the twelve takes only to inform his readers: "All the girls whispered that Joe improved with every one of them, and that should be enough for you. They said he was only colossal at first."

It turned out, the writer missed the big story (or wouldn't write it). One of the showgirls on that set was a Minnesota blonde, Dorothy Arnoldine Olson, who used the stage name Dorothy Arnold. Someone brought word to her that Joe DiMaggio would like to meet her.

"Who?" . . . She'd never heard of him.

"He's a Yankees slugger!"

"So what?" she said. But she went over to meet him anyway. And that was how Joe first broke his smart rule about love.

IT HAD TO BE A SHOWGIRL FOR JOE, of course: Gomez was married to a showgirl—June O'Dea, the song-and-dance artiste. Lefty had seen her in a Broadway musical in '32—and had to meet her. Now they were the fraternity's idea of the perfect couple. June was fun, and quite a looker. You could almost hear a buzz through the Stadium when she'd arrive, in her picture hat and makeup, and settle herself in the club seats behind home plate. She understood about nightlife, too, so Lefty still got around with the boys—even in New York—and didn't disappear with a ring through his nose, like a lot of those poor, henpecked shmoes. (Like, for instance, the dutiful and uxorious Herr Gehrig.)

The way the writers had it figured, Joe did everything Lefty did—from the start, since Joe came up and Gomez adopted him, when the kid didn't know *nothin'*. ("What do I do with this jock strap, Lefty? It's dirty." . . . "Put it in the basket, dummy. And go tell Pete, 'I need a jock.' ") Joe would show up with a beautiful new suit (he was always in a beautiful suit now), and everybody knew that it came from Lefty's tailor. Lefty was a bug about fit and finish in clothes—had to be perfect! You'd see them together at the Garden for fights—that was Joe's favorite night out, the fights—or after a big bout, at Dempsey's bar, and Gomez would be introducing Joe around like a broad. Lefty knew everybody in the New York sporting scene. They all loved him, told stories about him, or retold his: Lefty was good for a party, even when he wasn't there.

And what a welcome new member of the club was Joe! He couldn't tell jokes like Lefty, but he liked a good story, and he'd listen all night. He liked the fight game and the tough-talking boxing guys. Pretty soon they were inviting him; they'd save him ringside seats . . . of course, as their guest—*they insisted*. That was the point they wanted to show: they knew him—the new star in town. The sporting scene was a betting scene; and with bettors, big players, you were in the know, or you were really a shmoe.

One of the "players" who latched on to DiMaggio was Joe Gould, a sharp operator who was manager to the heavyweight boxer Jimmy Braddock. Gould had an eye for talent—unschooled talent: he'd found Braddock, for instance, on the docks, and made him into the heavyweight champ. (Gould would also make the deal with the mob in Detroit for Braddock's bout with Joe Louis—the bout that would make Louis the champ.) It was Gould and Braddock who squired Joe to Billy Lahiff's bar one afternoon, and introduced him to the headwaiter, Bernard "Toots" Shor. Toots was a Philadelphian—he'd only been in New York since 1930—but, by the time Joe walked into his joint, he was already a famous Broadway character—built like a bear, loud, insulting, and beloved. He'd run a couple of speaks for the mob— Lucky Luciano was his boss—and after repeal he bounced in and out of saloon jobs. (No place could afford him for long.) He was actually running Lahiff's—running it into the ground. Toots took it as an insult if any of his friends tried to pay.

Toots always had a three-way problem: sports, friends, and money. Sports and friends were the only things he cared about—money was just for throwing around. But his friends cost him a fortune. And the way Toots bet, sports cost him even more. For instance, Joe's first year, '36, Toots had ahold of Lahiff's (ready access to the cash in the till), and he was riding a beautiful streak with his first love, the Giants, as they took the pennant in the National

League. Toots was sixty grand up on the season—clean at Lahiff's and fifty thousand dollars in the bank. So he put it on the Giants in the Series . . . which, of course, the Yankees won. By the time Toots met DiMaggio, Joe simply had to be his guest. It was a perfect example of the three-way problem: How could a guy with class, like Toots, worry about a bar tab between friends? Especially when that friend's *a champion!* And a champ who already cost Toots *Fifty Large!* . . . No, Joe couldn't buy a peanut in his joint.

Joe was everybody's favorite guest: quiet, mannerly, never any trouble, self-possessed but never full of himself. Wherever he went, he gave the place distinction—as long as they didn't make a show, introduce him from the stage or something like that. If they did, he was out of there. But in New York there were plenty of places that could take care of a guy in a quiet way. And plenty of people took care of Joe.

Polly Adler, for example, ran the best whorehouse in New York: beautiful appointments, gorgeous girls, the best food, best booze, satin sheets in every room—everything the finest, and most discreet. Joe's new Broadway friends used to bring him in, thought he'd love it. But Joe happened to mention, he had a complaint. It was those shiny sheets—his knees kept slipping! Well, not for nothing Polly was the best madam in New York. Immediately she sent out for a set of plain cotton sheets. Those were kept in a closet, at the ready, and called ever after the DiMaggio Sheets.

The fact was, the writers had it only half right: Joe did learn from Gomez. But Lefty, in truth, wasn't out on the town quite as much as they thought. And pretty soon, Joe was getting around to places even Lefty didn't go. Maybe Joe would have been better off if he'd stayed at Lefty's knee. For when Joe started talking to his new pals about things that concerned him—money, the Yankees, the sports business—well, of course, they helped out with a world of advice. And Joe took on, as his new brain trust, Joe Gould, Jim Braddock, Toots Shor . . . a mob-connected boxing tout, a heavyweight champ on his way down, and the most spendthrift barkeep in New York.

JOE BACKED OFF GRACEFULLY FROM his quest for Ruth's record. In August, as his pace slowed, DiMaggio confided to Dan Daniel, he'd be happy if he got to fifty home runs. He said he was more interested in runs batted in: "My goal is to sweep the sacks," he was quoted. ". . . I get a thrill in sending runners home." Privately, Joe groused that he could have hit seventy homers, if he played in a park that was fair to right-handers. And he might have, too: he hit at least a score of huge drives—four hundred feet to left center, four-ten, four-twenty . . . that were just loud outs in the grand Bronx ballyard.

Even so, his forty-six homers led the league—led both leagues, and handily: Hank Greenberg (with forty) and Gehrig (thirty-seven) trailed in the AL; the closest National Leaguer was Mel Ott, with thirty-one. DiMaggio finished with an average of .346, leading the league in runs and total bases; he was second in hits and runs batted in. And after the Yanks had disposed of the Giants in a lopsided Series—five games, it was never close—Joe fell only four votes shy of the highest individual honor in baseball: Most Valuable Player. (He was aced out by the sentimental vote for Charlie Gehringer, the esteemed Detroit second baseman, a veteran of fourteen years who'd won the batting crown with .371.)

No one in the history of big-league ball had broken in with two years like DiMaggio's. In fact, you had to know where to burrow in the books to find two consecutive years as spectacular—from any man, at any time. No less an oracle than Connie Mack, the septuagenarian sage of the A's (who'd seen his first ball-games during the Civil War), said Joe could be the greatest ever—and was already the greatest drawing card: "He has attracted a new type of fan to our games. He has made the Italian population baseball conscious." At twenty-two, with a baseball lifetime ahead of him, Joe was money in the bank.

So where was his?

After that '37 season, Joe and Tom did open a big new restaurant at Fisherman's Wharf. (They'd found a partner—but still, there were a thousand costs to get Joe DiMaggio's Grotto open and up to speed.) . . . And then, too, Joe spent almost his whole salary to buy the family a new house in the Marina District. That was a major league move for the DiMaggios. The old neighborhood of North Beach—the four-room flat on Taylor Street—lay only a mile away. But the Marina was another world. There, his mother would have her first living room, over the garage *(a garage!),* a washing machine, an electric icebox, a backyard, and only the finest neighbors. They didn't bring a thing from Taylor Street; not one chair. It had to be new: furniture, carpets, draperies, new kitchen things, new bedding—a new life.

Joe had responsibilities now—and he wanted to be paid like the greatest in the game, too. So, at the start of 1938, he didn't just send back Barrow's first contract, he asked for a meeting, face-to-face with Col. Ruppert. Joe said he was headed back east anyway—you know, to pick up a couple of awards, and to see his pal Jim Braddock fight Tommy Farr at the Garden.

It's possible that Joe thought, if he could fairly present his record (just man-to-man, you understand), the beer baron might take an interest, and offer a contract that made them both look good. Or it's possible Joe believed that just as no pitcher could stand up to him, no owner could either.

But no man on the mound ever kept Joe waiting six days before throwing him a pitch—which was how long Joe had to cool his heels in New York, before Baron Ruppert found time to see him. And when Joe finally did get an appointment, he was iced outside of

Ruppert's office for an additional forty-five minutes. Worse, Joe was stuck with a gaggle of newsmen who were after him the whole time for comments and pictures. *(Hey, Joe! Stand over there and make like you're rappin' on the door to his office.* . . . Bravely smiling, Joe did.)

The papers were all over this story. And why not? Gehrig wasn't signing, DiMaggio wanted a talk. It looked like the World Champs might come apart over money. Some of the newsmen wrote that DiMag would hold out for whatever Gehrig got. (Joe denied that.) One writer bid for a huge scoop when he wrote that Joe had already signed: his "holdout" was actually a Yankee trick to keep Gehrig from asking for the moon. (Joe hotly denied that, too.) DiMaggio was so busy denying, correcting, and explaining his case that Ruppert and Ed Barrow were already miffed: that upstart was trying to make the club look bad in the papers! The much-heralded meeting lasted only minutes. Ruppert, Barrow, and Joe looked grim as they emerged. The gap between them was "substantial" . . . and Joe went back to San Francisco with nothing in his hand.

Ruppert had warned DiMaggio to stop discussing his demands with the writers—but the Baron coyly broke his own silence. "I suppose there'll be no end of wild guessing among you fellows," Ruppert said. "So, I might as well tell. It's $25,000 and I think that is a very fair salary. I don't intend to go any higher." . . . With a top-drawer dinner ("in the French manner") advertised at a buck and a half, with a new V-6 Chevrolet retailing at $648, with the papers complaining that the average WPA "dole" had risen to $33 a month . . . Ruppert knew his offer sounded like a fortune.

And when it emerged that DiMaggio wanted *forty thousand dollars,* the word "greed" started cropping up in the papers. No third-year player had ever been paid like that. Gehrig was approaching two thousand straight games, and his last contract was thirty-six thousand dollars. After Lou's '37 season—a .351 average, thirty-seven homers, and a hundred fifty-nine runs knocked in—the Yankees offered Gehrig a three-thousand-dollar raise. And he took it. Lou settled for thirty-nine thousand. And Joe wanted forty? *(Who does this kid think he is?)*

Worst of all, news of DiMaggio's demands came to the writers from his pal, Joe Gould. *So, that's his brain trust! Aha! . . .*

(Bravura was Gould's bargaining style. For instance, one year before, when Gould was trying to put Braddock in the ring against Max Schmeling, Gould went into public negotiation with Adolf Hitler and Joseph Goebbels. Gould announced his three demands: 1) five hundred thousand dollars on deposit in a U.S. bank, 2) an American referee, and . . . 3) stop kickin' around the Jews. Of course, that deal never got made, either.)

All through February DiMaggio kept his heels dug into the San Francisco hills. Some writer would get under his skin—suggesting, perhaps, Ruppert wouldn't go any higher. "That's what he thinks," DiMaggio would snap. "I won't accept $25,000, and I'll stick right here until I get what I want." Then he'd fall silent for a week or so, and there'd be photos on the wire of Joe in an apron, cooking spaghetti at DiMaggio's Grotto.

By the end of the month, the Yankees were assembling in St. Petersburg. And no DiMaggio. Joe said he still had his unsigned contract. He'd mail it back, "when I get around to it." He never did get around to it. When next he was asked, he said that contract was "gone with the wind." Gone where? . . . To the city dump.

Everything he said got him in deeper. But the truth was, Joe was right. In any given baseball game, he was every bit as valuable as Gehrig. And for the first time since Ruth retired, the Yankees had drawn a million fans. Wasn't Joe their hero? . . . But that wasn't how the big game was played.

"DiMaggio is an ungrateful young man, and is very unfair to his teammates, to say the least," Col. Ruppert said, as he boarded his private railroad car for his annual visit to the training camp. "I've offered $25,000 and he won't get a button over that amount. Why, how many men his age earn that much? As far as I'm concerned that's all he's worth to the ballclub and if he doesn't sign we'll win the pennant without him."

To the fans in New York, that was still unthinkable:

the Yankees without DiMag? . . . But Ruppert might have made good his threat. The Yanks were better all around than the club that couldn't win before Joe showed up. If DiMaggio chose to cook spaghetti in San Francisco, the Yankee outfield still had George Selkirk (who had hit .328 the year before), Myril Hoag (who would hit .352 that spring), and a terrific kid right fielder, stolen from the Cleveland farm clubs, Tommy Henrich, who had joined the Yanks in '37 and hit .320 in his rookie year. Still, Joe didn't believe that the Yankees would give up on him and let him rot all year in San Francisco. He just *couldn't* believe that . . . until he read in the paper what Joe McCarthy said. "The Yankees can get along without DiMaggio. And that $25,000 is final."

How could McCarthy say that? His skipper! How could he take sides? That day, a wounded DiMaggio retorted in the press: "Well, maybe McCarthy knows what he's talking about. Maybe he doesn't. But they're going to pay my price, or else."

Or else what?

Joe had been spending his days at the Seals' training camp, trying to get in shape, or just to keep busy. Lefty O'Doul was still managing, and glad to have Joe around as inspiration for the kids. Charley Graham, the owner, was more than glad: he arranged for Joe to get extra BP before the games—then Graham would advertise a "Special Hitting Exhibition by the well-known Major League Star . . ."

But now Joe dropped that charade. He didn't want

to be on exhibition. He didn't want to be seen. Now he had come to believe that the Yanks really might forget him—his new life could be over—and that was the only thing that ever caused him fear. He went to ground in his new house—well, his parents' new house. He didn't show up with the Seals, or at the restaurant. There were no more cute photos. The Yankees started north. Writers called the new house in the Marina. *"No, Joe da home . . ."*

He didn't know how to climb down. Losing gracefully was an art in which he'd never had to train. Four days before opening day, reporters staked out the San Francisco station. If DiMaggio was going to throw in the towel, it would take him three and a half days to cross the country. But Joe didn't show at the railroad station, or anywhere else. Grimly, he read of the Yankees' opening day loss in Boston. Grimly, Ed Barrow, in New York, squelched the hopeful rumors that kicked up among the press and public: "We have received no communication from DiMaggio that he has changed his mind. . . . All I can add to this is that if he doesn't accept terms ten days from today he will, under baseball law, become automatically suspended."

On the third day of the season, DiMaggio folded. He wired Barrow at the Yankees office: "Your terms accepted. Leave at 2:40 P.M. Arrive Saturday morning." Ruppert released the wire to the press.

Graceful denouement was not the Baron's specialty, either. In a series of triumphal announcements, he revealed that DiMaggio would get the proffered twenty-five thousand dollars: no bonus clauses, nothing extra. And Joe would not get a dime till he got in shape at his own expense: about a hundred fifty a day in lost wages. Meanwhile, if he wanted to travel with the club, he could pay his own train fare, hotel, and meals. Said Ruppert: "I hope the young man has learned his lesson."

What could Joe do but swallow it down? The Yanks went on the road and DiMaggio worked out at the Stadium, with the baseball clown Al Schacht as his BP pitcher. With the boys Joe had rounded up to shag flies—amongst them Joe Gould, the boxing fixer, and one of his middleweights, Walter Woods—DiMaggio felt like a clown act himself. And he'd never trained for that either. The indignity (and the $1,850 he lost trying to get in shape) would rankle him forever. But what could he do? . . . Joe hit until his hands bled. Still, two weeks passed before he could rejoin the Yankees in Washington. And at that point, things got worse.

It wasn't that his game had suffered: he would hit safely that first day back with the club (and in the eight games to follow). But he was totally unprepared for the boos, the jeers—the hate. (They threw things at him from the center field stands.) . . . On that first day back, Joe ran in on a pop fly, and Joe Gordon, the second baseman, came streaking out—*Thukk!* They collided head-to-head, with a sickening thud that silenced Griffith Stadium. Both fell unconscious on the outfield grass. Both stayed in Garfield Hospital overnight. DiMaggio was back the next day, but Gordon was out of the lineup with shoulder pains. . . . And then the fans really let Joe have it: he wasn't just a greedy prima donna, but a *menace,* too selfish to train—he might have killed poor Gordon! And it wasn't just in Washington, but everywhere around the league—even in the Bronx, all he heard was raspberries. . . .

"I hear the boos," DiMaggio said. "I read in the papers that the cheers offset them, but you can't prove that by me. All I ever hear is boos. Pretty soon I got the idea the only reason people come to the game at all was to boo DiMaggio. And the mail! You would have thought I'd kidnapped the Lindbergh baby, the way some of the letters read."

Joe had learned lessons—but not the ones Ruppert intended. He'd learned that the fans could turn against him, and couldn't hear (or didn't want to hear) anything about it from him. Maybe if he could talk like Lefty, he could josh the boos away or explain himself. But how, to whom? The writers were all in bed with the club—Joe was convinced of that—they'd turned the fans against him. So, Joe would make statements the only way he could—he would be ever more perfect on the field. And to hell with the fans. They'd cheer, if he won.

And there'd be no more holdouts: not public ones—never again. Now, Joe understood: they would never pay him what he was worth—not fairly, not willingly . . . and he couldn't make them pay. Now Joe knew, he was hired help. No one ever made hired help rich. Now he knew, if he was going to get the dough (and by God, he would), he would have to take care of business himself, inside of baseball—or outside. Outside, no one would have to know a thing.

Joe DiMaggio's Grotto, Fisherman's Wharf, San Francisco.

The center of attention: Dorothy Arnold at Yankee Stadium.

**Joe and Dorothy out for a slap-up supper—
courtesy of Richie the Boot Boiardo—
Newark, New Jersey, 1939.**

CHAPTER 8

◆

WHEN JOE DIMAGGIO CAME TO NEW York after his holdout, in April 1938, he knew all the writers would be at the station waiting for his train. So he got off across the river, in Newark, New Jersey, and dodged them. He knew their game, now. He would wall off those writers as he would wall away the booing fans, the hateful mail, the oversolicitous teammates who tried to support and befriend him. He'd make his own friends. He wasn't a bashful big-eyed kid anymore. He was twenty-three. He was the best in the business, and that wasn't pattycake.

Now, his teammates began to note that Daig wasn't around so much, sitting in the locker room or in the lobby. If a new player made the club, someone would take him aside with a brief explanation: "Just cause Dago don't talk to you, that don't mean anything. It's the way he is. Just leave him alone." Even established players—if they talked to Joe, it was a baseball matter; other than that, it was "Hiya, Joe!" "S'long, Joe." You wouldn't even see DiMaggio in the hotel dining room, eating with the rest of the team. Joe wasn't paid to be a spectacle for the fans in that restaurant. Why should he have to smile and sign napkins while his food was getting cold? In Gomez's famous phrase, Joe became "the King of Room Service."

Gomez was the exception in DiMaggio's regimen of solitude. No one had to show Joe the ropes anymore, but Lefty still took care of his roomie. And Joe did his best to reciprocate—as Gomez recalled for Maury Allen, in *Where Have You Gone, Joe DiMaggio?* . . .

"This one time I had pitched in Cleveland against Bobby Feller and I went thirteen innings and I got beat 2–1. Well, if you got beat, McCarthy didn't want you to blink your eyes. You just spent the rest of the day being quiet and thinking about it. We got on the train after the game and we were going on to Detroit. I really felt down after that game. I had pitched as good as I could, as long as I could, and we still lost. I was really feeling sorry for myself. Now DiMaggio comes along and he asks me to go up to the dining car for dinner. I told him I didn't feel like going up to the dining car for dinner. I just wanted to sit on the train and look out the window. Joe was trying to get me interested in something and forget about the game. Usually I was always talking to him after he had a bad day and trying to make him forget. This time he was helping me out.

"For some reason or other, McCarthy always put me near his compartment on the train. I guess he wanted to watch me. Well, anyway, DiMaggio is trying to get me to go with him. I'm in no mood to go. All of a sudden he says he wants to show me something. 'Lefty, it's something I've just learned.' He puts his thumb and his first finger on the end of that big nose of his and he begins tweaking it—bong, bong, bong, bong. 'Don't I sound like a banjo?' Well, I started laughing out loud. Hell, he did sound like a banjo. He's going on like that and I'm laughing like hell and all of a sudden McCarthy sticks his head out of his compartment and starts screaming at me, 'I bet you think you pitched a hell of a game today, Gomez.' Well, before he could remind me that I had lost the game I said, 'Well, it wasn't bad.' DiMaggio starts laughing like hell now and McCarthy's face is just getting red. He really didn't know what the hell else he could say to these two lunatics he had on his team so he just slammed the door of his compartment. I think it rocked the whole train."

That was another difference with Joe: he wasn't the Skipper's perfect boy anymore. Not since McCarthy said he'd get along without DiMaggio. And that was after Young Joe had done everything for McCarthy: ran his laps for McCarthy, shagged his flies for McCarthy—everything McCarthy's way—well, no more. Now the Skipper could try to get along with him. McCarthy was the boss. Joe wouldn't disobey an order. But that wasn't the same as striving to please. That was for kids. And Joe walked away from the kid in himself as firmly, finally, as he'd walk away from anyone else who'd let him down.

In those days, Joe was listening to another old baseball mentor, in his hometown: Ty Cobb. Cobb had helped DiMaggio even before Joe went to the Yanks, with his contract, some career advice. But Cobb's hard-eyed view of the game made more sense now, when the glare of the big time had baked away Joe's illusions. For instance, Cobb had counseled (and now, Joe agreed) that even a strong young hitter should change to a lighter bat around August, so the stress and wear of the long hot season wouldn't slow him in the stretch, when the money was on the line. Joe also took Cobb's counsel on daily outfield practice—forget it! Stop shagging flies and sit in the shade. You could catch a million balls in practice and not one would show up in your paycheck.

It was an accident of geography, timing, and the needs of the press that made Joe "the heir to Babe Ruth." But Joe had nothing in common with the overweight, roistering, How-Bouta-Beer Bambino. He was always more like the game's other icon, Cobb. The Georgia Peach was all business in baseball—all about winning, no sentiment in sight. He was Joe's kind of leader: distant, demanding toward teammates, and toward opponents purely venomous. The difference was DiMaggio would kill the opposition coolly, without a word, and with apparent indifference. Cobb meant to show he hated your guts. He'd open your shin with his spikes, sliding in, even if the play wasn't close—just so you knew where you stood (and you'd think twice about tagging him, next time). Cobb played against the A's second baseman, Jimmy Dykes, from 1918 to '28, and never stood next to him on second base, never passed him between innings, never once saw Dykes before, during, or after a game—*for eleven years*—without snarling: "You stink."

It's tempting to think Cobb was just vicious, an accident of nastiness, a "sport" in the genetic sense, but he wasn't far from baseball's mean main street. Nobody got to the majors, or stayed, by exercise of sweet reason. This was a rough set of boys, mostly poor, uneducated, and possessed of powerful wills which they enforced by intimidation and physical dominance. Every once in a while, like a camel through the needle's eye, some college boy might arrive in the bigs. On the sports page, he'd forever be linked with his alma mater; but in the dugout, he'd be busy showing that he could be just as know-nothing-tough as the meanest miner's son. In New York, for example, the Giants employed a summa cum laude second baseman, Frankie Frisch, forever known as the Fordham Flash: he must have written his thesis on tagging a sliding runner in the teeth. When Frisch's intellectual gifts won him elevation to a manager's job, he earned eternal fame in St. Louis as skipper of the Gashouse Gang, the most dementedly combative ball team ever loosed upon the league. (In one spring training, just to set the tone, Frisch's mound star, Dizzy Dean, got annoyed when the Giants scored seven runs off him, and hit seven Giants batters in a row.)

The Yankees weren't rowdy like the Cardinals,

they weren't alley fighters like the Tigers, or loud and daffy like the Brooklyns. But they were just as tough. They weren't born to those suits and ties, swank hotels, and Pullman cars. Red Ruffing, the big sorrel-haired son of the coal fields in Nokomis, Illinois, might have become one of the great power-hitting outfielders of the age if not for a mine accident that robbed him of four toes on his left foot. So he became a pitcher, the sort who'd fire a fastball at your chin if you looked at him funny with a bat in your hand. Ruffing wasn't going back to those coal mines. . . . Spud Chandler, the other big right-hander, was such a nasty competitor that no one would go near him on days he was supposed to pitch. In the year of Joe's holdout, Chandler pitched most of the season with bone chips in his arm. After he pitched he'd sneak out of the clubhouse without a tie, his shirt collar open, because he couldn't raise his arm to fasten a button. But he wouldn't go for an operation till he'd finished the year—at fourteen and five. . . . Early in Joe's rookie year, the catcher, Bill Dickey, almost died from kidney damage after a collision at the plate. But Dickey came back to hit .362 that year. And in the field, Dickey gave as good as he got: when the Senators' outfielder Carl Reynolds tried to run him over at home plate, the quiet gentleman from Little Rock stood up and broke Reynolds's jaw with one punch.

There were a number of ballparks in the league with only one tunnel from the clubhouse to the field—often that led through the home team dugout.

But that didn't mean opposing players would stop and chat, or nod hello as they took the field. Guys on the other team were enemies, pure and simple. By the end of the 1930s, Commissioner Landis turned custom into law with a baseball edict, "The Non-fraternization Rule." If you had something friendly to say to a player on another team, you could say it after the season. Meantime, you were at each other's throat.

That's what it meant to play for keeps. There were four hundred jobs in the major leagues. You fought to keep one. Gomez used to tell the story of Burleigh Grimes, the old spitballer who came over from the National League to the Yanks at the age of forty. He was warming up in Detroit, and the next hitter, Goose Goslin, was leaning in from the on-deck circle, trying to get a good look. So Burleigh threw one at Goslin—twenty feet in foul ground! Decked him! . . . Sure, Burleigh was near the end. But you were gonna have to pry that job out of his dead fingers.

It wasn't all lovey-dovey with your own team, either. Every kid who came up from the bushes had to fight his way into the batting cage. And even if he made the club, that didn't mean you were going to cuddle up with him. What if he got hot and took your spot in the lineup? One day, Selkirk complimented Gehrig on the way he started a three-six-three double play. "Nice goin', Lou!" Said Gehrig: "Shuddup, you fresh sonofabitch." No one was going to bump stomachs and slap high-fives all around the dugout because he laid down a proper sacrifice bunt. There were no group hugs on the field when you won, or kneeling in a circle to pray when you lost. You want to pray? Go to church. It was a big deal if someone on the bench shook your hand. If they shook it where anyone from the other team could see, you might as well walk up to the plate with a neon sign, flashing: "HIT ME."

Now, surely it's too much, and too mechanical, to say that Joe took on the hard edge of the business in which he throve. He'd only been in the league two years. But it would also be a mistake to ignore how precocious he was in the ways of baseball—how he drank it in.

It would be a mistake to underestimate the living crammed into each baseball year—experience of a high-wattage sort. There was the constant scorekeeping, when a win was affirmation for you, your team, and the city as a whole—and loss was condemned in thunderous judgments, printed in fist-high headlines by the millions every day . . . the joy, the rush, when mastery on the diamond gave your every act a godly grace—till a slump, an error, bad luck, or incapacity plunged you into hopeless, worthless woe . . . the physicality, the body shock, when you'd hurl yourself across dirt and stones, kicking for the base, while skin flayed off your thigh and hip till they were pinkish red like a tropical fruit (they called this, in fact, a strawberry), and the trainers would slap on alcohol till it burned like hellfire—but, of course, you'd do it all again, next day . . . the confrontations—how many battles?—every day, every play, every minute, between the pitcher and batter, batter and fielder, fielder and runner, runner and baseman. . . . How could they not make his model for living, when that was the only living on his own that Joe DiMaggio had ever done?

Why wouldn't he see life from his own point of view, the position in which he spent his most alive moments, that perch with the whole world that mattered before him—that was center field. It was a special place—not just that vastness in the Bronx, but every center field: the largest suzerainty in the game's realm, it had to be patrolled by a prince. He was the man on the field most unconstrained by others; he had the greatest distances to roam, and the farthest from home. Perhaps that's why Joe so often was the first to burst from the dugout, running, head down, on a beeline, with the other men spraying out behind, as if they'd been pulled, uncorked by the Dago's force. In center field, he had every twitch of every play in front of him: the bent back of his pitcher, the batter's swing and the ball-jump, and the crack of the bat to confirm his first step, with the infield in scurry, and the ball in flight, past their upturned faces, up, up . . . till it hung at the top of its arc, dead still in his sky for an instant, because he was moving perfectly toward its path, to intersection, yelling "I got it! Mine! Mine!" (In center everything he could reach was HIS!) . . . and slowing, now, to the glide that would let him leisurely raise his glove and bare hand (always two hands, to take care of business) and put it away . . . so he could trot in, ball in his glove, deadpan, confident, controlling, gathering teammates ahead of him homeward, a strong shepherd, to the dugout again.

That's how fast things were moving for Joe: now he led them out, he brought them in, he led without anyone having time to notice that DiMaggio had taken over. Now, in '38, as McCarthy fretted through a long Gehrig slump, the Skipper made a change: Gehrig would bat fifth. The new cleanup man for the Yanks was DiMaggio. It just made sense. No one said a word. No one much remarked when the season ended, and Joe had posted another splendid year: .324, one hundred forty runs batted in, thirty-two home runs (and only twenty-one strikeouts). There were even some suggestions that Joe had been a tad off his game, a bit disappointing. You know, he hadn't led the league. (Expectations were moving fast, too.) . . . But another World Series ring muted the critics. How could anyone argue with three in a row?

Even Joe himself could not quite keep up—the changes in his life all happened so fast. Or maybe it was the one big change. In New York, his life was like center field—anything he could reach was HIS! . . .

In his rookie year, Joe used to write home to his friend, Ciccio LaRocca, about this girl he'd fallen in love with. She was gorgeous, blond, a movie actress—Madeleine Carroll. And of course, Joe had never met her, never been anywhere near her. He was like ten thousand other guys in other towns—hayseeds, clerks, and gas-pump jockeys, dreaming in dark theaters—just a boy with a screen crush.

Now, after twenty-four months (some three hundred games as a Yankee) Joe had found another movie actress—blond, beautiful, only twenty-one—with riveting gray-blue eyes, and a girlish smile that made the camera love her. But this one he knew—she was as real as rain . . . and she wanted *him*.

IT WAS AMBITION THAT TOOK DOR-othy Arnoldine Olson from Duluth, Minnesota, first into vaudeville around her home state, and then to Chicago, New York, and (who could tell?) maybe a big break. Perhaps she didn't have the overwhelming talent that would make her name (the name she chose, Dorothy Arnold) a prayer upon a million lips . . . but she was always in demand as a model; she could sing and dance, she was sure she could act. She had the all-American idea that she could do anything she set her mind to. That's why she thought she could make a life with Joe.

There was a candid can-do air about Dorothy from the time she was a little girl. She was always ready to entertain for her schoolmates, their parents—for anyone who asked. And from that first day, when she sang and danced at a party for the neighbors, and they passed the hat, and she came home running with her big grin and that money in her hand, and she was so amazed, delighted . . . well, there was candor to her ambition, too. She wanted to be a star.

Her father was a railroad man; the Olsons were all working people. Even so, the way Dorothy went to work on this show business gave her parents pause. She was enrolled in Mrs. Geraldine Butler's School of Dance, where she met another Dorothy—Dorothy Tetsman—and the two girls made up a peppy stage act: "Dot and Dot (With a Little Bit of Dash)." Mrs. Butler wanted to take them around to dance their buck-and-wing at hotels and clubs, parties and smokers. That seemed a bit racy to Dorothy's mom. "You'll never get to heaven on a dancing floor," Mrs. Olson used to say. "But you'll dance to the devil's door."

There was another moment's pause, when vaudeville scouts from Chicago saw Dorothy's act in Duluth, and asked her to join the *Bandbox Review*. She was only sixteen, still in school. But she begged, cried, cajoled for the chance. She'd make up the school, or take the tests early. The teachers just had to let her graduate!

Her determination won out at every turn; she was that sort of take-charge girl. Once at a club in Duluth—she was performing in a New Year's Eve show—the straps on her bodice broke. Dorothy didn't even pause, but danced and sang through the act, clutching her breasts, and got the heck off stage. In Chicago, and on tour with the *Bandbox Review,* it

was three shows a day, six days a week, and sometimes buses or trains all night. But the grind never
wore her down. She just wanted something more.

She wanted to be a movie star; and that brought her
to the Paramount Acting School in New York. She
made her way in the city with odd jobs of the showbiz sort: modeling assignments, advertising shoots;
she was a staff singer on the radio for NBC and appeared in some Twentieth Century Fox short subjects. She was meeting so many people—young
actors, comedians, writers, promoters; her enthusi-
asm drew them, her smile was contagious. She was
particularly friendly with the publicists and columnists, and you might see Dorothy out for dinner with
her pal Dorothy Kilgallen, or out at the Stork Club
with Walter Winchell—though with Winchell (that
hound—and twice her age) it couldn't be just dinner.

When she met Joe DiMaggio on the set of *Manhattan Merry-Go-Round,* Dorothy didn't even have a
speaking part. But she was a young woman on the
rise. It wasn't long before an agent named Mort Millman arranged a screen test in Hollywood for her, and
she was signed by Universal Pictures as their *Oomph
Girl.* (You know, like Ann Sheridan was Paramount's
Oomph Girl? . . .) But then, things got serious with
Joe, too—and Dorothy had to decide where to put her
oomph.

It never was an easy courtship, not with Dorothy
trying to work in Hollywood and Joe in New York. Or
if Dorothy came back to New York, Joe might be on

the road with the team. They'd told each other that things would get easier after the season. But after the season, things never slowed down. Joe would go home to San Francisco, and then back and forth to L.A. Or Joe would have to go back east for an award, or some appearance that was worth money to him. There was always some reason to go. What was he supposed to do, sit around in Hollywood?

For a while, Joe wasn't sure if a steady girl wouldn't just be trouble, the sort that didn't go with a baseball life. Even Lefty Gomez and June O'Dea— Joe and Dorothy's double-date pals—couldn't seem to make it work. June was suing for divorce. She said Lefty went for an off-season visit to California, and he never came back. He shacked up with some actress out there, wouldn't even answer June's letters. Then Lefty was in the papers contending that June was frigid. She charged that he was a violent drunk, and hit her. Lefty said that June's mom hit *him*— with a chair! . . . Of course, this was fodder for the sporting press all through the winter, and most of the '38 season. For Joe, it was exemplary: exactly what he didn't want—but his hesitancy only drew Dorothy on.

It was darling how Joe was so bashful—so many people in her world would just paw a girl before they said hello. Joe didn't even try to sleep with her at first. When he did try, that was even better. (She said they were always wonderful in bed.) Dorothy had never played baseball, but she loved sports (she'd been a champion swimmer), and dove into the New York sporting scene—all the boxers and promoters, bootleggers-turned-bookie, wiseguy fixers, odds-makers, umpires, ticket-brokers, writers, dandy little jockeys, and stout millionaire owners. When Joe's loud friend, Toots Shor, opened his new restaurant, just west of Fifth Avenue on 51st, the whole sporting world tried to squeeze into one room. Two rooms, actually: the front was all one big circular bar with men standing three and four deep at the rail, shouting and drinking and laughing. Behind the bar was the big, bright dining room where Joe and Dorothy would sit. Of course, when she walked in with Joe, she was royalty—always the special table in the corner, and everyone would come to pay respects, say hello, tell a story. The only sad part was, Joe preferred to go alone. He was old-fashioned that way: boxing matches, some saloons, most discussions with men—Joe thought they just weren't right for a girl.

That was one of the ways they differed (or, as Dorothy liked to say, they *complemented* each other). She was the small-town girl, three years younger and newer to the city, but more open to anything modern, experimental, or odd. "Intelligent people," she used to say, "don't moralize." Dorothy valued intelligence. She was a reader, always working on a book. For Joe, it was still the sports page (and the clandestine *Superman* comics). She was the life of any party, a social All-Star. DiMaggio looked at any new acquaintance as a potential misery, or worse still, a mortification. (What if he said something wrong?)

That's how Dorothy knew she could help Joe. People thought Joe was aloof, too high and mighty to speak to them. But she thought he was just terribly shy—if he thought he might look bad—he had to look perfect. And if he didn't know how, he just had to leave. So many times, she felt sorry for him, that year, when they started dating in earnest, and Joe was being booed all over the league. People actually wrote that Joe didn't care. Dorothy knew he couldn't stop caring. He had to be that perfect player they wrote about before.

That's why she arranged for her friend Dorothy Kilgallen to do an interview with Joe. That would show his human side. In a syndicated article, Miss Kilgallen led with the news that DiMaggio had "wonderful brown eyes," and followed up with description of his widow's peak (like Robert Taylor's), "and quizzical eyebrows, to say nothing of eyelashes a yard long."

"Goodness," she exclaimed, "he's divine!

"Maybe there is something in this baseball at that. Of course, I have a lot to learn but with a little help from Joe, say a couple of hours a day—I think I could catch on to some of the fancier plays.

"I had lesson one today, but I'm afraid I'll have to go all over it again because I became rather confused—I might even say flustered—at the part where Joe was helping me hold the baseball.

" 'This,' he said, looking meltingly at the ball, 'is what we call the stitched potato, or the apricot, whichever you like.'

" 'I like you,' I said dreamily. . . ."

The surprising part was, Joe took right away to that lover-boy image. Of course, he laughed and shrugged it off with his fellow players. But he didn't do a thing to discourage that rep. If people saw him around town with that beautiful young actress, and talked him up as some debonair lady-killer . . . well, that was okay with Joe. It went with his determined attention to his new suits—he'd go back to the tailor a dozen times, till everything was perfect—that put him on the list of the Ten Best Dressed. It offered a harmless explanation for the way he would kill a couple of hours after games—standing in front of the locker room mirrors, working on the knot of his tie, or the part of his hair. *(Look out! Dago's got a hot date tonight!)*

It was better than harmless, actually, because the reputation brought its own fulfillment. Once the idea took hold that Joe D. was quite a hand with the ladies, well, what do you know? Ladies started showing up—presenting themselves. (They'd read in Walter Winchell's column: Joe knew how to show a girl a good time.) The best part was, Joe began to believe it himself—or at least to consider that people really might want to spend time with him, that he wasn't just the dumb Dago slugger. . . . But isn't that the way with love? Joe could see himself better when he saw himself through Dorothy's eyes.

The way she looked at him, he was terrific. And if there was room for improvement (say, with the way he spoke or wouldn't speak), that was just the proof that she was needed. Years later, people would ask why she had given up on movies for Joe. But the way Dorothy saw it, she wasn't giving up a career—just taking on a new one. The way she saw it, Joe simply hadn't had the benefit of schooling. But there were books to teach him all the words he needed. And for the rest, she could show him how to mingle socially, how to act at ease. It all went back to something Joe said that first day, on the set of *Manhattan Merry-Go-Round*. "The toughest part about this whole business of acting," he said, "is being nonchalant. That's a pretty tough thing to be."

But Dorothy knew how—she seemed perfectly at ease. No one from Joe's world ever remembered Dorothy displaying a moment's anxiety—except a couple of Italian girls in Newark, daughters of one of Joe's friends, who walked in on Dorothy after dinner, in the ladies' room. There was the golden girl starlet bent over the bowl, with her finger down her own throat, throwing up her dinner. Dorothy did it all the time. No one in those days knew the word "bulimia," or thought about that sort of thing as sickness. Dorothy would have laughed at that—a girl had to keep her figure.

BY HAPPENSTANCE, NEWARK WAS A big part of their social life. Somehow, that soot-stained New Jersey town offered the relaxation that DiMaggio never could find across the river in towering Manhattan, nine miles away. In New York, Joe was under the eye of public and press, prey to Gotham social lions who thought he ought to know them, visiting dignitaries who wanted to meet him, people who wanted to do him favors, people who acted like they'd done him favors, friends of the new friends he could barely keep straight—and more on the way, always more coming at him. . . . Newark was quiet, smaller, more manageable in every way. For Joe, it was like going back to North Beach. Everybody knew everybody, everyone knew who was who—especially in the First Ward, the Italian *quartiere,* where Joe was treated like a visiting Pope. (Well, not exactly like the Holy Father: Newark was small but it yielded to no town in the worldliness of its delights.)

No one could remember how Joe came to Newark for the first time. Some people said he had cousins in Jersey, but no one ever produced the cousins. He might have come for official Yankees business. The Pinstripes kept their number one farm team in Newark—the Bears, of the Triple A International League. Or Joe might have come with another Yankee player. In those days people came across the river to take in a certain show, to hear some music, or especially to eat at the Italian restaurants on Eighth Avenue, the heart of the First Ward.

But everyone agreed: when Joe first caught on in town, that was the doing of Jerry Spatola. That was one of Jerry's talents, spotting brilliance—as he'd done, for instance, with Abbott and Costello. They were just a couple of local comics—used to do their routine on the corner, standing in front of the trolley—nobody paid them any attention. But Jerry thought they were a knockout, a scream. And everybody with a radio knew the rest of that story. So Gerardo was well known for spotting the best of the best, and for him, the sun didn't rise until DiMaggio woke up.

You could almost call Spatola himself brilliant—though that's a word seldom heard about a mortician. But the way Jerry looked at it, he was only in that business by accident. His grandfather had gone to City Hall one day for a dog license. But the old man didden talka too gooda de English—so he walked out with a livery license, a permit to operate a horse and cart. Well, in those days, there were two ways into the funeral business: either you were a carpenter and had coffins to sell, or you had a livery license and could carry the dead out of town to their graves. Enough said. The Spatolas became the morticians of choice for the First Ward. Even so, their mortuary business didn't come to full flower until the passage of the next generation—with Jerry, so to speak, undertaking affairs.

It wasn't just that Jerry was professional, though he was—he'd gone to school for embalming and everything. The key was, this younger Spatola understood that a great burial involves being buried *by somebody*. That's where Jerry was a standout—he looked like a million bucks. He had those suits, made for him by his tailor on Fifth Avenue. (Not Newark's Fifth Avenue, the one in New York.) Plus, he had the latest in hearse equipment, with side-loading liftgates that could lower a coffin like a mother puts a baby to sleep. One of Jerry's hearses had a *Victrola,* so you could have Caruso singing *Ave Maria* right there in the graveyard, which raised the Spatola name to a new level of modern mortuary excellence—despite the one time Jerry got the neighborhood boys to clean up the cars, and the next dear-departed went into the ground to the tune of "A Tisket, A Tasket (A Green and Yellow Basket)." Even that was notable, which was more or less Jerry's goal.

Everything he did raised the family name in Newark, and the glory of the town itself. It was a Spatola (Jerry's granddad) who ordered from Italy the splendid statue of San Gerardo for St. Lucy's Church on Sheffield Street. Now, Jerry would continue the tradition, by bringing Joe DiMaggio to Newark for a slap-up dinner at Vesuvius on Eighth Avenue—to which dinner Spatola would invite other *prominenti,* and for which dinner, of course, Spatola would pay. Jerry was a great one for grabbing checks. He might not be paying his coffin suppliers, but it would be dishonor if so great a *paesano* as DiMaggio was to pay for even one *spaghetto*. And that was, of course, a comfort to Joe—still smarting from his holdout and the pay he'd been docked while he got in shape.

The other great comfort was that Joe didn't have to say a word. People used to marvel how Jerry Spatola could talk with anyone. But there was this simple explanation: Jerry talked—whoever else was around, that was an accident. So Joe (or these days, Joe and Dorothy) could enjoy dinner among the *prominenti* and listen to Jerry's tales of his trade and town. Who'd have thought an undertaker had so many stories? There was the time the shoemaker, Russomanno, came to him to make a funeral for his pet canary. Poor grieving cobbler wanted the works—a tiny satin-lined casket, a procession, flower cars—an orchestra! Problem was, Russomanno wanted a church funeral. But the priest balked. How's he gonna give a bird the sacraments? . . . So Jerry fishes up a C-note, tucks it into the Padre's cassock. "Oh," says the priest, "why didn't you tell me this was a Catholic canary?"

DiMaggio was a Spatola family project. Jerry would pick Joe up after games at the Stadium, and drive him to Newark. Sometimes there'd be a visit to one of the Italian social clubs, or the Victory Bocce Club; everyone wanted to honor DiMaggio. Sometimes it was a big festive dinner at Vittorio's Castle— top-of-the-line in Newark, a place with turrets, painted murals, statuary (profusely cascading grapes)—and then off to a show or a club, or Jerry's home, where his wife, Rose, would serve peaches and cream. The Spatola kids would show Joe their scrapbooks with all the clippings about him. (Above a funeral home, you've got to have quiet hobbies.) And when Joe got tired, or full, or bored, he'd jerk his head and Jerry would make for the car to take Joe back to New York. One time they planned to go out to a club after dinner, but Joe spilled wine on his shirt. So they went back to Jerry's, where Joe put on one of Jerry's shirts (Joe had five inches of wrist past the cuff) and Rose set to washing out the stain. They understood—Joe had to look perfect. The more perfect he looked, the better for them.

After a while, DiMaggio was a First Ward project—almost an ornament to the city as a whole. Jerry organized Joe's visit to the Crippled Children's Home, and then there was a testimonial dinner—had to be the biggest night of '39. Gehrig, McCarthy, Bill Dickey all came; along with the ex-champ Jimmy Braddock; the comic Jimmy Durante, screen star Jack LaRue; Miss Dorothy Arnold of Hollywood, seated with Mrs. Rose Spatola (Joe and Jerry, of course, were at the head table), along with a thousand honored local guests who so admired DiMaggio that they gave him a diamond-encrusted watch—five hundred dollars' worth of timepiece—and a new car.

For Joe this was a watershed. He'd just, warily, come to accept that people of attainment might want to be with him. Now he had to learn to accept their

tributes—and to speak about it. At the Newark testimonial, Joe would have to stand and deliver—more
than just "thank you." He obsessed about that for
weeks. Dorothy was consulted, dismissed, and recon-
sulted. Sportswriters were enlisted as ghostwriters
and then ignored. In the end, Joe spoke for about two
minutes. As the *Newark Ledger* reported:

"Betraying his usual nervousness behind a stiff
shirt, DiMaggio was brief in his thanks, and expressed the wish that the friendships he has made in
Newark and Essex County will always be among his
most valued."

Under inspection, it was a peculiar sentiment:
DiMaggio hoping that he would not someday kiss
these people off. But it went over fine, and when Joe
concluded his remarks—"And I thank you"—he was
cheered as if he'd just smacked a grand slam. When
he sat down he had attained, in one evening, emolu-
ments equivalent to a year's work for his dad. From
the adoration of these Jersey faithful, he had re-
couped for two minutes' talk just about as much as
he'd lost in his holdout. Clearly, there was money to
be made without even lacing on a pair of spikes: people would pay him just to be Joe DiMaggio. If he had
to learn to accept—well, he was learning. It started
with that big testimonial in Newark. And it would
continue at other dinners—at Vittorio's Castle, with
Richie the Boot.

THE WAY JOE FIGURED, HE EARNED
everything he got that year. Before the start of the '39
season, the Yankees once again showed DiMaggio
the back of their hand and sent him a contract without
a raise—as if they meant to insist he *still* wasn't
worth more than twenty-five thousand. But this time
there would be no histrionics. For one thing, Jacob
Ruppert took sick and quickly died. For both the Yankees and their center field star, it would have been un-
seemly to scrap about money over the Colonel's
grave. For his part, DiMaggio was determined to sign
early, to give himself (for once) a real spring training,
and a full season to prove he was the greatest in the
game. Alas, he only made it through the first six
games before he was hurt again: his calf muscles torn
away from the bone near his ankle. DiMaggio would
be laid up for more than a month.

Much worse for the Yanks, the spring training
jokes about Gehrig's old muscles turned to horror as
the season began, and Gehrig couldn't answer the
bell. He couldn't get the bat on the ball, and when he
did he hit weak grounders. He couldn't make the
plays at first, couldn't turn, catch, throw hard—and
couldn't hide those ugly facts, certainly not from
himself. Gehrig had played in every Yankee game
since 1925. But by early May 1939, the proud captain
had twenty-eight at bats, and only four hits. In Detroit, after two thousand one hundred and thirty
straight games—a record, it was said, that would

stand forever—Gehrig went to Joe McCarthy and took himself out of the lineup.

The Yankees had now lost the heart of their attack, lost Gehrig, their captain, and DiMaggio, their star. Another team might have folded, or at least bided time. But the day Gehrig sat down, the Yankees beat the Tigers 22–2. The Yanks then won twenty-eight of thirty-two games.

This was the high-water mark of the McCarthy-DiMaggio era, and maybe the best Yankee club ever. (Dan Daniel, for one, rated the '39 Bombers superior to the Murderers' Row of 1927.) Babe Dahlgren, who took over for Gehrig, was much better than competent at first—and hit fifteen home runs, knocked in eighty-nine. The rest of the infield—Joe Gordon at second base, Crosetti at short, Red Rolfe at third—was without weakness. (Gordon and Rolfe, along with DiMaggio, pitcher Red Ruffing, and catcher Bill Dickey, were named by *The Sporting News* as the best at their positions in either league, any league: they were the best, period.) And that year, baseball's best outfield—DiMaggio, Henrich, and Selkirk—was made stronger with a strapping rookie from Maryland, Charlie Keller, who announced his arrival with a batting average of .334.

By June, once DiMaggio emerged from the hospital, the Yankees weren't just beating the other clubs often, but badly. One Sunday in Philadelphia, the Yankees hit thirteen home runs in a twin bill, and drubbed the A's 23–2 and 10–0. The Pinstripes were running away with the pennant—winning three of every four games. The writers dubbed the other AL clubs the Seven Dwarfs. The only thing that stopped the Yankees was the All-Star Game—and even that was a Pinstripe party. It was held, aptly, at Yankee Stadium. The AL manager was Joe McCarthy, the AL captain was Lou Gehrig. DiMaggio and Selkirk started in the outfield, Rolfe and Gordon in the infield; Ruffing was on the mound, pitching to Dickey . . . the rest of the league only fielded three men. And it was Joe D.'s home run that put the game away for the Americans.

In 1939 DiMaggio played ball with a ferocious efficiency that left even other players in wonder. At the start of the season, he let slip his conviction that this would be his big year. His goal was the batting crown, nothing less. And nothing was going to get in the way: not pitchers—no matter how good they were (Tom Henrich described DiMaggio standing in against Feller: "Joe was bearing down—*criminy*—veins were standin' out on his neck") . . . not friends from other teams, other years (Dario Lodigiani, one of Joe's pals from the San Francisco sandlots, then with the Philadelphia A's, tagged DiMaggio out at second base—nothing on the line, a normal day, normal play. "He knocked me ass-over-teacups," Lodi recalled. "Then he got up, brushed his pants a couple of times and never said Doo, hello, shit, or nothin'—

just ran off to the dugout") . . . and nothing outside the game would be allowed to intrude. Joe went along through spring training, while the writers spun out stories on his deliciously modern, fabulously expensive, nightly long-distance telephone romance with Dorothy Arnold. (Fifteen dollars a coo, the writers figured.) But when Dorothy let some Hollywood writers know that she and Joe had gotten engaged— she said they would marry that summer—well, Joe hit the roof, and denied it all. Next day, he thought better and admitted the engagement, sort of: "We may be married next winter or the following winter. But the wedding definitely will not take place while the baseball season is on."

Nothing must stop him—not while he was hitting over .375, and still climbing. He'd get a hit in ten or twelve straight games, and then he'd take the collar for a day or two. Everyone would sigh and forget about Joe and his average: it was bound to sink, he was only human (last time anybody hit .400 was back in '23, Detroit's Harry Heilmann) . . . and the next time anybody noticed, Joe had hit in fifteen straight again. Mid-August, when the heat was supposed to wilt the flowers and statistics, Joe embarked on a road trip to the western provinces, and over twelve games hit for an average of .509. Then it was eighteen straight again. In the *San Francisco Examiner*'s daily DiMaggio box, the headline suggested a cure for all those new troubles in Europe:

They Ought to Hire DiMaggio to End the War, Hitting .408!

In the field, DiMaggio was incomparable, or compared only to bygone greats. The name most often linked to Joe's was Tristram Speaker, the Grey Eagle, said to be the classiest fly-chaser in history—though now, some writers suggested, Joe was rewriting history. At last, someone made bold to ask the aged Hall of Famer himself: Did Tris think Joe was a better center fielder? In the printable portion of his response, Speaker snorted: "HIM? I could name fifteen better outfielders!" The problem was, nobody else could name even one. (Finally, sheepishly, the Great Grey Immortal conceded to Bob Considine that he couldn't name fifteen current outfielders of any sort.) For his part, DiMaggio wasted not a word in response, but put on a center field show that seemed to settle the question. In one game at Yankee Stadium, DiMaggio registered ten putouts, one shy of the all-time record, and stole at least three hits from the Tigers. Next day, as the Yankees were losing 7–2, the great Detroit slugger, Hank Greenberg, came to bat in the ninth, with Pinky Higgins on first base. The Yankees always pitched Greenberg away and DiMaggio was shading him to right center. But Greenberg launched a howitzer shot to deepest left center field. DiMaggio turned and took off at a dead run toward the monuments—and he ran . . . Higgins ran from first base, around second, and then around third . . . the lumbering Greenberg made the turn at first with the thought that the ball would bounce around amid the plinths and plaques, and he'd have an inside-the-park home run . . . but DiMaggio still ran. Once, he glanced up at the ball, but mostly he kept his head down, and ran. He ran past the monuments, past the flag pole in front of the fence where the numbers 461 were painted, and then, behind the flag pole, at the edge of the world, he twisted his head, flung up his left hand, and at the edge of his reach, still at a dead run, caught the ball and brought his hands down to brake his run at the fence. Then he turned and trotted in with the ball—and that was the only mistake of that sort that anyone could remember Joe making: there was only one out when Greenberg came up. DiMag could have doubled Higgins off first. But somehow, his lapse just confirmed what every spectator felt: with that catch the inning *should* have been over—nothing more to be said.

Of course, the sportswriters were just the men to say it. "He is the greatest player in baseball," wrote the normally understated North Dakotan, the *World-Telegram*'s Pat McDonough. "Not alone as a hitter. His fielding has been marvelous, his throwing grand." The AP's Gayle Talbot took the case nationwide (and into history): "Every time you see Joe DiMaggio take that effortless swing of his or race back against the boards to rob some luckless batter of a triple, you can't help getting a sneaking feeling that here, perhaps, is the greatest all-around ball player there has been."

But sadly, at the season's end, it was Joe who went luckless. An infection invaded his left eye, swelling it nearly shut. That puffy blurred eye was his lead eye at the plate, so Joe expected McCarthy to sit him down, until he could see the ball. But day after day, Mc-Carthy wrote Joe's name on the lineup card, and DiMaggio was too proud to ask for a rest. Day after day, Joe went hitless; his .400 average melted that September like a snowman in May. In the season's last three weeks, Joe lost thirty points. Still, he finished atop the league at .381, more than twenty points better than the runner-up, the Red Sox first baseman, Double X, Jimmie Foxx.

More than fifty years later, Joe was still complaining that the Yanks had already clinched the pennant, but McCarthy wouldn't let him rest the eye, even for a day. More and more, through those fifty years, it would gall Joe that the subject of batting .400 called to mind not his name but that of his hated rival, Ted Williams. (Ted would hit .406 in 1941.) More and more, Joe would insist (to friends—never in public or print) that he could have hit .400, too, if only Mc-Carthy had let him sit. But that wasn't McCarthy's way. After the season the Skipper volunteered (Joe would never have asked) his reason—such as it was: "People might've said you were a cheese champion."

Joe took that explanation in silence. What good

would it do to protest? And at the time, he was too busy to look back. There was the pressing matter of the Cincinnati Reds, and DiMaggio's fourth World Series. Once again, in the game that would live in the lore, DiMaggio made the difference. That was Game Four, after the Yanks won the first three. To stave off elimination, Cincinnati put its ace, Paul Derringer, on the mound—and the game was a tight affair. DiMaggio saved a run in the second by racing back to pull in a long drive from the Reds' catcher, Ernie Lombardi. In the third, Joe sprinted to the wall again to rob Billy Werber of an extra-base hit and keep another runner from scoring. Still, it was 4–2 in favor of the Reds as the Yanks came up in the ninth. Keller led off with a single, and DiMaggio singled him to third. When Dickey bounced a ball to second base, Joe wiped out the shortstop, Buddy Myers, who dropped the throw—Keller scored, DiMaggio and Dickey were safe. Then, on Selkirk's fly to right, DiMaggio tagged up and made third—and that was the crucial extra base. Because the next batter, Gordon, chopped a ball to the third baseman, Werber, who gunned it home . . . but DiMaggio slid around the tag to tie the game, and send it on to extra innings.

In the tenth, a walk to Crosetti, a sacrifice by Red Rolfe, and a bobble on a grounder from Keller put Yankee runners at first and third—with Joe at the plate and all the money on the line. Joe didn't make any show, or try to power the ball—just spanked it on a line into right field, a sure single, to score Crosetti.

But the right fielder, Goodman, charged so hard that the ball got past him, and Keller kept running all the way around third. The throw from the outfield got to home plate at the same time Keller crashed into Lombardi, who dropped the ball—and Keller was safe. Lombardi lay on the ground, stunned, till he saw that DiMaggio had never stopped: he was racing around third like a mad Little Leaguer. Lombardi lunged for the ball and launched himself, glove first, toward the plate. He got his glove there ahead of Joe, but DiMaggio came up with a slide no one had ever seen: he twisted his body to the first-base side, and hiked his lead foot into the air. He *air-mailed* his right foot over Lombardi's glove, then dropped it onto the plate as he slid past. It was the most instinctively brilliant baserunning that players, coaches, fans, or writers had ever seen. Lombardi was mocked for his "snooze" through the rest of his career. Of course, that was unfair: Lombardi wasn't napping, he couldn't move—after Charlie Keller kicked him in the nuts. But the winners write the history, and the Yanks were winners, 7–4—and winners in their fourth straight World Series, a feat no team had ever pulled off. Joe was the only man in history who was a World Champ his first four seasons.

As a consequence, Joe was busy through October with awards, prizes, and gifts. This time the MVP balloting was no contest: Joe got the trophy from *The Sporting News* in a landslide vote from the baseball writers. Some of those voters were now billing him in print as "the all-time great centerfielder," or "America's No. 1 ball player." Joe was more than that—bigger than his game. When he accepted the Golden Laurel Award at the 1939 New York World's Fair, an eight-foot-tall portrait of Joe was mounted on the wall of the Academy of Sport, dominating the vista for millions of visitors. DiMaggio was Sport. And even Americans who never looked at the sports page knew about Joltin' Joe: from the cover of *Life* magazine or the newsreels on the Ten Best Dressed, or the boxed "bright" on the front page when DiMaggio's salary passed FDR's. Now, for good measure, he would debut on the society page—as America's number one bridegroom-to-be.

By that time, Joe's engagement was the real thing; had been since July, when Dorothy showed up in her hometown with a four-and-a-half-carat diamond shining on her left hand like a locomotive headlight. As her sister recalled, "It was *humungous!* . . . We'd never seen a ring like that in Duluth."

Of course, the nice folks in Duluth had no idea where that grand stone came from, save what Dorothy said: it came from Joe. If they had thought about it, they might have guessed Tiffany's, or Harry Winston, or some other great Fifth Avenue jeweler. They never would have thought of Newark, New Jersey. And they'd never heard of Richie "the Boot" Boiardo.

RUGGIERO BOIARDO WAS ACTUALLY a Chicago boy who'd moved to Newark before World War I, and found a job delivering milk in the First Ward. While he was stopping house to house with the milk, it was very little trouble to pick up the numbers: that is, the bets that the housewives placed on the local policy game—what police used to call "the Italian lottery." Actually, they could have called it the Jewish lottery, the Irish lottery, or half a dozen other names. It depended on the neighborhood and who was running the racket. At first, young Richie used to lay these numbers off with a local "banker," but soon he began to handle the action himself. He was ambitious that way. And being from Chicago, he had a knack for handling disputes. For instance, there was the "banker" who complained that Richie wasn't bringing him his action anymore—until something lamentable happened, and the banker ran into a bullet. So there was no more dispute.

Over the years, Richie became well known for that sort of story, the kind with a sudden and lamentable ending. He got so famous, matter of fact, that *Life* magazine did a photo spread on him and his house— actually, his compound. By that time, Richie had moved out of Newark to a large and private spread in Livingston, New Jersey. The *Life* feature ("House of a Mobster") showed the mansion (made of stones brought from Italy), and the grounds (with an outdoor barbecue grill—big like a furnace), and the sculpture grotto, with statues of Richie's kids and the grand statue of Richie himself on a horse, like Caesar, or Garibaldi at least. . . . By that time, Richie had become just like Joe, in one particular way: the more famous he got the more misinformation, or disinformation, seemed to surround him. In later years, there were people—even local people—who maintained that Richie was a famous mafioso who was nicknamed the Boot because of some heavy-footed way he disposed of his gangland foes . . . which just went to show, as Joe and Richie always agreed, how wrong and mean-spirited public talk could be. Because everybody who truly knew Boiardo knew that he disposed of his gangland foes in that big barbecue (more like an incinerator than a furnace, come to think of it)—and if you got on Richie's wrong side you could, lamentably, get cree-mated. . . . As for "the Boot," there was a simple explanation. Richie got the name back in Newark, in the early days, when he couldn't get or couldn't trust a private phone in his Newark row house. Like many residents of the First Ward, he took care of business from the pay phone at the candy store where no one could listen in on account of the glass enclosure thoughtfully provided. So, in those days, if you came to Richie's house, and asked for the boss, the muscle on the door would say, "He's not here. Siddown if you wanna wait." And you'd say: "What do you mean he's not here?" And they'd say, "Relax, will ya? He'll be back in a minute. He hadda make a call. He went down 't'da boot." (Of course, you shoulda known—*da phone boot.*)

In those days Prohibition was making Boiardo wealthy and powerful—but only in the First Ward. Richie might have shipped beer and whiskey all over the city; he had the ambition, he had the idea. But he encountered a more established supplier named Abner "Longy" Zwillman, who came from the Jewish Third Ward—and something lamentable happened: Richie went for a walk on Broad Street, one day, just as eight bullets were coming by. And Boiardo ran into them all. It was a sign of God's favor that Richie the Boot lived.

The amazing part of the story was, after that, Longy and Richie made peace and even went into business. That odd turn of events was owed, primarily, to Zwillman, who was that rare sort of mobster who saw the strategic value of cooperation. In fact, Longy would later extend that radical idea to mobsters of the entire region—he was the man who formed the Commission with Bugsy Siegel, Meyer Lansky, Joe Adonis, Lucky Luciano, and the great brain of New York crime, Frank Costello. In those days, they were called the Big Six. Later they would extend cooperation and control out to Cleveland, Detroit, Chicago, and of course, Las Vegas. In a way, that was all Zwillman's doing. There was no one bigger or smarter than Longy.

Zwillman put the "organized" in organized crime because he understood it was a business: turf wars, shooting sprees, and tit-for-tat assassinations did nothing but weaken all parties and bring unwelcome scrutiny upon affairs that would ripen to more profit in private. Longy was a peacemaker by temperament. Contrary to speculation (which he did not altogether discourage), he did not get his name for his sexual equipment. Rather it was because he grew to full height (six feet two) by the time of his bar mitzvah, and became the defender of his neighborhood. When the Irish kids would swoop down upon the Jewish merchants—turning over their pushcarts, yanking their sideburns, or knocking their yarmulkes off— the merchants would start hollering, in Yiddish: *"Reef der Langer!"* "Fetch the Tall One!" . . . And thus, young Abner became the Longy.

By the time he had to deal with Richie the Boot, Longy's methods were well developed. He could have finished off Richie's gang while the Boot, still lamentably perforated, languished in a hospital bed. But at what cost? Let Boiardo run the First Ward—it needed running, anyway. So Longy made peace. To mark the occasion, Richie threw a dinner that lasted two days. And in commemoration of their solemn accord, Longy gave Boiardo a gift: a huge diamond-studded belt buckle that Richie would wear forever after. (Years later, that gift would save his life, when Richie ran into another bullet—but the bullet hit the buckle and never entered the Boot.) . . . Longy took the trouble to research what Richie liked. Richie liked diamonds. In fact, another name on his police rap sheet was "Diamond Boiardo" (which, as a handle, never caught on).

But the point was, by the time Joe DiMaggio showed up in Newark . . . showed up not as a stranger, but as a friend of the well-known Jerry Spatola . . . showed up not anonymous but already possessed of a great name (you could call it the greatest Dago name in the country) . . . showed up with that league-leading average and that World Series ring on his finger . . . showed up with his quiet unassuming manner, with his physical grace, with his gorgeous dark suits, with that beautiful blond broad on his arm . . . showed up not just around town but amid the cascading grapes *at Vittorio's Castle,* which Richie himself had built as his palace, which he owned, and which he ran—in everything but name (alas, the Boot was legalistically ineligible to hold a liquor license, on account of some minor felonies, so the Castle was held in the name of his son, Tony Boy Boiardo) . . . the point was, by the time Joe DiMaggio showed up, Richie the Boot and Longy Zwillman had been at peace for years, running Newark for fun and fortune, unchallenged, unassailed in their hyperprofitable lines of work, which included the rackets, protection, whores, narcotics, numbers, betting parlors, and untaxed liquor. The point was, there was no one in Newark who could show Joe DiMaggio a better time than *Don Ruggiero Boiardo;* no one who could bring to bear such splendid resources for making Joe D. his friend, an honored guest and ornament to the operation. There was sure as hell no one else with a safe containing drawers full of jewels, piles of precious cut stones—mostly diamonds (still Richie's favorite); no one else who knew that Joe was thinking of marriage, who could take Joe from his table at Vittorio's Castle, back to the office, who could throw open that safe . . . and say: *"Take any one you want Joe. For the ring. Whatever you like."*

A four-and-a-half-carat emerald-cut diamond: it was a small price to pay—no, not a price, but a pleasure—for the honor that Joe brought to Richie in Newark. You could almost see Boiardo swell with pride when DiMag came around. Richie never liked to have his picture made—especially at the Castle, which was not supposed to be his, and where he was not supposed to hang around too prominently. But just let DiMaggio grace a chair with the back of his suit pants . . . and there was Richie, sitting next to him, smiling for the camera. Those photos were never meant to go public. No one outside had to know a thing. Richie's people knew.

And the way Richie treated Joe, it just confirmed for everybody who saw, the worth, the stature, of these two giants: Joltin' Joe and Richie the Boot. Nothing was too good. Whatever Joe wanted, Richie wanted to have offered it yesterday. More often, it was something Richie thought of without Joe asking one word. That car Joe got at the dinner (sure, Richie helped with that)—he was gonna need someone to drive him, wasn't he? So how 'bout Peanuts?

Peanuts was Jimmy Ceres, who was always around Richie's place, always available for jobs. Driving—

sure; personal security; help in a thousand ways: that was Peanuts. Soon, he was always with Joe around Newark, or driving him back and forth from New York. Peanuts would drive Joe's Cadillac to Florida, so the Clipper could have a car to carry him around in spring training.

Of course, what with Peanuts driving, Joe had less time for the Spatolas. As a matter of fact, Jerry Spatola tried to take Joe aside and explain to him that maybe Peanuts Ceres and Richie the Boot (and, for that matter, Mr. Abe Zwillman) did not exactly constitute the kind of crowd Joe should hang around with. Peanuts, as they used to say in the Spatola household, never had a job he paid taxes on. And Richie, well, the Spatolas weren't feeling too friendly about the Boot, either, because Boiardo had decided to help out the mortuary industry. *(What a shame if something lamentable should happen to that nice hearse!)* . . . Richie had invented "The Car Owners Protective Association." He was leaning on Spatola to join up and pay his dues.

But it didn't matter what Jerry said. Joe would pick his own friends. If they were friends he couldn't talk about, that was no hardship. When Joe was ready to announce his engagement, the big celebration was held in Newark—hosted at the Castle by Richie the Boot.

Jerry Spatola would have to wait till that autumn, after the season, to recoup his status as Newark's Number One DiMaggio Fan. He would wait till November, when he and Rose would ride the train three and a half days out to San Francisco to attend Joe and Dorothy's wedding and reception—and then, that same night, they would board another train to ride three and a half days back to Newark . . . holding in their laps, paper-clipped in a tent of waxed paper, a piece of Joe and Dorothy's wedding cake.

As for Richie the Boot, unhappily the press of business kept him from attending the wedding. Longy Zwillman, too, was occupied and could not attend. But in time, Longy would also become a good friend to DiMaggio. And Longy being Longy, he'd find a way for Joe to be a friend to him, too.

A GIRL FROM DULUTH DIDN'T HEAD for New York, thence to Hollywood, to run away from the limelight. Dorothy didn't mind the fans in the restaurants, photographers outside the nightclubs— she'd never learned to hate the fuss like Joe did. For one thing, she'd never had a chance to get fed up with it. (They'd gone together for two years, but seldom in the same city.) What they'd had together was a lot of dates . . . and all the adulation, the public commotion—that was part of the fun.

She'd wanted her life to be like that for so long— seemed to her forever—and now it was happening. The first time she announced their engagement, the studio called up the very next day, and gave her the lead in that horror serial, *The Phantom Creeps*. And then, when Joe finally set a date, there was her picture in all the papers, everybody coming up to say hello, to meet her, congratulate her, get to know her . . . everybody was *wonderful*. Days before the wedding, in San Francisco, Dorothy came out of a downtown shop, her sister and mom alongside, and people *applauded*. How could she know that from the wedding day onward, Joe would expect her to run away from the attention she craved?

For that matter, how could Joe know that this lovely young starlet who was so helpful to him in social situations—she was always friendly and outgoing—could embarrass him at home by being so brassy? Dorothy did everything that could be expected: took her instruction in the Catholic faith, made her conversion, and vowed solemnly to bring up their children in the One True Church. She even set herself to learning Italian, so she could have a proper conversation with her new mamma and papa. But the more she did, the more Joe wished she would just . . . *pipe down*. Not till he saw her in the murmurzone of the DiMaggio household did it dawn on him that she was loud. (Christ, she laughed like a man!)

In November, a week before the wedding date, the DiMaggios sent out eight hundred invitations. They could have saved the postage. Everybody in North Beach was coming, anyway. The grand Cathedral of the West, the Church of Sts. Peter and Paul, could hold two thousand faithful. But Sunday afternoon, November 19, 1939, the church was nearly full before the first invitee appeared. People had staked out the pews that morning. They'd sat through two or three Masses already. The wedding was scheduled for two P.M.; by one, there was standing room only.

Parking? Forget it. Traffic was snarled for ten blocks around. The street in front was packed with people like Times Square on New Year's Eve. There was scaffolding on the front of the cathedral—where sculptures and decoration were still incomplete (fifteen years after the church was opened)—and now the boys of the neighborhood swung from the beams, whooping and calling to the earthbound, below. As the hour approached, there were thousands who couldn't push onto the street at the base of the church steps, so they spilled out behind, into the park. Inside the cathedral, the side chapels were all full, the choir loft had been taken over; the standees had pushed all the way to the front, past the communion rail, and were threatening to overrun the altar. Kids were perched on confessional roofs—like boys who climbed trees near the ballpark to watch the game. Save for vendors, this was a stadium crowd: happy, noisy, ungovernable. "Remember that you are in the house of the Lord," Father F. Parolin scolded from the altar. "I beseech you, be calm, be still, be quiet. I ask you in His name to be silent!" The padre might as well have dummied up himself.

One North Beach *signora* collapsed trying to squeeze through the front door. Happily, this was the first wedding in San Francisco history to have a city ambulance on standby—a gesture from the health commissioner, who was a guest. Even so, a flying wedge of policemen had to use nightsticks to beat a path through the crowd for the fallen matron's stretcher. The inside ushers were plainclothes cops, too, a gesture from the police commish, who was another guest—as was the sheriff. And at 1:55, the last shards of solemnity were shattered for good when sirens blared for several minutes as motorcycle cops forced a passage to the door for the Honorable Paesano, Mayor Angelo Rossi . . . newly reelected to another term, with the endorsemenet of San Francisco's greatest *prominento:* "Mayor Rossi has been batting nearly 1.000 in the toughest league in the country—the old government circuit," said the statement from Joe DiMaggio. "Let me tell you now that I am for the Mayor until his last inning is played!"

DiMag, the political heavyweight, was already in the church, waiting with his best man and elder brother Tom. The newest property of the Boston Red Sox, little Dominic, had also come to church early, with the family, all suited up for duty. As usual, Vince had to shift for himself, and got trapped outside, where the cops wouldn't let him through; he had to bull his way in through a side door. Still, two o'clock came and went in the noisy church, and there was no bride. The Olsons were in a car, pinned at a standstill by traffic.

"When the bride comes in," Father Parolin tried again, "don't jump on your seats, don't talk, don't get excited. Remember you are in God's house." Still there was a cheer, low, throaty, and expectant, like the ballpark crowd when the home team takes the field . . . as the big doors at the rear of the church swung open—a half-hour late, Dorothy's car had arrived.

And there she was, behind Joe's four sisters—Nellie, Frances, Marie, and Mamie—and then her own sister, Irene, who was the maid of honor . . . there, in a Hollywood gown of white satin, with a sculptured bodice and a five-yard train . . . behind a coronet veil of gauzy lace, tied with filigree of gold . . . bearing orchids and gardenias in her hands, and a spray of orange blossom on her forehead . . . twenty-one years old, on the arm of her father, and as she would recall, "scared stiff" . . . but looking up, smiling bravely and, as one Duluth newsman noted, "so utterly beautiful that it just hurt to look at her."

No wonder North Beach cheered. Their guy, their Joe, had gone from this altar to the wide world, and now he'd come back a conqueror, a hero. One look at this American girl, with her golden skin, golden hair, trumpeted his triumph—just as clear as if a parade of chariots filled with treasure had rolled up Columbus Ave.

Now, Father Parolin's Latin gave way to orotund accented English: "My dear friends, you are about to enter a union . . ." It was noted that Dorothy's bouquet trembled. A tear was descried on Mother DiMaggio's cheek. Somewhere in the back of the church, a girl's voice broke into hysterical giggles.

Joe DiMaggio remained stone-faced. Father Parolin was speaking: "Joe Paul DiMaggio? . . ."

"I do."

It took the DiMaggios ten minutes to get out the church door, twenty minutes more amid the police wedge to get across the sidewalk, while yellow spotlights glared, flash powder splashed lurid blue-white over all, movie cameras whirred, and people clung and shoved, tried to grab Joe's hand, tried to touch Mrs. Joe's gown, and roared a thousand times, *"AU-GURI . . . CENT'ANNI . . . BRAVU GIUSEPP'."*

The wedding couple had to stop at the photographers, in the approved North Beach manner. But for the rest, it was down the hill to Joe DiMaggio's Grotto, where the family was laying on a buffet, open bar, orchestra, Italian tenor—a spread like those neighborhood folk had never seen. As Ciccio LaRocca, one of Joe's groomsmen, remembered: "They had ice—the first time I ever saw something like that—I was in awe, you know? I couldn't believe what I was seeing—ball players sculptured *in ice!*— and you could see them getting smaller and smaller as the night goes. They just melted away, you know? It was beautiful."

Joe wouldn't hang around for the melting—not in that crowd. He got to the restaurant, right away he wanted the cake cut. So the orchestra played, they wheeled out a cake three feet high—and Dorothy cut it. Cut her finger, too. Joe was upset. He wanted to get going, take off for the honeymoon.

He was cagey about that: wouldn't tell where they were headed. "Down south, toward Hollywood first, I guess," Joe said when reporters quizzed him. "Then maybe to Mexico. And maybe across the country to Miami . . . and maybe New York." Mostly he just wanted to go. What with the hoopla over cutting the cake, and the music and drinks and the mountain of food, very few people saw them slip away. But Ciccio was there to help.

"She drove," Ciccio remembered, "Joe's blue Dodge, the '38. He was in the back.

"No, not the back seat—way in the back, where they had the rumble seat. He didn't want to talk to her. I don't know why. But he was mad. They weren't talkin'."

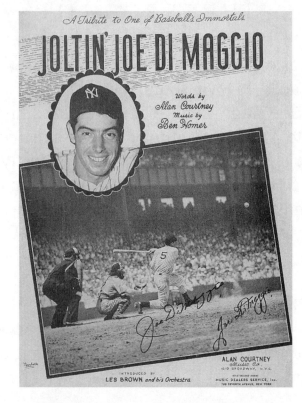

Number one on the Hit Parade, 1941.

Joe, Joe, Joe . . . will you sign my book?

Griffith Stadium, 1941.

CHAPTER 9

◆

ONE OF THE BOYS ON THE SCAFFOLD-
ing in front of the church was Dino Restelli. He was
ten years younger than Joe and lived in Valparaiso
Alley, just around the corner from Joe's old Taylor
Street home. He had the same rangy frame, same build
as DiMaggio. He played center field at the Horses' Lot
(and later for the Seals and the Pittsburgh Pirates). He
tried to run like DiMaggio, and catch the ball like
DiMaggio. He stood at the plate like DiMaggio. Of
course, everybody on his team stood at the plate like
DiMaggio. Every kid with a dime for the movies saw
Joe in the newsreels. They'd be acting out his slide that
same afternoon. After that, it was a short dream to
where they were him, in the brilliant World Series
they'd win that night as they fell asleep.

And it wasn't just San Francisco, or major-
leaguers-to-be. Three thousand miles across the
country in East Harlem, Salvatore "Sonny" Grosso
would grow up to be a New York cop (one of the hard-
boiled heroes who'd take down the French Connection drug ring). Still, the pole star in his boyhood sky
was DiMaggio. When Salvatore played ball he had to
be Number 5; football, he was Number 55. That was

since he could remember, since that first day his father took him across the Harlem River to the Bronx, to Yankee Stadium. Papa Grosso had box seats, but he sold them off so he could buy bleacher tickets. He and Sonny would be close to Joe D.

The connection to DiMaggio was more than a rooting interest. It had little to do with the Yanks, and went beyond hometown loyalty. In St. Louis (in the interstice between Medwick and Musial) the hero was DiMaggio. On Dago Hill, half the boys stepping up to the playground plate had their hands jammed down on the bat knob, feet spread wide, deadpan stare, as they tried to hold their bats still with DiMaggionic menace. One of those boys, a promising catcher named Joe Garagiola, remembered DiMag as a figure of such godly goodness, "it wouldn't have surprised me if I'd gone to church and they had him in the Litany. They'd have said: *'Joe DiMaggio,'* and we'd have said, *'Pray for us!'* "

For older *paesani,* DiMaggio transcended baseball: his virtue was success, and vice versa. On a cash-poor farm upstate in Garrison, New York, just across the Hudson from gray West Point, Frank the Mason (so he was known by the locals) used to punctuate his laboring days with the periodic comment, to no one in particular: "Joe DiMajj he getsa fifty tousan' dahll' for t'row da ball." An organization of Italo-Canadians sent word to Yankee Stadium that they were changing the name of their club to *Davedi,* so it could bear one precious syllable from each of history's three greatest Italians: *Dante . . . Verdi . . . DiMaggio.*

For kids (especially kids at Ground Zero, New York City), DiMaggio-love hit with such heat that it could blister away even tribal distinctions. Saturday afternoon in East Harlem, at the Fox Star Theater, 107th and Lexington, a shout of joy would greet DiMaggio when he showed up on the *Movietone News,* and hysterical applause echoed from the theater walls, while he ran the bases after his home run, or gunned down a runner from center field. It didn't matter that 1940 was an off year for the Yanks. (They would finish behind both Detroit and Cleveland.) It mattered not at all that the Fox Star was uneasy neutral turf between Italians and Puerto Ricans. The shouts for DiMaggio came from all sides. The Puerto Ricans didn't have a lot of models of their own. And Joe, he looked right, he had that "o" at the end of his name. He was Latin. He was their guy, too.

Those were the days when the newsreel cameramen were working out their own tricks. (Just because a newsreel was news—kinda—that didn't mean it wasn't also showbiz.) They'd get to the Stadium early, get close-ups of DiMaggio, and maybe the pitcher, maybe one or two other big names. And then, when DiMag did something in the game, they'd cut to the close-up, like the camera had caught him *just at that decisive moment.* That also meant DiMaggio was much more likely to be the hero. Once they had the close-up of his face, they might as well make his hit (or his steal, catch, throw . . .) the turning point of their story. The other effect was that Joe's cool persona was reinforced with every close-up. As far as the newsreel viewers could figure, they saw Joe's face just at the instant he was going to take that pitcher deep, or he was just heaving that ball home . . . and he looked as calm, matter-of-fact as if he was waitin' for the M-1 bus.

The point was, they were always going to sell Joe—because Joe sold. Of course they were going to show his face. That was the face that had graced the cover of *Life* magazine, one face on the ballfield that everybody knew. That's the same reason Joe was on the cover of the *Baseball Register.* It wasn't just that he had a big year, he was MVP, or a World Series winner. It was that face, that persona—that picture *was the story.* They could have run the portrait and left off the name of the magazine. That face *said* Baseball.

Radio built its audience with hero power, too—and with its constant repetitive flow, it cut deeper in the streambed of consciousness. That day in '39 when Arch McDonald thought of that new Pan American airplane, with its unequaled power, range, and style, and linked it to the center fielder: *"Batting clean-up, Joe DiMaggio—the Yankee Clipper . . ."* that was just one of a dozen nicknames with which Joe had been festooned. There was Dead Pan, the Wallopin' Wop, the Roamin' Roman, the Little Bambino, Dago, DiMag, Joe D., Big Giuseppe, and the most propitious, Joltin' Joe, or the Jolter. But Mc-

Donald had the power to make a nickname stick: specifically, fifty thousand watts on WABC, where he broadcast the Yankees' (and Giants') home games.

Now, on summer afternoons, the boys of the neighborhood would break from their own pickup game or stickball game, and gather on someone's porch, a front stoop, or in someone's kitchen, whence the radio transported them to Yankee Stadium. It was almost better than going to the park—where, of course, not everyone could buy the best seats. This way, they could see every play, every pitch in their heads—and they all went to the game together. Big games, it was like the whole city went. You could follow the action down any street, from the candy store, to the butcher shop, the tap room and restaurant, all the service stations, any garage, and of course any appliance shop. You could get an update on Joe's doings (in English or Italian) from almost any produce man; or simply find a quiet spot to loiter and listen: *". . . the White Sox will have to bring the infield in. They can't afford to give the Yanks anything more here. And here's DiMaggio striding to the plate—the Yank-Key Clipper! . . ."* The name, the image was now in the ether.

For working men who couldn't listen during the day, WHN started *Today in Baseball,* a seven-fifteen P.M. re-creation of the day's action—a whole game covered in fifteen minutes. Ward Bond started as the host, but by 1940, the mike was turned over to a popular local athlete-announcer, Marty Glickman. Soon, the show was such a hit, they'd do doubleheaders, two of the three New York teams every night. It was all done from a studio, with turntables for sound effects—one for steady crowd noise, and one for rising crowd noise (say, when the New York team scored a run). Glickman had a mallet to smack on a drummer's block for the sound of the bat on the ball. And he had the notes of what happened in the game. DiMAGGIO 2B HIT. NY 6 CHI 3.... *Whack!* (Glickman would smack that mallet down) ... *"DiMag hits a scorchin' drive PAST third base and Solters will haveta dig it out of the corner. Gordon has scored, Henrich is making the turn at third, and HERE HE COMES! Throw cut off and fired to second, but DiMaggio is IN THERE with his fadeaway slide!* (rising crowd noise) ... *And the Yankees lead SIX to three!"* ... Now, as a matter of cold, hard fact, there may have been no play at second, and DiMaggio's double might have been a pop-up that the right fielder lost in the sun. But not on that show. Glickman pumped up Joe's at bats, because Joe pumped up the show. People tuned in to hear "What'd Joe do?" and by God, they were going to hear something good!

The nicest part, the comfiest part, was that after *Today in Baseball* and the stories for the A.M. papers went to bed—say, seven or eight o'clock at night—then the hero machine was at rest, too. Actually, most of the men in the business went out to play, straight from the ballpark. They'd hand over their stories to the Western Union man, and head downtown: maybe say hello to the wife, maybe not; and by eight o'clock at the latest, they'd be at Toots Shor's, two and three deep around the circular bar, trying to catch up. Hell, by that time the early birds already had half a load on. *"Hey, Ziggy! Make it a double!"*

LOOKING BACK, YOU COULD SEE that as the last moment when the sports business was at human scale, a club where everybody knew who was who. If a player went to Shor's for a couple of belts and a nice free steak, he could relax and say what he wanted, without fear of it coming back to haunt him in print. Maybe there were two hundred guys in the joint, but he knew them—or he knew they were known. They understood the rules, or they wouldn't have been there. (Tootsie'd see to that.) They all knew what everybody thought about everything. If anybody thought something odd, well, that didn't last long. He'd be outvoted, outshouted, or mocked into compliance. For example, Toots himself might bellow (in the most insulting way): "Gehringer better than th' DAGO? Don't advertise yer ign'rance!"

Shor was the final arbiter on any topic worth his notice. Still atop the list were his problems: sports, money, friends. But now, in his own saloon, 51 West 51st, he had fistfuls of cash, his worries weren't pressing, and Toots had time for other subjects—for example, food. Toots got along with three basic tenets: "Good food." And "plenty." But "nuttin' fancy." Shrimp cocktail, steak, baked potato—if you didn't like them, why'd you come to his joint?

There was the more complicated subject of booze, which Toots researched more or less continuously, beginnning every day about eleven A.M., and finishing at closing time, four A.M.—unless there were regulars who cared to stay, in which case Toots would lock the doors and drink with them till they got their full load on. For a week or ten days every year, Toots teetotaled and took the baths in Hot Springs, Arkansas. Other than that, he drank every morning, afternoon, and evening (save for New Year's Eve, which he scorned as "Amma-cher Night"). From his beloved patrons (his "pals") Toots expected a professional drinker's decorum: no sloppiness, no puking, and show up on time the next day for work. If you didn't drink, you weren't a pal. And no nursing one lousy beer all night. "Any bum who can't get drunk by midnight," as Shor used to say, "ain't tryin'."

With his best pals ("our guys") Toots indulged in epic bouts—like the one with Jackie Gleason, when the comic maintained he could drink more than Toots. Toe-to-toe, drink for drink, they squared off before lunch, they drank through the rest of the day. Scotch for Gleason and, as always, fifteen-year-old brandy for Toots—and each was well into his second fifth, still trading insults, as evening drew nigh. Gleason was making a point at some length to the growing crowd at the circular bar—a point that Toots evidently found tiresome, for he interrupted to say: "You have the face of a pig." Gleason replied equably: "And you got the body." Then he turned back to the bar crowd and finished his point. It was after six P.M. when Gleason made murmur about the men's room, arose, and started across the floor. He fell with a mighty crash directly under the arch between the bar and dining room; he lay with an awful stillness in the path of every waiting diner—under the maître d's velvet rope. A captain and a waiter rushed to help the Great One up. "LEAVE HIM LIE," Toots roared. "I want 'em all to see what happens when ya mess wit' the champ."

The contests, the comradeship, all the lore from loads past fed into the most complicated subject— the matter of class. In the world of Toots Shor, class was a man's greatest attribute, albeit elusive, hard to handle in words. Toots could explain it only obliquely: "Class is a thing where a guy does everything decent."

It had nothing to with social class, though Toots did embrace the millionaire blueblood Jock Whitney, owner of the Greentree Stables. That wasn't for Whitney's breeding, but the way he bred horses: Toots respected a champion. (Toots admired Whitney so much, he wanted to send him a birthday gift, but what do you give to a Whitney? Finally, Toots sent a Western Union money order for ten bucks. "HAPPY BIRTHDAY," the wire said. "IF YOU NEED MORE CALL ME.") Even so, in Toots's joint, class was more than professional achievement. Toots wouldn't think twice about snubbing some tony corporate president and all the yes-men he brought with him. "Jeez," he'd mutter with audible disgust, "creeps are comin' in from all over." The Hollywood titan Louis B. Mayer fumed when he and his party had to wait twenty minutes for a table: "I trust the food will be worth all that waiting." Said Toots: "It'll be better'n some a your crummy pitchers I stood in line for."

No, to sun oneself in Shor's approval, you had to match success in the outside world with largeness and true feeling for him and his pals. Only thus could you become the highest sort of man—*a champion with class*—forever welcome with Toots . . . and what a welcome that was. "YOU CRUMB BUM!" he'd bellow, as his eighth-of-a-ton disappeared you into a hug. "YA CREEPY BUM, WHERE'YA BEEN? I LOVE YA!" . . .

Now, the Dago was a champion with class. And although Toots insisted that was the highest a man could go, in practice, DiMaggio stood even higher. The way Toots saw it, there were only two guys who could walk into his joint and everything stopped. Jack Dempsey was one, and Daig was the other. And even within that class of two—well, Dempsey was old, and had his own joint on Eighth Avenue. Joe D. was still fresh, in his prime, and all Shor's. He could've been Tootsie's kid, the way the old bear took care of him: fed him, talked to him, taught him, protected him.

There were days when DiMaggio had one of those games: he missed a ball in the field, or popped up a fat pitch when the Yankees needed runs, or the team lost a tough one (they were losing too many in that 1940 season) . . . right away, Toots was worried for the Dago. It wasn't worry about Joe's hitting, his fielding—nothing like that. But how would he feel? *(Joe could take it too hard, get all worked up. He might not come to dinner. He might not eat! Toots would have to send food to his hotel.)* . . . That night, Toots would be holding forth in his dining room, when the captain would appear to whisper: "Mr. DiMaggio is outside."

Toots would run out the door. Joe wouldn't come in—wouldn't want people to see him. So Toots would have to walk with him, 'round the corner, down Fifth Avenue, back and forth through the side streets. Neither one would talk much. Toots might ask: Did Joe eat the food he sent? Or maybe he'd tell Joe something that happened in the saloon. But after that, they'd walk in silence—half an hour, an hour, maybe two—till Joe felt better, till he could go back to his hotel and lie down.

Toots—well, you could call him sentimental. (His friend Rags Ragland used to say: "You can make him cry with card tricks.") . . . But how could Toots not love a kid like Joe, who needed him like that?

IT WAS A MEASURE OF HER CAN-DO spirit that Dorothy learned everything she could about baseball—went to the games, tried to keep up on the statistics: she plunged into the baseball life. What else would they talk about? She told her friends about the time Joe fell into a slump, and his average was slipping, and she told him that she didn't see the 5 on his back the way she always used to when he swung. The 5 was in a different place now. And Joe said that helped him, and he did start to hit again, and his average went back up, and pretty soon he was in the hunt for the batting crown for the second straight year, which was bound to happen because really there was nobody like him, and since that time when she helped him he was batting actually better than last year, more consistently, and she always said that batting was consistency more than anything else. . . . It was a measure of her self-involvement that she couldn't see this was driving him nuts.

He couldn't see why she wouldn't just be Mrs. Joe DiMaggio, why she had to be the center of attention. They were great together, the way she looked when they went out. The way she dressed, classy—he loved that. But sometimes they'd have to go home three times in one night, to change for different shows or parties. She ought to be able to see they couldn't do the town every night in the season. Some nights he'd rather just be quiet, with the guys, maybe get a steak with Toots. (Was there anything wrong with that?) Or if he stayed in with her, he'd rather just listen to the radio and get some rest. He had to be right the next day. That's what paid the freight. That's why they never had to worry for money. That's why she never had to work.

She never *could* see why she had to give up work. She'd had her own life—and so many friends! What did she have now? Why should Joe get upset if she spent the day with her agent, Mort Millman? Of course, Mort would try to talk her into some audition or a movie role—keep her career alive—that was his job. But what meant more to Dorothy was that Mort thought she was special. He always said she had that—well, that *something* that would make her a star. Dorothy loved to hear it. And Joe wasn't the kind who could scratch that itch for her. He'd leave in the morning, and sometimes by the time he got back—if he didn't get a hit, or he'd struck out once, or even if he was perfect and the Yankees had lost—he didn't want to talk. And if she talked, well, a lot of times he didn't want to hear it. If she kept it up, he'd get so furious, he'd walk out and she wouldn't see him that night, maybe nights on end. Then what was she supposed to do—Mrs. Joe DiMaggio? It would all be different if they had children. She knew that would tie her hands for a while. But, surely, Joe would settle down if he had a real family.

Why couldn't she just settle down? Joe wasn't against her working, not really. But he couldn't run around the country after her. She'd told the world she was giving up the movies for him. And now all she talked about was going back to work. Joe knew about the casting couch—or thought he knew. She didn't buy that mink coat she had—he'd bet ten to one. Before they met, Dorothy used to go into the Automat and buy a little pot of boiling water, the kind they sold for tea. Then she'd pour in ketchup, and that was tomato soup—for a nickel. (So, where'd she get that mink?) . . . No wife of his was going back to that sort of life. Joe thought, it would be different if they had kids—she'd have her hands full.

It was Dorothy who made the plan; she was always the planner—and by that September, 1940, it was clear they would have the autumn to themselves. As it turned out, Joe did win his second batting crown. She was thrilled. But he acted like that whole season was a failure. That was the first time, 1940, there was no World Series for Joe—and no tours, parties, banquets: that didn't happen for third-place ball clubs. Joe didn't even want to show up at Shor's, where everyone would talk about the Tigers or Cincinnati. No, Joe said they ought to just head west, to San Francisco; they could stay with the family, wouldn't cost a dime. He could spend some time at the Grotto. That would please brother Tom, be good for the business. And on the way back, Dorothy planned the visits to her kin in Minnesota, and Rice Lake, Wisconsin. The way Dorothy figured, that's where she was going to make it happen: a few weeks after New Year's, in Minnesota or Wisconsin. She had it all worked out: they'd conceive in late January—so the baby wouldn't be born until after next season. Joe wouldn't want a distraction.

That visit to Rice Lake would be the Olsons' first chance to see the marriage at close quarters. There was terrific excitement when Joe and Dorothy said they were coming. So it wasn't just her sister Joyce, and her husband, Les, awaiting them. Sister Irene also came to visit, along with Dorothy's parents and her grandfather, too. Joyce's small apartment had beds stuck everywhere. And then, Les's boss asked if he could meet Joe, and Les said, "Why not?" So the boss, Lindy Milbreth, and co-worker, Bob McKeon, came by that first evening, and the place was packed. Of course, they were chatting in a voluble way, as you'd expect folks could do in Rice Lake, in wintertime. Les, Bob, and Lindy were all great talkers: they were the divisional sales force for the Seal of Minnesota Flour Company. And they wanted to know all about their famous guests. Well, as usual, Joe was quiet, so Dorothy talked for them both. Joe got quieter. But Dorothy, as ever, was the life of the party. Joe was silent. Still, everybody had a wonderful time . . . until Joe stood up and marched out the door.

Well, of course, they were shocked and concerned—though it wasn't exactly concern for Joe. No one could get lost in Rice Lake. But as Joyce whispered urgently to Les, someone had to get Joe off the street. People would think that Joe didn't want to be with them. As Joyce explained to Dorothy: "We live in a small town. We just can't have this." So Les went out and found Joe. He was sitting alone in a tavern. They talked for a while, and Joe came back.

How could Joe explain it, to Les or anyone else? He wasn't envious of those flour salesmen—or any other man, really. He wasn't jealous of anyone in Rice Lake, except maybe Dorothy herself. Sure, he saw the men, the way they looked at her (couldn't not look). Okay. But the one he couldn't watch was her. She was so outgoing, beautiful, charming. She was turning herself inside out, for those . . . bush leaguers—that's what Joe couldn't stand. She was his.

Even that had its good side. For though this wasn't the sort of thing much talked about in Rice Lake (at least in those days), everybody in the family thought that was the night it happened. To be sure, Joe and Dorothy made something happen that night—clearly, you might say loudly (even in matters intimate, Dorothy was excited by an audience). And the way the family figured, that was the start of Little Joe. (Fifty years later, sister Joyce remembered: "We called it the shot heard 'round the world.")

By the end of spring training, 1941, Joe and Dorothy knew they were expecting; and then things got done on the double. They got their own apartment—thoroughly big-league: the penthouse at 400 West End Avenue. It was just a few blocks away from June and Lefty Gomez's West Side penthouse. (That way, Lefty could drive Joe to the Stadium every day.) Dorothy went into decorating as she went at everything: whole hog. Peanuts, Jimmy Ceres, was humping Joe's Cadillac all over town, bringing tubs of flowers for the terrace, house plants, gilded chairs, embroidered pillows, wallpaper books, and bolts of cloth—at Dorothy's beck and call. She started entertaining right away: called her friends Lou Costello and Bud Abbott to come over for her specialty, chicken *cacciatore.* (Dorothy maintained every Swedish girl could cook.) And it felt to her now *(at last),* she and Joe were starting a real life together.

BUT NOTHING COULD FEEL SOLID TO Joe if things weren't right on the field. In the end, eveything came from baseball—depended on the Yanks, who depended on him. After the Bronx Bombers finished third in 1940, heads were bound to roll. Crosetti was adjudged to be too old to play every day, so the Yankees brought up a kid named Rizzuto. Little Phil looked like he belonged in American Legion ball, but he'd burned up the Triple A's with Kansas City, and deserved a shot with the big club. They brought up another kid named Gerry Priddy to play second base. Joe Gordon, the established second baseman, would now try his hand at first. And Babe Dahlgren, the first baseman who'd stepped in and saved the Yanks when Gehrig crumbled—*Well, thanks very much for your efforts, Babe.* . . . Dahlgren was shucked off to the NL's miserable Boston Bees.

Now, no one on or off that club, inside or outside of baseball, could imagine the Yankees making any move to dislodge or disquiet their center fielder. DiMaggio had led the league in batting with an average of .352. He'd hit thirty-one home runs, and knocked in a hundred thirty-three. It was a measure of how Joe saw himself that he felt his job was on the line. The Yanks were paying him thirty-five thousand dollars a year—to win. If they didn't play better in '41, if they finished another year out of the money, who could tell what that bastard Barrow would do . . . or what McCarthy would do? It seemed, these days, a couple of losses could drive the old man around the bend. There were days (no one talked much about this) that the Skipper wouldn't show up until game time—coaches ran everything till then. And when McCarthy did show, he might be (as the players whispered) "a little shaky today," or more aptly, "riding the White Horse." That was the name of his scotch.

By mid-May '41, the whole team felt shaky: the Yanks had sunk to third, then fourth place—and falling. "A non-stop flight toward the second division," the *Herald Tribune* called it, after the Yanks lost five in a row. The reasons, as with all losing clubs, were depressingly various: Gordon was a mutt around first base. The pitching staff could be good one day and monstrous the next; no one knew if Jekyll or Hyde would show up. Henrich was supposed to be the everyday right fielder, but he looked so lost at the plate McCarthy had to sit him against left-handers. Rizzuto started out fine, but then he stopped hitting, like someone had flipped his switch to off. Priddy never hit at all. And worst of all, DiMaggio was in a slump like he'd never known. It started April 22, against the Philadelphia A's junk-baller, Lester McCrabb. Joe had some bad swings, lunging for balls he could never reach, and started pressing. Then he couldn't get back on track. His average for the young season dropped two hundred points in three weeks. In those twenty games he was batting .194—and living under a cloud.

The sporting press also offered multiple explanations for the Yankees' and Joe D.'s swoon. Maybe the Jolter had a case of nerves about impending fatherhood. (There was his gorgeously swelling bride in the club seats, every home game.) Or maybe the Big Guy was bothered by the unsettled lineup around him. (Now, McCarthy shook it up again, benching the rookies Rizzuto and Priddy, restoring Gordon and Crosetti to second and short. Another rookie, Johnny Sturm, would take over first base—unless he caught the bug and stopped hitting, too.) Some writers insisted the Yanks were simply mediocre without Lou Gehrig. Others, of a more psychological bent, said the Yanks were dealing with their grief over Gehrig's illness and his certain demise. (One writer, Jimmy Powers, suggested in the *Daily News* that Gehrig had spread his disease to other Yanks—for which accusation Powers was widely reviled, frozen out in the clubhouse, shouted down by rival writers, and finally sued by Gehrig. Actually, it was Lou's lawyers who spurred the suit: at that moment, as the papers revealed, Gehrig lay so near death, he couldn't even hold a smoke for himself.)

And one way or another, every analyst (in print or at the corner tavern) had to gauge the unsettling effect of the news from the wider world. Hitler had already gobbled up Europe—save for some out-of-the-way bits of gristle, like the Balkans, or Portugal; now, with Nazi bombs raining on London and U.S. ships dodging U-boats across the Atlantic, no one could be sure next September would bring a pennant race. Maybe all these Yankees would become Bombers for Uncle Sam, or trade in their bats for GI rifles. Surely the fans could feel the war coming, a chill breath of dread. *The Sporting News* offered a new baseball feature: "From the Army Front." There were strange new statistics to keep track of: Bob Feller's low draft lottery number; Hank Greenberg's new salary (a lousy twenty-one bucks a month) as the Army's newest buck private at Fort Custer, Michigan. The Yanks' GM, Ed Barrow, was already wailing about the draft: it would decimate his roster, and ruin baseball! But for the most part, the Baseball Nation wrapped itself in the red-white-and-blue and leapt to voice support for America's martial honor, for the armed forces, for FDR and his war aims against the fascist bullies. Here, for example, was the Secretary of State, that Yankee Doodle Dandy Daniel, writing of his thoughts as the National Anthem echoed over the diamond, and into the press box: "... *'Whose broad stripes and bright stars'* ... The stars are blacked out over there, and the broad stripes are the lash-marks on the backs of men in Poland. Starvation stalks and children die where the waltzes of Strauss used to be the theme song of *gemütlichkeit* which has fled the world. . . . *'And the home of the brave.'* . . . The Yankees take the field and the first batter comes to the plate. They are dropping bombs again over London. . . . 'Protect us by thy might, great God, our King.' . . . *'Play Ball!'* "

(Jeez, and we weren't even in the war, yet!)

One explanation that no one could offer was DiMaggio's own. Even by DiMaggio standards, Joe was hard to talk to that May. He'd slipped into Sicilian-fisherman mode, asking nothing, asserting nothing, warding off inquiries, well wishes, and any chance of advice. In the clubhouse, no one would say a word, except for quiet greetings, as they padded by the stool where he smoked and stared.

"Hiya, Joe." "Howsa goin', Daig?"

"Fine," DiMaggio would answer. "Fine."

What was he going to say? That someone got him with the evil eye? That no matter what he did, it came out wrong? Take, for example, the May 15 game—he finally got a hit, a solid single, drove in a run. But the Yankees lost again, lost hopelessly, 13–1. And who opened the gates to let the White Sox score? Joe D. He tried to throw out a ChiSox runner, little Billy Knickerbocker, racing for third. But Joe's throw hit Knickerbocker on the arm, and of course he scored. Joe got charged with the error—unfairly—his throw was straight to the bag. But he wasn't going to whine, or curse his luck aloud. That would sound like an alibi.

So, the next day, against the White Sox again, DiMaggio made a statement his way: he smashed a drive so deep into the left field bleachers that only one man (Private Hank Greenberg) had ever hit one there before. In the ninth, Joe hit another shot that banged off the left field wall for a triple, started a rally that gave the Yanks a 6–5 comeback win. That made two games in a row Joe got a hit—though no one said a word about it. It was more than a month, nearly two months later, when people tried to remember that game back in May, those two cannon shots Joe hit to beat Chicago. By that time DiMaggio had hit so many shots, in so many games, that all the players, writers, fans—all the Baseball Nation, and most of the American nation—were listening every day for news of him, or grabbing newspapers to read about him, or crowding into ballparks to scream his name, to be there as he made history, or simply to get a look at the man of the hour. By that time, it had become a giddy national derangement, DiMaggio-mania. . . . Joe gave America just what it needed: something apart from woe and war to talk about—a summer craze.

It was only after the fact that The Streak shone as portent of America's brilliant rise to superpower, and made DiMaggio her poster boy for valor, victory, and God-given grace. Through World War II, and the Cold War that followed, as America bulked up on her mythos and missiles, DiMaggio was said to exemplify the great melting pot, which turned immigrants from a hundred lands into one unbeatable nation. Here was the son of an impoverished fisherman, from a country we fought in war. And yet *(by the miracle of our society),* Joe was as American as ice cream on the Fourth of July. And with freedom, ambition, aspiration—those blessings bestowed by his new land—he could shoot for the stars (and get there). In history's foreshortened rearview mirror (with The Streak and Pearl Harbor clumped together in '41), DiMaggio showed up as more than our diversion from war: he seemed our answer to war. *He steeled the nation for its greatest test! He stood, he persevered, he excelled, even as the shadow of Hitler drew nigh! . . .*

The funny part was, if DiMaggio had been forced to carry, or had even been aware of one tenth of, this grand historical baggage, he'd never have made a streak of ten days. But in the event, he knew one thing: he had to hit for the Yankees to win. He was acting like a real immigrant's son. He was trying to keep his head down and do his job.

WITH A STREAK, IT'S THE LENGTH that makes it a record. We venerate Joe's feat today for its fifty-sixhood: that is, for the amazing number of times (two full months of games) that the same thing happened: Joe got a hit. But in the doing, it was nothing like the same thing over and over. In 1941, The Streak was formed not of months or weeks, but moment to moment—this at bat, that pitch, this swing . . . and every instant, every instance, with its own fingerprint, unique.

Take, for one instance, the fourth game. The White Sox had left town (after spanking the Yanks two out of three), and the visitors' dugout was taken over by the St. Louis Browns. Before a festive crowd of more than thirty thousand who showed their colors at the Stadium for "I Am an American Day," the Yankees walloped the Browns 12–2, and DiMaggio posted a perfect afternoon: three-for-three, with three runs scored. It would seem natural to regard this as a continuation of the hard-hitting heroics Joe had flashed in game two against the White Sox. But that was far from true. The first time he came up, Joe hit a dribbler to third base, where the Browns' Harlond Clift nudged the ball around for a while. The official scorer, Dan "I Am an American" Daniel, made all his compatriots happy by giving the Jolter a base hit. In the second inning, DiMaggio came up again, and launched a languid pop fly into the right field corner. Chet Laabs was the Brownie in charge of that real estate; he ran under the fly ball but, unluckily, it hit him in the glove. Laabs dropped the ball and Daniel credited DiMag with a double. Joe came to bat again in the fourth and popped up again, this time toward third base, where Clift actually caught the ball. But Joe's bat had nicked the glove of the catcher, Hans Grube. Interference was called and, by rule, Joe was awarded a single.

At that point, neither Joe nor the crowd cared if he

got a few gift hits. The fans were only waiting, hoping, for DiMag and the Yanks to get going—consistency eluded them still. The next day, Joe got a
double in his last at bat, but that was one of only four
Yankee hits and the cellar-dweller Browns won the
game 5–1. Day after that, the Pinstripes squeaked by
10–9 with the aid of six Brownie errors. DiMaggio
got a single in the eighth—one-for-five for the long
day's doing. No wonder no one made much of Joe's
hit. Bill Dickey, the catcher, who was pounding the
ball at a .391 clip, drove in three runs on three base
hits, to extend *his* batting streak to twenty-one
games.

The Yanks took two straight from Detroit after
that. Joe hit safely in both of those games—though
Bobo Newsom, who pitched the second contest, hypnotized DiMaggio through three at bats. Only after
the other Yanks drove Big Buck from the mound did
Joe awake to slap a seventh-inning single off the lefty
reliever, Archie McKain. The next day, the Boston
Red Sox came calling, and Joe wore the collar till the
eighth inning—once again, his last at bat; once
again, a paltry one-for-five. With one more game,
May 24, DiMaggio's streak would break into double
figures. But in the *Telegram,* Daniel was still trying to
elucidate the woes of the Yankees, their skipper, and
their slugger.

"Joe McCarthy now is concentrating on the hope
that Joe DiMaggio will snap out of his protracted and
inexplicable slump. . . . DiMaggio has contributed

only half a dozen hits in his most recent 21 trips to the plate, has seen his average whittled to .319."

In later years writers would marvel at the way The Streak snuck up on the press: no one paid attention until Joe had pushed past twenty straight games. But Professor Michael Seidel, who wrote the definitive *Streak: Joe DiMaggio and the Summer of '41*, noted that The Streak was mentioned in print as it passed a dozen games. More to the point, Seidel recounted the rataplan of world-shaking news that made Joe's base hits seem like small potatoes. In the first weeks of DiMaggio's streak, front pages featured (just to list a few stories): the mysterious flight to Scotland by Rudolf Hess, Deputy Führer of the Third Reich; news that the Germans sank the Egyptian steamship *Zamzam,* with one hundred thirty-eight Americans aboard (thirty-five of them kids); the surrender of Italy's Africa corps of thirty-eight thousand men to the British; the German conquest of Crete (and expulsion of the British); Roosevelt's electrifying radio address, known as the "Unlimited Emergency" speech; and the British hunt for, attack upon, and triumph over the world's greatest battleship: on May 27, they sank the *Bismarck.*

By the end of the month, the Yanks were in Boston for a return engagement with the Red Sox, and in the Memorial Day doubleheader, DiMaggio's streak pushed past fifteen games. Even so, Joe wasn't the headliner with the bat. That distinction belonged to the Bosox beanpole left fielder, Ted Williams, who improved (with a three-for-five afternoon) on his season's average of .429 (almost a C-note higher than Joe's measly .330). Williams was riding his own consecutive-games streak—one game longer than Joe's—and during his streak, Ted was hitting over .500. Alas, that day, the news of Joe had nothing to do with his hitting. A stiff neck and shoulder changed him from the embodiment of grace into an outfield menace: he posted four errors, including two throws so exuberantly wild that they overflew every available fielder and rattled up against the Fenway box seat rail. Of course the crowd made known its derision—though finding the proper insult was a challenge: the Boston leatherlungs couldn't imprecate Joe's nationality (their own center fielder was Italian, too), nor even his parentage (their own center fielder had the same parents). Professor Seidel quotes the fans as yelling, "Meatball! Meatball! . . ." But it is also possible that this holiday twin bill marked the genesis of the Fenway grandstand anthem (sung to the tune of "O Tannenbaum"):

He's better than his brother Joe . . .
Dom-i-nic Di-Maggio . . .

A failure in Boston was doubly galling, precisely because of brother Dom—and Ted Williams. Joe resented all comparisons to Williams, whom he thought of as a brat—Teddy Tantrum. And the way Ted played outfield! How could they be mentioned in the same breath? "He throws like a broad," Joe said, "and he runs like a ruptured duck."

Joe's attitude toward Dominic was more complex—a changeable admixture of fondness, family loyalty, and resentment. Dominic maintained in his memoir, *Real Grass, Real Heroes,* that Joe was ever the loving big brother. "He called me 'Min' sometimes, for the three middle letters in my first name, and he told one of his friends in Boston, 'Take care of Min—he's my pet.' " But Joe was not above suggesting that Dom was too small to be a great player, and got to the big leagues on the strength of his name—that is, Joe's name. Withal, when Min started stealing hits from big brother, well, that was not so amiable.

Joe often told the story of how Dominic almost stopped The Streak (and robbed him of a sure triple), when he flagged down a long drive in Yankee Stadium, and turned it into just another loud out. In point of fact, that never happened—or never happened during The Streak—but it satisfied Joe to think it did. The subtext of all his Streak stories was the same—no one was cutting him any breaks. The stories were fuel for his own performance. It was Joe, against all comers.

IRONICALLY, THAT WAS THE MOMENT the Yankees became DiMaggio's team, finally and without a doubt. On June 2, 1941, Lou Gehrig died. At that point, the Yanks were playing in Detroit. The manager, McCarthy, and Lou's closest Yankee friend, Bill Dickey, would fly to New York for the funeral. DiMaggio would stay behind to lead the team— which he did: though the mournful Yankees lost 4–2, DiMaggio's home run pushed his streak to twenty straight.

Right on cue, Joe was shaking off the pain and stiffness in his neck and shoulder, starting to hammer the ball. He was the intimidator in the middle of the Yankee lineup, and for his teammates, a beacon and spur. Sure, the club was in fourth place, but if Dago stayed hot, better times would surely follow. Next game, Detroit again, a triple for DiMag. But Tom Henrich also stepped up, with a homer to tie the game in the ninth. (Henrich had literally taken his cue from Joe; he'd broken a slump of his own by switching to one of DiMaggio's D-29 bats.)

The Yankee train arrived in St. Louis: three hits for DiMaggio, five Yankee runs in the ninth to win; and this time, it was Charlie Keller who stepped in with a home run.

A twin bill in St. Louis on Sunday: Joe had two home runs in the first game, another homer and a double in the second. And now all the Bombers fired away in fusillade: Henrich and Red Rolfe joined with homers in the first game, a 9–3 Yankee win. In the second game, 8–3 Yanks, Keller and Joe Gordon matched long balls with DiMaggio.

Next day, the venue changed to Chicago, Comiskey Park, but the result remained the same: the

New Yorkers ran away with the game 8–3, this time on the strength of a homer from Keller and a grand slam by old Frank Crosetti. The New York writers were noting a new streak: it was the eighth straight game that some Yankee had poled a ball out of the park. For Joe, it was a day of struggle against his erstwhile sandlot teammate, the White Sox third baseman, Dario Lodigiani. First time up, Lodi grabbed a hard hopper and threw Joe out at first base. Second time, Joe came up with a man on first, hit another hard shot to third, where Lodigiani collared it and slung the ball to second for the fielder's choice. When Joe came up, oh-for-three, in the seventh inning, Lodigiani backed up a step, on the balls of his feet, ready—or he thought he was. Joe hit another smash toward third, this one so hard that Lodigiani could only block it with his body. Then he pounced on the ball, fired across to first, and was relieved to see he'd nipped Joe by a hair—a quarter-step. *"SAAAFE!"* yelled the ump at first. . . . But the scorer couldn't give Lodi an E on that play. DiMaggio's streak climbed to twenty-five games, while the Yankees climbed into second place, four and a half behind Cleveland.

Of course, Lodigiani wanted to stop Joe. All the players wanted their picture in the papers—they're the guy who stopped him cold. And, of course, it was pitchers, most of all. One day, the young Chicago right-hander Jack Hallett, he'd had enough. First the Bostons had come through town, and Dominic DiMaggio hit everything Hallett threw. Now, it was the Yankees, and *big* DiMaggio already had two hits on the day. Hallett was steaming: "How d'you get these fuckin' DiMaggios out?" Lodigiani looked over at the on-deck circle and there was Joe with two bats, grindin' 'em together. He said: "Why'ncha hit the big bastard on the Number 5?" And Hallett, he was hot enough, young fool enough, to do it. He fired a fastball so far in, Joe could only turn around and take it in the back. (And Hallett was a big kid, threw a heavy ball.) Of course, Joe didn't say a word: dropped his bat, ran to first. On the White Sox bench, the old coach, Muddy Ruel (who'd been in the majors since 1915), announced to the team at large: "Hallett don't know it yet, but he just made a big mistake." Sure enough, next time up, Joe hit another bullet off Hallett—made it three for four that day. "Guys like that," as Ruel pointed out, "you don't wanna wake 'em up."

Joe would later say he didn't wake up to The Streak till it ran well into the thirties. That was another polite fable. It wasn't just the papers writing up the Big Guy each day—now the team record (twenty-nine straight by Roger Peckinpaugh in 1919) was in his sights. All the men in the Yankee clubhouse could see, they could feel Joe digging in, digging down, to keep it going. Of course, they couldn't say anything— wouldn't be the one to put the whammy on Daig's chances. But they all knew. After Chicago, the Yanks went home to face the first-place Cleveland Indians (led by their manager, Roger Peckinpaugh)—who had a streak of their own: they'd won six straight. And the Indians would lead with their ace, Rapid Robert Feller, who at that point had won his last eight straight. More than forty-four thousand fans filled the grandstand—even Babe Ruth showed up—to see if the Bombers could keep their homer string alive (they'd hit round-trippers in nine straight) and gain any ground in the pennant race. But mostly, that crowd turned out to see DiMag hit Feller. Joe was about the only right-hander who'd dig in, wouldn't give an inch to Feller. Feller was bearing down, too— trying to bust the fastball in under Joe's hands. But Joe wouldn't flinch, he'd just take it. In the third in- ning, Joe ran the count to three-and-oh; Feller had to throw a strike. He fired his heater out over the plate, and DiMaggio let loose, brought his bat through the zone in a blur. He slashed the ball on a line to right center, where it rolled up against the fence, drove home a run (that would be the game-clincher) . . . and DiMaggio, poker-faced on second base, busied himself brushing dirt off his pants while the crowd screamed his name. Feller's win streak would be un- done that day, 4–1; as would the Indians' team streak—obliterated, more like it—by three Yankee wins in a row. In fact, the Bombers would make it eight straight wins (with a home run by some Yank in every one of those games), to let the world know: they were back in the hunt; the whole team was going to ride this streak. But that hardly required any more announcement, once manager McCarthy flashed that hit sign for the Dago on Feller's cripple, three-and-oh. They might as well have put it on a billboard: DiMaggio's hit streak was now official Yankee business.

Joe took over the franchise record in the first game against the visiting White Sox, on a bit of good fortune: his grounder to short took an odd bounce and hit Luke Appling in the shoulder on its way into short left field. DiMaggio would call it the luckiest hit of his streak—game number thirty. Next day, Appling couldn't quite glove Joe's bloop past shortstop, and ended up holding the ball in short left again, staring across the diamond at Joe D. on first base. A couple of the writers essayed a few quips—Appling must be Joe's "cousin" (heh heh). But there was no indication that Joe took that as a laughing matter. In the final game with the White Sox, he could have brought the drama to a neat close, when he faced the left-hander Eddie Smith—the pitcher against whom he'd started The Streak, thirty-two games back. But Joe wasn't interested in a tidy roundness: he treated Smith just as he had the first time—with a solid single in the first. In fact, Joe would post a perfect three-for-three, including a home run to push the team's streak (or, in Danielese: "their circuit-spree") to fifteen straight games. In the locker room, with the writers buzzing in and out on streak story errands, there was open talk, now, about the home runs, and Yankee wins, and most of all, Joe's hits. He didn't seem to mind. "Heck, no!" the Jolter was quoted in the *Newark*

News. "Hoodoos aren't going to stop me—a pitcher will." Daniel wrote that Joe's streak had taken over the clubhouse and—"like the man who came to dinner"—it wouldn't go away. Most writers were stacking Joe up against the modern major league record: forty-one games by George Sisler, in 1922. But Daniel insisted on the all-time record: forty-four straight by Wee Willie Keeler—back, for God's sake, *in 1897,* before foul balls were even counted as strikes.

Still, no real pal would talk to Joe about the records. The trick was to take his mind off all that—talk about anything else—and keep him entertained. There was a new player on the '41 squad, another Coast League grad, Frenchy Bordagaray. He tried to play around with Joe, chatter at the table while Dago had dinner, or get him a beer on the train, run out for the papers—whatever Joe wanted. Mostly it was just to stick with Joe in public—so no one else could get to him. Bordagaray didn't mind playing bodyguard, or playing the fool to amuse Joe. Frenchy was a cutup, anyway. And he'd figured out what other marginal Yankees would discover in later years: if Dago talked to you, you belonged—simple as that.

Mostly, it was still Gomez who'd squire Joe out to dinners, or shows—if the place was good and dark, and they wouldn't make a fuss about the Great DiMaggio being in attendance. If Gomez was scheduled to pitch the next day, he'd make sure Joe got home early—to get plenty of rest, get some big hits tomorrow. Lefty tended to Joe's well-being like a second job. The night before DiMag's three-for-three against the White Sox, Lefty and Joe went out to the Polo Grounds for the fight of the year: Joe Louis v. Billy Conn. In fact, that bout would be called one of the greatest of all time, after Louis stalked Conn for thirteen rounds, and finally caught him, knocked him out, and held on to the heavyweight title. Even that grand spectacle couldn't divert Joe entirely from his own outsized athletic fame. When he and Lefty came in, just before the first bell, all other activity at the Polo Grounds stopped, as the crowd of fifty-eight thousand fans rose and roared approval for DiMaggio. "Joe always seemed more than just a baseball player," Lefty was quoted, in *Where Have You Gone, Joe DiMaggio?* "He seemed like a figure, a hero, that the whole country could root for. . . . He got up to thirty, thirty-five games and that was all anybody in the country seemed interested in. Joe was the biggest news there was. They moved him from the sports pages to the front pages and I had to tell a lot of strange stories to hide Joe from all the people that wanted to shake his hand or be with him in those days."

Within the Yankee clubhouse, there was pride simply in being with Joe. As his streak climbed through the thirties, everyone connected with the club was more notable every day, for having been with DiMaggio, for having seen him up close, for having talked to him—well, they didn't talk to him. But they watched him, admired him, learned from him. Maybe he wouldn't say ten words. But just by the way he was, the way he did business, the standard he set for himself—*by being Joe DiMaggio*—he made them all better players. Johnny Sturm would more than hold his own at first base—in the only season he ever stuck in the major leagues. In the Yankee home run streak, ten different players knocked balls over the fence—even little Scooter Rizzuto poled one out. Players whom no one thought of as great Yankees put up great Yankee stats: the fill-in catcher, Buddy Rosar, had a batting average of .374. The pitcher Red Ruffing became the best pinch hitter in the league. (He would hit .303 for the year.) . . . Pride of the Yankees was a concept so winning, Hollywood picked up the title for the new Gehrig bio-pic (filming that summer), with Gary Cooper in the lead role. But at that time, in the real world, the Pride of the Yanks was Joe. More than that, he was the meal ticket: the man who put fans in the seats. He was the motor of their pennant progress: now, they were breathing down Cleveland's neck. If Dago kept hitting every day, he might haul every player in that clubhouse to another World Series windfall. Why wouldn't they do *anything* to help him?

On June 26, the Yankees woke up in first place—for the first time in two months. They had won their last five out of six. They had just set a new major league record for a team home run streak: they'd passed the 1940 Tigers' mark of seventeen straight games. DiMaggio's hitting streak stood at thirty-seven games. And it looked like an easy series ahead. Time, tide, and the AL scheduler had washed into town (and the visitors' dugout) the bottom fish of the league, the St. Louis Browns. Normally, DiMaggio feasted on this chum. (In his streak he was hitting .500 against St. Louis.) But Joe was worried by one Brownie pitcher, the submariner Eldon Auker, a veteran cuss who'd feed you garbage all day, and you'd never get a damn thing to hit.

Sure enough, when Auker greeted Joe in the second inning, he offered ball one, ball two, ball three—until, in desperation, Joe reached for ball four and hit a weak fly to left field. In the fourth, Joe hit a grounder to short, where John Berardino couldn't field it cleanly. The scorer, Dan "I Play No Favorites" Daniel, signaled an error—no hit for Joe—and the crowd lustily booed the scoring. Joe Gordon leapt out of the dugout, and let Daniel know how the Yankees felt about it—with what the papers called "graphic gestures" toward the press box. In the sixth, DiMag hit a weak grounder to third base, and that made him oh-for-three on the day. It wasn't that the Yankees were in trouble—hardly: Henrich, who always hit Auker like a drum, smacked a home run in that same sixth inning, to put the Yanks ahead 3–0. And up to that point, the Yankee pitcher, Marius Russo, was throwing no-hit ball. But even Russo realized, no one gave a damn about his pitching. Joe had to get another chance.

Eighth inning, it was now 3–1, as the Yanks came up for their last at bats. (No one could even imagine the Brownies would rally to tie, and help out.) . . . Joe was fourth in the order, so someone had to get on base to give Dago a chance. Sturm, alas, popped up for the first out. Red Rolfe hung in for a gritty at bat, and worked a walk that brought Joe out on deck, and brought the crowd to a fever. Henrich was next up. But he was seized with a horrible vision: he might hit into a double play and leave Joe bereft! Henrich checked with the Skipper, McCarthy: "Would it be all right if I bunt?" Of course, McCarthy saw instantly. "That'll be all right," he said. Henrich laid down a sacrifice bunt. He was thrown out at first. But that brought up DiMaggio for a last lick at Auker—and Joe wasn't going to miss this chance. He wasn't going to let that underhanded bastard nibble around off the corners this time. First pitch, a low inside fastball—Joe golfed a bullet over third base, into the left field corner. Joe would later call it the hardest-hit ball in The Streak—but maybe he meant the hardest hit to get. Anyway, the Stadium erupted in cheers like the Yanks had just clinched a World Series. The whole squad leapt out of the dugout—clapping, whooping, pounding bats on the steps. Auker was all but forgotten for the moment, staring down at the dirt of the mound; his bid to enter the hero game had fallen one out short.

NOW, DIMAGGIO WAS ONLY THREE games short of Sisler's modern record, forty-one straight games. Every paper in the country was running Joe's doings—some in a daily box on the front page. Radio stations were breaking into music programs, quiz shows, detective dramas—didn't matter what was on: when Joe got his hit, that was a bulletin. For their trip south to Philadelphia and Washington, the Yankees had to put on an extra train car to carry all the visiting writers who arrived to watch Joe's assault on the record.

Most of them were writing about Johnny Babich, the Philadelphia A's right-hander, who vowed he would put an end to Joe's streak. Babich had history with the Yankees, and a score to settle with DiMaggio . . . from that Coast League game in '33—Joe for the Seals and Babich for the crosstown Mission Reds— when DiMaggio (in the midst of his sixty-one-game rookie streak) broke up a 0–0 tie, took a shutout from Babich, and made him a loser. Of course Babich never forgot, as he never forgot when he subsequently tried out with the Yankees—and they sent him packing. In 1940, then established with the A's, Babich had beaten the Yanks five times; by some accounts, he'd personally cost them the pennant. He liked his reputation as a "Yankee-killer," and told the other A's pitchers he knew how to handle DiMaggio. That June, 1941, Babich told the Philadelphia writers: he'd stop the big Dago, sure. He'd get DiMaggio out once, and then— well, he'd walk him three times if he had to.

More than thirteen thousand living souls material-
ized in Shibe Park (where the ghosts of champions
past usually dwelt undisturbed). Joe came up in the
first with two Yankees already aboard. With the count
three-and-one, Babich fed him a pitch he could hit.
Joe turned, whipping his bat through, and finished in
his trademark high follow-through. Alas, the ball
went straight up in the air and came down in the glove
of the shortstop, Al Brancato. The Yankee rally was
held to one run. Babich had won the first duel—just
as he'd predicted—and now, he could pitch around
Joe all day. But the rest of the Yankees would give
Babich no peace. (No bush-league .500 pitcher with
a grudge was going to get famous on Dago's back.)
The Bombers plated two more runs in the second,
and in the third Joe DiMaggio would be leading off.

Babich wasted the first pitch, high and wide—no
one could have reached it. The second, he threw well
off the outside edge. But DiMaggio lunged, almost
stepped across the dish. He caught the ball with the
fat of the bat, and drilled it straight back at the Babich
family jewels. The shot went low, through the
pitcher's legs. If Joe had hit the ball a few inches
higher, Babich would have been a hurling soprano.
DiMaggio compounded the insult by steaming nonstop into second base, where he slid, dusted himself
off, and regarded the Yankee-killer on the mound:
"Babich," as Joe later gloated, "was white as a sheet."

By that time, DiMag wasn't in the pink himself.
The Yankees made for their train, south to Washing-

ton—where, in a doubleheader, next day, Joe would have his chance to tie and surpass Sisler's modern record, forty-one games. The special chartered cars were packed with hungry writing press, but DiMaggio never showed among them. In fact, Joe and Lefty caught a different train, seven P.M., and snuck into the Shoreham Hotel. In the swampy misery of a Washington summer (a local headline announced: "Heat Kills Three . . ."), DiMaggio normally would have whiled time away in the lobby—where at least there was some air. He might have listened in, after supper, as Joe McCarthy smoked his cigar and held court for the writers. Or Joe and Crosetti might have staked out adjoining armchairs and sat, silent, watching the traffic all evening—till Joe could go to sleep. But now, Joe was simply too famous for the lobby: he was pinned in his upstairs bedroom, flopping around on sweaty sheets. His stomach was killing him— twenty-six years old and acid was eating away at his guts. Sleep? Forget it.

But that was no fuel for the hero machine: the writers couldn't U-turn now, and say Joe was human. *How 'bout it, Lefty—how's he sleepin'? . . .* "You could hang him on a coat hanger in the closet and he'd fall asleep," Gomez assured them. And so they wrote it: "Nerves of steel" . . . "Joe was probably the least excited guy in America." . . . "Cool as a Good Humor man in Alaska." For quotes, the press made do with the rest of the Baseball Nation, all talking about Joe. From the Brooklyn Dodgers, the nasty right-hander and maestro of chin music, Whit Wyatt, opined that DiMaggio would not have come close to a record in the National League: "In our league he would have to do most of his hitting from a sitting position."

From the halls of baseball history, Ty Cobb weighed in with his take on Joe: "DiMaggio is wonderful," the Peach allowed. But of course, Tyrus Raymond Cobb had put together *his* batting streak (forty straight games, in 1911) with a mushy hard-to-hit ball. Could DiMaggio have hit the dead ball? Anyway, Cobb didn't care much for hitting streaks—they hurt the team. "When a team's leading hitter is after a batting streak record, I don't care how good a competitor he is, he's thinking about himself more than usual."

The most gracious comments came from George Sisler—the man whose record was under attack. "I would like to see Joe break my record. I'll be the first to congratulate him." But Sisler also knew it wouldn't be easy on DiMaggio: "You can't imagine the strain," he was quoted in the *Daily News*. "The newspapers keep mentioning the streak. Your teammates continually bring it up. You try to forget, but it can't be done. It's in your head every time you step to the plate."

At Griffith Stadium, Joe couldn't even get to the plate before the start of the doubleheader. Fans invaded the field and besieged him, trying to slap him on the back, yelling encouragement, asking how he felt, begging for autographs. They were hauled off the field by D.C. police, who then formed a wall with their bodies athwart the home plate cage, so Joe could take BP. Meanwhile, more fans stood in long lines that snaked around the ballpark. Thirty-one thousand tickets would be sold. The Associated Press found fans from New York, Philadelphia, Baltimore, and points west and south of the District. "The capacity crowd we have is due to Joe, and nobody and nothing else," said the Senators' skipper, Bucky Harris. "Why, we couldn't even draw flies for a few games before the Yankees came to town."

In the first game, Harris sent to the mound the Senators' ace, Emil "Dutch" Leonard, the game's foremost knuckleball artist. When he had his good stuff, even he didn't know how the ball was going to dip and dance—and that day, Leonard had his blue-ribbon best. "Dutch had as much stuff as I've ever seen him have," said the plate umpire Johnny Quinn. "He was pitching out of a background of white shirts, too." . . . In the second inning, Joe jumped at the first pitch, caught a knuckler with the fat of the bat, and drove a liner over second base. But it carried in the air to the center fielder, Doc Cramer, who put it away amid a groan from the crowd. In the fourth, Leonard tried to tempt DiMaggio with three dancing knucklers, but Joe wouldn't bite and he got ahead, three-and-oh. The third base coach, Art Fletcher, flashed the hit sign from the Skipper, and DiMaggio stood in to take a rip, if he got a fastball. And he did get one— but a beauty, on the inside corner. Joe could only catch the ball on his thin bat handle, and he popped it up to George Archie, the Senators' third baseman. The crowd, which had sat in expectant stillness while Joe took his shot, exhaled another audible moan. In his book about Joe's "Golden Year," the editor of *Sport* magazine, Al Silverman, wrote of the strange crowd noise with DiMaggio at bat:

"First, there would be that loud buzz, like a squadron of queen bees descending on a cache of honey. Then, just before the ball would leave the pitcher's hand, the buzz would stop and there would be that deathlike silence—that hush. . . ."

In the sixth, Joe waved at a knuckler that dove away from him, low and outside—strike one. Then, he took a change-up inside, to even the count. At that point, Leonard took a risk: if he could sneak in a fastball (while the Jolter was looking for the knuckler), then he'd have DiMaggio one-and-two—with three chances after that to make him chase the dancer. So Leonard threw a near-perfect fastball—knee high, over the outside corner. Just as Leonard had hoped, it froze Joe for an instant. But an instant wasn't long enough. DiMaggio's dark bat smacked the ball right out of catcher Jake Early's glove. The ball shot on a line to the left center field gap, where Cramer and the left fielder, George Case, converged to cut it off. Too late again: the ball kicked off Case's glove and rolled to the 422 mark on the bleacher wall. DiMaggio could trot to second base—now tied with Sisler as best of the modern age.

The crowd exploded in joy: *He did it! He did it! It was history! They saw it!* . . . But for Joe, the squeeze only got tighter. The second game would tell the tale, whether he would set his name alone, at the top of the list.

In the first inning of game two, Tom Henrich was on his way to the batter's box to take his first licks, when he was frozen by one syllable—"TOMM!"—hurled from the on-deck circle.

As Henrich recalled the story half a century later, his head still ducked between his shoulder blades—like the voice had attacked him from behind.

"I said, 'Jeeminee! That's DiMaggio!' And I turned around to him, I says, 'What?'"

"He says, 'You got my ball bat!' (Henrich growled out the line like an accusation.)

" 'Joe,' I walked to him, and I says, 'Joe, I got *one* of your ball bats . . . ' " Henrich was still using the bat he'd borrowed from Joe in the first days of June.

Joe almost ripped it out of Tom's hand. "Lemme see it!"

DiMaggio glared at the bat he now held in both hands, his big fingers clenched white around the dark wood of the D-29. But he could see, right away, it wasn't his streak bat. It turned out, someone had stolen Joe's bat out of the dugout rack between games. Joe shoved Henrich's bat back to him—with the bad news: "Somebody took my ball bat."

Joe tried a brand-new bat in his first attempt against the lanky right-hander Sid Hudson. But the right fielder, Buddy Lewis, snared DiMaggio's line drive. It was entered in the records as a sacrifice fly—Rolfe scored—but that was cold comfort for the Clipper. As he trotted out to center field, Henrich heard him muttering: "If that'd been my ball bat, it would have been in there."

Of course, that was superstitious—but so are ballplayers. The whole Yankee club was shaken by the bat's disappearance. Sure, they were winning the game two–zip, but they made four errors in the first three innings. Everybody had the willies.

DiMaggio took another shot in the third—and what a shot! Hudson twirled in a sidearm curveball that sat on the inside corner till Joe creamed it with the new bat. Alas, the line drive instantly disappeared into the glove of the shortstop, Cecil Travis, who didn't even have to move. What further evidence of the evil eye did anyone need? Joe was snakebit.

By the time Joe got his third at bat, the Senators had a new pitcher, Red Anderson, another big right-hander, six foot three, who worked Joe up and in, low and away. First came the fastball under the chin. Then the sweeping curve, outside. Then, another fastball. DiMaggio swung. But he caught it on the handle and Cramer gloved the looping fly ball in short center. Joe was oh-for-three.

In the dugout, Henrich once again pressed Joe to take back his old bat, the one he'd lent Tommy. "Here, try it! This one feels good." DiMaggio was out of ideas of his own. In the seventh inning, facing Anderson again, Joe took Henrich's bat for what might well be his last chance. Once again, Anderson backed him off the plate with a barber shot under the chin. But then, as if God had laid hands upon the big pitcher, Anderson threw the perfect pitch—perfect for Joe: waist-high, over the middle. DiMaggio's eyes must have grown to saucer-size. *Craack!* . . . The fans all leapt up yelling. There wasn't any doubt about this liner: no fielder could touch it till it bounded two or three times in the left field grass. At first base, DiMaggio rounded the bag, for form's sake, but his legs probably couldn't have carried him to second. Anyway, he was trying to tip his hat to the screaming crowd. And the first base coach was slapping him on the back. And then the Senators' first baseman, Mickey Vernon, stuck out his hand—in the middle of a game! And Joe shook it. What the hell, this was bigger than the game.

On the train back to New York that evening, everyone was talking at once about Joe and his streak, and his record and his stolen bat. Joe didn't say much, of course, but his teammates could see he was happy—now the record was his. He was almost easy with his smile. And he bought everybody a beer.

WITH THAT TWIST, THE MYSTERIOUS missing bat, the story was pushed into mythic realms: *fate dashed the hero's sword from his hand, and yet—lo, even still, was the dragon slain.* . . . And it wasn't over! There was still Willie Keeler's dusty record, and after that, who could tell? As they used to say in newspaper city rooms, here was a story with legs.

And this wasn't a story just for newspapers, for radio bulletins, or theater newsreels. The first picture magazine, *Life,* had been joined by *Look, Collier's,* and the *Saturday Evening Post*—now they all had to have Joe in words and photos. In fact, *Life,* which only two years ago was marveling that Joe didn't talk with an accent, or smell like garlic, now adjudged him too classical a subject for mere silver nitrate. The editors commissioned a portrait in oil—Joe in the perfection of his follow-through—which would be reproduced in a September issue. Meanwhile, the flagship of the company, *Time,* humphed out the news in stentorian iambics: "The Yankee Clipper left in his wake the broken fragments of one of baseball's immortal records."

Some air of immortality—a whiff of All-Time-Greathood—had wafted around DiMaggio from the start of his career. But in 1941, the affect of classical perfection—and permanent importance—attached to him entirely: he would never lose it again. Joe's story, his glorious deeds, seemed to say something wonderful about America (and just when America needed to hear it). In Hollywood, where a man could make millions just by humming at the national pitch, one well-known film nabob, Nat Goldstone, was promoting a cinematic immigrant fable, *The Great DiMaggio*—which would feature the baseball brothers (as themselves) in a story that revolved around *Papa Giuseppe* . . . who, as Louella Parsons reported, had "made great sacrifices" so his sons could play the American Game.

Everybody wanted in on this story for the ages. In the summer of '41, so much of the world was out of control—there were new signs every day that nations, their wealth, machinery, and men were all disturbingly disposable—there was hunger for something that would endure. . . . Small wonder the producers of another (more successful) Hollywood project, *Casablanca,* chose for its musical centerpiece "As Time Goes By"—which was a ten-year-old song, but which, nevertheless, spoke to the lament of the moment:

> It's still the same old story,
> A fight for love and glory
> A case of do or die . . .
> The fundamental things apply
> As time goes by.

By the time that movie came out, Joe's own song had shot up the charts to number one. Les Brown and His Band of Renown recorded "Joltin' Joe DiMaggio," just when Streak Fever was most contagious (and the rest, as they say, was Hit Parade). The refrain—*Joe, Joe DiMaggio! We want you on our side!*—became a national mantra of homage. The songwriter was a New York disc jockey, Alan Court-

ney, who (talk about the same old story!) wrote out
the lyric on a nightclub napkin. At least, that's what
he said. But he thrummed the welcome chord of permanence—immortality—just as neatly as if he'd
worked it over for years.

He'll live in baseball's Hall of Fame
He got there blow by blow.
Our kids will tell their kids his name:
JOLTIN' JOE DIMAGGIO . . .

There were plenty of New Yorkers—being New
Yorkers—who didn't care that much about our children's children. They wanted Joe right now. They
wanted him, for instance, for that billboard that blew
smoke rings over Times Square, and a picture ad,
with a tasty smoke asmolder in his fingers
("Camels—they're milder!"). They wanted him to
smile around a big spoon, behind a heaping bowl of
Wheaties, and to pose with a grin over the wheel of a
Dodge car. They wanted him to stop by their restaurant for a free meal, or to be seen around town in their
brand of shoes, or to bring the wife to the jewelry
shop—she can have what she likes! And come by the
Lionel plant, to cheer on the crack softball team.
(And how 'bout a picture, playing with these toy
trains?) And stop by the boys club ("The kids are
wild about you, Joe!") or show up for a picture at the
Chinese Relief Fund. He had to stop by Newark and
pick up the handsome shotgun they wanted to give

him—along with the key to the city. And how about that radio spot for New Jersey's Vacation Traffic Accident Prevention Program? ("Whether at bat or on the curb, always be prepared to step back from the fast ones that may come too close!")

And those were just a few of the outside appearances. That didn't count the day-to-day doings at the ballpark. "Joe! Just a coupl'a shots! Could you make like you're warmin' up with three bats?" "Joe, who would you like to have pitching when you break the record?" "Can we get a shot of you and the postmaster general?" "Joe, do you think the streak is actually hurtin' your average?" "How 'bout a picture in the shower, Joe?" ("Hottest Man in Baseball Cools Off!"). . . . And no one could count the daily dozens (or hundreds) of pleas from fans—for autographs, for balls, a bat, Joe's shirt, his shoes. One fan ran into center field and swiped the cap right off of Joe's head. . . . *Would he authorize a candy bar? . . . How 'bout Yankee Clipper Comics? . . . "Joe! Oh, Joe! JOE! HEY, JOE! Would you sign my cast? . . ."*

There wasn't any way to stop it: the business of being a hero was too big, out of control. On the road, Joe and Lefty always used to have breakfast sent up to the rooms. Now, they were penned up there for dinner, too. (Otherwise Joe would never get to eat.) They'd tell the front desk: no calls—and don't give out the room. Never worked: people knocked on the door all night. Kids, a lot of 'em. But women, too. You wouldn't have thought God made so many eager

American women. But it seemed like every one He
made had a friend on the hotel switchboard, or went
to school with the bellboy's sister, or got the room
number somehow. Sometimes, they'd call from the
lobby. "Yeah, come on up," Joe would say into the
phone. And any other fellows who were visiting
would know, Daig was going to be tied up for a while.
When she got there, Joe would take her right into the
bedroom and, as he said, "give her a good pump."

So many people wanted to get in good with Joe,
take care of him, make a gesture of friendship: a broad
was always a welcome gift. Big guys with interest in
the business—for example, guys who made book all
over town—they were making fortunes off DiMag
and his streak. There wasn't any Dago in the whole
city (the whole *country)* who didn't want to put a couple of bucks on Joe—either to get another hit, or this
was the end, or to get his hit by the fifth inning, or it's
two hits today . . . in those days you could bet on the
Jolter down to the inning, down to the pitch. A guy like
Joe Adonis—he was booking millions—he wanted to
show appreciation. But without a lot of fingerprints.
He couldn't throw a dinner at the Waldorf for Joe
DiMaggio and a thousand bookies. That would make
a bad appearance. But Adonis had broads—houses
full of broads. So . . . he took care of the Slugger.

A guy like Adonis was quiet and careful. For example, Adonis was a pal of Toots. An investor you
could call him: all of Shor's money was mob. But you
wouldn't see Adonis lording it around Shor's sa-

loon—not with the sports guys that were Toots's
bread and butter. . . . One time, Toots was out in
Louisville for the Derby. (He always rented a couple
of floors of a hotel, and railroad cars to bring out the
shrimp, beef, cases of booze, and all his pals.) He
was at the track when he spotted Adonis. Of course,
Shor rushed right over. "JOEY, YOU CRUMB BUM!
WHERE YA BEEN?" And he gave him a hug. "I
AIN'T SEEN YA! WHY DON'CHA COME IN MY
JOINT?" Adonis pulled away and looked at Shor
gravely. "Tootsie, if I come in, do I help you or hurt
you?" . . . Anyway, in those days, the mob wasn't
such an issue. No less an authority than J. Edgar
Hoover was insisting that there was no organized
crime. Whenever he came to New York, Hoover used
to come in for lunch at Shor's—oftentimes, right
across the room from Frank Costello.

Still, all the favors made DiMaggio nervous: outside New York, there were guys who couldn't hide any
better than a circus elephant. In Detroit, Cleveland,
Chicago, they didn't even try. In Chicago, during The
Streak, there was a black limo, half a block long, waiting for DiMaggio. Head of the mob sent his car for
Joe. So Joe said to Frenchy Bordagaray, "You come
along." They got in the Cadillac and it took them to a
nightclub. More than fifty years later, Frenchy could
not remember the name. But he remembered the rest:
"We come in, they got all the girls in the whole place
lined up. They say, 'Joe, you pick out whoever you
want.' Then, they look at me. 'You, too.' So Joe picks

one out. And I pick one out. Then they throw him the keys to the Cadillac. 'Go wherever you want, Joe!' But Joe doesn't like to drive. He says to me, 'You're drivin'.' I say, 'All right, I can drive it.' So I open the door, I slide in the front seat. Then I see both girls get in the back with Joe! . . . They're taking turns . . . so he gets the girls, and I get the mirror."

Of course, there were writers with the team in Chicago who saw Joe DiMaggio go off to play in the mob limo. For that matter, Frenchy had never been famous for keeping a good story to himself. But no writer wanted to put that kind of thing in the paper. You'd be finished—washed up with DiMag, probably non grata with the rest of the Yanks—and maybe with the mob, too. Anyway, with kids all over the country marching around, singing the song *("From coast to coast that's all you hear—of Joe, the one-man show!"),* and keeping notebooks with each page numbered for a game of The Streak *(43—July 1— ground ball single to third base, line drive single to left field!)* . . . with strangers talking to each other on the streets, asking anybody with a radio: *"Did he do it?"* (everybody knew who He was) . . . who'd want to spoil that? Who would dare to break the heart of little Tony Morella?

It seems that Little Tony Morella was a terribly sick boy, ten years old, in Philadelphia's Jefferson Hospital—"SPLEEN REMOVED. LIFE OR DEATH," as the telegram to Joe exclaimed. So after the last game in Philadelphia, Joe and Lefty ran over to the hospital. That's why they'd missed that train to Washington—Joe went to cure the Morella boy, who was at death's door until his hero appeared. "You be listening to your radio tomorrow, Tony," DiMaggio was quoted at the bedside, "and hear me break that hitting record for you. That's a promise, kid." So, when the papers ran the story on Joltin' Joe breaking that record, there was the story of the Morella boy's hero-cure, right alongside. It was unfortunate only for the Associated Press (which had to sweep up after the exuberant New York writers left town)—and for little Tony himself—that his name was actually Norella, and he was actually, well, dead, before the record-tying game began. But the point was, everybody loved that story—that was the sort of story you wanted. The point was, our heroes were good—as were we. Even the spoilsport AP assured readers around the country that Tony died happier, because he knew his friend Joe would be a man of his word.

Whenever Joe came home, there were telegrams of entreaty, gifts for good luck, sacks of mail. Everybody knew where Joe lived; his penthouse address was printed in the *New York Times,* along with the rent: an astonishing three hundred dollars a month. That was part of the coverage now. Our heroes had good home lives, too. One time Joe got home and found the penthouse occupied by visitors from the *New York Post.* Their cameraman wanted Joe to pose reading his mail, keeping up with the fans' concerns. There was another photo with Joe lying back on a daybed, in a silk robe, with Dorothy leaning in to light his cigarette. The American people wanted to see that Mrs. Joe did her part.

Dorothy was happy to show. She bloomed under the national spotlight. The truth was, DiMaggio had given up on answering his fan mail, he'd given up on reading it—never looked through the sacks. But Dorothy looked over every envelope. Who could tell? Maybe there'd be something for her. She'd already done one national ad, for Swift's Premium Frankfurts *("As a dinner meat they're a real winner!" says Mrs. Joe DiMaggio.)* And she thought she could do a lot more, after the baby was born. She told the papers that she never talked to Joe about The Streak—didn't want to be a jinx. Fortunately, most days, Joe didn't want to talk. He was "even-tempered," Dorothy said. "And all he seemed to think about when he came home from the ballpark each day was digging into the eats." On the other hand, she was so nervous, so busy biting her nails at the ballpark, she hadn't even found time to decorate their apartment. But in the photos, the apartment looked wonderful—and so did she. It all looked, not by happenstance, like the American dream. As the *New York Post* feature writer mused in print: "Upon one thing do Joe and the missus agree. When a boy from Fisherman's Wharf, San Francisco, and a girl from Duluth, Minn., can marry and live in a penthouse because he has the crowd-pleasing ability to hit a ball with a bat—America, she is wonderful."

By the time Joe attempted to pass Willie Keeler—
at forty-five straight, Joe would stand alone, with the
all-time record—Dorothy was thought to be such
good copy that reporters were assigned to the Stadium club seats, to watch *her* through the game. Actually, they couldn't spend the whole game with her,
because she arrived, with her parents in tow, during
the third inning. (A girl needs a bit of time to prepare,
when she's going to be photographed.) She came
bustling in, asking "What'd Joe do?" and was informed that hubby had been robbed of a sure double
when the Boston right fielder, Stan Spence, ran back
and leapt to grab a drive in right center. "Too bad,"
Dorothy said. Joe came to bat in the last of the third,
and Mrs. Joe leaned forward in her seat. On the second pitch from Dick Newsome, DiMaggio slammed
a ball down the left field line. Dorothy leapt to her
feet, her bright red handbag tumbling to the floor.
Joe's drive hooked a mile into the seats—and foul.
"Gosh darn," Dorothy was quoted. On the next pitch,
Joe grounded out to Jim Tabor, the Red Sox third
baseman, and Dorothy slumped in her box seat to
await the next chance.

In the fifth inning, Joe took two balls outside.
Now, Newsome had to throw a strike, and Joe was
ready—maybe too ready. The next pitch, a high fastball, might have been ball three, but Joe whipped the
bat head through, caught the ball out in front of the
plate, and launched a high arching foul pop into the
second deck—where a struggle for the precious sou-

venir ensued. Even before most fans turned away from that scrap in the seats, Newsome pitched again, and—*Crack!* Joe lined a rifle shot to deep left field, where Ted Williams took a step back, gave up on running and turned, ready to play the carom. But the ball cleared the wall and disappeared from view. It all happened so fast, no one had much chance to react till Joe, in his quick trot, was around third and headed home. Then the huge crowd at the ballpark was on its feet, cheering, clapping, straw hats went sailing through the air. Even writers in the press box broke their cardinal rule of decorum and applauded. Joe DiMaggio had made history for them. The Yankee players poured onto the grass in front of the dugout, whooping and waiting to shake the Big Guy's hand. They were winning their sixth in a row; they were three up on Cleveland—in first place. Joe DiMaggio had hauled them there. In the club seats, Dorothy was shouting, clapping and laughing with Mom and Dad, even after Joe disappeared amid the back slaps on the Yankee bench. Then, she turned with a radiant smile. Joe had made this spotlight for her! She said to the press, who would print her words by the millions: "Beautiful, wasn't it?"

WHEN JOE DIMAGGIO LOPED PAST Keeler, and a standard of consistency that had stood for forty-four years, he was pushing into territory unknown—not only beyond the records, but beyond

conventional reckoning. As the Baseball Nation prepared for the All-Star break, July 7, the midpoint of
the '41 season, no one had been able to stop DiMaggio for almost eight weeks. He had faced every big-
name pitcher in the league, along with also-rans,
rookies, relievers. And still he was hitting. Writers
started diving into the old box scores, looking for
some statistical undertow, to explain how DiMaggio
could swim for two months against the tide. Here's a
bit of salvage they brought up from that ocean of
numbers: at that point, DiMaggio had not struck out
since June 8. In fact, over the course of his streak—
two hundred twenty-three official at bats—DiMaggio would strike out a total of five times. There had
been in the game only a handful of men who were
that difficult to strike out—but they were singles hitters: guys who choked up on the bat and tried to slap
the ball through the infield. In the history of the
major leagues there had never been a hitter like
DiMaggio, who struck out so seldom, and at the
same time, in the same streak, hit *fifteen* home runs.
What it meant, in theory: DiMaggio was assumed to
have complete and otherworldly mastery over his bat
and balance, his swing mechanics, his thoughts and
emotions, and of course, the strike zone. When, in the
tension of one record-tying game, DiMaggio actually turned his head to question a strike call, the home
plate umpire gulped and blurted out: "Sorry, Joe, it
was right over!" . . . What it meant, in practice, was
this: the thirty, forty, fifty thousand fans who now

crammed into ballparks to see this phenomenon could rest assured that with each new chance, each at bat—each time they saw him bend to scoop a bit of dirt to rub between his hands, and then step in with his strange, still stance—they were three times more likely to see DiMaggio hit a home run than to whiff and walk back to the bench. As for hits: they were *eighteen times* more likely to see him get a hit. . . . And especially when the Yankees were on the road, it also meant that the much-prayed-for third strikes were rarer, and as thrilling as any hit. Fifty-five years after the fact, there would be people who still remembered: *they saw DiMaggio strike out!*

Now, in the Baseball Nation, there was everyone else, and there was DiMaggio. No one had achieved that colossal Otherness for a couple of decades, since the Maestro of Mash bestrode New York. There were other great players, but that was something else. This was about star power, and Joe was unchallenged. For example, in that All-Star Game, Bob Feller took the mound for the Americans, and Ted Williams won the game with a thrilling last-ditch home run. But what people talked about was: *They'd seen DiMaggio!* (And he got a hit in that game, too!) Whatever Feller or Williams did—that was a part of the game. Seeing DiMaggio was an event in itself. Dan Daniel was at such pains to make this distinction that he could barely pause for breath: "Bob Feller has pitched 16 victories in 19 starts for Cleveland. Ted Williams is hitting around .400 for the Red Sox. But Bob, Ted and all the rest of the little army of major leaguers were forced into a shadowy background against which DiMaggio's sustained string of batting feats were intriguing fans from coast to coast and dramatizing the major league situation with a thrill it had not experienced since Babe Ruth hit his 60th home run in 1927."

After the All-Star break, the Yankee train pulled into St. Louis, to find that the town had been papered with handbills:

Sensational

JOE DI MAGGIO

Will Seek To Hit Safely In His
49th
Consecutive Game.
Thur. Nite, July 10
AT ST. LOUIS

Browns vs. Yankees
Sportsman's Park—8:30 P.M.

Charlie Keller, a quiet Maryland farm boy, knew a traveling circus when he saw one. "It looks," Keller said, "as if we've landed with the fat woman and the wild animals." The hoopla did help the Browns at the gate, but in no other way: the Yanks took three straight (that made it twelve wins in a row); DiMaggio hit safely in all three games (for an average of .583).

In Chicago, more than fifty thousand fans packed into Comiskey Park for a Sunday doubleheader: two chances for the Pale Hose to put themselves in the history books—if they could only stop DiMaggio. But there'd be no such luck for the Midway moundsmen: Joe went three-for-four in the first game, sliced one clean single to right in the second—and the Yankees won both ends, to push their team streak to fourteen straight. You could say the whole team—in fact, both teams, everybody in the ballpark that day—was now on unfamiliar turf. For the Yankees, this was the longest winning streak in the decade of manager McCarthy. For Chicago, this was the largest gathering of baseball fans since the very first All-Star Game was played at Comiskey, in July 1933.

As for Joe, he was also being pushed onto strange new ground. Back in New York, that same day, the *New York Times Sunday Magazine* published its account of Joe's record run, by the Pulitzer Prize–winning author Russell Owen. There wasn't much new about Joe's doings on the field—everybody knew that stuff, already. But how was he in the clubhouse? What did he say to teammates? Why was he always drinking coffee, smoking Camels? What did he do at night? As always, Gomez had run interference, tried to explain the silent star. But in the effort to protect

Joe D., Lefty let slip about the loneliness, how Joe couldn't go anywhere—how he spent his nights with *Superman* comics. And there was Joe, wanly protesting, "I like westerns, too." DiMaggio had become a "personality" for us.

It wasn't that the writers were trying to nose into his business—quite the reverse. There was still plenty in Joe's world that writers wouldn't touch. For instance, there was the return of his bat. It seems that Joe's man Peanuts, Jimmy Ceres, along with Joe's friend the funeral genius, Jerry Spatola, found Joe's stolen bat somewhere in Newark, or maybe it was Lyndhurst, New Jersey. Or in some versions of the story, they simply heard about the bat in New Jersey, and then had to travel somewhere to get it. The *Newark News* played up the amateur sleuthing— Peanuts, so the *News* claimed, spent five days investigating in Washington, before he tracked "the prized bludgeon" to New Jersey. Some writers said the bat had been returned willingly by the thief, who'd meant no harm. Others wrote about the thief's change of heart, after he heard how much Joe missed his bat. Still others hinted that Jerry and Peanuts had to buy the bat back, or they took the bat back. And Newark papers said Joe had to give the thief some tickets to Yankee games. The point was, nobody ever found out—and nobody much asked. At least, they didn't ask in print: Who stole the bat? How was the thief found? How did it happen that a middle-aged funeral director and a gofer for Newark's First Ward rackets

boss turned into such enterprising gumshoes? No . . .
the point on the sports page was, Joe got his bat
back—end of story.

Well, not quite the end: it turned out Peanuts and
Jerry Spatola had done a service for the *nation,* because when "a courier" showed up at the Yankee
locker room with Joe's "Betsy Ann" (i.e., his bat),
then Joe was able to ship out for auction the old bat
he'd lent to Tommy Henrich. After all, that was the
bat with which he'd broken the records—which was
what he'd promised (for the benefit of the USO). So
Joe autographed Henrich's bat, then turned it over to
Mayor La Guardia, who then staged a City Hall ceremony, during which *he* would turn over the bat to
Polly Carpenter, a stewardess for United Airlines,
who would personally transport the sainted swat-
stick to San Francisco (where the *Examiner* would
note its arrival "at 8:16 A.M. today"). There it would
be turned over to representatives of the USO, who
would raffle it off at Seals Stadium. With raffle tickets fetching twenty-five cents apiece, Joe's blessed
bastinado (actually, poor Henrich's bat) would earn
one thousand six hundred and seventy-eight dollars
for the welfare of U.S. servicemen all around the
world.

The treatment of Joe's relics was the surest sign of
his new saintly status. It wasn't just the bat. Over the
funeral parlor in Newark, Geta and Bina Spatola,
Jerry's daughters, were already saving Joe's wine-
stained shirt (alas, Mamma Rose had been unable to

lift the spot). "You keep that," Joe said, "as a remembrance of me." Soon, the Spatola girls would receive the shoes Joe wore during the Sacred Streak—or as Geta insisted upon calling them, "The Spikes." The two girls would have their coffin-maker fashion a beautiful encasement for The Spikes, which would then rest, in perpetuity, on rolled and tufted velvet, such as is seen in only the finest coffins. From time to time, over the years, the girls would bring out the velvet-lined encasement, so that Little Leaguers or Legion ballplayers (who were playing for the Spatola Funeral squad) could rub The Spikes for good and godly effect. But mostly The Spikes would remain in the reliquary of the Spatola home—that was the closet, where the DiMaggio-Arnold Wedding Cake was still perfect (not one ant!) in its tent of waxed paper.

But in July 1941, The Spikes were still digging into batter's boxes, pounding through the grass in center field. For there remained one last act of the passion play—the finale that seals a sainthood—a proper martyrdom. The setting was Cleveland, in the gloomy and outsized Municipal Stadium, where some sixty-seven thousand congregants, the year's largest crowd for any baseball game, assembled on the evening of July 17, to watch Joe push his streak to fifty-seven games.

In the aftermath of that famous night, people said there were signs: Joe was tired, or he'd started hitting into bad luck. Gomez said it was a Cleveland cab driver who put on the whammy, as he drove Joe and Lefty to the ballpark. Gomez quoted the cabbie—in suitably Delphic tones: "Make sure you get your hit the first time up," the driver warned. "If you do not make it then, you will be stopped."

Actually, all the signs for DiMaggio were good. After he broke Willie Keeler's record, Joe said he meant to chase down "that Williams" and win another batting crown. Since then, Joe had been batting at a .540 clip, and now trailed Teddy Ballgame by only twenty points. The previous night—against that same Cleveland staff—DiMaggio had posted three-for-four. And tonight's starter would not be the Tribe's ace, Bob Feller, nor even the righty curve-baller, Mel Harder (who, for DiMaggio, *was* always harder), but Al Smith, a lefty who held no particular terror. So much for the omens: they said Joe DiMaggio was doing fine.

He almost got a hit in his first chance—a screamer headed for the left field corner. But the third base-man, Ken Keltner, was playing so deep that he snagged the drive on a hop, near the chalk in short left, and from the grass in foul ground whipped a long throw across to beat Joe at first base. In his second at bat Joe drew a walk (as Smith was lustily booed by his home crowd). For his third chance, Joe hit another hard shot toward Keltner—who was now playing even deeper—and again, Joe was narrowly nipped at first. After that, he didn't come up again till the eighth—when he almost squeaked through. A

bouncer toward Lou Boudreau at short took a bad
hop and almost went into left field—but not that
night: Boudreau got his glove up, grabbed the ball
and whipped it to second base to start a double play.
Even then, there was still hope in the stands. The
huge crowd screamed for the Indians to tie the game,
send it on to extra innings—and another chance for
Joe D. In the ninth inning, Cleveland closed the gap
to 4–3. The tying run, Larry Rosenthal, was on third
base—with no one out. But the Yankee reliever, Fireman Johnny Murphy, wiggled out of the jam. The
Yankees won, closed it out in nine innings. DiMaggio's chances, and his streak, were no more.

In the mobbed visitors' clubhouse, DiMaggio said
he would have liked to beat his own minor league
mark of sixty-one straight. But at least the pressure
was off now. Yes, Keltner had made great plays. Yes,
Boudreau was a great one, too. Yes, those Cleveland
pitchers did great. . . . Joe was polite to all question-
ers; he even posed for the cameramen with his thumb
and index finger forming a ring (to denote the goose
egg). Then he escaped to the shower room, and
stayed there for a long while.

There were thousands of people waiting outside
the players' gate. Keltner and his wife had to walk
through the crowd with police protection. (You never
knew, with some of them Dagos, said the Cleveland
cops.)

Joe waited hours before he would chance it. By the

time he, at last, poked his head out the door, the only Yankee left with him was the rookie Rizzuto.

"After the reporters left, Joe asked me to wait for him," Rizzuto told Maury Allen, for *Where Have You Gone, Joe DiMaggio?*

"I don't know why, I guess to keep some fans away. Lefty had pitched the game and he was gone. Now Joe gets dressed and we walk out of the gate together. He doesn't say a word. We just start walking back toward the Cleveland Hotel. We go about two blocks. I don't know what to say to comfort him so I say nothing. Finally he looks up at me with a little smile. 'Do you know if I got a hit tonight I would have made ten thousand dollars? The Heinz 57 people were following me. They wanted to make some deal with me.' Then he reached into his back pocket. 'Son of a bitch. I forgot my wallet. I left it in the park. Phil, how much money you got?' I reached into my pocket and pulled out my wallet. I had eighteen dollars. 'Let me have it.' I gave it to him and he turned toward a bar. I started in and he turned back toward me. 'No, you go on back to the hotel. I want to relax a bit.' I just left him and walked back."

Joe would say later that the deal with Heinz 57 was just talk. But maybe he did believe, that night, that he'd lost ten grand. (That Heinz outfit knew how to promo: they once mounted a fifty-foot-long green neon pickle high above Madison Square.) The way Joe figured, they could have done the deal if they'd wanted to: as he would later note, somewhat peevishly: "I hit in the All-Star Game, too."

But all that ballyhoo was over for him. That was the good part. Now he could do his job. Now, Joe vowed, he would make the pitchers come to him—he wouldn't have to reach for bad balls, trying to avoid a walk, trying to swat at *something:* "Now," Joe said, "I'm really going to do some hitting." And so he would. In fact, he would begin only sixteen hours later, by touching up the fabled Feller for a single and a double in the next day's game. After that—well, why not?—Joe would hit in the next fifteen games, too, to stretch his hit-streak summer spree to seventy-two out of seventy-three. Not bad for two and a half months' work.

And meanwhile, during The Streak, the Yankees had won three out of every four games. They were now in first place by six games. Joe had carried the mail. But no one would ever hear that from him.

It would be up to the other Yankees to say that. But now, they went quiet, too. It seemed like they didn't want to bring The Streak up—might bother Joe (or spook his new streak). The teammates lay low through August, till they had their pennant wrapped up—all except for the ribbons. And even the Dago, who'd turned his ankle, was taking it easy, sitting out a series with the Senators in D.C. On the evening of August 30, Gomez and Joe were headed out to dinner—when Lefty, inexplicably, started dawdling around. "C'mon, Lefty. I'm starved," DiMaggio was complaining. Finally Lefty said: "I just gotta stop in Selkirk's room for a minute."

"Jesus! Meet me in the lobby."

"No, you come with me—I'll only be a minute."

When DiMaggio pushed open the door—the Shoreham Hotel, Room 609D—all the Yankees (and their writers) were present. The coach, Art Fletcher, yelled at DiMaggio: "Where the hell you been? Why can't you get here on time?" Joe was stunned, confused, and suddenly pink around the cheeks and temples. Fletcher led the team in the song, "For He's a Jolly Good Fellow." And Crosetti led a "Hip, Hip, Hooray" for Joe. The rest of the Yanks had glasses of sparkling burgundy wine, and now Johnny Murphy offered a toast:

"Joe," he said, "we just wanted to let you know how proud we are to be playing on a ball club with you, and that we think your hitting streak gave us the pennant we're winning."

Then, from a table, Gomez picked up a package and handed it to Joe. Inside was an elegant Tiffany humidor, in silver, engraved with the signatures of every man on the team. On the lid was an engraving of Joe D. swinging a bat, flanked by the numbers 56 (for the games of The Streak) and 91 (for the number of hits). And on the front, there was an inscription: *"Presented to Joe DiMaggio by his fellow players on the New York Yankees to express their admiration for his consecutive game hitting record, 1941."*

Joe was lost for words: "This is swell, fellows," he

said. "Only, I don't deserve it." Then he went around the room, with a little grin: "Cigars? Cigarettes? . . ." Everybody could see, Joe was blushing. "I think he cried," Henrich remembered, ". . . and said something I'll never forget: 'I didn't know you guys felt this way about me.' Here was the greatest player in the game on this incredible streak and helping us win again and again and he didn't think we cared that much about him."

That must have been what Joe was trying to say in his own version of the story, in *Lucky to Be a Yankee:* "It's nice to know that the guys you work with think you're a regular guy, too."

In the end, it proved to Joe that if he took care of business—took care of it his way—on his back alone . . . then he would be admired. As Joe saw it: he did his job. He'd won. And he wasn't done yet.

The last month of the season, the Yankees were only marking time (they'd win their pennant by seventeen games). The spotlight turned to Ted Williams, who was fighting to finish with a .400 average. No one had pulled that off for more than ten years—and no one would even come close for the rest of the century. On the last day of the season, Ted went into action with a batting average of .3995. That would have been rounded up to .400 if Ted had taken his skipper's offer to sit the last day out. But he didn't—wouldn't coast to the record: he played a doubleheader against the A's, went six-for-eight on the day, and finished at a gaudy .406.

Still, in the ballot for the MVP, the nod went to Joe DiMaggio. Ted's reaction was characteristically generous. "Yeah, awright," he said. "But it took the Big Guy to beat me!" Joe's reaction was characteristic, too: in public, he gave bland thanks to the MVP voters, his teammates, and his manager. In private, with his pals, Joe said of Williams: "Sure, he can hit. But he never won a thing."

The World Series that year was a feverish New York affair: the first time the Brooklyns ever had a chance to win the brass ring. But they would have to pry it loose from DiMaggio's fist. The Dodgers had the Yanks tied at one game apiece, when the action shifted to Ebbets Field. In Game Three, the Dodger pitchers held the Yanks scoreless into the eighth—until DiMaggio broke up the shutout, knocked in Red Rolfe with a single, to put the Yanks in the lead. As it turned out, one run would make the difference—the Yanks would win (and lead the Series) 2–1.

The most famous play, and the turning point of the Series, occurred the next day, in Game Four, with the Dodgers leading 4–3. The Yankees were down to their final out, as Tommy Henrich stood in against the Brooklyn fireman, Hugh Casey. On a three-and-two count, Henrich swung and missed for strike three—but then the ball slipped by the Dodger catcher, Mickey Owen. Henrich sprinted up the baseline, Owen scrambled after the ball, but Henrich ended safely on first base. Police now stood at the edge of the grass: they'd thought the game was over, and they'd rushed out to protect the field. Now DiMaggio strode to the plate, and the Brooklyn crowd keened with something like a wail of dread. DiMaggio lined a single to left; Henrich stopped at second, DiMaggio on first. The next batter, Keller, launched a high fly that bounced off the chain link screen, atop the concrete right field wall. The Brooklyn right fielder, Dixie Walker, ran into position to field the carom, but the carom didn't come—until the ball had dropped straight down and bounced off the flat top of the concrete. Meanwhile, Henrich scored easily from second base . . . and DiMaggio, as the winning run, now roared around third, dirt flying from under his spikes. As Henrich remembered:

"I've already scored. I'm standing there watching Joe comin' in. And he slid, he hit home plate—and I think his body, I think his body went by *six feet* past home plate! That was the speed of him. In other words, 'I WILL SCORE ON THIS PLAY.' . . . But, that's the way he played ball."

That was the run that broke Brooklyn's heart. Game Four ended as a 7–4 Yankee triumph. The next day, Brooklyn couldn't even make much noise as they bowed in the clincher 3–1. The Bombers were champions again. In their clubhouse, the third base coach, Art Fletcher, led the boozy anthem: "Roll Out the Barrel." The only time they sang it was for World Series wins—but still, with practice in five out of six years, they were starting to sound good. DiMaggio didn't sing, just sat on his stool, smoking and watching with a little smile. It was different for them, the rest of the guys: they'd all go home (even Lefty was leaving town) to do whatever they wanted with that extra six grand in their pockets . . . and they'd have a big time all winter. Joe, for his part, wasn't looking forward to that winter at all.

He'd be stuck in New York while he (and all the writers) waited for Dorothy to have the baby. He'd be left alone in the fishbowl. The way he said it was, he couldn't go home at all.

Sure, he had his New York apartment. But that was her place. And not exactly peaceful. That penthouse was all very nice—it was beautiful—but he had no idea how to make himself at home. Heading into that winter, into fatherhood and his twenty-seventh birthday, Joe DiMaggio was ulcerated, smoking too much, coffee-jangled, and sleepless.

He had legions of would-be pals, he was the idol of millions. But save for the coterie at Shor's, he was friendless. Of course, he couldn't go out alone, either. He'd have a million fans on him all night. . . . He was the most famous man in America, a man at every moment watched. But there was so much about his life that he didn't want anybody to see.

Joe's back in love—and off to the war.

**Joe and Joe Jr.,
1943.**

**With the Seventh Army Air
Force, Honolulu, 1944.**

CHAPTER 10

◆

ON OCTOBER 23, 1941, JOE DIMAGGIO came into Toots Shor's saloon to hand out cigars. Joe DiMaggio, Jr., had arrived. The fellows said they'd never seen Daig so happy. There were a lot of pals in the joint who wanted to buy a round, raise a toast. *"Hey, Joe! You're one-for-one—he'll be a slugger, too!"* So, Joe stayed for a belt with the boys. Mother and son were in the hospital, everybody was fine.

Actually, Dorothy wasn't fine. She'd asked a half-dozen times, but they wouldn't bring the baby to her. "I want to see him right now," she demanded. "He's my baby, not yours." As Dorothy recounted the story to her family, a nurse brought the infant, completely hidden in a swaddling blanket—and carefully un-wrapped the baby's head and face. Dorothy was pan-icked. There were angry red marks on his face and head, like big strawberries. "Mrs. DiMaggio, you re-quired a high forceps delivery, and this is a condition that sometimes develops." They assured her the sores wouldn't stay, wouldn't scar. But alone in that room, Dorothy was still scared. She wanted Joe to tell her it was all right. But Joe was tied up.

"A child was born today at the Doctors Hospital,"

the *Journal American* reported, "—a possible future president, clerk or another Joe DiMaggio. Joe was a little excited when he announced it . . . far more excited, in fact, than he was this year when he broke the consecutive hitting records of all time. Weighed 7 pounds, 11 ounces."

In time, Dorothy would come to see this as a pattern: the baby was a feather in Joe's cap, and her problem to deal with. Assuredly this was the year's most publicized baby. All the papers had to have pictures. Sometimes, they'd wrap the baby's tiny hand around a tiny bat, and they'd take a picture of Junior, asprawl in the crook of Dad's arm, with the bat propped up next to his lolling head.

The old San Francisco sportswriter Abe Kemp wrote a column naming Little Joe as "the most photographed child in the United States." As Kemp also noted:

"In some pictures, Dorothy wears a wistful smile, as much as to say, 'Here you, that is as much my baby as Joe's.'

"Somehow, the camera men do not seem to think so.

"It is always Joe who is holding the child.

"It is always Joe who is showing the little tyke how to hold a baseball bat. . . .

"It is always Joe who is pinning the diapers on the baby."

When the cameras weren't present, the Yankee Clipper wasn't as enamored of child care. He would ask in perplexity, and some annoyance: "When he's changed and fed and he still cries—what do you do, Dottie?" When the baby was fussy, Joe would get annoyed at her. Mostly he'd stay out of the apartment. He didn't want to get in the way, and it was impossible to relax there.

At Shor's he'd always find his crowd, men who knew how to keep him company. Joe was funny that way: he was such a solitary person—fundamentally alone, no matter who was around—but he always wanted somebody with him. In part it was a habit of self-protection. If he *looked* to be alone people were emboldened to approach, to engage him. But if he seemed to be with someone, people were more likely to leave him alone. So Joe would be shown to his table, the one with banquettes in the front right-hand corner of the dining room. From that position, he could see everybody who came in. Better still, no matter who came at him in that corner, the table would obtrude between them and Joe. No one could ever get behind him.

No one who meant to bother Joe could even get near. Toots and his staff would see to that. But those acceptable to the Clipper could stop by his table to pay respects. Joe might be sitting with his old pal, the ex-champ Jim Braddock. And, of course, Toots would spend time in that corner. And some of Shor's writer pals might sit down to tell a story or two. Bob Considine would be welcome, as would Granny Rice, Frank Graham—they were name players—or

Toots's guy, Ernie Hemingway, who was so big in the novel racket. (You had to respect a champion.)

But the writer who got closest, and became Joe's hang-around buddy, was the bard of the New York tenements, Jimmy Cannon. Cannon was the most writerly columnist in New York, a star attraction in the *New York Post.* But his friendship with DiMaggio was based on simpler things. Cannon was a bachelor who lived in hotels—never had to run home to someone else. Joe never wanted to go home, either. And if he met a broad somewhere, Cannon's hotel suite could come in handy. Cannon was on the wagon, a coffee drinker like Joe. Neither one could sleep, and they'd stay together through the wee hours while the rest of the guys faded off to their beds. Sometimes they'd hook up with the city's best known insomniac and the nation's most famous columnist, Walter Winchell. The three men would ride around the sleeping city in Winchell's car, with its police radio, chasing after murders and muggings. Winchell was glad of the company, glad to be the majordomo at the wheel, and especially glad if it brought him a Yankee Clipper item for his column—anything on DiMaggio was worth a few lines.

Cannon also found in DiMaggio his perfect subject: he idolized DiMaggio, a natural hero of innate grace, raised up (as was Cannon) from poor city streets. This was a patented Cannon story, the tough-guy romance he wrote over and over: the poor kid who became a king, the unlettered man who knew more than professors, the eloquence of the city's silent souls. It was as if DiMaggio was put on the planet, and brought to New York, to confirm Jimmy Cannon's beliefs about the world. But Cannon was cautious and sparing with DiMaggio columns. He understood right away: if Joe got the idea that Cannon was reaping advantage from the friendship, then that would be his last night with the Dago. Jimmy would go a long way to avoid that. He worked at being Joe's perfect companion: funny, irreverent, irrepressibly talkative; and at the same time careful never to repeat anything Joe said.

In some ways Cannon was like a lot of guys Joe went around with: short, stubby, not much to look at. But Cannon (you had to hand it to him) had style. It started with those black-Irish bushy eyebrows, and then the glasses, the wide-brimmed hats, the plaid jackets, striped ties, and fancy fifty-dollar shoes. He was a clothes horse, like DiMag, but without the Dago's restraint. Sometimes it looked like Cannon was trying to wear *as many* clothes as he could. Sometimes his writing was the same way: Cannon had a bursting wardrobe of words; in supply and quality they were splendid. But at times, he'd pile up so many, you couldn't appreciate a single one before it was buried under fifty more.

Still, he was so quick-witted that talking to him in a barroom was just as good as reading him. He had the gift of the great line that seemed to spring spontaneously from him. For example, Toots Shor's food had suffered sallies from a lot of comedians. (One was Shor, who described his own kitchen rule: "Buy the best of everything, and let the help try to spoil it.") Jackie Gleason used to sit down at one of Shor's tables and command the waiter to bring a phone—so he could order in pizza. But the classic on the subject came from Cannon, who was eating at Shor's when the lights flickered out for a moment. In the sudden silence, Cannon's voice echoed solemnly around the room: "They electrocuted the cook."

Joe's other new companion was a wit as well, though underappreciated by the world at large. George Solotaire was well known on Broadway as a ticket broker—proprietor of the Adelphi Theatre Ticket Service—and counted among his clients millionaires and nabobs of national renown. He once obtained for J. P. Morgan the same ticket to the same show, *in the same seat,* for seven successive Saturday nights, when the tycoon went sweet on a girl in the chorus line. But even more impressive, Gentleman George was ticket-broker-enough to supply all the freebies Toots Shor threw around. All of Shor's pals, pals of pals, and the families of pals could call Toots anytime and say what show they would like to see, and Toots would have their ducats waiting when they came in for a belt or a snack on the way to the theater. Solotaire handled all that in a friendly way—same way he turned tickets into envelopes stuffed with cash for a player like Joe DiMaggio, who might otherwise end up with too many seats for the World Series.

For DiMag, Solotaire would do anything at all—run out to get him a sandwich, pick up his suits at the tailor, sit with him all night. George had been married for years; had a home, family, and everything—but no one knew it: he always kept a place in a midtown hotel, too. Of course, Dago was welcome there, anytime. After half a lifetime in and around show business, Solotaire had other famous friends. But for Georgie, the Dago was more than a pal—he was a devotion. One time at the Stadium, when fans stood up and craned their necks to see Clark Gable leaving his seat, the faithful Solotaire was enraged. As one columnist reported the scene: "He wagged furiously toward the Yankee outfield. 'If you want to see a real star,' George bellowed at the crowd, 'look out in center field. That's a REAL star—Joe DiMaggio!' "

In a way, stardom was Solotaire's business: it was the ticket broker's root skill to know what (or whom) the public would want to see, in what numbers, and for how long. (Only thus could he estimate how many tickets to stock, and for how many weeks or months in the future.) On Broadway productions, George was uncanny: he could predict, almost to the day, how long a play would run. He was right so often, *The Hollywood Reporter* started printing Solotaire's capsule reviews—usually a rhymed couplet, which

Georgie composed in his theater seat, while the play ran, opening night. For example, when his friend Ethel Merman opened in her latest musical—a particularly weak excuse for a play—Georgie struck a nice balance with his instant review:

The show's infirm.
But it's still got the Merm.

But even with his growing fame as a poet, Solotaire's wit was still undervalued. He was, for example, the inventor of one locution that entered the American language—the *ville* school of description. A pair of lovers who fought and broke up were, according to George, "splitsville," or at least no longer "living in lovesville." A show that fell apart after the first act, in Georgie's view, "went to dullsville." And where was that play going at the box office? "Nowheresville," of course. He also had his own system for discussing the delicate subject of age. Say a man was approaching (as was George) his fortieth birthday. In Solotairese, he was "almost at the Metropolitan Opera." (The Met was at 40th Street.) Seventeen years later, that man might or might not admit that he was about to turn fifty-seven. But Georgie would be sure to say, that fellow was "pushin' Carnegie Hall." Solotaire would never say his tickets were in Row G. No, he was "sitting with Gladys." Or perhaps one row closer to the stage: i.e., "with Freddie." No wonder Walter Winchell "borrowed" for his column George's "splitsville," "dullsville," etc. Half of George's friends talked just like him. His delight was contagious.

That was the gift that brought him to Broadway. When Georgie got you tickets, it was as if he'd invited you to a party. The great drama critic Walter Kerr once wrote about the way Solotaire would materialize on some theater sidewalk, just as the intermission crowd burst forth. There was George scanning the faces of the ticket holders with a small smile of complicitous delight. As Kerr described it: "a bright, wistful smile, as if to say, 'It's another good one, isn't it?' I never knew a knowing man to be so cheerful." . . . That was the smile Georgie wore as he followed Joe, or Joe and Dorothy into a restaurant, a nightclub. All the other customers would be nudging one another, whispering, "That's DiMaggio! DiMaggio and his missus!" Joe played it like he didn't hear a thing. Dorothy was learning to act that way, too. But George would confirm with that little smile: *Yes! Here he is—isn't it exciting?*

Georgie was always looking to pump the excitement about DiMaggio. Didn't matter that Joe D. was the most famous man in the country (short, maybe, of FDR). Georgie was convinced that people didn't really know how great DiMag was. Toots was the same way—except he made Solotaire look subtle. Toots always argued that DiMaggio could be the biggest in history—bigger than Dempsey, bigger than Ruth.

The only thing that held Dago back was he ran off to San Francisco every winter. Now, with the baby, Joe was finally going to stay around town. So Toots showed him off, made it a program. Once Dorothy was up and around, Toots bought dinner every night for a month—every night, a different joint: Joe and Dorothy, Toots and his wife, a former dancer whom everybody called Baby (save for Toots—he called her Husky). Toots was the advance man, squaring things with the owner or maître d'. "Joe DiMaggio's comin' in here, but he don't want a lot of fuss made about it." Of course, with Toots assigned to keep things quiet, they might as well have hired a brass band. *Did you hear? DiMaggio's coming in tonight!* . . .

Joe said he made the rounds for Dorothy—she liked to get out. But Dorothy told her friends she wasn't having much fun—Toots was so loud. And she was tired of all that crum bum stuff. Still, when she'd go out alone, or with a girlfriend, no one pointed, whispered, said a word—and that was worse. In later years, when people talked about Joe and Dorothy, they would say he was jealous about her career. But that was true the other way around, too. It infuriated her, the way Joe was such a big deal, and he never lifted a finger for it. And unless she was with him, she was . . . well, nowheresville. One time, she was out with her friend, Lillian Millman, the wife of her theatrical agent, and they stopped for lunch, and the maître d' put them at an undistinguished table in the back. Dorothy complained to Lillian: "Don't they know I'm Mrs. Joe DiMaggio?"

It was a bitter pill when she found out his glory was not transferable. It was so male—and solitary, too. That was one reason the Clipper caught the hero breeze in his sails: Joe walked up to that plate alone, faced the opposing team alone. A hero doesn't appear in the midst of an army. No, it has to be one knight with only his magic sword (against the fire-breathing dragon); one cowboy with his six-shooter (against a legion of bad guys on some dusty cowtown street); one fighter pilot (low on fuel!) against a squadron of Messerschmitts in the skies over England . . . or one man with a bat. Single combat matched Joe's style to a T.

And the way he saw it, sometimes Dorothy just got in the way—or talked too much, or flirted too much—or was just too goddamn present. So he went out alone. If she got on him about that, he could walk away for days. He could always find a hotel room. He'd come home if he had to—for a magazine story on the baby, or an interview (she'd do the talking), or photographers, anything like that. He would never embarrass her.

"Little Joe . . . is now a sturdy young gentleman of 15 pounds," observed one Sunday magazine writer early in 1942. "The contentment which has been observed on his face is only the reflection of that which is to be seen on the faces of the elder DiMaggio and his wife, the former Dorothy Arnold. The two have made a big go of marriage. They have a luxurious penthouse in uptown Manhattan. Like their baby, they have a formula—only theirs is for happiness. The DiMaggios believe in home. They do not adhere to the widely prevalent Manhattan theory that home is merely a place to change one's dress between night clubs. While it is to be true that their Samba and Rumba are possibly a bit rusty, it is equally true that their marriage is as shiny as new."

One night at Shor's, in the spring of that year, the boys were all lifting their glasses to another champ, and another new dad—Eddie Arcaro, the brilliant jockey, had just become sire to a six-and-a-half-pound filly. "Come over to the house some night, Eddie," DiMaggio said, by way of bonhomie, "and I'll show you how to hold a baby." All the fellows thought that was a grand and classy offer. Very few were close enough to hear Mrs. Joe, whose blue eyes held a cold glint of scorn, as she said under her breath: "Whose baby are you going to use for teaching?"

THE WAR BEDEVILED DIMAGGIO even before the start of the '42 season. Ed Barrow sent a contract without a raise—not even ten bucks. Joe had carried the Yanks to a championship; he'd been named the MVP, player of the year, *sportsman* of the year, named everything except God-incarnate.

He'd put more people in the seats than Ruth did, when Ruth was making eighty large a year. DiMaggio filled the grandstands in St. Louis and Washington, where they hadn't drawn a parkful for twenty years. What did a guy have to do for a raise?

But Barrow said, "Doesn't he know there's a war on?" Why should DiMaggio get a raise on his salary—thirty-seven thousand five hundred dollars—when so many young men had put on uniforms of olive drab for one one-hundredth the pay? Was DiMaggio so much better, so much more valuable, than those brave boys who'd give their lives to defend our shores?

Of course that was a specious argument—immaterial, underhanded, insulting. It called into question DiMaggio's patriotism, when Italian-Americans were in a ticklish spot. The fact was, DiMaggio knew plenty about the war. In the weeks after Pearl Harbor, he got word from his brother Tom that the restaurant on Fisherman's Wharf was dead—might as well lock the doors. Tourism was a thing of the past. Local people stayed away from the Wharf. (A Japanese attack was expected any day, now.) Even men who'd spent their lives at the Wharf were restricted—they couldn't come near. The whole California coast was a military zone—off-limits for "alien Italians." Most of the old papas (like Giuseppe DiMaggio) had never got U.S. citizenship—they couldn't read or write. Now they were illegal anywhere within a half-mile of shore. There was a curfew every night, eight P.M. to six A.M. The "suspect aliens" couldn't travel more than five miles from home. They weren't even supposed to have radios. Hundreds of the *immigranti* were carted off to guarded camps in Montana. Some of the old North Beach families could no longer live in their homes. Fishermen couldn't get to their boats. And old Giuseppe could no longer get to the family restaurant.

For the past five years, that restaurant had been Giuseppe's joy. He made it a point of honor to prepare his *specialità,* the spicy fisherman's stew, crab *cioppino,* for all the visiting baseball people. He'd give them big bowls, a towel for their hands, and urge them on—*"Mangia, vai!"*—no silverware required. But now, Giuseppe had nothing to do but sit around his house. Even when he was visited there by the baseball press, he could barely manage a smile. There had developed a tradition in San Francisco—a preseason pilgrimage to Papa Giuseppe, who would then predict how many "homa run" his boy Joe would hit that year. The old man wasn't a bad savant. In '37, for example, he'd invited jeers with his confident prediction: "forty-fi homa run." But Joe finished that year with forty-six (and if the season had been one day shorter, Papa would have been on the nose). Alas, by spring of '42, Giuseppe was too sad to play along.

" 'Itsa no use,' " he was quoted in the *Examiner.* " 'I no can do.'

". . . Best we could get out of him was the admission Joe might hit 'one homa run' this year. 'One is gooda 'nuf,' he said.

"There was a note of resignation in his voice.

"We took it to mean he just didn't give a hoot."

There was a similar want of joy in another DiMaggio household, this one three thousand miles east, in a rented beach house in Florida. Joe had gone down early, he said, for a few weeks of "fishing and loafing." Actually he meant to be on hand, to go to camp with the Yankees once he and Barrow had come to terms. The last time Joe was branded a holdout, it cost him almost a grand in docked pay just to get himself across the country. This time, Joe was going to be ready, if negotiations got nasty—and it looked like they would.

A few big guns like Bob Considine—the national columnist for the Hearst chain (and, of course, a Toots Shor pal)—had weighed in on Joe's behalf. Considine called DiMag "the $80,000 a year ball player who'll probably sign for half that sum." But when Barrow sent a contract for precisely half—an even forty G's—Joe steadfastly refused to sign. Barrow's comments about the war hadn't wakened Joe's spirit of cooperation.

When the New York writers arrived for spring training, they tracked DiMaggio to the beach house. "There he sat playing cards while McCarthy burned," wrote Dan Daniel. "Not even Bill Greene, World-Telegram cameraman found asylum in the DiMaggio homestead. 'I will not pose for pictures or talk to any-one,' Giuseppe insisted. 'I have not signed my con-tract, so I do not belong to the Yankees, and you can't make me pose for you,' DiMaggio vehemed. The gentle knight of the lens was flabbergasted. 'Maybe in a couple of days there will be something doing,' DiMaggio added, as he returned to his gin rummy with the newly arrived Toots Shor, his No. 1 confi-dant."

Clearly, in wartime, the Secretary of State had to take a stand for the Baseball Nation. Joe, as Daniel said, was "a full-fledged hold out. . . .

"It's an old role for him, but somehow it doesn't become him quite as well as it did before. . . . Peo-ple just don't like to hear a ballplayer grumbling over being asked to work for a paltry $37,500 a year when the base pay for privates is 21 clackers per month."

Barrow knew how to push a winning hand. Within days, he arrived in Florida, went to Joe's house that same night, and signed his star for forty-two thou-sand. What else could Joe do? Three months after Pearl Harbor, he wasn't risking just accusations of greed, but of cowardice, too. He was booed once be-fore. This time, he'd be branded as a public enemy. So Joe smiled for pictures as he signed his contract. He professed himself "well satisfied." He announced that he'd be putting five thousand dollars into war bonds right away. And he predicted that '42 would be his best year ever.

THAT WAS NOT TO BE. JOE STARTED off in a slump, started worrying—and then things did get nasty. Even when he seemed to break out with a couple of homers against the A's, there was an invidious tone on the sports page. Daniel, for example, wrote him up as "Joe ($42,000) DiMaggio," and could not fail to mention Joe's "emaciated" average, .213.

Well into May, Joe was still struggling: convinced that he had to lead the club, but for some mystifying reason unable to achieve any consistent hitting. It seemed like his great streak had used up his luck. Or at least that was one cause the writers considered. Or maybe the Jolter was bothered by the uncertain times, the war news, or the draft. . . . But Joe was still classified 3-A—married, father of one—in no danger of imminent call-up. One way or another, the draft was hanging over every man on the club—and the rest of the fellows were doing fine. The Yanks were winning two out of every three games and running away with the pennant. The second baseman, Joe Gordon, was leading the league with the bat, hitting homers, driving runners in—having exactly the sort of year that everyone expected from DiMaggio.

Of course, there were comparisons. As May turned to June, Daniel took stock of the strange Yankee season: "Past the quarter pole, eight lengths in front and breezing, the Yankees today had adapted themselves to a change in field leadership which might well endure through the season. . . . Going into the June campaign with Giuseppe hitting a lack-lustre .253, and their new bellwether Joe Gordon, who had batted successfully in 18 straight games.

"In the Sunday double-header in Philadelphia . . . in eight trips to the plate, Joe achieved one single. In his eight efforts, Gordon hit his sixth home run, a double, two singles, raised his league-leading average to .380."

That didn't do much for Dago's mood either: DiMag was worse than teammates had ever seen him—mean as a snake. One sweltering day in New York, Joe hit four huge drives. But in the big Bronx ballpark, they all turned into outs. Joe came back to the dugout and launched a vicious kick at a bucket of ice on the concrete floor. McCarthy wheeled around on the bench: "What the hell do you think you're doing?" And Joe started cursing out the Skipper. . . . McCarthy saw there was no margin in this fight. He said mildly: "I was just worried you might have hurt your foot, Joe." But that was about the last thing he'd say to DiMaggio that year.

Even Toots, who never had a bad word to say about Joe, conceded that Daig was "really tough to handle." As he remembered for Maury Allen, in *Where Have You Gone, Joe DiMaggio?*: "Then if Joe would have two oh-for-four days in a row and the Yankees would lose both of them, look out. . . . He would really sulk. Like I say, he felt the whole team depended on him. He never showed it, but Joe worried a lot."

In the hardest times, Joe wouldn't show up at Shor's; he'd try to stay home. But he and Dorothy would start scrapping, then screaming, or someone would slam the door and walk out. She used to make her agent come get her in a cab; she'd stay the night on the Millmans' couch. One night, she slammed out and took the elevator down to the lobby. And there was Joe, waiting for her. He'd run down the stairs— from the penthouse. (Dago could always cover ground.) . . . But now, with the baby, she couldn't just leave. And Joe couldn't go out—didn't want to show his face. So both of them were cooped up, and things got ugly on West End Avenue.

The Stadium crowds got ugly, too. DiMaggio was playing like a mutt—and the fans let him hear about it. They had no idea what was wrong with the Clipper . . . at least until June, when the papers reported cryptically that Mrs. Joe DiMaggio had returned home, and had no intention of divorcing her husband.

As the story dribbled out, it came clear that Dorothy had been for some weeks in Reno, Nevada—"where," as the *Mirror* helpfully noted, "women with grievances sometimes go to get divorces."

DiMaggio was on a road trip to Cleveland and Detroit—eight games, wherein he hit .172. He had not a word to say about his situation.

Then, it was even more vaguely reported that "the management had taken a hand" to rescue Joe from "his depression." Only later would Ed Barrow confirm on the record that he "had talked to Mrs. DiMaggio and persuaded her to come back home."

Now two plus two was starting to add up—to .257, which was Joe's woeful average. There were even veiled hints in the press as to why Barrow had stepped in: if Joe got divorced, he'd lose his deferment; the precious center fielder might have to *go to war.*

Well, then the fans climbed all over Joe's case—and stayed on it. They booed him every time he stepped on the field. They wrote letters: *Why didn't he go back to Italy with the rest of the coward wops?* Joe stopped reading his mail again. He tried to tough it out with the writers—he said, sure, he wasn't hitting, he understood the fans. The writers understood, too, and piled on.

"DiMaggio maintains they are entitled to boo if they aren't satisfied," wrote Whitney Martin, columnist for World Wide Sports. "Most citizens would be willing to let the fans stand outside their windows and boo all night if they were getting the $40,000 or so a year DiMaggio is supposed to be getting.

"Getting $40,000 a year and hitting .257? B-o-o-o-o."

There were two All-Star contests that year, and DiMaggio was booed at both. One reason was, he was only there for reputation's sake. He wasn't having an All-Star year. But the other reason was, in the big hero game, Joe was now on the wrong side.

The second game pitted the AL stars against an All-Star service team—major leaguers who were already wearing Uncle Sam's uniforms. Chief Boatswain's Mate Robert Feller took the mound against the AL—albeit without much success. The major leaguers beat the servicemen 5–0, and DiMaggio started Feller's woes with a single to knock in the first AL run. Nevertheless, as *The Sporting News* remarked, the Clipper "had nearly been blown off the field by jeers every time the customers got a look at him." After the game, Joe was "morose." He was quoted in the locker room: "I can't understand why the crowds should be on me. I do not know anything that I have done to deserve it."

Actually, it was what he hadn't done. He hadn't signed up for the armed forces, and the public patience was running out. Greenberg and Feller—big stars—they were in. Johnny Sturm was on that service All-Star team. Henrich had signed up. Dominic DiMaggio announced that he'd be going in, too . . . *so what the hell was wrong with Joe?*

Dorothy was telling him every day (or every day they were talking) that he ought to be signed up, that the boos were never going to stop till he enlisted. Joe said she didn't know a thing about it. If he got a few hits, there'd be nothing but cheers. Dorothy said that was the trouble with him, that's all he thought about. *(He had to broaden himself! . . .)*

Joe told his pals he couldn't figure her out. First she complained nonstop any time he wanted to get out of the house, have a cup of coffee with Toots, whatever. She said he didn't know how to be a husband, and left him—turned over his whole apple cart. Then, finally, he got her back, they were going to make a go at the marriage, he promised he'd stay at home . . . and then she wanted him to disappear for a year or two. They couldn't see eye-to-eye on anything.

One time that summer, they got an off day in New York, so Lefty and June planned an outing. Lefty would drive everybody out to Jones Beach, they'd spend the day, get some sun, have a picnic—it was gonna be great.

So, came the day—June and Dorothy had a hamper packed, everybody had a swimsuit, sunhat for Little Joe, basket, towels, everything. As Lefty recalled, it was a beautiful day. Joe was hitting again, and everybody was happy. So they got to the beach, unloaded the car, spread out the blanket. The boys ran off for a dunk in the water, the girls were going to lay out the picnic. Then, Joe came back and saw Dorothy's swimsuit—a two-piece beauty, bare midriff—it cost a small fortune, but it was quite the latest. "Put your blouse back on," Joe said.

"Joe, don't be ridiculous!"

"No wife of mine is going to wear that in public. Put your shirt back on."

"But Joe! It's beautiful!"

"C'mon, Joe, it doesn't matter here. Let her wear whatev—"

"You put something decent on, or I'm going."

"Joe!"

So Joe got the keys from Lefty, jumped in the car and drove away.

Fortunately, Lefty never met a stranger, so soon he had a new friend who was thrilled to help out a famous Yankee, and he'd give them a ride back to town, take everybody home, no problem. . . . Except, Dorothy said she wasn't going home. So she stayed with the baby on Lefty and June's guest bed.

He'll call, June said.

Dorothy said: he won't call.

In those days, Joe and Lefty always rode to the Stadium in Lefty's car. Lefty would get himself ready most days near eleven, eleven-thirty, and then he'd wave a colored towel from his terrace, which Joe could see from his window. So then Joe would be ready downstairs when Lefty swung by with the car. The day after the picnic—Tuesday, a day game—Joe had the car so he picked up Lefty. They drove to the Stadium in companionable silence. After the game, they drove home. Lefty waited for Joe to bring up Dorothy. But Joe didn't say a word.

Next day they drove to the Stadium again. Lefty was still waiting, Joe was still silent. Thursday, same thing. Dorothy was still on the guest bed. As Lefty remembered, he thought: *Friday—he's gonna ask about her Friday. It's not gonna go through the week-*

end. . . . But Lefty wasn't going to push. Joe would bring it up himself.

Friday, they drove to the Stadium. Joe said, "Let's take the West Side Highway." Then, he didn't say a thing.

They played the game, they won again. Joe took forever after a game. Lefty waited around, in case Dago wanted to talk. "Let's take our time and go down Broadway," Joe said. . . . Broadway was a million stoplights. Joe didn't even clear his throat. Finally, they were near home—and Lefty burst out with it:

"Well, don't you wanna know how she is?"

And Joe said, "Who?"

HE WAS RIGHT ABOUT ONE THING. He did start to hit and the jeering abated. Or he was partly right: people still made comparisons when his brother Dom enlisted in the Navy. There were scattered boos for DiMaggio on the day Tom Henrich was honored at the Stadium, before he shipped out to war. Joe never got back to the hero worship of 1941. It wasn't the same country, after all. It was hard to care who won the batting crown when the U.S. had just lost four cruisers at Guadalcanal.

The Yankees won the pennant going away, and prepared to face a bunch of no-name kids who'd won the NL flag for St. Louis. (Who'd ever heard of Stanley F. Musial, from Donora, Pa.?) The Yankees were two-to-one favorites, and why not? Of the last six Series, the Yanks had appeared in five and won them all. But this Yankee club was not the same.

It wasn't just that Henrich and Sturm were out of the lineup, Gomez and Russo absent from the mound. This club had lost its competitive heart: that was Joe DiMaggio. Oh, he was in the lineup—batting fourth every day—and the box scores looked fine: he ended up with seven hits, at .333 for the Series. But every hit was a single, and there was never that moment, that one big play, where DiMaggio did something to put the Yanks up for good, to break the will of the other team. DiMaggio and his Yankees had never lost a World Series. But the young Cardinals won this championship four games to one. From start to finish, '42 was not Joe's year—and sad to say, it wasn't yet over.

After the Series, Joe, with Dorothy and Little Joe, set out by train for San Francisco. Even in wartime, with the rail system overworked, with the Army commandeering half the rolling stock, the DiMaggios went first-class all the way. A clause in DiMaggio's contract required the Yankees to pay, not just for Joe's return to the West Coast, but for Mrs. Joe as well. In a way, that would be a fateful perk. Because soon after Dorothy arrived in San Francisco, she grabbed up Little Joe, and hied herself over the mountains, back to Reno. And this time, she filed for residency, which she would need for a Nevada divorce.

The way most papers covered the story, Joe was

taken completely by surprise. There wasn't any paper that didn't try to cover. Since the days of the The Streak, Joe DiMaggio was a public property. His marital troubles were fit matter for the nation's readers—like his Best-Dressed wardrobe, his recommendations on what to smoke, his friendships, likes and dislikes, or his counsel on the value of war bonds. As a matter of fact, in those troublous times, a hero plunging into hot water was more satisfying than a hero on the rise. *(Hey! Even up in that penthouse, the Great DiMaggio has his troubles, too! . . .)*

The San Francisco writers called the house in the Marina. "No, Joe da home!" . . . Or they stopped by Joe DiMaggio's Grotto, the famous eatery on Fisherman's Wharf:

"Is Joe here?"

"Joe who?"

Finally, they tracked him to Reno, where he was trying to patch things up with Dorothy. Not that he'd admit that—or anything else. The raffish *Examiner* columnist, Joe's old pal Prescott Sullivan, called Dorothy's Reno apartment and Joe picked up the phone. Sullivan asked how things were going with the missus. "That's my business," Joe snapped. Sullivan retreated to baseball chat: travel restrictions had forced the Yankees to schedule their next spring training in New Jersey—did Joe think he could get in shape there?

"Spring training," said DiMaggio, "won't concern me this year."

As Sullivan wrote the following day: "The remark brought our ears up like those of a jackrabbit.

" 'Wotcha mean? Gonna quit?' "

Joe knew he'd said too much, and dummied up. "Draw your own conclusions," he said. And so, Sullivan did. In fact, knowing both the slugger and the missus, he correctly concluded that a hitch in the service had somehow got entangled in the marital negotiations:

"One theory—yet untested—is that Joe figures his prospects of effecting a reconciliation with the fair Dorothy might be materially enhanced by the appeal of a soldier or sailor suit, in either of which he would be a dashing figure."

Within hours, the wires launched the news of Joe's planned enlistment, and retirement from baseball. The story was refueled in almost every paper in the country, before it landed as a certainty in the mind of every fan.

Of course, that story was a surprise to Joe's draft board, which had closed off enlistments. It was more than surprising to Ed Barrow, who was mailing DiMaggio's contract for 1943. And it was something near to shock for Joe, who didn't know what he wanted to do at all.

What should he do? Dorothy wanted him in the Army—she'd made that clear enough; otherwise it would be divorce. The thought that she would walk out on him pushed Joe to rage. She was *his*. Still, if he gave himself over to the Army, then nothing would be his to control. Who could tell how long this war would go on? Or what they'd do with him? He could get hurt, and that would be the end of baseball for him. He could lose everything. . . . So what should he do?

He screamed that he'd been misquoted.

"That fellow asked me a lot of leading questions, and placed the wrong interpretation on my answers," Joe told the International News Service. He'd never said the armed forces were in his plans. "All I meant was that I'm not worried about spring training. I've got other things on my mind."

And that was true enough. Because Dorothy said he couldn't go back now—they'd be finished. There was the story in every paper in the country: *Joe leaving baseball for the duration . . . DiMag to sign up with Uncle Sam.* If he backed out now, it would be like desertion. She had her plans to consider, too—and they did not include being married to a famous coward.

She was always the planner—and she had this all worked out: Joe wasn't going to get hurt, wasn't going to get near any war. Who was running the Army? Why, men—American men, of course. And every one a baseball fan. They'd do anything for DiMaggio! They'd carry him around like a maharajah! . . . So the first thing he had to do was ask for an Army posting in L.A. That's where Dorothy wanted to live. She was going back to work.

For the rest . . . well, you could follow the story

from the news bulletins over the next few weeks—starting with a gorgeous photo of the fur-swaddled Dorothy Arnold planting a smooch on the cheek of her husband, the patriot:

"RENO, Jan. 13 (AP Wirephoto)—Love Me and Leave Me. That's the theme song for this second honeymoon scene at Reno, Nev., yesterday. Being kissed, and loving it, is Joe DiMaggio, ex-ballplayer for the duration and almost ex-husband. On the high-voltage end is Mrs. DiMag, blonde, delicious ex-canary of night clubs and radio, who called off divorce plans. Joe said he's back in love, and off to the wars."

"NEW YORK, Jan. 13 (AP)—'I wish him Godspeed and good luck,' said Ed Barrow, president of the New York Yankees, when informed that his star outfielder. . . .'"

"LOS ANGELES, Jan. 18 (Special to the Examiner)—Joe DiMaggio arrived here today with a blunt denial he intended to enlist in the Army Air Corps ground crew at Santa Ana. . . . 'Why, I can't do anything without consulting my draft board, and that's in San Francisco.' . . . 'I'm here for a couple of days, but it's more of a pleasure trip than anything.' "

"SAN FRANCISCO, Feb. 17 (UP)—Joe DiMaggio enlisted in the Army at the San Francisco Armed Services induction center and was given a week's furlough. . . . 'I've been planning this since last season. . . .' "

"LOS ANGELES, Feb. 24 (UP)—Joe DiMaggio reported for duty today at Santa Ana Air Base. The announcement by the Army Air Force's West Coast training center headquarters did not disclose DiMaggio's immediate assignment."

The only part of the story that couldn't be divined from the press was the saddest part. Only Dorothy spoke about it, and that was long after. It was how she felt her heart shutting, finally, against her husband, Joe—when he concluded that he'd have to enlist, and he started to cry.

THE ARMY WASN'T THAT BAD, NOT AT first. Joe never had a problem with discipline. And as for the job, he was good at that, too.

Joe DiMag Slams
First Army Homer
Riverside, April 30 (AP)—
". . . His first circuit clout of the season came with two mates aboard and sailed over the 345 foot left-field wall as he paced the Santa Ana Air Base team to a 14–8 win over March Field."

It was almost like a regular season, except the travel was a little less, and the games could get sloppy. There were plenty of fellows he knew on the circuit. He might be playing center field behind Red Ruffing, same as always, or have Lodigiani as a teammate at third base. And there was Wally Judnich, another San Francisco boy who, in better times, played for the Brownies, and Mike McCormick, the gifted outfielder for the Cincinnati Reds. There were also plenty of fill-ins—kids who hadn't yet gotten to the majors or players who didn't have big-league talent. That was all right with Joe, as long as they kept their heads down, paid attention, and tried as hard as they could. If they meant to screw around, DiMaggio wanted nothing to do with them. It was still his job to win.

His attitude delighted his commanders. Every general seemed to have the screwy idea that the excellence of his ball team reflected on the excellence of his air base, his unit, his command, his own much-saluted self. They'd set a training table for the team (steaks like no civilian could buy), or they'd invite DiMaggio to dinner at their mess, or ask him to parties, ask if he needed any smokes, booze, beer. . . . They were taking such good care of him, he was putting on weight (up to two-oh-five) and he had to have his tailor work his uniforms over (fatigues, too, of course), so they looked just right. Weekends, he could always get a pass, to get off the air base and check in with Dorothy.

They'd rented a house near Toluca, out in the Valley where it was just fields and shimmering heat—easier for Joe to get home that way, and cheaper than Hollywood, or Beverly Hills. Fifty bucks a month didn't go far, the way Joe and Dorothy ran a house. If it wasn't for the restaurant—back in business, now that the shoreline was safe again, and probably paying Joe ten times his Army wage—he would have lost a fortune that first year. As it was, he was pressing about money. He'd get to the house, see something new, and his face would darken with anger: "Dottie! What are we spending money on?"

She didn't have much else to do but shop, no other way to get out of the house. One producer talked to her about a part on stage—a show called *Oklahoma!*—but she'd just got out to the West Coast, and had her heart set on motion pictures. Still, it was one of those Hollywood stories—Dorothy was so hungry to work, no one wanted to talk to her. Either that, or they figured she'd want the moon to sign. Mrs. Joe DiMaggio—loaded with dough, wasn't she?. . . So, Dorothy took care of Little Joe, and tried to inveigle friends to come visit in the Valley. She went for long drives if she could get gas, or long walks if she was out of coupons.

She had to save gas to take Joe back and forth from the air base. And if there was a weekend game, she'd take him there, too. She'd sit in the grandstand with Little Joe. At one ballpark, the two-year-old climbed over the box seat rail, and carried his toy fungo bat onto the field, calling, "Play ball! Play ball!" Little Joe was excited whenever Dad was around. Mornings in Toluca, while Big Joe shaved, Little Joe would be clinging to his legs. Big Joe was happy enough to see the boy, too—but not so much that he'd sit around the house and watch him.

Rugger Ardizoia, a minor league pitcher (and later a Yankee) who played on Joe's Santa Ana club, remembered the day all the stand-out players suited up and went into the city for Joe E. Brown's annual all-star game. They packed the Hollywood stands and donated all the money to buy sports equipment for the troops in the Pacific. DiMaggio was the star of the show: four-for-four with two home runs. After the game, the fellows went out together: Joe put a twenty on the bar and they drank all afternoon, telling old stories. Every fifteen, twenty minutes, Dorothy would come in: "Joe, it's time to come home, now. Joe, you've got to come home." As Ardizoia remembered more than fifty years later: "She was a nice, down-to-earth girl, but Joe didn't want anything to do with her, really."

About six months into Joe's Army hitch, Dorothy came to the same conclusion. She didn't run back to Reno, this time, but filed for divorce in Los Angeles. In open court, she accused Joe of cruelty. She asked for custody of Little Joe, with six hundred fifty dollars a month to take care of her and the boy.

Joe got the case delayed—he said he couldn't get a pass to attend. Joe could have a pass whenever he wanted. He was playing for time, trying to talk Dorothy into sticking it out. But this time, she was obdurate. After a month, she got her court date. And Joe didn't bother to show up. He wasn't going to show the world his dirty laundry. Let her have the courtroom to herself—and get it over with. As it stood, the papers were having a field day:

"He may have been the idol of the baseball field, but as a husband he was strictly .000. . . ."

"Bursting into tears in the witness stand as she told how when baseball star husband, Joe DiMaggio, home run king of the New York Yankees, made her a stooge and wrecked their marriage by his 'cruel indifference' to her blond beauty, Mrs. DiMaggio. . . ."

Joe was too proud to fight her in public. Either that, or they'd worked out a straight deal: he wouldn't fight, and he'd pay her the money. She wouldn't tell how she'd had him tailed by detectives, or show the gumshoe reports on the women in hotels. Still, Dorothy played to the hilt the only role she'd been able to land—the lovely and lamenting young wife.

"The beautiful actress drew her costly mink wrap about her as though chilled by the memory and wept as she told Judge Most how she had a baby thinking the advent of a child of his own might make Joe 'realize his responsibilities as a married man.'

" 'But the event of the baby's arrival didn't change him,' she said. 'He became ill-tempered, refused to talk to me for days at a time and several times asked me to get out of our home.' "

By May 1944, she had the judge convinced. "As a rabid baseball fan it is difficult for me . . ." said Judge Stanley Most. "But the evidence is so overwhelming it must be done." He granted Dorothy a lump sum of fourteen thousand dollars in cash, plus one hundred fifty a month for the care of Little Joe. In addition, DiMaggio would have to maintain a ten-thousand-dollar life insurance policy for the benefit of his son.

The way DiMaggio saw it, he had to write out a check for fourteen thousand—as much as he'd paid for his family's house—just for the privilege of paying more every month. And that money would come from his own pocket—he'd have no way to earn it back. There was only one piece of good news. What Dorothy had won in court was an "interlocutory decree." It would run for a year, during which time, Joe and Dorothy would still be legally married. The way Joe figured, that gave him one more year to talk to her, reason with her, promise her he could make things better. If she'd come back to him, that would end the money woes—and stop the churning in his stomach. He never knew how much he wanted to keep her until she'd walked away. He never gave up on what was his. One more year. . . . With the same quiet confidence that always marked his goals and plans, DiMaggio vowed he would have her back.

AND THAT WAS THE MOMENT THE Army chose to send Sergeant Joe DiMaggio off to Hawaii, to return—well, nobody knew when. U.S. soldiers, sailors, and airmen were fighting their way west toward Japan, and the despatch of their baseball heroes to Honolulu bespoke a couple of truths—sort of a good-news-bad-news thing. It testified, on one hand, to the safety of Hawaii: the Nipponese navy was on the defensive, maybe on the run. But the other truth was more ominous: it was still a long way to

Tokyo. So these baseball stars might be gone for years, playing for the tens of thousands, hundreds of thousands of American boys who would take and hold the islands across the Pacific.

Most of the big-time players were going: Ruffing, Judnich, Lodigiani, McCormick, were now joined on the Army Air Force squad by a good young catcher (another future Pinstriper), Charlie Silvera, along with a fine AL infield: the A's Ferris Fain at first base, Joe Gordon of the Yankees at second, and the Browns' Bob Dillinger at third. The Navy team that would serve as their main competition was also loaded with stars, including the Cardinals' Big Cat (and All-Star) first baseman, Johnny Mize, and Brooklyn's young Harold Henry Reese at short. Most of the fellows would sail together from Seattle, June 6, 1944. For any U.S. serviceman embarking on that fateful morning—D-Day at the beaches of Normandy—Hawaii didn't seem a bad destination. But DiMaggio wasn't in a mood to enjoy the voyage. Every day he was on that ship, for as long as he had to stay in Hawaii—for that matter, any day he was out of reach, out of contact with Dorothy—he was losing time, money, and hope. He was farther and farther from the life he wanted—the life he used to have.

The other guys acted like this voyage was a floating party, another big road trip. One of the brass gave DiMaggio a case of scotch to ease his sojourn in the islands. But Joe knew he'd never get it off the ship and onto the base without being discovered. So he broke up the case and gave each player a couple of bottles to bring ashore. By the time he asked for his scotch in Hawaii, there wasn't a single bottle left.

When their ship steamed into Pearl Harbor, they were taken from the gangplank directly to Honolulu Stadium, where almost twenty thousand fans were waiting. The guys from the boat were stumbling around on their sealegs, but that didn't matter. The pitcher and catcher were Eddie Stutz and Neil Clifford from the Seals. So they had to take care of their club's most famous alum. When Joe came to the plate, Clifford muttered: "Let's see how far you can hit one." And they grooved him a fastball that DiMaggio hit half a mile, over the left field fence, over the left field bleachers, out to the street that bordered the ballpark, where the ball almost killed a Honolulu homeowner who was reading his paper on the front stoop. Of course, the place went crazy; fans and players alike would remember the moment for the rest of their lives. But to Joe it was another testament: he was the best in the business; his time, his prime, was being squandered.

On the whole, you couldn't have a better war. The general was Brigadier William J. Flood, a terrific fan who spared his stars all the normal Army tedium. There was a beach for the Seventh Army Air Force, supposed to be R&R for the fliers. But the ballplayers had privileges, too. So, they'd play a game, or they'd work out at McClellan Field, then they'd loll in the sand and surf, get a tan, drink some beer, tell some lies. When the boys were properly toasted, or on those rare days when the weather wasn't postcard-perfect, they might hang around their Quonset huts playing cards. Joe spent most of his time playing pinochle for money. Either that or he was off to himself, on his cot, thinking about Dorothy. . . . *What was she doing now?*

It was torture knowing Dorothy had moved back to New York, not just because that was so far away. It seemed like she had his old life (with his money) and he did not. How the hell was he going to get back there and talk to her, see the boy? . . . Or what if she met someone else? Of course, she would! *There'd be a million guys after her—the lucky ones, still at home.* . . . It was only a couple of months before Joe was checked into the hospital—an acute attack of the ulcers.

That was his war, to live in the loss that he couldn't change—to swallow his failure. No wonder his stomach was on fire. He'd lie in a hospital bed for a week or two, reading comics, listening to the radio. Then, he'd think he was going to go crazy; he'd say his stomach felt better. He'd rejoin the team, suit up, take some BP, and play again. Half the time, some newsreel crew would show up, or the Army cameramen: *How do you like playing for Uncle Sam, Joe? . . .* "Well, it's fine," Joe would say. "I don't mind it at all."

But what was the point? The only difference when they won was the Army brass would rake in their bets from the Navy brass. Big deal! Joe didn't bet. Sometimes the Army stars would whip up on some hapless Hawaiian minor leaguers, 12–2 or 14–1. That was even more pointless—and unfair—it burned Joe up. Those bush leaguers were getting paid for this—and what was he getting? Fifty a month!

Dario Lodigiani recalled: "One night, we're lyin' around on the cots and DiMaggio says, 'Somebody's gonna pay me for all this time I lost.'

"I said, 'Well, Joe, the GI Bill of Rights says you get your job back, same pay and everything.'

" 'The hell with the same,' he says. 'They're gonna pay me. I'm gonna get a twenty-five-thousand-dollar raise.'

"I said, 'Good night! Twenty-five thousand, that's a lot of money, Joe.'

" 'Cost me three years. They're gonna pay for it.' "

There wasn't anybody else in that unit who hated his war like DiMaggio. They all had the feeling, it could have been worse. They'd win a big game, they'd get a pass; screw around for the night in Honolulu. One time, after a game, a dance was arranged for them. But DiMaggio didn't dance. As Jack B. Moore reported in *Joe DiMaggio: A Bio-bibliography,* "Instead, he reportedly sat in a car 'a couple of hours' by himself."

The main battle hazard was probably cirrhosis. Ruffing, for one, was in the bag from the moment he arrived. He flew in late on an Army transport—stinko already. Every man was supposed to have a canteen of water on his hip, but Ruffing's canteen had vodka and grape juice.

Most of the players would hang around with Bill Whaley—he'd played for the Angels. Now he was manager of the Primo Brewery in Honolulu. Guys would sneak off the base with an ambulance and go to Whaley's house after dark. They'd chugalug Primo Beer all night. You'd tip up a bottle, and everyone would count—*one, two, three, four* . . . the game was to see who was the fastest. Then after everyone was drooling drunk, they'd ride back to the base (guards would never question an ambulance), and straight through to their bunk. Ruffing was in a chair at Whaley's one night, chugging Primo as fast as he could go. People told him to slow down, but Ruffing was indignant: "Don't you bastards tell me how to drink!" Then he knocked one back—chug, chug, chug—his head tipped back and back and back, until he went flat backward, chair and all, over and out. They carried him to the ambulance. And he was a big guy—took five of them to heft him onto his bunk. Next day, they're up for the workout, but no Red. They found him in the hospital in the bed right next to DiMaggio.

Joe was in and out of that hospital like one of those new yo-yo toys. He couldn't stay out and he couldn't stay in. And he couldn't figure out which he hated worse. Long after the war, Joe would tell the editor of *Sport* magazine, Al Silverman, that the war years "never seemed to move at all." He thought "they would never end."

Actually, they would end for Joe in a matter of months. The rest of his unit pushed on, westward. Most of them had a real war, too: fueling and reservicing the bombers that would pound the Japanese into submission—from Guam to Saipan, Tinian, and finally on to V-J Day. But Joe's war had a victory of another sort. He finally convinced the Air Force brass to send him back to the mainland, send him to a hospital in California, to fix his stomach for good. And then he prevailed on the mainland brass to transfer him again—this time, February '45, to the Special Services in Atlantic City, New Jersey. That just happened to be the spring training home of the New York Yankees, who would gather there in a matter of weeks. And it wasn't too far from New York City, home to Miss Dorothy Arnold and the three-year-old Joe DiMaggio, Jr.

THE PHONE WOULD RING IN THE middle of the night, and she'd grab it, before the noise could wake Joey. Dorothy had only a tiny place in the Adams Hotel.

Of course, it would be him. "I can't sleep," Joe would say. And then he'd start in on her again, how they ought to be together now—she had to be his.

Dorothy thought, he could be so sweet sometimes, when he wanted to try. He'd call up just for nothing, and tell her about a pretty nurse in the GI ward—but not as pretty as her. Or when he was out of the hospital, that summer, he'd call up on a Friday, and say he could get a car. He could drive up and take her off to the country for the weekend, get some fresh air— what would she say to that?

What she said was, she wanted to be friends, for Joey's sake. Of course, they had to talk, they could see each other, take care of each other. But she wanted her own life. Their divorce was final now— the interlocutory decree expired in May 1945—and she was free. She'd hired a nanny, and tried out for several parts. Nothing had happened yet. But you never could tell.

In August, they sent Joe to another hospital, this one in Sarasota, near the Florida beach where they used to live together for spring training. In retrospect, those times didn't seem so bad. He called from down there, too, and wrote the sweetest letters—said he was thinking of her all the time.

Tell the truth, she thought about him, too. How could she not, with Joey, now nearly four, asking, asking: Is Daddy coming home from the war? Joey was thrilled whenever he saw Big Joe. Dorothy's friends thought Joey was a bit strange—he was a clingy kid, for one thing, and a biter. One time Dorothy bit him back, just to show him how it felt. But that didn't stop him. Another odd thing: he had a habit of looking up her girlfriends' skirts—they'd glance down, and his little fingers would be lifting their hems! But he could be sweet, too, and he'd light up if anybody paid attention—especially a man.

She had a couple of fellows on the hook, though she said it was nothing serious. One was no more than a boy, named Gary, and one rich guy, George Schubert—he was in stocks somehow—he kept calling her, too. But it wasn't the same as when Joe called. No, she wasn't past him—not yet—she freely admitted that. He called from Florida and said he might get mustered out. Maybe next month! Joe said he'd move up to New York, and get her a real place. They could have a real apartment again . . . like the old days, like the old high life—her life, as she'd started to think of it.

The papers picked up hints of Joe's imminent discharge. The sportswriters spun out fantasies—how the Great DiMaggio might come back this season, right now! Surely, he could help to make the Yankees champs again. Then, there were darker hints in the papers: how DiMaggio might get a break, just because he was a famous slugger. The grumbling grew so insistent that the hometown daily, the *San Francisco Chronicle,* jumped in with unusual truculence to defend him:

"Immediately, some one will yell, if and when he's discharged, that he was mustered out because he's a baseball player. For that reason we repeat what we have already said here several times. It is this: 'If DiMaggio were a truck driver, beauty operator or newspaper office boy he'd have been discharged for

medical reasons long ago.' Notice that, though we
have printed this statement three times, nobody has
ever denied it!"

By September, the news was official: DiMaggio
would get a medical discharge owing to duodenal ulcers. And he would head straight for New York—
though not to suit up for the Yankees. The club's new
president, Larry MacPhail, got out front with a public statement to take the press off DiMaggio's case:
he said he had counseled the Yankee slugger to attend
to his health, sit out till next season, and come back
strong in 1946. But it was clear, in the same stories,
that this was not all MacPhail's idea. The Clipper had
another sort of comeback in mind. "DiMaggio," the
AP reported, ". . . attended the first game of a doubleheader between the Yankees and the St. Louis
Browns with his former wife, Dorothy Arnold, and
their 3 year old son."

Well, why shouldn't she go out with him? It was
exciting! They went to the ballpark and everybody
cheered them. The cameramen all wanted her picture with him. Everybody asking what they would
do . . . it was wonderful! Joe wanted her to move to
her own apartment, right away. And though he
wouldn't get a dime from the team till next year, he
said he would help her. He said he could find a way
to make money, he had an idea. And that was exciting, too: Joe was going to *write a book*. Well, he
wouldn't write it all himself but with a pal, Tom
Meany, a terrific sportswriter, who would talk to

Joe and put the story down in his own words. And here was the clincher: Joe wanted her to help! He said: Dot, you always know what to say. Joe pointed out to her, she was the reader in the family. He said he couldn't do it without her.

He was so sweet. And so thin! He must have lost twenty pounds, poor thing. And he needed a home, needed her—for the book! . . . Dorothy often regretted that she'd never gone to college. (My God, she used to say, what I could have done with four years of college!) But she was always reading to improve herself. And now she gave one of her favorite books to Joe: *How to Improve Your Word Power.* It was a program—new words to learn every week. And the dear man was reading it all the time.

And he did sign up to write his life story, and Tom Meany came over and they worked together in her new apartment, a wonderful place on the East Side. Joey was so happy—and Dorothy, too. They worked side by side with Tom, every day. Joe put in the book, *Lucky to Be a Yankee,* the story of how Dorothy cured his slump. She saw the 5 on his back was different, and she told him! . . . Tom wrote all that down—Joe insisted. And afternoons, she had to run out and get something to cook. And decorating—she was hunting antiques in all the little shops. Though when her old friend Dorothy Kilgallen mentioned in her column that "poor Joe DiMaggio" sent his wife out for "second-hand furniture," Dottie was furious. That wasn't fair! Joe was so generous. He bought a ton of

Christmas toys for Joey—"Little Butch," as they called him. And Joe didn't even mind when her mother came to visit, and her sister, too. And if Dorothy didn't have time to cook, he was always ready to take them all out. One night, they strolled out, near 86th and Madison. And Joe said—the dear man—"Let's go to Longchamps and get some of their insatiable food." Well, they didn't even laugh in front of him, he was trying so hard.

Of course, he wasn't altogether different. She couldn't expect that. He'd still go out with Toots and the boys—he'd say he had to relax. And once, when her mother and sister were there, they were all going out for the evening, and Dorothy appeared in a new black dress, with a scooping sweetheart neckline. She looked spectacular. "Take that off and put something decent on," Joe growled.

"But Joe!"

"No wife of mine is going out like that. Take off that goddamn dress."

Well, she stuck to her guns, she wore it. But Joe didn't say another word all night.

Still, it was so clear, he wanted to be with her. He wanted them to marry again, make a home, be a family. And she wanted that, too. That's the way she was raised, what she thought was right. That's why she gave up everything for him in the first place!

By January Tom had the whole book written down. It would come out that summer, as the new baseball season heated up. Joe's thoughts turned also to the season ahead. And he wanted Dorothy to come with him to Florida. He wanted to get down there early: it wouldn't be easy getting in shape. And she would have gone along, she said, if it wasn't for that idea of home. She had so much to do on their place. "No, Joe," she said. "Let me stay up here and work on the house. By the time you get back, everything will be ready."

He wasn't upset—maybe even relieved: he wouldn't want distractions down there. Though he would never say it aloud, he couldn't be sure how his body would respond. He was thirty-one years old now, and hadn't played steadily for almost two years. He had the club's new management to deal with. This MacPhail, the new boss, wasn't Joe's kind of guy: a showman, a showboat—from the *Brooklyn Dodgers*. Well, he'd have plenty to learn about Yankee baseball. But they'd show him. They'd get the club together again. Joe was looking forward to this. Hadn't he done exactly what he'd planned with Dorothy? Well, he'd show them. He'd put it all back together. And '46 would be the year.

EVERYBODY TALKED ABOUT HOW he'd changed. Not the way he played, and not physically (though he was still ten pounds underweight). It was the way he smiled, laughed out loud, and talked about anything—Daig was tellin' stories! And chatting up the writers, and buying dinners: happy as a kid. Well, not like the kid he used to be. Some other kid, maybe, the kind you could talk to. Hell, he didn't even hold out, but settled on what MacPhail gave him. Same as his old pay: that's what the papers said.

It was the old-timers who were truly amazed, writers most of all. Abe Kemp, who had known Joe for three years before the kid could vote, now had such a pleasant visit with old Dead Pan that he felt compelled to tell his readers: "There is a polish and a savoir faire to Joe now that one cannot help but notice. He is an agreeable host, certain of himself and free in his conversation."

A writer for the INS wire, Caswell Adams, was more explicit about his surprise:

"For a fellow who met Joe DiMaggio when he first came roaring into the big league, to chat with him nowadays is indeed a novelty. A pleasant one.

"In 1936, Joe was a silent young man whose idea of a lengthy conversation with a sports writer was 'yop' or 'maybe.' He seemed scared of the writers . . . he resented any panning and took written praise with silence. He was about as chummy a fellow as an elderly clam.

"Seven years of great play as a Yankee and three long years in the Army have changed all that. He now is a swell companion, intelligent talker, and laughs easily."

The writers started calling him "the new DiMaggio." This was something more than "Word Power" from a book. For the first time, Joe would make the effort to connect with others. He was as purposeful about it as he was about good relations with the new club management; or patching things up with the Skipper, Joe McCarthy; or wooing Dorothy into remarriage. In fact, it was Dorothy's advice that launched him on this charm campaign. As he told the writer (later his biographer) Gene Schoor: "I'm tired of being called a sour-puss. I want people to like me and I try to like them. . . . I guess maybe, if I could relax and smile a little more, it would be better all around."

How could he be any better than this? . . . That red-headed wildman, MacPhail, decided he couldn't wait for spring training. The Yanks couldn't wait till Florida warmed up. No, he'd get an airplane, and whisk eighty players to the Panama Canal. They could work out in tropical heat through February, maybe play a few games against the U.S. service teams. Then all the boys could fly back to St. Pete, already tanned and limber. The war had brought a new age of airpower, a world made small: what was the point of doing things the old way?

The press played the trip for laughs, dubbed it "MacPhail's Flying Circus." A lot of fellows didn't like the flying. McCarthy considered the whole scheme a dangerous tomfoolery. There wasn't anything about MacPhail that McCarthy didn't hate. The war years—trying to field a team with cripples, senior citizens, and bush-league kids—had taken their toll on the Skipper. Then old Col. Ruppert's heirs finally sold the Yankees to a pair of high rollers, Del Webb and Dan Topping, whom McCarthy considered undesirables. In his view they were war profiteers, or worse. (He heard they had connections to Las Vegas!) For the last straw, they took a third partner—the loudmouth, MacPhail, who would run the team. McCarthy tried to quit, without avail: MacPhail held him to his contract. . . . Still, from the mainstay of the squad, there was not one squawk about Panama, about the airplane, the new owners—about anything. DiMaggio was all smiles.

He was working harder than anybody else, and hitting the ball harder, too. There was a Canal Zone tradition at the ballpark in Balboa. In each game, the first man to hit a home run would win a white linen suit. DiMaggio would come home with a trunkful. The Yanks would manhandle some "Canal Zone All-Stars" 10–3, or 14–2—what the hell, the game score didn't mean a thing. The news was in the agate type below the story: HR—DiMaggio . . . or in a headline above: "DiMaggio Again Clouts Home Run."

By the time the boys were airmailed back to Florida, all the new trappings didn't seem so threatening. It felt like the good old times were back again. The Yankees were loaded with returning stars: DiMaggio, Keller, and Henrich in the out-field; Rizzuto and Gordon were a peerless middle infield. And somewhere they'd find a place for the wartime second baseman, little Snuffy Stirn-weiss—all he'd done the year before was lead the league in hitting.

They rolled untroubled through some grapefruit games, and then went barnstorming—a zigzag through Dixie that would last for weeks. Red Smith called this "MacPhail's weird Chatauqua tours." But there was nothing mystical about the count at the turnstiles: thirteen thousand paid fans in New Or-leans, twenty-one thousand in Atlanta. . . . Their train would pull into some little Gritsburg, and the town fathers would let the schools out! There was a hunger in the country for things that were great "be-fore the world went nuts." . . . Eight thousand fans in *Beaumont, Texas.*

The press settled happily into good old traditions, too. In San Francisco, the columnist Prescott Sulli-van made pilgrimage to Fisherman's Wharf for a bowl of crab *cioppino* and a chat with one proud new citizen of the U.S.A.

"Citizen Giuseppe DiMaggio, only man ever to sire three major league centerfielders, spoke with cool deliberation, as he sized up the part the most il-lustrious of his sons, Joe, is likely to play in the forth-coming campaign. . . .

" 'Joe,' the old fisherman said, in a voice made

husky by years of combat with the tossing seas. 'Joe—he gonna hit thirty-six homa runs.' "

The New York writers also settled into their good old habits—counting up for fun and profit the statistics of the Jolter:

"Joe DiMaggio carried his batting streak through ten straight games . . ."

"Joe DiMaggio got his fifteenth homer of the spring in the eighth inning, after having made four singles."

(That was fifteen taters in thirty games!)

"DI MAG IN HIT FEST!"

At last, the Yankees came home to New York, where the real fest was supposed to begin. But instead, that's where the good times stopped.

It turned out Dorothy hadn't finished making their family home. There wasn't going to be any home for DiMaggio—not with her. In fact, she was going to make her home in the Waldorf-Astoria with that stockbroker, George Schubert. She and Schubert would be married that summer. Dorothy and Joe were quitsville.

IT WAS A LONG SEASON, BUT A SHORT story. Joe went in the tank, and the Yankees with him. Joe was like a fighter getting punched out: there wasn't time for his head to clear before the next haymaker landed. Dorothy was the start, or maybe the

cause, no matter how he tried to put her perfidy behind him. How could he see himself a winner at the
Stadium when he slept in failure at the Edison Hotel?

It was tough to feel right at the Stadium, too. So
many changes—that relentless MacPhail. More
seats hemmed in the outfield, more fans screaming
for Joe (but no, they wouldn't cut one inch off left
center, where so many of his best shots went to
die). The clubhouse was all new, and Joe got himself off in the corner, with an escape route to the
trainer's room, right there next to his locker. He
didn't want to sit around and answer: *Joe, what
went wrong?* . . . If he had the answer, it wouldn't
have gone wrong.

By the time the season had run for a month, the
streaking Boston Red Sox were already in front of
the Bombers by four and a half games. They came to
the Bronx for a showdown series, and that's when
MacPhail chose to spring his first "promotion"—
Ladies' Day! He papered the town with free passes,
gave away five hundred pairs of free nylons, and
staged a pregame fashion show, with models riding
around the field in open Jeeps. Jesus, the Yankees
took a raft of shit from the Bostons! *(Yoo hoo,
Rizzuto—Phillis!—what'sa matter? You forgotchur
fuckin' NYLONS!)* But with the powerhouse lineup
that their owner, Tom Yawkey, bought, the Red Sox
could also back up their talk. They won that day, won
two out of three, and left the Yanks five and a half
games back.

After that, things went from embarrassing to miserable. MacPhail chartered airplanes for their road trips: revolt in the clubhouse! Crosetti wouldn't fly, made his own way by rail, and took a group of grousers with him. The Crow, by that time, was almost a coach: he'd be thirty-six that year, and couldn't play much. Bill Dickey turned thirty-nine; he could barely bend his knees. They'd put him in to catch and (at six foot one and a half) he'd stand taller than the batters. The pitching staff was stuck together with kids. (And worse for Joe, Lefty Gomez was retired and gone.) Spud Chandler, the ace, got hurt (and just before he faced the Red Sox, who shelled him). Joe Gordon (.210!) couldn't hit at all. Rizzuto wasn't much better. Henrich had an off year, Keller was subpar . . . you could go on forever.

McCarthy started riding the White Horse hard. One trip out west, late May, there were games where McCarthy didn't even show up. When he did it was worse. On the travel leg between Cleveland and Detroit, all the guys had to stare into their laps, pretending that they didn't hear, as McCarthy stood in the airplane aisle and screamed abuse at the problem-child pitcher, Joe Page. "You know what I'm gonna do with you, don't you? I'm gonna send you down, back to the minors. How much money d'you think you'll make there? PEANUTS!" And that was just the start. McCarthy ripped into anyone he could see, or even think of—including that meddling SOB, MacPhail. When they landed, the Skipper went on a

Homeric bender, left the club, disappeared, and after
three days resigned by telegram. Dickey would be the
new manager.

It was also May when Joe noticed, rounding second one day, that pain in his heel: it wouldn't go away.
And then, about a month later—sliding into second
this time—he caught his spikes, sprained an ankle,
tore cartilage in his knee, and had to be helped off the
field. For the first time, he'd miss an All-Star Game.
(And worse, Dominic would take his place.) Joe was
only hitting .266—he would have been booed, anyway. They were booing him in the Bronx, which he
couldn't understand. *(Did they think he wasn't trying?)*

He pushed himself, came back too fast, still favor-
ing the knee, and the heel got worse. He wouldn't say
a word about that. Joe DiMaggio didn't alibi. "In my
case," he told one writer, "it generally looks as if
somebody had shortened the distance between the
plate and the box, and the pitcher is right on top of
me. The result is that when I swing, my bat is back
here when it should be out there and I'm not able to
get it out in time to meet the ball. I worry. My stroke
is off." . . . Worry was too mild a word.

He'd talk, if there was someone he could trust, who
wouldn't blab, who didn't want anything. One morning, on Chicago's South Side, the old Del Prado
Hotel, he stopped the young radio man, Mel Allen, in
the lobby. That was the first year broadcasters were

traveling with the team. (That was MacPhail, too.) "What're you doing?" Joe said.

"Uh—nothing." They had a night game, and about seven hours to kill before that.

"Come on," said DiMaggio. They sat in the coffee shop and drank coffee all afternoon. There was DiMaggio telling—almost asking—all about the troubles with Dorothy. Mel was pinching himself under the table. He was just a kid from one of those Gritsburgs in Alabama, didn't even have a girlfriend. And the great Joe DiMaggio was asking him about marriage? . . . Even fifty years later, Allen's voice held a tinge of wonder and sadness, as he recalled: "Joe was depressed. He just didn't want to be alone.

"Everybody knew they were going to get back together. And then she dumped him. And he had this kid and all. Joe had this great sense of loyalty. And the fame. . . . He hated to strike out—just put it that way."

As the summer wore on, Joe talked less. He clamped down, as if he could squeeze his life back together, if only he put on enough pressure. All he had now was baseball. But even the old baseball life was gone. There were the first night games at the Stadium, there was radio everywhere, and promotions, giveaways—like a cheap carnival. In and out of airplanes, losing, squabbling . . . the big comeback season had turned into a bad blur.

The Red Sox lead grew to double figures. Joe couldn't hit the ball out of a ballpark to save his life. That damn Ted Williams was a hundred points ahead of him. . . .

Dorothy married that moneybags, Schubert— there it was in all the papers. Well, Joe would make more money than any bastard broker. But how could he ask for a dime more, now—like this? Forget it! You had a bad year and MacPhail didn't know you. . . .

Sure enough, MacPhail wanted Gordon benched. Dickey wouldn't do it—he hated MacPhail, too. Dickey couldn't stick it out. The Yanks would get their third manager of the year: the coach Johnny Neun filled in for the last month.

The Pinstripes would finish in third place, trailing the Red Sox by a humiliating seventeen games. Joe would wind up his worst year ever, at .290, with twenty-five home runs. (Only five in the last half of the year.) Doctors told DiMaggio he'd need an operation in the off season to cut away a bone spur—that pain in his heel was a jutting shard of calcium digging into flesh.

But Joe didn't want to go under the knife. In those days, guys got an operation, maybe it worked, maybe not. He'd see if the pain eased after the season. And still he waited—he'd give it till Christmas. . . . His room at the Edison was stacked with toys for Butch, but he only saw the kid alternate weekends (Dottie's court order). . . . MacPhail had a doctor picked out at

Beth David. Probably got a deal. (Joe thought he had that bastard redhead figured out, now.)

Joe only found out later the deal that MacPhail really wanted: he tried to shuck DiMaggio off to the pitiful Washington Senators, in a trade for last year's batting champ, Mickey Vernon, who was three years younger.

And the Senators turned it down.

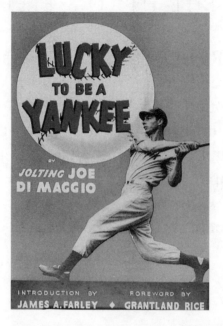

Joe's own story, written with
Tom Meany.

With "Spec" Shea: "Frankie, you pitched
a helluva game."

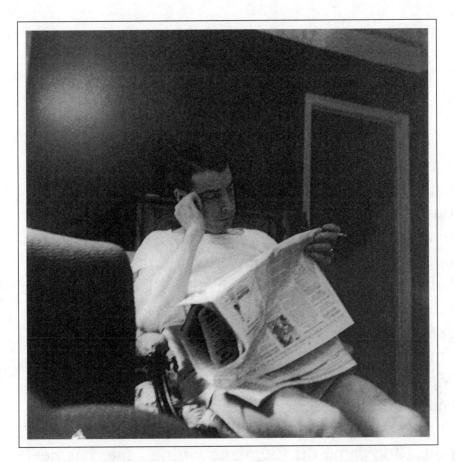

Alone at night, in Georgie Solotaire's suite.

CHAPTER 11

✦

THAT SPRING, 1947, IT WAS SAN
Juan, Puerto Rico; Caracas, Venezuela; Havana,
Cuba: MacPhail's Flying Circus was a three-ring ex-
travaganza. But *Los Yanqui de Nueva York* appeared
without *Número Cinco*. More than a month after his
operation, DiMaggio showed up with a five-and-a-
half-inch gash around his heel, still raw, and now
infected, oozing fluids. As Daniel wrote in the *World-
Telegram:* The Clipper had the "calcium chiseled
out," and it looked like that might have been the tool
MacPhail's surgeon used. The Yankees' new traveling
secretary, an eager young acolyte from Pittsburgh,
Frank Scott, picked up the Great DiMaggio at the airport. "Joe came off the plane with a cane. His heel
was grotesque. It was stitched up like a bad shoemaker had fixed it."

In San Juan, DiMaggio could only drag himself to
the ballpark—couldn't walk on the heel, much less
run or play. Sixto Escobar Field was just across the
street from the Normandie Hotel. Even so, Joe
needed a police escort: he was besieged by excited
fans, with only a carpet slipper to protect his
wounded foot. Every day, team doctors would cut

away more diseased flesh—the hole in his heel was growing. After two weeks, Joe was flown to Baltimore, and the Johns Hopkins Hospital.

The new wonder drug, penicillin, worked no magic upon the Clipper. Maggots were sown in his heel to eat away the dead skin. With opening day only a month away, the doctors at Hopkins wheeled Joe in for another operation. This time, a patch of skin from his thigh (as the AP noted, "a piece . . . the size of a Special Delivery stamp") was grafted over Joe's wound. Then, he had to lie around for two more weeks, while the doctors watched to see if the graft took.

With writers who made the pilgrimage to Baltimore, Joe put on his best Gary Cooper act (the quiet courage they expected from the successful author of *Lucky to Be a Yankee).* He joked about the skin graft. (He hoped it didn't grow hair on his heel.) He showed up in the Vanderbilts' box at Pimlico Race Track, betting with the easy élan that was expected from the hero: twenty dollars on the five horse—his number— whatever its name was.

But no one saw him awake in the wee hours, churning about his time, his season, his money. Almost as soon as he'd got back from the war, the IRS came calling. What about his income from 1942? Dorothy had the records, Joe had to scrape up the cash. He even sold out of the restaurant at Fisherman's Wharf. Of course they didn't give him what he should have gotten—his name made the place. So he fixed them good: he made brother Tom take the "Joe" off the sign (now it was just "DiMaggio's Grotto"). And he made them take off the neon baseball player at bat—even though it was Dommie who would buy out Joe's share. (That was Joe's stance!)

Ten years after he got to the majors, and he felt like he was starting from zero. Five world championships, two times MVP . . . all old news. He hadn't had a raise since the winter of '41 (Teddy Tantrum Williams was making twice Joe's pay). And at the moment, DiMaggio didn't know if he'd ever get another dime. How could he know if he would ever run on that heel? It could all be over already. How could he sleep on that? . . . When the Johns Hopkins doctors released him to travel by train to St. Petersburg, they told the writers to expect Joe in center field by June or July.

DiMaggio had other plans. There was only a little hole left in his heel. Two days after his train got to Florida, he'd ordered up a special padded shoe, and he was running. "This is my most critical year," he told Dan Daniel. "I've got to get going. I've got to make good—otherwise, where will I be? Where will I stand when it comes time to sign a contract for 1948? If it's up to me, you'll see me in there before May 1."

"Doubtless the most worried baseball player in the major leagues today is Joseph Paul DiMaggio Jr. of the Yankees," Daniel wrote on opening day. "Giuseppe sat on the bench in the Stadium while the

Bombers were celebrating Bucky Harris's debut as their manager by taking a 6-to-1 trouncing from the Athletics, undisputed candidates for the American League cellar."

The Yankee lineup was full of holes—they were in much worse shape than the year before. Henrich was hurt, and the "frightened" rookie Larry Berra was exploring the mysteries of right field. (Berra would also catch fifty games, relieving Aaron Robinson—that was an even more frightening experiment: the Yanks had to bring back Dickey to train him.) The infield didn't promise much punch: not one starter had hit over .260 the year before. The aged journeyman George McQuinn had been acquired for first base; Billy Johnson was the regular at third, and Stirnweiss, the utility man, would start at second (now that MacPhail had traded Gordon to the Clevelands for the no-name pitcher, Allie Reynolds).

This was the Yankee dynasty? . . . Nothing was settled, the team was all moving parts, and every name was still on the table. One night in Shor's, the owners of the Yankees and Red Sox, Dan Topping and Tom Yawkey, set in for a night-long drinking bout, during which they agreed to a straight swap— DiMaggio for Ted Williams. This would set the American League on its ear! The Splendid Splinter would get Yankee Stadium's short right field porch, and the Clipper could shoot for Fenway's Green Monster. They'd both break Ruth's record of sixty home runs—and both owners would be turning away fans at the gate. . . . In the morning pall of his hangover, Yawkey got cold feet—he'd be tampering with a pennant-winning club—Boston fans might kill him. He got Topping on the phone and called off the deal.

Five days into the season, the Yanks were in Philadelphia for a twin bill, when DiMaggio defied his doctors, and announced to Bucky Harris, "the boy wonder manager," that he was going back into the lineup. All he did that first game was break up the contest with a three-run homer—to show thirty-three thousand fans that the Yankees were back, starting that day. But in fact, it wasn't that easy. In the first game, the kid, Berra, bowled into right center and knocked DiMaggio on his ass. (He was roundly jeered by the A's faithful, who by that time thought of DiMaggio like some fragile Ming vase.) In the second game, one of the Yanks' rookie pitchers gave up the tying run in the ninth to bring on extra innings (which Henrich, fortunately, ended with an RBI double in the tenth). The fact was the Yanks were a .500 ball club—and even a month after the Clipper came back, every day was a struggle.

Harris was fine as a manager, easygoing in fact. But with MacPhail's fist still in the pie, it felt uneasy, like someone else's team—same as last year. Most of the pitchers (seemed like half the club) wouldn't show up for MacPhail's planes, but would hie themselves to train depots instead. When MacPhail demanded their attendance at dinners, charity events, and like promotions, a lot of guys simply didn't show.

The fourth outfielder, Johnny Lindell, told the rookies they shouldn't have to go. The new general manager, George Weiss—the kind of guy who'd lie to you just to keep in practice—now had the players tailed by detectives (to find out where they did go).

Late May, the sour bubble burst, when MacPhail sent cameramen—some "promotional newsreel" scheme Larry had—to shoot close-ups of the players, before a game. But the crew was late. DiMaggio was already in the batting cage, taking his licks. Of course, he told them where they could stick their lenses.

Well, that was too much for MacPhail. He launched a memorandum. (Didn't these boys know their contracts bound them to promote the club? MacPhail had inserted that clause himself!) . . . He would put an end to insubordination:

From now on, any man who didn't want to fly on Larry's plane could travel by rail—*at his own expense.* Meanwhile, Lindell got fined fifty dollars for telling the rookies they didn't have to show up. (Two rookies were fined twenty-five each, just for listening to Lindell.) Keller and Robinson would be fined fifty bucks each, for declining to pose for Larry's "newsreel." DiMaggio, as exemplar, got the big ticket: a hundred-dollar fine, to be docked from his pay.

And that was the turning point: every man in that clubhouse looked to DiMaggio to see what the Big Guy would do. And DiMaggio did nothing—didn't say a word. Writers milked the story for days—no, they tried for *weeks:* this *emotional affront* could wreck the Clipper's year, and the Yankees' chances. (You know, this could be like the missus dumping him—this guy's a stew inside!) . . . But DiMaggio acted like it wasn't worth talk.

What he did was his job: if he worried, it was about the job; if he talked, it was about the job. The job was winning. The players understood first: DiMaggio would not let a game end with a loss. Over the next two weeks, he hit for an average of .468, with six home runs, four of them game-winners. In the first series after the fines were levied, DiMaggio wrecked the hated Red Sox—nine-for-sixteen in a four-game Yankee sweep. The next week, in Cleveland, it was four hits and two home runs (one a grand slam) in a single game (a Yankee win, of course). At the next stop—with the league leaders, Detroit—DiMaggio had seven straight hits to put his name atop the list of AL batters, and haul the Yanks onto the Tigers' neck—only two games back.

It wasn't just what he did at the plate. His perfection in the middle of the defense anchored the machinery: suddenly, the Yanks were playing as a team. Berra only had to learn one thing about right field: "If I hear your voice," DiMaggio said, "the ball is yours." Berra could follow the logic: stay away from DiMag. "You had to play offa him," was the way Yogi put it. When Henrich came back, things were even smoother. "If I want the ball," as Henrich recalled, "then I call for it. And DiMaggio gives it to me every time. . . . But if I didn't open my mouth, get out of the way. Because that ball ain't going to drop. DiMaggio knows he's home free. Get out of his way, because he's going to get it."

With DiMaggio behind them, pitchers had a similar certainty. Spec Shea, who would become an All-Star as a rookie, remembered DiMaggio in center like faith in his own heart. "Joe's pet thing was: 'Make 'em hit the ball in the air. . . . I'll catch 'em.' "

That's just what Spec could do.

"It would be goin' over the shortstop's head, I'd say to myself: 'Get goin', Joe.' And I'd turn around and there'd be that big gazelle. Boy, he took them big strides, you know. And when he'd catch it, he'd catch it just so easy. There was nothin' to it."

When Spec couldn't do it just right, Joe would sit him down for another little talk.

" 'You know, we had a meeting before the game and you said you were going to pitch this guy inside,' " DiMaggio would scold him. " 'You pitched him outside a couple of times. And you had the outfield in the wrong position, the infield in the wrong position. And, therefore, we let that ball get through us in the infield and we had to break our necks to get over to keep him from going to two bases—because you made the wrong kind of a pitch!'

"And, I'd say, 'Well, the ball got away from me.'

" 'It shouldn't get away from you! You're in the major leagues now. You're here. And this is where you gotta do these things perfect.' "

The point that every player got was, DiMaggio expected them to play like he did. McCarthy was gone.
Joe was the senior man on the field. He was the
keeper of the old-time religion. Maybe he would
make them winners, maybe not. But he'd sure as hell
make them Yankees. . . . No mistakes!

What DiMaggio gave to that team was his person—literally, in the case of Joe Page. Here was a
pitcher who had everything he needed: talent, size,
power—a fastball that could knock the bat right out
of an opponent's hands. No one knew where Page's
fastball was going to move. Alas, Page didn't know
either. And the way he thought, he'd never get it over,
he'd never make the right pitch, he'd screw things up
. . . to make it short: Page was a head case. He was
also sure that all the other Pinstripes reviled him—as
McCarthy had—as a guy who'd never make it as a
Yankee. And Page made his own predictions come
true: he'd drink till he was blind, drink ugly. (He'd oc-
cupy two or three of Weiss's detectives all by himself.) And sure enough, he wouldn't be worth a shit
for his next start. . . . Even the mild Bucky Harris
had to demote Page to the bullpen. Page, of course,
figured his next stop would be back to the coal mines.
Then, DiMaggio took him as his road roomie. Page
became Joe's project, his number one hang-around
buddy—and his number one gofer.

See, Gomez was gone, and there was no one to
take care of the Dago—run out for his papers, get
him a beer, stay with him on the street . . . DiMaggio

needed someone to protect him. Page was perfect: he had no friends, except DiMag. If he wasn't with DiMaggio, the only thing you'd hear him say was, "Where's Daig? Did anybody see the Dago come through here?" If Joe went to a movie, Page had to go, too. If Joe was going to sit around a hotel lobby, Page had the next chair. He dressed like DiMaggio—carried a trunk, with a dozen suits and as many pairs of custom-made shoes. And of course he had to superintend Dago's bag, too. In the clubhouse, they made up names for Page: "The Shadow," "The Porter," or "Joe's Bobo." Page would never answer back. He'd be busy at his locker (next to Joe's)—boning Joe's bats.

"It was a strange, pathetic relationship on Page's part," wrote the *New York Post* beat writer, Milton Gross. But there was something DiMaggio was doing for Page that perhaps the others didn't see. At the Stadium one day, the Red Sox menaced a Yankee lead with two men on and nobody out, when Harris called Page in from the bullpen to face the fearsome Ted Williams. Page strode in, handcuffed the heart of the Red Sox order—three outs, inning over . . . Page was out of the doghouse. The other Yankees couldn't believe it. The Problem Child started mowing 'em down. He became the American League's number one reliever—fifty-six appearances and fourteen wins. Page was unhittable, and more: he became a threat that every other team had to fear. He became the man that the Yankees and their fans could depend on. What he'd absorbed from DiMaggio was the faith: Joe Page could be a hero.

That's what DiMag gave back to the Yanks, that year. It was the sense of what they could be. Spec Shea lived in the Edison Hotel, too, and he went to school on DiMaggio all year. "I used to go to the fights with him and Milton Berle and Toots Shor and them. Joe used to bring me along. He'd say, 'Come on, we'll go to fights.' I'd say, 'Where are you going to get the tickets?' He'd say, 'Don't worry about the tickets.' We'll have them, you know. . . .

"And on the way up, he'd see somebody on the side of the road, and he'd say: 'You see that, Frank?' (He always called me Frank, never called me Spec.) 'You see that? That guy could never be in the Yankee organization, because he wouldn't live up to the standard. You got to live up to the standard.'

"He told me, he said, 'One thing you always got to remember'—he used to tell me all the time: 'If you're going to do something, do it so it's done perfectly right or don't do it at all.' And, boy, I'll tell you what, he was a great guy. A real great guy."

Frank was another special case with DiMaggio. For one thing, Shea (in his new Hudson) would drive Joe every morning, from the hotel at Times Square, up to the Stadium in the Bronx. They'd breakfast in the hotel—Joe would always pick up the tab. What the hell, it was cheaper than a cab. Then Frank would bring the car around:

"Which way we goin' today, Joe?"

"Let's take the West Side Highway, Frank."

Frank would head for the highway, Joe would open his mail. "He'd open up a check from Chesterfield cigarettes, for like twenty-five hundred, or from a T-shirt company for fifteen hundred. And one morning, I remember: ninety-two hundred dollars he got in checks that day. Most of the rookies were makin' like five thousand. He got more than any one of us ever made for two years."

When Joe walked into the locker room, it was like the lights came on, as if a voice on the PA had announced: *the team is here.* Of course, he was impeccable: not just in a suit and tie, but the best suit and tie in America. He had a pal from Seventh Avenue who'd make the suits—whatever Joe wanted—and his tailor, of course, to put the finishing touches. And no hat: might obscure the face. It was funny about that face: the same features that had seemed so sharp and outsized in '36—now he'd grown into them, they gave him distinction. A committee of artists actually named him on a list of America's "ten most interesting faces." But it wasn't just the nose, the chin: what they saw was something that had marked DiMaggio even while he was a hatchet-faced boy. It was the composure—that sufficiency in his face—he needed no one to tell him who he was.

He'd stride in, across the new carpeted clubhouse, with the paper under his arm. If there were fellows already getting dressed, Joe wouldn't stop. "Good morning." "Good morning, Tom," he'd say as he passed—like an executive greeting secretaries on the way to his office. By the time he had his coat hung perfectly (now, it wasn't just the old metal lockers—the Yankees had new wire-mesh cubicles—big, like a closet), Pete Sheehy would be running with the "half-a-cuppa-coffee." Joe didn't have to ask, anymore.

DiMaggio would sit in his undershirt with his half-a-cup and a smoke, one leg thrown over the other. He'd open up the paper. The other players would sneak glances, to see if Dago was gonna say anything. They'd never talk to him first. Mostly they'd see his broad back—thick with muscle, like the withers of a racehorse—"like a dome of muscle," as one Yankee described it. Other players would filter in, attending to their rituals and chores. There was a big table in the center of the room, with boxes of baseballs arrayed. Those were for the club, the owners, or some bigwigs. All the players had to sign them, except for the Dago. Pete Sheehy would sign for DiMaggio—perfect, just like Joe's grade school script.

The Big Guy could sit in stillness till he was ready to visit the trainer, get himself taped. After that, it was BP. Joe hit first. When Joe stepped into the cage, that's when BP started. The pitchers all knew: Joe wanted the ball on the inside half, pecker high. Anything else, he'd let it go by. Players on opposing teams would linger in their dugout to watch him drive a few balls into the left field stands. Other Yankees, once they took their licks, they'd run to the outfield to shag some flies. DiMaggio would sit in the dugout shade. He knew how to catch. And he didn't need any extra throws. His arm was hurting him enough already. After BP, the Yanks would return to the clubhouse, to put on fresh shirts—crisp, clean, like Yankees. Then, they could come out for the game: all the players, and then, DiMaggio.

"Joe came out last, so he'd be alone," his old sandlot pal Lodigiani noticed. "And all the people sayin', 'There goes DiMaggio.' 'That's Joe DiMaggio!' He made it a point to come out last, see."

But that was part of his job, too: to be Joe DiMaggio. If he gave the Yankees back their swagger, he also taught them how to back it up. Around the All-Star break, Joe hit safely in twenty-five of twenty-seven games. In one three-week stretch, he averaged .493. The Pinstripes took over first place in mid-June—and they didn't just rest there. From June 19 to July 17, DiMaggio's Yankees won nineteen straight. No team had ever done that, since the Cubs in the year Nineteen Ought-Six.

The Yanks ran so far out in front that when his legs swelled up and started hurting, DiMaggio agreed he would sit out a week or two in the August heat. But he hated being forced to the bench—made him feel like a cursed nobody. "I wonder if I ever will play again," Daniel quoted Joe, when the idleness got to him. "It seems as if a jinx has set out to ruin me."

The Yankees clinched by September 15—they'd finish twelve games up on Detroit, fourteen games ahead of Boston. Still, in September, there was DiMaggio, pounding across the grass in center field. See, it was on that field where the self-possession came to him. That was where perfection started. One time, Jimmy Cannon asked Joe why he was out there every day, when the pennant was all locked up, the games didn't mean a thing. Why was he pushing himself so hard? As Cannon quoted Joe: "I always think, there might be someone out there in the stands who's never seen me play."

Millions saw him for the first time that October: the first televised World Series. Joe DiMaggio was everywhere—in that little box!—at the same time he was in the Bronx, playing the Dodgers! In East Harlem, that famous future cop, Sonny Grosso, was coming home from school when a guy from the corner tavern invited him in to see Game One. . . . "It wasn't in nobody's house. But this guy had, like, an experimental television. And I remember, trying to figure out how I was seeing this game that was being played as I was seeing it. I could not comprehend that." When Sonny told his friends, no one believed him. But the doubters soon saw for themselves the new glowing engine for the hero machine.

In New York, that Series was a fever of excitement. The 1947 Brooklyn Dodgers were a formidable outfit, with their rookie star, Jackie Robinson, the most talked-about man in the nation. They had speed, defense, pitching—and they had something to prove. (No Dodger team had ever been champs.) . . . But in

Yankee Stadium, they would have to face a team without doubt.

In the first game, the Brooklyn ace, Ralph Branca, had matters all his own way—a no-hitter till the fifth—when DiMaggio beat out a ball to deep short, and the Yankees were awakened to score five runs that put the game away. In Game Two, the Yanks beat a tattoo on four Brooklyn pitchers, while the Yankees' Allie Reynolds struck out twelve—Yanks 10, Brooklyn 3. The Bombers looked to have a grip on the Series, two games to none.

But when the teams moved across the city, to Ebbets Field, Brooklyn clawed back. In Game Three, DiMaggio hit a single and a homer, knocked in three runs—but it wasn't enough. The Pinstripes used up five pitchers in a 9–8 loss. The fourth game could have been a crusher for the Yankees, when their big right-hander, Bill Bevens, took a no-hitter into the ninth, and then lost the game on a two-out Cookie Lavagetto double that drove in the winner for Brooklyn.

With the Series even 2–2, and the fifth game scheduled, once again, for Ebbets Field, advantage swung to the Dodgers. But DiMaggio made his own odds: he crashed a fifth-inning homer, while Spec Shea threw a four-hitter, for a squeaky 2–1 Yankee win. Joe was so happy in the clubhouse ("Frankie, you pitched a hell of a game!") that he posed for pictures, giving Shea a kiss on the cheek.

In Game Six, there were six Yankee pitchers in an

alley fight in the Bronx. It was 2–0 Brooklyn, 4–0 Brooklyn, 4–4, 5–4 Yankees, and by the sixth inning, 8–5 Brooklyn. In the bottom of the sixth, the Jolter got his chance to do that one big thing that would break the will of the other team. With two on and one out, he came up against Brooklyn's premier left-hander, the seventeen-game winner Joe Hatten. DiMaggio smashed a high line drive straight for the 415 sign, where a low chain link fence walled off the Dodger bullpen from the outfield. You could say he had launched the game-tying homer right at the Dodger pitchers out there: *Here! You boys keep this one for a souvenir!* . . . As DiMaggio rounded first, he could see the outfielder Al Gionfriddo dancing a spirited tarantella—unsure where to run, which way to turn, how to get under the ball. Joe was digging for second base, when Gionfriddo, in an act of God, stumbled under the ball, stuck his glove over the wire fence, and—*Cazzo! Figlio di putana!*—stole the home run away from DiMaggio. Seventy thousand fans in the ballpark and three million watching that miraculous little box saw DiMaggio do what he'd never done before. In frustration—disbelief—he kicked at the dirt in the basepath near second. The sports pages wrote it up like the Pope had pissed on the floor of St. Peter's.

"The Catch" might not have burned Joe up, if Gionfriddo hadn't been out of position, clueless in that outfield, and a busher in the first place . . . but he was, he was, he was. And this was Joe's ballpark. That was his moment. This Series was his stage. After the game, he didn't answer questions, and told the photographers: no pictures. The next day, when one cameraman asked Joe to autograph a picture of that home run theft, DiMaggio snarled him away: "Whyn'cha get the other guy? He made the catch."

That was the day of the seventh game, with everything on the line. Joe didn't get one hit—not even a loud foul. The Brooklyns jumped out to a 2–0 lead, but the Yanks kept banging away at the weary Dodger staff: a single run in the second, two in the fourth, one in the sixth, one in the seventh—they scratched their way to a lead of 5–2. Problem was, the Yankee pitching staff was all but played out, too. MacPhail had offered a thousand-dollar bonus to any pitcher who could make the start. Spec Shea took the challenge—but he only lasted one and a third. Then Bad Luck Bevens got a measure of revenge: he shut down the Dodgers for two and two thirds. By the fifth inning, Bevens was spent, too. And the skipper, Bucky Harris, went to the best man he had. For the fourth time in that Series, Joe Page strode in from the Yankee bullpen. He started in the fifth, got through the sixth. In the press box the writers were asking aloud—how long could he go? Page threw the seventh inning, then the eighth—Brooklyn still scoreless against him, the Yanks holding on at 5–2. On guts alone, Page pitched the ninth, all fastballs—and Brooklyn never could touch him. For five innings, he had stopped the Dodgers with one hit. Joe Page was the man who won the World Series—he was the hero.

And in the clubhouse after, that was his moment. They mobbed him, poured drinks on him, they kissed him (and not just for pictures). Scores of writers surrounded Page, yelling questions: *How'dya get through it? How'dya keep going?* . . . Page said it was because of the Big Guy—there, at the next locker.

"I knew I had to do it for Joe."

Topping, Webb, and MacPhail rented the ballroom of the Waldorf for a grand celebration. Now the war was really over, all was right with the world: the New York Yankees were champions again. . . . The place was all aglitter, a big swing band playing, more champagne than you could drink, and everybody in their finest—wives, too, if you had one to bring. And right at the beginning, the party kicked into high gear when MacPhail announced he was selling out his shares in the club. Just like that—MacPhail was *gone.* So the guys all relaxed and really had a good time.

"Maybe two hours into the party," as Spec Shea recalled, "the big doors open up. And there's majestic Joe DiMaggio. Right there, with two broads—two blondes—one on each arm. They're about two inches taller than he is. And he's six foot one. They were beautiful women. They walked in with him, all dolled up in nice evening clothes and everything, and walked over to a table which they had reserved for him.

"And he called all the guys over, and he was introducin' them to, you know, the girls and everything. And it turned out to be a gala affair, I'll tell you. Because everybody, you know, that wanted to dance, or something, the girls were there and Joe didn't care whether you danced with them or not."

(Spec maybe didn't just mean, you know, dance.)

"But he had a good time, that night, too. . . . Oh, Joe was very happy, very happy."

**Sinat, Toots, and Joe admire the
new portrait.**

Joe and Joe Jr. grace the
first issue of *Sport*.

Yankee Stadium: the hero,
alone.

Exiting the hospital,
on crutches, in
camel hair.

CHAPTER 12

◆

FOR THE SECOND EDITION OF *LUCKY to Be a Yankee,* Joe brought Tom Meany back to make a few revisions. The first thing was to take out all that bullcrap about Dorothy telling him how to hit. But there was also an addition to the text—a new foreword by the popular New Deal postmaster general, James A. Farley. He was a Toots Shor pal, and the reigning boss of New York politics.

Farley wrote that DiMaggio's book told the story of America. Because of his ability to play ball, Joe not only saved himself from the hard life of a fisherman, he enabled his father to stay off the boat and take it easy, too. Farley might have put at risk a few votes from fishing folk, but he was no slouch at gauging a mood. Depression was gone, the war was history: people didn't want to hear about hard times anymore. We were at peace, strong and rich. And right on cue, here was our hero, the exemplar of power, wealth, ease: America had found her first Broadway Joe.

In New York, where everything big happened, every event was bigger, big-time, when DiMaggio was there. The only men who could match him for size in the public imagination were the great prize-fighters. But even with a boxing crowd, Joe might have outranked them all. In '48, when Rocky Graziano fought Tony Zale for the middleweight title, Frank Sinatra walked into the packed arena to polite applause. Walter Winchell, the nation's most famous newshound, got a few cheers, too. Then, suddenly—as Mel Allen described it:

"There was heard a vocal outburst from one of the distant entrances. You knew, of course, that some noted personage was arriving. All eyes and ears were trained and strained on the sector, as the mingled applause and cheering, like a raging forest fire fanned by a brisk breeze, increased in crescendo until it became a single contagious roar. Is it Jack Dempsey? Is it Gene Tunney? Is it Joe Louis? No? Well, this one time it can't be Superman. But it was the nearest thing in sports clothes to that legendary hero. It was Joe DiMaggio."

It never mattered who else was there—Joe was the Big Name. One time, Ernest Hemingway accompanied DiMaggio to the fights. Maybe Joe was hoping the novelist would protect him. Didn't work: fans were on Joe all night. One guy finished gushing on the Jolter, and then he saw Hemingway: "You're somebody, too—aren't you?" With a nod toward Joe, Hemingway said: "Yeah, I'm his doctor."

Of course, that found its way into print: Big Names were news. Put a couple of beauties together, like the Clipper and Papa (the Clipper and whoever) and it didn't matter exactly what they did. Mostly they were enjoying themselves. People liked to read about Big Names having big times. Now, the nation's readers were just as likely to get the latest on DiMag from the nightlife columns as they were from the sports page. Joe went to a club to hear some singer—that was an item. Joe was in some restaurant for a bowl of spaghetti—that was an item, too. If there was a broad across the table, that was a headliner. That's one reason Joe always wanted a guy to go around with him. The protection he needed wasn't just from fans.

It wasn't that he begrudged the columnists: he didn't mind his name in the paper. And, hell, he'd known them all for years: Winchell, Len Lyons, that nosy Kilgallen broad; even the battle-ax, Louella Parsons, used to write up Joe like an old friend. But the problem was he couldn't be sure what they'd write. And their cameramen, *at any moment,* firing away with the flashbulbs—*what if Joe didn't want that picture? . . .* That's why a guy like Peanuts came in so handy. They weren't going to write about Peanuts— Jimmy Who?—if he got loud, showed a temper, told some photographer to go fuck himself. Joe would never have to raise his voice—and never have to ask for a break. Joe DiMaggio didn't ask for favors.

Peanuts was faithful and he'd do anything. Joe liked to have a car at spring training, but why should he drive all the way to Florida? So, Joe could fly, or ride the train. Peanuts would drive Joe's Cadillac down. Or say there was someplace Joe shouldn't go: to be precise, someplace Joe shouldn't be seen. For instance, there was the dog track near St. Pete, where of course there was betting. And of course, the commissioner of baseball didn't want to see any players in there. Joe wouldn't go in. Instead, he'd have Peanuts park the Caddy outside the fence on the backstretch—whence Joe could see fine. If the Clipper wanted to bet, Peanuts could run in, put a couple of bills on the five-dog. No problem.

The road secretary of the Yankees, Frank Scott, was even better for certain tight spots Joe ran into. Frank was a college man—the University of Pittsburgh was where he'd fallen in love with sports. And he had manners, an eager affability that smoothed out some situations (where rough-house from Peanuts only would have made things worse). There was, for example, the night in St. Pete—spring training '48—when Joe got trapped in his room at the team hotel. The Hotel Soreno was one of those elegant pastel piles, built in the 1920s, when the truly rich and newly rich all came down for the winter season. The Yankees had used the place since old Col. Ruppert's day, and of course they were expected to act like proper guests.

Joe had been properly Joltin' a showgirl named Gregg Sherwood on and off for some time. Pretty girl. No big deal. He was friendly with a lot of girls. He might even have had one in his room that night. That wasn't the problem. The problem was, Gregg Sherwood was not in the room. She was in the hall outside Joe's door, slammin'-off-the-walls drunk, and yelling at the top of her lungs. Scott was awakened at two A.M. by a call from the hotel manager. He ran for Joe D.'s room . . . and there was Gregg, on her knees, arched against the door like a parenthesis—her belly at mid-curve, pressuring the wood. That and her fists, as she pounded and screamed: "Goddammit, Joe! I'll do anything you want, Joe—LET ME IN! . . ." Well, if Frank hadn't had those manners, he could have got maimed by Ms. Sherwood's fingernails as he pried her, yowling, off the door, and cleaned up the mess outside Joe's room. Of course, the Clipper never had to come out, or say a word. Frank wouldn't say a word, either. That would have made an item, sure—would have been embarrassing for DiMag. And it was Frank's job to take care of the Big Guy.

In Frank's case, that was more than a job: he did it for love. Or you could say, he was in love with the job—the most exciting he'd ever had, the most exciting he could even think of. He was the kind of guy who never was big enough, fast enough, strong enough to play—so he helped out the coach. That's how he'd started, at Pitt, just a few years before. And to think, now, the Great DiMaggio would ask him, Frank, if he would come along to the movies, or sit and have breakfast, or walk with him, help him out with a crowd . . . well, that was Frank's dream come true—even if there had been no paycheck. In fact, the following year, when the GM, George Weiss, would take away Frank's job (just because he wasn't Weiss's own man), Scott would become the first professional sports agent. Not for contracts with the team—agents were still taboo there. But he'd work out endorsement deals, appearance fees, that sort of thing. He'd take care of DiMaggio for the next four decades. (And the dream was still coming true: for forty years he'd never get a paycheck from the Jolter, either.)

Things went even smoother for DiMag once the team moved up to New York, where a network of helpers and protectors was on alert, full-time, for the Clipper. In those days, the network coordinator was Solotaire. By '48, Gentleman George had moved Joe out of the Edison, and (talk about full-time!) into his own suite at the Elysee Hotel. That way, Georgie could take care of things more efficiently—pick up the Jolter's cleaning, or bring him a nice sandwich from the Stage Delicatessen, or make sure that no one who was out to take advantage could get close to DiMag. See, Solotaire knew more people than Joe would ever meet in his life. George got along with almost all—but he could always tell who wanted what. In their sitting room at the Elysee, Georgie and Joe would talk into the wee hours—in a casual way, they were refining their list: who was an asshole.

In general, refinement was the way George helped out with the business of being DiMaggio. Not that Solotaire spoke like the Duke of Windsor, or knew the best years of Bordeaux. But in the business of stardom, he was a sophisticate. Here was the man to handle a columnist—Georgie knew the Big Name game better than any writer. He could trade with them: he'd give 'em two Gwen Verdons, if they'd clean up one item about DiMag. But with Georgie it was more than practical protection: he understood what Joe wanted, what Joe had to be. He understood living up to the standard: everything about Joe ought to look like a million bucks. Solotaire also brought discernment to the ticklish topic of women. After all the years on Broadway, he knew every working showgirl—better still, he knew the girls who were out of work, might have some time. He was always alert to possibilities for the Clipper, who liked a nice frisky looker, blond, young, who didn't mind a bit of inconstancy. Solotaire knew how to disappear, if Joe and the girl were going to, you know, stay in. And of course George would go along, if Joe and the girl were going to go out. Joe would want someone along to talk.

Naturally, there were times George was tied up. (He'd have a review to rhyme on opening night, say; or he'd have to be at the office, or at home—he did have the wife and kid.) So Joe would let some other guys take him to lunch: there was Ben Barzone, the tie salesman; Harry Moss, the blind jeweler; Henry Blank, who'd close his garment firm and take Joe around all afternoon. They'd buy. And they'd sit for hours, and talk about him: "That homer in the fifth game, Joe. I knew you'd do it—but that was really a thrill. . . ." At night, Joe could always take his ease at Toots's, or he'd ask Jimmy Cannon to go along to some other joints. (That was perfect: Cannon talked all the time.) Or on the off chance Cannon was absent, there'd be some other pal, who'd drop his own plans for the evening. To be in the network, you could put nothing ahead of the Dago.

One guy who'd drop it all for the Jolter was Lou Effrat, a sports writer for the *Times*. How Louie ever hooked on with the Great Gray Lady of 43rd Street was a mystery of the newspaper business. He was a Brooklyn boy, largely unlettered, a wiseacre, a gambler. If he came to the Stadium to fill in for Jim Dawson (the regular *Times*man on the Yanks), Louie's primary interest was in asking every trainer in the league about his own bad back. ("Trouble with my sacroiliac . . .") Professionally and personally, he was most at home at the track (thoroughbreds in the afternoon, trotters in the evening), where he was affectionately known as Tap-Out, on account of his prodigious losing. Louie didn't lose just often, but legendarily. He bet one horse who, while leading around the final turn, fell down dead. In reaction, Louie uttered one of his most famous laments: "I bet not to win, but to live."

He was a fount of one-liners, as much quoted as he was beloved. His style was strictly New York street-smart: very hard to impress. He might, for example, pause in the doorway of a recital hall, where some twelve-year-old Chinese prodigy was demonstrating her virtuosity on the violin. Louie, who couldn't even whistle, would turn away and shrug: "Eh! A Heifetz she's not." . . . But the Dago, the Big Guy, that was another matter. DiMaggio hung the moon, and scattered the stars, and shone like the sun, and—well, mostly, it was that DiMag picked Lou for a friend.

Here was palship: say, for example, the Clipper was at Shor's, when some broad would be brought to his table to meet the Great DiMaggio. Joe would modestly shake her hand—that was all . . . until he called for Lou. When Effrat got to Joe's corner, DiMaggio would murmur, "See that blonde in the black dress? Take her to the late show at El Morocco. Tell the maître d' you're at my table." Louie would race to a phone and call Brooklyn—eleven P.M. or midnight—he'd wake his wife, Alice: "I'll be late. I'm going out with the Dago!" She knew he'd have to squire some girl around for DiMaggio. But she didn't protest. She could hear the fever in his voice. Then, Lou would leave with the girl. ("Joe will be along to meet us, in a while . . .") Sure, there might be a columnist—photographers for sure—working the floor at El Morocco. But if anybody asked, it wasn't Joe had a date with the girl. No, Effrat had the date.

When the Yankees would leave town for a western trip—St. Louis, Chicago, Cleveland, Detroit—sometimes Lou would be away for two weeks. Alice and the other wives in Brooklyn would get dressed up, the day the boys were coming back: they'd go to Manhattan ("into the city," as they said in Flatbush); they'd all meet for dinner at Shor's. Joe would be on the banquette in his corner. Lou and Alice would be sitting at some unranked table in the middle of the dining room—and just about to tuck into their steaks, when a waiter would approach with a whisper for Louie: "He wants you." Nothing more: three words. Lou would trot to the corner, where DiMaggio would speak to him briefly. Lou would tell Alice what Joe said, later: "Get rid of her." . . . Meantime, she knew, from the moment that waiter appeared: she was going back to Brooklyn in a cab—and soon. Lou would bustle her out to the curb. "He needs me."

How could Alice complain? Lou would always come home. They weren't just married, but locked together for life—ever since she was fourteen, and running into a house, late for a high school sorority meeting . . . when she fell on her face. She'd tripped over Louie, who was on his knees in the hall, shooting craps. She knew his friendship with the Great Man was the most glorious thing in Lou's life—his distinction. Effrat dined out for years on the story of his visit to DiMag at the Elysee. He was talking to Joe about a trip to Florida, when Louie reached for the ashtray, and—*Wouff!*—his sacroiliac went out again.

"Lay me down! Lay me down! Jesus! Just get me on the floor . . . Ooh! Oufff!"

The Dago says, uh, he's got an appointment.

"That's okay, Joe. Lemme lie here. Just don't move me! I won't bother anything."

DiMaggio says: "Look Lou, sick or what, you gotta get out." Then, as Lou told it in his memoir, *I Was There:*

"Suddenly, the doorbell rang and in walked a beautiful showgirl friend of Joe's. . . ."

Beautiful? *She was a knockout*—with her nylons near, at Lou's eye level, her perfume wafting in his ample nostrils. Dago's got better things to do than tend to him—Lou understood. But there he was, in the middle of the floor in his soup-stained sports coat. *Ahhgg!* . . . He couldn't move.

Well, it all ended happily. Daig and the girl closed the door to the other room. Three hours later, Joe and Peanuts carried Lou out to the elevator. Tom Meany wrote the yarn up for laughs—but Meany changed the girl into Joe's accountant: DiMag had an appointment with his CPA. . . .

That was the part Joe didn't like about pals. No matter who the guy was, sooner or later he'd want something. Louie was in the suite that day trying to get Joe in on some junket to Florida—charity for sick kids, something like that. *Second year in a row, Lou was asking.* . . . Of course, Joe said he didn't want to go. Then, Louie said: "If you don't come, I don't get the trip!" People acted like Joe owed them.

The thing they couldn't seem to keep in mind: an appearance by DiMaggio was valuable—money in the bank. By '48, it was literally money in the Bowery Bank, where Joe's mob friends had established a trust account for his benefit. Here's how the system worked: say Joe did end up, with some photogenic broad on his arm, at El Morocco for the late show—or at the Copacabana, the Stork Club, or the Cotton Club. That was promotion, it gave the place class. Of course, he was never going to see a tab. That went without saying. But shouldn't Joe get something for lending the glamour of his presence? Sure, he should. . . . So all the managers of all the clubs knew, if the Clipper made an appearance, they should put a little something—say, a couple hundred bucks—into the trust account, next day. It was the gentlemanly thing to do; it fostered goodwill; it was clean and quiet.

All those clubs (and a dozen more) were mob-run, mob-owned, or they had mob money in the mix. Didn't matter whose name was on the license: every one of those clubs, one way or the other, was under the protection or control of Frank Costello—and he was fond of Joe. He was proud of Joe. DiMaggio was exactly the kind of Italian-American hero who should be put forward—especially in light of the terrible publicity that Italian-American business was getting. It seemed, by 1948, a proud Italian business-man could hardly do anything at all without some government snoops taking an unhealthy interest. Even J. Edgar Hoover, who was an old pal, now acquiesced in the witch-hunt on "organized crime." Hoover couldn't let the reputation of his outfit slip. In those days, FBI meant "Forever Bothering Italians."

DiMaggio had to be extra-quiet: the commissioner of baseball had his snoops, too. That's why it was a trust account: all the money for Joe would be at his disposal after his retirement from the Great Game. Until then he could say (truthfully), he never had a dime from "unsavory elements"—those other Big Names who were news for all the wrong reasons.

And that's why it had to be the Bowery. That was the bank of choice for all the Names in town. Not just for the mob—politicians did their business at the Bowery, too. All the big boys from Tammany Hall (Jim Farley's men) had their nest eggs there. (Unless they were from Brooklyn—then it was the Dime Savings Bank.) Tammany was the Bowery's protection. In those days (with Democrats always in the White House) New York never had to suffer federal intrusion. Even when there was some huge scandal, New York would take care of its own investigations. Some Blue Ribbon Panel would be empowered from Albany—noisily, with fanfare: hearings might go on for years. . . . But somehow, despite all the furious sweeping "to clean house," the Blue Ribbon brooms never reached into the Bowery. (As the bank's most famous pitchman would later assure us, money at the Bowery was "safe and sound.")

Joe let those thousands and tens of thousands pile up, untouched, and for the most part unmonitored. He didn't want to know more than he needed to; he couldn't know anybody he ought not to. Sometimes, DiMaggio would depute the mannerly Frank Scott to talk to some big mobster (especially the Jewish mobsters—Big Abe, or Meyer Lansky), to ask them not to pal up to Joe so publicly. "Don't ever say I don't want to talk to them," the Clipper would remind Scott. "Just say I don't think this is the place to meet." But Costello—"the brain" of the New York syndicate— understood perfectly. So, late at night, when Solo-

taire and Joe would reconvene at the Elysee, Georgie
might mention, by and by: "Oh, and I saw Frank. He
said to tell you he appreciates everything you been
doing. He's watching closely. And he wanted me to
pass on his respects."

Joe understood the bargain perfectly, too. Or to put
it another way: he understood the bargain with perfection. He could have honor, our adulation, the
glory of the Big Name . . . he could have men to sit
with him, take him around, buy for him, do for him
. . . he could have any woman he fancied—fresh or
famous—and no questions asked . . . he could have
all the money he needed, and a tidy pile left over,
growing in a dark place. He understood: *we would
give him anything*—if he would always be the hero
we required.

AT LAST, THE YANKEES HAD ALSO
concluded, DiMag was money in the bank. Postwar
prosperity had doubled attendance at the Stadium:
the '47 club that brought the World Series rings back
to the Bronx had also brought in two million fans. In
January 1948, DiMaggio got his first raise since before the war. Seventy thousand dollars a year would
leave only Feller and Ted Williams ahead of him. And
among his own coterie, Joe vowed to overtake
Williams soon. "He may out-homer me," Joe told
Lou Effrat. "But I will out-percentage him, I can out-
throw him, I can out-run him, and out-think him."

Another operation before that '48 season took loose chips of calcium out of Joe's elbow. Maybe his throwing arm would finally be right again. The spur in his left heel was just a small hole in the flesh: nothing to keep Joe from digging in at the plate. And the ball was jumping off his bat with a glad *thwack*—heard from a million radios. First series of the year, in Washington, D.C.: DiMaggio loosed a blistering throw from center field to snuff Mickey Vernon at third base. In the same game he hit a monster home run—maybe the longest in Griffith Stadium history (and that went back to 1911). DiMaggio told an AP writer that Ted Williams had better watch out for his batting crown: a .350 average should capture that title—Joe DiMaggio's .350. "I'm really looking forward to a fine year, one of my best."

For the public DiMaggio that was a remarkable speech—as near as he'd ever get to thumping his chest. He was in high spirits: he was on his way to New York to receive his award as last year's MVP, in front of an adoring crowd at the home opener. Even so, you could hardly say DiMaggio was culpable of baring his pride in the public prints. What Joe wanted for himself wasn't just to finish ahead of Ted Williams, a batting title, a .350 year. His ambition couldn't be described with a line of numbers in a record book. He wanted to be, in any year, any town, on any day, any field—in every game, on every play, no matter who else was there—the best player in the park. He wanted to be the man in whose hands the fate of the game would rest.

He expected to deliver that game, every game, to his team. He expected to dominate, not by doing something right but by doing everything right. Here was the difference between Ted Williams and DiMaggio: Ted wanted to be the greatest hitter who ever lived (and at times, he was cruelly mocked for saying so). But Joe's ambition was more astonishing: he wanted to be perfect, not at something but everything—to abide, in other words, as a god.

And more amazing was how close he came. That was the springtime when the New York press elevated DiMaggio off the ballfield, to hover in the pantheon of general genius. "A Cezanne with a finger-mitt, a Van Gogh with a Louisville Slugger," the *World-Telegram* columnist Joe Williams called him. And that was a near consensus among the New York critics. The harbingers of physical breakdown, the reminders that DiMaggio was working all this while with only a mortal body, like theirs . . . made his story somehow more prodigious, with an elegiac edge of sadness that pushed the writers over the top. That was also the time when the elegant Red Smith, of the *Herald Tribune,* received his only reprimand from the sports editor, Stanley Woodward. "Walter!" said Woodward, peering over Smith's copy, and freezing him (as a parent would), with his given name. "You are *not* writing about deities. Stop godding up the athletes." Of course, the column was about DiMag. But if Smith, Williams, and others overreached, it was because they were on unfamiliar ground. They weren't just trying to write what Joe did on the ballfield. They were trying to write about who he was.

DiMaggio fueled their efforts with a stoicism that did seem otherworldly—more likely Old Worldly—when his body could not keep up with his will. The operation on his elbow went fine. But the shoulder was still lame, and always would be. DiMaggio might get off one good throw in a game. After that, he'd lob the ball in, if he could—and hope nobody noticed. And then, a week and a half into the season, he felt a pain in his right heel—*the other heel.* A new spur was growing there, and stabbing him with every step. DiMaggio went back to the padded shoes. But he wouldn't say anything about that either.

Of course, his teammates knew—but that knowledge didn't bring them closer to the man. That was the season when admiration in that clubhouse turned to awe—DiMaggio was not like them. They'd talk to each other about the Big Guy's arm, his stiff back, or his bum wheels . . . but not where the Dago might hear. They'd sneak glances, as he dressed in his corner. Eddie Lopat, the great lefty junkball artist, who came over from the White Sox to the Yankees that year, was stopped in his tracks when he saw the rings of raw flesh on DiMaggio's flanks. "He had these sore marks, almost donuts on him—and it was because he slid so hard—always, his hips." Charlie Keller would watch the doc, Sidney Gaynor, working on the Dago before a game. "He would be in that training room getting taped or swallowing some pills to kill the pain," Keller recalled for Maury Allen, in *Where Have You Gone, Joe DiMaggio?* "And we wouldn't know if he was playing or not. All of a sudden he'd be on the lineup card and on the field, like nothing was wrong."

Even Spec Shea, who knew Joe liked him, would never push—he'd only ask in passing:

"How's the heel, Joe?"

"Fine, Frank. It'll be fine."

The skipper, Harris, wouldn't ask at all: he just kept writing in the Clipper's name at cleanup. Only DiMaggio took himself out of the lineup. And Joe wouldn't sit: the Yanks were playing catch-up from the first week on.

The Indians ran the table in April—didn't lose a game in that month. By the time the Yankees clawed their way up the standings to where they could even see Cleveland's back, the no-name Philadelphia A's started reeling off victories—and shoved the Yankees into third place. Then, in the unkindest cut, the Boston Red Sox—under their new manager, Mr. Joe McCarthy—caught fire around the All-Star break. Boston went 24–9 in July, and sailed past everybody into first place. . . . Meanwhile, the World Champs were hanging on by their fingernails—never out of the race, but never on top. How could DiMaggio sit for one game?

Well, he sat for exactly one game, the day before the All-Star break. And he took himself out of the

All-Star lineup: he only appeared to pinch-hit (and drive in a run) before he tucked his aching legs under the pine again. Still, on the train back to New York, he told John Corriden, an old Yankee coach, that he wanted Harris to start him again in a day and a half, when the season resumed. Joe wouldn't tell Harris himself. The skipper might want to talk—and Joe didn't.

What he did was, he hauled himself out to center field, day after day, pounding after balls in the gap, and when he got them, throwing as hard as he could. (He couldn't tell a runner: *Hey, stop, my arm hurts!)* . . . He ran the bases, same as he always had. (He was *supposed* to score from second on a hit to the outfield. What did it matter if the photo of his slide at the plate showed his bared teeth in a snarl of pain?) . . . He hit the ball, whenever he could, harder than he ever had:

Late May, Chicago, DiMaggio drove in six runs himself with two home runs, a triple, double, and a single, as the Yankees buried the White Sox 13–2 . . . "DiMag on Rampage!"

Three days later in Cleveland: three home runs in one game—two of them off Feller—to silence seventy-eight thousand Tribe fans, and drive in all the Yankee runs for a 6–5 win. ("He showed his wand had not lost its magic . . .")

The problem was, he couldn't hit as he expected to—as he was supposed to—all the time. It took him two months of grinding will just to push his average

up from a pathetic .268 in May, to the barely respectable .300 at the end of June. There were days
(felt like weeks) when he couldn't seem to hit at all.
He couldn't get his bat around in time, or his stroke
was off somehow: he'd get a pitch to hit and . . . *just
miss it.* That was the worst: if the Yankees lost and Joe
took an oh-for-four, then—watch out for the Dago.
You couldn't smile around him, or talk—*forget it!*—
you didn't want to be in the same train car with him.
No wonder he was hitting titanic home runs—slamming balls out of the park more often than he had
since 1937. Whenever he did get ahold of one, his
swing had the force of cold rage behind it.

Joe had no idea what his trouble was about. Was it
over for him? *At thirty-three years old?* Joe Page remembered waking up at five A.M., at the hotel in
Chicago, and seeing DiMaggio at the mirror, practic-
ing his swing. Or more likely, that was the hour when
Page got back to the room. That was one reason
DiMaggio threw Page out—and told Frank Scott to
book him a solo room from then on. Page was abject
in his sorrow—he still loved the Dago. But when
DiMaggio walked away, that was it. One year *(half a
year)* in the hero game, and Page had puffed up, he'd
put on weight, he was drinking, he wasn't pitching
well. He'd go into a bar and announce at the top of his
high voice, "I'm Joe Page of the Yankees." That
wasn't up to the standard. If you had to drink—okay,
drink: but don't drag the club into it. Page had gotten
sloppy. DiMaggio couldn't room with a slob.

DiMaggio had teammates, but no mates on the team. His outfield partners, Keller and Henrich, had standing with Joe, and respect. They were serious players with serious talent—good Yankees, with tenure that stretched back before the war. The press always said they were Joe's friends. But you'd never see Joe with them at night. They were married guys—that was part of it, but not all. People might get confused and think of the three of them all in the same breath. And that wasn't going to happen—Joe DiMaggio didn't have peers. Henrich played next to DiMaggio for eleven years. He recollected later that they'd never even been out to dinner.

Sometimes, Joe would grab some rookie, and keep him by his side all night. Of course, the kid was thrilled. If Daig even said hello, you'd made the grade. Some of them thought he must want to talk, so they'd pepper him with questions—and that was their last invitation. The smart ones just had a few laughs, made no demands. You could go with DiMaggio to dinner, then out for drinks, then a midnight movie (some dumb western) . . . and by the end of the night, he hadn't said twenty words. Joe took care of the bills. (With ballplayers, he grabbed all the checks.) If they tried to chip in, he'd slap away their money. What were they making—five grand? "No!" he'd command. "You eat with the Dago, the Dago pays."

He might spend time with the writers, too, if everything was off the record. The knights of the key-board were as thrilled as the rookies—they stuck to the rules. One night, Lou Effrat recalled, he asked DiMag a question, something about his contract. "What're you," Joe snapped, "turning into a newspaperman?" That was the end of that. In that summer of '48, Jimmy Cannon observed Joe in his hotel, mincing painfully down the stairs, left leg first, one step at a time. But Joe told him not to write it, and the story died there. There was no hint in the New York press of DiMaggio's pain, confusion, anger. It took a visit from an old San Francisco pal, Curly Grieve, sports editor of the *Examiner,* to put a picture of DiMaggio in trouble into print.

Grieve came east and had a chat with Joe before a doubleheader in St. Louis. He had one question for DiMag: what's wrong with you? Then he used a whole column to quote Joe's answer. Even to Curly, Joe insisted that his body was "a hundred percent better than last year. . . .

"And yet, I'm in the worst slump in my ten active seasons in the big leagues. I've had only two good days all season. Am I over the hill? Am I just another hitter? Is that my best figure, .290? I don't think so because I know I've lost something that I can regain. I've lost my timing. I'm not getting that bat around as fast as I should. I'm swinging behind the ball. I hit some balls as hard as I used to. But not nearly as many. I'm fouling off the ball I should be hitting. Is this going to continue all year? What's the cure?

"I've said it once and I insist it's true. We just don't get any batting practice. I never get a chance to iron out my swing. What happens before a game? Well, today, I had to take ten or fifteen pitches before getting a ball I could hit. One would be under the chin, another on the outside. I was ducking and weaving and getting madder by the second. The batting practice pitcher then started to press in an effort to get the ball over. He was worse than ever. You know, we don't call it batting practice any more. We call it pitching practice. Some of those pitchers actually try to develop new pitches during batting practice. And they pitch to spots instead of grooving it. I used to hit a couple over the fence in batting practice. Now I'm lucky to get ahold of it.

"Why don't I do something about it? I would if I could. I've tried hustling kids and getting out in the morning when I'm at home. But it isn't effective. They can't groove the ball either. Last year, just before the World Series, Frankie Crosetti came out to the park and pitched to me for a half hour. He was perfect. That tuned me up for the World Series. My swing was back where it belonged.

"I'm convinced that's what I need now. I guess I'll have to hire a batting practice pitcher myself."

Then, Joe D. went out and hit three more home runs to sweep two games from the Browns. The third of those homers was the one Joe would remember. It was the two hundred sixty-eighth of his career, which pushed him past Rudy York of the Red Sox, and past every other active player—Joe was alone at the top of the list.

Next day, in Cleveland, Joe hit another round-tripper. But that one was like dust in his mouth. Spec Shea, on the mound, couldn't hold back the Indians, who won 5–2 and shoved the Yankees three and a half games back. Shea was another guy who couldn't follow up on his one great year. With that loss in Cleveland he was three-and-eight for the season. So Joe wasn't talking to Frank as much, either.

He couldn't understand why these young guys couldn't buckle down on themselves: *pay attention to the goddamn job.* In those years, the divide in that dugout was always prewar or postwar, McCarthy-men or after-McCarthy. It was the old guys who judged and enforced the Yankee ethic. Chandler would keep the pitchers in line (before that bastard, Weiss, gave Spud his walking papers at the start of '48). For the everyday players, the high court consisted of Keller, Henrich, sometimes Lindell (he'd come on in '42, but he was squirrelly half the time, too). Rizzuto was prewar, but Scooter was still like the mascot: someone was always stuffing worms in his glove, or stuffing him into an equipment trunk. Of course, the Dago was the Chief Justice.

The other guys might get in a kid's face: "Hey, Rook! You're fuckin' around with my money." But DiMaggio would turn on the offender with one glance of icy disdain, and the kid would be mindful for a month, after that. Lopat remembered one day in Detroit, in '48, when Berra popped up, and jogged disgustedly toward first base. But the ball fell in. If

Yogi had been running, he could have made second. "Instead he gets into first, and because of that he doesn't score, and we lose the game. I'm down in the runway below the dugout with Joe DiMaggio. Joe had a coffee and a cigarette between every inning. And Yogi comes back and he's putting on his catching gear, and Keller says to him: 'Yogi, are you feeling all right?' And Yogi says, 'Yeah, I'm feelin' all right. Why?' *Then why the hell didn't you run it out?'* Yogi looks at DiMaggio, as if to say, HELP. And Joe gives him this really cold look. Then Lindell and Henrich came in, and they join in. And I'm thinking, 'Now I know what makes this team. Now I know what makes this special.' "

Yogi was a case worth Joe's attention. True, he didn't look like a Yankee (he won instant nomination as captain of the all-ugly team). Maybe his catching still looked sort of homely, too. But with a bat in his hands, the kid was beautiful. He didn't know *nuthin'* about the strike zone. Pitch in the dirt, pitch over his head—didn't matter: he'd hit the tar out of it anyway. He was on pace to knock in a hundred runs that year—and he wasn't even playing every game. As Joe saw it, that was part of the problem.

August, a doubleheader in Washington: hot as hell, and you couldn't even get a drink of water on the bench. They thought it was bad for you. They'd give you what they called "Florida water"—a towel soaked in ammonia to drape over your head. You could lose ten pounds in one afternoon. Guys would lose it all, and wake up on the trainer's table with smelling salts under their nose. The Yankees won the first game, but the scoreboard said Boston won, too. Yogi caught that first game, but after that he was pooped. Harris wanted to rest DiMaggio for the second game, as well. But the Dago overruled him, and went out to play. Boston, Cleveland, and the Yankees were in a mortal fight, and the pennant hung on every game. But the Yankees lost the second game. At the end, Lopat and Allie Reynolds almost carried DiMaggio back to the clubhouse. That's where he saw Berra—fresh as a daisy, after riding the bench. "Whatsa matter you TIRED?" DiMaggio almost spat out the word at him. "You're twenty years old! What kinda fuckin' bullshit is this—YOU CAN'T PLAY TWO GAMES? . . ." There wasn't a sound in the room, except the Dago's voice. He took the skin off Berra for ten minutes straight. If a look from DiMaggio lasted a month, this was a hundred times worse. Over the next eight years Berra would play an average of one hundred forty games—more than any other catcher in the league.

But the everyday toll on DiMaggio was frightening. He confessed to friends, back in New York, that his right heel felt "like an icepick was stabbing me." He ran on his toes and his knees swelled up. Then he got a charley horse in the left thigh: after games, he couldn't lift that leg into a cab. But he'd be back next morning, extra-early for extra tape. *How's the leg, Joe?* . . .

"Fine."

The only respite from the pennant race was sorrow: on August 19, six thousand mourners filled St. Patrick's Cathedral—and seventy-five thousand, who could not enter, stood out on Fifth Avenue in a soaking rain—to pay respect and mark their bereavement at the passing of Babe Ruth. Cancer had taken the Great Bambino at the age of fifty-three. Baseball had lost the greatest icon of the game's joy. For the Yankees, it felt like even the glory of their past was under attack, and being worn away. The team was represented at the final rites by DiMaggio. But even that occasion betokened for him no pause. At the close of the funeral, he borrowed a limousine (Toots commandeered it, from the boss of CBS, Bill Paley) and raced to La Guardia, whence a plane flew him through the storm to Washington, D.C., where he took the field in the bottom of the third. His Yankees had a game to win. And the Senators led 1–0.

Joe soon took care of that. He came up in the top of the fourth, and stroked a single that ignited the Yankees. *(Dago's back!)* They scored six runs in the inning, and that was the end of the contest. . . . After that, he went on a hellacious tear, and the Yankees did, too. He was lining shots off the outfield walls (over the wall seven times), he was driving home a run per game—and the Yankees would win twenty of their next twenty-three. It was the same sort of furious streak on which he'd led the Yanks a decade back— 1939, after disease took Lou Gehrig from the club.

But Joe didn't feel like he did ten years ago. When he wasn't on the field, he could barely walk. Special shoes with high arches couldn't stop the stabbing: he was on painkillers all the time—and he was exhausted. Every day Doc Gaynor had to wrap his thigh with a tight cinch of gauze and tape, and then another cinch around his midriff, to hold up the one on his leg. . . . But what could Joe do? The Indians and Red Sox wouldn't fold. In fact, McCarthy's Red Sox were winning twenty-two of twenty-six. For three weeks, into mid-September, the Yankees played .860 baseball—and didn't gain a game in the standings.

September 10, Boston: last game of a showdown series, and the Red Sox had already won two games. If the Yankees couldn't take one back, they'd be dead—four and a half games behind. But it seemed like no one could take that game. It went to extra innings, with the score 6–6. Top of the tenth, the Boston reliever, Earl Caldwell, didn't know where the ball was going: he walked two and hit another. But the Yankees couldn't touch his fireball, either. Keller and the kid right fielder, Hank Bauer, both struck out. DiMaggio came up with two outs and the bases loaded. Caldwell had to throw a strike, and Joe was on it: his body whirled in the batter's box, his bat was a blur, and . . . he missed it: a pop foul over the grandstand, onto the roof. Strike one. Caldwell threw another. Joe turned and smashed this ball—up, up, toward the Green Monster, the left field corner—*out of the park* . . . and foul. Strike two. The Boston fans took breath again, as Caldwell tried to make Joe chase, outside. DiMaggio didn't offer. The pitcher threw another off the outside edge. DiMaggio just stared at him. Caldwell didn't have another pitch to waste. He threw a fastball on the outer half, and DiMaggio swung again. That ball took off for the center field flagpole, soaring for an instant in a sudden silence. No one could even yell for brother Dominic, who was racing back, back over the grass . . . then, Dommie stopped, and watched the ball land halfway up the bleachers in dead center field. Grand slam, four runs—and the same old story: the Yanks were alive, as long as Joe was there.

But now, the rest of the story made it into the press, too. There was a column in the *New York Mirror* that said DiMaggio was planning to hold out next year for *one hundred twenty-five thousand bucks*—and anyway, he'd likely be lame: he was already "playing on one leg," and was sure to need another operation. When the beat writers tried to follow up, DiMaggio was enraged: the salary number was a fiction, he said. About the operation, even he didn't know. One by one, he ticked off the places where he had to be taped: his charley horse thigh, the cinch around his midriff, a patch on his hip for a strawberry, a bandage on his left hand. "I'm playing," he said. "I feel like a mummy." *But did they have to let the whole damn league know?*

There never had been a pennant race like it: one week before the season's end, Cleveland, Boston, and

New York were tied. Nobody even knew what to do—how could they run a three-way playoff? In the end, no one had to try. The Yankees were one game behind their rivals when they arrived in Boston for the last two games of the season. If the Yankees won both, they had a chance for the pennant. If they lost even one, they were finished.

Ted Williams made the end short and sweet; at least for him and the Sox. In the first inning, he hit a two-run bomb that gave the Bostons a lead they'd never lose. (With that homer, Williams also clinched another batting crown—he was pleased DiMaggio was there to see that.) Joe drove in the only Yankee run with a double off the Green Monster. But the rest of the Yanks could do nothing. Boston won the first game 5–1, to eliminate New York.

That might also have ended DiMaggio's season. There was no reason for him to play the last game—except Boston had to win one more, to get a share of the pennant. And his brother played for Boston: people might say he sat to give the pennant to Dom—or to his old skipper, McCarthy. . . . Of course, no one who said those things could have known Joe DiMaggio. The evening after that Yankee loss, Joe got a ride with Dominic to his home in the suburb of Wellesley. Dom was going to be married, right after the season. Mamma and Papa DiMaggio had come east for the occasion. There was to be a family dinner that night.

As Dom told David Halberstam for his classic *Summer of '49,* most of that ride passed in silence. At length, Joe turned to his brother, and announced: "We'll get back at you tomorrow—we'll knock you out. I'll take care of it personally."

Dominic, who had suffered a lifetime of being known as "DiMaggio's brother," now took the occasion to remind Joe: "I may have something to do with that . . . I'll be there, too."

Dominic was as good as his word: next day, he hit the home run that started the Sox on their winning rally. (Boston would win the right to meet Cleveland in a one-game playoff for the pennant, next day.) But Joe had meant what he said, too. He didn't just suit up: he personally kept the Yankees in that game. Two singles, two doubles . . . one of his shots hit the Monster so hard, Dommie thought the ball would go through it. With his single in the ninth, Joe would finish at four-for-five, but the game was beyond reach: 10–5 Boston, the scoreboard said. Harris sent out a pinch runner to take Joe's place on the first base bag. Head down, DiMaggio limped across the grass toward the dugout. And the Boston fans startled even themselves by standing—thirty-five thousand in that packed house, on their feet—to cheer their greatest opponent.

As Dominic told his co-writer, Al Hirshberg, for the memoir *Real Grass, Real Heroes,* he couldn't believe what he was hearing: "Out in center field, I listened, thrilled, fascinated and astonished. . . . My glasses clouded up and, as Joe reached the top step, I did something that, to me, was as involuntary as breathing. I reached up and took off my cap."

That year, Joe DiMaggio had played in a hundred fifty-three games out of a hundred fifty-four—played hurt in almost every one. He finished at an average of .320. He led the league with thirty-nine homers, and a hundred fifty-five runs batted in. Those were his greatest totals since 1937. But his impact couldn't be measured by a line of numbers. In fact, his impact didn't end with the Yankee season.

The following day, in the playoff, the Red Sox took the field behind a right-hander, Denny Galehouse. No Red Sox fan (and no Red Sox player) could figure out why Galehouse got that start. He was only eight and eight that year, and had never scared anyone. He didn't scare the Indians, either. They piled on him early and often. They won the playoff 8–3. And Boston cursed the name Galehouse, ever after. There were curses for McCarthy, too—the Skipper had put Galehouse out there. But the truth was even more pathetic. The previous day, in the season's last game, McCarthy was so scared of Joe DiMaggio that he kept a right-hander heated up in the bullpen for six innings straight. That exhausted pitcher was Denny Galehouse.

The day after Cleveland beat the Boston Braves to win the World Series, the Yankees once again became the talk of the Baseball Nation. The GM, Weiss, had fired the gentlemanly Bucky Harris. (A manager who couldn't win with DiMaggio must not be tough enough.) The Yankees gathered the sporting press at the 21 Club, the famous speakeasy-turned-richman's-restaurant, to introduce their new skipper, Charles Dillon Stengel.

It was an inexplicable choice, a Galehousian mystery: at fifty-eight years of age, Casey Stengel had experience, but mostly of the wrong sort. He'd played outfield—with middling success—for five teams, all in the National League. He'd managed two NL clubs, Brooklyn and the Boston Braves, for a total of nine years—but never finished better than fifth place. His combined percentage as a big-league skipper was .439. The last time the Yankees had finished that badly, Babe Ruth was still pitching for an orphanage in Baltimore, and the Austro-Hungarian Empire owned half of Europe.

What fame Stengel had garnered in the Great Game came mostly from his clowning. As a player, his most memorable act occurred when he caught a bird in left field, and tucked it under his hat. Then, when he made a nice running catch, he acknowledged the cheers with a tip of his cap—and the bird took wing, to the crowd's delight. He entered briefly into Yankee lore when, as a member of the New York Giants, he hit a home run against the Yanks in the 1923 World Series—and trotted the bases thumbing his nose, and then blowing kisses, toward the Yankee dugout.

Now this old Yankee-hater (steeriiike), this entertainer (strike TWOO), this loser (YER OUT!) . . . was revealed as the Bombers' new commandant. No wonder the writers and cameramen (unappeased by a splendid 21 Club lunch) took the news as a bad joke.

No wonder the club management asked DiMaggio to take the stage at Stengel's side: the presence of the Yankee Clipper would dignify the proceedings, and forestall any speculation that the players might revolt. Alas, it also guaranteed that Casey would be asked how he felt to be managing an all-time great, like DiMag. "I can't tell you much about that," Stengel replied, "being as since I have not been in the American League so I ain't seen the gentleman play, except once in a very great while."

That answer (and DiMaggio's scowl) indicated two truths about Stengel. First, he would talk quotably and at any length, even if the answer boiled down to, "I don't know." Second, and more important: he had no idea how to get along with his star.

The Yankee owners, Topping and Webb, had a pretty good idea how to get along: they were going to make DiMaggio the highest-paid player in baseball. Bob Feller, the Cleveland ace, was making eighty-five thousand a year. So the Yankee management had in mind ninety thousand for Joe. That would raise him, for the first time, past Babe Ruth (who topped out at eighty G's)—in fact, past every player in the history of the game. It was Toots who cornered Topping and Webb in his saloon one day, and convinced them to make it an even six figures—*the first hundred-thousand-dollar man!* That would be history!

That was promotion! Wasn't that worth an extra ten large?

Sure it was. Now, the only lingering question was whether the Big Guy could play. DiMaggio did his part. By November he showed up in Baltimore for another operation at Johns Hopkins. The surgeons had no trouble with the spur on the right heel. The jutting bit of calcium was excised, the wound was neatly sewn, Joe emerged with a cast and crutches, and said he would answer the bell, March 1, when the Yankees convened in St. Petersburg.

So he did. He reported on time, without fuss. No one would get a chance to say he was undermining the new regime. But Stengel had to show how tough that regime was going to be: he ordered double work-outs—even that first day. Joe did the work with the rest of the guys: did his stretches, ran in the outfield, shagged flies, took his licks in the cage, and . . . by March 2, DiMaggio could barely walk.

This time the Yanks wouldn't wait for God to breathe His balm on the Clipper's heel. That day, DiMaggio was flown back to Baltimore. The sages of the Hopkins examined Joe and announced that he had broken adhesions in his right foot. They saw no need for another operation. Joe was back in camp the next day. Now, Stengel had seen a sobering vision— his last chance as a major league skipper, flying away with DiMag on that plane. Suddenly, Casey wasn't quite so tough. He told Joe to get in shape at his own pace, in his own style: *Whatever you commence to wanna do, Mr. De-Madge.*

That suited Joe to a T. That sojourn in Florida would be exactly his style. That year, Joe wasn't joined in St. Pete by Jimmy Ceres—Peanuts was off the list. Solotaire had convinced Joe, that didn't look right. Joe needed someone with class. So, Gentleman George went south with DiMag.

In the mornings, Solotaire would drive Joe to Miller Huggins Field, and come with him into the locker room—make sure the Dago had everything he needed. Usually, Georgie would hang around the clubhouse or the grandstand, while DiMag did some light work in the A.M. session. Joe would take all his hitting—and more: no one else got into the cage until Dago'd had enough. He'd take a few grounders in the infield, maybe a few fly balls just for timing. But no running, no slides, no sudden stops or starts. He was wearing sponge insoles, designed by his doctors, to keep his weight from landing on his heels. But the insoles caused blisters on his toes. The newspaper stories from St. Pete read like a primer on podiatry.

Oftentimes, in the afternoons, Solotaire would show up at the clubhouse alone. All the fellows knew that meant Joe was "tied up"—with female company, back at their rooms. George went on ahead as a lookout, to make sure no one remarked too much about the Dago's training schedule. One time the phone in the clubhouse rang: a call for Solotaire. George lis-

tened briefly and hung up with the glad news: Daig
was on his way. Of course, Georgie said it in his own
famous style:

"I jus' got the flash—

"He's done with the gash."

At night, George would take Joe out to the dog
track—not to sit in the car on the backstretch—they'd
walk right in. And take along some of the other players, too. Hell, Stengel said Joe could run his own
camp. And DiMaggio took him at his word.

When Stengel was confronted with the news, he
had to crack down. He ruled that every man had to
live with the team in the hotel. There was a new midnight curfew, and a seven-thirty morning call. But on
the subject of DiMaggio, Casey was mild: "I'll handle this situation in my own way." That meant a
friendly chat with the Clipper. Stengel imposed no
penalties, and no fine. "DiMaggio admits he feels
badly about it."

What worried Stengel wasn't Joe's betting, but the
way he was playing ball. He still couldn't dig in at the
plate, couldn't turn on the ball, couldn't play a full
game, and couldn't, or didn't, run.

And Dago was only the biggest hole in the cheese.
The All-Star outfield that Casey was supposed to in-
herit turned out not to exist. Keller had a banged-up
leg, and his back had never fully healed from a disk
operation two years before. Henrich, the old pro in
right, was trying to learn to play first base. And the
best of the backup kids, Hank Bauer, had an injured

ankle. Yogi was going to catch full-time, but he got in a car wreck and screwed up a knee. Rizzuto, the shortstop, was underweight. Casey would likely have a rookie (and a shortstop), Jerry Coleman, starting at second base. At third, another untested kid, the bonus baby and med school student Bobby Brown would share time with last year's regular, Billy Johnson. And first base—well, if Henrich didn't work out, there were only rookies and retreads.

One of the young writers, Len Koppett, remarked to Stengel: "I see you got four first basemen . . ." Said Stengel (with the terseness that marked him when he had something to say): "When you got four first basemen, you got no first baseman."

The worst news was confirmed when the Yankees broke camp to barnstorm through Dixie. On April 9, at Beaumont, Texas, DiMaggio singled . . . and when the next Yankee batter stroked another single, DiMaggio kicked it into high gear and raced for third. From there, he hobbled straight to the dugout. The pain in his heel was back, and big-time. Next day, he couldn't make it to the third inning, before he sat down.

Then, the real nightmare began. He was flown to Dallas where an august orthopedist diagnosed a "hot condition" in Joe's right heel. It wasn't from the surgery—this was something like an infection. He could literally feel heat in the foot. DiMaggio would have to be hospitalized. And New York fans would get the dire headline they had cursed for eight of Joe's eleven seasons: "DiMaggio to Miss Opening Day."

DiMaggio thought the curse was on him. He was flown from Dallas, through thunderstorms, toward the East Coast, all afternoon and through the night: three different airplanes, four takeoffs, four landings. Each time, the plane would bounce around the thunderheads. Passengers were throwing up—Joe among them. He looked awful—ashen, his eyes were hollow—as he remarked to his reflection in the airplane mirror, he even needed a damn haircut. And every time he landed, the press was at the airport, with bulbs going off in his face, and writers yelling: *JOE! ANY COMMENT ON RETIREMENT? . . . JOE! D'Y'THINK YER FINISHED?*

To one gaggle, DiMaggio replied: "I am not going to retire from baseball. There's a lot of folks who'd like to see me retire. Sadistic people . . ." Then, he refused to answer more questions.

The last leg was a cab ride from Washington, an hour north to Baltimore and the Hopkins Hospital. At two A.M., they strapped him down on a gurney. They were wheeling him off for shots in his foot. Suddenly the hospital hall went lurid white with photographers' flashbulbs. DiMaggio strained at his straps, trying to sit up, cursing a blue streak. He screamed at the cameramen: "WHY ARE YOU DOING THIS TO ME?"

"Why" was in short supply for DiMaggio. The doctors at the Hopkins couldn't tell him why the heel had become inflamed now—or why the pain wouldn't go away, or why he ought to stay there. The pain would stop: they promised him. But when? They were stumped on that one, too.

He asked for a placard for his door: "Do Not Disturb." But the sign did no good. Other patients would stump right in on their casts, or crutches; wheelchair patients would roll in and gawk. They'd bribe the nurses to pester him for autographs. One time, he woke from a nap, and there were two citizens of Baltimore standing at his bedside, staring. By the time he was fully awake, they'd disappeared without a word. *Jesus! Did he just imagine them? Was he goin' nuts?* . . . No, he was a public freak show.

For two days, he took it. Then he tried to sneak away. He made the lobby on crutches, and there was the press—like a posse from hell—with their lenses pointed . . . his roar echoed off the vaulting lobby arches:

"DON'T YOU THINK YOU'VE GONE FAR ENOUGH? YOU GUYS'RE DRIVIN' ME BATTY! . . ." His crutches scattered the posse, on his way to the door. "Can't you leave me alone? This affects me mentally, too, you know." One of the newsmen protested: people wanted to know about the most expensive ballplayer in history! . . . Joe snapped: "I got to think of myself! This is tough on me." He ducked into a car at the curb, and disappeared.

Opening day, he sat in the Yankee dugout in a dark blue suit and camel hair overcoat. He looked perfect—and felt perfectly useless. That was about his only appearance. He holed up in the Elysee. Georgie and Toots would bring in food and news. Joe would sit and read the papers, smoke and drink coffee all day. Then he'd limp around the suite all night. Meals were no solace. His ulcers were back. He'd turn on the radio. Then turn it off. The television was better. He could stare at that for hours. But TV quit at night. How was he supposed to sleep? He'd be up till dawn, then asleep till lunch. Georgie would come in with a sandwich from the Stage, and DiMaggio would swing his legs tenderly out of bed. He only had to touch his heel to the floor, and he knew: *it was still there.*

The doctors said only time could cure the pain. But time wouldn't move. April finally dragged into May, and at last, Joe got news—bad news. His father had died in San Francisco. Then it was planes across the country again, the brothers, the family, old friends . . . and every damned one asking, "How's the heel, Joe? When you think you'll be back?" He couldn't even be a pallbearer for the old man. His mamma kept looking at him like— What had he done to bring the evil eye? And the hometown writers, with their sympathy—*like he was the one who died.* He couldn't wait to get back to New York. . . . And May went on, like the war, forever.

The few friends who got in to the Elysee to see him reported that Joe was on edge and snappish. When hints of his mood made the papers, Joe told the hotel: no more visitors, and no calls—except for Georgie and Toots. But every week, George Weiss would announce a new date when Joe would be back—as if that meddling skinflint knew! He was only trying to sell tickets. But the writers all had to use the announcements. And all so cute! "Joe DiMaggio, the Yankees' $90,000 invalid" . . . "The $100,000 bench warmer will don the Yankee pinstripes for the first time this season . . ." It wasn't just kids on the ball club, now; there were a lot of kids in the press box, too: They'd bury DiMaggio happily, for a good story—as a hundred-thousand-dollar joke.

Solotaire would try to tempt Joe with tickets. "Come on! We'll go out, get some air, see a show." That was a banner season on Broadway, with the major league musicals that Joe used to like: *Annie Get Your Gun, High Button Shoes, Show Boat . . .* and the blockbuster of that spring, Rodgers and Hammerstein's *South Pacific*—with that lyric in the "Bloody Mary" song: *"Her skin is tender as DiMaggio's glove"* . . . Even that brought no joy, just called attention to the way he was now—people in that theater, staring at him—he didn't want to be seen.

He tried watching Yankee games on TV. But the camera distorted everything. As he told David Halberstam, for *Summer of '49,* he'd see a pitch come straight down the middle—and the ump would call it a ball! He'd wait for Yogi or Stengel to protest, but no one said a word. *Christ, now he's losing his eye!* He'd end up even more depressed. . . . Things got so bad he even called Dorothy—to ask if she'd let Little Joe come over. She had split up with that Schubert guy. (Lost all her money with him, too.) She wasn't even cold to Joe, and sent the boy right over in a cab. That was good for a few afternoons. Joe got Lionel to send over a toy train. Joe and the kid played on the floor. Little Joe was eight—in a good private school—nice kid. But it made Joe think about Dorothy. *Why was she being so nice?* Joe thought she must feel sorry for him. *Well, he didn't want her pity.* And he didn't call for Little Joe anymore. . . . A couple of times, he got so stir-crazy, he called the Stadium, to tell them he was coming out. Maybe he could take a few swings, see some pitches. But Weiss would leak that, right away, to the writers: *DiMaggio will take batting practice!* It worked out great—for Weiss: May 23, thirty-seven thousand fans filled the grandstand for a game with the hopeless St. Louis Browns. But their roar when they saw DiMaggio in uniform only embarrassed Joe. He took a few swings, got blisters on his hands, and limped off to disappear again. After another year, May turned to June.

The Yankees were doing fine. (Did that make Joe feel better, or worse?) They weren't running away, but they held on to first place—with Boston, the big threat, leading the pack behind them. The papers still called them the Bronx Bombers. But that wasn't how they were winning games. The only real Bomber they had left was Henrich—who was batting cleanup in the Big Guy's absence. There never was a better clutch hitter than Henrich. That's why Mel Allen gave him the nickname: "Ol' Reliable." Alas, the nickname was apt on both ends, now: Tom had already turned thirty-six. Still, he'd never had a springtime like this. In the first sixty-five games of that season, Henrich had sixteen home runs, and twelve were game-winners.

But what really kept the Yankees on top was the pitching. Stengel was being acclaimed as a genius for the way he juggled the lineup each day—platoon at third base, outfielders *du jour,* four or five different first basemen. . . . But with the starters (and Joe Page in relief) Casey was as regular as Army chow—Reynolds, Raschi, Lopat, Byrne—just as automatic as Joe "Push-Button" McCarthy was, in the old glory days.

Not that Stengel didn't try to screw around with the pitchers. (No one was more convinced of Casey's genius than Casey.) That springtime, he'd stand on the dugout steps, yelling at Berra to look over for the next sign. But Raschi and Reynolds, the big right-handers, put a stop to that. Reynolds, the Superchief (he was an Indian from Oklahoma), would stand on the mound, yelling just as loud: "Yogi! You look over there one more time, and I'll cross you up." Berra didn't know what the hell to do. Stengel would be waving dollar bills in his hand, threatening to fine him, if he didn't look over. But Yogi was as scared of Reynolds as the batters were. If he hit you with a fastball, he could hurt you bad. Raschi, if anything, was more menacing—with that game face on the mound—looked like he could bite through a bar of iron. "Yogi, goddammit, LOOK AT ME." By May, Yogi wouldn't ever turn to the dugout.

Lopat and Byrne were as screwy as left-handers were supposed to be. Byrne never knew where the ball was going—but neither did the hitters: no one dug in on him. "As wild as he needed to be," was how the papers wrote him up. He'd walk three and strike out three, and stroll off the mound, whistling. Lopat walked a lot of guys, too. But he was nibbling with that junk he threw: fifteen pitches, fifteen different speeds: slow, slower, and Mississippi milk train. Hitters would mutter to Berra, in protest: "Don't this sonofabitch ever throw a fastball?" "Don't look at me," Yogi would answer. "He never t'rows what I call, anyway." Lopat used to drive Stengel crazy. One day, late innings, a tight game with Boston, the Red Sox slugger Vern Stephens was coming up. Now, Junior Stephens was no one to screw around with. He would hit thirty-nine home runs that year, and lead the league in RBIs. Of course, he was right-handed, so Stengel thought maybe he should get Lopat out of there. And Stephens was mad: he was oh-fer-the-day on Eddie's junk. He was yelling at Lopat as he walked to the plate: "You fuckin' Polack, get the goddamn ball up here. You haven't got the guts to throw a fuckin' fastball!"

So Lopat—Jesus, Stengel went white—fed Stephens an itty-bitty fastball. (There were better fastballs thrown in BP.) But of course, Lopat put it six inches inside. Stephens crushed it, four hundred feet—foul.

"Is that the best you got? I can hit you, fuckin' Po-lack! . . ." Stengel was standing on the steps of the dugout—he wanted Lopat to see he was ready with the hook.

Lopat threw another fastball, more pathetic, and two inches farther inside. Stephens flattened it—*four hundred fifty feet*—foul. Stephens was grinding his hands on the bat, spitting abuse. Stengel was on the top step, clutching his heart—as Lopat threw a humpback, spinny-winny-weeny-whatsit-it'll-never-get-there . . . strike three. And remarked, as he ambled into the dugout, "He couldn't hit me in a month."

It all looked fabulous in the next day's box score—as long as the pitchers never hit an off day, as long as the Yankees could score a couple of runs . . . but if you leave too many games close, you're bound to drop a few. That was why the Yankees couldn't pull away. That, and the fact that Boston was loaded. It wasn't just Stephens, Ted Williams, Dom DiMaggio. But Goodman, Pesky, Doerr, Zarilla—every one a .300 hitter. There wasn't any rest in that lineup. And good young pitchers: Parnell and Kinder were as tough as they came. They weren't even playing well yet, and they were still in the race: five games back, and the Yankees had to come to them, in Boston, for three games at the end of June. That was where they planned to make their move.

But that was when it happened—just a few days before that Boston series—DiMaggio swung his legs out of bed, brushed the floor gingerly with his heel, and . . . nothing. He stood up, he walked around the suite. Nothing! No pain. Gone! He felt the heel with his hand. It was cool. He got himself dressed up. He went out and walked around the block. *"Autograph? Of course! I'd be delighted . . ."* He went out for lunch and dinner, too. In between, he made calls—to Al Schacht, the baseball clown, who still could throw pretty hard, and Gus Niarhos, the backup catcher, who was injured and stayed behind in New York while the Yanks went west on a road trip. Schacht and Niarhos would meet him, next morning, at the Stadium. They rounded up some neighborhood kids to shag flies. DiMaggio hit until his hands were bloody. Blisters weren't a problem. The heel was his problem—and his problem was gone. Niarhos hit fly balls—and DiMaggio ran under them. He cut off the workout after an hour, and went back to the hotel. Tomorrow morning would tell the story. If the heel was still cool, if it didn't hurt to walk, they would meet again, the next day, and the next.

When the Yankees came back from their road trip, there was DiMaggio, in uniform at the Stadium. Nobody asked how he felt, what he was doing there. They could see it on him like the glow around a light tower at night. Dago was back!

The Yanks had an exhibition coming up: the annual charity game with the Giants, the Mayor's Trophy Game, June 27. Joe said he'd test the heel that day. Thirty-seven thousand New York fans cheered him, the minute he walked onto the field. When he popped one over the wall in a pregame home run derby, the ovation shook the ballpark. But in the game, his timing was nowhere. He drew one walk and popped up four times: never got a ball out of the infield. But he played nine innings. And he didn't hurt.

After that game, the Yankees left for Boston. Joe said he didn't think he could make it. They went for the train, and Dago stayed behind. And he might have sat out that series, if the next day's game had been a normal afternoon affair. But it was a night game. And by lunchtime, Toots was working on the Dago— while he fed him on the cuff, of course.

"You oughta go, Daig. You know you wanna."

"Well, maybe . . ."

"Why not? You look better strikin' out than any of those crumb bums hittin' the ball."

DiMaggio caught a plane to Boston at three-fifteen P.M. He'd go out to Fenway. Maybe he'd suit up. At least he could be with the guys. Stengel saw the Dago, and stopped filling out the lineup card. He was waiting for the word. He kept sneaking glances across the locker room. DiMaggio was dressing deliberately, pensively—as if the feel of his socks would tell him whether or not to play. Stengel waited, and stalled the press: "I'm commencin' to think about it," he said. Finally he got the nod from the

Dago. The genius manager had thought it through—
and he wrote DiMaggio in at cleanup.

In the Red Sox dugout, the players watched
DiMaggio gingerly warming up. He still seemed to
have a hitch in his walk. His shoes had no spikes on
the right heel. One of the young Red Sox offered the
opinion that Joe wasn't going to beat out any infield
hits. "You don't know him," said McCarthy darkly.
The old Skipper couldn't seem to shake his conviction that the Yankees were somehow tougher than his
boys. McCarthy's fear did his ballclub no good. But
in those days, it hovered in the air around him, along
with a vaporous hint of scotch. Once, when his outfielder Sam Mele couldn't run down a long drive to
right, McCarthy muttered, all too audibly: "Henrich
woulda stuck that in his ass." (And he shucked Mele
off to the Senators.) . . . With DiMaggio, McCarthy's
convictions were almost religious. He turned on his
young players now, and announced: "You watch him
the first time there's a chance for an infield hit. You
watch how he runs."

The first inning was scoreless. Reynolds for the
Yankees and the young Sox fireballer, Mickey Mc-
Dermott, both had their good stuff. DiMaggio led off
the second: McDermott tried to throw the ball by
him. And he almost did. With two strikes, McDermott kept firing at the outside corner, and Joe
couldn't get around. He hadn't faced a real heater
since April. But he wasn't giving in to any snot-nose,
either. With two strikes, he kept fouling balls off to

the right. Late every time: foul ball, foul ball, foul ball—six pitches spoiled . . . until McDermott fired one that caught more of the plate, and DiMaggio lined it over shortstop for a single. They were on their feet clapping in the Yankee dugout. And not just for sentiment's sake: Lindell walked, Bauer hit a home run, and the Yanks led 3–0.

Next inning, Rizzuto led off with a single. DiMaggio came up again. This time, McDermott dispensed with trying to get a ball past Joe on the outer edge. He tried to come in, and DiMaggio turned on the pitch and launched it over the wall—a home run into the screen atop the Green Monster. As Joe rounded third base, Rizzuto waited at the plate, jumping up and down like a kid at Christmas. There were thirty-six thousand fans in the place. (Capacity was listed at thirty-five.) Half were cheering the Great Man. Half were as lustily booing.

The Red Sox wouldn't lie down. They hung in, like it was a World Series game—maybe this was their Series. They nicked Reynolds for two runs in the fifth, and chased him in the eighth, with another. They were playing as tough as even McCarthy could demand. Every time there was a play at second base, someone would try to kick the ball from Rizzuto's grasp. The Sox second baseman, Bobby Doerr, simply ran over the Scooter, knocked him on his ass. But now the Dago was back. In the Yankee eighth, he got on with a walk, and when Berra hit a grounder to the right side, Doerr flipped the ball quickly to second, to start the double play. DiMaggio came into second base like the Broadway Limited *(You watch how he runs)* and threw himself into a slide on his right hip, left leg up. The shortstop, Stephens, was flattened like a penny on the tracks. He never even got off a throw. DiMaggio's business was done. He trotted off to the dugout.

In the bottom of the ninth, Page on the mound, the Red Sox scored their fourth run. And now they had the tying run on third base. And Ted Williams at the plate. Williams got hold of a Joe Page fastball and drove it, high and handsome—it soared through the night, four hundred feet, to the deepest part of the park, the triangle in right center . . . where it disappeared in the glove of the waiting Joe DiMaggio. Game over. Game one to the Yanks, 5–4.

The next day, Joe took over in earnest. No one could stop him when he was right. And he knew he was right, now. The Red Sox were determined to avenge game one. They jumped all over Tommy Byrne—he never made it through the first inning. By the fifth, the Sox led 7–1 behind the cocky (and talented) Ellis Kinder. But in the fifth, Kinder got sloppy and walked Rizzuto and Henrich. Then DiMaggio drove the first good pitch he saw out of the park in left center field. The Yankees were back in the game, 7–4. By the seventh, McCarthy was so furious at Kinder that he yanked him in favor of the club's top reliever, the veteran left-hander Earl Johnson. But New York's backup outfielder, Gene Woodling, dou-

bled off Johnson with the bases loaded. And the Yankees tied the game. That didn't last more than one inning, till the eighth, when DiMaggio came up with a
man on. Johnson tried to fool him with a low-inside
curveball—at least make him hit it on the ground.
But DiMaggio golfed it over the Monster—his second homer of the day, third of the series. He had now
driven home six runs—and had put game two away
for good. As Joe touched home plate and turned toward the dugout, Stengel emerged, hands high in the
air. Then, he backed away as Joe approached, bowing
and salaaming to the potentate.

And Joe wasn't even embarrassed. It *was* like after
a Series. They were hugging and whooping in the
locker room—kissing each other, throwing towels.
Every man on the club came over to Joe to shake his
hand, or slap him on the back, before they opened the
doors to the press. Only Spec Shea brought up the big
question: Any pain? . . . Said DiMaggio: "Nothing
hurts when you play like this." Only once did Joe's
face darken in a scowl. That was for Rizzuto, who
thought he'd had a pretty good game—drove in a run
himself. "What'sa matter with you?" DiMaggio
snapped, and the noise in the clubhouse died. "Are
you try'na steal my RBIs?" Then the hooting and
cheers redoubled. Dago's makin' jokes!

Only one more chance for the Red Sox remained.
They would take the field for game three behind their
ace, Mel Parnell. He'd already won ten games that
year—and must have broken a hundred bats. He

didn't pitch like other lefties: Parnell was always on
your hands with the heater, or hard slider. No one on
the Yankees liked to face him. Of course, the Yankees
had their ace up, too. Vic Raschi already had eleven
wins that season. But he didn't have his great stuff
that day, and the Red Sox would touch him up for
twelve hits. Still, Raschi battled on, holding by will
to a one-run lead. The Yankees were leading 3–2 in
the seventh, when Parnell fell into hot water. Stirn-
weiss got on first with a single. But Parnell got two
outs. Then he tried to get cute with Henrich, but Ol'
Reliable made him pay with another single. Two men
on, and DiMaggio up—once again with the game on
the line.

There was an ominous rumbling from the packed
grandstand—as if the fans were muttering: this could
not happen to them again. Parnell was going to make
something happen on his own terms: he threw his
heater on the outer half, and DiMaggio popped it up.
The crowd roared its relief, as the first baseman, Billy
Goodman, got under the ball in foul ground . . . *and
he dropped it.* The noise sank to murmurous unease
again. Strike one. Parnell squared himself and threw
the same heater, same spot. This time DiMaggio
squibbed it foul on the ground. Now the crowd came
back to life, urging Parnell on. He had DiMag at
oh-and-two, just where he wanted him—and he
threw a pitcher's pitch: a perfect fastball, inches off
the outside corner. DiMaggio didn't even flinch. He
was waiting for Parnell to come in. And Parnell knew

it: so he threw one just off the *inside* corner. DiMaggio moved not a whit. Now Fenway was filled with an unholy noise, high and plaintive: the Boston Irish were keening. There was nothing left for Parnell to do but throw DiMaggio a strike. Parnell reared back and threw his best. And DiMaggio hit it—so hard, so high, so far . . . it didn't just clear the Monster, it didn't just sail over the screen on top. *Whanggg!* It smashed, with the sound of hammered steel, off the top of the light stanchion that loomed above *everything*.

Three runs. End of contest. Yankees win, 6–2.

DiMaggio would later say the noise of that crowd built in his head until the roar was everywhere—like he was underwater—that roar was all over him. But Parnell would recall for David Halberstam: the noise he heard for the next few minutes was the clang of that ball off the steel light tower. He stood on the mound, his back to the plate, looking up at that tower and the sky behind it. It seemed like heaven itself had turned against the Red Sox—from the start, from the moment that game had begun . . . when from out of that sky, across that heaven, a little biplane had drawn into view and had flown around Fenway, trailing this message: "THE GREAT DIMAGGIO."

That day, the writers barely made the locker room—and barely made the train out of Boston that evening. They were still in the press box pounding on their Underwood keyboards. There wasn't time enough, or words enough, to write that scene, that game, that series, and That Man . . . who'd lifted himself from his bed of pain, to triumph . . . no, to *conquer* . . . no, to *vanquish!* . . .

Good Lord, it was too big to write.

This wasn't New York news, but world news. It wasn't about what pitch the Clipper hit, nor his slugging percentage, nor even three games; nor about old Joe McCarthy, in fury, grabbing his pitcher and shaking him in the tunnel, screaming abuse about that lousy pitch. This wasn't about Boston eight games back—it wasn't about the pennant race. This wasn't just baseball! It was the greatest comeback in the history of sport! This was—*this* . . . was . . . divine.

Later, in days to come, Joe would attend to the godly overtones. ("I don't want to pose as 'Holy Joe' or anything like that, but I'll tell you, I feel that someone's got His arm around my shoulder.")

Later, he would deal with *Life* magazine, and its offer to pay him more than a working man made in a year (six thousand dollars!) for his picture on the cover and a ghost-written story, "My Greatest Comeback."

There'd be time, in the interim, to work out his aw-shucks lines ("I got lucky and a few balls dropped in.") in the aptly titled column: "Jimmy Cannon Says."

For the moment, Joe wasn't worried about any of that. First time in months, he wasn't worried. And he had nothing to say about heaven, history, or the Greatest Comeback. On that train out of Boston, he was leaning back in a corner of the dining car, half a dozen Yankee kids jabbering around him, his hand around a bottle of Pabst Blue Ribbon, his face around a small smile. Joe knew what was back. As one of the rookies, Jerry Coleman, remembered, all Joe said was: "Can't beat this life, kid."

NOW THAT GOD HAD A HAND IN THE pennant race, it had to happen: the season came down to two final games—Yanks against Boston—for all the marbles.

The Red Sox had finally picked themselves up off the canvas, and started punching out wins. In August, Boston went 24–8.

Still, the Yankees could not be overtaken—not while they had DiMaggio. For once, even Stengel saw nowhere to apply his genius. He'd fill out the lineup card, then sit on the bench and watch. "When I had him, Joe," as Stengel told Maury Allen, "you didn't have to look at center field and see he was lined up. He knew how to line up right. The others looked at him. If he moved, they moved. If he stood there, they stood there."

As did Stengel . . . until September 18, with the Yankees still two and a half games ahead. But God's little viruses were already at work. Joe's summer cold had turned into the flu, and then pneumonia. That day, he rode the bench with a temperature of 102.

Then he was in the hospital, shot full of penicillin,

while the Yankees lost the next two out of three. Boston was only two games back. Then the Yankees had two in Boston—but they all looked sick at the plate: Kinder threw a 3–0 shutout, and the next day, Parnell mowed them down, 4–1. Now the Sox and Yankees were tied. Both teams traveled back to New York for one game, to make up a rainout. DiMaggio was still in a Manhattan hospital. Boston won in the Bronx. That put the Red Sox into first place—one game up—for the first time that year. Both teams had five games left. Boston would have three against the Senators, the Yankees three against the A's. Both teams would win two out of three. Both would be back in New York for their last two: if the Yankees won both, they would have the pennant. If Boston could win one game, they'd scuttle the Yanks for the second straight year, and redeem '48's pathetic playoff.

DiMaggio had disappeared again into the Elysee. George Solotaire and one of his pals, a press agent, Bernie Kamber, were nursing the Big Guy around the clock. DiMaggio's face was gray and gaunt. He had lost eighteen pounds. He'd walk around the suite and then have to sit down. If he had to say more than ten words, he was out of breath. Still, Joe ordered Kamber to get him downstairs and into a cab, the day of that first game with Boston. Joe was going to the Stadium. Maybe he could play a few innings, maybe not. But he'd be there. After the Greatest Comeback, Weiss had scheduled .this day, October 1, as Joe DiMaggio Day.

Toots Shor was frantic with worry for the Dago. If Joe couldn't play right, if he made a mistake, didn't look right, it would kill him. As Joe and Kamber rode north to the Stadium, Toots was on the phone to the Yankees' front office. "Don't let anybody shake hands with him," Shor was pleading. "He's too sick. That'll take all the strength away from him."

But there was no choice. His mother had come across the country to be there, the mayor was there, the cardinal, Jim Farley . . . and seventy thousand fans, whose donations and gifts for Joe piled up on the field one after another, as Joe stood near home plate and listened to speeches—went on forever—from all the bigwigs who'd come to shine in his light. And there were telegrams and messages to be read out—like this one, from New York's most famous barkeep, Toots Shor: "You have given me more thrills than all the rest of the champions put together. You always won the Big Ones and never knew how to choke up. You are the biggest guy I know and the biggest thing about you is your heart. You gave us baseball fans the greatest moments we have ever had but something more than that, Joe, you gave me your friendship." At length, Joe's mother was introduced, and the crowd gasped as she came onto the field and walked right past Joe—to the Boston dugout. (She'd seen Joe, but she hadn't said hello to Dommie.) Then, Dominic came out, too, and stood next to Joe. Joe put his arm on his brother's shoulder, and Dom could feel Joe's weight. He always worried that Joe would think he was bathing in Joe's starlight, so he whispered: "Do you want me to leave now?" Joe rasped out one word. "No!" Dom was the only thing holding him up. And still, there were more gifts: a car, two cars, free taxi service, a Chris-Craft boat *(The Yankee Clipper)*, a watch, two watches, three watches, a college scholarship for Joe Jr., three hundred quarts of ice cream, five hundred Joe DiMaggio T-shirts, a case of lima beans . . . They said it was fifty thousand bucks' worth of stuff. Joe only wanted to sit down. But he had to speak. He had dreaded that speech: three or four pals wrote it, three or four times. But it turned out Joe's remarks would be brief. He got to the line "I'd like to thank the Good Lord for making me a Yankee." Then he burst into tears.

He'd told Stengel he would play three innings. But he struck out the first time up against Parnell. It couldn't end that way for Joe DiMaggio. Or for the Yanks. By the third inning, the Bostons had knocked Reynolds out, they led 4–0, and Casey had to call for Joe Page. After that inning, DiMaggio sat in the tunnel, sucking down a Chesterfield. He signaled to Stengel in the silent Yankee dugout, and held up five fingers. He would play at least through five.

He came up in the fourth. Parnell had been unhittable. He was working DiMaggio away with hard stuff. Weak as Joe looked, Parnell knew he'd never get around fast enough to pull the ball—hit anything with power. Joe knew it, too. So he lashed a ball on the outer half on a line into right field. The ball bounced once and went over the short fence. DiMaggio jogged into second base. And the Yankees were up in their dugout, and shouting. Bauer singled DiMaggio home with a line single to left. Lindell hit another rope to left and the Yankees had first and third. Coleman hit a sacrifice fly to Dom DiMaggio, and the Yankees were back in the game 4–2.

Next inning, Rizzuto started it with a single. Henrich followed with a ground single into right—Rizzuto to third. Then Berra singled, Rizzuto scored, and Henrich went to second. The Yanks had two men on, for Joe DiMaggio. In the Boston dugout, the fearful Joe McCarthy made another move that Boston fans would forever bemoan. Parnell was his ace. He'd won twenty-five games. But the Skipper wouldn't let DiMaggio face the lefty again. He brought in the right-hander, Joe Dobson, to get the Clipper out. But DiMaggio greeted Dobson with a shot that almost knocked him over: a line drive right back at the mound. Dobson could barely react in time to knock the ball down—it dribbled away, and he raced after it. By the time he straightened up with the ball in his hand, the Yankees had the bases loaded. And that made all the difference: Dobson got the next man, Billy Johnson—got him good, on a grounder for a double play. But Henrich scored from third, and the Yanks had tied the game 4–4.

And they had Joe Page, who was mowing Red Sox batters down. Page wasn't fooling around with any breaking balls, or change of speeds. He was throwing

it by 'em. He'd held the Red Sox through the fourth
and fifth, while the Yankees drew even. And now he
blew through the lineup again: sixth inning, seventh
and eighth—not a loud foul. At that point, it was only
a matter of time. Johnny Lindell hit the homer for the
Yanks in the bottom of the eighth, and that was all she
wrote. The Yanks won 5–4, and they were celebrating
again. In the clubhouse, they were singing and splat-
tering beer on Lindell. The writers were clustered
around Page—more like fans than scribes. "You were
the boss out there!" "I said in the press box, they'd
never touch you!" Page had one question: "What did
Dago say?"

Joe only had one thing to say. "Let's win tomorrow." And that calmed down the celebration. The
Yankees and Red Sox were tied again, with one game
to go.

The next day Joe looked even worse. But who
could tell Dago to sit? He suited up slowly and went
out to center field. Both clubs played their remaining
aces: Kinder for the Red Sox, Raschi for the Yanks.
And those pitchers put on a clinic. The only big hit
was Rizzuto's triple in the first inning. After that, Ol'
Reliable, Henrich (who hated to face Kinder—never
could hit him), choked up on the bat and hit a twenty-
six-hopper to the right side, to Doerr at second base.
That was real Yankee baseball: a tiny grounder that
brought the run home. The Yankees led 1–0. And
that's the way it stayed, for seven innings straight.

DiMaggio could do nothing with Kinder. He'd

come in each inning, get a smoke and a coffee, and stare at the floor of the tunnel until he had to go out there again. He felt like it took all day just to trot to his position. His legs were cramping. There was nothing in him. But the game was still 1–0. DiMaggio went to center field.

And then, in the eighth, once again, McCarthy made a fear-filled move. He pinch-hit for the furious Kinder, and brought in the exhausted pitcher from the previous game—Mel Parnell. Henrich, who'd rather face anyone than Kinder, greeted Parnell with a home run. It was 2–0. DiMaggio came up with a man on first, and again the skittish McCarthy waved a new pitcher in. Tex Hughson got DiMaggio to hit into a double play. But then he couldn't get anyone else. Lindell singled. Johnson singled. Cliff Mapes was walked to get to the rookie, Jerry Coleman, who fought off a high, tight fastball, and nudged a little pop fly out to right field. The second baseman, Doerr, raced back. The right fielder, Zarilla, sprinted in and dove. The ball hit inches from Zarilla's outstretched glove . . . and bounced away for a triple. Now, it was 5–0 Yankees—with the ferocious Raschi still on the mound.

Once again, one last time, the Red Sox tried to come back. Raschi was tired. With one out he walked Ted Williams. Then Stephens singled to center. DiMaggio had to come in on the run to keep Williams at second base. The next man, Doerr, hit a long fly to center field. It was well hit, but there was room out there—just the kind of long fly that DiMaggio would be waiting for, as the ball dropped into his glove. But this time he turned, his legs wouldn't go. He stumbled and the ball went by him for a triple. Boston had two runs, a man on third. DiMaggio held up a hand and called time. He waved to Stengel in the dugout. He was taking himself out of the game. He trotted in, to a standing ovation. That was Yankee baseball, too. He was not going to be the one to lose this game.

Mapes moved into center field, and promptly caught a fly ball from Zarilla. Goodman singled for one more Boston run—5–3. Birdie Tebbetts, the catcher, was coming up for the Red Sox. From first base, Henrich walked the ball to the mound, to buck up Raschi. "You only need one more out!" Tommy said. But Raschi turned on him and snarled, "Get the hell out of here and gimme the ball." Henrich walked back to first base, grinning. No way Tebbetts was gonna hit Raschi. Tebbetts managed only a pop-up to the right side. Henrich called everybody off, and squeezed it. The Yankees had the pennant.

They would have to face Brooklyn in the World Series—probably the best Brooklyn team in history. It wasn't just Robinson and Reese now, but Snider, Furillo, Hermanski in the outfield, Hodges on first, and Campanella behind the plate. It was a Dodger club without any weak spots—but an unlucky club. Because, once again, they'd have to play a Yankee team of destiny—men who knew they couldn't lose.

Joe played in that Series by force of will and nothing else. He was weak at the plate: two-for-eighteen. But he played, through five straight games—four of them wins. He managed a homer in the last game, when the Yankees had to slug it out 10–6.

After the Series he took his mamma out to La Guardia Field, to put her on an airplane for San Francisco. And he promised her, he would follow soon. She didn't like the way he looked. Nor did he. He'd just take care of a few business things—appearances, paid magazine stories, endorsement ads—the money was too good to ignore.

He would spend the next two weeks in New York. But they were quiet weeks. He didn't want to go out. He'd try to eat in a restaurant, and the minute he picked up a fork, some fan would be there. Didn't matter if Joe was with someone. They'd hang over him while he ate. "Joe, you look great!" "You'll kill 'em next year." "How 'bout those Red Sox—bums, huh?"

And Joe was tired. He didn't have anything to say to them. He was tired of them looking at him. First time in years, he just wanted to go home. So Georgie packed Joe's trunk and he went home, to San Francisco—where the local fans met him with a parade.

**One big happy family—with Stengel, and
the rookie, Mantle.**

**Handshakes for his homer—
the World Series, 1951.**

"I'm never putting on that monkey suit again."

CHAPTER 13

◆

DOUBT AND DIMAGGIO HAD SELDOM kept company. But after that season, they were seldom apart. Joe talked to Topping about retirement. "Don't even think about it," the owner told him. He wanted Joe to come over for dinner—at his place, 405 Park Avenue. Topping was married to Sonja Henie, the skating star, and he liked to impress her: Dan and his hundred-thousand-dollar man. Anyway, Topping could read the numbers: with tickets, concessions, parking, radio, and TV, his World Champion Yankees probably made three million dollars that year—with one .300 hitter, a part-timer named DiMaggio, at .346. Topping wanted Joe to know he wasn't going to lose a nickel, just because he'd played in only half the games. He could have another hundred-thousand-dollar contract right now—just say the word. Joe wouldn't say the word. "Take some time off," Topping insisted. "Relax, go home, rest up. You'll feel different."

In San Francisco, Joe did feel different—stronger for one thing, week by week. His mamma was cooking every night, and he lost the hollows in his cheeks and ribs. But it wasn't just bulk, the pounds he recovered. His legs came back. He could go all day—never think about his legs—like he used to when he was a kid on those hills. His old skipper (and guide to the big time), Lefty O'Doul, finally had persuaded him to try his hand at golf. Joe had always thought it was a game for rich old farts. Well, O'Doul reminded him, he was just about qualified, on all counts. Joe was thirty-five that November—the same month golf became a passion.

They'd go out early to the city course at Salada Beach—or any one of the country clubs. Lefty never bothered with memberships. There wasn't any golf pro in Northern California who didn't know Lefty and want him at his club. O'Doul and DiMag? If Lefty would've called ahead, they'd have strewn the first tee with rose petals. . . . Most days, the boys would play thirty-six holes. Lunch in between rounds. Maybe a steam at the Olympic Club after. If they didn't play two rounds, they'd still be out all day. They'd go to the country, and wander. Lefty called this hunting. But they never shot much. They'd tramp the brown hills in the sunshine for a couple of hours, and finish at some hick-town bar where Lefty would buy rounds for every man in the joint.

When Joe would come home, to shower and dress for the evening, there would be Mamma in the kitchen, waiting. She'd been cooking for him all day—pasta with the sardines, roasted peppers with the olive oil—then how about a nice steak? . . . This was the life, the life he'd been raised to. Or the life that he imagined all the money would have brought him—should have brought him. His mamma was old, now. He could see her strength fading. Joe's sister Marie lived in and helped her keep the place. But to cook for her boy—no, not a boy, but the man of the household—that was Rosalie's pleasure. After his coffee, she would make sure his suit and tie looked perfect, before he went out for the night.

In fact, Joe hauled the freight for two households—though in one, he wasn't a hundred percent welcome. That November, Dorothy went back to court in New York, suing for more money. Little Joe's private school cost a fortune, and a hundred fifty dollars a month just didn't make ends meet. She wanted six-fifty. The lawyer Joe got steered to, a guy named Rosenblatt, called the suit "an outrageous action, without moral or legal basis." But Joe had to hand it to the broad: she had spunk. At least they were talking again. Tell the truth, he'd missed that.

Did Little Joe like the train he'd sent?

She said he didn't want toys. He wanted Big Joe to teach him how to hook-slide.

Well . . . that was his boy! She was his, too—always would be. That December, he piled up toys to send to Little Joe anyway. He sent along a little something, in fur, for the boy's mother. And before Christmas came, he gave them both another gift: the lawyer, Rosenblatt, informed the court, the suit had been settled. Terms were confidential of course—but mother and son shouldn't worry about money in the years to come.

Nighttimes, in San Francisco, Joe would have a couple of belts with his pal, the bartender Reno Barsocchini—couldn't do enough when the Clipper came in. Joe told Reno, he might be seeing Dorothy again.

That's great, Joe. Beautiful girl . . .

Pretty good, Joe would say, for an old guy like him.

You look great, Clipper. 'Nother belt? . . .

When George Weiss called the house in the Marina, late January, he and DiMaggio came to terms without any fuss. DiMaggio boarded a plane for New York, to appear at the Yankees' midtown office, and pose for pictures with Topping. Joe had his signing pen in his hand, and a big grin on his mug. He looked great.

Everything was coming back to him. He didn't have to push for the money—or anything else. People knew who Joe DiMaggio was. . . . That off season, there was the AP story on the vote for the Comeback of the Year. Joe won in a walk. (The second-place winner was the New York Yankees.) Joe was also the Christian Athlete of the Year. *The Sporting News* polled all major-leaguers on the player they most admired: more than eighty-five percent named DiMaggio. The Yankees were polled on the player they most admired *in the history of the game*—Joe won that, too. And those were only the formal tributes. How about Louella's Hollywood column—on all the excitement about *The Joe DiMaggio Story*? ("Joe is looking good enough to play himself, but I doubt if he will.") And there was Earl Wilson's column, *It Happened Last Night.* ("When he came in with his pals, Gentleman Georgie Solotaire and Bernie Kamber, the diners . . . quit eating and cheered him. . . . It remained for me to tell Joe that the NY Custom Designers will name him one of the ten Best Dressed Men of the Year.")

Everywhere he went it was the same: "Joe, you look great." (That's when Toots made his famous prediction: at Dago's funeral, twenty thousand people are gonna file by the casket—and every one of 'em says, "Joe, you look great!")

That was the season Joe's press agent pal, Bernie Kamber, was going to pick him up in the hotel lobby, when all of a sudden he saw Helen Hayes. She was the biggest name on Broadway—and she wanted to know, what's Bernie doing there? Then, of course, she wanted to meet DiMaggio. And so did her friends, who came in to meet her—Lillian and Dorothy Gish—these were legends! So Bernie called upstairs and told Joe, "There's some bobby-soxers down here who wanna say hello to you." And Joe and the ladies went off together, for coffee and a nice chat. (No, Bernie never knew what they talked about—he guessed it was about being famous.)

That was the season Joe and Jerry Coleman flew together to spring training. Joe went back to San Francisco, where Marie and his mamma got his things together. Then the two Yankees left from San

Francisco airport. Even with planes, it was still a tough trip. They would fly to L.A., then to Fort Worth, then to New Orleans, and finally to Tampa, where they'd get a cab across the Bay, to St. Pete. But Joe was in a good mood—telling Coleman: no more New York winters for him. San Francisco, every year. The way he felt now, he could play forever. Next year, maybe he'd bring, you know, the family. . . .

But the part Coleman would remember best—remember forever—was the stop in Fort Worth. "Joe said, 'S'gettapaper. . . .'

"He always talked quick, you know—sharp. He didn't spend a lot of time communicating. So, okay, Joe. We start going through this airport. Now I don't know how many people had television sets in those days. Not many. . . .

"But we're going through this airport to the newsstand and it was like, I guess, a prince or somebody. The attention. The eyes. Everybody knew who he was. And I'm thinking, 'That's the last time I travel with this guy.' You just couldn't be alone. . . . But it was like a president was walking through the airport."

But that was also the season of another incident with impact on Joe. He wasn't there. It happened in Phoenix. The other owner of the Yankees, Del Webb, always wanted the Yanks to train in the western desert. He was the biggest developer out there—and he could bring his Vegas friends, and show off. But it was too hard to move the whole spring training. So the Yankees just ran a one-week rookie camp.

Stengel showed up. He loved young players. And these bush-leaguers were the future of the Yankees. His future. His Yankees. Casey had also spent the winter hearing how great he was: the way he'd made the Yankees champs again, with all those kids—shuffling platoon players in and out of the lineup—*what a genius!* And he commenced to agree. That's when he modestly reminded the New York sporting press *("my writers,"* as he referred to them): "I couldn'a done it without my players."

Anyway, it happened late in this rookie camp, with a kid so young, so green and unknown, that no one had given him a glance at the start. Just a freckle-faced boy: he'd played only half a year—at Class D McAlester, Oklahoma. Maybe this year he'd make Class C, Joplin. In the sprints, he'd timed out the fastest in camp. But he was a shortstop who'd make you wince on every ground ball. (And his throws—*Jesus, take cover!)* Then, on the fourth day, there's an intrasquad game. The boy shyly steps in, batting right-handed—and hits a ball farther than anybody's ever seen a ball hit. Next time up—new pitcher, he turns around, left-handed—and blasts off another A-bomb, even longer. All of a sudden, Stengel's out of the dugout, running. First time most of those rookies ever saw him. The old man runs on his bandy bow legs right onto the field, with a fungo bat in his hand, waving it and stabbing, like a picador with his sword. And he's pokin' the kid, chases him—*what'sis name? Mantle?*—from home plate past the mound, past second base. "He's not playin' any more infield," Casey announces. "I'm personally gonna teach him to play center field."

IT WAS MOSTLY BOYS IN ST. PETERS-burg, too. Joe had to look around to find anybody he knew—a real Yankee, one of his guys. Stengel and Weiss had shuffled Charlie Keller off to the Tigers. They seemed to want a ball team where no one could remember past last year. (Soon, they'd shuck Snuffy Stirnweiss, too—to the Browns, for the bullpen pitcher Tom Ferrick. And Johnny Lindell they'd sell off to the Cardinals, for a pocketful of cash.) Tom Henrich was there—though Stengel now treated him like a coach. ("Mr. Hendricks, you can commence to show my outfielders how to make a throw.") . . . The only player from before the war who still had a spot was the shortstop, Rizzuto. And then there was Joe.

Everywhere else, there was someone new—or more than one: Casey had at least two for every spot on the diamond. Jerry Coleman, only in his second year, was suddenly splitting time with a pop-off Casey had managed in Oakland, a snot named Billy Martin. Third base, Billy Johnson was already pla-tooned with the med student Bobby Brown. The kid first baseman, Joe Collins (only got into seven games last year), was supposed to split time with the Big Cat, Johnny Mize (who'd come over from the Giants). In the outfield, it was all fresh legs—or just fresh: Bauer,

Mapes, Jensen, Woodling, Workman . . . they should have had name tags. And then there was Joe.

Stengel had the bit in his teeth—and he was going to prove true all that stuff "his writers" put into the papers, about his uncanny handling of kids, the masterful juggling, the brilliant platoons. The truth was, he was better with kids: they were so anxious to be Yankees, and stay Yankees; they were so grateful if he gave them a chance—if he *did* put them in, if he'd just *let them play* . . . they'd overachieve, and make him look like a genius. He liked kids because they'd sit still for his manipulation—and never utter a protest. He liked kids because they didn't care if he ever learned their names. (He'd walk down the dugout, stop in front of Hank Workman, and send him in to bat: "Jerry! Get up and hit one!") He liked kids because he liked writers better—and no writer would spend ink commending some twenty-three-year-old for his brilliant understanding of the game. No, there would be one Great Brain in that dugout. Twenty-five moving parts—one master mechanic.

And then there was Joe.

Fact was, "the Big Fella" was screwing up Stengel's act. Visiting writers would come in flocks to the spring camp of the World Champs, and the Ol' Perfesser (as they had dubbed Stengel) would hold court all day. He'd rewritten his history, to show he'd always been a Great Brain. Those other managin' jobs he'd had—why, they weren't even ball teams: "They was like golf courses," Casey would say. "One pro to a club." . . . He was rewriting last year's history—about that tough game with them Boston sluggers, where he seen his big Indian didn't have it, so he commences to remove him from the mound—which Mr. Rennels is unhappy: he wants to stay in. "So I tell him, 'I'd love to leave you in, but I got too many married men in the infield.' "

Mostly, Stengel was at pains to explain how genius worked: "When a man is aged and you rest him" (as Casey was quoted by one of his writers, the noted author Roger Kahn), "he will get limber again with his muscles and he runs faster and he becomes quicker with the bat. You do this, rest him good, and then his legs is fresh for five or six days. Platoonin' is also good for the young players, which they is the last to agree, because they get to come along at a slow pace. Now it is possible to see a young player who thinks he can hit any pitcher, which he did in the minor leagues. And he goes to the plate and gives it a great fight but those balls comin' in have too much stuff for him to handle, too much curve, because the pitchers are more expert, which is not even talking about the change of speeds. After a while the young player don't think he can hit any pitcher anymore. When a young player loses confidence in hisself, that is a terrible thing. I have seen them, good ones, blow up in a single season. They never make it back. They have been humiliated in professional baseball and will go somewhere else for their livelihood. You platoon the players depending on the pitcher and so forth but you also platoon them when they are gettin' distressed. You platoon them for their mental condition. . . ."

After hours of this, the writers would go off for a couple of minutes with DiMag—who'd tell them, this year, he planned to play every game.

And what would they write?

Yank Hopes on DiMaggio

". . . The way I feel now," he said, with an air of self-confidence, "I'm going to play a full 154 games, something I've been able to do only once in eleven years. Honestly, I never felt better in my life."

. . . The $100,000 salaried star has worked as hard as the most eager rookie in camp.

Worse still for Stengel, his New York writers would come and tell *him:* DiMaggio wasn't going to play today. He had a blister. Or Dago's left shoulder popped—he was gonna sit out . . .

(Who was runnin' this club?)

Roger Kahn quoted the Ol' Perfesser in another conversation—this one with his number one (maybe only) advisor, his partner for the last twenty-five years:

" 'I got this fella,' Stengel remarked to his wife, Edna, 'who sucks up all the glory and plays only when he feels like playing. I never had one like that before. What am I gonna do?'

"Edna Lawson Stengel was a practical person. 'Let him play whenever he wants to play, dear.' "

But in this case Stengel would not take her advice.

JOE STARTED IN AT A LATHER—AND the Yankees with him. Opening day, April 18, Fenway Park, was just like last year—all in one game. The Bombers spotted the rival Red Sox a 9–zip lead (with Parnell on the mound) . . . and then, the show began: DiMag blew away a runner at third base with a throw that could have come from a cannon; when he raced to the bullpen wall for an amazing over-the-shoulder catch, even writers in the press box were shouting. At the plate he smashed a triple over brother Dommie's head, and then threw in a single and a double, as the Yankees scored nine runs in the eighth—and a win, 15–10.

But after that, he cooled off just as fast. Twice in those early weeks, he suffered droughts of oh-fer-thirteen. He'd get it going for a game or two—he'd smash two or three over the wall, he'd be driving in runs by the handful . . . then, he'd founder through the next ten games with nothing more than a single. By the time the season was six weeks old, the Yanks were struggling for first place with the Tigers. And DiMaggio was just struggling—at an average of .243.

For the writers, this was a mystery that required explanation. Most of them—the young ones—worked the story in the trainer's room. Joe said he felt fine. But those Depression dinosaurs always said they were fine. What about that pulled back muscle? (Was the Clipper still wearing that girdle?) . . . What about his left arm that would pop out of his shoulder socket whenever he took a big cut? (Hadda hurt like hell, right?) . . . But the medical detectives found no satisfaction.

They'd troop into Stengel's office and ask him. But Casey would commence to talk. ("Well, the Big Fella, you haveta say, he knows where the ballpark is, and he knows when to get there, and that's the first thing ya haveta consider. Now there's some ballplayers—and you could look it up . . .") And after an hour, he hadn't said a damn thing.

They'd ask their pals on the club—players their age. But if Joe said anything past Hello, those kids just stared like deer in the headlights. (He spoke to them!) As for asking—well, maybe, if a few guys were sitting around, after a game or on the train, maybe they'd ask the Dago about some play, or a pitcher, or something they were doing. They sure as hell weren't going to ask what was wrong with *him*.

And the couple of coots in the press box, they were no help, as usual. Dan Daniel was still up there, in his vest and suit coat, still trying to tell the whippersnappers what Babe Ruth used to say about a slump, or what the great John McGraw once told him. But nowadays Daniel could also fall silent, with his head down, chin covering his tie, as he caught a snooze through the middle innings. . . .

The fact was, there were few men anywhere around the Yankees who knew what was eating at DiMag. Maybe a couple of coaches (the old Yanks— Dickey, Crosetti): they were the ones who were advising Stengel, don't say anything about the Dago. The fellows in Joe's network knew: Cannon probably, and Georgie for sure. Frank Scott knew, and Toots, of course. But they wouldn't speak. That was how they stayed in. That, and they'd sit up with Daig into the wee hours—sympathizing.

How could the broad do this to him?

Sure, he went in the tank the minute the Yankees came home from Boston: that's when Dorothy gave him the word—*thanks for the dough, and adios*—she wasn't moving back in with him. She wasn't even going to stay in New York. She was tired of New York—and what about her career? She was singing with a band again. Now she wanted to be in pictures. She was going to take the kid—soon as school was out—and move to Los Angeles. And not a damn thing Joe could do about it.

What about San Francisco? . . .

She laughed at him.

THE FIRST NOISE HE HEARD CAME from Dan Topping: "Joe, we want to make a little change . . ." That's what finished DiMaggio and his manager: Stengel wouldn't talk to him, man to man.

In June, the Yankees had fallen out of first place—they went to Detroit and lost three out of four. Stengel was frantic. But how was Casey going to be a genius with his center fielder batting .250—and at cleanup? . . . Casey had kids who could hit—or they might hit. But all outfielders: *How could he play 'em?* What he didn't have was a first baseman. Henrich had a knee that never would be right again. Mize couldn't throw. Collins couldn't hit. . . . But if Stengel put DiMaggio at first base, he'd get Bauer, Woodling, Mapes in the outfield, the bonus baby, Jensen, to fill in. Then, he'd have bats in the lineup, fresh legs in the field—and he'd have kids. Casey had commenced to think the unthinkable.

So Topping had to tell the Dago. Beginning of July—*why don't we have lunch?* . . . Topping signed Joe's checks. If you counted meal-money, that was eight grand and change, every two weeks. . . . So what could Joe do, but agree?

The experiment would begin July 3, at Washington. The writers were in an uproar. ("DIMAG MOVES TO FIRST BASE!") Stengel told them all how he'd talked this over with the Big Fella—of course: "And DiMaggio is going to give it a try because he is that type of player. When I asked him whether he'd try playing the bag, he replied, 'Certainly, I'll play anywhere you want if you think it will help the club.' " For his part, Joe stuck to Gary Cooper lines: "Now, if someone will show me where first base is . . ." But when he left the locker room, and found photographers jostling for position at the first base bag, the role stopped there. No, he wouldn't pose.

But he played it. And the papers said he did fine. He handled thirteen putouts without an error, and "looked as comfortable as a veteran first-sacker." The players knew different.

Tom Ferrick pitched that day. There was a swinging bunt down the first base line. Ferrick hustled over. Joe raced in—but Ferrick yelled: "I got it!" . . . And DiMaggio put on the brakes, tried to scramble back. He fell near the bag, on his hands and knees. He almost got stepped on. . . . "He almost got hurt," as Ferrick remembered. "But I knew it was shame. He was so furious to look clumsy. He was enraged."

Henrich could tell from the dugout. He knew first base—and he knew the Dago. He could see Joe trying to think his way through . . . and burning. "He's worried all over," Henrich said. "He's afraid of making a dumb play—because he's not familiar with first base. It would have *killed him* to make a stupid play."

The other thing Henrich remembered was Joe's exhaustion, after that game. You could always sweat in Washington. But in the locker room, Joe was wet. His T-shirt was soaked. And that gray road-flannel must have weighed five pounds.

And just as Joe feared, the following day all the papers carried pictures of the Yankee Clipper, crawling around in the dirt. . . . Even so, fortune had smiled on

DiMaggio. In that game, Bauer had sprained an ankle, sliding into second base—he'd be out of the lineup indefinitely. So, the next day, Joe was back in center field.

But Stengel was still thinking.

ONE WEEK LATER, JOE PLAYED IN the 1950 All-Star Game: his twelfth straight selection, he had to show up. But he didn't start. He didn't deserve to. Anyway, he wasn't right. Had a pulled groin muscle—that's what they said. So he sat in the White Sox dugout in Comiskey Park, until the very end of that game—which was a thriller, extra innings. The Nationals had tied it in the ninth, and the two leagues matched zeroes till the fourteenth, when at last the Nationals pushed across another run. The AL had one more chance—and they got a man on—then, DiMaggio came up. He grounded into a double play, and that was the game. Joe was the goat.

That night, the locker room story out of Chicago was headlined:

DiMag Lonesome
Dejected Figure

"They wanted me to swing and I did," said Joe, sitting alone and dejected in front of his locker. "Blackwell served up a slow curve ball, I went for it and just didn't bite into it enough, that's all. I don't feel so good about it."

But the rest of the stories were worse. This was the chance for the national press to tee off on the Great Man's slump.

"The brutal truth," wrote the AP's sports feature writer, Whitney Martin, "is that the Yankee Clipper hasn't much wind at his back as he sails toward the end of his career. Joe suddenly has been taken old."

By the time Joe got back to New York, the Yankee writers had the news that DiMag had aggravated his pulled muscle, trying to beat out that double-play grounder. The Ol' Perfesser said a few days' rest should put him right.

So DiMaggio was sitting in the Yankee dugout, too. For four games he sat, and watched Johnny Mize batting cleanup—where the Big Cat went on a spree (thirteen-for-fifteen, with five home runs). . . . When Stengel put Joe back in the lineup, Mize was still listed as the fourth batter. Joe DiMaggio, who'd batted in the cleanup spot since 1939, was shoved down the order, to number five.

Toots was in his box at the Stadium that afternoon. He saw the lineups posted on the scoreboard, and his heart ached for the Dago. "If Casey wanted to embarrass him by dropping him down in the lineup," Shor recalled for Maury Allen, "he should have done it on the road, the dirty son of a buck. . . . I started to get up and leave when I saw the lineup. The fans wouldn't have known but the writers would have. They would have written about it. Casey never said nothing to Joe. He just put Mize in there against this right-hander and Mize hit two homers. Joe got two hits and came in that night and he's knocking over a belt.

" 'Sore, ain'tcha?'

" 'Yeah, I'm sore. The least he could have done was explain it to me.' "

Now, it was war.

Curt Gowdy, the young broadcaster who was side-kick to Mel Allen in the Yankee radio booth, was out with his wife, Geri, that night. And of course, they wandered into Shor's. Toots had always been friendly to them—ever since they'd arrived in New York, with the Big Sky of Wyoming still in their eyes. But on that night, as Gowdy remembered, Toots went nuts—started shouting at him:

" 'YOU AND THAT SON OF A BITCH . . .' "

Gowdy said he finally figured out, Toots meant Stengel. "I said, 'Hey, it wasn't me!'

" 'Ah, you're all with him!'

"Toots was all about choosing sides," Gowdy said. "He was in the DiMag camp."

For his part, DiMaggio essayed a silence so total and fearsome that it chilled the whole Yankee clubhouse. He would not acknowledge Stengel by word or deed. If Joe was in the dugout, and Casey started talking, DiMaggio would turn on his heel and walk away.

In fact, a number of players didn't want to talk to

Stengel. Or didn't want to get caught talking to him. It would look like they were brownnosing. Everybody knew he played favorites. It was almost disloyal to your teammates if you sat and *let* him talk. Of course, there were times it couldn't be avoided. Stengel would call a clubhouse meeting and talk for an hour and a half straight—like he was hungry to talk—like the silence just made him talk more. Even some writers walked away.

"Eh! He's a bore," Louie Effrat said.

But some of them listened—his writers:

"DiMaggio is sulking like a sophomore," wrote Joe Trimble in the *Daily News,* on August 3. "No one denies this great player the right of his pride. But he is carrying things too far when he refuses to talk to the manager, curtly cuts the newspapermen who have been his friends for years and maintains a stony silence toward all but a few of his teammates."

DiMaggio's silence toward Trimble would last the rest of his life.

But if Joe thought he could make Stengel buckle with the icy stare, the evil eye . . . he was about thirty years too late. "So what if he doesn't talk to me?" said Stengel with the clear concision that always signaled his bottom line. "DiMaggio doesn't get paid to talk, and I don't either. He gets paid to play ball. I get paid to manage. If what I'm doing is wrong, my bosses will fire me. I've been fired lots of places before."

The real bottom line with Stengel was that all the clowning, the eagerness to entertain, the monologues and mispronunciations, the practiced old stories and "you could look it up" . . . all were accreted and deployed for decades to disguise a leathery survivor's soul. He'd seen ballplayers come and go for forty years. But Stengel was still there. More than just there: he was in that All-Star dugout as manager of the World Champs, while the rest were home listening in on the radio—for instance, Joe McCarthy, who'd just got fired by the Red Sox . . . and some had to yell to the nurse to put the game on . . . and some, as Casey often pointed out, were "dead at the present time." It would take more than DiMaggio's evil eye to run Stengel out of his game.

The players got the picture little by little, in flashes, clear and hard. There was the day in Casey's first year, when the Yankees were riding the train out of Philly after losing three straight to the woeful A's. Some kids were at a dining car table, playing Twenty Questions. "I got a question," Stengel said as he passed. "Which one of you clowns ain't gonna be here tomorrow?" Henrich got the message later that year, when he raced back on a long drive to right, ran out of room and slammed into the outfield wall. He lay on the ground (as it turned out, with broken ribs), as Casey ran out to the wall on his old bandy legs. "Stay down," Casey murmured softly, as he bent over his fallen player. "Just stay down." Jeez, he really cares, Henrich thought. Still, he tried to get up. "Stay down, dammit," Stengel ordered, "until I get somebody warmed up."

But Joe DiMaggio, along with the rest of the startled Baseball Nation, got the picture that August 11,
1950, when for the first time in his career, the Yankee
Clipper was benched. This time, there wasn't the fig
leaf of a pulled muscle—or anything else. Joe wasn't
hitting. (Four-for-his-last-thirty-eight.) Simple as
that. And he was on the pine.

Stengel said DiMaggio would sit for the next six or
seven games. No, he hadn't talked to the Great
Man—and didn't need to. New York was still three
back of Detroit. The Yanks had lost six of their last
nine games—during which the Bombers had hit
.186. "The way we're hitting," Stengel said, "I should
bench the entire team."

So Joe sat for six games, in silence. And he
burned. And while he sat, the Yanks fell four behind.

God bless Bauer. He got hurt again—beaned by a
throw as he slid into third and he had to be carried off
the field. The next night, August 18, DiMaggio
started in center field, and batting cleanup against the
A's. The game stayed tight into the ninth—a 2–2
squeaker . . . until DiMaggio caught a pitch from
Lou Brissie and drove it into the left field seats—
upper deck. A dozen Philadelphia kids jumped out of
the stands and mobbed Joe at third base. He had to
fight his way to the plate. The Yankees won 3–2.
DiMaggio was back.

The next day it was 6–2 over the A's again. This
time DiMaggio got a double, two singles, and drove
in two runs. Day after that . . . well, God was back in

His heaven, and all was right on the sports page again. The Yanks would win ten of their next eleven games. They would take over first place from the Tigers. In those games DiMaggio would hit at a .400 clip, slamming shots off the walls, and over the walls, leading the club in runs batted in, in homers, doubles, slugging percentage . . . until his knees gave out. Then, he had to sit again.

He came back again in September—and he was still on a tear. He would hit in nineteen straight games. He had pushed his average through the .260's, .270's, and into the .280's . . . another man would have been delirious with joy. But there was no joy for DiMaggio. The Yankees weren't winning consistently—like Yankees—winning every game they had to win. A week into September, they lost three in a row and let the Tigers climb back into first. Worse still, two of those losses were to Boston—now, the Red Sox were only two games back. And whatever Joe did now, he was kicking himself. It wasn't enough.

No matter how tough Stengel was, no boss was tougher on Joe than Joe. He admitted no ease. He'd get to bed late and wake up too early. He'd get to the locker room early, take off his pants, hang them in his locker, light a smoke, accept his half-a-cup from Pete Sheehy . . . and then just sit there—for hours—until he had to get taped. After games, he'd sit for hours again, sip a couple of beers and stare at the floor. Like the game had left him no strength to get dressed. There was no place he wanted to go. He stayed out of

Shor's. Any other joint was out of the question. Georgie would get him a sandwich at night. Often, Joe wouldn't eat it. He had always spent two or three hours after games—until the kids with their autograph books had gone home. But now, it was longer—and it wasn't the kids. After one night game, he stayed till two-thirty A.M. Sheehy always stayed with him. When Joe finally got ready to leave, Pete walked with him across the empty diamond and silent outfield to the center field gate—kids never figured that out. A cab would be waiting on the empty street, to ride Joe back to Manhattan.

Now, his isolation wasn't so much forbidding—more like foreboding: Joe was in a fight that no one could help him with. The young Yankees would have done anything for him—they'd tell each other, or their friends, family, writers, what a thrill it was to be on *his team* . . . but they couldn't tell him. Wouldn't presume.

The one exception was that pop-off, Billy Martin. He was all presumption, anyway. Martin had gone back to the minors, mid-season. But now, in September, he came back, brash as ever. He'd walk into the clubhouse, and hang his pants in his locker (always the pants first)—and call to Sheehy: "Half-a-cuppa-coffee, Pete!" Sheehy would've thrown the coffee on him . . . but DiMaggio would just look over with a wan smile.

It was after games Joe couldn't smile. If the Yankees didn't win, he'd lost that game. If he got two hits, he should've had three. If he got three, he wanted that fourth so bad he could taste it. What he wanted was a .300 average—except for '46, after the war, he'd never hit below that. If he couldn't hit .300, it was over for him.

On the bench, they'd hear him swear at himself from the tunnel, where he sat and smoked. Hank Workman, the fifth outfielder, only got in a couple of games that year. But he had another job: as each inning ended, he had to light a Chesterfield, take one puff and have it burning for the Dago when he came in from center field. After Joe finished his smoke, he'd resume his place at one end of the bench, legs crossed, back against the dugout wall, arms crossed in front of his chest, as he muttered through his private war. Henrich was next to Joe one day, as they watched Bobby Brown knock a single through the right side of the infield. Brown always had bat control, and he was smart: got a lot of hits that way. Joe said softly, without turning his head: "How come his fuckin' grounders go through?"

Then Joe would go to the plate and try to hit the ball through a wall. September 12, in Washington, DiMaggio hit three out of Griffith Stadium—first time anyone had done that, in the history of that old boneyard: it was four hundred and five feet *to the left field corner* . . . and he threw in a double and a walk for a perfect day. The 8–1 Yankee win brought the Bombers within a half-game of Detroit—and raised Joe's totals for the year to twenty-seven homers, with more than a hundred runs knocked in—for the ninth time in his career. (Joe even went out for dinner that night.)

But next day, a doubleheader, there he was muttering again: for Joe, it wasn't what you did one day, but every day, every play. Even in his private struggle there was something instructive in his every act—or the way he cared about his every act. One day in that stretch run, he came up with two Yankees on and hit a shot over third, a screamer . . . and the third baseman leapt into the air to make one hell of a catch. Just another loud out. Joe trotted back to the bench and launched a swift kick at the empty ball bag that hung in the Yankee dugout. There were always two leather bags hanging there—one full, one empty. Problem was, Joe made a mistake, and kicked the full one. It had to hurt like a hammer-blow; he could've broken his foot; there were balls rolling all over the field. A deep blush spread across DiMaggio's cheeks. And there was silence—save for a couple of snorts—as the Yankee kids tried not to laugh. But that was the game: the Yanks erupted for a half-dozen runs, and put it away.

September 14, still a half-game back, the Yankees went to Detroit for the showdown series—three games for first place. In the first game, Joe hit his twenty-ninth home run, and the Yankees won 7–5. The next day they lost, and fell behind the Tigers once more. So on the third day, the Yanks would have one last chance to take over first place. . . . Fifty-six thousand Detroit fans packed Briggs Stadium to cheer on their big right-hander, Dizzy Trout. The Yankees took the field behind a rookie southpaw who'd been called up from the minors in July. He was just a runt, at five foot eight (though the Yankees made it five ten in the program). But this kid—they called him Eddie Ford—had plenty of guts, and brought to the mound all the moxie of the New York streets where he'd learned to play.

They matched zeroes for five innings: one of those games that could go on forever, and no one would have any fingernails left. But in the sixth, DiMaggio hit a ball four hundred twenty-five feet to left center—gone by a mile—and gave Whitey Ford a 1–0 lead. He held off Detroit through the sixth, and the seventh. But in the eighth, disaster—back-to-back doubles—and Detroit was even at 1–1. Ford was the first scheduled batter in the ninth. He figured he was gone for a pinch hitter, for sure. But lately Joe Page hadn't been worth a damn—and Stengel hated him. So he let Ford hit, and Whitey drew a walk. That was the beginning of the end for Trout. The end of the end was DiMaggio, who came up with bases loaded. This time Joe didn't try to knock down walls—but lined the first pitch he could reach for a single into left, for two runs, and the game. The Yankees would score seven times in that inning. Ford would finish as a winner, 8–1. That night, he would run out for the papers that announced in bold, black headlines: "Ford, DiMaggio Beat Tigers." (He'd buy fifty, and mail 'em all home.) That night, the Yankees would leave town with first place in their grasp. And the Tigers would be also-rans for another year.

Only Boston could threaten now. The Red Sox were coming to the Stadium for two games, September 23 and 24. They were two games back. They'd have to win both. But they never had a chance. First inning of the first game, Mel Parnell let one Yankee get on—and that brought DiMaggio to the plate. He hit a two-run homer, and that was all Lopat would need. The Yankees won the first game 8–0—won both games tidily, in fact—and Boston was finished. The Yankees would clinch another pennant without any more trouble.

In six weeks since Joe had come off the bench, he had hit for an average of .376, with eleven home runs. He had knocked in thirty runs just in September . . . but it wasn't enough—or might not be. The Yankees were supposed to be loafing through their last games, just tuning up for the Series. But Joe was still at war.

"There was a game in Philadelphia," as Jerry Coleman remembered, "right at the tag end of the season, maybe two or three games to go. And Joe was at two-nine-nine-point-six, or three-oh-oh-point-four— right on the borderline. Now, to me, .300 would have been, 'Oh, that's wonderful!' If I hit .298, well, that's good, too. DiMaggio was .300 or nothing. Because that represented great baseball.

"And he hit a line drive to Eddie Joost, who was

playing at shortstop for the A's, and it was caught—last out of the inning. Now, I'm out at second base, and Joe comes by, out to center field. And he was mumbling. He always talked to himself a little bit. And he said, 'How'd I look? How'd I look?'

"I said, 'Joe, you look great.'

"And I'm thinking—my first reaction was: 'Why's he asking me? I can't even hit .300.'

" 'How'd I look?' . . .

"But I think he needed this confidence-builder from anybody, anywhere. You know, he just needed that comment, to hear that. *'Joe, you look great.'* And I did say that."

The Yankees would face the Whiz Kid Phillies in a World Series that was over in a blink. DiMaggio would beat their ace, Robin Roberts, with a home run in the tenth . . . and that was all she wrote. There was another game the Yanks had to win in their last at bat, and Raschi had to win his start 1–0. But there was never much doubt who was going to win—in the end, it was four straight.

And for a second straight year, the Yankee players had to hold a tribunal to decide how to divvy up the Series shares. (Fifty-three hundred dollars for a full share!) . . . Dago was the chief judge, as always—final authority. A few guys started joking around: maybe they'd cut Stengel to half a share! But the joke died. Daig didn't join in. Most of the fellows didn't know—hadn't heard, with all the whooping and the singing after that last game—how Casey had come to the Big Guy in the clubhouse. Now that "Stengel's Yankees" were in the record books as champions two years in a row, the old man went to DiMaggio's stool, and told him: "Joe, we couldn't have done it without you."

And those books would also show: DiMaggio had finished his '50 season at an average of .301.

NO DOUBT AND DIMAGGIO WOULD spend the off season together. Before he left New York, he told the writers, he didn't know if he'd be back to play next year. He also gave them to understand, he didn't much like the question. So nobody pushed. He said he'd see how his knees felt—they'd tell him whether or not to come back. . . . But he knew his knees wouldn't tell him a thing. He'd tell his knees. It was will that made DiMaggio.

The odd fact was, it was only because he'd had a bad season that he wanted to come back. He didn't want the fans to remember him struggling. He wanted at least one more good year.

He had the rest of his life to consider. And he was still counting cards. By that time, he'd tucked away a few aces for the long game. During that year, he'd signed up with CBS radio, for fifty thousand a year. He'd only done a weekly fifteen-minute show—answers for kids who wrote in with sports questions. But it wasn't bad: Joe would speak his answers into a studio microphone, while the engineers cut a record of his voice. If he messed up, he could redo the answer. He did each one until it was perfect. . . . Between Frank Scott, the pioneer sports agent, and another new lawyer (this one was Rosen*thal),* Joe had more endorsement offers than he could handle. He was already doing cereal and cigarettes, a line of toiletries, T-shirts, sport shirts, rubber balls with his autograph stamped on, baseballs, baseball gloves and bats. (Lefty Gomez had a sweetheart arrangement with the Wilson Sporting Goods Co., and Joe knew he could have one of those deals in a minute—a matter of one phone call.) . . . He and Tom Meany were already under contract to do a new chapter for another edition of *Lucky to Be a Yankee.* DiMaggio had recorded an album of boys' baseball stories—the ineptly titled *Little Johnny Strikeout.* He'd signed with Metro-Goldwyn-Mayer to play himself in a movie called *The Angels and the Pirates.* And he was holding MGM's feet to the fire on terms for *The Joe DiMaggio Story.* (He didn't mind being flown to L.A. for meetings with the movie bigs. That's where Little Joe was in boarding school—and where Dorothy Arnold lived. DiMaggio hadn't given up on making them part of his future, too.)

In sum, he was fully involved in the business of being DiMaggio. The New York writers filled the winter sports pages with speculation on DiMaggio's knees, his back, his heels, his shoulder, his batting eye . . . his relations with the skipper, with the owners, with George Weiss.

Would he get another contract of a hundred thousand dollars? . . . Did he want to be a manager? . . . How could a man walk away from the money and the glory of the Great Game? . . . But they mistook the game Joe was playing.

In November, Joe went with Lefty O'Doul on a goodwill mission to the troops in Korea. They were flown around to hospitals near the front, where Lefty would tell funny stories and Joe would sign autographs. There was a slap-up lunch and extravagant bonhomie from the commander of the U.N. forces, General Douglas MacArthur. There were medals for Lefty and Joe . . . and then a flight to Japan, where *O'Doul-san* was a Big Name.

Lefty had first sailed to Japan to spread the gospel of the Game in '31. Except for the war years, he'd made an appearance there almost every winter—more or less like Santa: he was Father Baseball. In 1950 Tokyo, where all things American were considered to be modern, correct, and highly fashionable (more than fashion—almost a state-sanctioned religion) . . . baseball and *O'Doul-san* were hugely admired.

But what startled Joe was the adulation for *DiMaggio-san.* In Japan everybody seemed to know him. He was, for one thing, the spiritual son of Father Baseball (who had trained him, as a youth, with the Seals of San Francisco). But also, he was a great and victorious warrior of the diamond in his own right. Was he not the heir to the immortal *Bay-ba Ru-tu?* Was he not

the exemplary samurai of the champion Yankees? . . .
"DiMaggio! Banzai!" ("A thousand years!")

By the time he returned from the Orient, Joe had a
trunkful of gifts, pottery, parasols, dolls, swords, and
silk kimonos . . . he had medals and certificates at-
testing him a hero from the U.S. armed forces, the
U.N. fighting forces, the governments of South Korea
and Japan . . . he had a new and larger sense of his
place in the world. He'd also lost about ten pounds.
He thought he'd have a couple of months of golf with
O'Doul, nights with his San Francisco pals, easy living with his mamma cooking, at home in the Marina.
Then he could decide what he wanted to do. But
things had changed while he was gone.

Rosalie DiMaggio had taken sick. Doctors said it
was cancer—not much they could do. Dominic came
out for a while before Christmas. But he couldn't
stay. He had his own home and family now, in
Boston. For that matter, Vince, too, had a happy marriage and a family of his own in the East Bay: he was
still out of the Marina picture. Tom and Mike had
their lives at the Wharf. Tom was still running
DiMaggio's Grotto. Mike was still fishing, going
after salmon—sometimes he'd be away for months.
If Joe stayed, he'd be the only one with nothing to do
but watch his mother die. When Dan Topping called
to wish Joe a Happy New Year, they came to an understanding within minutes. Weiss would send a contract a few days later—the standard hundred large.
Joe was going back to his life, at the Stadium.

He would join the club out west that year: Del Webb had finally gotten his way. The Yankees and Giants had swapped spring training camps. The Giants would train for the season in St. Pete. The Yankees would move for the first time to Phoenix. There they would enact the familiar and comfortable rituals: pictures of the Clipper, signing up for the new campaign (he'd actually mailed in his autographed contract from San Francisco, without delay) . . . glad welcomes from Stengel, Weiss, and the owners (who all predicted a fine year for DiMag and a third straight pennant for the Yanks) . . . and brave vows from Joe ("I'm out to surprise those who believe I am finishing up my career") as he reassumed his accustomed place as the jewel in the Yankee crown.

But it soon came clear, there would be little else familiar or comfortable in that spring of '51. It had been four months since Joe and the Yanks had dispatched the Phils in the World Series. In this case too, things had changed while he was gone.

"WAIT TILL YOU SEE THIS KID FROM Oklahoma," the soft-spoken coach Bill Dickey told the Yankee players. Dickey had seen players come and go to and from ball teams since the mid-1920s. And he was not, by nature, given to tall talk. But he'd been at the Yankee rookie camp in 1950. And he'd been saying ever since: "Just wait till you see this kid."

"There's never been anything like this kid which

we got from Joplin," Casey Stengel told his writers. "He has more speed than any slugger and more slug than any speedster—and nobody has ever had more of both of 'em together."

The final authority, Pete Sheehy, did his talking with the Pinstripes. He'd been Clubhouse Boy since the Babe's broad back bore the Number 3. Gehrig, of course, wore Number 4. Pete gave DiMaggio Number 5. And for that spring, Mickey Mantle would wear Number 6.

Well, the writers took it from there. By the time the Yankee camp opened officially on March 1, Mickey Charles Mantle was The Story. He was still listed as a shortstop—but all the writers knew he was moving to the outfield. (And the boldest among them suggested center field.) . . . He'd played only one full season at Class C, Joplin—but everybody knew he'd hit .383 there. (And home runs that never came down: they were still aloft over southern Missouri.) . . . Any normal nineteen-year-old would have to spend at least a year at finishing school—the Yankees' top farm, Triple-A Kansas City. (But on that subject, Stengel was quotably coy: "Don'cha think he'd be safer spendin' the summer with me in New York?")

Here was the replacement for Joe DiMaggio.

Mantle, for his part, was cooperatively spectacular (or vice versa, from the writers' point of view). He'd step into the cage (righty, lefty, didn't seem to matter), pull his cap down over his blond brush cut, take a stance that was natural, balanced, relaxed—and then just *crush the ball* . . . over the field, over the stands, off the training ground. They disappeared! These were not the fierce, slashing line drives that DiMaggio was wont to hit. No, they were huge, soaring grandiosities—astonishing in their excess.

Same way in the outfield, under a fly ball . . . well, no, take it back: he wasn't under any fly ball. A fly ball would be dropping, when young Mantle, knees pumping up and down in a blur, would streak across the grass (at a pace none of those writers had ever seen on a ballfield) . . . to spear the ball before it hit the ground. Once again, this was nothing like the loping spare stride of DiMaggio, as he arrived to tarry, elegantly, at the place where the ball would come down. Mantle had no idea where the ball would come down. But he'd get there, with the raw muscular speed of those jet-cars on the Bonneville Flats.

Here was the baseball star for the age of tail fins and the V-8.

DiMag? . . . He hadn't hit a solid line drive yet.

He was also heartily sick of the stink about Mantle from the moment he arrived. Seemed like that was all he heard from the writers: *What about the kid? . . . Joe! You think Mickey could play center field?*

Actually, they all seemed to have three questions—not one of which he cared to discuss:

What about Mickey? . . .

Does anything hurt, Joe? . . . and:

Hey, Joe! How you doin' with the wife?

That's what they mostly wrote about DiMag. It

turned out, Dorothy Arnold wasn't all that busy in Hollywood. She turned up in Phoenix, to watch the Yankees train. The Yankee writers might have given Joe a pass on that story—but not while they were getting scooped in papers across the country. . . .

DiMag Hints
Reconciliation
Ex-Wife Is Good Friend
He Tells Louella
(By Louella Parsons)

. . . I telephoned Joe, who is a good friend, to ask him if he and Dorothy were planning to reconcile and marry.

"Not on this visit," Joe said, "but there is a strong possibility that there may be a reconciliation later.

"Dorothy and I are still very good friends. She will bring our son to visit with me in New York this summer, and it is very possible we may remarry then. However, it is a little premature to discuss this matter now."

The two people who have worked ceaselessly to bring them back together are their very close friends, Mr. and Mrs. Lou Costello.

No wonder Joe decided he was news for all the wrong reasons—and he ought to make some news of

his own. It was still early in the training camp—
nighttime, at the hotel in Phoenix. Joe and Georgie
Solotaire had knocked back a few belts apiece. They
saw Benny Epstein, of the *Mirror,* in the lobby. They
grabbed Ben and a guy who was with him—Jack
Orr, from a little paper called *The Compass.* Then,
they rounded up Jim Dawson from the *Times*—to
give the story heft in New York. They didn't call any
other reporters. That might have alerted Joe Trimble
from the *News.* DiMag would have eaten dirt before
he gave Trimble a story. Screwing Trimble was what
made this such a good idea . . . well, it seemed like a
good idea. Dago and Georgie took the writers off to a
room—and made news:

This, said DiMaggio, will be my last year.

He might as well have dropped a bomb on Times
Square, the way those papers ran with the story. And
the rest of the writers (Joe had shafted eight metropolitan dailies) were all rattled by "rockets" from the
home office—telegrams or phone calls: *What the
hell's going on out there?* They followed up like
they'd been goosed with a cattle prod.

Weiss was wakened in his room at dawn. He didn't
know a thing about it—except that he didn't like it: the
biggest draw in the country was gonna take his marbles and go home? "DiMaggio has not discussed this
with any official of the club," Weiss said. "We regret
to hear anything like this, and we hope he will have the
sort of season that will cause him to change his mind."

Stengel was pinned at breakfast—he knew nothin'

from no one: "What am I supposed to do, get a gun and make him play? I don't own him."

But Stengel wasn't altogether displeased. He was tired of playing hostage to the Big Fella's moods. And he'd seen a center fielder—his center fielder— under that blond brush cut. Now, Stengel took Mantle aside in the dugout for a fatherly chat:

"Kid, you wanna play in the major leagues?"

"Yes, sir," the boy replied.

"Well, do yourself a favor. You see that fella out in center field there?"

"You mean DiMaggio?"

"Yeah," said the Perfesser. "You go out and have him teach you how to play that position. Because you'll never be a shortstop."

"Yes, sir."

There was only one problem with Casey's scheme: the nineteen-year-old pride of Commerce, Oklahoma, couldn't ask DiMaggio to teach him anything. Couldn't approach DiMaggio. Couldn't look at anything but his own shoes if DiMaggio happened by. . . . Years later, the great Mickey Mantle would have his own reputation as a hard man to talk to—as difficult an eminence as DiMaggio, in his way. But in that camp, he was just a shy kid, trying to find a spot for himself. He had no idea how to speak to DiMaggio, unless the Great Man spoke first—and as Mantle would recall (again, years later) that wouldn't happen until October.

In April, the Yankees broke camp and went barn-

storming—for the first time west of the Rockies. They
packed the Pacific Coast League parks. It should have
been a tour of glory for DiMag, in his old haunts, with
fans who remembered when. But there was only one
glorious story with the Yankees that year.

As the other prime rookie on that club, Gil Mc-
Dougald, remembered: "Mickey hit one out of Seals
Stadium—over the bleachers, off the property. . . . In
the L.A. Angels park, Mickey hit a line drive toward
right center. The center fielder took off toward right
center to grab it. But it never came down. It just kept
rising. The guy jumped, but the ball was twenty feet
over his head—and still going up as it left the park—
home run. The center fielder was in a state of
shock. . . .

"Mickey," as McDougald said, "had a spring training like a god."

At the University of Southern California, Mantle
hit one over the field, over the fence, and over the
field house behind the fence. It must have gone six
hundred feet—no one could even measure it. But
after that, at every stop, Stengel would tell a new
flock of writers: "I have my outfielder, Mr. Mantle,
who hits balls over buildings."

Joe? Well, they wrote history about him . . . they
wrote about him and his wife . . . there were pictures
when he visited Black Foxe Institute and posed,
showing Joe Jr. how to hold a bat . . . and they wrote
his brave assertions that he felt fine. But mostly—no
matter what he said—they wrote that he was quitting.

Joe had been trying to tone down that story since he woke up the next day and found the writers buzzing like mad hornets outside his door. He'd only meant to say, *right now,* this looked like it would be his last year. He said he'd see how the season went. He said his knees would tell him. Finally, he said, he wouldn't talk about it, till after the season—and maybe not then. But he could have saved all that breath. The only thing he'd accomplished was to add a new insult to the litany:

What about Mickey? . . .

Joe! Y'gonna get back with the Missus? . . .

How's the heels (back, neck, arm, knees, legs, eye)? . . . and:

Joe! You really think you're washed up?

IT WOULD NOT BE A HAPPY SUMMER for either of the Yankees' big stories. Mantle got to the grand Bronx ballyard, took a look at the towering tiers of seats, the monuments to Huggins, Gehrig, Ruth in the vastness of center field, the pennants and World Series flags fluttering in rows atop the scalloped balustrade . . . and he stopped hitting atomic home runs. In fact, he was trying so hard to crush the ball, to be the miracle advertised, to hit as he believed a New York Yankee must hit (harder, surely, than *he'd* ever hit) . . . he couldn't hit a thing.

The Yankee fans got their first look at him, and decided—well, he could strike out from either side. And being New York fans—who expect their miracles right away—they took to booing, which made the boy try to crush the ball harder.

In the outfield, Mantle had learned a lot from the Yankees' newest coach, Tom Henrich. In fact, Henrich was delighted with his pupil. Henrich had worked for days with young Mick, teaching him to catch the ball and *get rid of it*—all in one move. It's a matter of footwork: you set yourself to catch the ball coming down on your back foot, so you can fire it, right away, with your body in the throw. Then, in a game with the White Sox, Jim Busby was on third base when Mantle caught a fly ball, came down onto his right foot, and fired a BB to the plate. And right over the plate—a strike . . . that got there so fast, Busby stopped halfway home and fell down trying to get back to third. Henrich still laughed about it forty-five years later. "When Mickey came in, I says, 'You got that down pretty good. I think that's the best throw I ever saw!' "

But still, in 1951, Mick was green as the grass in right field: he'd never seen these batters—had no idea how they hit, where to play. And Henrich hadn't quite drummed home the crucial instruction: *you play off DiMaggio.* Joe was like a Univac out there. He not only knew every hitter in the league; he knew what every Yankee pitcher would throw; and he'd see, right away, if their curve wasn't biting, if they'd lost a couple inches off the fastball—then the hitter would get around just that much faster, and Joe would be shading two or three steps into the alley where that hitter would pull the ball (right into DiMaggio's glove). Every other kid on the Yankees learned: *Watch the Dago—if he moves, you move.* Not Mantle. He wouldn't look at DiMaggio. Maybe he couldn't. Joe would be flicking his glove at the kid, like he was shooing a fly—move over! Mantle would stare in at the plate until the ball was hit, and then he'd chase it to the wall.

Stengel hadn't done the boy any service by bringing him to New York that year. Within a couple of months, Mantle would be so shaky that Stengel would have to send him out to Kansas City. (And there, Mick would come within an inch of quitting.) . . . By that time, DiMaggio had decided Mantle wasn't worth all the talk. Not that he'd spent any talk on the kid. Joe told Lou Effrat (who, of course, wouldn't write it): "He's a rockhead."

By that time, Joe had problems of his own—and unlike Mantle's, these could not be cured by experience. His big comeback, his grand finale, was passing in a bad blur. He wasn't even out of April before his shoulder and neck went stiff and started aching. He could barely swing, couldn't throw without pain, and had to sit out. He came back in mid-May, played for about three weeks, until a pulled muscle put him out of the lineup again. He was still riding the pine, June 16, when Dorothy arrived in New York, with Joe Jr. To the waiting press at La Guardia Field, she called it "a Father's Day visit." Joe clearly hoped it would be more.

But the next day, he got word from San Francisco: Rosalie DiMaggio had slipped into a coma. And he went back to La Guardia, to catch a plane—alone. Maybe if Dorothy and the boy had come with him, things would have been different—his future and his hopes. But he flew by himself across the country. Dominic flew from Boston all that night and into the day, but arrived minutes too late. Joe got there while his mother was still breathing. But that was all. She never regained consciousness, and died that morning, June 18, 1951.

The aftermath of her death was so much louder than her life that she probably would have been embarrassed. The newspapers called her "Rose Dimaggio, the sturdy Italian peasant woman whose three sons grew to baseball fame and fortune." All her boys were there, of course: the three famed outfielders, big Mike, and her eldest, Tom—all carried her casket past the crowd, down the steps of the great Sts. Peter and Paul's, where she had slipped unnoticed into early Mass, so many mornings, for so many years. For a few days, they would all be home, with their four sisters—together in the old Marina house, as mourners. Only later would anyone realize: that would be the last time they'd be all together, home. It turned out, without Rosalie, it wouldn't be home.

Joe flew back to New York to take his place again at Yankee Stadium. He hadn't hit worth a damn yet that year. Couldn't play the outfield without pain. His back was so stiff, his shoulder so tender, Rizzuto or Coleman had to run halfway out to the fence to take his cutoff throws. It hurt Joe even to bend over, to scoop up a ground ball. But he wanted to play. Now was when he needed his place. And that was his place. . . . Alas, no one thought to remind Casey Stengel.

July 6, at the Stadium, a big crowd, a big game with Boston. The Yankees weren't playing well—in the midst of dropping five out of six (including three losses to the Red Sox), the Bombers were stumbling out of first place—and Stengel was snappish. In the first inning, DiMaggio had misplayed a ball in the field, while Boston runners circled the bases—and the Yanks had fallen behind 6–1. Now, as the second inning began, DiMaggio was at his post in center field, when Johnny Hopp, the veteran National Leaguer who'd come over to the Yanks that year, emerged from the dugout. Hopp trotted toward the outfield, to tell DiMaggio he was out of the game. Stengel wasn't waiting till the end of the inning. In the most visible and humiliating way, he was going to yank the Clipper right off the field. Joe's face darkened in fury, and he waved Hopp back to the dugout. "I'll tell Casey when I want to come out." As Phil Rizzuto remembered: "When that inning was over, DiMaggio came back to the bench and went right past Stengel, into the clubhouse without a word. I don't think they ever talked again. From then on, things got worse. Casey couldn't wait until DiMaggio quit."

There was an uproar in the sporting press. Jimmy Cannon—who had always spoken for DiMag—fulminated in his column: "There has only been one truly great baseball player in this generation. Some one should remind Casey Stengel the man's name is Joe DiMaggio. . . . It was a mean little decision. It was a thoughtless act of panic and insensitivity. It was nasty and petty and follows the pattern of cheapness which has assumed shape since Lonesome George Weiss, the friendless General Manager, took charge. The prestige of the Yankees diminishes rapidly."

The Yankees had to issue a statement denying all intent to insult the Great DiMaggio—and denying any feud in the Bronx clubhouse. Stengel played dumb: claimed he only meant "to rest the Big Fella." He said he tried to make the change before the inning began—but gosh, he looked around and Joe was already out on the field. . . . Stengel tried to make amends by naming Joe to the All-Star team—even though the fans hadn't voted DiMaggio in with their ballots. But then, Stengel said Joe was injured—and stuck him on the bench for the whole game. That took the story national.

Dissension was the sportswriter's stock-in-trade now. And even some of Joe's erstwhile boosters took this chance to pin the Yankees' slide onto the back of Number 5. Not just for his woeful hitting—his average bouncing around the .250's. . . . No, it was the Cold War that Joe had brought on with his silence.

The lead Yankee writer for the *Post,* Milton Gross,

told his readers: "I did recognize a profound difference in the personal climate which surrounds
DiMaggio and the Yankees this season. It is a frigid
one, all because Joe, who always was a strange man,
difficult to understand, is now living in a shell that is
virtually impenetrable."

After that, the Cold War extended to most of the
writers, too. If they were headed across the locker
room toward his stool, Joe would get up, turn his
back, and leave. It was only two steps to the passage-
way that led to the trainer's room. They weren't allowed there. Joe could wait 'em out, until his pal,
Bernie Kamber, arrived to drive the Dago downtown.
That summer, Bernie left work every day at four P.M.,
to get to the Stadium with his big Chrysler—and
make sure Joe was protected as he left for home.

Home was still George Solotaire's suite at the Elysee. Joe was the only Yankee who still lived in a midtown hotel. Most of the young guys, who'd just
gotten to New York (and couldn't be sure if they'd
stay), lived at the Concourse Plaza in the Bronx. It
was cheap, clean, and safe up there—and they could
walk down the hill to the Stadium. More and more of
the established Yanks—Rizzuto, Berra, Bauer—had
their own houses in New Jersey. That was the postwar
Yankee style: a nice new house in the Jersey suburbs.
It wasn't Joe's style—not by a long shot. But of
course, all those guys were married. And now it
looked like Joe never would be. For a long time, he'd
kept a picture frame—one of those folding double

frames that opened like two pages of a book—
propped open on the dresser of his room. One side
had a picture of the kid, the other side was Dorothy in
a glamour pose. Now that frame was folded up in a
drawer. That was the surest sign the reconciliation
was *finito*.

Now, his room in the Elysee was as bare of personal affect as if he'd moved in that morning. If he
took his clothes from the drawers and closet, some
businessman from Milwaukee could have checked in
that afternoon without a hint that Joe had ever been
there. Oh, and he would have had to move his Victrola, too. That's what he did late at night, when the
TV quit, when sleep wouldn't come, when he sat and
smoked, smoked and sat. He'd play his song, over and
over. He wore the grooves of that record into ruts.

There's a somebody
I'm longing to see . . .

It was an old Gershwin tune, sung simply, over
mournful strings, by Frank Sinatra—or Sinat, as he
was known to all the pals at Toots Shor's.

Won't you tell her please,
To put on some speed,
Follow my lead.
Oh, how I need
Someone to watch over me . . .

Solotaire and Kamber were there to watch over
him, to feed him, get his things at the cleaners or the

deli—or they'd grasp his arm and pop it back into the shoulder, as Joe would grunt and sweat with the pain. But they couldn't put the fun back in him—or the appetite. He didn't want to go out to eat, or see a show, take in a club—not even if they were paying into the account. Joe thought, he'd done enough for those wiseguys. And it wasn't safe anymore. Half the time he'd turn on the TV, some hood he half-knew would be runnin' his mouth to Kefauver and his posse of snoops—trying to send Frank Costello up the river. (Joe would grunt up out of his chair and turn the channel, try to find a decent western.) In those days, you couldn't even get Dago up for a girl. He'd been spooked off broads, when one went crazy and started writing him notes every day—how she was going to kill herself if he wouldn't love her, come to her, be with her. . . . Joe didn't even want to see the guys at Shor's. Fact was, he wouldn't talk to Toots. In a way, that was about broads, too.

Look magazine got a broad of its own, by the name of Isabella Taves, to root around into Joe's love life. Then, they promoted her story like a circus-come-to-town. "A facet of his personality we never suspected," as the press release from the magazine claimed. "Joe is a heart-throb, a lady-killer, the ideal male from the feminine point of view!

"Just bashful enough to be effective . . . Joltin' Joe is so attractive to women he has to wait in the clubhouse after each game to avoid being mobbed.

"And yet, for all his devastating charm, DiMag,

Miss Taves reports, remains a shy kid at heart. He still blushes at the sight of a pretty face and his best friends are men, notably Toots Shor. To Mrs. Shor, Joe is 'Toots's Other Wife.' . . .

"Oh, fudge! That's enough for us. If you want more, read Miss Taves in *Look.*"

Well, that sent Dago around the bend. Fudge her! And Toots, too! Where the hell did he come off? *(Toots's Other Wife!)* . . . But the part that put Toots into the deep freeze was a blind quote—had to be Shor, who else?—about how Joe couldn't hit one year, because he was mooning for his faithless wife. *Toots had no business talking about that.* . . . It just confirmed what Joe had been thinking—late at night, when thinking was all he could do—how Toots had made himself a big man, a Big Name, on Joe's back. It was that spring, it all started to figure—about the time of those pictures in the paper—Toots, with his arm around his pal, Mickey Mantle. . . . After that, when Shor called the suite, Bernie would answer, and silently mouth the word: "Toots." Joe would shake his head, no. And Bernie would say, smooth as silk, "He ain't here, Tootsie."

There were days when Joe seemed like his old self—you could see it at the Stadium, the way he hit the ball. Or maybe it was the other way around. He'd get a few hits, maybe smack one over the wall, and he'd feel like himself again. The Yankees had been trailing the White Sox half the season . . . until a doubleheader, end of July, when DiMag woke up and started smacking their pitchers around. Two home runs, five runs driven in—that took care of game one. Game two was tighter, a pitchers' duel, but DiMaggio broke the Chi-Sox' back when he raced from first to third on a single, and then slid around the catcher's tag on Gil McDougald's squeeze bunt. The Yankees won 2–zip, took the double-dip, and swept the series. Chicago would never threaten again.

The Yanks might have put away Cleveland and Boston with the same dispatch, if DiMaggio could have kept it going. But that consistency—the weeks-at-a-stretch when no one could get him out—that's what he couldn't seem to find. He'd have a good game or two. Every at bat a shot to left: *bang, bang, boom* . . . he might even smile, if one went out. Then, next day, he'd show up, same as always, and all he could do was pop up a fat pitch . . . or a stinkin' grounder on a checked swing (a doubter doesn't pull line shots) . . . then, he'd be mumbling in the tunnel again. One time, that August, it got so bad, he actually told those Yankee kids how he used to hit a ball so hard—he could hit it dead on the third baseman's glove, didn't matter—it would *handcuff* the guy. Joe said he wasn't trying to brag, but no one could field those shots. One time (it was just a couple of years ago), he hit that goddamn ball so hard—right at the Tiger third baseman, George Kell—it broke his fuckin' jaw. No lie. . . . The kids couldn't believe it—not the part about Kell—but Dago talkin' about old times.

But he couldn't turn on the ball and power it to left now. And those kids couldn't look at him without hurting for him. . . . Sometimes, even though he was late, he'd catch a ball clean, and hit it out toward the short right field fence—two or three, he hit over that fence. The Yanks would gather to greet him on the dugout steps. *"Attaboy, Joe!" "Way to go, Daig!"* But DiMaggio bridled at the praise. "People don't pay to see me hit to right." He called them "piss homers . . . I could piss 'em right over that wall."

Many more of his hits were just flares to right: they'd kick up chalk on the line behind first, or drop because the other team was playing him to pull—they hadn't caught on yet. But word got around, sure enough, that summer. Then all the pitchers were killing him with fastballs. (What were they supposed to serve him? Tea and cookies?) DiMaggio didn't expect sympathy. No, he said his swing would come back. By will, he was going to make it come back.

One day, batting practice, he came out of the cage—Daig still got first licks in BP—and Bauer was waiting there. DiMaggio sidled up. "What am I doin', Hank? What am I doin' wrong?"

Bauer thought: Why's he asking me? But Bauer wasn't one to mince words. "I think you can't get around anymore."

"Bullshit!" DiMaggio barked. He walked away, stiff with indignation. "Load-a BULLSHIT."

AT LEAST STENGEL WAS PLAYING HIM steady—and batting him cleanup. Maybe he had to. Someone upstairs may have sat on Ol' Case.

Before a twin bill against Philadelphia, the rookie Gil McDougald came into the dugout after infield practice, to check the lineup and see where he was hitting. There it was: McDougald at cleanup, and DiMaggio fifth. The kid went white, turned to his coach, Frank Crosetti. "Crow, he musta made a fuckin' mistake."

Crosetti looked like he had a bad stomach. "No. He didn't make no mistake."

McDougald was almost pleading. "Anyplace but that."

Crosetti said grimly, "No. You're cleanup."

So Gil batted cleanup—went four-for-four, drove in every runner he could find on base. And he was thinking: "This is it!"

Game two, he ran in from infield to see where he was hitting. He was eighth. Dago was back at cleanup. McDougald looked at Casey—and he could see the rage in the old man.

So the Yanks played on toward autumn with DiMaggio at cleanup—batting .260, leaving his teammates to wither on base—with two lousy homers in the whole month of August. No wonder the Yankees still trailed the Indians (by a game, two games, two and a half—depending on which day you checked). And by September, Boston was right on their necks, too. No wonder Stengel was looking so sour—as Cannon once wrote, "like an eagle that had just flown through a sleet-storm." No wonder DiMaggio was lunging at the plate, trying to smash every pitch through a wall somewhere. It was his job to carry the Yankees. And he felt like he was a weight on their backs.

He felt the weight on him, every time he took a swing—like an unseen hand was pressing on him, making him slow. He changed his bat from his old thirty-seven-ounce, down to a thirty-five-ounce—a Babe Ruth model—then he sanded the handles, trying to put the whip back into his wrists. But he wasn't fighting the weight of his bat. It was the weight of his expectations and doubts—and those he could feel from the dugout and press box, from the stands, from fans in New York and every other town . . . everyone (as he imagined, as he *knew*) watching, judging him, concluding that he wasn't what he used to be. For the first time, the game was humbling him—as it did every other man.

That September, as the Yanks left town on the train, McDougald and Rizzuto wandered into the dining car. There sat DiMag, alone at a four-top table, with his mail spread out in front of him. Of course, they went to another table. "Hey, come over here," DiMaggio said.

They sat across from him, their hands in their laps. DiMaggio glanced down at his mail. "Here," he said, and flipped a sheaf of papers across the table. They were all offers—a hundred thousand for this or that, fifty a year for three to five years—to be vice president, do the ads, be the spokesman. . . . And Dago said: "I wish I could give one of these to you, and one for you. Then you could forget about this goddamn game."

But how would he forget, if he left it a loser?

September 16, the Indians arrived in New York for two games. The Yankees were now one behind—they'd have to win both. And the first game, they'd be up against Bob Feller (best in the league, with twenty-two wins). At that point, Casey couldn't sit still—he'd rather be fired. He shook up the order, top to bottom. Mantle was back from K.C. for the stretch run. He would lead off. (Let him use them fine young legs to beat out a hit.) Rizzuto was demoted to eighth. McDougald was moved up from eighth to third. And Yogi Berra would hit cleanup. DiMaggio was shoved down behind him, to fifth.

At the start, Casey looked like a genius again . . . when Yogi's first-inning triple gave the Yanks a run—and they scored two more to take a 3–0 lead. But like all the great ones, Feller only got tougher. Cleveland started chipping away against Allie Reynolds. It was 3–1 when the Yanks came up in the fifth. And then Feller would make a mistake—not with his arm: his head did him dirty.

Mantle got on with a drag bunt down the first base line. He was bunted over to second base. McDougald took a good shot at driving Mantle home, but the Indians' Sam Chapman robbed him at the left field wall. So Berra, the cleanup batter, stepped in with two outs and Mantle on second base. That's when Feller started thinking . . . and walked Yogi intentionally—to get to DiMaggio.

There were seventy thousand fans in the Stadium, booing to the skies, baying imprecations at Feller and plaintive encouragement to Joe—who stayed on one knee, motionless in the on-deck circle, until Berra got ball four. Then, Joe walked to the plate, scooped a handful of dirt and spent, perhaps, one extra moment, rubbing it into his palms. He was staring at nothing. His face was expressionless. You had to be a Dago-watcher to note the veins, like cords on his neck, and the ominous darkness around his eyes.

Feller had pitched against DiMaggio since '36. And DiMaggio had hammered him—plenty of times. But Feller figured he wasn't facing that DiMaggio—just a .260 hitter, who couldn't get around. Feller got one quick strike with the heater. Then, he threw one ball. He came back with the heater, and Joe hesitated—it ticked off his bat for a lousy check-swing foul, and Feller had him set up, one-and-two. He only had to blow one more by him . . . so Rapid Robert reared back and fired. And DiMaggio did what no one thought he could do anymore: he pulled Feller's best—hammered it on a line, into the deepest reach of the Stadium. It shot past the center fielder, Larry Doby . . . and rolled, and rolled to the base of the wall, where the numbers 457 were painted. Mantle and Berra trotted home. DiMaggio pulled up at third base, and bowed his head slightly under waves of frantic fan-roar. Cleveland was finished for that day. The Yankees won 5–1. They were tied for first.

Next day, another tough customer—Bob Lemon took the mound for the Indians. The Yankees had their smart junkballer, Eddie Lopat. Those two pitchers battled through the game . . . to a tense and terrible 1–1 tie in the ninth. The Yankees came to the plate with their cleanup man, Berra, scheduled as first batter. But Yogi topped a tame ground ball, for out number one. That brought up DiMaggio. The Stadium crowd was wailing for him. There was no Joe Page in the Yankee bullpen anymore. How long could Lopat go on? . . . DiMaggio stepped in, cocked his bat once, and stood still. Lemon fired the hard stuff that had got him past DiMag all day. But this time, Joe was ready. He turned in the box, his bat a blur, and smashed a shot down the line. It was right at Al Rosen, the Tribe third baseman. He could barely get his glove across to knock the ball down—it was simply hit too hard to field. Dago had *handcuffed* the sonofagun—and Joe was on first base, with the winning run, and the Yankees were up in the dugout, yelling. Woodling stepped in and stroked a single into right. DiMaggio turned it on around second base and slid into third as the ball came back to the infield. Lemon walked Bobby Brown to load the bases, and then little Phil Rizzuto stepped in. As Lemon wound up, DiMaggio streaked for home: *a suicide squeeze!* Lemon was no dummy. He fired that ball high and tight—a pitch that was all but impossible to bunt. But Rizzuto was the best bunter in baseball. He yanked the bat up, with the barrel at his cheek, and dropped the ball down the first base line. DiMaggio blew by the catcher, standing up—with the run that made the difference. And the Yankees stood alone in first place.

That finished Cleveland: they would fade to five games back. But once again, the Yanks would have to clinch against Boston. They'd have their shot, September 28, in a doubleheader at the Stadium. If the Yankees won both, they would be champs again. Game one, Allie Reynolds left nothing to chance. He threw a masterpiece—a no-hitter—and the Yanks won 8–0. In game two, Boston got up off the canvas to take an early 3–0 lead. But then the Yankees came on like killers. It was 7–3 by the fifth, with the Red Sox hanging on, trying to stay in the game—have a chance to slug it out in late innings. But they'd have no chance. Two on and two out, DiMaggio faced the lefty Chuck Stobbs, who was careful—he worked the count full, three-and-two. Then he had to come in, and DiMaggio put him away: home run over the left field wall. Three runs. End of contest. And the Yankees had their third straight pennant.

In the clubhouse, there was a big celebration—whooping, hugging, everybody wet with spray. (In the Topping years, champagne had replaced Col. Ruppert's beer.) But DiMaggio sat quietly on his stool. He was holding a ball—brother Dom had hit it to Gene Woodling for the final out. And Woodling ran in with it, to give it to the Dago. Joe said he'd keep that one. "My tenth pennant . . ." In the history of baseball, only Babe Ruth could ever say those words. But Ruth had won three of his with the Red Sox. For the Yankees, only DiMaggio had ten.

NOW THE YANKS HAD TO WAIT, WITH the rest of the Baseball Nation, while the Giants and Dodgers fought it out for the NL flag. The Giants had staged a comeback for the ages. From thirteen back in the middle of August, they played near-perfect baseball for the next month and a half (won thirty-seven games and only lost seven) to finish in a flat-out tie with Brooklyn. Then, there was a three-game playoff that ended so famously with Bobby Thomson's homer, bottom of the ninth—The Shot Heard Round the World (and televised, for the first time, across the country). . . . So, for the first time, these Yanks would have to face an *opposing* team of destiny, a club that knew it couldn't lose. There it was in all the papers, next day, when that World Series began: God must be a Giant fan!

Sure enough, that afternoon, the Giants could do nothing wrong—not even in Yankee Stadium (where so many NL champs had gone to die). In fact, the Giants made the Yanks look slow and stupid—from the very first inning, when Monte Irvin stole home. Meanwhile, the Giants' fourth starter, a lefty named

Dave Koslo, looked like Cy Young that day—he went all the way and beat the Yanks 5–1. DiMaggio flied out four straight times.

In the second game, Steady Eddie Lopat hypnotized the Giants with junk. And though the Yanks couldn't do much (DiMaggio took another oh-fer), they squeaked out a 3–1 win that brought the Series even. But still, that game brought more woe upon the Bombers. Disaster struck in inning five, when the Giants' phenom, Willie Mays, lifted a pop fly to short right center. Mantle came racing across from right field—in full jet-car mode. As Mantle described it to his co-writer Mickey Herskowitz for the memoir *All My Octobers:*

"I knew there was no way DiMaggio could get to it so I hauled ass. Just as I arrived, I heard Joe say, 'I got it.' I looked over and he was *camped* under the ball. . . ."

(Mantle would tell friends, he thought—"Oh, shit! I'm gonna hit DiMaggio. I'll put him in the hospital. They'll never let me play again!")

". . . I put on the brakes and the spikes of my right shoe caught the rubber cover of a sprinkler head. There was a sound like a tire blowing out and my right knee collapsed. I fell to the ground and stayed there, motionless. A bone was sticking out the side of my leg."

It was a terrible price, to learn at last: *you watch the Dago—play offa him* . . . and to hear DiMaggio speak to him for the first time.

"DiMaggio leaned over me and said, 'Don't move. They're bringing a stretcher.' I guess that was about as close as Joe and I had come to a conversation. I don't know what impressed me more, the injury or the sight of an aging DiMaggio still able to make a difficult catch look easy."

(It was Mantle on his way to the hospital. But his knee—them fine young legs—would never be the same. Mantle would never again have that Bonneville speed. In later years, among friends, the Mick was neither so stoic nor impressed by the Clipper. The way Mantle figured, DiMaggio wouldn't call that ball until he was damn sure he could make it look easy. Joe had to look good . . . but Mickey would never play another game without pain.)

In that Series, the loss of Mantle put the Yanks in real trouble. And their troubles got worse at the Polo Grounds in Game Three. On a play at second base, Eddie Stanky, the bantamweight second baseman, kicked the ball from Rizzuto's glove and ignited the Giants—they pounded Raschi for a 6–2 win. DiMaggio went hitless for the third straight game. These Yanks had never been behind in a Series. They had never been beaten up by a team as talented and tough. And for Game Four, the Giants had their best, Sal Maglie, ready to shove the Yanks into the hole for good.

But a day of rain intervened. (Maybe God still loved the Yanks a bit.) Joe spent the day with Lefty O'Doul, who'd come to New York for the Series. And

O'Doul told Joe to try an even lighter bat—and swing easy—Joe was lunging at the ball.

Game Four, DiMaggio ended the Yankee first when he took strike three from Maglie. But it was strike one that sent a jolt around the Polo Grounds: the Clipper had crushed a ball down the left field line (out of the park but clearly foul). The game was tied 1–1 in inning three, when DiMaggio stroked a single to left—his first hit for twelve at bats in the Series. But he died on first, when Maglie got Woodling on a pop to left. By inning five, the Yanks had scratched out another run, and led 2–1—when Berra singled to right. Now, the scowling Maglie had to put away DiMaggio, and wasn't going to let him turn on another pitch—like that line single, or the one hammered foul in the first. So Maglie worked him away, away, away. But DiMaggio wouldn't lunge. The count went to three-and-one. Maglie came in with a low curveball—and DiMaggio flattened that ball, but good. It shot on a line between third and short, out to left field, and kept rising . . . Monte Irvin, in left, had turned and started racing back—but he stopped after a couple of steps. The ball was already over his head, still climbing—as it cleared the wall, and slammed into the left field seats. When Joe trotted home, Berra was bouncing up and down at the plate. He almost jumped into Dago's arms. The Yanks had lost Mantle, but they had the Big Guy back.

That was the game—and the Series, as it turned out. The next day, Joe had three hits, and McDougald broke the Giants' back with a grand slam, as the

Bombers won in steamroller style, 13–1. Day after that, back at the Stadium, it was Koslo again—but not Cy Young. The Yankees touched him up for four runs. DiMaggio had a double in two at bats. (And the Giants had seen enough—Koslo walked him twice intentionally.) . . . When Sal Yvars's liner to right disappeared into Bauer's glove, the Giants' last comeback of the year fell short . . . and the Yanks won the Series in six games.

The clubhouse was just like old times: packed with happy hangers-on, wet with spray, and loud with song. (It was a new generation, but still "Roll Out the Barrel.") . . . DiMaggio had never sung along, and he didn't now. He sat on his stool, amid a ring of writers—answered some questions ("Yup, a thirty-four-ounce bat . . .") and ducked the big one ("I have no announcement on my plans."). Bernie Kamber hovered at the edge of the ring, in case the Big Guy needed anything. And it was Bernie whom Gil Mc-Dougald took aside.

"I just wanted to tell him what it was like to play with him—what it meant to me."

What he really wanted was for Kamber to tell Joe. Gil could never tell the Big Guy himself.

Other Yankees did talk to Joe. One by one they came, to say congratulations, and shake his hand. But it was much later—the crowd was gone, the clubhouse was quiet—when Spec Shea sat down next to DiMag, and softly brought up the big question: "What about it, Joe? . . ."

Just as quietly, DiMaggio said: "I've played my last game."

Then, all the players came back to him—they came out of the showers, came over from their lockers. A few brought balls, then some brought bats—and hats, T-shirts, their own gloves . . . they clustered around him, like boys, and asked for his autograph.

THERE WAS STILL HOPE—AT LEAST in the papers. Topping said Joe might change his mind if he got a good rest in the off season. Weiss drew up contracts for another hundred G's. Daniel had a piece in the *Telegram,* totting up the Clipper's World Series records: most Series games, most for one team, most Series at bats . . . and the one Joe valued, the last one—most times as a World Champ. In the history of the Series, only DiMaggio had won nine times. Then Daniel offered this intriguing coda: *"It is believed that DiMaggio will come back in 1952. . . ."* (Believed by whom? Did the old coot know something?)

And then, hope faded, when the new *Life* hit the newsstands one week after the Series. The magazine had obtained the Brooklyn Dodgers' scouting report (prepared when the Dodgers still thought they had the pennant, and a World Series with the Yanks ahead). Andy High, an old and able judge of baseball talent, had written about DiMaggio:

"He can't stop quickly and throw hard. You can take the extra base on him. . . .

"He can't run and won't bunt. . . .

"His reflexes are very slow, and he can't pull a good fastball at all."

It was a brutal assessment, and damn near true. (The only thing High missed was how DiMaggio could still beat you, somehow.) . . . The good part for Joe was, he didn't have to answer. He was on an airplane, bound for Japan with Lefty O'Doul and fifteen other "U.S. All-Stars"—and a two-month schedule of exhibition games.

Their plane made the Tokyo airport at dusk. Magnesium flares lit the skies to signal the arrival of the diamond gods. They were driven in a cavalcade of open cars to the middle of town—the Ginza—where pandemonium ensued. A storm of paper scraps fluttered down from windows on all sides. Raking spotlights and a fusillade of flashbulbs lit the startled Americans in stroboscope freeze-frames. College boys and high school girls flung themselves onto the cars. Lefty and Joe were in the lead convertible, which was finally stopped dead by a million screaming fans: *Banzai DiMaggio! Banzai O'Doul!* . . . Japanese police and U.S. soldiers had to plead with the crowd to let the car move.

Joe played a few games, then left the tour early, to fly home alone. Even the Japanese fans—the way he figured—were cheering only for what he had been. (At that point, he couldn't know: that screaming Tokyo crowd was a harbinger of his future, too.)

When he got to the West Coast, he made his arrangements to meet the Yankee owners, Webb and Topping. He'd tell them his decision and announce it in New York. He flew east in early December, and Topping was ready with his last-ditch offers. Joe could have his hundred grand. He could play when he wanted—fill in, pinch-hit. If he didn't want to travel, he could play only home games. Joe answered: "I'm never putting on that monkey suit again." . . . The Yankees scheduled a press conference the following day, at the club's midtown office.

Of course, the papers knew what was up. A few doubters—Daniel in the lead—pointed out that Joe was barely thirty-seven. He could easily play another year or two. True, he'd hit only .263 last year—but his career figure was still .325 . . . and he was still, in Daniel's phrase, "the equal of any center fielder in the league." But the writers closer to Joe knew, "equal" was only an insult. They limbered up, with elegiac columns on the Jolter's history, his impact, grace, and style. The chief topic was "class"—that ineffable quality they'd chewed over so many nights at Shor's. Class, they concluded, made DiMag the greatest in the game; class would make him leave it, while the memory of him was bright. Cannon stepped out in front of the choir: "If you saw him play, you'll never forget him."

The story was too big for one press conference. So

many writers, radio men with microphones, television cameras, and newsreel crews packed into the club's Fifth Avenue suite that it took four rooms to stage the Clipper's final bow. His writer pals had typed out his statement, and the Yanks' PR man, Red Patterson, handed out carbon copies for the pencil press. In another room, Joe read aloud for the radio and camera crews:

"I told you fellows last spring I thought this would be my last year. I only wish I could have had a better year, but even if I had hit .350, this would have been the last year for me.

"You all know I have had more than my share of physical injuries and setbacks during my career. In recent years these have been much too frequent to laugh off. When baseball is no longer fun, it's no longer a game.

"And so, I've played my last game of ball."

Joe thanked the Yankees, the game, and its fans. He answered questions from the writers for an hour. He posed for pictures till the newsreel spotlights blew a fuse and plunged the Yankees' suite into darkness. When the lights went back on, DiMaggio was gone.

"SO HE TURNED HIS BACK ON THE $100,000 and abruptly walked away," Arthur Daley wrote for the next day's column, *Sports of the Times.* "Only a man with character and an overwhelming pride could take a step like that. The Yankee Clipper has always been a proud man. That's why he was such a great ballplayer. He was never satisfied with anything less than perfection."

Those were the other big topics of the day: perfection, pride—and money. From within the game, it was mostly money. Frank Crosetti, now a Yankee coach, said DiMaggio had pushed the salary standard higher all over the major leagues. Now that he was gone, every player would suffer. . . . Gene Woodling, the young Yankee outfielder, was already making little enough—he got by on his annual World Series shares. "Please, Joe, come back next year," Woodling pleaded in print. "I need more money to buy shoes for my three kids." . . . Frank Lane, GM of the White Sox, said DiMaggio's retirement would cost his club some five thousand fans—twenty-five thousand dollars—for every game the Yankees played in Chicago. That meant every team in the league would lose, perhaps, a quarter-million dollars. (For some clubs that was the whole team payroll.)

But for fans, the story was Joe's own money. *How could a guy turn his back on a hundred grand?*

Actually, DiMag and Topping already had an agreement. The club would pay Joe his hundred G's to move into the broadcast booth, to do the interview show after every Yankee game on TV. The announcement of that deal (one day after Joe's retirement) would diminish the mourning in New York—and put paid (with a satisfying flourish) to all the talk about Joe's money.

Withal, the real story was never announced. And the few men who knew it were not much for talk. (In fact, the man who knew best, Frank Costello, was already in the federal slam for failure to talk when Kefauver came calling. Now, the feds were threatening to strip his citizenship, and throw him out of the country. Costello still wouldn't talk.) . . . So, nobody ever wrote about the money in that Bowery Bank trust account—money Joe would have in his hands, when he retired from the game. And even in the mob, there were few men who knew how that money had grown. But a handful of *i grandi* in East Harlem, a couple in the East Bronx, at least one in Brooklyn, weren't at all shocked when Joe hung up his spikes. (Nor would they be surprised, one year later, when Joe would dump that stupid broadcast job.) They knew he didn't need the money—never would. As they said around their own kitchen tables, Joe DiMaggio didn't walk away from a hundred grand. He was walking into more than a million in cash—all safe and sound, at the Bowery.

With that sort of money, you could have a nice quiet life—just what Joe always said he was after. . . . And he did leave town, soon after his announcement—headed home, as he said, "for some peace and quiet."

But he didn't stay around his old San Francisco haunts. No one could find him at Reno Barsocchini's.

Nor at the Grotto. Nor at home. He flew two or three times to L.A. The official story was "business meetings"—that, and Joe Jr. was down there in school. But it soon got around among his San Francisco pals, Joe had some girlfriend down there. Still, no one knew much . . . till one day that spring—as Dario Lodigiani remembered.

Dario had played golf in a charity tournament at the Merced Country Club. After that, all the guys went out to a bar. Dominic DiMaggio was partners in that bar. And Reno Barsocchini was serving drinks— just to help out. "Hey, Dario!" Barsocchini called out. "Go down that hall and turn left, the first door you come to. There's a guy down there who wants to see you."

"So I walked down there," Lodigiani remembered, "and I turned left, walked in. And there in a chair, there was Joe DiMaggio! And there, on his lap . . .

"I said, 'GOOD NIGHT!' . . . Talk about a beautiful gal! . . . And of course, that was Marilyn Monroe."

BOOK III

FAME

1952–1962

✦

Marilyn shows off her arm—introduced by Ralph Edwards, at L.A.'s Wrigley Field.

"Kiss 'er, Joe!" . . . San Francisco City Hall,
January 14, 1954.

CHAPTER 14

✦

YOU COULD SAY THEY MET FOR THE
sake of her fame—it was one of her press agents who
set up Marilyn's "blind date" with Joe. And fame was
so tied up in this love story—her fame, and his, and
theirs, such a mess of fame—it was both a joy and the
sorrow, from the start.

Even those words, "blind date," didn't really make
sense, in that spring of 1952. By that time, only the
truly blind—a man with a white cane, officially
sightless—would not have seen a picture of Marilyn Monroe. She had appeared in five films (and
would make five more that year). At twenty-five,
she was Hollywood's hottest young honeypot—
subject of a full-page feature in *Collier's* (with cover
shoots for *Look* and *Life* in the works), and she was
already lighting up the nation's magazine racks as
cover girl for *Photoplay* ("Temptations of a Bachelor
Girl").

In fact, a few million American men had seen her
picture (seen her whole) before they ever knew her
name—almost before she had that name. In 1949,
when she was still unfamous, out of work, and poor
(two studios had signed her and dumped her al-

ready), she'd posed nude for fifty bucks. And although those calendar photos weren't pinned on her for three years, she was the number one pinup girl in gas stations from coast to coast, and for American troops around the world.

It was precisely her photographs (these were the "clean" sort, studio sanctioned) that drew Joe in that spring. The publicity mill at Twentieth Century Fox had "borrowed" the Philadelphia A's handsome young slugger, Gus Zernial, to make some photos with their rising star. Marilyn showed up at the A's spring camp, and took "her stance" in a halter top, very short shorts, and very high heels. Zernial was told to wrap his arms around her, and show her how to hold the bat. It was a winsome photo—made all the L.A. papers . . . and pissed Joe off, right away. "How come that fuckin' busher gets to meet a beautiful girl like that?"

DiMaggio was in town for a charity game—a team of retired California stars against the A's—and that's when Joe asked Zernial about her. Gus gave him the name of the "business manager," David March. Joe had a pal call March, right away, and the "date" was set up for two days thence.

For propriety's sake, it was a double date: March and another actress were going to tag along. It was set up for dinner—seven P.M., at the Villa Nova, a dark Dago joint on the Sunset Strip. March and his date were there on time. Joe came by cab, fifteen minutes later. Then, another hour expired in uncomfortable near silence, and still, Miss Monroe didn't show.

March had to excuse himself—he called her at home. She was vague about whether she was coming, at all. She hadn't been keen about meeting a sports star. "I don't like men in loud clothes, with checked suits, and big muscles, and pink ties. I get nervous." But March told her, Joe wasn't like that. And this dinner was all set up—for her own good.

She was two hours late, when she floated in. DiMaggio stood as she got to the table. He was so different than the man she'd imagined, it shook her up. As she recalled for the writer Ben Hecht, when he was attempting to compile her memoirs:

"I found myself staring at a reserved gentleman in a gray suit, with a gray tie and a sprinkle of gray in his hair. There were a few blue polka dots on his tie. If I hadn't been told he was some sort of ball player, I would have guessed he was either a steel magnate or a congressman.

"He said 'I'm glad to meet you,' and then fell silent for the whole rest of the evening. . . . I addressed only one remark to him. 'There's a blue polka dot exactly in the middle of your tie knot,' I said. 'Did it take you long to fix it like that?'

"Mr. DiMaggio shook his head. I could see right away he was not a man to waste words. Acting mysterious and far away while in company was my own sort of specialty. I didn't see how it was going to work on somebody who was busy being mysterious and far away himself."

She was seated next to DiMaggio, but had no idea what else to say to him. (As she later recalled, she'd never seen a baseball game.) So she chatted to March about the picture she was shooting by day, *Monkey Business.* In fact, all the talk was about the movie business—and all excluded Joe—until Mickey Rooney spotted the Great DiMaggio across the dining room, and pulled up a chair at the table.

Rooney was an ardent fan, and started asking Joe about his famous feats. What about that huge home run off Sal Maglie? . . . What about the comeback in Boston, in '49? . . . What about that day you broke the record—remember, in The Streak?—when your bat got stolen? . . .

Marilyn was still a bit vague on who DiMaggio was. (Baseball? Or football? . . .) But Rooney, she knew, was somebody big. In fact, he had been Hollywood's number one box office draw, before the war, when she was the miserable little foster-child, Norma Jeane Baker. In those days, her guardian, Grace Goddard (the woman who came closest to a parent in her life), had stowed her every afternoon in some darkened cinema palace, and fed her relentlessly on the fantasy that someday she—Norma Jeane—would be a great screen star, too. The decade since had mostly been a narrow, all-excluding quest to make that fantasy into fact. Marilyn was painfully aware that all her life had been around Hollywood, about Hollywood—and nothing else. That's why she'd signed up for a literature course at UCLA—and why she was always broke: if she had cash, she'd spend it on "great books." Now that the dream of her girlhood was coming true—or starting to come true—the wider world she'd never known was her new hunger. And as the great star, Mickey Rooney—and for that matter, her friend, David March—turned their eager attention upon this dignified stranger from that wider world, it came clear to Marilyn that this was somebody big, too.

As Marilyn remembered for Ben Hecht: "The other men talked and threw their personalities around. Mr. DiMaggio just sat there. Yet somehow he was the most exciting man at the table. The excitement was in his eyes. They are sharp and alert.

"Then I became aware of something odd. The men at the table weren't showing off for me or telling their stories for my attention. It was Mr. DiMaggio they were wooing. This was a novelty. No woman has ever put me so much in the shade before.

"But as far as I was concerned, Mr. DiMaggio was all novelty. In Hollywood, the more important a man is the more he talks. The better he is at his job, the more he brags. By these Hollywood standards of male greatness my dinner companion was a nobody. Yet I have never seen any man in Hollywood who got so much respect and attention at a dinner table. Sitting next to Mr. DiMaggio was like sitting next to a peacock with its tail spread—that's how noticeable you were."

Near eleven P.M., she rose and said she had an early call. DiMaggio stood, as well. By her account, she startled herself by offering him a ride home. But they didn't go to his hotel . . .

" 'I don't feel like turning in,' he said. 'Would you mind driving around a little while?'

"My heart jumped, and I felt full of happiness. But all I did was nod and mysteriously answer, 'It's a lovely night for a drive.'

"We rode around for three hours. After the first hour I began to find out things about Joe DiMaggio. He was a baseball player and had belonged to the Yankee Ball Club of the American League in New York. And he always worried when he went out with a girl. He didn't mind going out once with her. It was the second time he didn't like. As for the third time, that very seldom happened. He had a loyal friend named Georgie Solotaire who ran interference for him and pried the girl loose.

" 'Is Mr. Solotaire with you?' I asked.

"He said he was.

" 'I'll try not to make him too much trouble when he starts prying me loose,' I said.

" 'I don't think I'll have use for Mr. Solotaire's services on this trip,' he replied.

"After that we didn't talk for another half hour, but I didn't mind. I had an instinct that compliments from Mr. DiMaggio were going to be few and far between, so I was content to just sit in silence and enjoy the one he had just paid me."

Joe told her that he'd seen her photos in the paper. That's why he'd wanted to meet her. She said she couldn't understand why. He must have met so many more famous people. Joe thought for a moment, and said—well, he'd met Ethyl Barrymore, and Douglas MacArthur. Then, he added shyly: "But you're prettier than them."

That's what fetched her into the boat. Joe never did get home that night.

And it never occurred to him to ask why she'd wanted to meet him—why did she agree to that dinner date? . . . He had, at that moment, no way to know how she was making up her life on the fly, and why, suddenly, he fit into her fictions. Joe didn't know how she'd talked it over with her friend and advisor, the gossip columnist Sidney Skolsky—who would reveal to the world Joe and Marilyn's liaison in the column he'd write the following day. It was Skolsky who'd told her how DiMaggio was so hugely admired, how his name—a really Big Name!—bespoke for the public dignity and class. It was Skolsky who told her Joe was a hero . . . just what she needed for her problem, now.

The problem was, the news was out that Marilyn Monroe was the naked girl on those scandalous calendars. In 1952, nice girls didn't pose nude. When a UPI reporter, Aline Mosby, alerted the brass at Twentieth Century Fox, the boss, Darryl Zanuck, hit the roof. Zanuck was a buck-toothed and bumptious tyrant who demanded obedience, and enforced it with rage. He wanted Marilyn to deny that was her—deny everything! It was Skolsky who advised her to tell the truth, and tell it exclusively to Mosby (who had written, some months before, a syrupy account of Marilyn's childhood—the "little orphan girl" who'd made it big).

So despite Zanuck's threats (Her career would be ruined! He would exercise the morals clause in her contract—and cut her loose!) . . . Marilyn went to lunch with Mosby, and took her to the ladies' room of the restaurant, to offer her tearful tale: she'd been broke, scared, and hungry—otherwise she never would have done it. But that fifty dollars was the only way to pay the rent! . . .)

Mosby's scoop would hit the papers that March 13—the day that Marilyn signed on for dinner with Joe. The way Skolsky (and Miss Monroe) had it figured, if the most admired hero in the country thought her a nice, decent girl, worthy of his company (in public—and in hyper-public print) . . . well, what more did anybody need to know?

As it turned out, Marilyn's dangerous "scandal" would become an enormous public relations triumph—one of the building blocks of her legend. And, at the cost of his own lifelong heartache, so would Joe.

STILL, THAT COULDN'T EXPLAIN why she went out with him the next night, and the next, and the next . . . in fact they were together every night he was in town—which was just about every night, till he had to go east, that April, to take up his job in the Yankee Stadium broadcast booth.

He was so different from all the chattery men who buzzed around her in Hollywood. He was a fascination. It wasn't that he didn't have anything to say— just that he didn't have to say it. Like he already knew everything that they were always talking about. Even about her.

He wasn't mad about that calendar—or about the next crisis, when the papers found out she wasn't "a little orphan girl." (Her mother was very much alive, and just released from a state mental hospital.) Joe knew all about making up your own life story. He didn't judge her for that. And he knew why she did it. He seemed to understand (without a word said) how she wanted to be a star—had to be the biggest star, a perfect star. That's what was wonderful: this man, who was so solid, rich, strong, assured, admired . . . still, he knew everything there was to know about hunger.

He wooed her sweetly, and gave her respite from the fever of appearing that was the rest of her life. (Joe was just as happy to spend an evening on a couch in a darkened room with on old movie on TV, while she resumed the habits of her girlhood and curled up next to him, to dream while some celluloid fantasy played out onscreen.) Withal, he bound her to him with the only cords that could ever keep her—those of her own ambition. She wanted to learn to be like him.

What she saw, what she wanted to learn, was the same thing two generations of Yankees saw, and tried to learn, from Joe. That was the certainty of his own stardom. She saw, she thought she had to have, the same thing the kids on the old North Beach Playground wanted, when they looked at Joe: the sufficiency in himself that made him quiet at his core. It was enviable, it was maddening. Marilyn and Ben Hecht tried to put it into words:

"I was always able to tell what it was about a man that attracted me. Except this time with Mr. DiMaggio. My feelings for this silent smiling man began to disturb me. What was the use of buzzing all over for a man who was like somebody sitting alone in the Observation Car?

". . . I thought, 'You learn to be silent and smiling like that from having millions of people look at you with love and excitement while you stand alone getting ready to do something.'

"I only wished I knew what Mr. DiMaggio did."

What Joe knew was, here was the most beautiful creature he'd ever seen. He knew a lot of broads—beauties, sure—but no one, nothing, like this girl. It wasn't even the same category. He'd been around the block a few times in Hollywood. And not just with Dorothy—but big stars: Marlene Dietrich, for instance. (Joe didn't like her. She had bad breath.) But Marilyn put them all in the shade. This girl had beauty shining out from inside.

It wasn't her stardom that made her shine—though it pleased Joe that everything Dorothy hungered for, strove for, *dumped him for* . . . Marilyn already had all that (effortlessly, as he imagined), and by age twenty-five. She was just a kid! . . . And it wasn't only her looks—though, what a looker! When she'd get dressed up (finally!) and made-up (second or third time, when she was satisfied), they'd go to some joint and she'd stop the place cold—like everybody else in the room disappeared. He loved that.

But he loved it more when it was just for him—or even better, when they'd get to her place, and she'd drop that dress on the floor (there was never anything on underneath), and scrub all that shit off her face, and drop the towel coming out of the bathroom, lit perhaps by one bulb behind her, or the blue of the TV he'd flicked on . . . and there she was, his girl, so pale, past vanilla, it was white in her young skin—dairy milk—and perfect, tiny-boned, delicate, like a twelve-year-old virgin, childlike as her giggle when he grabbed her, then, covered her with him, filled her, crushed her, sometimes (Christ forgive him) he was trying to kill her . . . God, he never wanted to jolt anybody like this girl.

Maybe she did know a bit about baseball—or she was learning fast. She called Joe her "slugger." Years later, when her friend (and the great profile writer of the age) Truman Capote asked her who was the best, she brought up Joe's name, and added: "He can hit home runs." Capote understood—and, as usual, he understood why: he entitled his profile on Marilyn Monroe, "A Beautiful Child."

By the time April came, Joe didn't want his job on TV, and didn't want to leave for New York. He felt like his real life—his aliveness—was with Marilyn. He'd known her three weeks.

Still, what he wanted was to leave with her—take her away to San Francisco, which was always the stage set in his mind when he cast himself as head of household. He didn't push. He didn't want to scare her . . . but he had to ask: did she ever want—you know, a real family? Kids? . . .

Oh, yes—more than anything! (Marilyn always said that.)

It made perfect sense to Joe. What didn't make sense was to leave her now—here, in this town full of worms. What would happen when he left? Nothing good. (He could feel the acid-ache in his stomach, already.) But he had to leave. She told him she was going to come east that summer, to film on location at Niagara Falls. She could come to New York then. He could show her his town. She loved New York! . . . He made her promise, then promise again.

What happened when he left was a bellyache of the worst sort—Marilyn was hospitalized with acute appendicitis. On April 28, she was wheeled into an operating room at the Cedars of Lebanon Hospital.

From New York, DiMaggio sent wires and mail, called at all hours, day and night. Every day, he sent flowers—roses, always. (Marilyn had told him she loved roses. If she died, she wanted him to put roses on her grave every week—just as William Powell did for the great Jean Harlow.) . . . DiMaggio filled her room with roses.

In her own way Marilyn, too, tried to be true to what she'd told him—or what she always told herself. When the OR staff lifted her hospital gown to reveal her belly where the incision would be made, they found a note, taped to her skin:

Most important to Read Before *operation.*
Dear Doctor,
Cut as little as possible. I know it seems vain but that doesn't really enter into it—the fact that I'm a *woman* is important and means much to me. Save please (can't ask you enough) what you can—I'm in your hands. You have children and you must know what it means—*please Doctor*—I know somehow you will! thank you—thank you—for Gods sakes Dear Doctor No *ovaries* removed—please again do whatever you can to prevent large *scars.* Thanking you with all my *heart.*
Marilyn Monroe

As her British biographer *(Goddess: The Secret Lives of Marilyn Monroe),* the relentless digger, Anthony Summers, confirmed with her surgeon more than thirty years later, there was no collateral damage, no ovaries disturbed (and just a normal small scar) when Marilyn's appendix came out. A week later, she was back on the set, to finish *Monkey Business*. Her makeup man, Allan "Whitey" Snyder, promised he would make her the picture of good health. (Anyway, he said, if she keeled over and died, he'd make her look great in her coffin. Marilyn laughed, and made him promise that, too.)

In New York, Joe was delighted with her good news. The way he figured, as soon as she finished that picture (When? A week? Two weeks?) . . . she'd be coming east to start on *Niagara*. He called every night (though it was late in New York) to see how she was, what she'd done that day—and to fret about his own job (it was stupid, and nerve-wracking). She was always sympathetic. He was just shy, like her—she was always scared to death in front of a camera. . . .

It did him so much good to talk to her, Joe never realized that all her good news (She'd be working once again with Howard Hawks. . . . She'd met an agent, a big-time agent—Charley Feldman—he came to see her, himself! . . . They were talking about her for *Gentlemen Prefer Blondes*!) . . . every good thing that happened was carrying her farther from the life he saw for them. The life he thought she saw, too.

"She's a plain kid," Joe told his pal Jimmy Cannon.

"She'd give up the business if I asked her. She'd quit the movies in a minute. It means nothing to her."

LAST WEEK IN MAY, SHE ARRIVED in New York, and that's where she fetched Joe into the boat forever. It was like life came back to him—and appetite, excitement, fun. Even within his network of pals, no one had ever seen him like this. Jesus! Daig was grinnin' all the time!

He'd had such a rotten month—with that little pissy job. He knew it should have been easy. There was a pregame warm-up show—five minutes at most. And then after the games, fifteen minutes more: just an interview with one of the guys, five or six questions (the writers would have them all written out), then give the final score again, and goodbye. . . . It should have been a walk in the park. But it ate him up. He knew he looked bad.

Even the brevity of it was a problem. It was like a whole day leading up to one at-bat. And then you got up, there were only two pitches (that you never saw before, and neither one worth a shit) . . . how could you hit 'em out of the park like that? He'd show up every day—every hair in place, beautiful suit, perfect shirt, gorgeous tie, pants creased, shoes shined—and wait (That was another problem: wait, wait, wait! What's he supposed to do? Chat?) . . . while something got screwed up. He'd stand in front of the camera, waiting ten minutes, stiffer every minute (he could feel it in his back) . . . twenty times, he'd unbutton his coat, cram his shirtfront back into his pants, hold the microphone in front of him again, then look down—*his fuckin' shirt was wrinkled!* . . . Then, he'd look up again. *Where's the goddamn CUE CARDS?* One time, he threw a total fit, roaring curses—he refused to go on—because the producer lost the first cue card. They calmed him down in the nick of time—wrote out a new card in block capitals:

HI, I'M JOE DIMAGGIO.

WELCOME TO THE JOE DIMAGGIO SHOW.

For contract purposes, it was called *The Buitoni Show.* That was the sponsor, the big pasta company. That was another problem. Joe liked the guys from Buitoni fine. They treated him with total respect. And their checks were good. But still, he wasn't thrilled about being the front man for an all-Dago band. He'd sit down in a restaurant, and smart-ass fans would start making jokes: how come he wasn't eating Buitoni macaroni? . . . And then there was the hokey end they wrote for the interviews. They'd bring out a bowl of spaghetti—like Joe and the guy he was talking to were going to chow down, after the game. One time, he had Jerry Coleman on the show—they bring out the big, steaming dish of spaghetti . . . and Joe's supposed to wind it up by asking Coleman, "How's the spaghetti?"

Coleman's supposed to say it's good—"Great!" And that's that. But he says, "How do I know, Joe? I haven't tasted it yet."

Then what the hell was Joe supposed to say? . . . After the show, he was furious at Coleman. *Sonof-abitch showed him up!*

It was like being in a slump all year. Couldn't get his timing . . . couldn't just *hit it* . . . and spending every night with the worry that always made it worse. He'd go out at night, have some belts to unwind, and the pal he was with would tell him he was fine—all he had to do was relax. That was like a slump, too: same meaningless advice. "Just go up there and be yourself! . . ." What the hell did they know about it?

But when Marilyn came, she told him he looked wonderful. And he was so cow-eyed—from her he half-believed it. (She was the one who looked per- fect—to him.) And, after all, this was the kind of thing she did know about. The way the camera stared at you, like a million eyes in one, when you knew everything about you was wrong. Yes, she did under- stand. . . . She told him about the tricks she'd learned—the breathing lessons she received from her coach (Natasha. Oh, she was brilliant!) . . . Joe even said he'd try those, too.

He would've stood on his head if she'd told him to—or tried, or said he would someday . . . if she'd just stay with him. All his troubles disappeared. He took her around to his New York haunts. Dinner at the

Colony, and next night, Le Pavillion . . . and she loved them. She must have said five times, there wasn't anything like this—nothing close—in Los Angeles. She hated L.A. . . . and New York loved her. Everywhere they went, she stopped the show. Or she and Joe did. There was no one who didn't look, and whisper to friends, or poke a companion so he could look, too. And no one who didn't start to smile, the minute they saw them—those two looked so . . . perfect! There were plenty who came over for autographs (natch). But Joe even smiled through that. Of course, he'd sign—glad to—"But don't you really want her . . . ?"

The papers fell into the love-fest, too—couldn't get enough of this dream couple. Mr. and Miss America! . . . Or maybe it was Mrs. (There were immediate rumors that wedding bells were in the offing—or maybe they'd already tolled! Winchell, for one, insisted that he had information . . . about *Mr. and Mrs. DiMaggio.)* Marilyn, who was always thrilled by publicity, reveled in the excitement of this. Sure, she was (or she was getting to be) a big deal in Hollywood. But this was amazing! There was her photo— their photo—in a dozen papers, all in the same day. She couldn't understand why Joe was so suspicious about that. He warned her repeatedly to watch out for the writers—and watch what she said around them. It was like he didn't want her to enjoy herself . . . and just forget. But she knew he was only trying to protect her. He was so sweet. He rented them two rooms at the Drake—made a big show about that—in case anybody asked. (They did.)

There was in New York's glee an element of civic ratification. Competition with "The Coast"—Tinseltown in particular—hadn't heated up to a fever yet. But still it was satisfying that *their hero* (forget where he was born—wasn't he always the Yankee Clipper?) . . . had sallied forth from his Manhattan cave and clubbed to (radiantly happy) submission this golden girl of Hollywood. It was as good as the Yankees dashing the hopes of the Red Sox again. (Better! Who gave a shit about dowdy old Boston?) . . . And, of course, being New Yorkers, both writers and readers assumed that anything that happened in New York had happened for America, once and for all. "They are folk idols," Jimmy Cannon announced, "Marilyn and Joe, a whole country's pets."

That wasn't quite how Joe would have said it—he wasn't interested in being the national poodle. But, still, he couldn't argue the point. With the Hero Machine artillery firing barrels of ink from both coasts *(Photoplay* shot first, among the monthly cannoneers—with "He's Her JOE! The Romantic Score on the Pin-up Girl and the Yankee Clipper.") . . . the nation as a whole was soon splattered. Seemed like a dozen times a day, now, Joe had to "no comment" some writer or columnist, or send Georgie out to tell the shutterbugs to back off. And not just through that first visit—but weekends, all through June and

July—she'd fly down from Buffalo, Friday night, when her shooting was done. DiMaggio steadfastly refused to discuss Miss M. in print. Except to deny they were married (when he'd settle for the blandly suggestive demurral: "No. We're just good friends.").

But what was also suggestive was, he wasn't hiding her—or hiding himself anymore. He took her happily to Yankee Stadium where, to the delight of the sporting press, she coached him in the interview studio in the basement tunnel behind the Yankee dugout. Before the games, she'd wander down to the box seats, and all the young Yankees would flock to the railing to meet her, and get her autograph. (That part, Joe wasn't happy about: did they have to crowd her like that? Jesus! *Why didn't they just climb in her lap?*)

And the surest sign of his newfound ease: he took her to the cannoneers' HQ—what Red Smith used to call the Mother Lodge—after dinner, they'd show up at Toots Shor's saloon. Joe had finally forgiven Toots, and resumed his place on the banquette in the corner. What the hell, it was only a fight about broads—and Dorothy—that was all over now. Joe didn't have any more problems on that subject. In fact, he took a positive delight in showing Toots how he'd worked out his worries. (Who's moonin' now?)

And for his part, Toots was so abjectly grateful that the Big Guy had come back (God, Toots cried like a baby when Joe got mad, it was like losing a son) . . . he woulda thrown everybody else on the street, locked the doors—leave the crumb bums on the curb!—if Joe and his girl wanted the joint to themselves. But that was the beauty part. Joe didn't want anything special. That's why Tootsie had to love him! Joe walks in with a broad—*she's so gorgeous a train would stop* . . . and says he don't want to disturb anybody. That is a champion with class!

Of course, in the event, what happened was, they walked in and the place *was jolted*—bigger than Dempsey, Sinatra and Gleason, and Joe Louis all rolled into one—the place went electric, like everybody found a plug and stuck their fingers in, and you could feel the lights flicker and come on brighter. Then the noise: like the air had come out of them all at once—*whhouff*—and then a rumbling male approbation (the sound at the Garden when a champ lands a big hook to the head), louder and louder, as they're shouting, "It's Dago! Hey, Joe! There he is, the Clipper!" And then they came over—a parade to the corner: "You look great, Daig! Y'gonna introduce me?"

The funny part was, Joe had told her that's where they could go to get away from the columnists, photographers, fans—where they wouldn't be bothered. But she loved it anyway. And it was funny. Joe was laughing. He looked so happy. All these strange, loud, adoring men, clapping him on the back like he'd just won the big game. "Joe! You look great! . . ." He'd shrug, and say through his grin: "I'm just with her."

For Joe, in this happiness, there was more than an

element of ratification. Maybe he would always be a stiff on TV. Maybe center field now belonged to Mantle—and (despite the mistakes that Joe had pointed out to Marilyn that afternoon) maybe the rockhead would do fine. Maybe the Yanks (in first place, and coasting) could even be champions without the Dago. . . . But with this girl on his arm, Joe was, once again, the Big Guy in the Hero Game. Without another word said—from her, or him. And didn't matter what they did! Simply, in her person, she affirmed him—made him once again what he was (what he thought he'd lost) . . . He loved what he was in her eyes—and in the eyes of the world, with her. He was Joe DiMaggio again.

THE CLINCHER WAS, HE KNEW HE could help her. Here was someone he could watch over. She was just a sweet kid. She could get eaten alive—everybody wanting a chunk of her. He could see that already, the way she was with the writers, and photographers—it was like they owned her. Stand here, do this, hold that . . . and she'd jump. All excited. They wanted to make her picture! The kid didn't know the ropes, how to say no.

Joe knew. And he was trying to teach her. By August, when she was back in L.A., he was on the phone every night, with advice, encouragement, warnings, like a long-distance manager. See, now, she had three pictures out that summer—*Clash by Night* in June,

We're Not Married in July, and now, in August, *Don't Bother to Knock.* . . . Now, she was going to have *Monkey Business* and *Niagara* in the can. How was she ever gonna get more money—put the studio over a barrel, if she already gave them everything they wanted? They had a backlog on her—they were using her, see?—so she'd never be able to hold out against them.

They were using her up! (Take it from him—Joe had been through this.) . . . They had her on a seven-year contract, and of course every year they picked up the option—and what could she do? What were they paying her now? Seven hundred fifty a week. Chump change! She was making real money for them. And they were treating her like a piece of meat.

Of course, she explained to Joe how she'd got into this, two years ago, before anybody knew who she was. . . . Her first agent (and champion, daddy-figure, lover)—Johnny Hyde (he was such a wonderful man, the first man who promised to make her a star—and he wanted to marry her!) . . . Johnny had worked out that seven-year contract, and then, a week later, he was dead. That's why she was still with his agency, William Morris. But nobody there took care of her now.

Jesus, Joe almost jumped through the phone. *He would take care of her.* . . . The whole story fed his certainty that this kid needed someone—a strong man, a guy who'd been around—to wrest her from the clutches of those Hollywood assholes. He'd be out there, right after the season . . . don't sign with Feldman. Don't sign anything!

For Marilyn, this was an accustomed role, familiar and comfortable—or at least well practiced. In her marriage (into which she'd been placed, at age sixteen, more or less like another foster home), the best thing about her husband, Jimmy Dougherty, was he was five years older, and had a mustache. She called him Daddy. After she divorced him, in 1946, all her serious relationships had been with older men, strong and shrewd men. She played waif to their protector. Now, her Slugger signed his letters, "Pa."

But she also knew, Joe was right. Or he might be right. He was from outside—he wasn't all caught up in the tangly web of Hollywood friendship and power, loyalty and fear—he was only loyal to her. He did know about bargaining and contracts. (They gave him more money to play in a baseball game than she ever made in a week.) . . . But it wasn't the money she cared about most. What Joe was really talking about was control: about her deciding when to make a picture—and what picture. *That should be up to her!* Joe had such certainty, and pride. And what she loved most was his pride in her—his certainty that she was great.

Sometimes, she wished he wouldn't watch over her so constantly. There was the time that September, when she came east again, for the premiere of *Monkey Business,* and to serve as Grand Marshal for the Miss America Pageant in Atlantic City. She dressed for the occasion in a gown of black chiffon, with a neckline . . . well, no, it never got near her neck. Instead, two orphan folds of chiffon were born apart, somewhere near her shoulders, and made acquaintance with each other, down the road, near her navel.

"It was an entirely decent dress," Marilyn was still protesting to Ben Hecht, years later. "You could ride in a streetcar in it without disturbing the passengers.

"But there was one bright-minded photographer who figured he would get a more striking picture if he photographed me shooting down. I didn't notice him pointing his camera from a balcony . . ."

(Well, gosh! A girl can't keep track of everything!)

The scandal erupted, predictably, with the next day's papers. And predictably—expertly—she turned it to her advantage. If there was still anybody in the country who knew nothing about Marilyn Monroe . . . they got an eyeful in their paper that morning—and probably an earful, that Sunday, in church. In short, it worked out just like she wanted— except for Joe. Joe was awful.

He was furious. He was screaming at her. Like she'd done the whole thing to embarrass him. She tried to explain, it was publicity, it was part of her job, she had to show herself.

"SHOW 'EM NOTHING!" Joe just shouted her down.

But that was the dress she got from the studio!

"WEAR YOUR OWN GODDAMN CLOTHES . . ."

But she didn't have any clothes!

He was so unfair. He was hateful. He said they made her look like a whore. And she was in tears on the phone.

Thing was, Joe couldn't stay mad at her. At least, he couldn't stay away. He had to talk to her. Late at night, there was nothing else he wanted in the world. Except he wanted to be there with her. . . . But she couldn't shrug off the hurt from him—not that fast, not with what he'd said. She shrank away from him. Let the phone ring. (Or maybe she wasn't there! . . . *What was she doing? . . . Who was she with?*) . . . Marilyn fixed his wagon, but good. She didn't have to take that from him.

So, Joe had to fly to L.A.—come to her—middle of September, with the season still on. What else could he do? He was so contrite. He wanted her so.

And that was the pattern: she'd shy from the pressure of his grasp . . . and he'd come on, to woo her, care for her, convince her. Then, his hold would get so tight, she wanted to scream—had to do something—and Joe would be hurt, offended, enraged. It wasn't really for herself she had to act out. (God, no! If nothing else, her life had taught her to make do.) But she had to do something for the beautiful creation she'd made—for Marilyn Monroe—the girl the whole country was falling in love with. In those days she would linger, examining, fretting, fixing, redoing, in her dressing room, or some ladies' room mirror—she'd be in there for hours—till someone would have to come get her.

What are you doing? . . .

"Looking at Her."

That was the girl she had to protect. Sometimes, Joe wanted to kill Her.

But she wouldn't, or couldn't, shrink from Joe forever, either. He was so lonely without her. And so hurt, if she said she didn't care to see him. He was so real! And he did what he said. After the Yankees won the World Series (it was exciting: Mickey Mantle hit a home run to win the seventh game!) . . . her Slugger did come back—Joe came straight to Hollywood, to take care of her. And the first thing was, he took her shopping, to buy some clothes of her own.

OF COURSE, EVERY OUTFIT HAD A neckline right up under her chin. But they were darling, and so was he—the way he sat there and helped her pick them out—and then he paid. She promised she'd wear them, if he'd try to be more patient with her. And he promised, too—he would try. They had a deal.

After that, he dived into the rest of her life, like a busy superintendent. How come she didn't have any money? Marilyn didn't have any idea. But there was rent, and her car, and she had to eat something, and books, and singing lessons, and acting lessons— Marilyn paid her acting coach, Natasha Lytess, hundreds of dollars every week for private lessons. Joe couldn't figure that. Wasn't Natasha the studio coach?

Why, yes! Marilyn had even made the studio give Natasha a raise. She would never do a picture without Natasha.

Well then, Joe said, let the studio pay her. (He never paid Crosetti to pitch extra BP.)

But Natasha would be hurt—and terribly upset!

Joe barely bothered to shrug. Next time Natasha called Marilyn at home, it was Joe who picked up the phone. "If you want to talk to Miss Monroe," said DiMaggio, "you'd better call her agent."

(Of course, that sent Natasha right up the wall. And Marilyn couldn't, or wouldn't, go on without her. So she had to make the studio promote Miss Lytess to *chief drama coach*—and give her another raise.)

There were a lot of things about Marilyn's life that Joe couldn't figure. (To be precise, he thought he had them all figured. He just couldn't figure why she didn't.) . . . Publicity, for instance—what was in it for her?

As she recalled for Ben Hecht, Joe would sneer at her excitement when some magazine was giving her a big picture spread.

" 'Yes, but where's the money?' he asks.

" 'It's the publicity,' I yell back.

" 'Money is better,' he says in the quiet way men use when they think they've won an argument."

There was the subject of punctuality. Why was she always late? Ten minutes late from traffic, sure. But two hours? Three hours? What got into her? . . . She'd say something like her hair was a wreck, and she had to comb it out, but she needed color, so she just couldn't get it to look right. Or she had nothing to wear, because her outfit was at the cleaners, and she was at the studio, and by the time she got out . . .

That was another thing! She wasn't shooting on a film that day. What was she doing at the studio? And who was she with? (That voice coach who ate her up with his eyes? That greasy designer who made her dress like a whore? . . .) She was always at the goddamn studio.

She'd have plenty to wear, if her clothes weren't in a dirty ball, where she dropped 'em. Joe couldn't understand that, either. Why did she have to be such a mess? . . . Marilyn wasn't just untidy. It was more like unconscious. The great director Billy Wilder (another man with a European sense of all things in their place) remembered a time when he caught a ride with Marilyn, and got a good look at her car. "Such a mess you wouldn't believe," as Wilder described it. "It is like she threw everything in the back helter-skelter because there's an invasion and the enemy is already in Pasadena. There's blouses lying there, and slacks, girdles, skirts, shoes, old plane tickets—old lovers, for all I know—you never saw such a filthy mess in your life. On top of the mess is a whole bunch of traffic tickets. I ask her about them.

Tickets for parking. Tickets for speeding, passing lights, who knows what? Is she worried about them? Am I worried about the sun rising tomorrow?"

Mess was one of the reasons Joe always paid for a room of his own (or maybe he didn't pay, but he made some kind of arrangement) at the slightly-less-than-top-of-the-line Knickerbocker Hotel, on North Ivar. Still, that wasn't much of a place to entertain Marilyn, if they were going out (or staying in) that night. Sometimes, his pal Bernie Kamber would have to come out to the Coast. Bernie's on the cuff, of course, so he's staying at some nice hotel. Plus, Bernie had to have a TV—he'd schmear the bell captain, three-fifty a day. So Joe would say, "Hey, Bernie, you got a TV, right? I got a date with Marilyn tonight. Can we use your place?" And that worked out fine. . . . But still, a lot of nights, as that winter drew nigh, Joe would end up at Marilyn's place. She liked that—she was lovely about that. But Joe could only take it so long. She'd have to get up in the morning, so by midnight, she's alone in the bed (with her face greased like a wheel bearing, in a half-inch of Vaseline), while Joe's wandering around in the mess. No wonder, every week or two, he discovered that some business required his presence in New York or San Francisco.

For almost twenty years, he'd had a rhythm to his life. A week or two at home (or some hotel that passed as home). And then he'd have to get going. What was he supposed to do in Hollywood forever? . . . It'd be different if she wasn't working. He'd grouse, sometimes: Why did she always have to be working? It was like Marilyn didn't even hear him. It was *Gentlemen Prefer Blondes*—and she's the blonde! She'd have to sing, and dance (how was she ever going to do it?). . . . But this was her biggest film ever.

The times she hated were holidays, when there was no work. She'd always hated them. It'd be different, if she had a family. Never did. Holidays, she was just at loose ends. Thanksgiving, what was she supposed to do? There was as much chance of a turkey cooking her. Joe said, forget about it—he'd take care of that. He'd take them to the Brown Derby, and they'd have Thanksgiving dinner. And Bernie happened to be in L.A., so Joe was happy about that, too. Joe and Bernie got to the restaurant by three-thirty, or four P.M. Joe wanted to be early—insisted on it—so they could get a table in the back, where they wouldn't be bothered. Naturally, Marilyn was coming on her own from the studio. *(What the hell's she doing at the studio, Thanksgiving?)* Except she didn't come. And didn't come, didn't come. A half-hour, an hour, then two hours. By the time she showed up, Joe was so mad—he was rigid! He'd talk to Bernie. Marilyn, he acted like she wasn't there. Then, she was hurt, so she wouldn't talk to Joe. She only talked to Bernie, too. And that was the holiday (which just confirmed how awful they were).

And Christmas was always the worst. Everybody else had someone. And Joe wasn't even in town. Marilyn went (she had to appear) to the studio Christmas party. But that only made her feel more empty—she left early, and went home, alone. Home, in those days, was a suite at the Beverly Hills Hotel. She was a star now—and ought to live like one. But what was the good of that, on Christmas? She unlocked the door, and there, on a table across the room, was a little Christmas tree, with a card propped up against the bottom of it. She ripped open the envelope, and read:

Merry Christmas, Marilyn
—Joe.

There were tears in her eyes as she looked up, and there he was, sitting silent in a corner of the room. She ran to him. "Nobody ever gave me a Christmas tree before," she said. "Joe, I love you." There was dinner he had ordered in, and champagne. They got a little tight and danced to an Ella Fitzgerald record, before they left it all, and went together into the next room.

THE TIMES JOE LIKED WERE WEEK- ends, when she didn't have to get up, and they could lounge around all day. Or they'd ride in the country in his blue Cadillac, with the license plate JOE D. (No, he wasn't hiding anymore. Why should he?) . . . Best of all, they could ride out to the Black Foxe Institute, Joe Jr.'s school, and take him out for a day, show the boy a big time. Then, Joe felt like he had everything taken care of—all the eggs were back in his carton.

Of course, little Butchie was thrilled. Well, he wasn't so little now—almost eleven years old—and every boy in his class knew very well who Marilyn Monroe was. (And he got to meet her!) It made him an object of high regard among his classmates. It was almost as good as being tall (which he wasn't), or cool and dismissive and funny (no, he wasn't) or a star on the baseball team (alas, he wasn't that either). In fact, being friends with Marilyn Monroe was one of the very few ways that Joe DiMaggio, Jr., ever felt he fulfilled the expectations raised by his name.

It was terribly complicated, that name. A lot of times, he wished he could get rid of it. It wasn't just baseball—though that was heartache enough—that's why he always said he liked football better. He wasn't even great at that (or big enough, strong enough)— maybe he could be the kicker . . . that would have been okay, if he'd had a lot of stories to tell about the Yankees, or times with his dad, or anything about him. But he didn't. So he cultivated silence about Big Joe—like the other boys wouldn't understand. But that was only good for a while—like when he changed schools, and people didn't know him, which his manner more or less enforced, but it would have been nicer if they did know him—if it was *just him* they wanted to know. . . . It was complicated even to explain, sometimes.

But Marilyn (he liked using just her first name)—

that was a name like a smile. "Marilyn told me . . ." Nothing complicated about that!

And she did tell him things. She liked him! She was so nice. She'd just talk like a regular person. ("Naw, she doesn't have that whispery voice," he'd assure his schoolmates, in days to come. "That's not her, really. Not with friends . . .")

Marilyn always got along with kids, because she would just talk to them, as equals. And she got such a kick out of how they really thought—they were all fears and delight (not airs and posturing of unconcern, like grown-ups). They were like her.

It was Marilyn who'd steer Big Joe off his nervous plans—a big-deal lunch, and then get some ice cream, and shopping, then the boy can go bowling, and then . . . it was Marilyn who'd say, let's just go home. They'd hang around the pool at the hotel— whatever hotel it was now, that didn't matter. It was great.

And then, even Big Joe was fine—once he relaxed. In fact, he'd just sit there and smoke, and smile, watching Marilyn and the boy. Satisfied. Or if he wasn't satisfied, it was just about him, and he'd go off and get a coffee or something. Or he and Marilyn would go off for a little while—and come back laughing. Big Joe was nicer than Butch had ever seen him. For once he didn't ask about the teams, Junior's marks, his clothes, his friends (did he have friends?). Joe Jr. was usually so scared of putting his father in a bad mood, failing to live up (to what, he never did quite know) . . . it was like any visit started with a quiz, and the price of failure was an ice-bath for the day. If the visit was with Mom *and* Dad, that was impossible. Then, his father always asked more questions, like he wanted to find out something bad. And his mom would go wacky, too, hugging him all the time—like showing off their love.

He did love his mom. But that was complicated, too. It was fine, if it was just them. But with anybody else—even one of her boyfriends—she'd get switched on, loud and eager, and there wasn't any way to calm her down. She was beautiful and everything. But couldn't she just be Mom? Even if he brought friends home from school, it was like she'd put on a show. Now that Butch was older, it made him embarrassed. One time, he brought guys home and she had to show how she could do a handstand—she did it, and she didn't have underpants on, or anything! The friends thought it was great—or said they did. Joe Jr. wanted to die.

But this was different, with Marilyn. She just was okay with him—and they all were. It was just nice. Until he told his mom about it. And she went nuts.

Dorothy Arnold got a lawyer, and went to court in Los Angeles. She filed a petition to limit DiMaggio's visitation rights. It was "entirely inappropriate" to take Little Butchie to "adult places." Why couldn't Joe just take the boy to movies, a circus, bowling— someplace like that? Instead, she had to read (in gossip columns!) that her son, her ex-husband, and

Marilyn Monroe were lounging around the Bel Air Hotel pool, where there was "a lot of adult talk." (And by the by, Dorothy wanted more money, too. She couldn't make ends meet on three hundred a month. Why not make it a thousand?)

The newspapers played it big—and wrote it as a catfight over the Great Man: the ex–Bride of Clipper against the future Mrs. Joe. What a tasty little *contretemps*! . . . But Dorothy insisted she had nothing against Marilyn. "I'm only trying to make a better father out of Joe," Dorothy told the papers. "Joe has never really exercised his privilege to see the child. When he did, he never spent more than a few minutes with him, sometimes shoving him off on his men friends to take him to the movies." The pool scene with Marilyn was just the last straw—"although, good heavens, I'm not a jealous woman!" With her own family, Dorothy was more candid. She told her sister, maybe Marilyn was a sweet, darling person. But they'd put Butchie in the pool, and then they'd go shack up in a bedroom somewhere!

This time, DiMaggio wouldn't give her a pass in court. He hired a lawyer of his own, by the name of Loyd Wright, Jr. And Joe took the stand, to reveal he was going to seek custody of his son as soon as his own situation was "more settled." He was already paying the boy's school fees—and the cost of summer camp. He had already given Miss Arnold more money: even last year he sent her two thousand dollars when she said she'd have to sell the fur he'd given her as a gift. He'd sent a piano for the boy. Miss Arnold sold it. . . .

It got pretty gamy in the courtroom—down to the matter of who bought the boy his baseball glove. But it was always clear who was winning this fight. Judge Elmer D. Doyle knew a hero when he saw one: he commended DiMaggio for showing on the witness stand the same fine sportsmanship he'd always shown on the ballfield. Then the judge asked Dorothy: "He's been pretty nice to you, hasn't he?"

In the end, Judge Doyle called Joe Jr. into chambers for a two-minute conversation, and then came out to give Dorothy the bad news. Her petition was denied. Joe DiMaggio would have visitation rights every other weekend. And no more money. The judge told Dorothy she'd made a mistake by divorcing the Great DiMaggio in the first place. "It's too bad we don't have more men like this coming to this court," Judge Doyle commented, "trying to make good American citizens of their boys."

In the aftermath, it came clear who was the big loser. Joe said it had been torture in court. Lawyers and a judge—*and the papers*—picking through his life. (They hadda run the story big, so they could run Marilyn's picture. Joe knew their game.) . . . But he was on alert, now. That would never happen again.

So there weren't going to be any more lazy days with Marilyn and Butchie around the pool. And Joe Jr. knew he'd ruined everything again.

WHAT BIG JOE LIKED BEST WAS TO take Marilyn out of her town—north to San Francisco. There, he wouldn't have to be on alert. And, of course, she wouldn't have to work. They could make up each day as it came.

There were afternoons when Joe would tell her to put a scarf around her head, put on some slacks . . . and he'd take her to the shore. He would teach her how to surf-cast. Joe could throw a line until it disappeared out over the water, and landed in the deep pools, where they might catch a striped bass, or a salmon (that's what he said). He taught her to throw it, too. But it wasn't the same when she did it. She liked to watch him. He was beautiful, the way he moved, and so strong. And then they'd stand, staring out at the sea and sky and the soaring birds, and the only sound came from gulls above and the water at their feet, and the dull, distant grumble of engines in the city behind them. They'd stay for a long time, and then finish up at some bar near the water, that always turned out to be owned by a cousin, or a cousin of a friend, or a friend of a cousin. And they'd bring drinks, and little cups of crabmeat with crackers and sauce that tasted like heaven, and there was never any bill.

Joe seemed to know everybody, or even if he didn't, they seemed to know him. But she noticed that in San Francisco, when you knew somebody that didn't mean you talked. It meant you didn't talk. One time, Joe said he'd show her the sights, and he got a cab, and they rode all over, up and down the hills, with the Bay sparkling in the distance, and Alcatraz that looked like a huge brown bread baking in the sun, and through the smells of Chinatown, down to the Embarcadero, and up to that tower thing . . . with Joe telling stories of what he used to do there. Then he'd tell the driver some other place—it went on for half a day. And when they finally stopped, there wasn't any bill for that either. The cabbie was a cousin's friend, or a friend's cousin. And Joe hadn't talked to him at all, for four hours!

He asked his friend Dario Lodigiani to go out fishing with them. It was Joe's boat, *The Yankee Clipper,* that he'd got on Joe DiMaggio Day. They motored back and forth in the Bay all morning—and Marilyn hooked a big one—a striper that grabbed her line and took off with it.

"Hold on!" Dario encouraged her. "When he lets up, that's when you reel him in a little, see?" But Marilyn could barely hold on to her pole. The fish seemed to be twice as strong as she was.

Dario said to Joe: "You better help her, Joe. She's having a hell of a time with that."

Joe said: "She hooked it. Let her bring it in."

"And boy, she was struggling," as Dario recalled. "She had that thing, the pole, stuck under there with her arm around it . . ."

Marilyn couldn't hold on with her hands, so she'd

hugged the pole to her body with her left arm, while she tried to reel in with her right hand. She had the pole mashed up against her ample breasts, which were pretty well mashed up by some half-bra, anyway . . . to Dario, it looked like a near overload.

"Joe, you better help her out. She's gonna pop one of them things!"

Joe got such a boot out of that, he threw back his head and laughed.

But she did bring in that fish. She was a gamer. She finally fought it back to the boat, where Joe and Dario netted it in. It was a beautiful striped bass. But then, Marilyn dropped that pole, and wouldn't pick it up again. She wanted no part of it anymore.

Joe seemed to like just looking at her there. Not only on the boat. . . . They'd stay upstairs in the old Marina house. Sometimes she'd wake up, and Joe would be standing with his coffee, in the doorway, watching with a little smile. Until she figured she must look funny, and she'd jump up, to do something with herself. Or, afternoons, she'd be standing with his sister Marie, at the stove, watching how she made tomato gravy for the noodles, and talking idly—until something made her turn, and there was Joe again.

Marie lived downstairs (with her daughter, Betty) and took care of everything in the house. She was seven years older than Joe, and had grown up taking care of all the younger kids. She'd had a marriage that didn't last—and since then, she'd always worked. She hooked on with Western Union, and worked her way up to branch manager. After that, she got a real estate license, then an insurance broker's license, beautician's license. She worked at DiMaggio's Grotto, then a friend's restaurant, and then a hotel. . . . There was nothing Marie couldn't do—though she was just a tiny wisp of a woman. She said their dad, Giuseppe, used to tell her to put rocks in her pockets, so the first good wind wouldn't blow her away. Marilyn thought it must have been wonderful to have a father home all the time. Marie laughed and said, well, good and bad.

For Marilyn, the feeling of family around her was half the joy in San Francisco. It was like Marie's food: strange, spicy, delicious. In June 1953, when Joe's big brother Mike was found dead—floating between a dock and his fishing boat, in the water of Bodega Bay—Marilyn rushed north with Joe, and stayed with him upstairs in the old house on Beach Street. The house was filled with sadness—mourning cousins, crying aunts, and what seemed like hundreds of strange small men, talking in Sicilian downstairs. It went on for days, before and after the funeral—the men drinking wine, smoking little cheroots; the women in the kitchen nonstop (it seemed like another full meal every hour or two), the marathon of cooking interrupted only for new arrivals (another aunt, another cousin), which would set off another bout of weeping and hugs. They were even hugging her—and tut-tutting over her, how thin she was, and how pretty . . . and telling her about Joe (such a boy—did she know he bought this house for his mamma?) . . . and laughing when she blushed, as they said she and Joe ought to make some babies. It was the closest Marilyn had ever come to the comfort of a family of her own. When she got back to L.A., she told her confidant, Sidney Skolsky, that visit had opened her heart to Joe.

After that, San Francisco, the Marina house, became her refuge, too. Having Marie there was like having a big sister for the first time. (Marilyn did have a real half-sister, Berniece. But they'd grown up a continent apart, and had only seen each other once or twice.) . . . Now, the neighbors would see them setting off down Beach Street, Marilyn and Marie— the two *Signorine* DiMaggio—all dressed up to go shopping. In fact, it was Marilyn who looked the more old-worldly. She wouldn't put on makeup, and she'd swaddle her white-blond hair in a black scarf, and wear some high-necked black dress (one of those things Joe bought for her)—and giggle with the fun of it: she was *incognito!* . . . Of course, no one was fooled. Not with four-inch heels, and her famously alluring walk—she was instantly recognizable, especially from the rear. (As the columnist James Bacon wrote, "her derriere looked like two puppies fighting under a silk sheet.") . . .

In fact, every day in San Francisco felt like hiding out. And for the first time in years (years she'd worked so hard so everyone would know her) Marilyn embraced that. That year, 1953, she was truly (finally!) at the crest of a great wave. She and Jane Russell had been such a hit in *Gentlemen Prefer Blondes,* the studio put Marilyn right away into another girl-buddy comedy, *How to Marry a Millionaire.* (That one would be literally huge—in wide-screen CinemaScope—and equally popular.) Everything Marilyn had dreamed of and worked for was coming true. That was the year she and Jane Russell knelt in front of Grauman's Chinese Theater, to place for all time their handprints and footprints into the cement of Hollywood Boulevard. Marilyn's song, "Diamonds Are a Girl's Best Friend," was such a winsome success, she got her first recording contract with RCA. That year, she would make her first TV appearance—for twenty million viewers, nationwide, on *The Jack Benny Show.* No wonder there were moments when she felt it couldn't (she couldn't) go on—that the great wave might turn, and engulf her. After *Gentlemen,* Marilyn was getting twenty-five thousand fan letters a week.

MARILYN HAD BOXES STUFFED WITH letters from a year ago, and two years back. (Joe's advice? Throw 'em in the trash. But she could never do that.) She'd hired her old guardian, Grace Goddard, to file, or try to answer some—just the most important ones. Sometimes, Marilyn and Grace would work half the night, with Marilyn signing hundreds of photos (for big wheels—the studio would provide a list), and Grace stuffing envelopes, to send them off to the favored fans. Grace Goddard was hardly a professional business manager. But she knew who was who. She'd toiled around the studios forever (since the 1920s, when she'd worked in the film labs with Marilyn's mother, Gladys Baker—that was how she had come to know and care for little Norma Jeane). It was Grace who first told the wide-eyed girl that she would be a star, Grace who made the movies "more real than real life." So this was her dream come true, as well.

And who else did Marilyn have? Who else would be loyal to her? Natasha, by that time, was only feeding Marilyn's uncertainties about her own worth. On the set of *How to Marry a Millionaire,* Marilyn would finish a take, then instantly shield her eyes from the lights and squint through the darkness beyond for Natasha. Until she got the nod from her coach, Marilyn would demand retake after retake— for hours—till everybody else was limp and disgusted. "Well, I suppose that wasn't bad, dear," Miss Lytess would say, with disapproval soaking every word. "But I thought you could do better." It was like some pathetic hostage scene—with Marilyn powerless to break free. And this tired drama was replayed on every film: sooner or later, the director would banish Natasha from the set. Then Marilyn could not go on—she was unable even to leave her dressing room.

She'd send out word that she was ill, and production would stall . . . until Natasha was reinstated—always at a higher wage.

As the agent Charley Feldman summed up the problem of Marilyn and her coach, in a memo to his staff: "First of all Monroe cannot do a picture without her. I am convinced of this. . . . Incidentally, Lytess wants a helluva lot of dough."

Feldman tried earnestly throughout that year to act on Marilyn's behalf—though he had no contract with her, and no guarantee he would ever see a dime for himself or his company, Famous Artists. She'd dumped her old agent-firm, William Morris, but still, mysteriously (inexplicably, from Feldman's point of view), avoided signing the new agency contracts he had (gently) proffered three or four times. When Marilyn's mother had to go back into a hospital, Feldman loaned "the girl" money (that didn't do the trick); he stepped in to get Natasha reinstated (no help—save to Miss Lytess); he adjured his staff to "stay with this girl and see her as often as possible. Don't wait for her to call you, but call her and discuss her matters with her. . . . Too much attention cannot be given to this girl at this critical stage of her career, and she will need it."

What C. K. Feldman saw in "this girl" (this client—or not quite) was, to a man of his town, trade, and stature, irresistible. Here was a new fascination on screen (already, as he reminded his staff, "the most important personality on the lot") who had nobody to represent her interests. Here was an emerging megastar whose three films in release that year would bring almost thirty million dollars into the till at Fox—who was "being grossly underpaid, and up to now there has never been any indication from the studio that they want to adjust her contract." Here was, withal, a young actress who was painfully confused about her future (she didn't want to be the next Betty Grable—why, Feldman couldn't quite figure) . . . who would answer her own phone when he called at night, talking like she was underwater (she had to take pills to get any sleep, after she'd worked through her lines with Natasha) . . . who was in tears, exhausted, in ill health, when one of his agents came to see her on the set (she'd pushed herself to the breaking point for three months on *Gentlemen Prefer Blondes,* and Feldman had to send a man to the studio to get her four days off between pictures).

Like other men of his age and attainment, Feldman cast himself as Marilyn's protector. "We must concentrate our efforts in talking with this girl at all times and constantly seeing her," he wrote in a memorandum to the staff. ". . . We can be very forceful and direct with the studio in this situation. We can be the heavy. . . ." But as Feldman gradually learned, that role was taken.

Joe DiMaggio didn't like to go to the studio with Marilyn. All he could do was stand around all day, drinking coffee, while the crew pestered him for autographs. He liked even less accompanying Marilyn to some movie business party or banquet. That would be just another crowd of phonies. If he was in L.A., Joe preferred to hang around her two-room apartment on Doheny Drive (he'd moved her out of her hotels—photographers always lurking around) . . . stretched out on the couch, smoking, watching TV, and waiting for his girl. Nevertheless, he had particular and definite ideas about her business. In fact, with Joe they were certainties.

They were giving her lousy parts. They just wanted her on screen to wiggle her ass in front of the whole country. They dressed her like a slut, and gave her come-on lines to say, and made her act like she didn't know what she was saying. They worked her all the time, they didn't care about her. They were using her. She was making millions for them, and where was hers? She wanted respect—money was respect. She ought to marry him and quit the goddamn business. But if she didn't, she had to stop being a chump. . . .

Little by little, Joe's contempt for the business, steady as the drip of an old faucet, wore the shine off her pride in all her achievements. Over time, an acidulous drip like that can cut through rock—and Marilyn was no rock. By the summer of 1953, his certainties had become her anguished fears. As Marilyn's most recent biographer, Barbara Leaming, pointed out: one thing Joe and Marilyn shared was "a thick streak of suspiciousness."

If Charley Feldman wondered why Marilyn

wouldn't sign on as his client, he need only have asked what her Slugger advised. *(Why should that guy make a buck off your life?)* . . . Or if Feldman couldn't figure why she didn't want to be the next Betty Grable, it was because he'd never heard Joe on the topic. *(They used up Grable until she's too old. Now they want to put you into her spot in the lineup.)*

By the end of that summer, Feldman had figured out that the best way to get "the girl" to consider an idea was to tell it to "her lawyer," Loyd Wright. But Wright was, in point of fact, DiMaggio's lawyer. When Wright and Feldman cooked up a deal for Marilyn to buy the screen rights to a novel, have a script written from it, and then make the studio buy it at a huge profit, it was Feldman who'd have to put up the money (for the rights, and the writer). But the man who would select Marilyn's first screen property was that noted judge of literature, Joe DiMaggio. (Maybe he read the book, *Horns of the Devil*. More likely, he got Georgie to read it, or Jimmy Cannon.)

In August, Marilyn was on location in the Canadian Rockies for her third picture that year, *River of No Return*. When she ran afoul of her director—it was actually the Marilyn-Natasha drama that pushed Otto Preminger to ugly rage—Marilyn fell back on her oldest trick. (Oh, darn, she'd hurt her leg! It might be broken! She'd have to wear a cast. She couldn't work.) . . . This time, she also called Charley Feldman to intervene with the studio. But the first call she made was to Joe DiMaggio. She complained that the

picture was stupid and they were horrible to her—
they threw water on her all day and screamed at her,
and she was in tears. . . . So, the Yankee Clipper
showed up in Jasper, Alberta, with the lame explanation (for the waiting press) that he was just on a fishing and hunting trip, with his friend Mr. Solotaire.
(Georgie had never hunted anything wilder than a
corned beef on rye. But he didn't mind a little camping. For Georgie, anything outside New York—even
Pittsburgh—was camping.)

Now that Joe had the girl seeing things his way, he
moved in as full-time *consigliere*. He would stay as
long as it took in Jasper—and then move on, with
cast and crew, to Banff—to make sure Miss Monroe
wasn't bothered. (He also meant to make sure she
didn't get too chummy with her co-star, Robert
Mitchum.) . . . Joe would stay till location shooting
was finished. It was he who would fly with her back
to L.A. And when the studio shooting was done, by
the end of September, it was he who'd whisk her out
of town, to San Francisco. There would be no more
motion pictures for Miss Monroe that year. Joe
would see to that, too.

THE STUDIO BOSS, DARRYL ZANUCK,
wanted to put her, right away, into another musical.
The Girl in Pink Tights was the title this time. Everything else was an unformed mess. The working story
was particularly harebrained: Marilyn would be a

prim schoolteacher who needs money to launch her boyfriend's career, so (Gosh!)—she ends up singing torch songs as a cabaret artiste. Marilyn spotted it right away as "another Betty Grable part." (It was, in fact, a remake of a Grable pic from 1934.) Marilyn didn't think it was good for her. But Joe was adamant about it: they were just going to put her out there half-naked, and make her look stupid again. If she would only marry him, she could tell 'em to shove pink tights up their ass.

He was as certain that they must marry as he was about everything else. . . . In San Francisco, there was no counterbalance to Joe's will—except her own hunger for respect. Joe told her, you talk about respect—how about the money? Sinatra's the boyfriend in that picture. Sinat's getting five grand a week. And they're paying you a quarter of that—twelve-fifty. Fuck 'em and feed 'em fish! . . . In Los Angeles, Famous Artists sent word to Twentieth Century Fox that Miss Monroe would have to see a script before she could consent to do the picture. And that sent the boss, Darryl Zanuck, marching around his office, swinging his polo mallet in fury. Why show her a script? He had picked the scripts that made her a star! She couldn't refuse an assignment. They had a contract! . . .

But Joe had Loyd Wright working with Feldman to rewrite Marilyn's contract entirely. Now she was the biggest star at the studio—they needed her—it was time to cash in. Marilyn wanted control of her scripts, directors, cinematographers. (And, of course, she wanted her coach.) But DiMaggio wanted money for the girl—big-league dough. And fewer pictures: they worked her like a slave. Joe was in this deal up to his elbows, had to know everything—and no mistakes! It had to be just right. He wanted her new contract done in February. That's because the book he'd picked out for her, *Horns of the Devil,* was bought in August. She had to hold the rights on that book for six months, before the studio bought it from her—so the money would be a capital gain (a lower tax rate)— that was important. (To Joe, taxes were like publicity: a little bit was unavoidable, maybe even a good sign, but anyone who walked around looking for more was a busher.) . . . And, in the meantime, there would be no *Pink Tights*—no pictures at all! . . . Why should the studio negotiate, if they had a backlog of her movies to release?

Marilyn agreed with everything he said—while he said it. But it scared her, too. No pictures? . . . It wasn't that long ago when she didn't have anything, and "no pictures in the works" was the story of her life. In November, Marilyn had to go to L.A. for the premiere of *Millionaire*—and some retakes in the studio for *River of No Return.* And the longer she was there, the more she wavered. Maybe she could do *Pink Tights* (if the studio would get Gene Kelly for her co-star) . . . or they could put her into another picture. She'd love to play the harlot, Nefer, in that big costume project, *The Egyptian.* (That sent

Zanuck into another rage: he was saving that part for his mistress, Bella Darvi.)

Feldman was no help. He was stuck in Switzerland, where his ex-wife was undergoing an operation. From there he sent memos to his staff—with orders to read them to "the girl." But he had nothing to say. He couldn't get her that *Egyptian* part, even if he camped at Zanuck's door twenty-four hours a day. As for *Pink Tights,* she could do the film, or not—either way was fine with Charley.

And Natasha was horrid. First, she tried to convince Marilyn that she had to do *Pink Tights.* Otherwise the studio would put her on suspension . . . and what would happen to Natasha's job? Then she demanded five thousand dollars—right away, or she'd walk! Marilyn had to sell the mink stole that Johnny Hyde had given her. (Even so, she could only raise a thousand—Natasha was still pressuring her.)

Strange to say, it was the holidays that rescued Marilyn from the griddle. She had to fly to San Francisco, for Thanksgiving—a real family Thanksgiving, this time. Marie was cooking for a houseful of DiMaggios . . . and three days later, when Marilyn flew south again, she had one with her. She brought back to L.A. her own cleanup hitter. And that would make all the difference.

When the studio ordered Marilyn to report for reheasals on *The Girl in Pink Tights,* Joe told Marilyn to ignore the call.

Two days later, Zanuck himself was on the phone

to Famous Artists—and in a famous rage. Monroe's contract had no script approval! What the hell did she mean by this? He'd made her a star! He threatened "drastic measures." Joe told Marilyn to let him stew.

The next day, Zanuck tried another tack: he ordered Marilyn in to redub a song for *River of No Return*. That was a serious matter—a film she had agreed to do, that had to be completed. But Joe said it was only a trick. And Marilyn stayed home.

Then, Natasha was on the phone to the agents, demanding that Marilyn report to work immediately. (Why yes, she'd had a visit from Mr. Zanuck, but that wasn't the point. The point was Marilyn's selfishness!) . . . The staff at Famous Artists dialed faster than Natasha, and got Marilyn on the phone. By the time Natasha got her call through to the apartment on Doheny Drive, it was DiMaggio who picked up, to inform the coach that Miss Monroe was unavailable.

Then, Zanuck dispatched a man from the publicity department, Roy Craft, to visit Miss Monroe at home. Marilyn always loved publicity. She would let Craft in—Zanuck was sure. But Marilyn didn't answer the door. DiMaggio answered it—in fact, he filled the door—and told Craft he could get the fuck away from it, too!

The standoff continued through most of December. By the time it was over, there were legal documents ordering Miss Monroe back to work; there was a nighttime escape (by Cadillac) up the coast to San Francisco; there were code names ("Mr. Robin calling") to alert Marie to put the agents through; there were retakes (whole new scenes!) for *River of No Return,* ordered by Zanuck, so Marilyn would have to come back to the studio. There were secret calls from pay phones, nighttime meetings with the agents on the street in front of the Knickerbocker Hotel, ferocious cables back and forth from Switzerland . . . and through it all, profuse threats from Zanuck. He was going to take this story to the press! Louella! Hedda! And all the rest. They would ruin the girl! "They will assassinate her! Even if I have to destroy an asset, they have got to do it!" Zanuck roared. (Of course, the asset was Marilyn.) ". . . This will be the Goddamnedest story I have broken in this Goddamn town! It will be all over the Whole Damn INDUSTRY!"

But all his splenetic bluster could not fetch Marilyn back to the fold. She was (and always had been) her own asset. When she was with Joe, she never doubted that—he wouldn't let her. By the end of December 1953, she made her escape, flying north *(incognito)* as Miss Norma Dougherty, to the safety of the house on Beach Street, San Francisco.

And it was wonderful, hiding out there, the way the family took care of her. Some brother or sister was always coming by, for coffee, or just to say hello. (And bringing kids!) . . . Marie turned away all the calls from reporters. Joe would go out for anything they needed. (Or anything Marilyn even talked about wanting.) . . . For Christmas—the best Christmas ever—there was a big tree, for her and Marie to decorate. And under it, on Christmas morning, Marilyn found her gift from Joe—a mink! And not a stole, like the horrid Natasha had made her sell— but a lustrous, enveloping black mink coat, from Maximilian—it must have cost ten thousand dollars. Just to put it on was an embrace. Marilyn modeled it all around the house, and said she would wear it forever.

But all the excitement (and all the DiMaggios) couldn't protect her forever. Right after Christmas, the agents called and said production was scheduled on *Pink Tights*. This wasn't a rehearsal call. On Monday, January 4, they'd be on the set, *shooting*. (Zanuck was pulling the trigger.) . . . And Marilyn was ordered to appear.

Joe said, what could they do without her? It's another trick. They'll back down. And Marilyn stayed in San Francisco.

Monday, the phone on Beach Street was ringing off the hook. All reporters . . . and Marie relayed their news—an announcement, from Twentieth Century Fox: Marilyn Monroe had breached her contract. Miss Monroe, her pay and privileges, and all her movie projects, were suspended.

She was all right that day, with the calls bringing news, and the radio announcing her name—and she had to think about the statement Loyd Wright would release to the press. (She wanted it known that she was not fighting over money—she just wanted to see

the script, to make sure it would be a good picture.)
. . . But in days to come, the house grew quiet. And
she was quiet, fearful.

She saw the terrible things they wrote in the San
Francisco papers. Louella Parsons was in there, with
a line about Frank Sinatra flying all the way from
Rome, to be on time. But not *La Monroe*—she
couldn't be bothered! . . . Marilyn knew the studio
fed that to Louella. They *were* trying to assassinate
her.

And she knew how they worked. They could make
her nothing! . . . What if they wouldn't make a new
contract? They could keep her out of work forever.
Or for four more years—she'd be old, *thirty-one!*—
everything could be over by then, for Her. Everything
she'd worked for could be gone, ruined. Maybe she
had ruined it already. Who was going to take care of
Her?

There was no one. She hadn't felt it coming—the
aloneness—it just happened: people left her, all at
the same time.

In September, poor Grace had found out she had
cancer of the uterus, and she'd swallowed a bottle of
sleeping pills. Grace was the first one who ever believed in Marilyn—now, she was gone.

And Natasha had shown she was a betrayer. (Had
she ever really believed in Marilyn, like she said?)
. . . Who did believe?

Now, there were only men, fighting about "the
girl." Charley Feldman had finally come back to

America. But only to New York. He called in and said he'd talked to the studio president, the money man, Spyros Skouras. But Skouras could do nothing about "the Coast." That was Zanuck—and he was vicious—he was trying to kill off Marilyn Monroe. There was Loyd Wright, but he mostly listened to Joe. And Joe—he didn't want her to be . . . Her. He never did. *He couldn't.*

He did love her. But he only wanted to marry her, bury her. That's why she never would—though he asked all the time. And she knew he was hurt when she said no. But how could she say yes? He didn't care about her acting, or the movies, or anything she'd done. He didn't care now, when everything was ruined . . .

He didn't understand.

But he did understand. And he told her about a time—it was fifteen years ago, in that same house— when he thought that everything he wanted, everything he had, all he had worked for, could be gone. They would take it away. Because he said he wouldn't go to play ball, unless they gave him what he deserved. And all of a sudden, all the things people said and wrote about him, all the big things he'd done— that all felt like it must have happened for somebody else. Because he was here, all by himself, and not so big, and scared.

She asked him, what happened? And he laughed and said he lost. . . . But he didn't lose for long. He came back bigger than ever. And they did pay him—

more than he ever dreamed he could have. And in the end, when he walked away they were begging him to stay and take more. He got what he wanted. And so would she.

And he asked her again, to marry him.

And she said yes.

IN THE LONG YEARS AFTERWARD, IT was fashionable (even among Joe's pals) to maintain they were always ill-suited. Marilyn and Joe—how could that ever work? . . . She knew nothing about his game; he had only contempt for hers. What could they ever have in common? . . . How could that old-world Italian—so conservative, shy, and inward—get along with a wife who didn't wear underpants?

But they missed the point.

Joe and Marilyn had one big thing in common. In fact, they may have been the only two people in the country, at that moment, who could understand each other. Because both were living inside the vast personages that the hero machine had created for them. And inside those personages—those enormous idols for the nation—these two, Marilyn and Joe, were only small and struggling, fearful to be seen. And alone—always. They were like kids, left in a giant house, and they must not be discovered. Or it would all come crashing down. In their loneliness, they might have been brother and sister.

Joe's insistence made them husband and wife.

LOOKING BACK, SHE REMEMBERED
it as mostly about her career—and what the public thought of the Giant Goddess she was supposed
to be:

"Joe and I had been talking about getting married
for some months," she told Ben Hecht. "We knew it
wouldn't be an easy marriage. On the other hand, we
couldn't keep on going forever as a pair of cross-
country lovers. It might begin to hurt both of our careers.

"The public doesn't mind people living together
without being married, providing they don't overdo
it. . . .

"One day Joe said to me:

" 'You're having all this trouble with the studio
and not working so why don't we get married now?
I've got to go to Japan anyway on some baseball
business, and we could make a honeymoon out of the
trip.'

"That's the way Joe is, always cool and practical . . .

"And so we were married and took off for Japan on
our honeymoon.

"That was something I had never planned on or
dreamed about—becoming the wife of a great man.
Any more than Joe had ever thought of marrying a
woman who seemed eighty percent publicity.

"The truth is that we were very much alike. My

publicity, like Joe's greatness, is something on the outside. It has nothing to do with what we actually are."

WHEN JOE GOT THE GREEN LIGHT, he turned it on like he would rounding first base— speed, smooth power, and no wasted motion. Reno Barsocchini got a judge who was a pal, Lefty O'Doul got another seat on the plane to Japan, Joe got three white orchids. Day and a half after she said yes, they were at City Hall. It was January 14, 1954.

Of course, there were about a hundred reporters and photographers, too. Someone tipped 'em. But Joe didn't mind. He kept them frozen in Judge Charlie Peery's outer office. Meantime, Joe and his girl signed the registry, and went inside. Joe entered his age, thirty-nine. But twenty-seven sounded old to Marilyn: she signed in at age twenty-five.

The wedding party was Joe's big brother Tom, Mr. and Mrs. Reno Barsocchini, and Mr. and Mrs. Lefty O'Doul. They were the only guests, too. The reporters were frustrated by the frosted glass in the judge's door. But one of them, Jerry Flamm, from the *Call,* was six feet four, so they hoisted him up, to peer through the clear-glass transom.

"Do you, Norma Jeane Mortenson Dougherty . . ."
Flamm was barking out a running play-by-play.
"Promise to love, honor, and cherish . . ."
(No obey!) . . .

Flamm kept it up, until Joe said, "I do." But when he saw the man from the *Daily News* sprinting for a phone, Flamm started hollering to get down, too.

It didn't matter—it was over in three minutes. Joe and Marilyn came out, and there were two hundred newsmen of every stripe, and court clerks, bailiffs, jury members, witnesses—five hundred people pushing in the corridor.

KISS 'ER, JOE!

They kissed for the camera.

DO IT AGAIN!

They kissed again. Marilyn made such a darling bride, in a brown suit with a little white Peter Pan collar (right up under her chin).

Y'WANT KIDS?

"I'd like to have six," Marilyn said.

"One." That was from DiMaggio.

WHERE YOU GONNA LIVE?

"Here, San Francisco," DiMaggio said.

"I'm going to continue my career," said Marilyn. Then she saw the look from Joe. "But I'm looking forward to being a housewife, too!"

As the *Examiner* reported: "Joe gave his blonde bride a playful pat, and almost growled, 'Let's go.' " He had to push through the crowd into the hallway— took a wrong turn and ended up in a dead end at the assessor's office, and had to turn back—running now, colliding with photographers, Marilyn behind him, trying to keep up—and giggling . . . as the elevator doors closed.

Joe didn't even have a smile. This was supposed to be a strictly private affair!

Marilyn knew better. An hour before she went to City Hall, she'd called the studio—the publicity department—and told the boss there, Harry Brand: "Harry, I promised I'd tell you first, if I ever got married. I'm being married to Joe this afternoon."

Marilyn understood publicity and its power. Within hours, Twentieth Century Fox had issued a statement, to wish the newlyweds well . . . and to announce that the suspension of Marilyn Monroe was now revoked.

By that time, Joe's blue Cadillac was parked outside the Clifton Motel, in Paso Robles—a little coastal town three hours south of San Francisco. Joe had rented a room for six and a half dollars. He said he wanted a double bed. And he wanted a TV.

"At home" with the troops in Korea, 1954.

Enough said. The *Daily News*,
October 5, 1954.

A very important scene, with her
attorney, Jerry Giesler.

CHAPTER 15

✦

AT THE TOKYO AIRPORT, JOE DIMAG-
gio and Marilyn Monroe could not leave the plane
on which they had arrived. In the early winter darkness, five thousand Japanese fans—mostly young-
sters—blew past the Japanese cops, stormed onto
the tarmac, and besieged the Pan American Strato-
clipper. U.S. Air Force MPs were called in to rein-
force the police lines, but Mr. and Mrs. America
were still pinned in the plane for forty-five minutes—and thereafter could only debark through the
rear baggage hatch.

(In point of fact, Joe probably could have walked
down the main stairs, and emerged with nothing
worse than an earache from the *Banzai* cheers. But
Marilyn was scared by that crowd—and with reason:
"If she had tried to go through that mob," a Japanese
police official told the International News Service,
"they would probably have torn all her clothes off.")

The plans called for a cavalcade in open cars,
down the Ginza, and on to the Imperial Hotel. But
Joe had been down that road—and after sixteen
hours in a plane (and that airport scene), he didn't
want any part of it. So he ordered the driver to take

another route, and stiff the hundreds of thousands of fans who'd lined the curbs, and waited hours in the February cold. Joe only wanted to get to the hotel—where, he was sure, they'd be safe. In the forty years since Frank Lloyd Wright designed that magnificent stone pile (and personally supervised its construction), the Imperial Hotel had withstood (without one broken teacup) an earthquake that leveled much of old Tokyo, and American bombing during World War II. But it would not survive unscathed the arrival of Marilyn Monroe. Two hundred Tokyo policemen guarded the hotel doors. But thousands of fans from the parade route had been denied their glimpse of the Honorable Buttocks-Swinging Madam (as Marilyn was known in the Japanese press) . . . and they could not be held back. They trampled through the koi ponds, broke the hotel's revolving doors, and—when those were jammed—crashed through the plate glass windows on either side. They were in no mood to be shooed away. They ringed the hotel, shouting her name into the icy night—until Marilyn (a bit snappish herself, by that time) was forced to make appearance on a balcony ("like I was a dictator or something," as she said) to wave, and blow kisses—by which gestures the crowd was calmed.

By that time she had to get ready for the press conference. More than a hundred Japanese and American reporters and cameramen were already jammed into a room at the hotel, waiting for her. In fact, they would wait two hours until the honored guest, in a clingy red wool dress, essayed her famous walk to the table and microphones.

"How long have you been walking like that?" one of the Japanese reporters called out.

"I started when I was six months old, and haven't stopped yet," she replied.

"Do you sleep naked?"

"No comment."

"We are told you do not wear anything under your dress," said another Japanese newsman. "Is that true?"

Marilyn grimaced slightly. This was supposed to be a press conference for her and Joe. But all the questions were for her—and questions likely to provoke an explosion, later that night, in the suite of Mr. and Mrs. DiMaggio. In the meantime, Marilyn was assisted at the front table by Lefty O'Doul. Joe was lurking unnoticed, outside the ring of newsreel spotlights, in a corner of the room . . . as Marilyn favored the reporter with a smile, and lightly sidestepped. "I'm planning to buy a kimono tomorrow."

The big question from American reporters was whether she would visit the troops in Korea. War against "the Reds" had ended (at least the shooting had stopped) a few months before. But there were still a million American men, stuck (and as they feared, half-forgotten) in miserably makeshift front-line camps. There was no one they'd rather see than Marilyn Monroe. And the brass had promised, she would be invited. Marilyn had no snappy answer on that; in fact, she seemed torn and tentative: "I'd love to go to Korea, and have been waiting to go for a long time—but I don't know if we'll have time on this trip." That was the only topic on which DiMaggio was quoted—and the wire services promptly shoved him into a face-off with the brave boys who fought for Uncle Sam:

" *'How can we go to Korea?' DiMaggio asked newsmen. 'Marilyn doesn't have an act.'*

"The response across the Sea of Japan from the troops in Korea was prompt:

" *'What does he mean WE? It's Marilyn we want. She doesn't need an act.' "*

Lefty O'Doul would say, years later, that trip marked the first time Joe realized what a big star his wife had become—she put DiMaggio in the shade, and that's when he turned surly. But Joe was well aware of Marilyn's fame. He just didn't like what she was famous for. What he learned on that honeymoon trip was how little influence he would have on the content of her stardom—and how inessential to it he was.

His mood did not improve the next day, when a U.S. Army officer came to visit at the suite, to press upon Miss Monroe an invitation to Korea, from General John E. Hull, commander of U.S. forces in the Far East. Actually, what made Joe sour was Marilyn's excitement. Joe was going off to coach baseball at the training camps for Japan's Central League. And Marilyn had it all figured: she could go to Korea then—wouldn't that be perfect?

"Go if you want to," DiMaggio said. "It's your honeymoon."

So it was. And within days, she got her shots and papers (an ID card that missed the point, entirely: "Mrs. Norma Jeane DiMaggio," it read) . . . and she was on her way to Korea, with a piano player and Mrs. Jean O'Doul.

By that time, her excitement was almost wild. From Seoul, she was choppered to her first appearance—a remote and primitive mountainside tent camp, habited by the men of the First Marine Division. As her helicopter swooped in, banking over the steep ground, Marilyn was thrilled by what she saw. Thousands of men had come out to see her. They were standing on an open slope, all looking up, waving and cheering. She shouted to the pilot to circle low, so she could wave to the boys. Two soldiers in the belly of the chopper slid the main door open. And she shouted to them to hold her feet, as she slid out the door on her belly, to hang in midair over the gimballing ground, waving and blowing kisses while the men below screamed their delight. Four times she circled that mountainside, till the Marines were in a fever for her—a fever that matched her own.

On the ground, she changed (in ten minutes!) from her flight jacket and combat boots into a plum-purple

cocktail dress and stiletto heels. She parted the
burlap curtains and fairly sauntered to the front of a
plywood stage, to caress the waiting microphone,
and breathe in her baby voice a greeting to the boys
who were whistling and cheering. Marilyn was unac-
customed to live performance. On a movie set, the
idea of facing the cameras could immobilize her with
panic, and she'd break out in hives. But she loved her
power to provoke want in men—and this was the
tops—she was without fear. To the accompaniment
of an upright piano, she sang "Diamonds Are a Girl's
Best Friend"—and the boys went crazy. The Marines
were dressed in hooded parkas and boots. Marilyn's
silk dress was held up by thin spaghetti straps. Her
shoulders and arms were bare. That didn't matter. To
the consternation of the general in command (who
feared a riot), she followed up with a Gershwin
tune—"Do It Again."

Oooohhh, do it again.
I may say, no, no, no, no—
But do it again.

Oooohh, no one is near.
I may cry, oh, oh, ohhhh—
But no one will hear.

As she recalled for Ben Hecht in her memoir:
"They were all yelling at me at the top of their
lungs. I stood smiling at them. It had started snowing,

but I felt as warm as if I was standing in a bright sun. Even the snowflakes falling on my bare arms felt warm.

"I've always been frightened by an audience—any audience. . . . My stomach pounds, my head gets dizzy and I'm sure my voice has left me.

"But standing in the snowfall facing these seventeen thousand yelling soldiers, I felt for the first time in my life no fear of anything. I felt only happy. . . . I felt at home."

For four days, the Marilyn Monroe show traveled by helicopter, airplane, and Jeep. She didn't see any of Korea—from one landing field to another, as she remembered—but at ten camps, she did see (by Army estimate) a hundred thousand American men . . . and she loved them all. She could never forget; it was the boys in uniform—thousands of letters from Korea to the studio—who convinced Twentieth Century Fox to give her a chance, her first good parts. Now she could return the favor.

One party at an officers club turned into such a bacchanal that Marilyn tried to cut a cake with a bayonet—and put a pretty good cut in her wrist instead. Then, of course, a surgeon was called—and for Miss Monroe, it was a surgeon general—who treated the gash, and then gave orders that the drunken party never had occurred. The newspaper *Stars & Stripes* was ordered to spike the story. Those in attendance had to surrender all photographic film—which was duly burned.

Another night, another officers club: the Signal Corps had hooked up a call to Japan—so Marilyn could talk to her husband—and both ends of the call would be broadcast over loudspeakers. "Do you still love me, Joe?" Marilyn's voice cooed over the camp. "Do you miss me?" And then the voice of DiMaggio—rather curt, it was thought. "I do. Yeah." Joe did not appreciate being a prop in her show.

But Marilyn was in her glory. She would call it the greatest experience of her life. ("This is what I've always wanted, I guess.") . . . And as she told one crowd of frenzied men: "I'll never forget my honeymoon—with the 45th Division."

By the time she got back to Joe and Japan, her fever was real. Doctors would call it pneumonia. But Marilyn was still exuberant. She had to tell Joe how wonderful it was. They loved everything she did! They loved her! Thousands of men, screaming her name. . . . "Joe, you never heard such cheering."

"Yes I have," he said.

For the rest of that trip, there were rumors of roaring fights in their Imperial Hotel suite. Marilyn very seldom emerged. The story in the papers was about the pneumonia—Marilyn had been ordered to rest. Still, more than one observer wanted to know what happened to Miss Monroe's hand—which was bandaged and held by a splint. Maybe it was that bayonet gash. Marilyn never talked about it.

She and Joe flew back to America, where she'd spend four days in Marie's care on Beach Street—

and thereafter, when they flew to L.A., Marilyn looked to be in radiant good health. Mr. and Mrs. DiMaggio checked into the Beverly Hills Hotel— and right away, Marilyn phoned her friend Sidney Skolsky, to come visit. She wanted to tell Sidney about the honeymoon—and what a dear Joe had been. "Wonderful and considerate," was how Skolsky quoted her. "I've never been so happy." Then, she went on at considerable length about how she sang to the boys in Korea.

As Skolsky wrote in his memoir, *Don't Get Me Wrong, I Love Hollywood:*

"After a while Joe excused himself and went downstairs to have a drink with one of his baseball cronies in the Polo Lounge. As soon as Marilyn and I were alone, she dropped a bombshell.

" 'Sidney?'

" 'Yes.'

" 'Do you know who I'm going to marry?'

" 'Marry? What're you talking about?'

" 'I'm going to marry Arthur Miller,' Marilyn said.

"I looked at her as though she were crazy.

" 'Arthur Miller! You just got home from a honeymoon. You told me how wonderful Joe was, how happy he made you, and what a great time you had! Now you tell me you're going to marry Arthur Miller. I don't understand.'

" 'You wait,' Marilyn said. 'You'll see.' "

DESPITE JOE'S BRAVE ASSERTIONS about San Francisco being "headquarters," he was a Hollywood householder within a month of the honeymoon. He and Marilyn rented a "Tudor cottage" on North Palm Drive, Beverly Hills—eight rooms, one reserved for Joe Jr., and a couple of extra bedrooms in case "little baseball players" happened to come along. Mrs. D. told Sidney Skolsky how she positioned Joe's favorite chair in front of the TV in the living room. Skolsky also got the exclusive on how she liked to iron Joe's shirts. (But just in case she didn't have time, there would be a house staff of three.) The truth was, for both her and Joe, there was little time for anything except her career.

Charley Feldman had opened negotiations with the studio—he said the news was good. Zanuck would drop *Pink Tights*. He wanted Marilyn to sing and dance in the Irving Berlin musical *There's No Business Like Show Business*. And after that, there was an even more tantalizing prospect: Feldman himself was going to produce a movie version of *The Seven Year Itch*—with the great Billy Wilder directing—and he wanted Marilyn to star as "The Girl Upstairs." In the meantime, Twentieth Century Fox would grant Marilyn her new contract—with a limit of two pictures a year. Fox would buy *Horns of the Devil* (whether or not Miss Monroe did the film) for $225,000. And they were close to capitulation on the "target price" for any new picture. It was a measure of DiMaggio's influence (Feldman wouldn't even report to "the girl" unless Joe was in town and could come along) that the "target price" was a hundred grand.

There was one problem: Fox wouldn't budge on creative control. Zanuck had approval on all Fox pictures—including scripts, directors, cinematographers—and that wasn't going to change. Marilyn would have to compromise, too. And so she did. She told Feldman she would only demand approval on her drama coach (she still wanted Natasha) and her choreographer. They were largely symbolic demands—to recognize her control of her own performance—even Zanuck would have to see that. And as a gesture of her goodwill, Marilyn signed as a client with Famous Artists, so when a new contract came into force, Feldman would finally make some money, too.

Marilyn was back in business, and her business was being a great star. At a press conference to celebrate her return to the studio, Marilyn said her representatives were still "working out details," but she expected to sign her new contract soon. To a question about married life, she said: "Ballplayers make good husbands. Joe and I want a lot of little DiMaggios." As the *L.A. Times* reported, that made the studio executives wince—but the reporters stood to applaud her. Then Marilyn swept off to Dressing Room M— the best and biggest on the lot, on the ground floor of the Star Building. As Barbara Leaming reported, in *Marilyn Monroe,* it was actually a suite, with a parlor in front—table lamps, and crimson upholstery on chairs fit for Queen Anne herself—and inside, a grand dressing space with full-length wall mirrors, and "a spacious dressing table . . . adorned with a small framed photograph of Joe . . . and littered with countless tiny prescription bottles from Schwab's." It was bigger than some apartments she'd rented, only a couple of years before. But it was like them in one regard: someone had been there before. Marilyn had inherited Dressing Room M—from *(she shoulda known)* Betty Grable.

Show Business was scheduled to start filming at the end of May. But Marilyn's second honeymoon at Fox would not last that long. On May 5, Feldman sent to Palm Drive the studio draft of her new contract. All the money was there, the limits on pictures . . . but Marilyn ripped through the document, looking for her guarantees on creative control. There was not a word. They were not going to give her *anything*—no Natasha, no choreographer—not even a nod of respect. They were treating her like the dumb blonde she played in the pictures they picked for her. To Marilyn, it was an affront, an attack—not just on her present and future, but on everything she'd already done. They were desperate to prove that they were the ones who'd made her a star. Well, she would show them—they were mistaken.

And then, Feldman also made a mistake: he recommended she sign it. His point was simple—and in a way, correct. In practice, she would have the control she sought. If the studio wouldn't give in on coach or choreographer, she could go back to her old tricks, simply fail to appear. Meanwhile, he said, he'd stay on it—maybe in the future, they could win an (oral) understanding, that in case of dispute Miss Monroe would have her way. Feldman didn't realize, at that moment, that he and Marilyn didn't have any future.

But the worst mistake was Joe's: he also said she ought to sign up. But he hadn't Feldman's gift of patter. Joe simply said the money was right. And for the rest, what the hell was the difference? For Marilyn that was confirmation of everything she'd feared. Joe had no respect for who she was. When he said he would help her get what she wanted, the only thing he meant was the money he wanted. At that point, she also knew, there was no future for her with Joe.

What he knew was, suddenly, she was spending all her time at the studio—with her handsome, dark-eyed voice coach, Hal Schaefer. She said she had a lot of work, to prepare her numbers for *Show Business*. But shooting hadn't even begun, and Marilyn was never home.

When the filming started, that was even worse. Wardobe assistants coming to the house, and hairdressers, publicity men . . . and Joe's pet peeve, Natasha Lytess, who'd sit all night in the house on Palm Drive, ordering Marilyn around—like *she* was the husband. And going over those stupid lines— over and over—it drove Joe crazy. He couldn't even hear the ballgame on TV. What kind of a home was that? Marilyn had told Joe she'd never trust Natasha again. But the minute she started another picture—*bang*—Natasha was back, and lording it around his house.

Even after Natasha left, late at night, Joe would be seething. Let Marilyn say one thing wrong, and he'd go off like a Roman candle. Sometimes, he'd get up and storm out, go into town, just get the hell away. If he didn't, he'd start yelling—and Marilyn would run upstairs to cry and hide. She was scared of Joe when he got like that. She'd lock herself in a bedroom . . . and phone Natasha. As the coach would recall, in an unpublished interview (later quoted by one of Marilyn's biographers, Dr. Donald Spoto), Marilyn might call two or three times a night when she felt in peril. She would call ". . . at two or three in the morning that spring, when DiMaggio was being so filthy to her, when he beat her. She couldn't stand being treated that way. I talked to her for hours, until my hand was clammy on the telephone."

And after that, Marilyn would gulp down pills to get some sleep before her early call. *Show Business* was the first film on which colleagues reported that Marilyn was "dazed," unable to remember lines, or speak them clearly. Sometimes, in the mornings, Natasha, Hal Schaefer, or her makeup man, Whitey Snyder, would have to march her around her dressing room—walking her, like an overheated horse—for an hour, or two, until her head cleared. Even then, it was anybody's guess whether she could make a scene work on film. The delays made everybody else half-crazy—and Marilyn was so apologetic, she pressed harder. By late June, she had collapsed on the set.

The studio publicity mill covered with the tired tale of Far East Pneumonia (Miss Monroe, the press releases now claimed, had never quite recovered) . . . but the sickness that beset Marilyn had less to do with her lungs than her heart. She felt trapped in her marriage, at that studio, and in that stupid movie. (No, she wouldn't sign her contract—not even if she had to sit idle for four years.)

She found solace in the coaching and company of Hal Schaefer—who was gentle with her, and thought she was wonderful. (Now he was helping not only with her movie songs but also songs she was recording for RCA.) . . . In the course of that summer, by Schaefer's account, she sought solace in his bed, too. DiMaggio's jealousy was so apparent it made the papers—as did Schaefer's awkward protest (which was, alas, not much of a denial): "It's ridiculous," said Schaefer, "that Mr. DiMaggio could be any more jealous of me than he is of other people working with Marilyn." That only fueled Joe's other suspicions.

He seemed to resent anybody she was with. Even with girlfriends, Marilyn conspired to meet them away from home, or get them in and out of the house while Joe was away, so he wouldn't get mad. Sometimes, it seemed to her, weeks would pass and she wouldn't see anyone. But Joe would still be mad about something, and he wouldn't talk to her either.

One time, she invited an old friend, Brad Dexter, to come to the house for dinner—maybe she and Joe could have a friend together. She'd met Dexter years before, on her first good movie, *The Asphalt Jungle*. He was a man's man—a poker player, a racetrack fan, a friend of Sinatra's—she thought Joe and Brad might get along. But as Dexter remembered, he was in the house with Marilyn when Joe walked in, and it was obvious DiMaggio only wanted to know what the hell Brad was doing with his wife. As Dexter said, the whole house went creepy with DiMaggio's suspicion. "So I pretended to have another appointment, and I didn't stay to dinner."

Marilyn kept herself going with the thought that soon she would fly to New York, for location shooting on her next picture, *The Seven Year Itch*. Strange to say, it was New York (Joe's town) that came to stand in her mind for freedom—escape. She was working, secretly, on a plan to get away to New York for good, and leave all her troubles behind: this picture, this studio, and Hollywood itself—with the house on Palm Drive, and the prison of her marriage. New York was where her new friend, Milton Greene, a still photographer, wanted to help her set up her own company—Marilyn Monroe Productions. (That was the only way she'd have real control.) . . . New York was where Lee Strasberg coached the nation's great actors, at the legendary Actors Studio. (His wife, Paula, had stopped by the set of *Show Business*—and told Marilyn that she'd be welcome to come and study anytime.) . . . And New York (this was the most secret part) was also home to a man Marilyn had met more than four years before, but had never forgotten—America's most celebrated playwright, Arthur Miller.

She couldn't let anybody know what she was dreaming up. (Skolsky was the one exception—he wanted to produce *The Life of Jean Harlow* as the first film for Marilyn Monroe Productions.) . . . On the set at Twentieth Century Fox, Marilyn had to act like the only thing she cared about was finishing her picture. (So she could get on to the next one, *The Seven Year Itch.*) . . . With Feldman, she couldn't have been friendlier—they never talked anymore about her contract. (She sent him on a fool's errand to get her loaned out to Samuel Goldwyn, to star with Marlon Brando in the film version of *Guys and Dolls.*) . . . And with Joe, if she talked about the future at all, it was just looking forward to the next vacation. (It was always "when this picture's done" or "after the next picture.")

But it may be that she told the truth to Hal Schaefer. (If she escaped to New York, she would leave him behind, too.) Or Schaefer may have sensed her slipping away. Or maybe it was true (as it was later reported) that Schaefer was being followed, and threatened in anonymous telephone calls . . . anyway, something made him desperate. On July 27, Hal Schaefer was found unconscious on the floor of his bungalow at Fox, with his stomach full of sleeping pills and Benzedrine (all washed down with a draught of typewriter cleaning fluid). He would barely survive—he would never regain his health entirely—and while he lingered in the hospital, his most frequent visitor was Marilyn Monroe. She didn't make any secret of that. Joe's impotent jealousy was discussed around Hollywood—and richly enjoyed.

That was another strange twist: just as Marilyn was plotting to leave Hollywood in her dust, the luminaries and powers of the town had decided that she was one of their own—a sweet girl and a great star . . . and the only thing wrong with her was her husband. Joe's contempt for the movie folk was well known; and now it was matched by theirs for him. By August, several industry columnists had mentioned Marilyn's hospital visits to Hal Schaefer—and some pointed out that Joe DiMaggio had never even paid one visit to his wife on the set during the entire production of *There's No Business Like Show Business*.

So, just before the film was wrapped up, on August 27, Joe paid a visit to the soundstage. He said Marilyn wanted him to come and watch. (And of course, Georgie Solotaire had to come with him.) That was the day for shooting Marilyn's big production number, "Heat Wave"—and if she had asked Joe to watch, that was an uncharacteristic miscalculation. Over and over, Marilyn writhed through the number, in her plumed headdress and a costume that was so elaborately skimpy that even her fans would be embarrassed for her when the film came out. DiMaggio wouldn't have to wait. He was embarrassed right away—standing in the shadows, sweating in his perfect blue suit . . . and muttering audibly about the assholes who made his wife look like a slut. When Marilyn saw him there, she seized up, forgot her lyrics, got her feet tangled, and fell on the floor. Technicians rushed in to pick her up, and make sure she wasn't hurt. Assistants fretted over her, patching her makeup, fixing her hair . . . and then, at the urging of publicity men, they led her over to Joe—*Could we get a photo?* But DiMaggio refused to be photographed with her. She wasn't properly dressed. (Later he was glad to pose with her co-star, Ethel Merman. That was different. The Merm was a friend of Georgie's. And anyway, she was a great star.)

When *Show Business* was finally finished, at the end of August, it turned out Marilyn wouldn't have any time for vacation between films. She had to fly to New York, right away, to begin *The Seven Year Itch.* Maybe that's the way she wanted it. She was flying toward a future that only she knew about—her great escape. Alas, four days later, DiMaggio would follow her across the country. And that was another mistake.

WHY DID HE COME? HE HAD TO SEE her—to be with her. Simple as that. . . . Well, it wasn't simple, but always the same: every time they'd have a fight, he'd blow up—she was driving him

crazy—until she went away from him. And then he
had to come. He told her he loved her. He always
loved her. He'd promise to be better, to make it better.
Maybe he'd go see the head-shrinkers, like she did.
(Marilyn had started therapy that summer.) Maybe
they could tell him why he got so mad. Joe would say,
he knew it could be better—he could be better—if
she just wasn't working. They could live together
quietly. How could he be calm in the middle of . . . all
this?

Marilyn was the news in New York—wherever
she went, the town stopped around her—the studio
saw to that. In fact, the trip was only for publicity.
(All the scenes shot on location in New York could
have been filmed more easily in Hollywood—and
most of them later were.) It worked out better than
the studio had dreamed. As one Fox publicist was
pleased to recall: "The Russians could have invaded Manhattan, and nobody would have taken
any notice." (For drivers, her week in New York
was a nightmare. The *Daily News* called her "a
roadblock named Marilyn Monroe.") Amid the
columns of newsprint under the daily photographs
of her, there were hints that her marriage with
DiMaggio had fallen on hard times, a victim of her
career. Marilyn's standard rejoinder—"No, everything's fine. A happy marriage comes before anything!"—never put the rumor to rest.

So, when Joe arrived, he had to tell Jimmy Cannon
about life in Hollywood. "My life is dull. I never in-

terfere with Marilyn's work. . . . I don't resent her fame. She was working long before she met me. And for what? What has she got after all those years? She works like a dog. When she's working, she's up at five or six in the morning and doesn't get through until seven at night. We eat dinner, watch a little television, and go to bed."

It was the need of the columnists that brought Joe out to watch Marilyn work. Walter Winchell (as he would later recall) knew it would make a good story. The studio had publicized a night scene with Marilyn, the papers trumpeted the news: "Miss Monroe's costume," Hearst's *Journal-American* announced, "is expected to be more revealing than the one she wore yesterday to stop the traffic." On a Wednesday at midnight, about fifteen hundred newsmen and fans, pro photographers and snapshot amateurs, turned out on Lexington Avenue, at 52nd Street, in front of the Trans-Lux Theater. But Winchell needed more than a street scene. (Everyone would have that.) That's why he hunted up Joe, who was having a couple of quiet belts with Georgie Solotaire, in the bar of the St. Regis Hotel. Winchell wanted Joe to come with him to watch Marilyn strut her stuff.

Joe didn't think it was a good idea. "It would make her nervous, and it would make me nervous, too."

But Winchell insisted. "Oh, come on, Joe. I have to be there. It might make some copy for me."

The scene they went to witness would produce one of the most famous screen images in history—Marilyn Monroe, in simple summer white, standing on a subway grating, cooling herself with the wind from a train below. But what sent Joe DiMaggio into a fury was the scene around the scene. Fans were yelling and shoving at police barricades as the train (actually a wind machine manned beneath the street by the special effects crew) blew Marilyn's skirt around her ears. Each time it blew, the crowd would yell, "Higher!" "More!" Her legs were bare from her high heels to her thin white panties. Photographers were stretched out on the pavement, with their lenses pointed up at his wife's crotch, the glare of their flashbulbs clearly outlining the shadow of her pubic hair. "What the hell is going on here?" Joe growled. The director, Billy Wilder, would recall "the look of death" on DiMaggio's face. Joe turned and bulled his way through the crowd—on his way back to the bar—with the delighted Winchell trotting at his heels.

That night, there was a famous fight in Marilyn and Joe's suite on the eleventh floor of the St. Regis. It was famous because none of the guests on that floor could sleep. And famous because Natasha Lytess was so alarmed by Marilyn's cries that she went next door to intervene. (Joe answered the door, and told her to get lost.) It was famous because the following morning Marilyn told her hairdresser and wardrobe mistress that she had screamed for them in the night. ("Her husband got very, very mad with her, and he beat her up a little bit," said the hairdresser,

Gladys Whitten. ("It was on her shoulders, but we covered it up, you know.") And famous because Milton Greene's wife, Amy, came to visit at the suite the following day (to try on Marilyn's mink), and was appalled to see bruises all over her friend's back.

And that fight would stay famous—as the end of Joe and Marilyn's famous marriage.

Years later, Marilyn would tell another hairdresser, Sidney Guilaroff, that she'd warned Joe clearly the first time he beat her up. "Don't ever do that again. I was abused as a child, and I'm not going to stand for it." But, as Guilaroff would write in his memoir:

"Nevertheless, after watching her film a sexy scene for *Seven Year Itch,* Marilyn said, 'Joe slapped me around the hotel room until I screamed, "That's it!" You know, Sidney, the first time a man beats you up, it makes you angry. When it happens a second time you have to be crazy to stay. So I left him.' "

She would file for divorce in Los Angeles, three weeks later.

AND EVEN THEN, THE PATTERN held. Joe was so sorry after that fight, he pleaded with her for another chance. He would go with her to Los Angeles. He would read those psychology books she had offered. He would never say another mean thing about her work . . . if she'd just stay—let him stay—together, married, at home. But even before she went to court, Joe's new home was the living room couch. He was not to come upstairs and try to see her.

When Joe went back east for the World Series (he had a broadcasting contract), she called Jerry Giesler, L.A.'s Attorney to the Stars, who was famous for stage-managing dramas of this sort like a veteran film director. When Joe came back early (he kissed off the last game—he had to see Marilyn), she called Billy Wilder and told him she couldn't come in to work. She was too upset—she was divorcing Joe. Then, the studio cavalry rode onto the scene. They would make accommodations for Miss Monroe to sleep on the lot. DiMaggio was quietly barred from the Fox property. (The studio was alert to the rumors that Joe had been slugging Fox's number one asset.) Meanwhile, the publicity troops were calling scores of columnists, reporters, and editors to announce that Joe and Marilyn had decided their marriage could not continue, "because of the conflicting demands of their careers." And hairdressers, makeup, and wardrobe assistants were scrambled to North Palm Drive. This would be—for Miss Monroe, for the studio, and the industry—a crucial scene. Joe DiMaggio was still a hero. One wrong move could gravely injure Miss Monroe's career.

By early morning, October 6, 1954, a hundred reporters and cameramen had staked out the lawn on North Palm Drive. At the curb, there were a couple of idling tour buses ("See the Homes of the Stars!"): they'd changed their itineraries so their patrons could witness this important scene, too. Upstairs, Marilyn's makeup man, her hairdresser, and dress designer were fretting over her person, while Giesler rehearsed her. He didn't want her to speak. She was to weep and, at one point, stumble—he would support her, and sweep her past the crowd to a car. Sidney Skolsky was recruited and schooled for his bit part. And although he didn't know it—he was downstairs on his couch of exile—there was a part for Joe DiMaggio in this drama, too.

Joe did his bit—or fell right into it—at ten A.M., when his pal from San Francisco, Reno Barsocchini, arrived to help the Clipper get his things out of the house. Reno loaded up Joe's Cadillac: a couple of suitcases, a bag of golf clubs . . . and then the Great DiMag himself. "Where are you going?" the newsmen were shouting.

Joe was trying to push through the crowd, without any rough stuff that would make news. "I'm going to San Francisco."

"Are you coming home again?"

"San Francisco's my home," Joe said, and he darted for the car. "It's always been my home. I'll never come back here."

Reno gunned the Cadillac, and Joe was gone. . . . Inside the house, Giesler was well satisfied. It was important for Joe to leave first, and visibly—to walk out of his own accord.

Forty-five minutes later, the star made her exit. (Why she had to exit was never explained—and never asked—it was strictly part of the scene.) The front door opened, the movie cameras on the lawn started whirring, and Marilyn's tear-stained face emerged. She wore a black sweater (not too tight), black skirt, black pumps, black leather belt. Billy Travilla, her designer (still upstairs), had gone for the funereal effect. The print press rushed forward and then parted as Marilyn made her way, on Giesler's arm, to a stand of microphones in front of the house . . . but she wept. Instantly, Sidney Skolsky emerged from the crowd, and ran to her side to comfort her. Then he turned, to announce: "There is no other man."

Giesler shot him an angry look, and stepped in, to take over. "Miss Monroe will have nothing to say this morning. As her attorney I am speaking for her, and can only say that the conflict of careers has brought about this regrettable necessity."

Then he steered Marilyn through the shouting horde. "I can't say anything," she sniffled into her hankie. She stumbled—and if Giesler hadn't been there, to catch her in her collapse . . . well, it was so sad. "I'm sorry," Marilyn sobbed, and patted her eyes with the hankie. "I'm so sorry." Then, she was driven away.

She was back at the house within a couple of hours, and next morning, appeared (right on time, and quite cheerful) for a good day's work on *The Seven Year Itch*.

AND EVEN THEN, JOE WAS SO SORRY. He stayed in San Francisco long enough to have his picture taken (and sent out nationwide, on the wire) . . . then he sneaked back to Los Angeles. He had to talk to her, to change her mind. He couldn't understand why she would divorce him. She *couldn't* be dumping him for that singing coach—but if it wasn't another man . . . then, why?

He thought if he could just talk to her, she would give him another chance. They could try to start over. He tried to tell her, all he ever wanted to do was take care of her. She didn't want to hear it. When reporters spotted Joe and asked about a reconciliation, Joe couldn't hide his confusion. "I can't understand what happened," he said. "I hope she'll see the light." But he would never fight her in court. When the hearing on her petition was scheduled for October 27, Marilyn listed one witness, her business manager, Inez Melson. Joe told Inez he didn't care what she said in court—Inez should say whatever Marilyn wanted. Joe didn't hire a lawyer for himself. "If she wants the divorce," he told the press, "she will get it."

Still, he couldn't understand—or walk away. Sidney Skolsky was terrified to receive a summons to Joe's room at the Knickerbocker Hotel. Sidney told his wife, Estelle, as she dropped him off for the interview: "If I get hit over the head with a bat . . . you know where you delivered me."

But as Skolsky wrote in his memoir, Joe didn't have any rage left in him: "It was about noon when I entered Joe's room. He pointed toward the bed and asked me to sit down on the edge of it. He drew his chair up close to me.

" 'You know everything. There's one thing I must know,' he said as softly as a torch singer squeezing the pathos out of every note.

" 'Is there another man? Why did Marilyn divorce me?'

"I felt awful. No man should be confronted by an idol on his knees, begging to have his clay feet examined. And I had no balm for them. . . .

"How could I tell him he'd bored her? How could I tell a man his ex-wife became ex because she found him dull?

"I spoke all around it, saying that Marilyn wasn't mature enough to be a wife, that she had failed before, that Marilyn's ever bigger ambition didn't call for a husband, that she didn't want to cater to Joe's likes and dislikes.

"Joe thanked me. I honestly don't believe he had the slightest inkling of what I had avoided saying.

" 'Can I give you a ride anywhere?' he offered, knowing I couldn't drive.

"I told him I had to go to my office at Twentieth Century Fox. Joe drove me there. Later I went on the set of *The Seven Year Itch* but didn't tell Marilyn about my meeting with Joe."

A couple of days before the court date, Brad Dexter walked into a restaurant called the Villa Capri for dinner with Frank Sinatra. Sinatra was already at a table, with a private detective named Barney Rudit-sky, and Joe DiMaggio. DiMaggio immediately apologized for his suspicion of Dexter the first time they'd met. ("Jesus Christ, I'm sorry about the other night. I didn't know who you were or what sort of guy you were. . .") Sinatra said to Dexter: "You gotta help Joe out." He explained that Marilyn was sleeping in her dressing room on the Fox lot, and Joe couldn't even get a call through to her. They'd dreamed up a scheme where Dexter would drive through the studio gates, with DiMaggio under a blanket in the back seat. Dexter didn't think much of the idea. But Joe was pleading, almost in tears: "I'd just like to talk to her . . ."

So Dexter walked into the kitchen of the restaurant (where, he knew, there was a wall phone), and called the Fox lot. He got Marilyn on the phone right away. "I said, 'Marilyn, I'm here at the Villa Capri with Sinatra and Joe, and he's a pretty unhappy guy. He'd like very much to talk to you.' And she said, 'Brad, I really don't care to talk to him.' I said, 'Well, if that's your desire . . . ' " Dexter went back to the table, and told DiMaggio, he couldn't help.

So, two days later, Marilyn told a Santa Monica court (and the world) that Joe DiMaggio's cruel in-difference had driven her to divorce. "Your honor," she told the judge, "my husband would get in moods where he wouldn't speak to me for five to seven days at a time—sometimes longer, ten days. I would ask him what was wrong. He wouldn't answer, or he would say, 'Stop nagging me!' I was permitted to have visitors three times . . . on one occasion, it was when I was sick. Then, he did allow someone to come and see me."

She told the court she had offered to give up her work—but even that didn't help. "I hoped to have out of my marriage love, warmth, affection and understanding. But the relationship was mostly one of coldness and indifference."

Inez Melson was called to corroborate: "Mr. DiMaggio was very indifferent and not concerned with Mrs. DiMaggio's happiness," she testified. "I have seen him push her away and tell her not to bother him."

After eight minutes, Judge Orlando H. Rhodes granted Marilyn her interlocutory decree. Her divorce would be final in one year. From San Francisco City Hall to that courtroom in Santa Monica, the famous marriage had lasted two hundred and eighty-six days.

AND THEN, STRANGELY, THINGS GOT easier—at least for her. She knew she could always call on Joe when she needed something, or someone. Ten days after her appearance in divorce court, Marilyn was admitted to the Cedars of Lebanon Hospital for a gynecological operation. (She was diagnosed with endometriosis.) So, Joe DiMaggio drove her to the hospital, sat and held her hand, filled her room

with roses, and (at her request) talked to the newsmen who had invaded the lobby.

Three months after she testified to Joe's cruel indifference, Marilyn had to go from New York to
Boston to talk to a potential investor in Marilyn Monroe Productions. So, Joe drove her to Boston, and
took her to stay at brother Dom's house. (That was
easy for her, though not necessarily for the Dominic
DiMaggio family. One of Dom's sons reported to a
playmate that things were kinda tight around the
house. "Aunt Marilyn never comes out of the bathroom!")

And eight months after her date in divorce court—
on her twenty-ninth birthday, June 1, 1955—Marilyn
had no one to squire her to the New York premiere of
The Seven Year Itch. (Her boyfriend at the time was
both famous and married—which made him unsuit-
able for duty as an escort.) So Joe DiMaggio put on a
headwaiter's suit and bravely walked her up the red
carpet, into the Loew's State Theater (where, of
course, he'd be treated to a replay of the subway grating scene). Joe also knew that after a premiere, there
should be a party. So he took her to Toots Shor's,
where the boys at the bar sang a rousing chorus of
"Happy Birthday to You."

But it wasn't ever easy for Joe. Not when he was
with her—and never when he wasn't. And when he
thought she was with someone else . . . well, watch
out for DiMag. Just a few days after the divorce, for
example, Joe was once again in the Villa Capri with

Sinatra and some of Frank's cronies. That's when Barney Ruditsky, the detective, called to say that his man who was tailing Marilyn had tracked her to an apartment house in West Hollywood. Ruditsky was working for Sinatra. He had a man keeping tabs on Marilyn as a favor from Sinat to DiMag. . . . If there was one man in the country who understood DiMaggio—understood what it was to be a Dago poor-boy who was (all of a sudden, the very next day) the toast of the nation and the target of a million eyes—that was Sinatra. Frank also understood how it was with Joe and broads. Frank had his own too similar troubles with Ava Gardner. His jealousy about her almost killed him—and maybe it still would, if he didn't kill her first.

So, when Ruditsky called the Villa Capri to say that Marilyn was holed up in an apartment at Waring Avenue and Kilkea Drive, Sinatra and Joe were on their way in a hurry. Frank was trying to calm Joe down. The landlady would later testify that she saw Sinatra and DiMaggio arguing outside the apartment house. At about eleven-fifteen P.M., everybody in the building heard a splintering crash, as Sinatra's men broke down the door to one apartment. The noise was most fearsome for Mrs. Florence Kotz, a fifty-year-old woman who was asleep, alone, in that apartment. When the door crashed down, strange men rushed in, taking pictures, shooting off flashbulbs—but their pictures would only show Mrs. Kotz sitting up in bed, clutching her bedclothes about her, her mouth open to loose an ear-splitting scream. . . . Meanwhile, through a door just a few yards away, Marilyn Monroe and Hal Schaefer left the apartment of the actress Sheila Stuart (another of Schaefer's clients)—and they got away clean.

Everybody almost got away clean. The cops wrote it up as an attempted burglary—and so did the papers. Mrs. Kotz brought suit for $200,000 against Sinatra and DiMaggio—but Sinatra's attorney, Mickey Rudin, worked out a quiet settlement for $7,500. The "Wrong-Door Raid" only came to light two years later, in a *Confidential Magazine* exposé. After that, a committee of the California State Senate launched an investigation, forcing Sinatra and the detectives to testify. Joe DiMaggio never had to tell his story. He sent a note of regret to the members of the Senate committee—he was, alas, unable to attend their hearings—and stayed in New York, or out of the country, out of the range of their subpoenas.

By that time, DiMaggio was hard for anybody to find. He spent a lot of time overseas. When he came to New York, he'd slip in quietly. He could always stay (just as quietly) in Georgie Solotaire's suite—which had moved to the Hotel Madison, and then the Mayflower. (Later, Joe got a deal of his own to keep a place at the Hotel Lexington.) But he was very seldom seen around town—even at Shor's. He didn't like to go out to eat—his ulcers were killing him. He looked thin, and haggard around the eyes. (Like a man under pressure—but what was he doing?) . . . And he'd never stay for long.

By that time, Joe had resumed his habitual rhythm of itinerancy, that was the life in which he'd come of age—a few days, maybe a week, at some home base, and then a pal would have to drive him to the airport: he was on his way to some other town, to some date, an appearance, or a golf tournament—some payday for being Joe DiMaggio . . . where another subnetwork of pals would spring to alert, to take care of the Clipper. The old Chicago Bears quarterback Sid Luckman (and his friends) would host DiMag, drive him around, and entertain him in Miami Beach. Eddie Liberatore, a scout for the Dodger organization, took care of everything for Joe in Philadelphia; Sam Brody, a clothing manufacturer, ran an arm of the network out of Chicago; a couple of mob-connected fixers, Harry Hall and Sugar Brown, would take care of anything Joe needed in Los Angeles; across the country—and across the great legal divide—Joe's lawyer and friend (an old Toots Shor pal), Edward Bennett Williams, was his host in Washington. But even at Williams's commodious home, Joe wouldn't be at ease for long. It seemed like he couldn't stay anywhere—and New York was the worst.

By that time, New York was Marilyn's town—she had made her great escape . . . and announced that New York would be her home ever after. With her photographer friend, Milton Greene, she had formed Marilyn Monroe Productions . . . and she had brought Twentieth Century Fox to its knees. Now she was the highest paid actress in the world—a hundred thousand dollars per picture!—with a new seven-year contract that only required four pictures for Fox, and guaranteed her control of script, director, cine-matographer, choreographer, drama coach, singing coach, costumes, makeup man, and hairstylist. Still, most of the time, she preferred to stay at the small apartment rented by Marilyn Monroe Productions, just off Park Avenue, in the Waldorf Towers.

(The door of that building was often staked out by the rabid members of her local fan club. And the most rabid of them—a boy named Jimmy Haspiel—used to stand on that street for hours, just for a glimpse of her. Sometimes, Haspiel would notice another lurker—across the street, in the shadow of an entry-way . . . there was Joe DiMaggio, also watching that door.)

By that time, Marilyn had been adopted by New York (as she never had been in Los Angeles). She had taken up studies with Lee Strasberg at the Actors Stu-dio—in fact, she had become Strasberg's most fa-mous pupil, his personal project, his frequent houseguest, and a favorite among his circle of ac-quaintance—actors, directors, and playwrights . . . one playwright in particular.

By that time, late 1956, Joe had watched, with the

rest of the nation, as the celebrated dramatist Arthur Miller blew up the latest congressional commie-hunt ... by asking for the return of his passport, so he could travel to London with Marilyn Monroe—"to be with the woman who will then be my wife."

Edward Bennett Williams recalled for Maury Allen, in *Where Have You Gone, Joe DiMaggio?* ... "I was with Joe when Arthur Miller was called to testify before the House Un-American Activities Committee. Joe and Marilyn had been divorced but, of course, Joe was still carrying the torch.

"... Marilyn volunteered to testify for Miller at the hearings. She got up before the committee, defended Miller vigorously, and said, 'Arthur Miller is the only man I ever loved.' I knew that would hit Joe like a brick wall. I figured he would cancel our dinner date that evening. He didn't. He went straight ahead with it and never said a word about Marilyn all night."

EVERYBODY IN THE NETWORK KNEW, you couldn't bring her name up, or the Clipper would be gone—maybe gone for good. It seemed like Joe was always walking out in those days, like there was nowhere that was his—and he was drinking pretty hard, too. Didn't do any good for his ulcers. Didn't do much good for his mood, either. He liked a guy to stay with him, belt for belt. But you couldn't get sloppy and say something wrong. It wasn't just her name you couldn't bring up—but things about her . . . and how were you supposed to know?

Roses, for example, could set Joe off. One time, a pal told the Clipper—this didn't have anything to do with broads, it was about a stupid dinner in Cleveland—anyway, the pal says, "Joe, sometimes, you oughta just smell the roses." And DiMaggio goes nasty, his face gets dark, he says: "What the fuck do you know about roses?"

Movie stars—it was better not to talk about them. You never knew when you'd step on a mine. Clark Gable: how're you supposed to know, Marilyn loved Clark Gable? She dreamed her father looked like Gable. Or Brando—bad name. Marilyn's picture was in the papers with Brando, and they were in the columns. ("MM, Marlon 'That Way' It Sez Here . . .")

That was part of the problem. She was always in the papers. Marilyn turns Jewish to marry Arthur Miller, that's in the papers. They go to England, they're back from England, they get an apartment, she shows up at his play . . . there's always something. Chrissake, she's on the cover of *Time* magazine. How's the Dago supposed to forget her? Sometimes you couldn't even mention the names of the papers. That would start Joe thinking, what they said about her—or about him. Some headline had burned into him from the time when she dumped him: "The Clipper Strikes Out" . . . "Joe Out at

Home!" . . . They made him a public joke. And any mention of that paper now could bring back his shame.

It wasn't like he didn't have honor. Nobody wrote bad about him now—anything but. When they put him into the Hall of Fame, the papers wrote about him as the All-Time Great—maybe the best ever. He was a legend. (But after that one time he went to Cooperstown to get his plaque, he hardly ever went back.) He'd show up, once a year, for Old-Timers' Day at the Stadium, and people treated him like God. They'd always introduce him last, and the fans would go crazy. And the papers were filled with the memories of him—all the writers wanted to interview him. He could have been in the papers every day, if he wanted. (When Hemingway put Joe in that old fisherman book, they wrote about people writing about him!) . . . But Joe didn't seem to want any of it—or said he didn't. He'd give a laugh like a snort, and say it was time for him to get out of town.

A lot of times, he got into the papers with some girl. In those years, that was his reputation—the big lover—like something sexy from Marilyn had rubbed onto him. Or maybe the papers were just in the habit of writing his love life—he was such big news with Marilyn, they didn't want to miss out on the next chapter. But there was something to the reputation, because in those years, more than ever, women just fell all over him. That was partly about Marilyn, too. Every female of a certain age in America had wondered what it would be like to be Marilyn Monroe. (A lot of 'em were willing to try it for a night.) But it was something about Joe, too—because he was so publicly, famously hurt . . . it gave him a softer edge, a vulnerability, that drew women in, like bears to honey—a lot of volunteers to fix his broken heart.

For instance, there was one girl—Lola Mason— she wasn't half Joe's age. She was, at that time, one of many girls in New York who wanted to get into show business. But she wasn't really tough enough to make it in that racket. So she ended up working in nightclubs, and publicity. She was just a beautiful nineteen-year-old girl, with soft blond hair and a soft sweet voice. Anyway, she was dancing one night at El Morocco, and the friend who took her (a male friend, but not a boyfriend) was asking why a lovely girl like her didn't have a steady man in her life. And she told him—she remembers—that the only man she really wanted to date was Joe DiMaggio . . . though she'd never met him, he was just the ideal man. Anyway, they finished a dance, sat down at their table—and who's at the next table? DiMag. And he was just as she'd imagined, so distinguished (with a bit of gray in his hair), handsome and quiet, courtly and perfect. He was there with the former Miss America, Lee Meriwether—but he wasn't with Lee for long. Lola he was with, on and off (whenever he cared to call), for the next five years. Of course, that didn't make much hay in the papers. Lola wasn't in it for her own publicity . . . and Joe never stuck with the ones who made the papers.

The dates that made ink were with girls who were names themselves—a lot of Miss Americas. Lee Meriwether was a perfect example. She was Miss California (in fact, she came from San Francisco), and then was crowned Miss America of 1955. She had just given up her title—she had crowned the next queen and had become (as the ladies of the Pageant say) "a former"—when she and her mother went back to Atlantic City to visit Lee's brother, who was working in a hotel. They were at the front desk of that hotel when they saw Joe DiMaggio. It was Lee's mother who started talking to him: "I don't know if you remember my husband, but he used to come into your brother's restaurant." Joe couldn't have been nicer—it was possible he remembered Mr. Meri-wether, but it was certain that Mr. Meriwether's daughter was on Joe's radar screen. He invited the whole family to dinner. But as it turned out, Lee's brother had to work, and her mother got too much sun on the Boardwalk. So Lee and Joe went out to dinner that Saturday night—as only a former would point out—"unchaperoned."

Joe took her to the 500 Club, which was the mob's best nightclub and headquarters in Atlantic City. "I've got to be interviewed there," Joe explained. "Is that all right?" (Of course, it was.) . . . Joe was going to be a guest on the radio show that was broadcast from the 500 Club—as a matter of promotion. He agreed to the interview as a favor to Paul "Skinny" D'Amato, who ran the 500 Club and its hyper-profitable backroom gambling—high stakes for big players. (Skinny was very close to Joe's old pal from Newark, Longy Zwillman.) . . . And for his part, Skinny would show himself appreciative of Joe's favor—by doing Joe the favor of handing him a grand or two, in cash.

So, it was a pleasant night. Joe's interview went fine—all baseball reminiscence—and at the 500, they ran into Walter Winchell, the famous columnist, and another guest on the radio show. Winchell insisted they go with him to the Cotton Club, where there was a dance act that he thought was a knockout. But first Winchell had to do his bit on the radio—where he spent a few minutes talking about what a wonderful fellow Joe DiMaggio was. "And did you see who he was with?" Winchell asked into the microphone. "The former Miss America, Lee Meriwether. I hear they're quite an item. Are there wedding bells in the future?"

In the cab on the way to the Cotton Club, Winchell's mug (and its cigar) turned around from the shotgun seat, toward Joe and Lee, who were sitting in the back—and the newshound said, "Thanks for the scoop."

"Ah, Walter, come on," DiMaggio said. "You know how long I know this girl? I mean, I knew her family . . ." (Lee was unable to help out. She was twenty years old, nervous and silent.)

Winchell said: "You mean, you deny it?"

"Aw, come on, Walter—get off it."

Winchell knew enough not to ask again. Two days later, in the *New York Mirror,* Winchell ran a copy of Joe and Lee's picture (taken at the 500 Club)—ran it full-page, under the headline: "TO WED?"

Lee, at that point, was the "Women's Editor" for the *Today* show on NBC, and Dave Garroway, the host, asked if she wanted to deny it on the air. Lee didn't know what was the right thing to do. But Garroway liked news—and this was news. So, that morning, she denied it, to about ten million people. She didn't see DiMaggio much after that—or hear from him—except one time, by phone, about two in the morning . . . when she picked up the receiver and heard through her sleep: "S'Joe DiMaggio, I need to talk to you."

As her head cleared, she could hear, he'd had too much to drink. "Where are you?" she said.

"Please can I come over?"

"What *time* is it?"

"I wanna come over."

Lee didn't like the way this was going. "But how do you know where I live?"

Then, Joe DiMaggio hung up.

EVEN WITH THE MISS AMERICAS, A lot of Joe's dates were business. There were a number of nights, for instance, when he was "out on a date" at the Stork Club with perhaps the most notable former, Yolande Betbeze, Miss America 1951. Yolande and Joe had both been paid to show up, and lend the place a little glamour. They'd appear on TV (the Stork Club had its own show)—and they were both good names for ink in the papers the following day.

But Joe was hardly Yolande's cup of tea. She was a woman of sophistication, and could talk like Joe could play center field. The only time she saw Joe, when they weren't just being seen, was when she was doing a good deed in Paris. Yolande had come from Mobile, Alabama, and there was a girl from her home state—another great beauty, some years her junior—who'd had a broken engagement and was teetering on the edge of a nervous breakdown. So Yolande took her to Europe, to get her mind off things. In Paris, they ran into Joe, who also favored the Continent to get his mind off things. (He could binge there without making news.) And Joe being Joe, when he ran into Yolande and her friend, he hit on the blond one, the wounded duck. So Yolande was treated (strictly as a spectator) to the sight of DiMaggio sitting on an upper-story staircase of the Hotel George V (those wonderful stairs that curve around the elevators), very late at night, trying to talk the wounded duck into his bed. The problem was, DiMaggio was so loaded, he could barely talk at all—so stinko, in fact, that his pants were open, with his member lying exposed upon his leg. ("And that," as Yolande would recall, "was the biggest thing you ever saw.")*

There was one Miss America whom Joe actually approached on his own. And he took her out on real dates, too. That was Marian McKnight, the five-foot-five-inch blond Miss South Carolina. Joe happened to be in attendance at the Atlantic City Convention Hall when she was crowned Miss America 1957 . . . after she wowed the talent competition with her impersonation of Marilyn Monroe. Joe went right backstage to meet her.

That was another pattern. There were a lot of Marilyn Monroe acts in those years, and if he could do so without making news, Joe took them all in. Here, for example, is the recollection of the burlesque artist, Liz Renay, from her memoir, *My First 2,000 Men* (Joe made the chapter called "Celebrities"):

"There were wild bed scenes with Joe DiMaggio. I'd won the Marilyn Monroe Look-Alike contest for Twentieth Century Fox. He and Marilyn were no longer together and, so his friends said, he kept trying to get glimpses of his Marilyn by looking at me.

---

* I told Yolande that I had always heard Joe's "Louisville Slugger" ranked only second to the big schtick of Milton Berle. But on this subject Yolande was firm. "Oh, no," she said. "Milton's was never that big."

"Joe DiMaggio was not only a good lover but a nice, likeable guy—a real gentleman. I had at least a dozen liaisons with 'Joltin' Joe' in various hotel rooms and especially in his Mayflower Hotel suite. He was a once-a-night lover, but as he so nicely put it, 'I only come once, but I last a long time.'

"Joe liked variety in his women. A delivery boy from the drugstore downstairs once whispered to me that just about every time he made a delivery Joe had a different girl in the apartment."

Things didn't work out quite so nicely for Dixie Evans—despite her well-earned reputation as the Marilyn Monroe of Burlesque. She'd got the name from Mr. Minsky himself (she was a Minsky Girl) in Newark, New Jersey. At that time, her act was a casting couch skit. Dixie was the actress. She took her clothes off, and got the part. Mr. Minsky said she looked like Marilyn, and she should use the name. Suddenly, she was a headliner.

By the late 1950s, when she was working Miami Beach, at the Place Pigalle (a beautiful club, with French motif—they even had murals in the bathroom), Dixie wasn't just the big name on the marquee. An airplane flew past the beach hotels—every day, four passes a day—towing a banner that read: "See the Marilyn Monroe of Burlesque, Place Pigalle." The plane always went by the Fontainebleau, where the celebs stayed, and they all came to see her. Sinatra, Bogart . . . Walter Cronkite came in every year with Chris Schenkel. Schenkel told her she should come to the Kentucky Derby. He'd announce her, coming in: *"Ladies and gentlemen, it's Marilyn Monroe! Oh, my mistake. It's Dixie Evans! She'll be playing at the Post and Paddock this evening."* (Wouldn't that be good advertising?) . . . Anyway, they all loved her act—which, at that point, involved Joe and his bat.

One night, the owner of Pigalle came to Dixie's table, to tell her Joe DiMaggio was in attendance, and he wanted to talk to her. So, Dixie excused herself from her companions, and was introduced to Joe— and to the famous sportswriter Grantland Rice, and Mr. Skinny D'Amato, of the 500 Club in Atlantic City. Skinny and the writer were pretty profane guys and they were slinging it around pretty good, but Joe was gentlemanly. He leaned over, and whispered in her ear, "Just excuse that conversation." She'd heard it all before, of course, but that was nice. And he was so handsome—with a little gray.

Pretty soon it was time to go on, but Dixie was thinking—Wait a minute! I don't want to do this act in front of Joe! . . . And she told him that. He said: "Why do you think I came here?" And he told her how he went backstage to meet some eighteen-year-old girl who'd done a Marilyn imitation at the Miss America Pageant. So, Dixie got up, and did her thing.

Her thing was this: She entered in a tight satin gown, a long scarf, and a Yankee cap, with a Number 5 on it—and crying, boo-hooing, which mood she explained in song:

Joe, you walked off and left me flat—
But I'm sure glad you left your bat . . .

There were a few lines about baseball, and
spaghetti, and how he'd stop in the middle of making
love to say, "What's the score?" . . .

But I know . . .
You'll still return my calls.
Why? It's simple—I've still got you
By your New York Yankee base— (badaboomcha,
strike up the band) . . .

Afterward, when she came out from her dressing
room, Joe stood up and motioned her over. She sat
with him all night. He didn't say much. He never
mentioned the act, or talked about Marilyn. But he
kept sneaking glances at Dixie, checking her out.
And he stayed until she'd done her last set, at a quarter to five. Then he invited her to breakfast. So the
four of them went to Wolfie's. The guys had ham and
eggs. Dixie had a fruit cup. "Izzat all you want?" Joe
kept asking. She said, sure. She was starving, but trying to be ladylike.

After breakfast, Skinny and the writer left the two
of them alone on the sidewalk. Joe took her makeup
kit and started to get a cab. Dixie said, "I just live
right across the park. We can walk." So Joe carried
her bag home.

Dixie's mother met them at the door. She was

wearing curlers, looked like a scared cat jumping up in the air. Dixie excused herself and went to her bedroom to freshen up. Dixie's mom hied to her room. And Joe paced the living room, picking up trinkets. When Dixie came out he gave her a long kiss. And, as she said, it was magic. With a lot of important men she had to invent the magic. But with Joe, it was real. Her knees went weak. And she noticed he was kind of aroused, too. The kissing got pretty heavy—but her mother was in the next room. So Joe said, "Do you want to go to the Flamingo Stakes?" (That was the big horse race at Hialeah.) And he told her to meet him at the Fontainebleau at twelve-thirty.

Well, then came the funny part, or the tragic part—she was never sure which. She rushed off to the beauty parlor, and was baking under a hairdryer hood, when the owner of the Place Pigalle rushed in and found her. "What are you doing?" he was yelling. "We're supposed to be in court this morning!"

"But I have a date with Joe DiMaggio."

"You have a date in court."

So she went to court, got stuck there, and stood up Joe DiMaggio. "He probably thinks I'm a rotten person," she says. "That's the last I ever saw him." (Years later, when her coffeepot broke, she called Mr. Coffee, and said she was a friend of Joe's. But she didn't get a new coffeepot—and he didn't call.)

EVEN THAT NEAR-DATE WITH DIXIE
at the racetrack was business for Joe. In those lost
years, business was about the only thing that held his
attention. Or you could put it another way: once Marilyn threw him out, the only way he'd be Joe DiMaggio was for the business of being DiMaggio . . . and
that's where Skinny D'Amato came in. Skinny cur-
ried favor with the biggest players by offering them a
chance to meet—to chat with, or sit with, to say they
hung around with—that legend in the flesh, the Yankee Clipper. It was more or less like a big casino hir-
ing a "greeter"—a former heavyweight champ, or an
ex–major leaguer—someone the suckers could talk
about: they'd met him, they shook hands, they had a
laugh together. But like all of Skinny and Joe's business, this was of the private variety.

That was one reason Joe liked D'Amato, for the
privacy that was Skinny's rule. Joe could go into the
500, and sit in the back room all day, maybe play a little cards. . . . It was bigger, fancier of course, but for
Joe it was more or less like LaRocca's Corner, back
in North Beach, when he was growing up. No one
would bother him in there. And if he did talk to one of
D'Amato's friends, Skinny would make that worth
Joe's while. . . . If he went down to Florida with
Skinny for a big race, Joe might lose twenty bucks at
the track. (He was a two-dollar bettor.) But Skinny
would give him a couple of grand, just for sitting with
some pals. If Joe would go out for a round of golf at

the Breakers with one of Skinny's big guys, that was a better payday—five grand at least.

(And Skinny took care of Joe, more or less like Toots always did. Any subject involving the Clipper's welfare, Skinny had opinions and an interest. Joe's teeth for example: Joe never got his buck teeth fixed until Skinny took care of it—put him with the Dentist to the Stars in New York. Everybody got their TV teeth from that guy—from the vice president, Nixon, on down—or up. . . . In Joe's case, that was the first sign that he might actually be getting over Marilyn. She'd always said she could never love a man with perfect teeth. But Joe went ahead and got a nice new grille, like a Roadmaster Buick.)

Of course, Joe knew who Skinny's pals were—or why they were pals. For instance, there was the man who went by the name of Walter Thomas. Joe had to have a talk about him with a pair of New York police detectives, and a couple of district attorneys. And for that sort of talk, the investigating officers later typed up a transcript:

"Q. You know a Walter Thomas, and did you make reservations for him at the Madison Hotel in 1957 at the request of Paul D-Amato?

"A. Yes, Paul De-Amato is the owner of a Five Hundred Club, Atlantic City, and when I am in Atlantic City I spend a lot of time there just sitting around. He called me about a Mr.

Thomas during the World Series of 1957 and
asked me to make reservations for him at the
Madison where I was living at that time. . . .

"Q. Where did you meet [Mr. Thomas]?

"A. When in Atlantic City I would sit around the
Five Hundred Club. I saw him there. I only
called him Tommy.

"Q. What business is Tommy in?

"A. I don't know.

"Q. If you had to guess what would you say?

"A. I would guess he was a gambler."

The reason Joe had that uncomfortable chat (it
went on for more than an hour) was because his pal
Tommy had taken him over to the Warwick Hotel to
meet three Cuban mobsters who wanted Joe to front a
gambling operation in Havana. And on the way up, in
the elevator of the Warwick, Joe's pal Tommy said he
had to stop by another room . . . so Joe went with him
to the room of Albert Anastasia, who was, at that moment, the boss of bosses in New York organized
crime. Unfortunately, those visits had come to official attention—because that was the day that Albert
Anastasia was lamentably shot dead in a barber chair
at the Park Sheraton Hotel. Joe was upset with his
pals for taking him to talk with the mob boss on the
day of his death. (What if the hit had taken place in
the Warwick?)

Of course, the way Joe tried to tell it to the cops,
the Cubans were only baseball fans—Joe only
walked across town and went up to their room to chat

about the World Series. And Anastasia—gosh, he didn't know who that was! . . . Joe also dummied up (nope, he never saw the guy) when the cops showed him a picture of Joe Adonis (with whom Joe and Georgie used to drink by the hour, in Adonis's own joint). And he could only shrug—never saw her, either—when the cops showed a picture of Liz Renay. (Funny, she seemed to know him so well.)

Thing was, Joe could say whatever he wanted to those cops—or any cops. Joe took the same tack when the FBI sat him down to inquire why he was playing golf with the boss of Chicago crime, Sam Giancana. Joe said, that was just a guy he happened to meet. He wasn't going to volunteer the fact that Giancana was a pal since Joe was playing ball. He wasn't going to say that Sam G. was always good for a broad, or a payday, in Chicago. Or that he got messages frequently, through Georgie Solotaire (who referred to that pal as "Sam from Chi"). Joe did not make an effort to explain that he was also friends with Giancana's girlfriend, Phyllis McGuire . . . and Giancana's younger girlfriend, Judy Campbell . . . and when Judy came to New York, Giancana told her to call Joe D.—and he'd get her into the Plaza Hotel. . . . Why should Joe tell them any of that? No investigation was going to lay a glove on the Yankee Clipper.

And that was one thing the mob guys loved about Joe. He didn't talk. And no one was ever going to make him talk. Why would the cops be bothering a hero? . . . That's what convinced Longy Zwillman that Joe was such a good, safe bet—just the man to help him with his problem. Longy had a problem with cash.

Actually, Longy had two problems with cash. For one thing, once the Kefauver snoops couldn't make anything stick on Zwillman, they got nasty and turned him over to the tax guys. And of course the tax guys, the way they were, started poking around trying to figure out what money Longy had, and how did he get it. But Longy couldn't explain all his money, in a nice federal way. The other problem Longy had was with his partners in the syndicate, on whose turf and in whose rackets Longy was continually poaching. So, even with his peers and associates, Longy couldn't explain all his cash. So what Longy used to do was to put some money in a suitcase—say, a couple of hundred G's—and he'd show up at your home with his suitcase, and explain, in his quiet way: "This is my money. When I need it I'll be back for it." Of course, no one touched Longy's "boxes" because bad things could happen. And about that time, Longy also figured out that the last guy in the country the feds would ever bother was his old friend Joe DiMaggio. So, after a while, Longy had thirteen "boxes" out with friends. And three of the boxes had been placed with the Yankee Clipper. Longy figured Joe had plenty of room in San Francisco.

It was that sort of figuring that convinced Joe he ought to have a real job. Not only would it help him, if he had to explain his own finances, but it might make him less available for the sort of deals that made him nervous. Also, he could use the money. (Joe Jr. was now going to Lawrenceville Prep, which cost Big Joe plenty.) . . . Sid Luckman, the old Bears quarterback, had a pal he wanted to put Joe D. with. And that was how Joe found employment with the V. H. Monette Co., of Smithfield, Virginia.

Come to think of it, it was the same job—just a different target audience. The Monette Company was the number one supplier of merchandise for U.S. military post exchange stores, all over the world. That was a business with a lot of work for a greeter. Joe and the boss, Val Monette, would turn up in Frankfurt, Germany (or Okinawa, Otranto, San Diego, Lakeland, Florida—wherever the contracts were coming up), to play a round of golf with the general in command of the U.S. base there—and maybe the colonel who ran the PX. Joe might coach some Little Leaguers on the base, or reminisce of an evening in the officers club. And that was all that was required. The generals and colonels were thrilled. They'd be talking about it for months. And Val Monette was thrilled. Business had never been better.

Valmore Monette had an instinct for promotion. Two things he thought were top-of-the-line—and two things for which his company was known—were Joe DiMaggio, and Miss Americas. Monette employed as many formers as he could. (Joe got to meet them all.) And Monette promoted DiMaggio's affiliation with the company by announcing that he paid the Yankee Clipper a hundred G's a year. (Joe was happy to announce that, too.) . . . In point of fact—on the testimony of one pal who saw Joe's pay stub—Joe's wage worked out to about thirty-five grand. But Monette threw in a suite at the Lexington Hotel in New York, and picked up all the tabs when he and Joe were on the road. It worked out great. In fact, Joe stayed with the company for almost three years—and even when he left, that was pretty good publicity, because Monette told everybody that DiMaggio resigned to go back with Marilyn Monroe.

And that may well have been what Joe told him. But it was also true that Joe didn't need to work anymore . . . because of a lamentable event in New Jersey. Longy Zwillman was found (alas, dead) hanging from the chandelier in his house. The cops in West Orange marked it down as suicide—poor Longy, the feds had hounded him to an early grave. . . .

(Actually, the cops put it on the logs as a suicide, before the body was even discovered. This was the kind of suicide that somebody phoned in. According to pals in New York, what happened was Longy had poached once too often. His boys had hijacked a truckload of beef that was destined for Petey Castellano, in Brooklyn. So Castellano got upset and sent three guys to West Orange, New Jersey, to hang Longy up like a side of beef. Problem was, Castellano's guys forgot the meathook—so what could they do? . . . They strung Longy up from his chandelier instead.)

But meanwhile, there was Joe DiMaggio, with three of Longy's "boxes"—and what was he to do with the cash? Take it to the cops, and say, "I found this?" . . . Probably not. Of course, he'd never paid any taxes on it, either—which also made it inconvenient to bring up. This was where his lifelong habitude of quiet came in handy. Joe kept the money in his storeroom at the Marina house, and never said a word about it, for years.

JOE JR.'S PROBLEM WAS, HE COULDN'T get his dad down to Lawrenceville, New Jersey, to visit at the new school—which would have done a lot to put Junior on the map. That was only one of Junior's problems. Another was, the schoolwork was hard. (As he wrote to his mom: "Algebra . . . Whew!") The major problem was, he was sixteen years old, and still not quite five feet seven, a bit of a butterball at one hundred sixty pounds. That put varsity football out of reach, for the moment—unless he could be the kicker . . . but in his first junior varsity game, Butch missed the extra point, and Lawrenceville lost 7–6. ("I guess you know how badly I felt . . .") So, he explained in a letter home to mom, maybe it was better that "J.D." hadn't come to watch.

That's how he often referred to his dad, or sometimes as "my father." It gave his references to Big Joe a weary and adult air that probably mirrored Dorothy's. As Junior noted in one letter home: "JD has tried to be charming in his miserable sort of way, but then I guess he's doing better than what I expected, and he knows no different so we bless him and give him our love."

In fact, in that fall of 1957, J.D. was trying to make the boy part of his life—which, in Big Joe's case, meant bringing him in as one of the guys. Here, for example, is Junior's happy recollection of Thanksgiving vacation in New York with J.D.

"Chuck Heller went with me because he is a long way from home and had no place to go.

"Wednesday—arrived in New York about 3:00. went to Toots Shors had dinner and Chuck and I went bowling. First game 109 second game 160. Then home went the two noble warriors. Asked J.D. for tickets to "My Fair Lady." Wound up sitting in 'house seats' (second row center) . . . Wow!! It was a great show, but I guess you can imagine. After the show we went to Dinty Moore's had a bite to eat then home. Bed.

"Thursday—after eating breakfast we watched the football games on T.V. Then over to Toots's home for Thanksgiving dinner. It was really good!! After dinner We went to see a new musical called Rumple. It starred Eddie Foy Jr. and we enjoyed it very much. Back to Toots's home where we met Frank

Gifford, Charley Connerly, and Kyle Rote, the players on the NY Giants football team. Afterwards home again. Bed.

"Friday—slept most of the day. Met another boy from school and the three of us plus George Solotaire and Dad went to the Colony for dinner! Great! Then we went out on the town and met a bunch of kids from school. Finally home to bed.

"Saturday—up at 7:30. Caught train to Phila. on our way to the Army Navy Game. 7 in our party. There were J.D., Chuck, Eddie Arcaro's son, Toots, his daughter, John Daly and myself. Sat in the rain. It was miserable but we had a great time, Lots of fun! Bad game! Home after the game. J.D. was feeling lousy because of the cold in his back so the two of us joined George Solotaire, his wife, son, son's wife and mother-in-law for dinner. Afterward I took Chuck to see Around the World in 80 Days. He enjoyed it. So did I. Had a couple of Hamburgers at Hamburger Heaven after the show. then Home!

"Sunday—up late! Ate breakfast and then we went to the Giants 49ers football game! Had to leave at the half so we could get back to school in time. Score 17–7. Finally got back to school."

He was very seldom alone with his dad, but it was more time than the boy could ever remember spending with Big Joe. And Junior loved it. He felt like he *was* becoming one of the guys—coming of age as a DiMaggio—though that wasn't something he would write home to mom. Nor would he write what he did talk about with his father, one of their major points of contact: Junior was in touch with Mrs. Arthur Miller. Marilyn had never stopped caring for Joe Jr. (She did like him—that was all real.) Joe Jr. could always call her on the phone, just to talk. And that was one thing that put him on the map with his dad.

The sad part was, from the time Joe Jr. came east to prep school—through all his years at Lawrenceville, in fact—the news from Marilyn wasn't often good. While Junior had that slap-up Thanksgiving with his dad, Marilyn was in slow and painful recovery from a miscarriage that plunged her into depression, and a suicide attempt that shook everyone around her. She wasn't talking, in those days, about her dream of becoming a great stage actress—she didn't talk about anything she was doing—and that first year Junior was in New Jersey, she didn't even make one picture.

By his second year, she did go back to work (on a picture called *Some Like It Hot)* but in the middle of filming, she was once again hospitalized for "nervous exhaustion." Everyone around her was exhausted *by her*—every scene was a million retakes, and sometimes, she wouldn't appear on the set till late afternoon. The gossip columns were filled with her problems, and resentful reactions from her co-stars and crew. Everything Big Joe read in the papers just confirmed for him what he'd always said: those phonies around her were going to ruin her. And he'd ask Joe Jr.—had he talked to Marilyn lately? . . . And did she ask about his dad?

The good news (at least for Big Joe) was she did ask about him. She had never cast him out of her mind—never worked at forgetting him. (For example, the combination lock on her jewelry box was still, and always, 5-5-5.) And her thoughts always turned to Joe in times of trouble—she was in trouble, now. It wasn't just career woes of the old sort. When *Some Like It Hot* finally did come out, it set box office records through the spring and summer of 1959—it would become the most successful comedy in Hollywood history. But Marilyn was in trouble with herself, in herself. All the dreams that were her life rafts had come apart as she clutched for them.

Her studies to become a stage actress had led precisely nowhere. That sent her back to Hollywood, for *Some Like It Hot*. Her role in that picture, and even its huge success, convinced her that the industry (and the public) only loved her as the ditzy blond bombshell (in this case, too dumb to see that Jack Lemmon and Tony Curtis were men). But how would she ever escape that role, now? She had broken her partnership with Milton Greene, and Marilyn Monroe Productions was now nothing more than a shell.

Another miscarriage convinced her that she could never be the wife and mother that Arthur Miller wanted. (His protests that the want of a child came from her, not him, did nothing to console her.) . . . Desperately, to show his love, Miller started writing a screenplay for her—*The Misfits*—that would finally give scope to her dramatic talents. But in practice, that only meant that Miller was squirreled away in his writing studio all day, every day—and Marilyn was left alone.

Now most of her days began around noon, in a lingering barbiturate haze. And even when she woke she would stay in her darkened room, drinking (first a stiff Bloody Mary, and then champagne all afternoon) . . . until she mustered courage to leave her bed. Her maids and attendants would hear Frank Sinatra on Marilyn's record player . . .

All of me,
Why not take all of me?
Can't you see,
I'm no good without you?

. . . as Marilyn made the trip across the room, to her closet, where, inside the door, there was a full-length picture of Joe DiMaggio.

NOW MARILYN'S LIFELINE WAS THE telephone. And according to her New York maid, there were two callers who could always cheer Marilyn up—two men she'd loved and left: Frank Sinatra, and Joe DiMaggio.

She hadn't told anybody when she started calling Joe again—except in the most cryptic way. She used to say: "I guess everybody I've ever loved, I still love a little bit." And there was another unintended hint to her change of attitude. Once, when a friend asked how she could be so bitchy to Arthur Miller—she'd berate him, and order him around in public (fetch her purse, get her mink)—Marilyn shrugged, and blamed it on him: "Why didn't he slap me? He should have slapped me."

Joe didn't talk about her calls, either—except to mention them happily to two or three fellows in the network. For one thing, she was still (nominally) Mrs. Arthur Miller. Joe didn't want it said he'd interfered in that marriage. And the last thing he wanted was the papers finding out. He didn't want any public pressure on their "friendship"—the way he saw it, that's what turned things wrong the first time.

(In fact, all through 1960, when Joe and Marilyn's conversations were more and more fond and frequent, the papers were nattering on about the new love of Marilyn's life, Yves Montand. The Frenchman had been the co-star in her film that year, *Let's Make Love.* She was said to be besotted with him—like a schoolgirl—that was Montand's recollection. The only thing Marilyn said, publicly, was that she considered Montand a most attractive man. In private, she said why—she told friends he reminded her of Joe DiMaggio.)

The odd part was, Sinatra's calls had to be secret, too—not only from Mr. Miller, but from Joe. He would have hit the roof. Since the Wrong-Door Raid, DiMaggio would have nothing to do with Sinatra. He thought Frank had set him up—so Sinatra could jump into bed with Marilyn. Sinatra, for his part, didn't take DiMaggio that seriously. He didn't even take Marilyn that seriously. That was one thing she liked about "Frankie." He didn't want to change her, fix her, rescue her. Frankie knew how to have a good time. In that, he was the perfect antidote to Mr. Miller.

Marilyn's faithful reverence for her playwright husband was a thing of the past. Now her attitude toward him swung wildly from pole to pole—oftentimes all in the same day. She might contend one minute that whatever she did was unimportant, as long as she did not disturb Arthur, who must be allowed to write—his work was all that mattered. And next minute, she might be crying and demanding that he pay attention to her—he had coldly abandoned her! That might be followed by a bout of self-loathing, and pity for Arthur: she was barren both as his wife and his muse—poor man! And soon thereafter, she might be screaming her scorn for him—he had produced nothing, while she supported them. There were times she suspected him of forcing her back to Hollywood—and dumb-blondehood—all for money. And when he showed her the pages of his great love offering, *The Misfits,* she found her character, Roslyn, to be passive, preachy, and in spots, "just lousy."

By the time *The Misfits* started filming, in the summer of 1960, Miller had been cowed into never-ending rewrites, night after night, on location in the

Nevada desert. The script kept changing with his atti-tude toward his wife—and neither one was getting any better. It was apparent to everyone on location that this movie—which Miller had begun as an affir-mation of his love—would end up putting paid to his marriage. Marilyn humiliated Miller at every turn, and at length exiled him from her hotel suite (she slept instead with her coach, Paula Strasberg).

But it was also clear that Marilyn's problems weren't likely to end with that marriage. Now, she wasn't just afraid of the camera, late to the set, fuzzy on her lines. She was taking so many pills (and injec-tions) that the cinematographer protested, he couldn't photograph her. (He could see it through his lens—her eyes wouldn't focus.) And once again, pro-duction was shut down, as Marilyn was hospitalized for a week. When *The Misfits* was finally finished, in November 1960—forty days and God knows how many dollars over budget—Marilyn was all but unin-surable as a motion picture star.

And after production the news got worse. One week later came the announcement that her marriage to Arthur Miller was over. (This time, she'd get a quickie divorce in Mexico.) A week after that, her co-star, Clark Gable, died of a heart attack. Marilyn and her maddening troubles were blamed for impos-ing too much stress on the King. By January 1961, the film had premiered—and was adjudged to be a dud. Marilyn was back in New York, in the East 57th Street apartment that she and Mr. Miller used to share. Now, he was gone (to their country house in Connecticut). Marilyn was alone with her staff, with her pills, and splits of champagne. She had no projects and no prospect of work—nothing to get her out of bed—except appointments with her psychiatrist, Dr. Marianne Kris. Marilyn wasn't sleeping well, or eating well—she wasn't well in any way. So, on February 5, 1961, Dr. Kris drove her to the Cornell University medical center on New York's East Side, where Marilyn checked herself in for a rest.

Immediately, she was taken to the Payne Whitney psychiatric division, where she was locked into a cell, on the ward for the truly psychotic patients. Her screams of protest, her demands to be released, were ignored (or taken as evidence of her sickness). When she broke the pane of glass in her (locked) bathroom door, she was threatened with restraint and watched day and night. And to whom could she appeal? Her doctor had betrayed her. For Marilyn this was the worst fear of her life come true—she was locked away like her mother—a prisoner in a loony bin. So, after three days, when she was finally permitted one call, she phoned to Florida. She called Joe DiMaggio.

He was there the next day, at the Payne Whitney reception desk—six feet one and a half inches tall, wide at the shoulders, glowering darkly, and in no mood for talk.

"I want my wife," DiMaggio said.

No one pointed out to him that he and Marilyn

Monroe had not been married for six years. Instead, they tried to tell him they had no authority to release Miss Monroe—to him or to anyone else.

"I want my wife," DiMaggio said, with menacing precision. His large hands gripped the reception desk. "And if you do not release her to me, I will take this place apart—piece of wood, by piece . . . of . . . wood."

Suddenly, the Payne Whitney staff discovered that Miss Monroe was free to go. Joe had Marilyn transferred crosstown, to another hospital, Columbia Presbyterian, where she could have a real rest—in a normal private room—which he would visit daily, and which he'd fill with roses.

In New York, 1961.

**Back all the way:
together in Florida, 1961.**

August 8, 1962, with Joe Jr. at his side.

CHAPTER 16

✦

WHEN MARILYN EMERGED FROM HER hospital rest, in March 1961, Joe flew her to St. Petersburg, where he was coaching at the Yankees' spring training camp. That was the first year Casey Stengel was gone—and the first time Joe had been paid the respect of an invitation. For DiMaggio that was vindication—a validation of all he'd meant to that club. His exile was over, he was back in pinstripes. And when Marilyn said she would meet him in Florida, then Joe was back all the way. He ran around for days before she arrived, getting things ready—as purposeful as a mama bird building a nest in the spring. He was in action again, and he hadn't lost his moves: he told his pals he was going to be tied up; he told the press precisely nothing about Miss Monroe; he told the road secretary of the Yankees that he wanted two suites at the Soreno—in case anybody asked. (They did.)

But it wasn't just the old moves. Joe was different, calmer about the little things. The old guys who'd come to camp noticed Daig didn't mind taking meals in the dining room—he'd sit after dinner, talking with the kids on the team, even if some fans interrupted. A couple of the old writers, Joe asked *them* to break-fast—just for the hell of it, he didn't have anything to prove. At that camp, he was a god, a *Hall of Famer*—and a relic. It wasn't just the players seemed like boys to him, now. The manager who'd invited him was a kid, too: Joe had seen Ralph Houk break in, after the war. Joe wore his age and distance from the modern game with grace—never scolded, never compared these kids to his guys, his day, his Yankee winners—and never tried to make himself a force upon this jet-age club. He cultivated his remove, as he did the handsome gray in his hair—never had a conversation without some offhand joke about that. He was as ele-gant (and bygone) as private railroad cars.

And with Marilyn, he showed no swagger of pos-session. In his years of exile, he'd learned a few things. He told her that she'd saved him by sending him to a psychiatrist. He hadn't stuck with the ther-apy long, but it was long enough to convince him that the rage inside him could ruin lives—his, first and foremost. Now, at the age of forty-six, Joe very sel-dom took a drink—maybe one beer with dinner. And after dinner, a cup of tea: the endless coffee was a thing of the past. He seemed to want to cultivate a distance even from his old self. With a rueful laugh, he told Marilyn that if he'd been married to that guy he was seven years ago . . . well, he would have di-vorced him, too.

He wanted her to feel safe with him—and that meant showing her he'd changed. He could take care of her without taking over. He didn't remonstrate about her habits, her friends—never said a bad thing about her work. Anyway, she didn't have any work. She didn't seem to have enough energy to get work, or even to want it. The years since their marriage had changed Marilyn, too.

In some ways, she was more womanly—that was a word the Hollywood writers used to describe her looks when *The Misfits* came out. Of course, she'd been so miserable then—overweight and drugged out and haunted around the eyes . . . that was probably just their shorthand way of saying she had aged. Now, as she neared her thirty-fifth birthday, she'd lost all that extra weight—she was, if anything, too thin. But still, the girlishness hadn't come back. Now, when she went out incognito (without makeup, with her black wig or a head scarf and shades) she didn't have about her the air of a waif—maybe a housewife, a bit washed out, too busy (or too hopeless) to put herself together.

She could still turn it on, when she took the time and trouble. She could be dazzling—she could be *Marilyn Monroe*—as she was the couple of times Joe took her to the St. Petersburg ballpark, and the boys on the club were so thrilled to meet her, to shake her hand, and get her autograph. (Joe didn't even mind that now.) . . . But that was an act of will on her part. That's what she didn't have the energy for—not often, anyway.

It had always been her will that made Marilyn

Monroe. And whatever else was wrong (a marriage, a movie, the studio, the industry) she'd always had that as her guide and spur—her own restless wanting. The real change now was she couldn't count on that. When she was weary or hurting, she found that reservoir was dry—she didn't want to be Marilyn Monroe, or anything else—and that was scary. While she was still in the hospital in New York, she'd had a visit from her friend, the poet Norman Rosten, and what he saw disturbed him ever after. "She was ill," as Rosten would later write, "not only of the body and mind, but of the soul, the innermost engine of desire. That light was missing from her eyes."

In Florida, Joe and Marilyn hid away, and took care of each other like an old married couple. She liked to do for him. She made his tea, and listened to his troubles. Joe Jr. had made it out of Lawrenceville, and was enrolled at Yale. But the boy wasn't happy, wasn't doing well, wasn't fitting in. He was drinking, and that made Big Joe angry. The boy had wrecked the car Joe bought for him—now he wanted another. *Did he think they grew on trees? . . .*

Joe tried to guard Marilyn's sleep, made sure she ate, and listened to her troubles. Her stomach was hurting her, and sometimes she had awful pain and cramps. She didn't know how she could find a psychiatrist in New York—she could never talk to Dr. Kris again. She liked her psychiatrist in L.A., Dr. Greenson, but she wouldn't move there just to talk to him. There was no one to talk to at night, no matter where she was, and sleep was impossible. *That's why those pills were so important. . . .*

She gave Joe not a whit of trouble. She made elaborate plans to sneak in a visit with her half-sister, Berniece (who lived in Gainesville, Florida). But then, Marilyn called Berniece in tears. She couldn't make the meeting. Joe had decided, that day was for fishing. Another day, he decided they had to hit the beach. So Marilyn (covered with clothes from her ankles to a large floppy hat) sat with Joe on a couple of deck chairs outside the hotel. One passerby stopped and asked for her autograph. Joe growled: "Leave the lady alone."

When the Yankees went north in April, Joe and Marilyn broke camp, too. They would be at the Stadium for opening day—honored guests in the press box. In fact, they were together almost every day and night, at the suite Joe used in the Hotel Lexington, or a few blocks away, at her apartment on East 57th— the place she used to share with Arthur Miller. Now that apartment was half-furnished. (Things Arthur liked had moved with him to the country house.) Some rooms had nothing in them but the white wall-to-wall carpet, with leftover stains from the basset hound, Hugo. (He'd moved with Arthur to Connecticut, too.) . . . Joe didn't like to leave Marilyn alone in that apartment. The way he figured, someone had to watch over her—and he was the man.

It was like he told her when he made his first gingerly push back into her life—that was a few months back, on Christmas night. As Marilyn recalled in a letter to Ralph Greenson, her L.A. psychiatrist, she was in the apartment with her new publicist, a woman named Patricia Newcomb, when a forest of poinsettia plants arrived. Marilyn asked Pat who they were from, but Pat said she couldn't tell: the card only read, "Best, Joe."

Marilyn said, "Well, there's only one Joe. . . ."

"Because it was Christmas night," as she wrote to Dr. Greenson, "I called him up and asked him why he had sent me the flowers. He said, 'First of all, because I thought you would call me to thank me,' and then he said, 'Besides, who in the hell else do you have in the world?' "

MOSTLY, SHE HAD HER STAFF FOR companions. They were at the apartment six days a week. There was her secretary (Arthur's former secretary), May Reis, a businesslike gray-haired woman who mostly kept to her cubbyhole office—an island of order amid Marilyn's oceanic mess. There was Hattie Stevenson, the stout cook, who arrived in the morning to poach Marilyn's eggs and mix her Bloody Mary, and spent the afternoon doing not much in the old-fashioned kitchen. And Lena Pepitone, the curly-haired Neapolitan seamstress and lady's maid, fought a losing battle for cleanliness in Marilyn's bedroom and closet. (Marilyn could rip thirty blouses off their hangers, before she found one that was not altogether terrible.)

Now that Joe was around, Marilyn often asked Lena to stay and cook supper—spaghetti with sausage, veal piccata . . . Lena cooked just like she did at home. And she was delighted to do it for Mr. DiMaggio, who was Lena's idea of the perfect man. "He may have been famous," as Lena remembered in her memoir, "but he was very sympathetic and easy to be with." She got him alone in the kitchen one night, and in Italian (for secrecy's sake), she brought up the big question on her mind. " 'Why don't you marry Marilyn again. She loves you. It would be wonderful for her.'

"Joe just shook his head sadly. He said that he loved her more than any other woman, that he'd do anything for her. But marriage . . . they had too many differences that just didn't work. He felt, as always, that her career was what was killing her." Then, Joe's rusty Italian ran out, as he brought up the word "Hollywood"—he made a face like he had a terrible pain, and held his stomach with both hands. . . . But Joe couldn't bring up that pain with Marilyn—not anymore.

The other subject Joe tried to avoid was Ralph Roberts, Marilyn's closest companion, confidant, and masseur. Ralph was a handsome, soft-spoken actor from North Carolina. He'd made a second career as Masseur to the Stars. But in those days, his career was Marilyn—Ralph would do anything for her. He'd show up in the middle of the night (or at dawn) if she needed a massage to get to sleep. He'd drive her to her doctors' appointments, or business meetings—whatever she had to do. He listened to her endlessly about her plans, her fears, suspicions, the scripts that came in the mail . . . the long and the short of it was Ralph loved her.

Joe didn't understand—or thought he understood too well. But it wasn't like he imagined. It was more innocent, and intimate. Marilyn could talk to Ralph about anything—almost everything. One evening that spring, Marilyn was telling Ralph about Joe's body—it was beautiful, rippled with muscle, but not bulky, every part in perfect form—like that statue, she said, Michelangelo's *David*. Then, she asked Ralph to walk with her to Joe's hotel. She got all dressed up—or dressed down, with her head scarf and shades—and they went to the Hotel Lexington. And there was Joe, who'd just come back from some dinner where Italian-Americans had honored him as Man of the Year, or Man of the Age, or something. And they'd given him, as Joe said, "a trophy for it"—which he showed to Marilyn and Ralph: a copy of Michelangelo's *David*. Joe started blushing and got mad when they burst out laughing.

But the Man of the Age couldn't push about Ralph's presence, either. Joe would grumble obliquely—like he had nothing against the guy, but . . . wasn't she taking advantage of Ralph? ("Oh, no!" Marilyn would say, "Ralph likes to do little things for me.")

In May, it was Ralph whom Marilyn took along to L.A., for meetings at the studio, and another procedure by her gynecologist (once again, for those cramps—her chronic endometriosis). Once again, Joe had roses delivered to her hospital room. And he sent letters—one of which was later found among her papers. Those three handwritten pages, on Hotel Lexington stationery, reveal a man who was trying to find common ground, without taking up too much ground himself.

Dearest, Had an early dinner at the Colony with George. Was able to relax and enjoy our boiled chicken as we were the only two people in the place. It's always nice to hear your voice and I well realize your phone bill runs into astronomical figures. I'd like to be able to tear mine up without opening the envelope this month—as I have talked to Joe [Jr.] quite a bit this month, trying to help resolve some of his present problems. You have been quite a help to me in so much as discussing Joe's affairs. . . . And dear, I want to thank you beyond words for helping relieve my mind. . . . I'm sure you're not interested about my every day activities . . . so I'll dispense of the boring details. However, I'm always interested in your activities. . . . It was nice to hear you say "you are gaining weight and

are slowly but surely rounding into form"
(WOW!!!!) Now I hope that the happiness
we all seek comes to you soon—so that friends
who give a damn will relish right along with
you. I better wrap this up as I feel mushi-
ness coming on. And so my dearest, good night!
My love, Joe.

BUT HOW COULD HE HELP HIMSELF,
when Marilyn needed him? He had to take care of
her. That was the role she cast him in. (As she told
one Danish journalist: "To know that Joe is there is
like having a lifeguard." And Marilyn always seemed
near drowning.) . . . That summer, back in New York,
she'd be wheeled into the Manhattan Polyclinic for
another emergency operation—gall bladder surgery,
this time—and once again Joe stood by as her protector in the hospital. (Marilyn wouldn't work at all in
1961, except one way or another on her health.)

In her weeks of recuperation after that surgery,
Marilyn would be joined in the East 57th Street
apartment by her half-sister, Berniece Miracle. The
house staff was also on duty, Ralph was back in New
York, on call. Marilyn's publicist, Pat Newcomb, flew
in from L.A. to be in daily attendance. And of course,
there were the doctors, who stopped by every afternoon to have a talk (and a drink) with Marilyn—and
they'd write her prescriptions for whatever pills she
fancied that day.

But as Berniece would remember, in her book, *My Sister, Marilyn: A Memoir of Marilyn Monroe:*

"The daily routine peaks for Marilyn when the doctor departs and Joe DiMaggio arrives for dinner. . . .

"Lena prepares a dinner each evening for four: Marilyn, Berniece, Joe and George Solotaire, a ticket broker in New York. . . .

"Sometimes when Joe and Marilyn were discussing something, George and I would go into the den to watch TV. We would watch a couple of programs and leave Joe and Marilyn alone. Joe acted as if he were still in love with Marilyn."

Well, that was true—and more: Joe was once again a man with love in his life. He'd put Marilyn to bed (he insisted, she had to rest), then he and Georgie would hit a few spots—it was always too early to sleep. They'd walk into a club to take in a late show, and a ringside table would materialize by magic—while the rest of the patrons applauded—the champ was back. At one exclusive *ristorante* on Park Avenue, Joe sat in for late supper with Eddie Arcaro and Rocky Marciano—and the place literally seized up with champions. (As Joe would remember with amusement, the headwaiter had to lock the doors.) When DiMag and the other Big Names made items in the next day's press, Joe didn't complain that it was time to leave town. In fact, he talked about getting a place in New York—an apartment of his own, home base—maybe it was time. When *Photoplay* followed up its first doubting salvo ("Will She Break Joe's Heart Again?") with a full investigation ("Marilyn to Wed?")—the magazine concluded: "Joe has changed in the years between. He is not the fiery combination of temper and brawn he used to be. . . . He's more understanding now, and he's eager for a home again."

But Joe's new understanding, his plans, his willingness to see and be seen, all rested on his confidence that Marilyn was safe and at home. When Marilyn suggested that she and Berniece could go out at night with him, Joe wanted no part of that.

"When she proposes the idea to Joe," Berniece would write, "he shakes his head determinedly. 'You'd be mobbed. Absolutely not.' "

During her two-week stay, Berniece and Joe got along fine. She found him "unpretentious . . . full of common sense and concern for Marilyn." Before Berniece went back to Florida, Joe even surprised her with a gift—an eight-by-ten glossy photo of himself in Yankee pinstripes—which he signed: *"To Marilyn's lovely sister, Berniece—whose pleasant company was appreciated . . ."* Ms. Miracle would save that photo ever after.

But she had only come to New York to help Marilyn—with anything, from changing bandages to walking Marilyn's new poodle pup . . . it seemed to Berniece that her sister had "so many problems!" And it wasn't long before Berniece discovered that one of Marilyn's problems was Joe.

"Dropping his second tea bag into the kitchen

trash can one night, Joe spies a discarded bill and idly fishes it out. He scans over the list of household supplies and wines that have been delivered in the afternoon.

"He grumbles loudly, 'This bill is not right! It's added up nearly double! Doesn't someone check these things when they are delivered?'

" 'I don't think that's any of your business,' Marilyn hisses, taking the bill from Joe."

Not long after that, Marilyn clued Berniece in on a couple of secrets. Number one was about that poodle puppy. The name was not Mop (as Berniece had first heard it)—though that name might have fit the shaggy ball of white fur. . . . But the dog was a gift from Frank Sinatra (no one was supposed to know that). And its name was Maf—which was Marilyn's joke about Frankie's menacing Italian friends.

The second secret, Marilyn said, was bigger. As soon as Berniece (and Joe) left town, Marilyn was going to Los Angeles—where she would be a guest in Frank Sinatra's house.

". . . To Berniece," as Ms. Miracle would write in her memoir, "this trip seems one of Marilyn's more tangible problems. Marilyn seems filled with apprehension because of Joe's jealousy, yet eager to go. 'You mustn't tell anyone,' she confides to Berniece. 'Especially Joe. I *am* going, nevertheless, because I need some total privacy.' "

As Ms. Miracle would also note: "Marilyn's desire

to avoid Joe's jealousy and her desire to hold his precious friendship place her on a tightrope of her own devising. . . ."

Of course, Berniece didn't know Frankie and his friends. If she had, she might have seen that Marilyn was walking on a tightrope with no net.

AS SOON AS JOE WENT ON THE ROAD for the Monette Company—in August 1961—Marilyn flew out to L.A. Her scar from the operation had healed, her strength was returning, she looked wonderful. She said she felt better than she had in years— and now, she was eager to work. She was happy to be back in Sinatra's town ("Frankie won't let me be lonely," she said) and even happier to be back with her psychiatrist, Ralph Greenson (she never had found another shrink she liked in New York). She had the air of a woman who was returning to her real life . . . and she was in trouble from the minute she landed.

She fell into the embrace of Sinatra and drugs with equal abandon. Just after she arrived, Sinatra took her out for a weekend cruise aboard his yacht. But Marilyn was becalmed on her own murky sea. In *Goddess: The Secret Lives of Marilyn Monroe,* Anthony Summers quoted Dean Martin's wife, Jeanne, who was also aboard that weekend:

" 'I remember going up to Frank's house before we

got on the boat. And he said, "Will you please go in and get Marilyn dressed, so we can get in the limo and go." She couldn't get herself organized.' . . .

"Jeanne Martin remembers Marilyn 'wandering around the dock, pitifully trying to find more pills. She'd be unable to sleep, and go lurching around half-dressed, trying to find someone who could give her "reds" at three o'clock in the morning.' "

By that time, it wasn't just reds—the sleeping pill, Seconal—but also Nembutal and phenobarbital (two other addictive barbiturates), or the knock-out drug chloral hydrate (what detective writers called "a Mickey Finn"), the tranquilizers Valium and Librium, or some combination of the above, recommended by one of her pals in pharmacopoeia—Sidney Skolsky, Monty Clift, or some other knowledgeable user. For quick action, Marilyn preferred to have her L.A. physician, Hyman Engelberg, administer a hypodermic "cocktail" of sedatives . . . or some days, it was a shot of tranquilizers mixed with speed to "revive Marilyn's energy." (Those were referred to as "vitamin shots.") Or if Engelberg wasn't around, there was Greenson, the psychiatrist, to offer more pills—Marilyn would poke the capsules with a pin to hasten the onset of oblivion.

Her relationship with Greenson had taken a turn away from standard Freudian therapy to something closer, messier, and more dependent. She saw him every day (phoned him day or night)—and not at his office—their sessions took place in his home. Greenson would depute his daughter, Joan, to take walks and talk with Marilyn before appointments. And afterward, Marilyn didn't go home, but stayed with the Greenson family for champagne, or dinner, or sometimes all night. For Marilyn, this was the caboose on the long train of older men who took her in and cast themselves as protectors. Greenson was the most dangerous of all—a trained psychological manipulator whom Marilyn obeyed as a patient, and revered for his degrees, his mastery of jargon, and his ready prescription pad.

By autumn 1961, Greenson had taken over her life. Friends, staff, colleagues were all "bad influences"—he was at war against all her other relationships. He counseled her to get rid of her agents, and sign up for representation instead with his brother-in-law (who was Sinatra's lawyer), Mickey Rudin. Ultimately, Greenson would even order Marilyn to send her best friend, Ralph Roberts, away. (Said Ralph Greenson: "Two Ralphs in your life are one too many.") . . . Greenson didn't even like the fact that Marilyn had her own home. (She'd rented another dingy one-bedroom in her old apartment complex on Doheny Drive.) Within months he would force her to buy a house near his (and like his, a Spanish colonial), where she would live with a companion of Greenson's choosing—in fact, with the woman who'd sold Greenson *his* house—a spooky gray-haired duenna-and-spy named Eunice Murray.

Of course, Greenson had sciency jargon to cover

all of these moves. (He was weaning Marilyn from *destructive sado-masochistic relationships.*) But in private, his language smelt of his own overspiced psychological soup. "This is the kind of planning you do with an adolescent girl who needs guidance, friendliness and firmness," Greenson wrote in one letter to a colleague, "and she seems to take it very well. . . . Of course, this does not prevent her from cancelling several hours to go to Palm Springs with Mr. F.S. She is unfaithful to me as one is to a parent."

By autumn 1961, even "Mr. F.S." had concluded that Marilyn was too much to handle. Sinatra backed away from their love affair. (Soon, he would announce his engagement to the actress and dancer Juliet Prowse.) But Marilyn was still a favorite with the members of Sinatra's "Clan"—and with a couple of adjunct members, the Kennedy boys from Washington, D.C. At the start of October, she was invited to dine with Robert Kennedy, at Peter Lawford's house (Lawford was married to Bobby's sister, Patricia). Marilyn had too much champagne that night, so the attorney general thoughtfully saw her home in his car. Later that month, Marilyn went again to the Lawfords' house, for dinner with her Commander-in-Chief, John F. Kennedy.

For four decades after, there would be speculation and debate about Marilyn's relationships with the Kennedy brothers. (One of them? Both of them? Both at the same time?) But in that season of Marilyn's dissolution, there wasn't much debate. Her affair with President Kennedy had to be the country's worst-kept secret.

Marilyn was so atwitter about "The President" (as she always called him, never "Jack") that she had to alert a couple of columnists—her pal Sidney Skolsky, and Earl "It Happened Last Night" Wilson—though, of course, they wouldn't use the item at that time. "I still find it grim to speculate," Skolsky would muse in his memoir, years later, "on what might have happened to me if I had tried to write about this romance in my column when it first came to my attention." Not that the pressure for silence came from Marilyn: as Skolsky remembered, she was so thrilled that *she* ("the little orphan waif," as Skolsky wrote) was involved with the Leader of the Free World—she could hardly *stop* talking about it. One night, early in '62, Marilyn was visiting at Bing Crosby's house in Palm Springs, and she phoned Ralph Roberts in the middle of the night to ask about a certain muscle in the back (the solus muscle, Ralph recalled). It turned out that the president, who was sharing her bed, had problems with his back, and Marilyn was sure the solus was at fault. She wanted Ralph's advice on how to ease that muscle—which advice Ralph offered . . . whereupon JFK took the phone to thank him ("Marilyn's told me good things about you . . .") and to wish him good night.

In Robert Kennedy's case, it's tempting to think there was more smoke than fire. His contacts with Marilyn in the fall of 1961 were mostly of a public sort—receptions, dinner parties, and the like. And Marilyn was so obviously working her agendas (for civil rights, and against commie witch-hunts), it was easy to explain why she monopolized Bobby's time whenever they were in the same room. His friends and staff all claimed that Bobby wasn't the philandering kind. And at one point, that autumn, Marilyn denied the affair to Ralph Roberts (to whom she told almost everything). She asked Ralph, one day, whether he'd heard rumors about Bobby and her. Ralph said, "You can't not hear. It's the talk of Hollywood." Marilyn said indignantly: "Well, it's not true. Anyway, he's too puny for me."

But by the spring or summer of 1962, Marilyn confirmed her relationship with RFK—this time to Greenson (to whom she did tell everything)—and in a manner so private and matter-of-fact that it is incontrovertible. By that time, Greenson was tape-recording Marilyn's free associations—these weren't regular therapy sessions, but simply Marilyn's thoughts—whatever came into her head. (Marilyn approved the taping, and ran the machine herself: she told Greenson he ought to patent the idea.) Greenson later played two tapes for John W. Miner, head of the medical legal section of the L.A. District Attorney's office. Miner made detailed notes at the time, and vowed to Greenson he would never reveal what was on those tapes. That vow Miner kept for thirty-five years, until the Greenson family released him from his promise, and he shared the contents of Marilyn's tapes with the dean of American diggers, Seymour Hersh, who was researching *The Dark Side of Camelot.*

In the two tapes Greenson played for Miner, Marilyn was speaking (as she said on tape) from her own bed, dressed only in a brassiere—taking breaks whenever she wanted, to go to the bathroom, or the fridge—directly addressing her psychiatrist, often in graphic language. As Miner reported: "There's no phoniness. There's no faking in the tapes."

She was reverent toward Greenson. ("Doctor, you're the greatest psychiatrist in the world . . .")

She was so grateful that he'd helped her to achieve—at last!—a true orgasm. (She said, if they really gave Oscars for the best acting in Hollywood, she would have won for faking it all those years.) Now, as she said, she wished Joe were with her, so she could "give him a real one."

Toward the president, she was devoted—not just as a lover, but as a political adherent and patriot. Near the end of the tapes, she spoke of herself in the third person:

"Marilyn Monroe is a soldier. Her Commander-in-Chief is the greatest and most powerful man in the world. The first duty of a soldier is to obey her Commander-in-Chief. He says do this, you do it. This man is going to change our country. No child will go hungry, no person will sleep in the street and get his meals from garbage cans. People who can't afford it will get good medical care. Industrial products will be the best in the world. No, I'm not talking utopia, that's an illusion. But he will transform America today like Franklin Delano Roosevelt did in the thirties. I tell you, Doctor, when he has finished his achievements he will take his place with Washington, Jefferson, Lincoln and Franklin Roosevelt as one of our greatest presidents. . . ."

But about Bobby Kennedy, Marilyn was worried. It wasn't the worry that conspiracy buffs always write about—that she'd threatened to tell the world about Bobby, or he'd threatened her with harm—because (drum-roll) *she knew too much.* . . . No, she was worried because she didn't know how to tell poor Bobby that they were, well—splitsville.

"I'm glad he has Bobby," she continued, about JFK. "It's like the Navy. The President is the captain and Bobby is his executive officer. Bobby will do absolutely anything for his brother and so would I. I'll never embarrass him. As long as I have memory I have John Fitzgerald Kennedy. But Bobby, Doctor, what shall I do about Bobby? As you see, there's no room in my life for him. I guess I don't have the moral courage to face up to it and hurt him. I want someone else to tell him it's over. I tried to get the President to do it, but I couldn't reach him. Now I'm glad I couldn't—he's too important to ask."

She said that with Greenson's help she would find the moral courage to tell Bobby the bad news herself. In Greenson, she'd found her savior. At one point on the tape, she told the doctor that after he had cured her, maybe he could adopt her—to be the father she had always wanted. And his wife, Hildi, would be her mother, and the Greenson children would be her brother and sister. As Miner reported, when Greenson listened to that part of the tape, tears were streaming down the psychiatrist's face.

DIMAGGIO VISITED IN HOLLYWOOD from time to time—whenever he wasn't working for Monette—and he didn't like what he saw. He didn't like the public part of Marilyn's life—she'd been ordered in for another picture with Fox, and that already had her half-nuts with worry. *Something's Got to Give* would be another stupid remake—Marilyn was panicky that it would be another dud. (In fact, Joe was told by Greenson that he thought she was suicidal: he'd ordered round-the-clock nursing care at Marilyn's apartment.) . . . And from what Joe knew about his girl's private life—well, that was worse. The way Joe told his L.A. pal, Harry Hall, Marilyn was drifting back to a life among people who didn't respect her.

Joe knew all about Sinatra and Marilyn—he could read the papers, like anybody else. But he'd also heard about the Kennedy boys—and he hated them worse than Sinatra. "Joe's attitude was, they didn't care about her," as Hall remembered. "She was a toy for them."

Harry Hall was a Chicago wiseguy who'd come

out to California before World War II. He'd known
DiMag since the early war years, when Harry gave
Joe a couple of paydays for exhibition ballgames in
L.A. Hall still had his mob connections in the early
1960s—but according to FBI records, he was working both sides of the street. (He kept himself out of
trouble by informing for the feds.) For DiMaggio, he
was simply a pal, part of the western branch of the
network. And as Harry remembered, at that time
DiMag was a pal in over his head—he didn't have a
clue what to do about Marilyn. One time, Harry gave
Joe a ride to Marilyn's place. She slammed the door
in his face. Joe just took it, and tried to shrug off his
embarrassment: "Well," he said to Harry, "one of
those days."

DiMaggio never knew where he stood with her
from day to day, or hour to hour. Joe showed up for
Christmas 1961—he may have been summoned by
Greenson—and that went great: Marilyn loved it, and
seemed to love him. (She always loved him at Christ-
mastime.) Joe put up a little tree, and they shopped
for ornaments in L.A.'s Mexican marketplace. (Marilyn was enamored of everything Mexican—Greenson's house was in the Mexican style.) Christmas
Day they spent at the Greensons', where the psychiatrist and his family treated Joe as the big attraction—
they talked baseball all day. New Year's Eve, Joe and
Marilyn stayed in, alone at the apartment on Doheny,
save for a visit after midnight by Greenson's daughter, Joan (and her date), who remembered Joe and

Marilyn curled up on the floor, roasting chestnuts on the open fire.

Still, the next time Joe arrived, February 1962, she stiffed him altogether. He came to L.A.—and Marilyn had gone to New York. . . . Two weeks later, Joe took her to the airport in Miami, whence she left for a shopping trip in Mexico—she wanted furniture for the new house Greenson had helped her pick out. Joe knew all about the house. In fact, he'd loaned her ten grand for the down payment. But he was mightily miffed when she came home from Mexico, not with furniture (that would be shipped later), but with a handsome young Mexican screenwriter named José Bolaños. DiMaggio got that news from the paper, too—when Marilyn showed up "tipsy" (as the papers phrased it), slurred of speech, and barely able to walk, wearing Bolaños (and not much else), to receive an award as the World's Favorite Female Star from the Hollywood Foreign Press Association. DiMaggio flew into L.A. the next day.

Bolaños was soon on a plane back to Mexico. He didn't have any other choice. Marilyn stuck him in the Beverly Hills Hotel—and then she never came back. The day after that awards dinner, she went to Greenson's house, and the shrink put her in a bedroom upstairs, under sedation and under his control. That's where Joe tracked her, after he flew in late that afternoon. Marilyn's biographer, Dr. Donald Spoto, got the scene from a student psychiatrist who was training with Greenson at the time.

"Joe DiMaggio came to the house, and Marilyn Monroe was upstairs. Learning that Joe had come, she wanted to see him. But Greenson forbade them to meet. He asked Joe to remain downstairs to talk with him, and after a while Marilyn began to make a minor fuss upstairs—like a person confined in a hospital against her will who wanted to see her family or her visitors. Nevertheless, Greenson insisted on detaining Joe, and Marilyn was eventually close to a tantrum. . . ."

Joe and Greenson had always gotten along fine. With DiMaggio's newfound respect for psychiatry, he'd never tried to argue with the doctor. And Greenson had treated him as a hero—and sort of a junior colleague. The way Greenson talked to Joe about Marilyn was a thorough breach of ethics. But DiMaggio was the exception to all rules, even those of psychiatry. Anyway, they agreed on Ralph Roberts, Sinatra, the Kennedy boys—on so many of Marilyn's friends—shrink and slugger were on the same side in those wars. But no matter what Greenson said (or how many diplomas he had on the wall) no one could keep Joe from seeing his girl.

"Joe excused himself," as the student psychiatrist remembered, "and insisted that he was going to go up to see Marilyn, and Greenson turned to me and said, 'You see, this is a good example of the narcissistic character. See how demanding she is? She has to have things her way. She's nothing but a child, poor thing.' "

Joe prised Marilyn out of Greenson's home, and got her back to the apartment on Doheny. Two days later, he was helping her move into her new house in Brentwood—on Fifth Helena Drive, near the Greenson residence. In the new place, Marilyn would be under the watchful eye of the "companion" Greenson had picked out—Mrs. Eunice Murray.

Mrs. Murray projected an unblinking calm and a constant grandmotherly disapproval. She could never be a real companion to Marilyn. Mrs. Murray never laughed at anything. But she seemed competent at setting up a house. And Joe was relieved there'd be someone on duty. It would be different, if he wasn't working. (He didn't need the money anymore—and he was getting tired of flying around the world on someone else's schedule.) If he could stick around, he'd keep an eye on things—he could be in the house, or close . . . at least he'd know what was going on. As it stood, Joe wasn't even sure about the lowdown he got from the shrink.

He had to know. That's why he hired L.A.'s celebrity detective of the moment, Fred Otash, to do reports on Marilyn. Otash had a big reputation—which he relentlessly promoted. But Joe's wiseguy pals said Otash could back up his talk. If Marilyn was running around with the wrong crowd, Otash would be the guy to find out.

IT WAS A ROLLER-COASTER RIDE, and Joe was hanging on. He never knew what the next curve would bring.

He'd fly into L.A. and visit at the new house, and Marilyn would settle into his arms like a kitten. She'd show him the new kitchen tiles, the brick path abuilding to the guest house in back . . . it was the first home she'd ever owned—she was in love with that idea, home—and Joe had helped her do that. They'd curl up on the living room floor (there was still no furniture—just white wall-to-wall, now stained with poodle pee) and Marilyn would muse about adopting a Mexican child—the orphans were so beautiful, she'd written a thousand-dollar check for them, and then she tore that up and wrote out ten thousand. *A real home with children, wouldn't that be wonderful?* Then, without pause, she'd be furious about her new picture—the studio idiots didn't know what they had. They'd had a perfectly good script from Nunnally Johnson (Joe and Marilyn's friend, who'd written *How to Marry a Millionaire*) and then they hired a new writer who wrecked it—she hated it. She hated them. They didn't want Marilyn Monroe! If she was going to do the picture, she wanted to be Marilyn Monroe—*and they didn't understand*. She should get out of pictures, never do another one. If she had another flop (she'd had two years of flops) she'd be out of pictures anyway—after this mess. But Dr. Greenson said she had to make the picture, and she was trapped, it was horrible. And she was broke—the house! (Why had she bought it? She cried at the closing.) But she felt better now that Joe was here. What she wanted was champagne. . . .

She always felt better when Joe was there—told him she did. He always told her she wasn't trapped. She could sell the house. She could quit the picture. She didn't have to do any of that. She could marry him . . . but he always said that with a shrug in his voice—to show he wasn't pushing, he didn't want to make her do anything, that's what he meant. And Marilyn didn't take it amiss. She never had a bad word to say about her exes—or to them—and marriage was a beautiful idea. But it was hard. She told Joe Jr. he shouldn't get married. He'd left Yale now— he'd joined the Marines—and he called from Camp Pendleton, whenever he was allowed to phone. He talked about proposing to his girlfriend, Pamela. But Marilyn was always against that. She told him, sometimes getting married just makes things harder— which, in a way, was the same thing she told Big Joe. But she loved him for asking—her Slugger.

Then, before he left town, Joe would meet with Otash, who'd give him his reports: Marilyn in meetings with the Kennedys at the Lawfords' beach house . . . Bing Crosby's house with JFK . . . a weekend with Sinatra's friends at Frankie's new casino resort, the Cal-Neva Lodge, on the border at Lake Tahoe. . . . One time, Joe made the mistake of getting the report before he saw Marilyn. He had to pick up Joe Jr. and the girlfriend, Pamela. And they all went to visit at Marilyn's house . . . until Joe brought up the name Bobby Kennedy—and the visit was cut short by an ugly fight.

On the road it was worse: Joe was on the roller coaster all by himself. More and more he chafed at his schedule—Air Force bases, naval stations, Army forts, *and what the hell did he care? . . .* Alaska to Florida, then over to Europe . . . that spring, Monette and Joe poked into Poland, and then they went to Moscow—because Monette wanted to see it. The only thing Joe wanted was the news from L.A. Of course, when he got it, his stomach would start to roil—every time he checked with another source, the news got more disturbing.

He'd hear from Joe Jr.—the boy had called twice last Saturday, but no luck—Marilyn wasn't home. . . .

In May, the newspapers were reporting trouble on the set of *Something's Got to Give.* Filming was delayed, as Marilyn Monroe failed to show—she was ill. . . .

Marilyn was back at the Cal-Neva Lodge, where Sinatra kept her hidden away in the private bungalows. (That news came from an authoritative source: Sinatra's partner in the Cal-Neva Lodge was Sam Giancana, who had brought in a manager—Paul "Skinny" D'Amato.) . . .

Big news from New York! On May 19, fifteen

thousand cheering Democrats filled Madison Square Garden (as Americans from coast to coast tuned in on TV) to celebrate the forty-fifth birthday of Jack Kennedy. And for the finale—to sing "Happy Birthday to You"—Peter Lawford introduced on stage . . . Miss Marilyn Monroe! Joe saw that even in Europe—couldn't get away from those film clips anywhere. There she was, in a skin-colored, skintight gown—rhinestones sewn in, shining from strategic spots (just "skin and beads," in the words of Adlai Stevenson) . . . and rubbing her hands up her thighs, across her belly, as she woozily breathed out her song—"making love to the president," as Dorothy Kilgallen wrote, "in the direct view of forty million Americans."

That's when Joe's thrill ride hit bottom. In his view, she might as well have told him to his face: he was only in line for sloppy seconds. As it was, she'd told the whole rest of the world: treat her as a toy and she'd put on a show for you—but love her all your life, like Joe DiMaggio did . . . *and she played him for a chump.*

He could count on one hand the times he'd given up—walked away from what was his. But he would walk away now. Enough was enough. In late May, on his last stop in Europe, Joe talked to Nunnally Johnson in London. Johnson's script for *Something's Got to Give* had by then been entirely rewritten, but his friends on the picture still fed him all the news—and Johnson said that Marilyn was in trouble. Most days, she didn't show up, and when she did she looked like she was walking underwater. Her shrink had left town, and she was sick, depressed, stoned all the time. If Joe didn't go to Hollywood to help her, Fox would shut that picture down. And Marilyn was going to be fired.

But Joe said he couldn't help. It wouldn't do any good for him to go to Hollywood. He'd try to phone—that was all he could do.

"I can't help the girl," Joe said. "I've tried."

But it wasn't that simple. He couldn't just will it to stop. If he could have walled away his heart, just by decision, it would have ended years before. But it never would end for Joe.

Marilyn did a scene naked for her movie. (Of course, that made the papers worldwide.) But it didn't help her. She got fired anyway. Fox shut down the picture and sued her for half a million dollars. Then the Fox publicity boys fed the papers on how she'd lost her marbles. Said the studio boss, on the AP wire: "She is mentally ill, perhaps seriously." Hedda Hopper had the quotes from Marilyn's director. "The poor dear has finally gone round the bend," said George Cukor. "The sad thing is the little work she did was no good. I think it's the end of her career." And with that, Cukor made his own prediction come true. No one would bankroll (or insure) a picture for her now. Marilyn Monroe was finished.

When Joe read those quotes in London, he caught a cab for the airport, he got on a plane—he flew straight to L.A. Picking up eight time zones, he could get there the same day. That was his chance. She was out of motion pictures. Joe went to Marilyn's house. She wasn't home. He waited . . . and when she came back, he told her: he would take her away. They'd get married. They could make a life! Now that movies were over for her—they could be happy.

And she looked at him like he was from Mars.

What was he talking about? No one was going to sink her! . . .

And then it turned into a terrible fight. (Marilyn would appear at her plastic surgeon's office the following day—she feared she had a broken nose.)

Joe left town as soon as he could—by the next day, he'd ended up in New York. He went to work on the ache in his heart like he used to go at it—he went to Toots Shor's. And as the regulars remembered that night, Joe wasn't drinking tea.

Toots didn't see Joe much in those days—still, he knew when Daig was sore. Toots stayed with him belt for belt. In fact, Toots was way ahead. Those were hard times for Shor, too—now that sportswriters, as he said, "were home watchin' TV and drinkin' malteds." Most nights, Toots was his own best customer. And that night, he had an excuse: his heart hurt for the Dago.

Joe and Marilyn hadn't talked since that fight. He couldn't even get her on the phone. She might be off with the Kennedys—how would he know? And the hell of it was, he wouldn't even care. He only wanted to tell her he was sorry. But, Jesus—she made him crazy. . . . Joe said, "What can you do with a girl like that?"

And before he thought, Toots said to his drink:

"Aw, whaddya do with any whore . . ."

He was sorry before it was out. But who could he tell? Before Toots had drawn another breath, Joe was up, and on his way out the door. Toots ran after him, calling his name—calling, "Joe! I'm sorry. I didn't mean it—JOE!"

But Toots would stay sorry. DiMaggio would never come back.

IT WAS ALMOST TWO WEEKS BEFORE Joe and Marilyn did talk. But then, it was like a miracle for Joe. He apologized. He asked her forgiveness for his anger, for his failure of control. He hadn't understood. And he promised to do better— if he could, if she would give him the chance—if she didn't hate him.

But she didn't hate him. It wasn't in her to hate him. She forgave him for the reason she always forgave him—and always came back to him—he cared so much, and never hid it. He couldn't hide it. He was so real.

She understood, he'd been mad. And God knows, she'd done some things to make him mad.

It was like her answer to her friend Ralph

Roberts, when he'd asked her, once, if Joe had ever hit her.

"Yes," she'd replied, "but not without cause."

And in that summer of '62, she thought Joe was right about so many things—big things they used to argue about. Some answers she spoke in interviews in those weeks might just as easily have come out of Joe's mouth. For instance, in her biggest interview, for *Life* magazine, she talked about fame:

"Everybody," she said, "is always tugging at you. They'd all like sort of a chunk of you. They kind of like to take a piece out of you."

On the topic of motion pictures, she was just as cool and world-weary: ". . . It might be kind of a relief to be finished with movie-making. That kind of work is like a hundred yard dash and then you're at the finish line, and you sigh and say you've made it. But you never have. There's another scene and another film, and you have to start all over again."

To Joe, she said maybe it was time to start over again. She was ready to change her life now. She had made a lot of wrong turns—she knew. She was ready to have done with the creepy Mrs. Murray— and maybe Greenson, too. (He'd shown his true colors when he met with the studio brass to offer his services—to deliver Marilyn Monroe for their film.)

Now, Marilyn told Joe, she knew who the people were who really cared for her. And Joe cared. She always knew that.

So, he flew across the country again, to visit in her new house—and that was wonderful. He came in late June, then three times in July. And it was easy, friendly, and full of fun. Fox wanted her back now, but she still wasn't working. They shopped. They went to the beach. They rode bicycles! At night, they'd bring in food and eat on her carpet— there still wasn't furniture. And then, they'd stretch out together, right there on the floor . . . and she told him—showed him—he didn't have to worry. In New York or Hollywood, picture or no picture, whatever else he might hear or fear, he was her guy.

And that July, Joe did what he'd never done with her, what he never could do before in his life. He told her it didn't matter what she wanted to do— about the pictures, or where they lived, or the shrink, or the pills, or the bills, or the . . . anything.

He *was* her guy—and he would stay with her.

He gambled with his life. He gave it to her. And he asked her to marry him again, and never leave him.

And she said yes.

JOE FLEW BACK EAST, THE LAST week of July. He saw Val Monette in Virginia, and told him the news. He was quitting the business as of July 31—Joe was headed back to California. He and Marilyn were going to be married again.

Marilyn flew into preparation for a new life. She was talking about a new movie—a musical with the songs of Jule Styne. (She made a date to talk with Styne in New York on August 9.) She shopped for furniture (Joe couldn't sit on the floor forever), and she called her lawyer, Mickey Rudin—she wanted to make a new will. But Rudin stalled her. He later said, he wasn't sure that she was of sound mind to make a will. But they agreed to meet on Monday, to talk about resumption of her contract with Fox for *Something's Got to Give*.

Joe had to fly back to New York and get his things from the Hotel Lexington suite. And he had to invite Georgie Solotaire for some "camping" next week in Los Angeles. Then Joe made preparations to fly west through San Francisco. He'd drop his stuff at the Marina house. And he had to make a charity ballgame appearance—on August 4, with Dom and Vince—a reunion of the famous baseball brothers.

Marilyn called the atelier of her designer, Jean Louis. He had famously dressed her some three months before, with the skintight, skin-toned, naked-save-for-sequins gown of scandal in which she had sung "Happy Birthday" to JFK. Now, Marilyn had ordered a new gown, but this one would be for Joe— her wedding dress. Marilyn scheduled the final fitting for Monday, August 6.

Joe called every night from the East Coast, and they planned the wedding for Wednesday, August 8—a true DiMaggionic affair: maybe fifteen guests in Marilyn's backyard—just the real friends—and not a word in advance to anyone who might talk.

Marilyn ordered new bushes and trees to be delivered Saturday, August 4. That day, she also talked to Ralph Roberts and invited him for supper, Sunday—they could barbecue steaks outside. She seemed fine to Ralph—a bit scattered, as always—she said they'd talk later to make firmer plans. But she spent all afternoon with Greenson, the shrink. And when Roberts called back after five P.M., it was Greenson who answered. When Ralph asked for Marilyn, Greenson said, "Not here," and he slammed down the phone. Two calls from Joe DiMaggio, Jr., also got refused. But on the third try, he got her—just after seven P.M. They talked for ten or fifteen minutes—she didn't mention his dad. It was Junior's news they talked about: he had broken his engagement with Pamela, his girlfriend. And Marilyn was delighted—she said he'd done the right thing. It was sad, she knew. But he was so young, and sadness would pass. She told him happily: wait and see—good things would happen.

When Big Joe showed up in San Francisco for that Saturday old-timers' game, he was happy, too—and the exemplar of discretion. Of course, he had to be interviewed—the reunion of DiMaggios was a municipal event. But he said not a word about Marilyn Monroe. And when his old pal, sports editor Curly Grieve, asked the Clipper if he was going to stick around in San Francisco, Joe said, sure—"for a while." What he meant was, he'd be leaving the next day. He'd told Marilyn they'd get together on Monday. He would fly into Los Angeles on Sunday night.

So he played three innings in the old-timers' game—took an oh-for-two—and took some razzing when Vince was the only DiMaggio to get a hit. But Joe took that fine. He was in good spirits all day . . . and through the night, into the wee hours of morning. Joe didn't get home to call Marilyn that Saturday night. After the game, he and Lefty O'Doul, with O'Doul's stepson, Jimmy, and a couple of Lefty's pals, went out for dinner, and then turned up at Bimbo's 365 Club—where they made a night of it amongst the showgirls, on Columbus Avenue—just like old times. Maybe Joe thought of that as his bachelor party . . . he could sleep in the next day, and still make the airport in plenty of time.

But Joe would not sleep in. Before eight A.M., his phone was ringing in the house on Beach Street. He woke, stiff and sour, grabbed the phone on the fourth ring. He could already feel in his back that the day would be gray, cold, and damp. "Mr. DiMaggio? . . ."

The voice was not familiar.

"This is Dr. Hyman Engelberg . . ."

Then he told Joe he was calling from Marilyn's house. There had been "a terrible accident." And the rest Joe heard in fragments, as his world fell apart.

". . . pronounced her dead this morning," the voice was saying.

". . . overdose . . . toxicology."

". . . claim the body . . . formalities."

". . . when you arrive. . . . I'm sorry."

Engelberg had pronounced Marilyn dead many hours before. Her lifeless naked body had been discovered before midnight. But after that, no one knew what to do. (The cops weren't even called until 4:25 A.M.) Meanwhile, Engelberg consulted with her lawyer, Mickey Rudin. But Rudin had never talked to Marilyn about "arrangements." Rudin consulted with her other attorney, the New Yorker Aaron Frosch—but Frosch also had no idea what to do. The mother was no help, locked away in an asylum. The sister lived—where was it? Georgia? Florida? . . .

Who in the hell else did Marilyn have in the world?

As Rudin recalled:

"We took the cowards' way out. We called Joe DiMaggio."

UNITED AIRLINES AGREED TO HOLD the nine A.M. plane. But Joe made the airport on time—and as the papers reported, "stooped by grief," "ashen," and "silent."

"Let's go," he said, on the steps to the plane. And then he didn't make another sound till landing in Los Angeles, near eleven A.M.

He would have to identify the body at the morgue. They slid her out of a drawer. She was nothing like his girl anymore. Her hair was thin and lank like an old woman's. Her face was flattened, bloated, sagging—after a pathologist had snipped the facial muscles to remove her brain. DiMaggio made a noise in the back of his throat and turned away.

She was gone. Everything he'd feared had come true.

They'd made her into a piece of meat.

They had killed his girl.

Tight-lipped, Joe nodded. He signed a form for the body to be released to the Westwood Memorial Park. His words were quiet, to the point, contained. Harry Hall drove him to the Miramar Motel, where Joe rented a room, locked the door behind them, sat down on the bed. Then the noise came out of Joe—like a roar from inside him—animal pain, it wasn't words at all. And he doubled over in tears.

THEY STAYED IN THAT ROOM ALL day. The front desk put through no calls. Telegrams piled up. Joe didn't read them. He sent a wire of his own to Berniece Miracle, asking permission to make funeral arrangements. Ms. Miracle wasn't home—and didn't know Marilyn was gone—till late in the day. When she finally got the news, and the wire from Joe, she gave DiMaggio the power to bury his girl.

News of the death hadn't made the Sunday papers. But the story was all over the radio. Harry turned it on. Joe turned it off. Then he turned it on again. The announcers called it suicide—or probable suicide. Police had already put out the word about her sleeping pills—empty bottles on the table next to her bed.

Even then, Joe knew that wasn't true. That couldn't be true. She had their life together to live for.

They had killed her. And Joe told Harry who they were: "the fucking Kennedys," as Harry quoted him. "Bobby Kennedy was the one Joe talked about. He hated him. And Sinatra—Joe cursed Sinatra, right that day, in the Miramar."

Even that Sunday, there were questions for police, for the newsmen and writers who'd flocked to the story. Mrs. Murray was quoted on the radio, saying she'd discovered Marilyn's body near midnight. But then the housekeeper changed her story for police, to put the discovery after three A.M.—

much closer to the time police were notified. There was also the mystery of the telephone receiver in Marilyn's hand. To whom was she calling with her final breath? (As the *L.A. Herald Examiner* would headline, next day: "Silent Phone Holds Key to Marilyn Death.") By that time the county coroner, Theodore Curphey, had acknowledged the questions and appointed a special "suicide team" to help determine a cause of death. Curphey appointed a psychiatrist and a psychologist from his staff to lead the inquiry. (He also assigned the deputy district attorney, John W. Miner, to secure an interview with Ralph Greenson—which was how Miner would come to hear Marilyn's tapes.) To the news media Curphey vowed "a thorough psychiatric approach," involving "all available evidence." But in the days that followed Curphey would, for some reason, take a dive on the case and issue a preemptive finding of "probable suicide." There would never even be a coroner's inquest. And the mysteries would fester for forty years.

Joe knew there was something wrong with that investigation within hours of his arrival in L.A. On that same Sunday, in the late afternoon—when he figured the newspapermen would have run for their offices to make deadline, and the gawkers would have gone home to dinner—Joe and Harry Hall went to Marilyn's house on Fifth Helena Drive. There was a sign on the door, announcing that police would prosecute anybody who entered. But the cops were still on scene, and of course, they let DiMaggio in. Joe marched straight into Marilyn's bedroom, barely glancing at the bed on which she'd been found. And he ignored the pill bottles that still littered the table. He went to her personal papers, which he flipped through hurriedly—but without avail. Later, he would complain to Harry that "her book" was missing. "It was her personal notes," as Hall remembered. Joe asked the police if papers had been removed. But no—they'd been examined on scene, in the search for a suicide note—and all left in place. "Joe kept looking for her book," Hall said. "But it was gone. He was hot about that." And Joe searched, also in vain, for her pearls. He had given them to Marilyn in Japan—they were his wedding gift . . . now he'd lost them, too. Stolen, he concluded.

But Joe did get a gift of his own from that futile search in Marilyn's house. It was a paper, folded once at its midpoint, and inserted amid the pages of her address book. Police had found it that morning. It was a letter to him. She must have started it Friday or Saturday, and when something interrupted her, she'd put it aside, tucked it away. Now it would be her last gift to him.

Dear Joe,
    If I can only succeed in making you happy,
I will have succeeded in the biggest and most

difficult thing there is—that is, to make *one person completely happy.* Your happiness means my happiness, and

WHEN BERNIECE MIRACLE ARRIVED on Monday, Joe quickly won her approval to make the funeral a strictly private affair. She and Joe, along with Inez Melson, Marilyn's old business manager, issued a statement that they all signed.

"... Last rites must of great necessity be as private as possible so that she can go to her final resting place in the quiet she always sought ..."

Apart from Berniece, Inez, and Joe (who would bring along Joe Jr. and George Solotaire) there would be only two dozen mourners—mostly people who had served Marilyn—a maid, her housekeeper, her secretary, her driver, her masseur Ralph Roberts, her psychiatrist Ralph Greenson (and his family), her publicist, her lawyers, a couple of hairdressers, and her loyal makeup man, Allan "Whitey" Snyder.

Years before—after her appendectomy, when she was only twenty-five—Marilyn had made Whitey Snyder promise that whenever she died, he would do her makeup. She would look as beautiful, as much a star, as ever he had made her look in her films. So it was Whitey whom Joe called, early Tuesday morning, when Marilyn's body had arrived at the Westwood Memorial Park.

"Whitey," Joe said, "you promised. Will you do it, please? For her?"

Joe didn't have to say any more. Whitey understood.

"I'll be there, Joe."

That afternoon, Whitey was there, to restore the world's most beloved face—while his wife-to-be (Marilyn's wardrobe assistant), Marjorie Plecher, tried to coax and pad Marilyn's embalmed body back to its famous form. When they finished, late Tuesday, that face and form were once again Marilyn Monroe. With a wig that she'd worn for *The Misfits,* a chiffon scarf around her neck, a pale green Pucci dress that she loved—she lay in repose in the bronze casket that Joe had bought . . . and she was as beautiful as ever.

Joe sat and stared at the face of his girl as Whitey and Marjorie left the mortuary.

When they came back, Wednesday morning, to touch up their work, Joe was still there in the same seat. He had spent all night gazing at her face, and talking to her, praying for her, crying. That morning, he simply stared, bent slightly forward in his chair—toward her—his hands wrung together in his lap . . . until he had to leave, to get dressed.

The funeral was scheduled for one o'clock that afternoon—Wednesday, August 8, 1962—the day Joe and Marilyn would have been remarried.

Joe and Joe Jr. rode to the chapel at the Westwood Memorial Park in a mortuary limousine. Junior was in his Marine dress uniform, Joe in a charcoal gray suit. In the limo, Big Joe started crying again—and without a word, he reached out, took Junior's hand—and held it all the way to the chapel. Joe Jr. would later say that was the closest he ever got to his dad.

Many in the crowd outside the gates were angry, as the hour of the funeral approached. Joe had excluded everyone in Hollywood—all the big wheels who wanted to say goodbye to Marilyn. People at the fence actually yelled at Berniece: *"There are people that really loved her out here!"*... *"Aren't you going to invite the Kennedys?"*... Inez Melson recalled that Frank Sinatra, Ella Fitzgerald, and Sammy Davis, Jr., tried to bull their way in with their own security guards. They claimed they had permission to go to the chapel. But they were turned away.... Peter Lawford complained that his wife *(the sister of the President)* had flown across the country from Hyannis Port, only to be barred from her friend's final rites. "It seems to be a concerted effort," Lawford said, "to keep some of Marilyn's old friends from attending." Even the lawyer Mickey Rudin, who *was* invited, protested to DiMaggio that he was keeping out a lot of important people—studio heads, directors, stars—and what was Rudin supposed to tell them?

"Tell them," Joe growled, "if it wasn't for them, she'd still be here."

In the chapel, a nondenominational minister

from a neighborhood church conducted the service. The funeral director's wife played the organ—one of Marilyn's favorite songs, from *The Wizard of Oz,* "Over the Rainbow." At Joe's request, Lee Strasberg, Marilyn's teacher, delivered the eulogy.

"Marilyn Monroe was a legend," he began. He was reading through tears at first.

"In her own lifetime she created a myth of what a poor girl from a deprived background could attain. For the entire world she became a symbol of the eternal feminine.

"But I have no words to describe the myth and the legend. Nor would she want us to do so. I did not know this Marilyn Monroe, nor did she.

"We, gathered here today, knew only Marilyn— a warm human being, impulsive and shy and lonely, sensitive and in fear of rejection, yet ever avid for life and reaching out for fulfillment. . . ."

Strasberg spoke for five minutes. His text was her talent—which, he assured them, "was not a mirage."

"Now, it is all at an end," he said.

"I cannot say goodbye. Marilyn never liked goodbyes, but in that peculiar way she had of turning things around so that they face reality—I will say *au revoir.* For the country to which she has gone, we must all someday visit."

At the close the mourners stood, and most turned toward the door for the walk to the crypt where she would be entombed—about two hundred yards away. But Joe DiMaggio lingered until the others who wanted to say goodbye had passed by her coffin. And then, before the casket was closed, he bent over her and placed three roses in her hands. And sobbing aloud, with his last kiss, he told her: "I love you. I love you. I love you."

HE STAYED IN L.A. FOR A COUPLE OF days. He didn't really know where to go. Every place he thought of had too many memories. But still, he'd have to go somewhere—out of her town. He could never turn around without seeing her there, in the corner of his eye.

And the papers there were full of her—with more and more questions fueling the fever. Peter Lawford came forward as the "mystery caller"— he'd talked to Marilyn that Saturday night—and he quoted her last words to him (or maybe he wasn't really quoting): "Say goodbye to Pat, say goodbye to the president, and say goodbye to yourself, because you're a nice guy." Then, she didn't hang up, but simply dropped the phone. That put the press back on the suicide theory. . . . But then came news that the autopsy had found no residue of sleeping pills in Marilyn's stomach. How could she have killed herself with bottlesful of pills—and there was nothing left of them in her system when she died? . . . And by the end of the week, the press got ahold of a fresh and evocative fact: Marilyn had ordered a thousand-dollar gown from her designer, Jean Louis . . . now, what the hell could she have been planning?

By that time, Joe had to get away. He and Harry Hall and their pal, Sugar Brown, were headed down to Mexico—where at least Joe wouldn't understand the news. So that Friday, two days after the funeral, he stopped by the cemetery office, just once more, to look over the cards and leaf through hundreds of telegrams, and see the piles of flowers that had been delivered. Joe had already arranged for his own flower deliveries—roses for Marilyn's crypt, twice a week—and forever. Just as Marilyn had asked, so many years ago.

When Joe was ready to leave, he wanted to stop by the crypt, to say goodbye or tell her he'd be back. But the cemetery gates were wide open, now, and fans had been streaming in—hundreds every day—and they'd kneel by her crypt, or feel her plaque, and leave notes or flowers. They were around her all the time. There were twenty or thirty of them over there now. Maybe that's the way it would be from now on—she belonged to them, after all.

With an air of dejection, Joe told the cemetery manager, Guy Hackett: "Well, I guess I can say goodbye now."

Hackett looked over toward Marilyn's tomb, and told Joe: "Just wait a moment."

Then he went to the fans, and explained that Mr.

DiMaggio would like to have a moment with his—
with Miss Monroe. And an extraordinary thing
happened: all the faithful around Marilyn parted,
and stepped back, as Joe DiMaggio approached.

Because they all knew, he was her worshipper.
He was the one who had burned for her. He was
the one who would come to her, to help her, to
carry her, or bury her—to the very end.

So, in the end, she was his.

That first time, it surprised him, pleased him,
and he was grateful. But in time, he would come to
see this as his destiny and due. And he would hold
on to Marilyn Monroe—as he would hold on to
everything that was his—for the next forty years.

Because in death, he did possess her—as he
never quite could in life.

BOOK IV

THE GREATEST LIVING . . .

1989–1998

✦

As an A's coach, with Governor Reagan.

Thumping the tub for Mr. Coffee.

**In the San Francisco earthquake,
October 1989.**

CHAPTER 17

◆

YOU'D THINK—WHEN THE LAND starts to shudder and roar, and splits apart to swallow bridges and cars . . . when the rocks of the earth smash together, heaving houses like toddlers' toys . . . you'd think all the people would be the same. An earthquake must send a shudder through every helpless heart. What is any man in the face of ineluctable tectonic force? You'd have to think—when every man must fear, with a wakening reptile-brain jolt of panic . . . that must overwhelm, at least for the moment, our small distinctions of self and style.

And people did think so—or at least said so—when the avid news crews of the western world started filming, after the San Francisco earthquake in October 1989. The city was packed with crews already, for the Bay Bridge World Series—the Giants against the local rival Oakland A's—first time in history, the town was in its glory . . . and then, just as Game Three was to start, the quake hit and the newsies jumped to it. Almost instantly, there were horrific aerial shots of highways crumpled, whole blocks afire; there were death counts, pleas and pronouncements from the mayor, the governor;

736

live shots of firemen, police, emergency room personnel; but mostly interviews—scores of witnesses, victims, helpers, neighbors . . . and all, or mostly all, expressing the same oddly ennobling thought: they had run out to the street, all the citizens together; they had fled with, huddled among, and clung to perfect strangers; and now everybody was helping everybody, because . . . *they were all in the same boat.*

But they didn't know Joe DiMaggio—though he was a neighbor, too. They might have seen him, that famous, dapper seventy-four-year-old who took his walks on the Marina streets. They knew his house. They probably thought they knew him, or knew things about him:

A very quiet gentleman . . .

So private since he'd left baseball!

And doesn't he still send roses to Marilyn Monroe's grave? . . .

They couldn't have known much. Joe had seen to that. No one really knew what it meant to have spent a half-century being precisely and distinctly DiMaggio—what we required Joe DiMaggio to be. No one knew, as he did, what it cost to live the hero's life. And no one knew, as he did, precisely what it was worth.

If the neighbors had known, they would have understood: DiMaggio had his own boat—his alone. No matter the emergency, he'd steer his own course—for him alone. They would have known—

even in an earthquake—DiMaggio would have his own destiny, apparently blessed from above.

TO UNDERSTAND YOU HAD TO SEE him, first, where he sat as the quake struck—to be precise, on the field of Candlestick Park, in one of the special seats installed for the Series in front of the normal box seat railing. This was appropriate because, if he'd been sitting in the stands—anywhere in the stands—he would have been in company with sixty-two thousand others in the stands. Or, more likely, he would not have come. To put DiMaggio among fans would have ignored his standing in the Great Game—to be precise, as Baseball's Greatest Living Player—which was the epithet he insisted upon, when he was publicly introduced. (But this was better: Joe had the Greatest Living Player's seat, and he wasn't introduced.)

He was sitting next to the Oakland A's dugout, which was proper because he was, as ever, an American Leaguer. Besides, the A's were one of his teams, the only big league club he'd worked for—apart from the Yankees, of course. In '68 and '69 he'd served as a coach (with vice president's rank) for Charlie Finley's Oakland A's. It was a not-quite-ready-for-prime-time ball club—and looked even worse in Kelly green uniforms. But DiMaggio needed two more years of employment to qualify for baseball's maximum pension (which pension he began to receive some five years later, and which he never touched, but piled up in a satisfying stack). Even thereafter, through the 1980s, the A's would call DiMaggio for special events, to come to their park, to be introduced, to be cheered by the fans as he threw out the first pitch—for a decent fee. More than decent, actually, because the A's did not cavil when DiMaggio asked for transcontinental first-class airfare back and forth from New York or Miami—when Joe was actually in San Francisco, which was a twenty-dollar cab ride . . . or would have been, if Joe hadn't brought along some pal, who'd ride him to Oakland for free.

He was sitting in company with Bobby Brown, third baseman for the Yanks in the 1940s, when Joe was the eminence in the old Bronx clubhouse. Normally, DiMag would not have sat with another player—he still wouldn't be "part of the gang." (He wouldn't even go to Cooperstown, where the players who gathered could be described as his peers.) But Bobby Brown was an exception. He had become a successful cardiologist, and now served as president of the American League. You could say he and Joe were friends. And Joe had his seat at Dr. Brown's invitation—Bobby gave him the ticket.

Of course, DiMaggio got tickets, too—all the baseball tickets he wanted, any game he wanted—All-Star games, playoff games, World Series . . . but he sold those. Like all his SuperBowl tickets: Joe could make a stack with the tickets he got from the NFL, from the clubs, from companies or the rich guys who owned them. Joe gave them to Ben Langella, who was a banker in a suburb south of San Francisco—and Ben would turn those tickets into cash. Ben took care of a lot of little things for Joe, and the Clipper would come to Langella's savings-and-loan, down near the airport, almost every day to give Ben some new job. Or he'd ask: "How you doin' with the tickets?" And Ben would say: "Good, Joe. Eighteen thousand dollars. I got 'em all sold." Joe would say, "Not so fast. I can get more." Tickets were a fat five figures for DiMaggio every year. And you couldn't say Joe wasn't grateful. Ben Langella had a seat on the Candlestick field, too—same row as Joe.

That was still how Joe paid off: his company was currency, sufficient to any cost. Now, in Joe's seventy-fifth year, that had become his modus operandi—as close as he came to an article of faith. One time, at Joe's house, a pal and business associate was needling DiMag about the money he'd made for him, checks he'd written to him, all the stuff he'd paid for—and what had Joe ever paid? Joe turned his poker face on him, and replied: "You're here, aren't you?" . . . In the old days there had been occasional moments when it pleased Joe to give away that currency—especially to people who didn't ask, or weren't in position to expect anything—like kids, or guys minding their own business in a bar or a restaurant. Joe would hang around, and even talk, so he wouldn't be alone—unless they asked for something, or called attention to *themselves with Joe* . . . then he'd get his back up and walk out. But lately, the marketplace kept pushing the value of Joe's company higher. By 1989, he was commanding forty to fifty thousand dollars a day for autograph shows and memorabilia sales. And for the most part, he'd stopped doing anything for free. As for friendship— well, the old pals he'd hung around with for fun were gone. New pals were in the business of taking care of Joe, somehow.

That day, in the special seats at Candlestick, there was Sam Spear, the PR guy at Bay Meadows Race Track, where Joe would spend some days. Sam would make sure Joe was comfortable in the press box or the Directors' Room, with a table to himself, so he could look at his mail or think about placing a two-dollar bet, and none of the fans could get near him. That was how Sam earned his World Series ticket—and, of course, he called himself Joe's pal. But DiMaggio had his doubts about Spear: he was getting to be like all the rest—presumptuous about the palship. (And Joe's doubts were borne out within a couple of months, when Sam threw a birthday party for Joe at the track. It was up in the Directors' Room; Sam had the place full—must have cost him a bundle—but Joe didn't like the crowd Sam invited. Then Sam put up on the big tote board that Joe D. was at the track, celebrating his birthday . . . DiMaggio threw a twenty on his table and walked out.)

Ben Langella had met Joe at the track, too. That was more than ten years ago, in the press box—Joe was going through his brown paper sack of mail. Someone told Joe that Ben ran a bank in Millbrae, and Joe got an idea. He turned to Ben: "Do you have anyone at your bank who could type some letters for me?" Ben smiled sweetly. "I can type, Joe." Joe was at the bank, nine A.M. the next day. Ben had been writing Joe's letters ever since. And Joe had been good for Ben. People came to Ben's office of Continental Savings Bank just to see DiMaggio napping in the armchair near Ben's desk. When Joe was in a good mood, Langella would slip him three or four balls to sign—Ben would hand those out to good customers. Langella got his branch up to $130 million in deposits that way . . . and that didn't count Joe's money in there. You couldn't really count on Joe's money. He favored hundred-dollar bills, in safe deposit boxes—like an old Papa who'd tuck cash in the mattress. Joe stuffed so many hundreds in his box that Ben told him, "Joe, don't put any more in there. We'll have to get 'em out with dynamite." (Like most jokes in those days, Joe didn't get it—or didn't choose to get it: "No," he said. "There's room for more.")

Langella had become a man of all work for Joe— chief of the San Francisco branch of the network—it wasn't just letters, now. Ben would field his calls, screen his offers, put him in deals, take him to lunch, ride him around. Langella would drive Joe's car—his Acura—to San Jose every six months, take Joe to the dealership, where Joe would sign balls for everybody who'd bought cars since his last visit. Then the dealer would give Joe a brand-new Acura. Joe would move his tape of Hemingway's *The Old Man and the Sea* (it was Spencer Tracy's voice: "I would like to fish with the Great DiMaggio. They say his father was a fisherman . . .") from the six-month-old Acura into the new Acura. Then Ben would drive Joe home again. And they'd always stop at a fishmonger Ben knew—a Greek named Manaidas, a beautiful fish place— where they were so honored by DiMaggio's visit that they'd load him up with fish, whatever he wanted. They'd pack the new Acura's trunk, and put some extra in the back seat . . . until one day Manaidas asked Joe to sign something, and Joe wouldn't do that—so Manaidas told him, no more fish. Now Ben was looking for a new fish guy. That sort of service had earned Ben his Series ticket.

Actually, Ben had half-a-ticket, once they got in the park—they rip everybody's ticket at the turnstile . . . everybody but Joe. DiMaggio wouldn't let them rip his ticket. A whole ticket was worth more in the memorabilia business. (And it would not escape Joe's notice—after the quake hit—that he had a pretty good item: the Only Series Game in History

Canceled on Account of Earthquake . . . and he's got the only mint ticket. Not bad.)

Anyway, it was just after five P.M., a half-hour till game time, and DiMag was talking idly with Bobby Brown—baseball chat—but staring straight ahead, with a look of doleful concentration, like he had to watch all the pregame stuff. Joe knew if he sat back, or smiled, or turned and looked around, that would give fans license to approach and ask him to sign things. If even one guy got to him, there'd be a million fans on his neck all day. So everything in Joe's countenance advertised that he was unavailable. He had his legs crossed with his arms across his knees— a bit of self-protection from his arms, on both sides. His shoulders were hunched—he was hunched all the time, now, with the scoliosis in his back. He had his great nose pointed out to center field, his dark eyes focused at a distance, as if he meant to descry the stitching on the color guard uniforms. "Look at that power alley," Joe said, shifting his stare to the left center field wall. "What's it say?" Brown grinned at the memory of four hundred sixty-one feet to left center in the grand old Yankee Stadium. Then he read out the number from the Candlestick fence: "Three eighty-five, Joe."

DiMaggio snorted. "That's a bunt."

But when everything stopped, what was Joe supposed to stare at? At first, he didn't know it was an earthquake. He didn't feel the stands sway: he was on the field—didn't feel a thing. *What's the hold-up? . . .* Then he was annoyed. He'd got a limo to take him to the ballpark. *Now they're gonna cancel the game?*

But word from radios was sweeping the stands—this was a bad one: the Bay Bridge was out! People started leaving, and DiMaggio relaxed. It was bad enough, no one was looking at him. Then, the announcement—please file out of the stands, onto the field. That got DiMaggio up in a hurry: *Sixty thousand fans, on the field with him?* . . . And then, from the radios: fires raging in the Marina. *That was Joe's house! . . .* Ben Langella had hustled off to call his family. So Sam Spear walked DiMag out to the Giants players' parking lot, where the limo waited. And Joe was on his way home before most of the fans even got to firm ground.

THERE WAS ACTUALLY A VOTE, IN 1969, for baseball's Greatest Living Player. It was for a dinner to celebrate baseball's centennial—baseball writers, mostly, and mostly New Yorkers. It wasn't official. There wasn't any nationwide poll. Of course, Ruth, Cobb, and Gehrig were (as Stengel used to say) "dead at the present time." But Ted Williams, the last man to hit .400, was very much alive in memory and person. The voters all had fresher visions of the modern greats—Musial and

Mantle had recently retired; Mays and Clemente were present-day All-Stars. . . . Still, it wasn't even close. Even dimmed by two decades' distance, one name, one man stood out alone. DiMaggio walked away with the honor, as he'd won every other accolade in baseball—without apparent strain.

Why? What was it about DiMag?

Well, you could keep it simple—call it the destiny of talent. Of the five things a ballplayer must do—run, field, throw, hit, and hit for power—DiMaggio was the first man in history who was brilliant at five out of five. (One time, when Joe complained about the fuss people made—"I don't understand all this limelight!"—his pal Eddie Liberatore said: "Look, Joe. God made Mozart and He said, 'You're gonna be a genius for music.' He made Michelangelo, He said, 'You're gonna be a genius for art.' He made you— 'You're gonna be a genius for baseball.' " . . . Joe thought that over, and conceded: "You might be right.")

Or you could talk about the only attribute that Joe would bring up: DiMaggio-as-Winner. In his thirteen years, his Yankees won ten pennants, and nine world championships. That was a record unmatched by any player in history. (As his teammate the shortstop Phil Rizzuto recalled: "You'd just turn around and see him out there—and you knew you had a pretty good chance to win.")

Or you could talk (as the voters did, at that dinner) about what DiMaggio couldn't do. He couldn't misjudge a fly ball in that vast Stadium center field; couldn't look bad on a low, slow curveball; couldn't ever rile an umpire against him, or act in an unbecoming way toward opponents. He never seemed to throw to the wrong base, never ran the basepaths stupidly—he just *couldn't*. For it wasn't that DiMaggio was often good, he was almost never bad. (All through the thirties and forties— every time he came to the plate, through six thousand at bats—fans were two and a half times more likely to see him smash an extra-base hit than they were to see him strike out.)

It was often said—for want of better—that Joe D. was "a natural." In fact, he was the un-natural: over a span of sixteen years, he'd stood against the humbling nature of the game. He excelled and continued to excel, against the mounting "natural" odds. He exceeded, withal, the cruelest expectations: He was expected to lead and to win—and he did. He was expected to be the best—and he was. He was expected to be the exemplar of dignity, class, grace— expected even to look the best. . . . And he looked perfect.

And, of course, that didn't stop with the forties, or with retirement—that wasn't about what he did on the field, but who he was—that was why he won that vote in a walk. You could also say that was where destiny ended, and gave way to a lifetime of doing. DiMaggio did for us—for the sake of our good opinion—through every decade, every day.

He was, at every turn, one man we could look at who made us feel good. For it was always about how *we felt* . . . with Joe. No wonder we strove for sixty years to give him the hero's life. It was always about us. Alas, it was his destiny to know that, as well.

THE OLD HOUSE ON BEACH STREET was the only home Joe had ever bought. What griped him was he had to buy it twice: first time was for his parents, after his second year in the bigs. But when Giuseppe and Rosalie died they left the house to all the kids—Joe had to buy out his siblings . . . and the second purchase cost more than the first. (After forty years, Joe was still grumbling about that deal.) Of course, now he could sell it for a million—but he wouldn't. That would bring publicity—and taxes.

Taxes had driven him out of San Francisco. He wasn't a resident anymore—not officially. He got a bug up his nose about the state income tax. They had the nerve to come after him for all the cash he took for ads, appearances, autographs . . . they wanted him to pay a million dollars. So, Joe screwed them down to four hundred thousand, and changed his residence to Hollywood, Florida. Of course, it was kind of a dump, but there was no income tax, no estate tax—and Joe wasn't sentimental about hometowns. In fact, he'd just had a

go-round with the first hometown, Martinez, California. Talk about a dump! . . . But Martinez was
always trying to make a big deal out of being the
birthplace—the Cradle of Clipperdom. So, lately,
they'd found his old boat—the Chris-Craft Joe got
on DiMaggio Day, 1949. A cousin in Martinez had
kept it for Joe—but the cousin was dead, now, the
boat was a wreck. The town fathers wanted to fix
it up, and put it in their new waterfront park. So
Joe said, okay, and they worked the boat over like
a pharaonic relic—restored the wood, buffed the
brass till it gleamed—and put it on a pedestal in
the park. They asked Joe to come for the dedica-
tion. DiMaggio took his $24,000 tax deduction and
told 'em to stick it up their ass.

But the house in the Marina was different. That
was about who he was. He'd put the house in his sister Marie's name—she still lived downstairs. Now,
she was more than eighty years old, with one heart attack behind her—but she still kept that place pin-
neat, mowed the grass in back, dragged the hose
around to water the garden. (Joe wouldn't spring for a
sprinkler system, or a power mower.) And still, Marie
took care of Joe's mail—kept the letters with names
she recognized in brown grocery sacks, and marked
the ones from autograph seekers or anybody else:
"No longer lives here." (She had a deal with the post-
man, so Joe wouldn't have to buy stamps to send
those back.)

When the earthquake hit, Marie had run out the

door—didn't even stop to grab clothes. She found her neighbor, Rose, amid the crowd on Beach Street. The dust, the smell, the noise was awful. Things were crashing in the houses. The house two doors away was coming apart, tumbling down. So Marie and Rose got out as fast as they could. (They would end up at Rose's friend's house, where they'd sleep for the next few days—politely declining the Red Cross food—till it was safe to stay home again.)

By the time Joe got to the Marina, the streets were a horror show: buckled pavement, crumbling houses, broken concrete, glass, wires, fires. Military police in cammo gear had been mobilized to cordon off the area. The firemen had rushed through and broken into houses to shut off the gas. Rescue workers were already hunting for survivors who might be trapped under rubble. Any extra men were pinned down fighting, or trying to contain, the fires. No one was allowed to go in there, except for firefighters, cops, the water main guys, gas and electric . . . and Joe. A fire captain and police officer broke away to walk the Jolter in. On his block of Beach Street, there were three houses down in ruin, an apartment building was cockeyed, menacing the rest of the buildings. And amid the chaotic destruction, Joe's house was . . . fine.

The front gate was twisted and the door was open where the firemen had to break in, but the building looked solid, the grounds were undisturbed. And inside there was, well . . . a bit of dust. Maybe there were new plaster cracks. But nothing crumbled. Nothing burned. Nothing fell. Not one dish was broken. There was his portrait of Marilyn on the wall of the living room. And the larger-than-life painting of himself in a shoulder-padded 1950s suit. There, in its place of honor on the TV, was his proudest new possession: the baseball signed by Ronny Reagan and Mikhail Gorbachev, when Joe was at the White House a couple of years before. And there, in its accustomed place on the fridge, was his proudest old possession: the silver humidor engraved with the names of his Yankee teammates, who gave that gift to Joe after The Streak, in 1941. Joe took a minute to go upstairs, to his private quarters, and came back with his big right hand around the neck of a garbage bag. No, no, he said, he'd carry his own. He left the house without another glance around.

He could see, everything was in its place, except his sister. Marie was gone, and he had no way to find her. He wasn't seized with fear for her. Panic was never Joe's style. It was more like the last egg in the carton—he couldn't close the lid until he knew where his sister was. The police and fire brass walked Joe out to the yacht harbor—the open space that the neighborhood folks called Marina Green. That's where the emergency management teams had set up shop, where residents had gathered—and the news crews, of course—who flocked to DiMaggio. And for once, he didn't duck.

There he was, full-frame in their cameras, standing so humbly, like all the other dispossessed. And look! The Great DiMaggio was dragging out a garbage bag. Uncomplaining—no, he didn't want help.

He was fine, he said to the cameras. He'd been at the ballgame. He'd find a place to stay. His house was not a worry. . . . But he'd like to get in touch with his sister.

Within minutes, the news was everywhere in San Francisco—TV, radio, police and fire scanners, the National Guard, the mayor's command post: *Joe DiMaggio is looking for his sister!*

That was classic Joe: grace is just another word for no wasted motion. Of course, Marie got the news, she called in, to say she was all right. Before full darkness fell upon the shaken city, Joe DiMaggio's world was back in place.

And Joe would be comfortable that night, too—at the Presidio Club. He was an honorary member—didn't have to pay dues. But he knew they kept a few quiet guest rooms upstairs. And he'd sleep well there—with the garbage bag, which held six hundred thousand dollars, cash.

THE ODD THING WAS, THE FIREMEN, police brass, the newsmen, everybody in Marina Green . . . when they talked about the earthquake, what they brought up was: *They saw DiMaggio*. Of course they felt better: wherever he went, everybody else was more notable for having been there with Joe—which had been his privilege and problem for fifty years.

That, and when they met him, they thought they knew him. That was the worst—the presumption of intimacy. Like the movie actor Aldo Ray, who walked up to Joe in the press room at the track in Vallejo—middle of a crowd of guys—and said, "Hey whatever happened t'that blonde you had? . . . I gotta blonde, too. She's the best cocksucker you ever saw—just like that one you had." Then he stuck out his hand, like him and Joe were gonna chew the fat about Marilyn. But DiMaggio was already on his way out the door, to the parking lot.

The real problem was, we all did know him, somehow—he'd been with us so long. In fact, you could say that in the nation's life, he was the first guy we knew like that—as a public person for all of us—and maybe we took liberties, as we would with any friend of our youth. It wasn't really his doing, but he came along just as we found the means to peer into our heroes' lives. It was only an accident of timing—small solace: you could say the same about a train wreck.

There were moments when he tried to protest—to tell the country and the world to back off—what we were looking for, he couldn't give . . . like the day in the 1960s, when a brilliant young writer named Gay Talese, on assignment for *Esquire,* tracked DiMaggio to the family restaurant at Fisherman's Wharf. Talese simply couldn't be ducked—and Joe got angry: "You are invading my rights. I did not ask you to come. I assume you must have a lawyer, you must have a lawyer, get your lawyer!" Talese wrote how he tried to tell Joe, he had come as a friend: "I don't want to cause trouble. I think you're a great man, and . . ."

"I'm not great," DiMaggio cut in. "I'm not great," he repeated softly. "I'm just a man trying to get along."

But Joe couldn't walk away from the hero game—not forever—what else did he have? He took a chance in the 1970s on TV ads—the Bowery Bank in New York, then Mr. Coffee, nationwide. Joe still wasn't comfortable on TV. But the money was good, and those were scripted spots. He could do each ad a hundred times, if he chose. And the agency men wanted exactly the DiMaggio he preferred to show: quiet, dignified, solid, and calm . . . a bit aloof even from the commerce that landed him on the screen.

It worked out brilliantly for everyone involved. The ad men and the companies thought they were pitching to an older demographic—solid citizens in their fifties and sixties (good credit risks, and coffee drinkers), who'd seen DiMaggio play ball. But they got much more, when younger folk, even kids, hooked on to Joe as a TV icon—it wasn't about baseball, or banking, or coffeepots. It wasn't about anything—except the power of that glowing box in the rec room. Joe became a TV *thing*—like Mr. Whipple squeezin' Charmin! He was as real as the Gardol Shield.

And that would turn out great for Joe, too. He found out (as a generation of pols found, at the same time) that with TV working for you—over and over, a million screens, a million times—not only could you make your own image (and enforce it) . . . but it *satisfied:* people stopped asking about anything else. They wanted him to be what they knew—to validate their time, their attention. They just wanted *that guy on TV.* . . . Talk about a safe remove!

And when that TV power was piled on a dusty history of real achievement—*a plaque in Cooperstown* . . . and there was Dad or Grampa, struggling for words to describe the grace of the Clipper in center field . . . and Mom approving, with tears in her eyes, the way that man buried poor Marilyn *(and doesn't he still send roses?)* . . . well, Joe had become bigger than ever—and more distant. He hadn't just climbed back to the top of the pile. There was the pile. And then there was Joe. It was beyond fame, to veneration. We put him in the pantheon—which, by his eighth decade, was his home address.

THE DAY AFTER THE EARTHQUAKE, Henry Bracco drove Joe to Ben Langella's bank. Henry lived north of the city, in Marin—the trip to Millbrae, in the south, was a trek. But Bracco was one of those guys who'd do anything for DiMaggio. He was a pharmacist and got Joe his pills: vitamins, arthritis stuff, heart pills, plenty—expensive ones, too—though Joe never paid a dime. Bracco used to drive Joe anywhere he needed to go, then stay in the car, have a nap—content just to wait for the Clipper.

DiMaggio wanted Langella to find a contractor—right now—get him over to the house. "It's gotta be a guy we can trust," Joe said. But Ben knew that: dealings with DiMaggio were, by nature, confidential.

Ben got a builder named Wally Baldwin—convinced him to get on the case right away. Wally was a rising commercial builder. Houses weren't really his business. (And his commercial clients were all calling in—they wanted their buildings checked out for quake damage, cracks, or cosmetics.) . . . "But we gotta take care of Joe first," Ben said. Baldwin said he'd look at Joe's house, that day.

But lunch came first—for the Clipper, anyway. Anytime Joe came to Ben's bank, Ben would take him next door to the deli—Leonardo's. When Continental Savings built Ben's branch in Millbrae, they created a strip mall around the bank. Lenny Baranti's

deli was a tenant. He'd make Joe a nice fresh sandwich—maybe turkey, with a touch of olive oil. Joe
didn't want anything fat, like salami—and no garlic:
it made your breath smell. Joe didn't want to smell
like a Dago. (He was punctilious about that, as he
was about his hair—no hair oil. He'd tell you, even if
you didn't ask: nothing but water on his hair. Of
course, now he was also using a special shampoo that
made his hair whiter. But that was a secret.) . . . Anyway, Joe's taste in food had grown simpler with age.
What hadn't changed was his method of payment:
Baranti's walls were studded with signed pics of the
Jolter—to enhance the glory of Leonardo's Deli.
Even so, after a few hundred lunches, Lenny had
protested to Ben—they never paid a nickel! So that
day, Ben had to pay for Joe and Henry Bracco.

They got to the Marina in the early afternoon—
Bracco drove, Ben had the back seat. Joe sat shotgun,
as he always did—so he got to run the heater. Joe
liked his cars warm. They were nice and toasty by the
time Bracco parked, as near as he could, and prepared
for a nap. Joe and Ben Langella walked in toward
Beach Street. Marie was at the house. She had a yellow card from the Fire Department that permitted
residents to visit their houses for an hour—in case
there was medicine, or some other crucial thing to
pick up. The unlucky residents got red cards: meant
their houses weren't safe even to visit. Green cards
allowed full access—they were hard to get. Joe
flashed his green card.

Joe sat Ben in the front room, across from the giant oil of the 1950s DiMaggio in the double-breasted suit. There was a striking opulence to that portrait—it wasn't just the size of the canvas. There was something about the half-smile on Joe's face and the look in his eye—a look at nothing in particular, nothing to give rise to that smile . . . so the look of pleasure was for Joe, in himself. And there was the suit, so richly built up at the shoulder, so generous about Joe's slender midriff. It was more than a 1950s fullness, it was regal, that ratio of raiment to man—like the fabulous garments borne by dead Sun Kings in the (similarly sized) portraits at Versailles. But there was nothing else palatial in the place—just the old stuff. And the old king couldn't sit still to regard the painting. He was pacing, full of projects for the house.

"This place hasn't been fixed up in a long time. We gotta get everything fixed up. We'll get these carpets cleaned . . ." There was wall-to-wall in the front room, the old sculpted wool, original to '37—that carpet wore like iron. "And we get this all painted . . ."

Joe walked past the little table with the phone for the house. There was the Pac-Tel bill—he checked that over. "Eighteen dollars! Marie! What are we spending money on?"

"It's all yours," Marie said instantly. She knew all his moods—knew that bill would cause an eruption. "I only make local calls."

The Clipper scowled, and set the bill down. He had

to check downstairs. He hadn't had time, day before, to inspect all his stuff there. "Come on," he said to Ben.

There wasn't any car in Joe's garage. There wasn't room. He parked on the street. For a while, he'd kept the Cadillac in there—the free Cadillac. That was classic Joe, too. He knew this guy named Cappy Harada—Japanese guy, kind of an operator—used to be an executive with the Yomiuri Giants in Japan. Later, Cappy was hustling in the U.S.A., on his own, promoting this and that. So, one time, Cappy got a contract for some ratty town in California—Santa Maria, or Margaret—Santa Something . . . they were going to have their sesquicentennial, and Cappy wanted Joe to show up. Big deal. Joe didn't even know where the town was. But Cappy was on him like a cheap hooker, and finally, Joe said okay. So he did go, he did hang around, and even talked for a minute after the big dinner. That was that. But two days later, into the bank, here came Cappy.

"Where's Joe? . . ." Joe was in his armchair, half-asleep. "Joe!" said Cappy. "Hold out your hand!" Cappy dropped a set of keys into Joe's palm.

"What is it?" Joe said.

"It's your brand-new Cadillac! I got it parked for you, right outside."

Joe looked from the keys to Cappy without sitting up, without a smile, without moving his head an extra inch. Joe said: "Did you fill it up with gas?"

So, Joe kept the Cadillac for a while, but then it

was his tank to fill, so he gave it to his granddaughter—actually, her husband. As Joe liked to say in those days, everything was for the grandkids. Anyway, the car was taking up his garage. Joe needed the room.

Now, the garage was lined with golf bags—neat, against the walls—must have been fifty golf bags. They were all new, each with a new set of clubs inside. A lot of famous tournaments, like the Dinah Shore, always gave the celebs a new set of clubs (and a bag, shirt, and shoes) automatically—with the tournament name—as a memento. Joe liked those. One time, Dinah herself called up to invite him—and Joe said, sure, he'd come. But he was going to bring a friend—so he'd need two sets of stuff, and all . . . and the friend was exactly the same size as him. When it wasn't automatic, Joe didn't like that. He didn't like to ask. He played for something like fifteen years straight in the American Airlines tourney, and every time, he'd have to tell the girl in the office that his bag was in Florida, or his sister screwed up, and it never got shipped—so he'd need some clubs, and shoes . . . but that was over, now. They stopped inviting him. Crandall, the airline president, got pissed off because if Joe didn't win and wasn't going to get a check he wouldn't even stay for the big Sunday dinner.

So Joe had his bags all lined up, with the shoes on shelves above, and on the floor, in front of the golf bags, he had the shirts—hundreds of shirts!—still in plastic bags. They had things like "Buick Open" or "Pebble Beach" embroidered on the chest where the pocket would have been. But you couldn't see what was what anymore. They were dusty before the quake—but now, Jesus! It was a quarter-inch of grime over everything.

And Joe was in a state—*who was going to clean all this shit up?* (He was going to pay someone to clean up dust?) . . . And then he saw the window. It wasn't in the garage, but behind, in a small room that led to the backyard patch of grass. There was a door back there—the old wooden kind, with six panes of glass. And the firemen had broken a pane, so they could reach in and open the lock, to check the house. There was glass on the floor.

"Cocksucker firemen! Lookit what they did here!"

Joe was stomping around the back room, looking at the glass like it was shards of Ming vase. And cursing the firemen up and down, back and forth . . .

"SONOFABITCH ASSHOLES . . ."

Langella was picking up shirts, blowing dust off. He came to look. He couldn't get upset. "It's okay, Joe."

"OKAY MY ASS . . ." Joe was inspecting a cliff-wall of baseballs, brand-new baseballs, American Leaguers, in boxes of a dozen. People sent Joe balls—sometimes he forgot to sign. Plus, any time he went to a locker room, they'd load up his car. Joe had at least a hundred dozen new balls in his stack.

"LOOKIT! I knew it! Those cocksuckers stole a half a dozen balls!"

"You can't tell, Joe. How can you tell?"

"I CAN TELL, GODDAMMIT! THEY STOLE HALF A DOZEN FUCKING BALLS!"

Silent, Ben went back to the shirts. He knew Joe would subside. Ben blew dust for a couple of minutes, then held up a Buick Open shirt. "Hey, Joe! This one's my size. Can I have it?"

Joe didn't yell. He was tired, hunched over. He tilted his head on his bent neck, but he couldn't really see the shirt . . .

"Put it back," he said. "I'll get you another one."

LOOKING BACK, LANGELLA NEVER did get the shirt. But it didn't matter—Ben was soon gone from Joe's life. They were all gone, sooner or later, the way Joe figured. Everybody he was close to, gone—and he was still here.

One day, a couple of years before the earthquake, DiMaggio got picked up at the airport by Bob Wuerth. Bob was the PR guy at Bay Meadows back then—and part of the Clipper's network. Whenever Joe was in San Francisco, Wuerth would drive into town in the morning to pick Joe up and bring him to the track. He'd drive Joe on off days, too—to appointments, lunch, to the club for a steam. After a day at the track, Wuerth would bring the Clipper home with him, to watch TV and share a bag of pretzels.

Anyway, they were driving in from the airport, and Wuerth asked Joe what he planned to do in San Francisco. "I don't know," Joe said. "All my friends are dead." Joe didn't see Wuerth's face—looked like he could've cried. He thought he was Joe's friend. But that didn't matter anymore, either. Now Wuerth was dead, too.

Joe didn't go to his funeral—didn't like that sort of thing. What was all the talk about? Guy was dead. (Now his friends would pester Joe all day.) Same way with Reno Barsocchini, and Lefty O'Doul. Of course, Joe wasn't real pals with them when they died. He'd figured out, years before: they were only inviting him to their bars so people would talk about their joints. That wasn't his job, to make them big names. Wasn't his job to sit in funerals, either. Same with Lefty Gomez—when El Goofo kicked the bucket up in Rodeo. Joe was afraid the family would ask him to be a pallbearer—that was no good for Joe's back. So he got somebody to drive him up the day before the funeral. He signed the book and got the hell out. Joe said he had to go to New York, next day. But he didn't.

A lot of fellows who were still around were out of Joe's life just as wholly, and finally, as if they'd been planted six feet under. Somewhere along the line Joe had decided, they weren't true pals, or they'd done something wrong . . . and he walked away. And when Joe walked away, that was it, you were gone. You could try to call, you wanted to explain—he'd hang up. Or you could wait: he'd think it over, he was bound to call, right? What about all those years of friendship? . . . But it didn't pay to hold your breath. Joe wouldn't call.

See, the way Joe looked at it, you were in it for your own reasons. Even if you just loved the guy, the man was your hero . . . well, then, that was your reason. You might've gotten along for years that way— did everything for Joe, put your life on call for Joe—and then one day, maybe you decided you had to get back some money you'd laid out—not a profit, just expenses. *Whack!* You were gone. . . . Or say you got a call from another friend—all he wanted in the world was to meet Joe DiMaggio. And you said, "Sure, come on over. He's coming here today." And DiMaggio walked in and saw someone extra there. So, he was gone, for good. . . . Or maybe you did something really stupid, and talked to a writer—you said you knew Joe. You should have said you *used* to know, because he'd never know you again. Writers were the worst—but it was the same logic. Joe looked at a writer, interviewer, biographer (they were all the same), and thought: *Why should this guy make a buck off my life?*

As a matter of fact, it was the same for everyone— family was not excepted. Now, Joe and Dom were the only two brothers left. But they didn't talk. Why? Who knew why, with that family. They were DiMaggios. Neither one would say. But the silence went on for years. Dom didn't even like to show up at baseball dinners, or All-Star Games—places where Joe was going to be. Joe would figure that Dom was trying to steal his spotlight—and that would set the Big Guy off, for sure. Money might have caused the trouble, at the start. Dom ended up with the building where DiMaggio's Grotto used to be—he made a fortune with that. (Dom made a fortune with everything, which always pissed Joe off.) Or sometimes, the brothers would fight about the sisters. There weren't so many of them left, either. When one of the older ones, Mamie, got too sick to care for herself, Joe was sitting in San Francisco, and he didn't lift a finger. So Dominic had to fly across the country, to put her into a nursing home. Dom wasn't happy about that episode. And neither was Joe. Because Dom flying all that way to take care of Mamie—that shamed Joe. And shame was what he hated worst.

In the end, it was shame that finished Joe and his son. Shame and money—a deadly combination with DiMag. Joe Jr. never did stop drifting, or drinking. One night—late 1960s (he was out of the Marines)—Joey was hanging around Miami Beach, and wandered onto a houseboat from which a nighttime radio show was being broadcast. It was a popular show—made a big name for the host, a guy named Larry King—who, of course, put Joe Jr. on the air, straightaway. As King told the story in his memoir, years later, he was shocked when Junior started to speak about growing up a DiMaggio:

" 'I never knew my father,' he said. 'My parents

were divorced when I was little, and I was sent away to private school, and my father was totally missing from my childhood. When they needed a picture of father and son, I'd get picked up in a limo and have my picture taken. We were on the cover of the first issue of *Sport* magazine when it came out in 1949, my father and I, me wearing a little number 5 jersey. I was driven to the photo session, we had the picture taken, and I was driven back. My father and I didn't say two words.

" 'I cursed the name Joe DiMaggio, Jr. At Yale, I played football—I deliberately avoided baseball— but when I ran out on the field and they announced my name, you could hear the crowd murmur. . . . When I decided to leave college and join the Marines, I called my father to tell him. You call your father when you make that sort of decision. So I told him, and he said, "The Marines are a good thing." And there was nothing more for us to say to each other.'

"DiMaggio, Jr. said that the closest he'd ever been to his father was in the car on the way to Marilyn Monroe's funeral. He said his father had always gone on loving Monroe, and that he loved her too. . . ."

Of course, Big Joe was furious after Junior told the world all that crap. What right did the kid have to talk about him that way?

As Joe saw it, whatever he gave, Junior pissed away. In 1970, Joe put the kid in a business making polyurethane foam. But the other guys who'd put money in yanked the rug—and forced both DiMaggios out. Joe always said Junior lost that business. Joe bought the kid a long-haul truck—a beauty, Peterbilt, seventy-five grand. Junior wrecked it (and screwed up his trucker's license, too). Big Joe told Ben Langella to give the boy a job. So Ben brought Joey into his bank, and asked him, what did he want to do? "Nothin'," Junior said. "I want to be a bum." By that time—the 1980s—Joey was doing drugs, on top of the drink. And he didn't want a damn thing from his dad. Back east, in New Jersey, Big Joe had a meeting with a man named Bob Boffa—friend of a friend, you could say—Boffa was very big with the Teamsters. And Big Joe asked Boffa to get the kid a job, in a quiet way—which Boffa did, as a favor to the hero. He got Joey signed on to drive a cement truck in Las Vegas. But it didn't last. Anyway, Junior had no place to stay in Vegas. So, while his dad was signing autographs for fifty G's a day, Junior was sleeping in an empty cement-mixer drum . . . and telling *his* friends—if his father called, they were to say they didn't know where Joey was.

Looking back, there was one chance, one time the kid might have turned it all around. Joe Jr. was in his late twenties when he met a woman named Sue—a single mom with two toddler daughters, Paula and Kathie—and Sue fell in love with Joey. They got married. And Junior adopted the two girls. He moved them all to California, to a town across the Bay from San Francisco. Junior was a head of household. He was working (making foam). He was pleased with himself. He took Sue with him to meet Big Joe at the American Airlines Golf Tournament—it was in Scottsdale, Arizona, that year, and a lavish affair, as always. Joey made one mistake right away: he came downstairs the first morning in a pair of jeans. Big Joe sent him right back to his room to get dressed properly. That night, Joe Jr. and Sue joined Big Joe, along with Frank Scott and his wife, Betty, for dinner in the resort dining room. Joey wore his best suit and tie. And Sue looked lovely. But she was tapping the table in time to the music. "Step outside," Big Joe said to Junior. "I want to talk to you." Joey came back and told his wife: "Come on. We've got to get out of here." She looked up. "Where?" Junior said: "Come on. We're going back to San Francisco." Betty Scott ran after them, and stopped Joe Jr. in the hallway. "Why you goin', honey?"

"My father said he doesn't want anything to do with her."

And after that, Joe wouldn't have anything to do with her. In fact, he did all he could to make sure the marriage didn't work. Not that Joey needed help—he didn't do well as a husband. By the mid-1970s his marriage was history. But it did provide Big Joe a chance to send the boy one last message. Because long after the marriage was gone, Big Joe decided that Sue's daughters, Paula and Kathie, were *his granddaughters* . . . and they would be his heirs. So the Clipper's fortune would never go to his son— who, after all, had not lived up to the standard.

By that time, all the Clipper's pals knew, Joe Jr. was like Marilyn—a name you couldn't bring up. Junior was a loss, and DiMaggio did not talk about loss. By that time, he had cut away everything that did not fit the picture—our picture of the Great DiMag. If that didn't leave much that we would call a normal life—well, he wouldn't say that. And we didn't really want to know.

By the late 1980s people always seemed shocked if they saw Joe in real life—toting his garment bag off a plane at LAX . . . licking an ice cream cone on Central Park South in New York . . . or walking down a South Florida street with an armful of dirty laundry (the machines in his apartment house took half a buck, but at the wash-a-teria it was only thirty-five cents). And when folks talked about those sightings (as they always did), the amazing part was, he was just . . . alone.

You could call that his bargain with the hero's life. Day to day, that was surely his doing. Or you could conclude it was just part of the package, from the start—Joe was sufficient to Joe. And no matter what else was going on—for one night, one vote of sportswriters, or through decades, twenty thousand days and nights—or in an earthquake . . . it was his destiny to stand alone.

IT TURNED OUT WALLY BALDWIN
was as good as his word: he got to the house even before PG&E could turn the power back on—and took
the whole thing in hand. He got a laundry list of
everything Joe wanted: the walls fixed, and that place
on the roof . . . check the plumbing, plaster, paint,
clean the carpets, clean up the garage—and that
glass! . . . the front gate straightened, the locks, the
service door, the stucco outside, bolts to the foundation . . . it came to a lot of work, a score of picky jobs.

But Wally was doing three million dollars that
year—ran a good union shop, knew everybody in the
business—subcontractors weren't going to tell him
no. And Wally called in his friends—the roofer, the
concrete man, the painter, drywall guys. He got the
best old-line German plasterers, Meiswinkle—used
to do every good job in the city, when real plaster was
the way to go—like when Joe's house was built. That
was Meiswinkle work. They came for Wally—for no
cost, or pretty near. "Hey, Wally, just get me an autographed ball outa the deal . . ." Wally would say: "No
problem." And he'd schedule them in.

A lot of small things, he just did himself—like the
tradesman's door, the side entrance on the front of the
house. He took the door off, threw it in his own truck
and took it down to San Francisco Door . . . that was
an old guy named Vic, and his son, Mike—Santini,
or something, was the last name. It turned out they

were cousins of Joe—or somebody married someone's cousin—anyway, one of those old Dago fishing families. They made the door brand-new—of course for free. It was Joe's door. "Just get me a ball."

Wally was at the house a million times—to meet the sheetrocker, glass guy, painter . . . to let 'em in, so Joe wouldn't have to be there. Wally would call Marie and clear the times with her, to make sure he wouldn't be disturbing Joe. Bolts in the concrete every four feet—he brought his own crew with hammer-drills for that—steel bolts with epoxy, eight or nine inches down. The front gate—he got an iron man, at cost. Then the door release with the buzzer upstairs—electrical was a whole 'nother thing. The work went on for a couple of months. The crews all talked about the same thing: how simple the place was, unfancy, low-profile . . . there had to be people in the neighborhood who didn't even know DiMaggio was there. And no Jacuzzis with gold-plated fixtures. Nothing like that inside. Wally made sure no one poked around too much. He knew DiMaggio had his private stuff upstairs, on the third floor. Wally never even went up there. And if Joe did happen to show up, it was always, "Hello, Joe," and that was it. Wally didn't try to make himself a big deal with the man. If he needed to talk to Joe, he'd ask Marie. Or Ben Langella would call from the bank, with new instructions. One time Wally went to the bank—Ben took him and Joe out to lunch at that deli next door. And they talked about the job. Wally told Joe how everyone was doing the work at cost, or free—all for an autograph. Joe liked that. He smiled.

See, Joe had insurance—no problem. They'd worked all that out at the beginning. But Wally didn't have to deal with the insurance. He just gave Joe an estimate at the start. It came to about sixty thousand dollars' worth of work. Joe sent that right in to the insurance company. (They sent a check for sixty grand.) And in the end, Wally just billed Joe at cost—basically materials—and whatever the subs sent in for their costs. It wasn't that bad, as Wally remembers—about twelve thousand. Joe liked the work. And Wally was proud: tens of thousands he saved for Joe. Wally felt good about the job, all around—even with the hassle at the end, about the balls.

That was later, when the work was done. Wally bought a box of new baseballs—perfect, American Leaguers. (Ben said Joe wouldn't sign any other kind.) Wally bought enough for the men who worked on the house with him, and sent them to Joe at Langella's bank. But Joe wouldn't sign them—and that put Wally into a bind with his subs.

So, Ben said he'd talk to Joe. And when Ben called back, he said, okay, Joe would sign—but he wanted the names, a name for each ball. Wally listed all the names he remembered. But he was worried. What if he forgot someone? (And sure enough, he did forget—Mike, Vic's son, at San Francisco Door!) So in the end, just to be safe, Wally asked for a few more balls, without "Best wishes to . . ." and just the auto-graph.

And Joe complied, finally. But it just confirmed for him what he'd suspected all along: that sonof-abitch was gonna sell those balls . . . and make a buck off Joe.

As for the money Joe made—say, forty-five G's of insurance money that wound up in Joe's pocket—well, no one had to know about Joe in the earthquake. That was Joe's business, strictly for Joe.

**Joe and Barry Halper at supper
in Cooperstown.**

The merchandise.

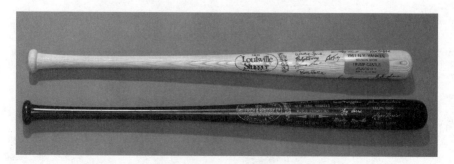

Joe's bats sold on TV for $3,995.

Joe regards his own memorabilia for photographer David Spindel.

CHAPTER 18

✦

IT WAS ONLY A FEW MONTHS AFTER the earthquake, turn of the year, 1990, when Joe pulled a sweet little holdout—on a baseball card company called Score. That was a deal like many others in his life: an admirer put him in. Barry Halper, one of the guys who'd do anything for Joe, was a founding partner of Score. So, DiMaggio signed their baseball cards—two thousand five hundred signatures—took him a day, maybe day and a half, and fetched a nice check: a hundred grand.

Halper was famous, in his own quiet way. He was a Jersey guy who'd done well, had a paper goods business worth a lot of money. But his life was baseball. He had a tiny minority stake in the Yankees—but that brought no fame. (There's nothing more silent than Steinbrenner's silent partners.) No, Halper was famous as the King of Collectors.

Plenty of guys had baseball cards. But Halper had thirty thousand cards, going back to the famous Honus Wagner card of 1909—that was a half-million-dollar item, right there—there were only four of those cards. Baseballs, everybody collected baseballs; but Halper had thousands of signed balls, home run balls and game balls—going back to a grungy brown spheroid said to be from the first organized ballgame (Hoboken, 1846). Bats: Halper had Ruth's last bat, which the Bambino signed as memento for Al Capone and the boys in Chicago. Uniforms: only big-time collectors had a signed uniform. But Halper had a secret wall in his house that swung open like a prop from a James Bond movie, and behind it whirred one of those automated dry-cleaner carousels bearing hundreds of historic uniforms.

The whole house was a stash of baseball treasure: equipment, photographs, programs, advertisements, magazines, diaries, player contracts—there was no end. When the house was packed, Halper filled warehouses. Everybody in baseball knew, the Hall of Fame in Cooperstown was very nice and all . . . but the Hall couldn't pay for stuff. And Barry could. What's more he would pay, quietly and with gratitude. No haggling. He'd tell you what an item was worth, and that, like his check, you could take to the bank. In a charlatan's business, Halper had honor; his stuff was real, and so was he. That's why he was King. But the jewel in his crown wasn't listed in any price guide. The jewel was Joe.

They'd met in the 1970s, at a Yankee Old Timers' Day—had to be the greatest day in Halper's life: the Yankee Clipper, talking with him! It was like everything Barry had done—all the history, all the things in his house, all of Barry's own passion came true—*came to life* . . . and asked him for a ride. What a ride Barry offered. Halper took care of DiMaggio everywhere—anytime, anywhere—squired him all over the country when Joe had to make an appearance (say, at the All-Star Game, or some other tribal rite). Spring training: Joe was living in Florida, a half-hour drive from the Yankee camp. But Barry would fly to Florida and rent a car, so he could take Joe to camp. If Joe had to show up at Yankee Stadium, he'd never have to mix and mingle—he'd sit with Halper, or Halper and Steinbrenner, in the owners' box. Meanwhile, back at the house in New Jersey, Barry's wife, Sharon, would be working up Joe's favorite dinner in her kitchen. Sharon went into cooking like Barry went into baseball: there was no end. One time she went to chef's school in Italy, so she could cook better for Joe. Barry took Sharon to the cooking school—and of course, he took DiMag along, so Joe would have a European vacation. That's how it was with Barry. He went into caring for DiMaggio—well, like Sharon went into cooking.

And in his way, DiMag took care of Halper. If a restaurant owner asked Barry (they'd beg him) to bring the Clipper by—well, Joe would go along, sign a menu, have a meal, maybe even have a good time. . . . In the house, Barry showed Joe everything he had—like Joe's '51 World Series ring. Joe had traded that away to an L.A. hotelier, in exchange for lodging. Barry had bought it from that guy's son. Now,

Barry offered to give the ring back to Joe. But Joe didn't want it. He signed a paper for Barry, affirming that was his ring. Joe signed thousands of items for Halper—stuff no one else would even show him, like the naked pinup of Marilyn—Joe signed, and Barry put it away. Joe knew Halper wouldn't show it around—that would embarrass the Clipper—or sell it off to make a buck. What they had between them was trust.

So, when Barry invested in that card company, it was a natural: he had to have DiMag. A hundred thousand dollars was real money to Score, but Barry and his partners thought Joe was good business. Joe's signed cards were slipped into random packs, so buyers would think, if they bought Score cards, they might get something special. And the managing partner, a marketer named Dan Shedrick, worked in another clever twist: whenever a DiMaggio card slipped in, so did another card, with an 800 number to call—so the buyer could "register" his DiMaggio autograph. What really happened was, Score registered the buyer's name, then publicized his lucky buy in the local papers. That way word got around, this was real.

In a small way, they'd got to the heart of the memorabilia business: the buyer's stubborn, clinging hope that if he spends enough, trades up, invests enough love, learning, attention, he is going to end up with something real from a hero. That's the root impulse, the deep, unthought source of joy—whether it's a kid pumping the air with his fist outside a dirty little card store at the strip mall, because he's just unwrapped his third Edgar Martinez card that he knows he can trade (three-for-one!) to his friend for the Griffey Jr. rookie card . . . or whether it's Barry Halper, buying Mickey Mantle's first-year minor league paycheck (at a hundred times the face amount). . . . If a packet of five picture cards representing five modern major league heroes was real enough to find a buyer, how much realer (and how many more buyers might seek) a packet with a Hall of Famer inside—and not just a picture card, but a card he himself had regarded, held in his hands, and authenticated with his pen. It came *straight from him.* And, of course, it didn't hurt that Joe's signed card could be resold (anywhere, that same day) for at least a hundred and fifty bucks—the sort of sum that, increasingly, measured America's joy in her heroes.

So it worked pretty well, that DiMaggio contract—well enough, alas, that the competition woke up, and started horning in. The Upper Deck company, makers of another card set, wooed and won Mickey Mantle: they were slipping his signed cards into their packs. And then, Upper Deck came after the Clipper!

Well, the boys at Score had to keep DiMaggio. They held a financial meeting and decided to make a preemptive strike. They would re-sign DiMaggio with a sweetheart deal: same number of cards—*for a hundred fifty thousand*. That was sixty a signature! It would set the industry on its ear.

Of course, they had Halper to make the approach—but, still, this had to be done right. There was the big New York baseball writers' dinner coming up, January 1990, and that was perfect. Joe would be there. Barry would be taking him, of course. If it all worked out, they could do the deal and leak it— get some ink—all in the same night.

So, the Score company went first-class. They didn't just buy a table at the dinner. Everybody did that. No, they rented a suite atop the Manhattan hotel that was hosting the dinner—a huge apartment—for a swanky pre-dinner cocktail reception. With a whispered word that DiMaggio would be there, they were sure to draw a solid crowd. And then Barry could take Joe aside, to another room—you know, get him out of the crush . . . then, they could talk about the deal.

Well, it all went like clockwork: place was sumptuous, no lines at the bars; splendid turnout, lotta hearty male noise . . . and Barry took Joe out of the crowd, into a bedroom. That's when it happened. They came out, ten, twelve minutes later, and Barry looked like his mama just took sick. Shedrick sidled over through the crowd: "What happened?"

"He won't do it."

"Whadd'he say? . . ."

"I don't know. He just said . . ." Barry was shaking his head, and he shrugged. "He won't do it."

"You want me to try?"

"Try what? He won't do it."

"I'm gonna try. Okay if I try?"

"Go ahead. There he is." And Barry retreated, still shaking his head.

Five minutes later, Shedrick and Joe emerged from the bedroom—big smile on Shedrick's kisser—had his thumb up in front of his belly, flashing the high sign at Halper, as he approached.

"Got it!" Shedrick whispered.

"He'll do it?"

"Done."

Barry didn't know whether he was happy or sad. He was happy for the card business—that would be him and Joe. But how could Shedrick make the deal, and he couldn't? What about—well, him and Joe?

Shedrick was already moving away, eager to spread the news. Halper stopped him for a moment. "Same deal?"

"Yeah," Shedrick said, with a little less excitement. "Only one thing: it's a quarter-million."

ONE STRANGE THING ABOUT DIMAG-gio in business: it drove him nuts if anybody else made money.

Naturally, Joe's price for an autograph had to be higher than anyone else's. Personal appearances, endorsements, licenses to use his image or name, all had to be the highest—regardless of circumstance. For example, in the mid-1990s, Ted Williams decided to price himself out of autograph shows. For one thing, Ted had suffered a stroke, and signing was difficult. For another, he hated the shows—always had—like a damn meat market, and he was stuffing sausage, to sell it before it stank. So Ted opted out, with one simple rule—he set his price at $350 per signature . . . and no one called him for shows.

Then, Joe had a problem. He was raking in plenty from autograph shows, selling thousands of signatures at $125, even one-fifty per. But he couldn't let Ted's price be higher. So DiMaggio made a rule, too: for a hundred and a half, he'd sign your baseball, or your picture of him (or him and Dom, or even him with Mickey Mantle). . . . But if you had a picture of *DiMaggio with Ted Williams*—Joe's signature would cost $375.

But that was just pride—that went without saying—and went back a long way. When he and Ted were still on the ballfield, DiMaggio wanted to be paid more, too. But with Joe, it wasn't just competition—it went much deeper than that.

There was in the mix his legendary disinclination to pay. In the business of being DiMaggio, Joe preferred to obtain all requisite goods and services for free. (That dovetailed neatly with his long-standing predilection for free food, clothing, and shelter.) Even in this new high-dollar era of DiMaggio business, Joe had found himself a small-time Florida lawyer who would do his contracts, taxes, and estate work without charging Joe a fee. Joe called the lawyer "my accountant"—or sometimes, "my friend"—that ought to be payment enough. And for his part, Morris Engelberg, Esq., announced at every opportunity that he "never made a dime" from the Jolter, his hero. But he was thrilled to ride around Hollywood, Florida, in a pinstriped van with the vanity plate, DIMAG 5—and to rename his strip mall office "The Yankee Clipper Center." Engelberg called himself not only "Joe's friend," but his "confidant." And then, too: "the son Joe never had."

Of course, for DiMaggio, that kind of fee structure went back a long way, too—to '36, his rookie year, when the affable Lou Gehrig offered to place Joe with his "business manager," Christy Walsh.

"How much?" Joe said.

Walsh took thirty percent.

Joe declined.

Even so, his was not a simple cheapness: it wasn't just paying that drove Joe nuts. It was even when he didn't pay, when he was getting money, even when he was *getting millions.* That's when he took it one step beyond.

What would happen to the rest of the money? Joe wanted to know the whole deal, from the cost of the item he was going to sign, down to the final price the retail buyer was going to pay. And every step in between . . .

Who else would make money in the deal?

How much?

Why should those guys make a buck off my life?

See, it was the guys he was in business with: if they were making money, it ate at Joe's stomach. That was *his money*—or should have been.

It didn't matter if they were friends. That was worse. Friends shouldn't make money off of Joe— not the way Joe figured, not if they were real friends. It made him wonder about their loyalty. Why did they want to be friends?

Consider Joe's deal on the sixteen-by-twenties: two thousand giant-sized photographs of Joe, signed by Joe—a nice piece, a nice friendly deal.

Ed Liberatore put Joe in. Eddie was an old Dodger scout, salt of the earth. He was trying to help some friends in his hometown of Philadelphia: a young sports marketer named Milt Beaver, and some part- ners were in it—all friends of Ed's. And of course, Eddie was helping Joe. Liberatore had blisters on his lips from kissing the ground Joe walked on. Thirty, forty years, he took care of Joe—like they were mar- ried. Well, in point of fact, Eddie had a wife, a home and all. But if Joe called, Eddie would move out of home, and into Joe's hotel, wherever that was, to be close. Sometimes they'd share a room, and hang a sheet down the middle so it was like two rooms. (Anyway, if they hung the sheet with a string, they could also hang their laundry to dry, so they didn't pay.)

But the deal: the way Joe worked it out, he'd get fifty dollars to sign each photograph. That made a hundred thousand up front. But the fellows in Philadelphia were going to sell these beauties for $350 each. So when they sold, Joe would get another $100 for every piece—or, in sum, two hundred thousand on the back end. But getting to the back end was the problem: that small, new company didn't have its channels of distribution worked out. It was an old story in that sort of business: the piece sold slowly; the partners got edgy; they pulled the money . . . and the company went belly-up.

So, then, in walked Jerry Romolt. Romolt was from Chicago, an experienced operator. He'd done deals with Joe before. Of course, he knew Liberatore. Beaver, he'd met. He liked them all, as far as that went. And he was going to help out by buying re-mainders. There were fourteen hundred photographs left. Romolt bought seven hundred right away—at distressed prices (basically at Beaver's cost). For the other seven hundred, he took an option. Then, he turned around, same day, and placed two hundred photos with the Hammacher Schlemmer catalogue people. They stuck those pieces in their spring book—*at $500 per*—and they were gone in a week. So, Hammacher called Romolt for three hundred more, for the summer catalogue: three weeks, and those were gone. . . . And Hammacher bought out the other nine hundred.

It was gorgeous! Beaver got his money out, Romolt got a beautiful new Porsche. Hammacher Schlemmer—they were extremely pleased.

And Joe . . . was livid. *They were all makin' money off of him*—and he was getting beat for a hundred a copy. Of course, he didn't say that. He said they were gouging his public: fans shouldn't have to pay five hundred dollars. But the way he figured, it was a million-dollar deal now. And they were cheating him: *he only got $50 per.*

So Joe was in the airport—Miami International— at the baggage carousel . . . and who was also waiting for a bag? This young woman: a nice Jewish girl—not a beauty queen, but sweet, and smart—she worked for Hammacher Schlemmer. She saw Joe, and she couldn't contain herself. Normally, she would never bother someone famous, but—she'd been working on his photographs!

"Oh, Mr. DiMaggio! You can't imagine what a thrill it's been to be working with you! I mean, Hammacher works with a lot of very—"

"Fuck you!"

That was just Joe's opener.

"Fuckin' cunt! Gives you the right to come up to me? Get the fuck away from me! You're too fuckin' ugly to talk to me in public."

Well, of course, she was upset. (She complained to her company—tried to complain to Romolt. "What do you want me to do?" Romolt said. "I didn't raise him.") . . . She didn't understand, it was just about money.

And she couldn't have known, it was worse for friends: that deal started the unraveling between Joe and Eddie Liberatore. Then, one time, Eddie couldn't come to meet Joe, or showed up late, or waited in the wrong place . . . Joe decided Liberatore was like all the rest. When Eddie finally found Joe, DiMaggio started yelling—at a dinner, in front of everybody— and then DiMaggio gave Eddie a shove, and almost knocked him over. Liberatore left the room in shame. And Joe never called again . . . which broke old Eddie's heart.

SO, THAT WAS THE GREAT THING about Joe's holdout with Score. After Joe drove the price up, Halper and his friends wouldn't make any money.

In fact, it wasn't long after that, Halper and his partners got out of the business, sold the Score company to a Texas group called Pinnacle. The new owners inherited the DiMaggio deal—which they weren't too happy about, but that didn't matter: Joe had a contract. DiMaggio and Engelberg, Esq. were particular about contracts. In this case, Pinnacle was going to pay Joe for two days of signing—or they could pay a quarter-million for nothing at all. It turned out Halper and his pals had done the smart thing: they'd sold out at the height of the memorabilia craze. But Joe and Engelberg went on, riding the hot wind. After he signed the

Pinnacle cards, Joe wouldn't do another card deal. Cards were too cheap. Instead, Joe would do a deal with a company called Score Board. And that really did change the business.

Score Board was the brainchild of a couple of New Jersey guys, big baseball fans: Paul and Kenny Goldin, a father-son act. In fact, Dad got the idea from his boy's card collection. In the mid-1980s, when the "value" of certain cards shot up, when the first price guides put dollar figures into collecting, the elder Goldin started on a simple scheme. He'd buy card sets from the manufacturers (like Topps, Fleer, or Upper Deck), he'd buy at wholesale. Then he'd pick out the cards with value, and repackage them for dealers at a handsome markup. Soon he was paying the featured players to sign his cards, and he was sitting on a gold mine. The elder Goldin took the company public and raised millions: Score Board Inc. was the industry leader, the Microsoft of memorabilia. Then, they went after Joe.

How else could they be the Big Dog of "the hobby"? Wasn't Joe *(by actual vote)* the Greatest Living Player? . . . What good was a Mays, Nolan Ryan, Barry Bonds—without the Clipper? Not good enough. So, in 1991, they signed the deal with DiMaggio. Joe would sign balls and "flats" (such as eight-by-ten-inch photographs) exclusively for Score Board—*at $150 per.* It was a new high for the industry (in fact, a nice round multiple of what anyone else was paid). Score Board and Joe were flying high.

Joe had to be a frequent flier, too. He required Score Board to buy from him *twenty thousand signatures a year.* So, Joe would get three million dollars a year, guaranteed. In fact, it was more than three million, because when Score Board wanted adjustments to the deal, they had to compensate Joe with Score Board stock options—thousands of shares—and they were flying, too. After the Goldins announced the DiMaggio deal (they said it was worth $10 million in new business), stock in Score Board Inc. climbed to $40 a share.

But that's how the Goldins had it figured: they'd established the value of Joe's autograph at an all-time high—pushed it into the stratosphere. But why shouldn't they push the value of that asset? It was their asset now. And if the company did well, Joe would do well. His stock would climb along with theirs. They were top of the line. The sky was the limit. They were in business with the Yankee Clipper!

So Joe started signing, every month, two days straight, in Morris Engelberg's office. And Score Board started selling—in its catalogue, in the industry paper, at every big card show, and on TV. They cut a deal with the Home Shopping Network, a DiMaggio exclusive: "The keepsake signed baseball, your own little piece of history!" For only $390.

Sure, it was a little high, but what could they do? The TV network took $190 a ball, and Joe was getting $150. So that only left $50 per for Score Board. (And they had to buy the ball.)

Well, it's a great and powerful nation that can suck up thousands of four-hundred-dollar baseballs. But America came through, month after month, all through 1992. Sure, it was a lot of money, but how many people had a baseball that Joe himself had held in his hands—and signed it so perfectly? . . . It was like a little piece of him!

Then, it was 1993, and business wasn't quite as rosy. The national economy was sour enough that we'd dumped one president for a younger, more vigorous model. The baseball economy was sour enough that owners and players were girding for a shutdown. (Even average players were making millions, and owners said they simply couldn't go on.) There were a billion regretful or outraged words on sports pages about the pernicious effects of money: it was wrecking the National Pastime! . . . And still, the shopping networks were hawking DiMaggio balls.

But not quite as many balls as before. True, Joe had a lot of fans, but how many had four hundred extra dollars in the fixed incomes of their golden years? . . . There were thousands of eager collectors, but there were thousands of hero artifacts, too. (How about that cunning resin model of Yankee Stadium, housed in a clear plastic dome and mounted on a handsome woodgrain base, with a genuine replication of Yogi Berra's genuine signature?) . . . Sure, people wanted a little piece of Joe. But how many wanted two?

So, Kenny Goldin, executive vice president and son of the founder of Score Board Inc., made pilgrimage to Florida to have a talk with Joe. Score Board was still very excited to be in business with the Yankee Clipper . . . but, couldn't they—possibly— make the excitement last longer? You know, stretch the business out?

No.

Maybe Joe could just sign, you know . . . an eensy bit fewer balls. You know—this month. No? . . .

No.

But what about the stock analysts: what would they say? Score Board's sales were leveling off, but inventories were climbing through the roof. (There were warehouses full of DiMaggio balls.) *If they downgrade the stock, we all get hurt. We're all in the same boat on Wall Street! . . .*

No, DiMaggio had his own boat. He had unloaded the stock the minute he was able. There was nothing in the contract that said he had to hold it forever. (Why should he be in business with them?) . . . And there was nothing in the contract that said he had to listen to a lot of whining.

In fact, nothing in that contract said he had to do anything—except sign balls and flats . . . and, hey! There was nothing in that contract to keep Joe from signing something else—*like bats* . . . Call Romolt!

SO, RIGHT IN THE MIDDLE OF THE Score Board deal, Joe signed another contract, this one with Jerry Romolt—and this one the Mother of All Deals. Romolt would commission Hillerich and Bradsby (makers of the Louisville Slugger) to make two thousand DiMaggio bats—strictly a limited edition. In fact, Romolt would issue a guarantee that only one thousand nine hundred and forty-one bats would ever be sold. See, get it? *1941—The Year of The Streak....* This would be about baseball's one unbreakable record, the sacred fifty-six games—a once-in-a-lifetime Joltin' Joe commemorative!

Romolt had a flair for this sort of business. He could manufacture rarity, just as he could manufacture sentiment, solemnity, authenticity, art. From the basement of his house in a new and treeless Illinois suburb, he'd made millions from the fans of the Great Game, because for his part, in his own heart . . . well, he didn't give a shit—he wanted the money.

All the memorabilia in Romolt's house was inventory, nothing more, nothing less. Jerry was not a collector. He dealt with a lot of sports heroes. If they wanted to be friends, fine. That didn't change what Jerry did. Romolt would make sure that every bat coming off the line at Louisville was perfect. That was a matter of his own reputation. He would prepare on bonded paper (with the salutation, in Italian:

"May You Stay Forever Young") an elegant Certificate of Authenticity. The retail buyer had a right to that. He would make sure there were pictures—no, better yet, video—of DiMaggio signing the bats. That way, no one could even suggest a fake. But most of all, Romolt would make sure he had every one of those bats sold, before he even paid his first plane fare to Kentucky.

Romolt would turn those bats around (at a substantial profit) to a New York company called Madison Sports. It was a new company, small, but with big plans. Madison had just started selling shares to the public. When they announced the acquisition of America's largest sports film library ("valued," said their press release, "at more than $10 million") their stock shares nudged above one dollar on the OTC Bulletin Board, and they were on their way. Now, Madison would buy Joe's bats and turn them around again, to the Home Shopping Network, where the bats could be retailed to Joe's many fans.

So, the whole deal was done in three or four months, more or less the time it took Louisville Slugger to make the bats. After that, it was clear sailing. DiMaggio and Engelberg, Esq. were flown into Kentucky. The Home Shopping Network brought a video cameraman. Romolt was on scene with a fistful of Sharpie pens. The Hillerich and Bradsby company had a splendid signing table, with a built-in rack to hold a bat. That way, Joe could sign a couple of thousand—he could sign all day—and his arm, his hand, wouldn't even get stiff.

Employees of the factory shifted bats in and out of the rack, each bat numbered, recorded, and witnessed by a notary on scene. With a fresh Sharpie, Joe could sign forty or fifty bats before the tip of the pen would splay. Then he might take a break for tea, or he might take a new pen, and keep rackin' up bats. It was August in Louisville, hot as hell in the factory, but Joe didn't mind. They brought a portable fan for him, but he shifted it away, to the notary, Jan Isaacs. The Louisville Slugger people all admired his diligence (and laughed when he wouldn't let them throw away the used pens). It took ten hours of signing—then, Joe was on his way—with more than three million dollars for his labor (and the used pens—hey, they still had plenty of ink).

Actually, the money was kind of a hassle. As it turned out, the Home Shopping Network only bought a few hundred bats—and Madison couldn't come up with Joe's cash. So Romolt had to step back in, and wire the rest of the cash into Joe's account. Romolt held on to the bats for security (and took a hundred bats for his trouble). Then Joe got mad—though he got his money—because at that point he realized, Romolt already had those bats sold. Romolt wasn't even taking any risk, and he was going to make a million! So, to calm him down, Joe got some extra bats, too. (For the grand-kids, as Joe said.)

And in the end, Romolt got his money back. It came in dribs and drabs from tax-cheater banks in Dubai, Panama, the Cayman Islands—and without any mystery about how it was raised. With the right whisper on the DiMaggio deal to Dan Dorfman (who wrote up Madison Sports in his popular *USA Today* column), Madison's stock climbed 500 percent in a year—it was nearly ten dollars a share.

Alas, it was a stock that was jacked up, just to come down. Within a year, the stock price had crumbled: it fell back to a dollar and change. The main problem was no one wanted the bats—not at four thousand dollars a pop on TV. The Home Shopping Network brought in Whitey Ford *(in a tuxedo)* to thump the tub for the Dago's bats. They said the bats "normally" sold for *eight thousand dollars.* (But tonight only, the chance of a lifetime, three thousand nine hundred ninety-five!) They had the bats carried on stage by a pair of armed guards (in white gloves) . . . and still they couldn't move the damn bats. Home Shopping couldn't even unload the few hundred they already owned, much less the remaining thousand that were weighing down Madison's balance sheet.

Madison had other problems, too. For instance, there were the two principal officers who jumped ship (one took the name Madison with him, and the other took a couple of hundred bats). There was the "nation's largest sports film library"—which, the company announced, might actually, umm, not exist.

And then there was the matter of the lawsuit from Score Board Inc., alleging that Madison was selling forged autographs.

Of course, Paul and Kenny Goldin at Score Board were generally in a sour mood, since their pal, partner, and asset, Joe DiMaggio, had swamped the market with some eight million dollars in new autographed merchandise (i.e., his bats). And meanwhile, they were sitting on five million dollars' worth of unsold DiMaggio autographs (i.e., his balls). The Wall Street analysts had by now discerned Score Board's problem, and the Goldins watched helplessly as the value of their company was cut in half. It killed the old man: he died in 1994. It was left to Kenny Goldin, the son, to deal with DiMaggio.

Actually, to cut off the deal. Score Board was glad to let its DiMaggio "exclusive" lapse in 1994. And Kenny Goldin also traded a bunch of useless baseball cards to the Home Shopping Network, in exchange for their leftover bats. Those bats, Goldin dumped on the market for about eight hundred bucks a copy. Why not? He'd gotten them for nothing, and he could raise some cash. But even better: it was a price so embarrassingly low that no one could miss the insult.

Joe's retaliation was instant, and lethal. He started carting his seventy-nine-year-old frame around to card shows, all over the country, and selling his own autographed balls at one-fifty, or one-seventy-five. He said he was trying to make sure the public could get his signature "at a reasonable price." But he also made sure Score Board Inc. would never make a nickel on its thousands of DiMaggio balls.

So what could Goldin do? Well, he dumped out the rest of his DiMaggio balls even lower than Joe would go. Why pay $150 to stand in line for the old bastard, when you could phone up Score Board's 800 number and have the same DiMaggio ball for . . . well, how 'bout a hundred bucks?

Of course, that didn't do much for the company. They were losing money on every ball they sold. Within a couple of years, Kenny Goldin had to jump ship, too. And soon after, Score Board went bankrupt.

And they never could really get at Joe. He'd got his money up front: close to nine million from Score Board, more than three million on the bats. And that didn't even count the shows. In the end, Joe and Morris were bragging to pals, how they'd been shorting that Score Board stock, all along. *(What's it tradin' now, five cents a share? Hah!)* . . .

It was never remarked that Joe's progress in business had carried him from Barry Halper, who loved baseball and adored Joe . . . through the Score Board boys and Jerry Romolt—they all liked baseball, but they loved a deal . . . and onward, to a cast of quick-buck artists who only loved a deal. What the hell—this was business. Why should they all have to be friends?

And it was never remarked how so many of Joe's

new partners were losers—goners, after a while: bankrupt, out of the trade, or ass-deep in trouble with the SEC. . . . Except Romolt: he was still on his feet. In fact, Jerry came through with another deal, the year after the bats—some serigraphs, an art piece— nothing huge, but a tidy six hundred grand for Joe. And Romolt came down to Florida, hung around the Yankee Clipper Center for the signing, mostly for old times' sake. Jerry even brought along a picture of him and Joe in Louisville, in the middle of all those bats . . . just as memento, a reminder of that chapter in their lives.

Joe looked at the picture and squinted up. He said, without a question in his voice: "You want me to sign it."

"Well, yeah," said Romolt. "If you would."

"Well, what would I say?"

"Shit, I don't know, Joe! How 'bout, 'To My Friend, Jerry Romolt.' "

Joe made a pained face. "Ahh, I don't know if I wanna go that far."

IT WAS JUST AFTER THE CIVIL WAR when writers and fans started fretting that money was ruining the great game of Base Ball. The mustachioed professionals of the Cincinnati Red Stockings had yanked the game (forever, it was feared) out of the soft hands of sporting gentlemen, and debased it. Soon (as it was balefully foretold) this noble pastime

would be nothing more than a grab for greenbacks—
for miners, farmers, factory hands, city rabble, and
immigrants.

By the turn of the century, baseball teams were
well-entrenched professional companies—with
owners, with capital, with physical plants (stadi-
ums) and workers who manned them. But still
America would not swallow the idea of baseball as
business. When the Philadelphia Phillies sued to
keep their (twenty-four-hundred-a-year) star, Napo-
leon Lajoie, from jumping to the new crosstown
Athletics (for a big raise—three thousand dollars!),
the Supreme Court of Pennsylvania ruled that poor
Nappy must remain in Phillie peonage. In any
other American business, a worker could seek employment wherever salary or whim might lead him.
But baseball would not be like any other business.
Even the grinding rigors of antitrust and contract
law had to yield to the dewy myth that baseball
was not about money.

In the decades that followed, baseball became an
even better business. And the myth that swaddled it
grew stronger, too. With the construction of steel
and concrete ballparks, the enterprise took on an
air of permanence—almost timelessness—and fed
the feeling that the Great Game followed ancient
dictates, some order handed down from gods in the
rosy, unremembered past. These great green
spaces—the same spaces, in the same cities (no
team had pulled up stakes since 1903)—were

decade by decade encrusted with memories so brilliant, and so tied up with the civic well-being that
it was possible (even while Joe played) to believe
that players spent themselves for the glory of their
team and town.

Every once in a while, some ugly scar of rock
would erupt amid these meadows. But all the gardeners of the Game (owners, promoters, sportswriters,
and the fans who believed them) would then con-
verge to cover over the telltale stone. In 1919, when
six hired hands who played ball for Chicago gave
away the greatest games of all *(They threw the World
Series—just for money?)* . . . the scandal almost shattered the industry, because it shook the central myth.
But the Baseball Nation responded with brilliant
vigor, by appointing a commissioner—a showboat
Republican judge, whose pose of incorruptible au-
tocracy, whose godly white mane of hair, and whose
thunderous name, *Kenesaw Mountain Landis* . . .
seemed sufficiently Old Testament to banish Mam-
mon from the public mind.

True, every winter, every spring, there was some
glimpse of the rock beneath the meadow—as some
star player in some town said he wouldn't play ball if
he didn't get more money. But as his only alternative
was to sit out the season (and get nothing at all), the
holdout usually folded in a matter of weeks, whereupon the gardeners of the sports page would cover
over the rock again, with fulsome features: how that
player had put all thoughts of money behind him.

Now he just wanted to smack that horsehide—and win the pennant for his squad.

If the holdout player went so far as to miss a game, he was roundly condemned by the Baseball Nation—and written up in the press not just for greed, but as some kind of head case, a problem child or troublemaker. Even Babe Ruth, for whom there were no rules, whose every other appetite was celebrated, was criticized when he showed himself hungry for money, too. There was the famous story from the Babe's holdout (for eighty thousand dollars) in the Depression year of '31. One writer harrumphed: Why should Ruth make more than President Hoover? Said the Babe: "I had a better year than him."

Like a body isolating and attacking some dangerous internal germ, baseball assailed any man who was open about the business as business—as Joe found out to his sorrow, in 1938. No man, no matter how talented, no matter how important to his club, was as crucial to the health of the game as the myth that protected it from public doubt. In fact, if Joe had played in some other town (New York, then as now, tolerated love of money); if the writers hadn't spent two years making him God's gift to baseball (even they couldn't manage a U-turn in the course of a month); if Joe hadn't made the Yankees champs for two years running (and could make them so again), his reputation might never have recovered. In the event, his chastisement was mild. But even so, it was never written that when he came back, every man in the clubhouse was with him. Every Yankee player knew Ed Barrow to be a sonofabitch. They knew Joe didn't get what he was worth. Nor did they. They knew every man in pinstripes played (and played as hard as he could) for the money. And not one could say a word about it.

In our day, we might call it a conspiracy of silence. We also call it the game's Golden Age. It lasted from April 1902, when that Pennsylvania court affirmed baseball's reserve clause in *Phila. Ball Club, Ltd. v. Lajoie* . . . for seventy years, until a speedy and daring outfielder named Curt Flood (who also didn't want to be a Phillie) took baseball and the reserve clause to the U.S. Supreme Court. "I do not feel," Flood told the court, "that I am a piece of property to be bought and sold irrespective of my wishes." With that enunciation, baseball was revealed as a business—an unfair one—and the wall of myth began to crumble. So, is Curt Flood a hero of the game? Not hardly. He was pretty much drummed out of baseball, for understandable reasons. The Pastime has been ill, infected with ugliness and greed—strikes, free agency, small-market weakness, guaranteed multiyear millions—money fights and money fretting, enough to break a fan's heart . . . more or less nonstop for twenty-five years, since Flood went to court.

Disgust with money in baseball reached its nadir in the early 1990s, when the basic labor agreement was expiring (each side wanted the whole pie), legalese filled the sports pages, attendance fell off a cliff, TV ratings were down (and still sinking), the commissioner's office was empty (no one who was anyone would take the job), and Bobby Bonilla (whom the Mets had to hide in the field) was leading the league with six point one million dollars a year. *Newsday* (the Mets' hometown paper) heralded the '93 season with a column by Bill Reel: "The spoiled modern ballplayer with his obscene salary and malcontent personality gets on my nerves. I wouldn't buy a ticket to a ballgame. Damned if I'll subsidize overpaid louts who complain harder than they play." And it wasn't just newspapers noting baseball's woe—there were dirges and whines in magazines, like *Esquire* ("The Dying Game") . . . from TV magazines, like *Frontline* ("The Trouble with Baseball") . . . and even a five-part nosebleed from Lou Dobbs on CNN's *Moneyline.* The Great Game had fallen into one of those public affairs "crises" that never seem to get better, and we're all supposed to be "concerned." They were chewing it over on *Meet the Press*—for God's sake, like Bosnia!

No wonder so many baseball fans froze their loving loyalties entirely in the past, in that timeless Age of Not Knowing, when pennants and glory were the currencies discussed, when smacking that horsehide seemed a good and truth unto itself. It was no accident that the years of baseball's monied discontent were also the glory years for the memorabilia trade. You'd see the fleshy men in the autograph lines, with reproduction Brooklyn ball caps hiding their pale pates, and they'd talk about two subjects. The first was the glory and grandeur of The Game, when they were there (not knowing) to see Branca face Thomson, or to watch Jackie Robinson stealing home, or to see the divine DiMaggio take Feller deep three times. *(Aw, they played the game right, then. Not like these assholes who get millions today. These guys were beautiful! Lookit 'im in this picture, this one I got for 'im to sign, right here.)* . . . And of course, the second topic was how much the picture would be worth, once he signed it.

When DiMaggio hit the autograph circuit after the Score Board deal, in '94, baseball truly had been wiped out by money. The big leagues were on strike. In the long lines that wound toward his signing table, Joe was held up as the embodiment of the Golden Age. The Clipper's desire, his dignity, his ethics, were a living reproach to the bratty players of the modern day. *(Six million, Bonilla won't run out a ground ball. Now, fuck him, he won't even play!)* . . . Sometimes, at the head of the line, some fan would try to share these feelings with the Great DiMag—and if the fan made it snappy, if Joe's mood was good, he might indirectly approve. "Well," he'd say, "we did work hard." But unlike other old heroes on tour, Joe wouldn't bash the current players or their pay. In fact, Joe wouldn't talk about money in public. Only amid his own network would he speculate on what he and the other players of his age would have done, if they'd had the power that players have now. "I'd walk into Steinbrenner's office," Joe told one friend, "and say to him, 'Hello, partner.' "

And even in those long autograph lines, there was only dim recognition of what Joe was doing now. All those fans knew they'd paid $150 or $175 for Joe's signature. They could see there were hundreds in line, and hundreds more whose numbers hadn't yet been called. Still, most of those fans seemed shocked to hear that weekend would net DiMag a cool quarter-million. And many just refused to believe that the highest paid major leaguer that year wasn't the Six Million Dollar Man, Bonilla. The highest (at age seventy-nine) was Joltin' Joe.

Which brought up the strangest thing about Joe and business. And that was: Why?

With tens of millions already socked away, it wasn't that Joe needed the money. And, he wouldn't spend it. So, what was it about?

"EVERYTHING IS FOR THE GRAND-kids," Joe liked to say. Paula and Kathie were grown up now—both married, with children of their own. They were the only family Joe dealt with, the ones he called when he was alone at night. Especially Paula, the blond one: that was a connection! She called him

Big Joe—and they'd fight like a couple of lovers. But he had to have her around. He made the autograph show promoters fly her across the country, or her and her kids (first class) so he could see her. The promoters didn't like it—plane fares on top of Joe's quarter-million—but what could they do? At the end of the show, Paula would count the tickets, like the cashier-wife at an old Italian fruit stand. And Joe liked that. He could count on Paula—after all, she had an interest in the business.

But Paula's life wouldn't be much different, if the trust that Joe bequeathed in the end was twenty million or thirty—or fifty. What would change? The short answer was, not much for Paula. Nor for Kathie. Nor for their kids. Every year they would get the interest from their portion of the trust. They would be well off. But they wouldn't be able to touch the big pile—unless Engelberg, Esq. allowed them to. That was how Morris drew up Joe's will. He (or his firm) would be the personal representative, trustee, and lawyer for the estate. In other words, the big pile would be in his hands.

So it wasn't Paula who was whipping Joe on to rack up the millions. Morris was Joe's business buddy, and they talked about the money every day, over lunch at the Deli Den in Hollywood—or sometimes all day, if Joe came into the strip mall office, to sign some pieces, to get some letters written, to plan out some deal, or just to hang around. It was Morris who would identify all the threats and schemes that beset Joe on every side—threats that Morris would then vanquish. It was Morris who'd remind Joe how he'd been cheated on that deal for the king-sized photographs . . . who'd point out how Joe had made Halper rich by signing all that shit in his house . . . who told Joe which of his partners and pals (pretty much all of 'em) were up to no good.

When Jerry Romolt came to Florida for that deal on the serigraphs, he and the artist, Carlo Beninati, sat all day in the strip mall, to keep Joe company while he signed. At one point Joe excused himself—Romolt thought Joe had to go to the bathroom. (With that Lasix diuretic the Clipper took, he might be in the can two or three times an hour.) But Joe didn't come back—for ten, fifteen minutes . . . well, maybe Joe had taken a break for tea. But then Joe came back with Morris, who announced with chortling glee that he'd sat the Clipper down with another client—and Joe had made thirty grand, signing flats during his break. "All I could think of," Romolt said, "was a hooker who goes to the bathroom, and turns another trick in the john."

If Joe ever strayed from the path of business, Morris was there to set him straight. One time, a kid came up to Joe with a scrap of paper, and asked—please—for an autograph. Joe had a soft spot for kids (as long as there weren't too many of 'em)—and even he could see, this boy wasn't looking for something to sell . . . so he signed. The kid was thrilled. And Joe was smiling, too. "You know what you just did?" Morris said, from behind Joe's ear. "You just gave away a hundred dollars—might as well just pull out a hundred and throw it away." The son Joe never had knew how to push the old man's buttons.

But Joe knew Morris was on his team. And, most of the time, DiMaggio didn't need pushing. The money was how Joe kept score. Measuring himself against the other guys from the Great Game, or the partners in his own deals—measuring against the whole damn country—DiMaggio was going to come out a winner.

That was why his teammates venerated Joe. (They honored him still, though he'd shown them his back for almost fifty years.) Maybe they couldn't be friends—okay. But they remembered: the Dago made them winners. No one could stay on Joe's team forever—but why wouldn't they try? . . . As the band used to sing in the chorus of that old song:

Joe, Joe DiMaggio, we want you on our side!

He was always a winner—for sixty-five years. If he gave that up, who would be with him?

WHEN JOE FINISHED SIGNING THE baseball cards for Pinnacle, there were two hours left on his contract. And the company had nothing more for him to sign.

But they got an idea. They would run a nationwide contest, a promotion with Toys "R" Us, and the winners would get to meet Joe DiMaggio. In fact, the five winners would come to New York for a baseball weekend: a skybox at Yankee Stadium, lunch at Mickey Mantle's restaurant . . . and a tour of Barry Halper's storied baseball collection, with Joe DiMaggio as their special guide.

Joe agreed: he owed them, by contract. So, Pinnacle ran the promotion, and brought the winners to New York. It was June 4, 1994. The tour at Barry's house was the Saturday morning highlight. They showed up in five limousines: five winners and their five guests. And the Pinnacle people showed up, of course, and a handful of suits from Toys "R" Us. So there were quite a few cars out front. By the time Joe got to Halper's door, precisely at ten A.M., Barry could see, the Clipper was in a foul mood.

"How many people here—a hundred?"

"Joe, it's just ten people."

"Ten! I thought it was five."

"Well, five and a guest, and . . ."

"All right, all right."

"C'mon, Joe. Sharon's makin' your favorite lunch with the shrimp . . ."

So Joe walked in, the tour began. But it was not to be. Joe kept looking around, until he saw it: one of the suits. He was taking notes. Toys "R" Us had brought a reporter from *Sports Collectors Digest*. They were putting Joe on display.

Joe stopped in mid-sentence, and made for the front door. Halper ran after him, out the door, onto the front walk. "Joe! I didn't even know! It wasn't my idea. Joe! Listen! . . ."

But Joe wasn't going to listen. That was in his contract: no press. He got into his waiting car—and he was gone.

Halper was off the team, too.

The Hall of Famer, Cooperstown, New York.

**With Hank and Nancy Kissinger at the *Time*
magazine seventy-fifth anniversary dinner, 1998.**

CHAPTER 19

◆

JOE HAD A PAL NAMED ROLLIE ROL-
ovich, an ex-cop in San Francisco. They'd met when
Rollie was on the detail for special events: anything
big that happened in the city, Rollie was out there—
like a Forty-niners football game. Rollie would
always look out for Joe, and get him in—get his car
into the lot right next to Candlestick Park.

Then Rollie took Joe to his cousin Mike Buscati's
restaurant. They went maybe a half-dozen times.
Buscati's wasn't the kind of place you'd know
about—a neighborhood joint on Lombard Street,
near the Marina—and the food wasn't great. But
when DiMaggio came, the food was spectacular.
They'd bring out the special oil someone had brought
back from Sicily, and make everything fresh—they
cooked like Joe's mamma. After the earthquake the
joint shut down, because the city closed that off-ramp
from Route 101, and the place was hard to get to . . .
but by that time, Joe and Rollie were pals—which
meant Rollie drove Joe around from time to time.

One time, he had to take Joe to Vallejo, to the track,
where they were having a DiMaggio Day, and the Joe
DiMaggio Featured Race. The Clipper didn't want to

go—people would be on him like flies—but he was committed. Rollie said: "Joe, don't worry. I know a way to get you in—no one'll see a thing." . . . And so he did. (That was Rollie's specialty.) He drove Joe through a back gate, across the auxiliary parking lots, to a side door of the clubhouse. And no one even caught a glimpse . . . until Joe got out of the car, and protested:

"Hey, wait a minute. They gotta know I'm here!"

Same way at the autograph shows: Joe would complain and haggle for months before a show—he wanted his own room, with special ushers to keep the customers in line, so fans couldn't crowd around, get behind his table and put their hands all over him while the wife or kid snapped their picture—Joe wasn't going to be on display! But he would also schedule his three hours of signing well after the doors opened in the morning—say eleven A.M., or right after lunch—when the place was full. And even then, he'd be just a few minutes late—so people would be in line quite a while, and expectation would build . . . until that moment when the organizer would grab the PA microphone, and everything in the hall would stop, as the news blared from overhead: *"Ladies and Gentlemen—now entering the building!—Baseball's Greatest Living Player . . ."* That was why the promoters paid Joe's quarter-million. When the Clipper walked in, their show was an event.

For example, there was a 1995 show called "Yankee Legends" at the Trump Taj Mahal, in Atlantic City. The promoters had a good lineup: Don Larsen, Yogi Berra,

Phil Rizzuto, all at a table in the big hall . . . and in the special side room, Reggie Jackson and Mickey Mantle. Mantle sat next to a pretty blond woman, talking with the fans, signing anything they had for him, listening with his head cocked while they told him about the games they'd seen. Reggie Jackson came alone, in a tight golf shirt, spent his day talking at length about his games, posing for pictures, signing a few things with whatever words the fans requested. But when DiMaggio arrived in his dark blue suit and tie, flanked by Morris Engelberg and his associate, Jerry Cantor—both of them in matching dark blue suits—then the serious business had begun. Joe's table looked like one side of the boardroom at a takeover meeting.

Large notices proclaimed:

Joe DiMaggio
RULES AND REGULATIONS FOR AUTOGRAPHS

Joe will *not* sign the following: Bats, jerseys, Perez-Steele cards, baseball cards, plates, multi-signature balls, original art, statues, lithos, gloves, albums, caps, cloth or wood items, flats over 16 X 20, books, items not related to baseball, photo or NL balls, equipment or personalizations. Joe has the right to refuse to sign any item that in his opinion fits into these categories.

PLEASE DO NOT BRING UP ANY ITEMS THAT JOE WILL NOT SIGN.

At the head of a long line, fans would present their articles to Cantor, who would accept or reject them. Rejected articles were handed back to the fan by an usher. Accepted articles were passed on to Morris, who would turn the piece into signing position and slide it under Joe's hands. If it was a proper American League ball, that would disappear into Joe's big left hand, with the '36 World Series ring gleaming toward the customer, as Joe's Sharpie pen rolled a perfect signature onto the sweet spot (with one dot above, and one below the last "i"—which was Joe's mark to guard against forgeries). Then the ball would be rolled down the baize toward another usher who was returning signed articles to their owners, and moving fans away. Few words were spoken. Joe wore dark glasses. He looked up only in annoyance. At the end of his three hours, he stood amid the last fans who were trying to engage him. "Morris!" he barked. "You comin'? Let's go!" They walked down an electric purple corridor of the Trump Taj Mahal, in the lurid glow of a neon sign directing gamblers to the "World Cash Center."

"Joe! . . . JOE! Wait a minute! . . ." This was from a man in a nylon jacket and a Yankees cap, steaming down the hall with a couple of large flats under his arm. His voice held echoes of New York, and desperation. "JOE! I PAID! WAITAMINUTE WILLYA?"

DiMaggio turned and froze the man ten feet

away. Joe's face was a gray mask, his opaque shades a slash of purple reflection. He didn't say a word, just stared the guy into a puddle of pleading. "Joe! I was in line. Two pictures! . . . Joe! I'm a collector!"

DiMaggio walked away. The fan stood rooted in the hall like the Clipper had glued him there. "Joe . . . !" People were staring at the fan as they passed. DiMaggio was already turning into the elevator bank. "Thanks, Joe! Thanks a lot, you asshole!" DiMaggio and Morris were laughing as the elevator doors closed.

EIGHTY YEARS OLD, AND PEOPLE were still desperate for him. And not just at shows. Joe would take along some guy to New York—say, an associate from Engelberg's office—and the man would talk about it for the rest of his life. They walked into the Carnegie Deli—everybody stopped eating and stood up to applaud! The fame made it fun to hang out with Joe. You were in a special world—on the inside—and there was nothing like it.

And stories—New York was the best for that— something had happened everywhere Joe went. If you asked him, of course, he wouldn't talk. But if you just went along, sooner or later Joe would bring up some name, or some tale: "You know, this place has a kitchen door . . ."

(Joe knew the back way in and out of every-place.)

"The night before a World Series game—it was my second or third year in New York—I was getting out through the kitchen door at three in the morning. And who do I run into? Walter Winchell. He said, 'Joe! Don't you have a game today?' And I said, 'I sure do, Walter. And I'm going to be just as keen as ever. If I'm not, you can write that you saw me here.'" ... That day, DiMaggio got three hits—and Winchell never wrote a word.

But it wasn't just old stories: the amazing thing about DiMaggio was, it was all still happening. In 1996, when a new generation of Yankees brought the world championship back to New York, Steinbrenner asked Joe if he would ride in the lead car in the ticker tape parade up Broadway to City Hall. So there was the Clipper—eighty-one years old, bent in the back, shrunken now to maybe five foot ten—but handsome still, in his perfect suit that didn't even roll at the collar when he lifted both his hands in his Pope wave to acknowledge the cheers of a million fans ... in a storm of cascading paper ... and riding next to New York's governor, George Pataki, who was hanging on the Jolter's every word, and laughing. Of course, those pictures were beamed around the world, too.

"Hey, Joe," one of his pals remarked, "it looked like you were having a good time riding around with Pataki."

"Good time!" said the Clipper. "Did you see all the crap they were throwing down? Big rolls of toilet paper. I told Pataki—'Hey, they're aiming at you, but they're hittin' me.' "

It was like that speech from the film *Field of Dreams* (one of Joe's favorites)—where James Earl Jones, in his godly voice, tells the hero, Ray Kinsella: "The one constant through all the years, Ray, is baseball. . . .

"America has rolled by like an army of steamrollers. It has been erased like a blackboard, rebuilt and erased again—but baseball has marked the time. This field, this game, it's a part of our past, Ray. It reminds us of all that once was good and could be again."

Except, in point of fact, baseball had been kind of up and down lately. The one constant through the last sixty years, Ray . . . was DiMaggio.

That was something special about being with DiMag, too. The old DiMag, especially. Because nothing stopped him—not even time. In the army of steamrollers, he was in the lead car. And always would be. And while you were with him, it was possible to think all the rules could be cheated—age, frailty, and the flight of fame . . . to hell with death and taxes—he even faced them without a flinch.

People used to cringe when Joe and Morris sat around in Florida talking about "the estate." Morris would tell Joe, he had to keep a diary every day—even if he only wrote down what he ate—and sign every page ... because every one of those pages would be worth hundreds when Joe was dead. And the checks—thousands of checks that Morris was keeping. They would fetch millions when Joe was dead. And the contracts—they would sell for even more. (Of course, Morris likely didn't tell Joe about the extra three contract copies that he made Joe sign—Morris put those in his own house—because then Joe would know how Morris planned to cash in. And the Clipper might walk, if he figured that out.) ... But visitors always got a creepy feeling when they listened in. How could Morris talk that way? Wasn't it a bit—well, insensitive?

Joe liked it. Because it proved to him that DiMaggio would go on, even after his lousy ticker gave out—or his lungs, after all those goddamn cigarettes. (Joe hadn't smoked since '69—but still, he was kicking himself.) ... It was Joe who'd bring Morris back to the subject—what to do with the money, after—especially if Joe was in a bad mood about Paula. If they'd had a fight, or he couldn't get her on the phone, or he'd got the idea, somehow, that she didn't care enough about him—then, he'd tell Morris how Paula was only after the money, and they mustn't let her get her hands on it.

(For his part, when Morris would run his mouth to visitors, he liked to call the heiress "that cunt, Paula." And he'd tell everybody how he could have her in bed in a minute if he chose—she was hot for Morris, as Morris imagined—and anyway, he never failed to add, without any evidence, her husband was a fag. But Morris couldn't let Joe hear him say any of that.)

For Joe, Morris himself was evidence that DiMaggio would go on. He liked it when Morris would tell about his greatest thrill in life—Morris often told that story—about when they stopped the Yankee Clipper van because Joe had to pee, so Morris got out, too, and both stood by the side of the road, and Morris knew he had arrived—*there he was, pissing with the Yankee Clipper!* . . . Joe liked the fact that Morris dressed like him. Morris always wore a dark blue blazer, or a dark suit stretched without a wrinkle over his tall frame and stooped shoulders. Or maybe Morris stooped because Joe was stooped now—it was hard to tell. . . . Joe liked Engelberg's absolute conviction that DiMaggio—the fame of DiMaggio—would never die. Joe would be like Elvis—bigger and bigger over the years. (And Morris would be Priscilla.) . . . Truly, Engelberg was convinced. He'd staked his fortune on that.

BUT IN THE LATTER YEARS, through the 1990s, Joe came more and more to New York, and left Morris at home. The way Joe's New York pals talked about it, New York was where Joe came to get away from business—to get away from Florida. (He complained that life was boring there—he didn't know many people.) . . . The fact was, sometimes, Joe got tired of talking about the money.

He had always tried to wall away one part of his life from another—say, his love life from his public life, or the public life from his business interests. Now, he was building a new life in New York that only a few people knew about. And there was no business in it. New York was where Joe came to have a good time.

He didn't have to fool with hotels anymore. Now, he had a pal, Dick Burke, who took care of the Clipper's lodging. Dick and Kathy Burke had a business in Atlantic City—a bar, restaurant, and hotel called the Irish Pub. But they also kept an apartment in New York, on Fifth Avenue, and Joe could use the place as his own.

He could call from Florida, to his friends Mario Faustini and Nat Recine—and ask what they were doing for dinner the following night. Of course, what they were doing was running their own restaurant—they had a big operation called Alex and Henry's, in Eastchester, just north of the Bronx. But when the Clipper called, Alex and Henry's would have to run itself. Mario or Nat, or often both, would drive to the airport, and bring DiMag into town, take him out to dinner, and to the Burkes' apartment to spend the night.

The next day, Joe might call Bill Gallo, the famous cartoonist for the *Daily News* sports page, to
ask what Bill was doing for lunch. Those two went
back almost as long as Gallo had been drawing heroes for the New York fans—that was forty years.
So, what Gallo would be doing for lunch, that day,
was sitting in a neighborhood Italian joint (the Foro
Italico on West 34th), while the mamma in the
kitchen spent herself to create her specialties, one
after the other, as DiMag and Gallo, *a tavola,*
talked about old times. (Bill had heard Joe's stories
five or six times—but he always laughed like they
were brand-new.) . . . After two or three hours, Joe
would be so relaxed, he might walk Bill back to his
office at the *Daily News*—where the city room
would stop dead when they walked in. Next time
he wrote a column, Gallo would mention the
visit—but Joe didn't mind. He knew Gallo didn't
want anything from him.

Or Joe might show up for lunch with his friend
Gianni Garavelli—at Bravo Gianni, a luxurious
hideaway on East 63rd. There, Gianni would present Joe's specialties. They weren't on the menu,
but DiMaggio had his own menu. First came the
minestrone, thick with vegetables (no pasta), and
with a bit of pesto in the broth, for tang. Then,
came the bow ties *(farfalle,* Joe's favorite)—with a
hint of garlic in the oil, fresh tomato, basil, and
sweet Italian sausage. Joe got to be so at home
with Gianni, he'd walk around from table to table,

to be introduced and shake the patrons' hands. One time, he was wandering past the phone as it rang. He picked it up and answered: "Bravo Joey!" The woman who was calling for reservations was confused. "Oh, I was calling Gianni," she said. "Yeah, but I'm Joe DiMaggio," said the Clipper. "S'not enough for you?" . . . (That night, when she told her husband—a supermarket magnate—of course, he didn't believe her. But when he came for his dinner, and there was DiMaggio to greet him at his table, he was so thrilled that the following day, he sent a pair of ruby earrings for Garavelli's wife. As Gianni would remember ever after: "If I had given twenty thousand dollars to this man, he would not have been so happy.")

But the pal Joe called every day was Rock Positano, Foot Doctor to the Stars. You probably wouldn't have known that *People* magazine's list of the "Fifty Most Fascinating" hid a hundred aching feet. But Dr. Rock knew. He knew them all—from the ground up, you could say. And he enjoyed them all. If he hadn't taken a wrong turn into med school, he would have made an all-star social director on the world's best cruise ship. He had the gifts of relentless energy and unflagging interest in the lives of his patients. You could talk to Dr. Rock about your heels, it was like going to a party. Maybe he could fix your feet, maybe not, but he was always a balm to the soul. That was how he met DiMaggio, who came in at the turn of the

1990s with a complaint about his ancient, aching heels. (They'd butchered Joe back in the forties, as Dr. Rock discerned.) . . . But after he'd come in about his heels two or three times, Joe showed up, one day, to ask: "You wanta have a cuppa coffee?"

In Joe's eyes, Rock was only a boy—thirty-one years old, when he met the Clipper. But as Joe also saw, Dr. Rock already had come a long way. He'd grown up poor on Brooklyn streets and had hauled himself through Yale Medical School, to the top of his profession—and to a glad welcome at a thousand doors. Maybe Joe saw something of himself in the kid. But Joe also knew a good time when he saw one—and in Dr. Rock, Joe had met fame's reward. In the doctor's fond gaze—and maybe for the first time in his life—Joe relaxed, without agenda, save to enjoy who he was.

So one day, Woody Allen was walking, with his wife-to-be, Soon-Yi, up Madison Avenue near 75th—just about where the old Sotheby's used to be—when he heard a voice call: "Woody!" And as he turned, he saw a limo at the curb, with a window rolling down and a hand extended, waggling invitation. "Woody! Over here!" . . . As Allen recalled, it was a good neighborhood, and a good car, so he went over and peered in, to find Dr. Rock and Joe DiMaggio—who, it turned out, was a Woody Allen fan. It also turned out that Woody was a fan of the Jolter . . . so when they said, "Let's have dinner!"—well, they actually did. They were both connoisseurs of New York—especially the old New York, where everybody was out all the time—Joe had been there, and could bring it to life in his stories. And for his part, Woody wanted to tell Joe how, at the age of ten, he'd read *Lucky to Be a Yankee*—and now, nearing sixty, he could still quote parts of it. (Which parts? . . . Well, for one, there was the advice about throwing the ball from center field on one hop—which made the throw easier to handle for an infielder or the catcher. Woody never forgot that—who could?)

And then, too, with some trepidation (this could have gone either way), Dr. Rock (and his limo) took the Clipper to the Carlyle Hotel to hear Woody Allen's jazz band. It turned out, Joe enjoyed that, too. And he was especially pleased to meet the producer of some of Woody's best-known films. That was Jean Doumanian, a smart and very comely woman, who was at the same show. (Dr. Rock happened to be her friend, as well.) Jean was startled by how handsome DiMaggio was, with that sparkle in his eye. As she said, "He could just win you with a smile." They went out to dinner at an Italian joint in Brooklyn. Joe was interested in everything Jean was doing. (He knew the entertainment business—and quite a few people in it.) In those days, she was producing an off-Broadway play, *Dinah Was*—a tribute to the late great singer Dinah Washington. So on opening night, Joe arrived to see the play. There were lots of notables in

the audience—but Joe was the star. And Jean, who
was, perhaps, half Joe's age, adored him. "So
courtly," she said. "I mean, he paid so much attention to you as a woman. Now I understand how a
woman can fall in love with a man so much older."

But old habits die hard—and Joe still played the
field. He was also very much taken with Elizabeth
Vargas, who was another passenger on Dr. Rock's
cruise ship, and a good-looking newswoman for
NBC. "Lizzie," as Joe liked to call her, hadn't yet
attained half Joe's age—which spurred the Jolter to
effusions of charm, and stories. "Now, Lizzie," Joe
said, "I've got a real cute one for you. Have you
ever heard of Alcatraz? . . ." And Joe explained
how the prison there had a ballfield—he'd played
against the cons—and at Alcatraz, when you hit a
ball over the wall, that was not a home run. It was
an out! Because they wanted to put the idea into
the prisoners' minds, see, that if you went over that
wall, you were going to be a loser. . . . After hours
of cute ones, Lizzie had to powder her nose—
whereupon Joe said to Dr. Rock: "Doc, she's a real
class act. Do you think she'd come out to dinner
with me again?" . . . Joe took her to Lattanzi's on
West 46th. (Kosher Italian—Joe loved it. And they
had a back room for him.) Joe told more stories.
And then, Joe saw, in the front room . . . there was
Paul Simon! So, to impress Lizzie, Joe told the
Doc to tell the maître d': "Eddie—Mr. DiMaggio
wants Paul Simon to come over."

Of course, the celebrated musician was one of Dr. Rock's, too . . . and an old friend of Joe's—since they'd talked about that song, with the famous lyric:

Where have you gone, Joe DiMaggio?
The nation turns its lonely eyes to you.

When he first heard about that, Joe wanted to sue. He thought those two singin' guys were trying to make him out like a bum. "I haven't gone anywhere," he protested. "I'm employed."

But now, he liked Paul Simon. And he liked the song. It was a memory for him—and another good thing: everybody still knew that song. "You know," Joe would say, when the subject of "Mrs. Robinson" came up, "that song will still be around after I'm gone."

But it wasn't his favorite Paul Simon song. Joe's favorite was "Bookends"—which he'd ask the driver to play, in Dr. Rock's limo . . . and Joe would sing along:

Preserve your memories;
They're all that's left you.

Tell the truth, that was half the joy with the girls. More than half, now. (Joe couldn't, you know, follow up like he used to.) But the memories they brought to him, brought from him, those were as strong, alive as ever—and Joe held on to them. They were his.

One night, Joe and his pals were closing out at the Waldorf—Peacock Alley (Joe liked the waffles)—after the big annual dinner for the Baseball Hall of Fame. All the guys were there—Mario Faustini and Nat Recine, Dick Burke, Dr. Rock, Bill Gallo . . . all grinning at each other as the octogenarian Clipper put the moves on this blond broad who wanted to meet him—TV star, or something—Susan Anton. Joe was all over her with stories, till it was quite late . . . and, finally, Ms. Anton had to go. The boys stood to leave, as well—to take the Clipper upstairs to the suite the organizers had rented for him. And Mario whispered: "Joe, why don't you take Susan upstairs, and—you know . . ."

"Nah," Joe said sadly. And he held his index finger in the air—but bent at the knuckles. And Joe didn't have to say more.

But on the way up in the elevator, Mario was startled to hear, just behind his ear, Joe's voice in half-whisper:

"Don't forget," said Joe. "There was a time I had the best there ever was."

IT WAS LIKE JOE HAD TWO NEW Yorks to visit—both had their joys, and both their bitterness. There was the New York that was alive now—and Joe wanted to see that—he was hungry for it. He never wanted to be in bed. But he got so tired now—sometimes, he couldn't keep going—*he couldn't walk four blocks* . . . that was hard to take.

But for him, that live New York stood shoulder to shoulder with the shadow town Joe knew. That was his New York, which had come and gone, leaving shadows everywhere.

The Waldorf, for instance—Marilyn had an apartment there. Joe had almost broken his hands one night, beating on the door of that apartment—trying to break it down.

No, not all the shadows were fond. . . .

A lot of them were whispers of loss. Fifty-fifth Street: Joe Adonis's joint, with the Strega bottles on the tables. Joe and Georgie drank there. . . . But Solotaire was gone, from a heart attack, twenty years ago.

Times Square—the Edison: Jimmy Cannon, poor sonofabitch, had a stroke in his apartment—they didn't find him for three days. And that street-tough Mick was *still alive.* But never the same. He could barely move. And it killed him, soon after.

That Sheraton—the old Americana: Joe stayed there free for years—the Yankee Clipper Suite. Frank Scott used to pick him up there, ride him to New Jersey for dinner with Halper. But Frank got to be like all the rest—asking Joe to sign stuff. And when Joe cut him off, Scott got bitter—said he had to carry envelopes with cash from Halper, so Joe would come to dinner. Well, those guys were past tense. Frank was dead. Halper had a stroke. But Joe went on.

Fifty-second—that was Toots's. Used to be. Toots got to be an old drunk at the end. And lost his joint. All the guys sent money. Joe wouldn't. Then Toots had a stroke, too. He was walking on canes. Joe saw him, the last time, in the locker room at the Stadium—Old Timers' Day—and Toots stumped in. Everybody made a fuss. Mantle, Martin, Berra, Ford all hugged him. But Toots only wanted Joe. Joe was in his corner. And Toots came across the room on his canes—or tried to come. Joe turned his back and walked away, into the trainer's room.

Sometimes, Joe wished the shadows would go away—the bad ones. Or he wished he could pick and choose. But they reached out for him . . . you could almost see it on him, when they took over. It happened more and more, when he was alone. You could see him on the street, sometimes—Fifth Avenue, or Central Park South—just wandering, with a faraway look in his eye. Like he didn't even see everybody watching him. Or they weren't there.

The writer Gay Talese thought that look was the consequence of fame. It was the same look that Talese had seen (on those same streets) in the eyes of Greta Garbo. Because when people got so famous that there was no one else on their level—no one else had a life at that pitch of hyperexistence—

then, it was like the other people didn't quite *have* existence . . . they simply weren't there.

But it might have been just the shadows. And maybe Joe was with others—who weren't there.

He would chase them away. He would call Dr. Rock. "What's going on? Do you wanta have a coffee? . . ."

And with Rock, something was always going on. "Hey, Joe! Would you mind if I introduced you to Isaac Stern? You know, he comes from San Francisco, too. . . ."

One day, DiMaggio was hanging around in Dr. Rock's office, when the Doc inquired if it would be all right if he brought in another patient—he was in the waiting room—would Joe like to have a talk with Henry Kissinger?

Well, that sounded fine to Joe. He had met Kissinger once before, in the 1970s, at the Stadium—Dr. K. was another denizen of Steinbrenner's box. But now, Hank and Joe had a good long talk.

It turned out young Henry was a Stadium bleacher bum—back in '38, '39, he was always out there—and never saw a ball get past DiMaggio. At that point, Kissinger was making eleven bucks a week, but he'd spring for a dollar-ten for a reserved seat when Bob Feller was pitching. Then, Kissinger would watch DiMag stand in, with that distinctive stillness—not a wiggle of the bat or twitch of a leg . . . until he hammered Feller's fastball toward a distant fence. Even then, young Henry was a student of power. And DiMaggio was his hero. "He was in a world by himself," as Kissinger remembered. "There was nobody who could take over a ballpark like he could."

In the present day they saw the world companionably, too. If DiMaggio wasn't a lifelong Republican, the Kennedy boys had driven him to forty years' fealty with the GOP. Joe approved of Kissinger. And enjoyed Kissinger approving him. When Kissinger brought baseballs, Joe signed them for Dr. K.'s nephews—Kissinger had no idea Joe didn't like to sign. Now, the two pals would arrange to meet in the Kaiser's skybox for big games. They'd sit together and Joe would hold forth. (Kissinger learned not to ask: Joe would talk if he wanted to.) One time, eighth inning of a World Series Game One—Atlanta was clobbering the Yanks—both Hank and Joe left their seats for a moment, and when they came back, the Braves' skipper, Bobby Cox, had replaced one left-hander with another. "New pitcher," Joe remarked. "Looks the same to me," said Hank. "No, look," Joe said. "It's a different arm angle. You gotta look for the release point. See this guy comes three quarters, he's gonna curve you on the outside—unless you move up a little, get the bat out to hit it before the break. See, watch, Doc—the second baseman'll move over a couple a steps . . ." And Kissinger was in heaven. "If you had told me in 1938 that I would be secretary of state, and I would be friends with DiMaggio, I would have thought the second was less likely than the first."

America she is wonderful—as the papas on the Wharf used to say. And DiMaggio was her favorite son. Or one of them, who knew all the rest. And he understood, at last, it didn't matter that Kissinger had written more books than Joe had read . . . Hank liked him. And they had more in common than not—all the big ones did, who'd been at the top. It was like those tables at the autograph shows, where they sold the stuff to the fans. There was Joe DiMaggio's signed baseball—a special one, three hundred bucks (because, you see how he wrote "Yankee Clipper" under his name there?)—which was next to the George Bush White House cuff links, and just in front of the autographed photo from Farrah Fawcett (that's when her hair was great)—and an original cel from the first Disney movie with Donald Duck. They were all a bit different from each other, sure. But they were all big.

And so, in 1997, when Joe had to show up to get an award from the Sports Broadcasters of America, he brought along a special guest to make a few remarks at the podium. *(Ladies and Gentlemen, please welcome the State Department's Greatest Living . . .).* Of course, the sportscasters were delighted. And then, too, Hank saved Joe at the big *Time* magazine dinner, in March of 1998.

Now, that was the World Series of collectible

bigs—when *Time* brought together the people who had graced its cover, to celebrate the magazine's seventy-fifth year—it was damn near all "the greatest living" at a supper (catered by the Plaza) for twelve hundred in Radio City Music Hall. It was Winona Ryder in a chat 'n' chew with the Gorbachevs, and Nicole Kidman and Kofi Annan, and Claudia Schiffer, Arthur Schlesinger, Jr., and Toni Morrison and Norman Mailer and Sophia Loren and Ralph Lauren and Lauren Bacall and the Drs. Kevorkian and Falwell and . . . well, you get the idea.

But Joe had a problem.

Bill Clinton wanted DiMag at his table. And DiMaggio loathed Clinton. Hated his politics. Hated his style. And that Monica Lewinsky! That was not up to the standard. (As Joe pointed out to some pals: "You know, we paid for that White House. He shouldn't be doing that there.")

So, Dr. Rock (Joe's escort) had to tell the *Time* bigs that Hank and Nancy Kissinger had asked for Joe at their table. And Joe had already accepted—the Clipper had made a commitment! (And Hank backed up that story for his pal.) A few gossip-mongers still wrote how Joe had snubbed the president. But that was only a little spray in the ocean of ink about that dinner . . . and Joe got to sit where he liked.

He liked everything about that night. Joe was radiant in his bespoke Pierre Cardin tuxedo. And amid the hundreds of movers and shakers, heads of state and movie stars . . . DiMaggio was the star of the show. From the moment he and Dr. Rock walked in through the lobby of Radio City, there was a line of bigs—a never-ending line—all stars-turned-fan, just to shake Joe's hand. Steven Spielberg, Sean Connery, Jack Lemmon, Kevin Costner, Tom Cruise . . . and Nicole Kidman, Sophia Loren, Mira Sorvino, Sharon Stone . . . and The Greatest, Muhammad Ali, came over and Joe took his boxing stance and made like he was gonna hit the champ with a right cross, and they mugged for pictures . . . and the writers and the newsies all crowded around—Mailer, Cronkite, Jennings, Rather, Mike Wallace, Tim Russert ("This," said Joe as he embraced Russert, "is one of the good guys." Joe never missed *Meet the Press*.) . . . It was only the call to dinner that broke up the happy crowd around the Clipper. Joe talked diplomacy— sitting between Hank and Nancy—when they weren't all telling stories about everybody else who was there. Dr. Rock sat across the table with Mel Brooks and Anne Bancroft—they were Joe's pals, too. In fact, they'd had lunch with Joe, just a couple of weeks before.

(It was only afterward Joe tried to figure out with Dr. Rock how the editors of *Time* went about deciding who would sit with whom. "Why do you think," Joe mused, "they put Brooks and Anne Bancroft with us?" Dr. Rock shook his head disgustedly. "Joe—get it? They sat DiMaggio with Mrs. Robinson!" . . . "You know, Doc," Joe said, "you might be right.")

And they sat all night, everybody stayed—nobody wanted the party to end. Joe least of all. Because for him, it was like his two New Yorks, his live pals and the shadows, too, all got dressed up and did the town together for one night. They got Bill Clinton up to make a speech—a toast, actually, to FDR—that was the last Democrat Joe liked. They got Gorbachev up to speak about leadership (and Joe told his story of how he got his ball signed by Gorby at the White House) . . . they got that computer man, Bill Gates, to make a toast about the Wright brothers, and Toni Morrison talked about Martin Luther King (Marilyn thought that guy was great) . . . scientists talked about scientists and editors about editors (that was kind of slow) . . . but then, Kevin Costner got up, and made his toast—to Joe.

"There are certain people's names that, when spoken out loud, are reminders of what men can be like," Costner said. "To this day, when I hear the name Joe DiMaggio, it is so much more than a man's name. It reminds me to play whatever game I'm in with more grace, and pride, and dignity. . . .

"He's a man who speaks to us about things men don't speak of—about how to walk through life, and how to receive the admiration that (only the famous can know) is half-deserved. And about how to wear defeat and disappointment as if it were just a passing storm.

"It's important for you to know that I never actually saw Joe DiMaggio hit a ball, or catch one. I was never at Yankee Stadium to see him run into center field, or step up to the plate. But when I step into the yard to play catch with my son—whose name is Joe—I think about the Joe we are honoring tonight. I wish that both of us could go to the ballpark and see him play. Because men like Joe DiMaggio are not just of their own time. They are men for the ages. And as the century comes to a close, and debates heat up about who is the man or the woman of the century, I know the list will be impressive. But it will not be complete unless Joe DiMaggio's name is on it. So, I'd like you to raise a glass to Joe DiMaggio, for showing us the way."

That set off the loudest and longest ovation of the night—a thousand stars on their feet to cheer. Joe tried to busy himself, looking down, setting to rights his spoon and coffee cup. But at last, he looked up with a grin, and raised a hand to his brow, as if the custom Cardin tuxedo came with a cap that he could tip.

THE NEXT DAY, JOE WAS AT ROCK'S office. "Hey, Doc, get a ball, will you? We'll send it to Costner's kid." So Rock found a baseball, and

Joe signed it—"To Little Joe . . . from your friend in sports, Joe DiMaggio."

But that was about all Joe did that day—that and wonder aloud where his energy had gone.

Dr. Rock wanted Joe to see a doctor in New York—the best specialists in the world, as Rock said—and he could get 'em all. Or whoever Joe wanted, or needed—that's what Rock was trying to say. Positano could see something wasn't right with Joe's health—and hadn't been right for more than a year. They'd be walking down the street, and Joe would stop. "Wait up, Doc." (It used to be, Positano would have to run to keep up.) "Doc, I don't understand why the hell I get so winded." . . . So, Positano pleaded with the Clipper—he could bring Joe in right now, to New York Presbyterian (where Rock was affiliated) . . . and have him checked out by the best—today.

Joe wouldn't do it. He didn't want to waste his time in New York. He didn't want to deal with it. He said he hated doctors ("No offense, Doc") . . . he'd get someone to check him out in Florida—at the Hollywood, Florida, Memorial Hospital. That was where Joe was affiliated. It was Hollywood Memorial that ran the Joe DiMaggio Children's Hospital.

That hospital had been good for Joe. He had lent his name to the children's wing when he was in that tax fight with California. It bolstered his claim to Florida residency—it showed Joe was involved with the local community, he was active in the civic affairs of South Florida—his new home. . . . And Morris would occasionally tell the newspapers that the money he demanded for Joe to appear— well, that wasn't just pay for the Clipper. Most of that money would be spent on sick kids.

It was all tax-true . . . which was to say, it hid the facts. DiMaggio never gave money to the hospital. Well, once he wrote out a check for a hundred bucks, at the request of his favorite great-grandchild—Paula's daughter, Vanessa. . . . But for the most part, Joe wouldn't give anything—not even a signed ball. If the hospital officials wanted autographed DiMaggio baseballs or signed pictures (for fund-raising purposes), they had to buy them on the open market—from dealers, like Jerry Romolt.

Still, Joe's name had been good for the hospital—and vice versa. There was a giant billboard looming over I-95, heading south through Holly-wood—a picture that was like a landmark now— a smiling DiMag holding up a smiling infant— with the clever copyline: "DiMaggio and the Babe." It lent a new tint of altruism to his aura, and displayed the Great Name (in letters six feet tall) for a new generation that never even saw a Mr. Coffee ad.

Joe could rely on the hospital staff to take care of that name—they had an interest in the business. And he could count on them to never breathe aloud the word he never wanted to hear—that was cancer. Joe had his generation's fear of the disease, and that awful word. To him it was like the evil eye—a curse that might descend upon him, if he even heard the word in a sentence with his name.

So, through the spring and summer of 1998, Joe's breathing grew more labored, his stamina diminished. He'd come to New York, and Dr. Rock would get on him. "Joe, at least let's find out what it is . . ." And Joe would say what he'd said for a year. He had a lung infection. "How long can you have a goddamn infection?" Positano asked in exasperation. But then he'd have to back off. Joe would dig in his heels—this was his affair. "Doc, I'm just more comfortable with the fellas in Florida." . . . Mario Faustini suggested to Joe in a gentle way, "You know, it doesn't hurt to get a second opinion." That was exactly what Joe didn't want. He'd talked this over with Morris. It was Morris who tended the relationship with Memorial Hospital . . . and Morris who warned Joe that in New York, he couldn't protect the name.

"Joe, if it's a matter of security," Positano said, "we had the goddamn Shah of Iran! . . . Look, if it's something—you know . . . put it this way: Would you rather have Sloan-Kettering, or a community hospital in Florida?"

But the papers could get hold of it. Then it would be a circus. Joe told Rock that he was going to have tests—he'd take care of it—with the fellows in Florida. End of September, he would have it checked out. But Joe wanted to come to New York one more time, before that happened. Joe said that Steinbrenner was going to put together a DiMaggio Day, at the Stadium—September 27, last Sunday of the season. It was all kind of an ad lib, a last-minute thing—but Joe said it was important.

And, hey—did Rock want to come?

BOOK V

THE
LAST DEAL

1998–2000

✦

In the skybox: the host, George Steinbrenner, has to sit in the aisle. Morris Engelberg (right) insists: "He has to learn his place."

The great name is displayed for a new generation, in Hollywood, Florida.

Without Joe's autograph, the special Yankee Clipper ball sold at $25—and slowly.

CHAPTER 20

◆

STEINBRENNER DIDN'T REALLY WANT
a Joe DiMaggio day that September. Or the
regulation Joe DiMaggio ball—or fifteen thousand free balls for Joe . . . that wasn't Steinbrenner's
idea. (And the copies of Joe's World Series rings—
that was Barry Halper's idea. He was still trying to
get back with Joe.)

Of course, in principle, a day for DiMag would be
fine—Steinbrenner had no objection. In latter years
G.S. and Joe D. had gotten along splendidly. And
Yankee history was an asset on Steinbrenner's balance sheet. The Clipper was Yankee history.

But in 1998, the Yankees didn't need a DiMaggio
Day. That year, the Pinstripes were winning more
ballgames than any AL club had ever won—that was
baseball history. The Yanks were the darlings of New
York . . . and the stands were full. Why not save
DiMaggio Day for next year—say, early in the '99
season? It could put some fannies in the seats (it
could fill the whole Stadium) on some solemn Sunday when Minnesota or K.C. was in town.

It was Joe who wanted to schedule his day before
the '98 season ended. Or, to be precise, the pressure

came from Yankee Clipper Enterprises, of Hollywood, Florida—YCE, as it was called by Morris
Engelberg, Esq., who ran it. . . . Joe told Morris, Di-
Maggio Day had to be this year, or never—and Morris jumped on the case big-time. Joe didn't tell
Morris why the big day had to happen now. Joe didn't
tell anyone, when he started coughing up blood.

WHAT MORRIS KNEW WAS, HE HAD
to come through. No mistakes! This was the biggest
payday he'd ever attempted for DiMaggio. Morris
ran the numbers in his head, over and over. If that special Yankee Clipper baseball (autographed by the
Clipper) could be retailed for four hundred dollars
(Morris was sure it could), this deal could add up to
five million bucks—or better. Even if they had to
wholesale Joe's signed balls (say, at two hundred a
pop), that would net three million. And there was no
Romolt in the mix this time, no one to look over Engelberg's shoulder—this one would be just Morris
and Joe. They'd been talking about this deal for so
long—since that day in 1995 when the Yankees un-
veiled Mantle's monument—and played the game
with a Mickey Mantle ball . . . Morris had been
working to create an official DiMaggio baseball *for
three years.*
    That was how Engelberg, Esq. complained of his
exertions to his new business buddy—Scott DiStefano, who was a young memorabilia salesman with

the Lakewood, New Jersey, firm called B & J Collectibles. By long-distance telephone, Morris was at pains to impress young DiStefano with the amount of work that had gone into this DiMaggio Day, with the importance of the DiMaggio ball, with the seriousness of this deal as a whole. "This is a very big deal, Scott."

"I know that," said DiStefano, who agreed with Morris often.

"I mean, you're selling two thousand balls that go for four hundred thousand dollars with no overhead and no cost."

"I know."

"It's major," said Engelberg.

"Major," said DiStefano.

"Biggest deal you're going to have for next year."

"I'm looking forward to it."

"Okay?" said Morris. "So, we've got to get this wrapped up."

No one was trying any harder than DiStefano, who saw this deal, and Engelberg, and DiMaggio (especially a dead DiMaggio) as a ticket he could ride into business for himself. Young Scott didn't want to flog baseballs forever for B & J Collectibles of Lakewood, New Jersey. In fact, he wanted out right now. (That's why Scott wouldn't tell his boss that he was doing deals on the side with Morris.) DiStefano had formed his own company, Atlantic Coast Sports. And he, too, had run the numbers in his head a thousand times. . . .

Morris said DiMaggio was sitting on ten million dollars' worth of autographed material.

Let's see—sales commission on ten million for the estate . . .

And that didn't count the stuff that Morris had squirreled away.

Morris would split the profits with Scott—as long as he kept Morris's name out of the sale . . .

"But what do you think," Morris was saying. "Can you make a hundred on your own?"

"I think so," said Scott. "I think so. If I keep doing things with you, yeah, absolutely."

Morris advised caution. He was fond of giving fatherly advice to DiStefano, his new protégé. Maybe Scott should keep a paycheck with B & J for a while. . . .

In the months to come, Morris would claim that he knew all about DiMaggio's illness. He just couldn't talk about it, because Joe insisted on privacy. Of course, that was when Engelberg was promoting himself as "Joe's longtime personal attorney, confidant, and closest friend."

But Engelberg didn't know.

Scott said he wanted to be in business on his own, so he wouldn't have to share the big windfall, when DiMaggio died.

"Yeah, but Joe's worth ten more years," Morris said.

That was why he and Scott had to make their money now.

YOU HAD TO UNDERSTAND, ENGEL-
berg had shadows, too—particularly one persistent
shadow in the shape of a doll, with a painted porce-
lain face . . . a Madame Alexander doll.

For years after Joe and Morris met (that was 1983)
the office of Engelberg, Esq. did not display a single
picture of DiMaggio. True, Joe D. was a client—but
all that meant was, Morris directed a CPA in the office, Paul Schneider, to prepare Joe's annual tax returns. Morris didn't deal much with DiMag. And in
the Engelberg inner sanctum, there were no signed
bats or balls, uniform jerseys, magazine covers, lith-
ographs of Joe . . . none of the collectible Clipper
flotsam in which Morris would ultimately wallow.
Through all the 1980s, in fact, Morris's office was
filled with dolls.

Because in those days, the meal ticket (and the big
payday of which Morris dreamed) was Beatrice
Alexander Behrman, who was known to millions as
Madame Alexander, and who was, by the mid-1980s,
pushing ninety years old.

Mrs. Behrman was the daughter of a Russian immigrant who ran America's first doll hospital—and
she had spent her life in the family trade. Her Alexander Doll Company had created the first licensed
character doll (Scarlett, from the movie *Gone With
the Wind),* the first dolls to honor living people
(England's Queen Elizabeth and the Dionne Quin-
tuplets), the first full-figured fashion doll (CissyJ),
with high-style (and highly lucrative) clothing out-

fits. . . . Mrs. Behrman's dolls were prized worldwide for their detail and workmanship. And they were prized in the office of Engelberg, Esq. for the millions they had brought to Madame.

For Morris had drafted Mrs. Behrman's will. And by the terms of that will, when she died (how long could it be, now?) . . . Morris—or his law firm —would serve as Madame Alexander's personal representative and as attorney to the personal representative (from which positions fat six-figure fees could be garnered) . . . and as preparer of federal tax returns for the estate (for which labor a percentage of the estate would go to Morris) . . . and that didn't even count the fees Morris could charge for disposal of property or litigation involving the estate. To put it baldly, when Madame died, Morris would be rich.

But then, disaster struck. Before Morris could wave goodbye to the beloved Madame on her way to doll heaven, Mrs. Behrman's daughter took over the old lady's care. And at the same time, the daughter also took a look at the arrangements for Madame's estate—and (to make a long and gamy story short) . . . a new will was drawn, and Morris was dumped.

To be sure, that did not stop the avid Engelberg. Within hours of Madame Alexander's death, Morris filed at the courthouse a document that he represented as the last will and testament of Madame Alexander. It was, in fact, the old will that would have made him rich.

Needless to say, litigation followed—during which Engelberg, Esq. was accused of a number of lawyerly crimes—for instance, filing a will that he knew to be false. The litigation was protracted, expensive, and surpassingly ugly. And in the end, Morris was paid a hundred thousand smackers.

Anyway, it should come as no surprise that 1990, the year of Madame Alexander's death, was also the year that the dolls disappeared from Morris Engelberg's office—to be replaced by the looming shadow doll that Morris would never quite shake. . . . That was also the year when a young associate in Engelberg's office, the lawyer Les Kushner, went to a baseball card show at the Hollywood Mall. Kushner was a baseball memorabilia fan, and he came back from that show with two sets of Joe DiMaggio pics—six photographic prints in all. Three of them he gave as a gift to Engelberg.

"Here, Morris," Kushner said. "Why don't you get Mr. DiMaggio to sign these? You can put them on the wall." And that was the first hint Morris had of the evocative grandeur (i.e., the dollar value) of the Yankee Clipper's likeness and image.

That also signaled a change of practice in the office. Now Mr. DiMaggio's affairs were not the sole province of Paul Schneider, CPA . . . but the personal business—nay, the life passion—of Morris Engelberg, Doctor of Laws. Now, not only did Morris take a copious interest in DiMaggio's business—say, for instance, in the contracts that wooed Joe to autograph shows—but Morris would go along to the shows, to make sure Joe was well taken care of. And soon, Morris was handling all of DiMaggio's business. In fact, everything about DiMaggio became Morris's business . . . at the same time that Clipper artifacts took over the tables, credenza, shelves—in fact, every available space in the office, where dolls used to abide.

But the larger shadow doll lingered—with the larger lesson that Morris couldn't forget: this one must not get away.

WHAT WOULD MORRIS DO TO KEEP Joe?

What would he not do?

Just for starters, Engelberg, Esq. undertook all of Joe's legal work, got him his Florida residency, got California off Joe's back, and made Joe compliant with the federal tax authorities. (That was a great worry off Joe's mind. He had fretted unceasingly through the investigation that busted Darryl Strawberry and Duke Snider—among others—for taking unreported cash at autograph shows and personal appearances. No one had taken more cash than Joe.) And Morris undertook those labors without ever sending Joe a bill.

Morris would name his office for Joe, and would park in front of it the van he'd bought with the pinstripes, and the DIMAG 5 vanity plate, and the words painted on—"Yankee Clipper." But the van would not be parked directly in front of the door. That prime space—"Number 5"—would be "Reserved for Mr. Joseph P. DiMaggio."

Whenever Joe cared to use that space, Morris would host him in the office for hours, and take Joe to lunch every day, and dinner maybe once or twice a week. He would make a great and talky show of involving Joe D. in Engelberg family events—for instance, the wedding of Morris's daughter Laurie to a young man named Herb Milgrim. (And Morris would complain for years—but never where Joe could hear—about Joe's failure to bring a gift.)

For almost a decade Morris would walk a tightrope between public celebration and private complaint about the Great Man. Morris would often boast that Joe held Laurie's baby boy for his circumcision—Morris had insisted on Joe as "Godfather." (Joe wasn't comfortable with that title—he knew more about it than Morris did.) But just as often, Morris would complain about how much it had cost him to confer that honor. He had offered his daughter ten thousand bucks to name the kid Joseph. At the end of negotiations, Morris paid Laurie five grand for the middle name—Montgomery Joseph Milgrim.

Morris would take Joe to the doctors. (Doctors mostly of Engelberg's choosing.) Morris would detail the women of his office to pick up Joe's dry cleaning, to get Joe's car washed, to go to Joe's house and clean it up. Ultimately Morris would get a free house for Joe in the gated community where Morris lived. In fact, Joe's new house would stand no more than fifty feet from Morris's house—so Joe couldn't open up his front door to get his newspaper without Morris knowing.

But mostly—most of all and constantly—Morris would have to make Joe money, and scheme for Joe's money, and talk about Joe's money, and pile up millions upon millions for DiMaggio. Morris would raise Joe's prices, and enforce Joe's prices, and make prices on things any other man might do for free. (A consortium of Reno, Nevada, promoters would be asked to pony up a million, guaranteed, for the honor of hosting the Great DiMag on his eightieth birthday.) . . .

But there was one more thing:

When Morris made money, Joe could never know.

So, Morris was on the phone again to Scott Di-Stefano, in New Jersey—beginning of September 1998—adjuring Scott to sell more DiMaggio autographed baseballs . . . but not for Joe. These were balls that Morris had socked away in his own house.

And, for all his efforts, DiStefano couldn't sell fast enough:

"Scott, I've got to get rid of these balls," Morris said. "They're taking up my whole closet. I can't hang up my clothes . . ."

"No problem. No problem."

". . . That's all I care about. I don't need the money."

What Morris needed—and the subject he returned to over and over—was secrecy.

"There's millions of dollars in this thing here if you don't blow it."

"Well, just plan it with me," said DiStefano. "I'll do it whatever way you want."

"No, I'm saying you can't mention my name to [the buyers] and these guys. It floats around the business. They tell Barry Halper, and it gets back . . ."

"Right."

". . . gets right back to Joe," said Engelberg.

"Okay. No."

"Who you tell, it floats around."

"Okay."

"Okay?"

"I got it," said DiStefano.

"Again, we've got to get those two thousand balls, Scott."

"I will get that."

"Okay," Morris said. "Take care."

"Bye-bye."

SEE, THE MOST IMPORTANT PART OF this deal for Morris was not Joe DiMaggio Day, nor the World Series rings for Joe—not even the fifteen thousand Yankee Clipper balls that Joe could sign and market for three million dollars or more. That would be Joe's three million. It would add to the estate, sure. And Morris was counting on a piece of that estate—but when? . . . Morris could not wait.

So the crucial part of the deal was the two thousand balls that Morris would buy, secretly, through DiStefano. And then, Engelberg, Esq. could mix those in, while Joe was signing. . . . And the price of those balls—say, a cool four hundred grand—would be all for Morris. . . . Or Morris and Scott—of course, Morris would share! (He wanted Scott to know that.)

"If I don't get those balls," said Morris, "I don't want to go."

"I know," said Scott.

"I don't want to do this," Engelberg said.

"I don't blame you," said DiStefano.

"I'm running all over the place with Joe. . . . I'm going to do four straight days with this guy."

"Good luck."

"Three days in Chicago and one day in New York. . . ." Morris wanted Scott to know: "It's a tremendous strain on me."

That was why Morris had to make sure this would be worth his exertions.

"Now, you've ordered two thousand?"

"Two thousand."

"Do you think you can sell these at two hundred apiece?"

"Yes."

"I'm talking about my balls. I'm not talking about

his balls. . . . But there are people you can sell wholesale, this ball?"

"Yeah, I've got wholesale people lined up."

"But not ten balls at a time?"

"No, like fifty or more. . . ."

"I'm only going to let go of maybe a thousand or
two for him, and my two thousand."

"Right."

"I'm going to make the money on my two thousand—not him."

"Oh, I know."

With the benefit of Morris's Socratic tutelage,
Scott knew very well what balls he had to get, and
what balls he had to sell first.

"There's no money being made on his two thousand," Morris said.

Scott knew that, too.

SO MORRIS SECURED HIS TWO THOU-
sand balls, and Joe DiMaggio Day was a go. In fact,
you could call it a DiMaggio weekend—that
last weekend of September 1998. It was a schedule
that few other men of Joe's age would have attempted. But for DiMaggio, it was more or less run-
of-the-mill.

Thursday, Joe and Morris would fly into Chicago
on American Airlines. Joe mostly flew American, because they'd upgrade him, gratis, and if possible to
seat 5D, which bore his number and initial. Then, a

stretch limo would transport the principals of YCE to the Chicago Hilton Hotel and Towers, where Joe's host, George Randazzo from the National Italian American Sports Hall of Fame, had secured a suite for the Clipper's comfort. In fact, it was the Conrad Hilton Suite—with its fourteen-hundred-square-foot parlor (suitable for stand-up receptions up to a hundred guests), dining room (for sit-down dinners of twenty), private kitchen, sixteen-foot-high lakeview windows, eighteenth-century tapestries, crystal chandeliers, oriental carpets, a baby grand piano, the library with bar and billiard table, and three Mussolini-sized balconies overlooking the lake and the city—and that was just the top floor. Down the circular staircase was the master bedroom with the king-sized four-poster canopy bed, master bath, also with a view of the lake, and a video panel over the Jacuzzi, and two other king . . . well, you could see it yourself for four thousand two hundred dollars a night. The good part was it had a TV, on which Joe could watch an old western, until he dozed with the remote in his lap.

Friday Joe would be out early to ring the bell at the Chicago Board of Trade, an honor often accorded to visiting kings and presidents, rescued POW's, moonwalking astronauts, and that sort of national pride-and-joy. Friday evening he'd be hosted to a party for Chicago's top *paesani.* George Randazzo had mentioned to Mel Bechina, a big-time trucking nabob, that DiMaggio was coming, maybe he'd like dinner.

"You got," Bechina replied, "whatever you want." That meant Carmichael's Steak House (which Bechina operated as a sort of hobby) would serve prime beef, pasta, Chianti, and all the trimmings for two hundred movers and shakers, including the mayor and governor—black tie, of course.

Saturday would mark the rededication of the Italian American Sports Hall of Fame in a new made-to-measure two-million-dollar facility—and at a new downtown location. The state of Illinois and city of Chicago had completely remade the corner of Bishop and Taylor streets, the heart of Little Italy—where, amid classical Roman columns, plashing fountains, pedestrian benches, tilework, greenery, ornamental lighting, an elaborate plinth would now support an eight-foot-tall bronze sculpture of Joe, with his bat in graceful and eternal follow-through . . . to mark the Hall of Fame's new address—*Piazza DiMaggio.* Saturday night would feature another dinner, this one strictly for big givers to the Hall . . . after which DiMaggio could doze again—until he had to rise at four A.M., to make the first plane out to New York, and Joe DiMaggio Day.

It was all more or less normal, because the city, the state, the Hilton, the Hall of Fame, its officers and givers . . . were all showing off for Joe. The black tie banquet, the Mussolini Suite, and the long limo parked outside (twenty-four hours a day) had nothing to do with Joe's needs—they were about what the other guys needed to show. On Saturday, Mayor

Daley would change his schedule to be with Joe, for the same reason that Sunday would be DiMaggio Day not just at Yankee Stadium but (by mayoral proclamation) in New York City as a whole. It was the same reason the commodity jockeys at the Board of Trade watched Joe whack their bell with his special bat, and they started to cheer. And unlike every other day (with anyone else ringing), the traders didn't lower their gaze to their screens and start yelling orders, but stood looking up at the bell and that man, yelling, "JOE D., JOE D., JOE D." . . . and the pork bellies, wheat futures, and carloads of copper *went untraded*—had to be ten minutes or more— for that same reason: he was the hero; and they wanted him to know who they were.

That was the way it had gone for sixty-five years . . . and to that weekend, which would be the last. Because from the moment he got to Chicago, it was evident that something was not normal with Joe. He was two months shy of his eighty-fourth birthday, and suddenly, he looked it. He was pasty and small, shrunken around a pain in himself—and couldn't manage the quiet equanimity and politesse with strangers that were the hallmarks of his public persona. When the president of the Board of Trade revealed Joe's Friday schedule—a tour, a luncheon, meetings—DiMaggio fixed him with the evil eye, and snapped: "Don't you know the difference between forty-eight and eighty-four?" When a big giver's wife came to flirt at Joe's table, and sat, with

coy self-invitation: "You don't mind, Joe—do you?"
Joe said he did.

"You wouldn't mind if it was Marilyn Monroe."

"You're not Marilyn."

JOE DIMAGGIO DAY WAS A ONE-thirty start with the Tampa Bay Devil Rays. The '98 Yanks had long since clinched—they were on cruise control, and waiting for the playoffs. The action for New Yorkers was on TV—where fans could watch the crosstown Mets scrambling for (and losing) a wildcard spot . . . or they could look in on St. Louis, where Mark McGwire would mash his sixty-ninth and seventieth homers of the year. . . . Still, fifty thousand faithful filled the grandstand and most of the bleachers in the Bronx.

But at one-fifteen, most of those fans were still walking in, or finding their seats, or getting food, when the big black scoreboard in center field came to light and life with three words: "Joltin' Joe Dimaggio." And the loudspeakers filled the Stadium with a strangely familiar sound—the voices of two young men, singing:

Doot do do do doot doo,
Doot doot do do do d'doooo . . .
And here's to you, Mrs. Robinson.
Jesus loves you more than you will know
(wo wo woh).

The big TV screen in right center frizzled to life, and there were video and film clips of Joe hitting, Joe sliding, Joe running, Joe waving. . . . And then, the gate at the old bullpen swung open—and there he was—riding a white '56 T-bird convertible around the outfield track and down the third base line . . . both hands lifted in the Pope wave, to acknowledge the cheers that swelled to a roar, as the fans caught on to what was happening. Joe DiMaggio Day had begun.

With the cheers and the music and the sunshine glinting off the car, it looked fine—a happy day at the ballpark. And you could count on one hand the people in the Stadium who knew enough to see how quickly this had been thrown together—and how it failed to live up to the standard. There was the car: the only person Joe knew with a T-bird convertible was Marilyn—Joe never liked that car. . . . Those three words on the scoreboard: no capitalization for the M in DiMaggio. . . . The film clips on the big TV: there was the newsreel footage from the day Joe got put out of Marilyn's house on North Palm Drive. . . . And the big problem: that bent old man, who looked frail and ill, as the T-bird drew to a stop at the Yankee dugout. Joe could barely get out of the car—and almost killed himself when he stumbled on the dugout steps.

But not many people could see how bad Joe looked—only the ones who got close, like Joe Torre, the Yankee skipper, who walked Joe out from the dugout, to the microphone behind home plate, where the big interlocking NY was limed onto the Stadium grass.

"He has been called baseball's greatest living player . . ." said the voice of the public address man, Bob Sheppard. "Please welcome . . ."

Joe was carrying a sheet of paper—a speech that Morris had written for him. Torre had come along to the mike to read Mayor Giuliani's proclamation for Joe DiMaggio Day in New York. But there would be no reading of the proclamation—and no speech. The microphone didn't work. So, all that was left was to bring out an officer of Major League Baseball, Paul Beeston, who presented Joe with a boxy frame, inside which was mounted one authorized and genuine American League baseball, with a blue number 5 printed on, with a picture of Joe swinging his bat in front of the NY logo, and with Yankee-blue stitching—the official Joe DiMaggio ball, to be used in that day's game. Joe took his ball and started back to the dugout. . . .

But wait! Bob Sheppard's voice on the PA introduced the Scooter, Phil Rizzuto, on whom the crowd rained cheers as he climbed out of the dugout, and stopped Joe—brought him back to home plate. And while the scoreboard flashed, one after the other, Joe's World Series wins—1936, 1937, 1938, 1939, 1941, 1947, 1949, 1950, 1951 . . . Phil handed Joe the box of replica rings. And Joe lifted it, as if to show it to the crowd. He would never wear any of them. He had his ring—from '36—but the great-grandchildren might enjoy seeing these. And then, Joe tottered off the field for good. DiMaggio's Day was done.

BY THE TIME ROCK POSITANO AR-rived in the fourth inning of the game with Tampa Bay, he could see it wasn't the normal hearty party around the table in Steinbrenner's suite. There was Joe, sitting in silence, with the Scooter, Steinbrenner, Barry Halper (still trying to mend his fences), and the opera singer Robert Merrill (who always did the anthem on big days). That wasn't an unusual crowd—but the air was unusually solemn. (Joe had been so furious about the dead microphone he'd cursed out a girl in the Yankee office till she was in tears—Steinbrenner had to send her home.)

And as soon as Positano walked in, Joe said: "You ready, Doc?" . . . which meant they were leaving without delay. They would drop off Engelberg in the city for his luggage. (His deal was done—he was flying home.) Joe wouldn't fly till the following day. So he and Rock would have one more night in New York. . . . But on that night, there would be no eager calls to gather the friends. Joe was exhausted, slumped in the back of Rock's limo.

"What do you want to do, Joe?" Dr. Rock asked. "Where d'you want to go to dinner?"

Joe wanted Bravo Gianni—he said he didn't know when he'd be back for another meal there. So they got

Joe his *farfalle*—and Joe ate, but he was terribly quiet. When they got back to the car he said he didn't want to turn in. Couldn't they just drive around? . . .

So Dr. Rock told his driver to put on Joe's CDs. (Rock always kept them in the car—Pavarotti, Ella Fitzgerald, Glenn Miller, Simon and Garfunkel . . . along with a copy of the book, *The Old Man and the Sea,* with the pages that mentioned the Great DiMaggio dog-eared at the corners, so Joe could find them.) . . . And in the quiet of the Sunday night streets, Joe and Rock rode across town to the West Side, and then up Broadway.

Dr. Rock knew something serious was wrong. Because the town Joe was pointing out was the shadow New York. And Joe never did that.

There was the Mayflower, Joe said. He had a good suite there. (But Joe hadn't stayed there for the past thirty years.)

And there was 400 West End Avenue. "Lotta good times in that place," Joe said. That was Joe and Dorothy's penthouse. (But Dorothy had died in Mexico, almost ten years before.)

On the CD player, it was Ella Fitzgerald, singing Gershwin songs.

Embrace me,
My sweet embraceable you . . .

"That's our song," Joe said. "Marilyn's favorite." He closed his eyes. And he was fading out. . . . And then, suddenly, he had his hands to his chest. And he was gasping to Positano. "Doc, I don't know what's wrong. I never felt this bad."

Positano stretched Joe out on the limo's back seat and told the driver to go east, across the park—and don't lose any time. Rock was heading for the hospital—New York Presbyterian—and praying silently that Joe would pass out . . . so Rock could have him admitted, right now—without argument. He'd get a pulmonologist and a heart guy on the case right away.

"Just lie back, Joe. Just take it easy. . . ." And in his head, Rock was screaming: *C'mon you stubborn bastard—give it up! Pass out!* . . . They were only ten blocks from the emergency door.

But Joe was too tough to give it up. He sat up. He said he'd better get to bed.

"Whyn'cha let me get you a bed, right here," Rock said, as lightly as he could. "We're near the hospital. It'll be no trouble."

But Joe didn't want that. No, he'd just get some sleep. He'd see a doctor he knew down in Florida, when he got back. Sure, some time this week . . .

BY THURSDAY OF THAT FOLLOWING week, Joe had seen that doctor he knew—and the news wasn't good. He would have to put up with more docs, and more tests. Joe said he wanted it done, right away—he had to be back in New York for the Series—when the Yanks got through the playoffs.

(And he had a dinner date with Woody and Soon-Yi.) ... Joe was snappish with the specialists—with everyone. He hated doctors. And he didn't want to be in Florida.

But Engelberg, Esq. couldn't have been in better humor. That Thursday, October 1, he was on the phone again to his partner, DiStefano. To be sure, Morris still complained about the rigors of DiMaggio Day. ("You don't know the aggravation I had ...") But that beautiful ball was going to sell itself.

And that was only the start! Now, Morris wanted Scott to sell replica jerseys. Of course, Morris already had done a deal with Jerry Romolt for jerseys—but that deal ran into problems. So, now Morris could cut Romolt out—do the deal himself, with Scott—and he was eagerly instructing his pupil:

"I know we can do four hundred jerseys, right?"

"Yeah, sure," said Scott, "eventually."

"You can do three hundred roughly at two hundred dollars, right—that's sixty thousand. All right?"

"Right."

"And you do a hundred at three hundred dollars— am I right? So you do another thirty thousand dollars," said Morris. "You got ninety thousand dollars there."

"That's perfect," said DiStefano. "I could take off for the year."

"No no no—I get half!"

"No—I know that!"

"That's forty-five thousand dollars . . . ," said Morris.

"That's what I get."

"Now, I put in the contract between Joe and you, our legal fee is fifteen. I offset that against my forty-five. See what I'm doing?"

"Yes. So then I would owe you thirty."

"Thaaat's it. Now that's a way of getting money to me."

And the beauty part was (as Morris often explained), when Scott paid those legal fees, that was deductible—it wouldn't cost anything.

(Of course—as Morris also explained—the best was cash: "When you give me green, there's no taxes." But Morris didn't like to discuss cash on the phone. "It might be tapped.")

The point was, they were going great guns, now, with the Rawlings Yankee Clipper ball and the jerseys . . . and Morris had a fortune in articles stashed in his house—two thousand balls, as he estimated, and bins full of other stuff—a huge closet under his stairs, chock-full! . . .

"Scott, I have, in canceled checks, millions of dollars."

"That's the key," said DiStefano.

"I have five hundred signed baseball cards—'Yankee Clipper.' "

"Whoa!"

"You know those plastics you have? The plastics we did? Mine are all signed 'Yankee Clipper.' "

"Wow."

"I'll have sixty—fifty . . ."

"That's okay, I know right where to go with them things."

"You think Paula knows there's twenty-three LeRoy Neimans there?"

"Probably not."

". . . Joe's memory is going, big-time. Big-time!"

Morris told Scott to get busy on the selling—the Rawlings ball and the jerseys. They had to get Joe signing on those jerseys, right away.

"I'm gonna tell him," Morris said. "I'm gonna take him to the doctor—four doctors tomorrow . . ."

TEN DAYS LATER, JOE WAS IN THE hospital—Memorial Hospital in Hollywood, Florida —though the Baseball Nation didn't find out for almost a week, till the World Series began, and Joe wasn't there to throw out the first ball.

"Joe DiMaggio has walking pneumonia," the Associated Press quoted Morris Engelberg ("attorney and longtime friend") . . . "He's had it three or four months. He's fine. He's eating like a horse."

In the days that followed there were further bulletins. DiMaggio was up, watching the Series on TV. He'd ordered in pizza. "He'll eventually be out . . . maybe three or four days," said ("close friend and personal attorney") Morris Engelberg. "He has six doctors. They aren't going to discharge this guy unless he's perfect."

The hospital refused all requests for information. "All inquiries regarding Mr. DiMaggio, at Mr. Engelberg's request, must be directed to Mr. Engelberg," said Lisa Kronhaus, director of public relations.

" 'He was sitting in a chair watching the news on television when I walked in,' Morris Engelberg, the Hall of Famer's lawyer and confidant told the Associated Press after visiting DiMaggio today. . . . The lawyer said DiMaggio would be hospitalized at least three more weeks. 'Then I hope to have him to dinner at my house for his 84th birthday, November 25.' . . ."

But Joe wouldn't be out for his birthday. He wasn't up to watching news, ordering pizza—and pneumonia wasn't his big problem. Except for the date of Joe's birthday, it was all lies. Two days after Joe was admitted, doctors operated to remove a cancerous tumor in his right lung. And Joe had never recovered. Infection set in. Then pneumonia beset Joe's other lung. X-rays showed Joe's lungs all whited out. He couldn't breathe on his own. A respirator pushed air into him through a tube in the base of his neck. He was fed through a tube in his stomach. He couldn't eat. He couldn't talk. And he often didn't know who else was in the room.

George Steinbrenner wanted to come for a visit. He was told to stay away. Joe wouldn't know him.

Dominic DiMaggio arrived to see his brother. But Morris lied to Dominic, too—and when he was called on the lies, he wouldn't tell Dom anything. Then he tried to keep Dom out of Joe's room. The fifty-nine-year-old Morris and eighty-one-year-old Dominic had a push-and-shove fight in the hospital hallway.

Still, the lies kept coming:

"DiMaggio's Health Improving . . ."

"Yankee Clipper Battling Back . . ."

"DiMaggio Gave Millions to Hospital."

"I'm being misquoted," Engelberg protested to the AP. The strain of being a name in the news was almost too much for Morris. "My [telephone] lines are being tied up. My practice has been hurt daily by what's happened." (Only later would Morris claim that he'd dropped his practice—to stay at the bedside—from the moment Joe got sick.) For a while, one of Joe's doctors (and Morris's pal), Earl Barron, took over the bulletins. Then, the news was different:

"Joe DiMaggio Had Cancer Surgery . . ."

"His Outlook Is Very Poor . . ."

"DiMaggio Family Holds Vigil."

But Morris had become a Big Name in another way—the way he'd always wanted to be. "Every ball," as the Internet offers informed potential buyers, "will be accompanied by a letter of authenticity, signed by Morris Engelberg, attorney for Yankee Clipper Enterprises." . . . News of Joe's cancer had kicked the memorabilia merchants into high gear.

Now, in the Christmas rush, prices were sky-high. And Morris himself had become a Signature.

As Christmas neared, Joe woke up from a coma that his doctors had feared was fatal. (Two months into Joe's hospital stay, they'd discovered that the antibiotics weren't getting to Joe's bloodstream—so they gave him the drug intravenously—and miraculously, Joe improved.) He was still in intensive care. He couldn't talk, unless they unhooked him from his ventilator—and even then it was only a rasping few words. ("No more news," he told the doctor, one day—and that put an end to the bulletins.) But in this case, no news was good news—or at least better than it had been. Joe needed less sedation. He sat up more. He knew who came into his room. He made signals with his hands.

Morris, for one, noticed Joe's hands were fine. Later, Engelberg would sell sixty-eight Yankee Clipper balls, with pen marks upon them . . . which were Joe's attempted signatures on the balls Morris gave him in the hospital.

AFTER NINETY-NINE DAYS IN INTENsive care, Joe DiMaggio was released from Memorial Hospital, January 18, 1999. The glad event was trumpeted around the nation. "Mr. DiMaggio is looking forward to opening day in Yankee Stadium," said a statement from "his spokesman and closest friend," Morris Engelberg.

"Joe will certainly toss out the first ball," said George Steinbrenner, in New York. "It's a wonderful moment for me personally and for the fans."

And maybe there were moments when Joe thought he'd be on his feet by April. He was so happy to get out of that hospital, he was even patient with the nurses and technicians who staffed his house around the clock.

There were two on duty at all times—on assignment from Memorial Hospital—a critical care nurse and respiratory tech. A therapist would come, by day, to try to get Joe up, help him take a step or two. At times, the duty staff could take Joe off the respirator—when he wanted to speak, or get out of bed—and they'd wheel him outside in a chair, to sit next to his pool. Joe could breathe on his own for a while, but after ten minutes, the oxygen level in his blood would sink below the point of safety, and they'd have to bring him in, hook the tube into the base of his neck, and "reinflate."

Ninety percent of the time, Joe was in his bed—a hospital bed installed in the "Florida Room" on the ground floor. (The living room, on the other side of the stairway, might have been more commodious—but it was stacked floor to ceiling with thousands of Joe DiMaggio baseballs.) . . . On Joe's left, as he lay in bed, there were two sliding glass doors that looked out on the Intracoastal Waterway. Also to the left of the bed stood the IV pole where Joe's bags hung, along with packs of nutrients that dripped down the

tube into his stomach. A few feet away from the foot
of the bed, there was a fifty-two-inch television. And
atop the TV sat the boom box, to play Joe's Pavarotti
songs, Ella Fitzgerald, or Michael Bolton. Next to the
bed, on Joe's right, stood his breathing machine and
four big oxygen tanks—along with a rolling console
that held dressing changes, gauze, bandages, baby
wipes, gloves, and creams.

Joe needed cream all the time. His skin was breaking down. His face was red and sore. Something was
wrong with his left eye—it wouldn't close. So he had
to have eyedrops constantly, or the nurses would tape
the eye shut. Then, Joe would rip off the tape. Joe
hated to be handled. Everything hurt. The scars on
his heels hurt when the staff barely touched them to
rub in cream. His ankles were tender. His right knee
was delicate. His left shoulder pained him. And his
back was always bad. Sometimes, when nurses (especially females) had to turn him over, or haul him
up, after he'd slid down with his ankles hanging off
the foot of the bed, Joe would wince and roughly bat
them away. (There were only two female nurses who
did well with him—they'd each had three sons.) Men
did better with Joe in general. When they had to do
something with him, he might be a sonofabitch about
it, but he wouldn't flinch—he let them do it. And he
never whined.

One man did better than all the others—that was
DeJan Pesut, who was the butler hired in from a
South Florida service. DeJan was a hearty, square-

jawed Slovenian Serb, with a brush cut and goatee, both tinged with gray. He spoke English with a Serbo-Croatian accent, and he knew some words of Italian. But from the moment he walked in, he seemed to know Joe.

It was always "Joe" with DeJan—never "Sir" or "Mr. DiMaggio." Or sometimes, when he'd get his face up right next to Joe, it was "boss," or "my man." And he wouldn't mince words or prattle about the weather—he'd tell Joe what was going on. "Joe! Hey! You gotta let 'em get the blood pressure now— and then you gonna take the medications, and then you gonna eat something. Okay? You gotta get this done now." Once the portly nurse had taken blood pressure and left the bedside, DeJan would be back with a growling whisper in DiMaggio's ear. "Joe— my man—she's weighing five hundred pounds that one! You want me to fire her for you?" Joe couldn't speak. But he smiled a little.

DeJan would try to feed Joe apple sauce or pudding—or a little ice cream—but Joe's throat couldn't separate the food from air. Still, DeJan would be back the next day with tomatoes from the local green market. "Joe! Looka these. You see that? You know I'm gonna make you *pomodoro.* You want the *pomodoro? . . .* My man! You gonna get better! You gonna be strong! *Siciliano!"* DeJan would lift his arms like a muscle man, showing off. And Joe would smile and nod.

But Joe wasn't getting better. And after a while,

he knew it. They'd take him off the collar so he could talk to a granddaughter on the phone, and after five minutes, he'd have to hang up and go back on the breather. As they got him settled and reached again for the ventilator tube, Joe said, "Is that thing keeping me goin'?" And they couldn't deny it. "S'no way to be," Joe said, before they hooked him on again.

People wanted to visit. Morris kept almost all of them out. Joe had signed a paper making Morris his "medical surrogate" under Florida law. (As Morris told one pal who wanted to see Joe: "I call the shots.") . . . But truly, Joe didn't want anybody to see him—not like this. DeJan brought potted trees to block the view from the Intracoastal Waterway. Joe thought people would sneak up by boat to take pictures of him. And he knew he looked bad.

When George Steinbrenner won consent for a visit, DeJan had to work Joe over for hours, with a haircut, shave, a crisp white shirt. ("Lookit my man! Like a bran' new Cadillac!") . . . But Steinbrenner was there only a few minutes before Joe got tired again. A couple of old Florida pals did get in to sit with DiMag. Joe Nacchio, who was a pal since the 1940s, came several times—and so did Al Tordella, who'd been Joe's steam room buddy at La Gorse Country Club for the last few years. Once, when Tordella came, Joe ordered everybody else from the room. (Only the nurse refused to go.) Joe had something important to tell Tordella. But by the time Joe got off the tube and shooed everybody out, he was exhausted and couldn't speak. . . .

Mostly Joe was alone, save for staff and the huge TV. That was how he could see his son—who did an interview with *Inside Edition* (for fifteen grand). Joe Jr. said there were no problems between him and his dad—they just hadn't talked for a few years. But Junior was glad the old man was better. . . . The granddaughters, Paula and Kathie, shuttled back and forth from the West Coast several times—as did their husbands, Jim Hamra and Roger Stein. But they had businesses and children back home (February was a school month), so they couldn't stay. . . . Dominic DiMaggio had a house in Florida, so he came more often—and he was admitted. Despite the silence between brothers that had lasted for years, Joe had ruled now, he wanted to see Dom. They were the last of the breed. And only a few months before, Joe had told Dick Burke, his New York pal, that he wanted Burke and Dommie to be his executors. But that was never going to happen. Morris was always there when Dom got in.

Morris would stop in on his way to the office in the morning, or on his way back home at night. If he allowed somebody to visit Joe, Morris would arrive with the guest in the afternoon. And he'd hang around to make sure nothing untoward was said. If Joe was safely alone (save for staff), Morris would issue a few orders and then walk across the street to his own house, for dinner.

Soon, Morris would begin to write the dramatic story—"five months spent away from my law practice to be at DiMaggio's bedside making life and death decisions in an effort to prolong the life of my friend and the nation's hero, Joe DiMaggio." (In fact, the saga of Morris's care for his friend would form a chapter in a book—a "tell-all," as Morris called it—that he would offer to New York publishers for a million and a half.)

But somehow, Morris still found time to take care of a few business details. For instance, there was some nasty correspondence to Jerry Romolt, warning him of dire consequences if Romolt continued to criticize the handling of DiMaggio's business affairs. . . . There was also, in those same weeks, a letter to inform Barry Halper that Joe had never really liked him. And by the bye, Morris accused Barry of stealing Joe's '51 World Series ring.

Morris also found time to do some business with Scott DiStefano, who was the front man on the sale of five hundred bats (all signed "Yankee Clipper") to the Shop At Home Network, which would offer them to Joe's fans on the Internet and on TV, starting at two A.M., February 14, 1999. Those were bats rejected as defects by Romolt, in his bat deal six years before. But now, as the Shop At Home Network announced: "Each bat comes with a certificate of authenticity signed by Mr. DiMaggio's personal attorney Morris Engelberg."

Maybe Joe was channel surfing in the wee hours,

and stumbled across the Shop At Home Network. Or maybe—as the staff assumed—he was talking in a daze, when he startled his nurse by rasping out: "Morris is an asshole. Let's get out of here." The nurse and the tech on duty tried to calm Joe—they told him to relax—this was his home. "I know," Joe said. "I want to get outa here." But by that time, late February, Joe knew he wouldn't get out. Or he'd get out only one way.

"I don't want to be like this anymore," Joe told the nurse one night.

To DeJan, he said simply, "It's no good. I wanna die." DeJan wouldn't hear it. "I don't wanna have this bullshit from my man. Where is my hand? . . ." And roughly, he grabbed Joe's hand, bent down and kissed it.

Monday, March 1, Morris brought in a nurse from Hospice Care of Broward County. That was Javier Ribe, a Spaniard who had worked for five years helping people to die in ease. Once hospice care began, either the respirator or the feeding tube had to be disconnected. In Joe's case, they pulled the feeding tube.

DeJan came down the steps of Joe's house wearing a chef's hat and waving an Italian flag. "Boss! You gonna eat!"

He cooked crab and *farfalle* for Joe, and Joe ate.

Next day, it was chicken. "Joe!" said DeJan, appearing with the chicken. "You gonna point it what piece you want. You touch the chicken what piece you gonna eat." Joe touched the chicken and ate what he could.

Third day, Thursday, March 4, was lobster. But Joe didn't eat. And he would not eat again.

Morris put the plan in place to "let Joe go" Saturday night. The doctor pals had prescribed morphine suppositories every other hour. The medical staff gave Joe one suppository and he slept for hours. They wouldn't give him more. It would have killed him. That was the idea—but they couldn't do that.

There was an uneasy feeling in the room. Dominic was there. But Paula and Kathy were both absent. Paula's husband, Jim, had just arrived, and Kathie's husband, Roger, had left. It was like some hockey team changing on the fly . . . with Morris "calling the shots." He ordered the staff to shut down the ventilator's pressure support. Oxygen would flow, but without pressure to fill Joe's lungs. When Joe's blood oxygen level fell into the seventies, Dommie couldn't help himself. He said, "You're killing him!" And the staff balked again—and turned the pressure back on, pushed in eight breaths a minute. Joe was brought back to life. That ventilator could have kept him going for years.

But the next night, nothing would be left to chance. The staff that came on at seven P.M. was asked at the start if they would have problems "letting Mr. DiMaggio go." The hospice nurse, Javier, was on scene. Dominic was excluded. Kathie had made the trip across the country. Paula was on her way. Her husband, Jim, was there, still. And Morris, of course, who arrived to give orders, after his dinner.

Javier Ribe sat in front of the breathing machine, holding Joe's hand. (Ribe said the human touch was a beautiful sensation that should never be denied.) For a while, DeJan took Joe's other hand, and talked to his man. "Joe, you leavin' us," he was whispering. "But you gonna be in my thoughts. I'm gonna dress up alla time, like my man!"

"How long will this take?" Morris asked the staff.

Pavarotti was singing "Ave Maria" at low volume, from the boom box. For once the TV was off. The lights were dim. Kathie and Jim were standing at the bedside, sniffly with tears. Morris bustled around the bed giving hush-hush orders. "Make sure you don't tell anybody about this till eight in the morning," Engelberg instructed the staff. "That's when I'm going to announce it. And I don't want a lot of press calling, waking me up." (He had a big day tomorrow—a will to file.)

Joe was lying on his back, propped up slightly, his head lolling to the side. He was out of it on morphine. He didn't speak. He didn't wake up. Javier would call it the most peaceful and beautiful death he had attended.

Joe lasted till midnight. Then he was gone.

When he died, Kathie and Jim couldn't look. They left the room, and talked quietly together.

Morris stood by. But he didn't approach, he didn't touch Joe. The nursing staff was preparing the body for the funeral guys, who were to arrive at two A.M., by prearrangement with Morris. The nurse had folded Joe's arms, and was about to wrap him in a sheet.

"Wait," Morris ordered. "You need to take that ring off for me."

"His ring?"

"Yeah, get that ring off."

The nurse reached for Joe's left hand, and pulled at the ring. But it wouldn't budge. He couldn't stretch out the finger and pull the ring at the same time.

Morris asked sharply: "Can't you get something to take that off?"

"Well, yeah—we could lube it up . . ." But just then the ring came free. "What is it?" the nurse asked.

"Thirty-six World Series, rookie year."

The nurse turned the ring over—"Can I look?" . . . But he had only a glimpse before Morris yanked the ring out of his hands, and left the room in a hurry. All the nurse would remember was the weight of the gold, the edges worn smooth, and on the face, the soft sparkle of diamonds.

**The Yankee old-timers, and
the Clipper alone.**

EPILOGUE

✦

THREE DAYS LATER, AT JOE'S FU-
neral in San Francisco, Engelberg was wearing the
ring. He would say Joe gave him that ring, on his
deathbed—before Joe died in his arms.

Morris didn't like the funeral. Dominic DiMaggio was in charge. All the other brothers and sisters
were gone. Marie was the last sister to go. She had
died in 1997, and since that time, the house on
Beach Street had stood empty and hushed. Joe's
funeral was quiet, too—only thirty people in the
church, mostly cousins. Dominic spoke the only
eulogy. In the "tell-all" book that Morris would
later attempt to sell, he would call it "the fiasco of
Joe DiMaggio's funeral. . . .

"DiMaggio's estranged relationship with his
brother, Dominick [sic], is detailed," as the book's
preface promised. "Especially the fact that Dominick DiMaggio was not at Joe's bedside when
he passed away and was not mentioned in his
Will."

Morris wanted it known that he was Joe's real
family. "I devoted the past sixteen years of my
life to the Yankee baseball legend, Joe DiMaggio,"

his book would claim, "and have been referred to by the media as 'the man behind the great DiMaggio,' 'DiMaggio's closest friend and confident [sic],' 'DiMaggio's attorney and close friend,' among others. DiMaggio divulged stories and facts to me relating to his life that this 'private man' never told anyone before. In reality, Joe was the father that I never had; the father I had always wished for and wanted, and in turn, I was the type of son he wanted but never had in his son, Joe DiMaggio, Jr."

Joe Jr. did attend his father's funeral. Joey had his gray hair pulled neatly into a ponytail. He wore a new suit, and a new set of teeth, that a cousin had bought him for the occasion. Morris told Joey that he'd take care of him now. Junior wouldn't have to live at that cousin's junkyard anymore. How about a nice condo in Florida? . . . Joey didn't want any condo. He took the money Morris gave him (from the twenty-thousand-dollar annual stipend specified in Joe's will). And six months after his father's death, Joey was dead, too—from an overdose of crank, heroin mixed with crack cocaine.

Morris did not attend last rites for Joey. Engelberg was busy as the personal representative and lawyer for the estate of the Yankee Clipper—under the terms of the will that Morris filed in Fort Lauderdale on the day of Joe's death. By June of 1999, he had sold "for a price in the millions" Joe's bats, balls, pictures, lithos, posters, pins, magazines, jerseys, baseball cards . . . to a North Carolina businessman (originally from Bayonne, New Jersey) by the name of Ralph Perullo. Engelberg told the AP that he knew Joe would not have approved "carving up his collection strictly for the money." That was why he'd sold it all to Perullo. "I know Joe is watching all the moves I make," said Engelberg. The next weekend, Perullo started retailing at an autograph show in Philadelphia, where the items that caused the most comment were sixty-eight Yankee Clipper balls with the wavering pen marks Joe had made in the hospital. "On some of them you can't make out his name," Morris told reporters. "But I know he signed them because I was there." And every item in Perullo's sale came with a certificate of authenticity with the personal signature of "Joe's attorney and closest friend."

But not all of Joe's articles made it to Perullo. There was one particular uniform shirt that Morris kept. He'd started talking about that shirt while Joe still lay dying. "Oh, yeah—Joe gave me that shirt," Morris told one memorabilia dealer in Florida. "I said to him, 'No, Joe, that's too much.' But he said if I didn't take that shirt, our friendship was over. So what could I do? . . ." That shirt would be offered for auction at Christie's—with a reserve price of more than a hundred grand. In fact, Christie's would run a DiMaggio event, with a number of "one-of-a-kind" sale items. There was the Florida license plate DIMAG 5, along with the Clipper's MasterCard, his health insurance cards (from the Screen Actors Guild and the American Federation of Television and Radio Actors), and his driver's license. Christie's, of course, advertised those items as DiMaggio's. But when pressed, the auction house revealed that the "owners" who would get the money from those sales were "employees of the law firm, Engelberg, Cantor, Leone & Milgrim, P.L., of Hollywood, Florida." Further inquiries were referred to Christie's newest consultant, Mr. Scott DiStefano.

Scott was out on his own, now—president of Atlantic Coast Sports, Inc.—but still in tow to YCE and the estate of Joe DiMaggio. Scott's reputation in the business depended on his access to DiMaggio memorabilia—and he'd sold most of his own stash (and put the money in a mutual fund, which nosedived). DiStefano remained doggedly loyal to Morris Engelberg, Esq. In an interview, Scott said he was sure that Joe had known everything Morris was doing. Sure, Scott had sold a lot of items for Engelberg—but "Joe probably gave Morris all that stuff." As to the special Joe DiMaggio baseball, Scott eagerly confirmed he had "set up the whole deal." But when he was asked about the two thousand balls that he ordered for Engelberg, DiStefano said he wasn't sure how many balls Morris or Joe had ever gotten . . . it was complicated and, gosh, Scott just couldn't remember.*

There was another big auction of DiMaggio memorabilia. Barry Halper had lost his taste for collecting, and sold most of his holdings at a Sotheby's event. But Halper reserved part of his treasure to be placed intact in the Baseball Hall of Fame, at Cooperstown, New York. (The Hall would even build a replica of the den in Barry's New Jersey house, to display the "Halper Collection.") And to Cooperstown, Barry sent his favorite likeness of DiMaggio—a statue of the Clipper in his famous follow-through, by the Italian sculptor Clemente Spampinato. It was Joe who had first told Barry about that statue, made in 1950—Joe said that was more like him than any drawing, painting, or photograph he'd seen. And after months of investigation, Halper located the sculptor's family and bought the bronze, so DiMaggio could see it again.

---

* Mr. Engelberg declined to be interviewed. He was informed that this book would contain serious allegations about his conduct in connection with Joe's memorabilia business, but he maintained his perfect five-year record and refused "contact and communication." For the text of the reply from Engelberg, Cantor & Milgrim, see the illustration that follows this epilogue.

Now, the Hall of Fame would display that likeness, as Barry's homage to Joe.

In the year after Joe's death, there were gestures of honor to his name from coast to coast. Chicago, of course, had jumped the gun—*Piazza DiMaggio* was already completed. . . . The Yankees wasted no time—a month after Joe's death, the club dedicated the fifth monument in Stadium history to the memory of the Yankee Clipper. Beyond the current field and fence, in the deepest reach of the old left center field (whose vastness he had cursed so often, when it stole his home runs), Joe's likeness would now stand shoulder to shoulder with those of Gehrig, Ruth, Mantle, and Miller Huggins. . . . The governor and mayor of New York got into a public scrap over which of them would have his way, honoring the Great DiMag. The governor wanted to rename for Joe the Bronx parkway that carried fans to Yankee Stadium. The mayor wanted to rename the West Side Highway in Manhattan. With the (unasked for) aid of Morris Engelberg, Esq., "attorney for the estate and the Yankee Clipper's oldest and dearest friend," Mayor Giuliani won out—and the ratty ruin of the road along the Hudson went onto the maps as Joe DiMaggio Highway. . . .

Joe's "dearest friend" and biographer-to-be got into the act himself in Florida. The city of Hollywood was considering a plan to rename for DiMaggio an actual landmark, the Presidential Circle, on the west side of town. Engelberg scotched that plan, with fury and bluster. He was going to name his own park for DiMaggio—in the gated housing development where he lived. There was an open space where the developers had been forced to put in a drainage pond. That would be Joe's park. Morris said he and Joe used to ride out there, in Joe's golf cart—and those were special memories. (That was the golf cart that was offered for auction at Christie's. Joe must have insisted that Morris accept that golf cart as a gift, too.)

In San Francisco, Mayor Willie Brown and the town supervisors settled on a plan to honor Joe D. by repairing, renovating, and renaming the North Beach Playground in his honor. After all, that was where Joe grew up, and learned to play ball. "An insult!" came the rejoinder from Engelberg, Cantor, Leone & Milgrim, in Hollywood, Florida. Morris insisted that San Francisco should rename the airport, or the Bay Bridge—not some rotten patch of cement. When San Francisco persisted, Morris threatened to sue. When Dominic DiMaggio approved the idea ("I feel certain in my heart, Joe would be pleased"), Morris told the *San Francisco Chronicle* that Dominic didn't know Joe. "Joe died in my arms, not his."

At the anniversary of Joe's death, matters seemed a bit calmer. The city said it would search

out a "legal means" to honor Joe in a manner all
parties could approve. For his part, Morris told
the *Chronicle* that he'd never really threatened to
sue. As the paper quoted Engelberg: " 'I'm not
going to take money from [DiMaggio's] grandchildren' to go to court." . . . So San Francisco went
ahead and renamed the playground. And Morris
filed suit.

Engelberg's complaint in federal court said that
San Francisco "should not be given carte blanche
to name the city junk yard, the city waste dump, in
this case the North Beach Playground, or any other
such facility after Joe DiMaggio without consent."
And in remarks to the press, Morris left no doubt
whose consent he meant:

"I control absolutely the use of the name Joe
DiMaggio, as long as I am alive."

Apart from the legal issues, there was a certain
logic on Engelberg's side. If you looked at Joe's
life the way Joe did, as a never-ending parade of
guys who tried to eat a chunk of his life, who all
wanted a piece of him . . . well, then, the natural
last step, at the end of that parade, was a guy who
wanted to eat it all. Morris Engelberg now owned
Joe's life.

But Joe likely wouldn't have pushed the dispute
to a face-off in federal court. Bad publicity, for one
thing. (And San Francisco could just give up—
and name nothing for him.) . . . In the end, brother
Dominic was probably right—Joe would have liked

his name on a sign over the tar of the North Beach Playground. The Asian kids who played there now would see it every day—and they'd remember him. . . . To paraphrase the words Joe used himself:

Hey, wait a minute. They gotta know I was here!

ENGELBERG, CANTOR & MILGRIM, P. L.

A PROFESSIONAL LIMITED LIABILITY COMPANY
ATTORNEYS AT LAW
YANKEE CLIPPER CENTER
3230 STIRLING ROAD
SUITE I
HOLLYWOOD, FLORIDA 33021
HOLLYWOOD (954) 966-3900
FAX (954) 981-2300

MORRIS ENGELBERG &
LAURIE E. MILGRIM, P. A.
―――
JERALD C. CANTOR, P. A.
RICK LEONE, P. A.
TAX COUNSEL

PALM BEACH OFFICE
125 WORTH AVENUE
PALM BEACH, FLORIDA 33480
TELEPHONE (561) 734-0440
―――
PLEASE DIRECT ALL MAIL
TO HOLLYWOOD OFFICE

July 13, 2000

VIA CERTIFIED MAIL
Mr. Richard Ben Cramer
Simon & Schuster Consumer Group
1230 Avenue of the Americas
New York, New York 10020

RE: Biography of Joe DiMaggio

Dear Mr. Cramer:

Your letter of July 12, 2000 to Morris Engelberg, Esquire, has been referred to me for reply. We have been requested to represent Mr. Engelberg in connection with your threatening letter which was clearly intended to intimidate Mr. Engelberg in regard to his personal and business relationship with Mr. DiMaggio.

Morris Engelberg, Esquire, as well as this law firm, represented Joe DiMaggio for sixteen (16) years prior to his death, and continue to represent Mr. DiMaggio's estate together with its legal and business interests. Mr. Engelberg and Mr. DiMaggio maintained an extremely close personal and business relationship. Mr. DiMaggio was fully and intimately engaged in all levels and aspects of his memorabilia business, and consulted with Mr. Engelberg on a daily basis regarding such dealings. All ultimate decisions were made by Mr. DiMaggio.

As you are aware, Yankee Clipper Enterprises, Inc. was involved in litigation, and/or disputes with certain individuals and businesses listed in your letter. These businesses and individuals, at different times, were adversaries of Yankee Clipper Enterprises, Inc. and Mr. Engelberg. Additionally, Mr. Engelberg is currently a potential material witness in a lawsuit involving Pro Sports Services against Mitchell and Ness. It is not appropriate for us to discuss or defend our positions against these former adversaries in your book since all issues have been resolved.

Mr. Engelberg's conduct in the business affairs of Mr. DiMaggio, Yankee Clipper Enterprises, Inc. and its memorabilia business was beyond reproach. Your reference to serious allegations about Mr. Engelberg's conduct in connection with the memorabilia business and Mr. DiMaggio's personal affairs is a vengeful and self-serving attempt to discredit Mr. Engelberg driven by your having been rebuked by both Mr. DiMaggio and him. Despite your repeated attempts, Mr. Dimaggio refused to meet with you, speak with you, and even to shake your hand. He instructed Mr. Engelberg to likewise refuse contact and communication with you. Mr. Engelberg intends to honor Mr. DiMaggio's instructions.

Your unsubtle threat to publish serious allegations about Mr. Engelberg's conduct will be treated as a malicious and intentional attempt to defame Mr. Engelberg which will not be tolerated. We caution you against printing any unsubstantiated allegations or comments regarding Joe DiMaggio, Yankee Clipper Enterprises, Inc., Morris Engelberg, Esquire, and/or our law firm. We will pursue all remedies available to us in connection with any false statements which may appear in your book.

Govern yourself accordingly.

Very truly yours,

JERALD C. CANTOR
For the Firm

JCC:neh
cc. Morris Engelberg, Esquire
    Mr. David Rosenthal, Publisher
     Simon & Schuster via Certified Mail
    Laurie E. Milgrim, Esquire

AUTHOR'S NOTE
AND ACKNOWLEDGMENTS
◆

I BEGAN THIS BIOGRAPHY OF JOE DiMaggio in 1995, with the sobering awareness that I stepped in with two strikes against me. The first came from the fact that DiMaggio was so often written about. It wasn't just a dozen books about him— nor dozens more about his team, his towns, his wives, the World Series, the sporting press, the broadcasters who covered his doings, and baseball in the Golden Age (DiMag took center stage in all of them). There were also hundreds of magazine stories, and newspaper stories by the thousands, going back to 1932. The problem wasn't simply volume(s) but a well-trodden sameness that had matted down the grass along a few practiced paths—the stories that were always mentioned—which were (not by coincidence) the stories of which Joe approved. The net effect of the vast and mostly shallow coverage was the creation of a character who was at once gigantic and at the same time curiously flat—there was so little about him that felt human and alive.

A second problem helped to explain the first—but

amounted to another strike against this book. That was: I could expect no help from Joe. The coverage of DiMaggio for sixty-five years was mostly flat because Joe would show nothing but a shiny surface of his own devising. Any attempt to penetrate that surface he met with silence (at best). Persistence only spurred him to more icy and obdurate exclusion. And if that didn't work, there was anger and threat. Moreover, he enforced a similar silence within his wide acquaintance. All the men and women who truly knew Joe were well aware they would face his exclusion or rage if he found out they had talked about him. Accordingly, to members of his family; to his employers, partners, colleagues, idolaters, lovers; to pals of his youth, his prime, and his old age; and to scores of people who served him, I owe gratitude not only for their information, but for their courage and their trust in me.

Despite these problems, there was in the story of DiMaggio an allure so sharp and fresh that there was never any question of stopping. There was, from day one, the joy of rediscovering the worlds through which he walked: North Beach and Fisherman's Wharf in the 1920s; the hard-knuckled business of baseball in the 1930s; the abundance and glamour of New York in postwar triumph; the rotten magnificence of Marilyn's Hollywood . . . here was a canvas as generous, colorful, and crass as the country that made Joe its hero. Withal, as the story pushed past the practiced paths, there was at every turn the excitement of history never told, of connections hidden for decades, of old mysteries answered. The story of DiMaggio the icon was well known. The story of DiMaggio the man had been buried.

Alas, excavation is slow work—slower still in this case because a shovel once misplaced would hit only rock forever. Digging into the world of DiMaggio was, from start to finish, a very Sicilian business. I soon learned I could not simply call up a fellow, explain there was a book in progress, and start asking questions. Instead, I was passed from source to source by hand and with evident caution. Then, if I hung around for a while, didn't ask much and didn't blab what I heard, I might over time learn something real. After two or three years, I had become the crypt of DiMaggionic data. As my patient publishers noted (but seldom aloud—for which I thank them), vast matter went in, but nothing came out.

When Joe died in 1999, this book was once again delayed—for several reasons. There was, of course, a final chapter to be reported and written. But every chapter that came before was enriched by information that came sluicing in—new recollections spurred by the event, new sources who felt free to talk, and old sources who wanted to talk—to remember the man who had touched their lives. Moreover, the book itself was changed. Now, it had to be written more amply, with more context, and perhaps with new calm. The chase was over. Journalism had turned into history. And the story was better for it.

Once again, I was grateful to my publishers for their extension of time and resources. For that generosity, and for the chance to try my hand at this project, I have to thank first and foremost David Rosenthal, publisher of Simon & Schuster, godfather to this book. It was David who told me in 1993 that if I didn't do DiMaggio he would break both my legs; and it was David who (six years later, when I still hadn't quite done DiMaggio) didn't break both my legs. In my house, he is *capo di tutti.*

I WAS BLESSED TO HAVE ON THIS book the help of three reporters and authors who are as exemplary in my trade as DiMaggio was on a ballfield: David Halberstam, Seymour Hersh, and Gay Talese. Every reporter reading these words will understand my feeling that I hit the trifecta. (As every horse player will understand, that sort of win is always dumb luck.) Halberstam in particular was so generous with recollections, advice, sources, and the notes from his splendid *Summer of '49,* that I shall always be in his debt. Hersh made available to me the voluminous files on Marilyn Monroe that he barely touched for *The Dark Side of Camelot* (wherein Sy had bigger fish to fry). Talese tried to give me the integral and intuitive understanding of DiMaggio that informed his "Silent Season of a Hero," which was written for *Esquire* in 1966, and which remains the seminal work on DiMaggio.

On the topic of Joe D. I was aided by generous help from Maury Allen, who got to the people who mattered for his 1974 book, *Where Have You Gone, Joe DiMaggio?*, and set down their words with economy and grace. I am also in the debt of Roger Kahn, who wrote extensively about DiMaggio in *The Era: 1947–1957*, and *Joe and Marilyn: A Memory of Love*, and who was kind enough to share his recollections. I benefited greatly from the work of Dick Johnson and Glenn Stout, whose *DiMaggio: An Illustrated Life* presented a matchless game-by-game narrative of DiMaggio's baseball career; from the work of Michael Seidel, whose *Streak: Joe DiMaggio and the Summer of '41* re-created the fever of Joe D.'s heroics on the eve of war; from the work of Professor Jack B. Moore, whose *Joe DiMaggio: A Biobibliography* surveyed DiMaggio's life and gauged its impact on the culture of his times. I also derived valuable information by mining *The DiMaggio Albums*, from reading Al Silverman's *Joe DiMaggio: The Golden Year, 1941*, and from books by three *New York Times*men: George DeGregorio's *Joe DiMaggio: An Informal Biography*, Christopher Lehmann-Haupt's *Me and DiMaggio: A Baseball Fan Goes in Search of His Gods*, and Joseph Durso's *DiMaggio: The Last American Knight*.

On the gnarly topic of Marilyn Monroe, I was guided by the work and helped by the kindness of authors who'd gone before. Anthony Summers, author of *Goddess: The Secret Lives of Marilyn Monroe*, was unfailingly generous and patient with my urgencies. Donald Wolfe graciously compared notes with me before publication of *The Last Days of Marilyn Monroe*. Dr. Donald Spoto, author of *Marilyn Monroe: The Biography,* directed me to his taped interviews at the library of the Academy of Motion Picture Arts and Sciences. Lena Pepitone (and her friend Renee Glicker) kindly met me to review the recollections in her memoir, *Marilyn Monroe Confidential*. James Haspiel, author of *Marilyn: The Ultimate Look at the Legend,* was helpful both with his own recollections and additional sources on Marilyn and her mythos. I also found valuable information on Marilyn's career in Barbara Leaming's biography, *Marilyn Monroe*. In addition, I was aided by the writings of Truman Capote, Billy Grady, Sidney Guilaroff, Fred Guiles, Ben Hecht, Hedda Hopper, Hans Jørgen Lembourn, Norman Mailer, Arthur Miller, Berniece Miracle, Louella Parsons, Norman Rosten, Sidney Skolsky, Steffi Skolsky, Susan Strasberg, W. J. Weatherby, Billy Wilder, and Earl Wilson. I am also grateful for recollection, information, and documents made available to me from Udell Hays, Mary Jane McCord, Louis Alhanati at Parisian Florists, Bob and Debby Slatzer, Jeanne Carmen, Mill Conroy; also from Dixie Evans, Liz Renay, Antoinette Giancana, and a special thanks to Mark Allen. On the topic of Miss Americas, I was charmed and informed by Lee Meriwether and Yolande Fox. I also found valuable the book *There She Is: The Life and Times of Miss America,* by Frank Deford. I thank Gus Zernial for sharing the memory of his meeting with Marilyn. I am also grateful to Brad Dexter for sharing the memory of his friendship with Marilyn. And I ended this book forever in the debt of Ralph Roberts, a great friend to Marilyn and a man of grace who died too soon.

On Joe's life in San Francisco, I am indebted first to his family: to Dominic and Emily DiMaggio, who were kind enough to put up with me, though they didn't want to help; to Mr. and Mrs. Dominic DiMaggio of Antioch, California, to Debby McKillop Shields, Jerri and Richard McKillop, Sam and Agnes Billaci, Donna Mather, Todd Mather, Gloria Rovegno, Joe Clima, Jr., Bob Marazani, Mike Fernandes, Joanne DiMaggio Webber, Marie DiMaggio, and especially to Betty Corbin. On the history of Italians in San Francisco, I was helped by Deanna Paoli Gumina and Russ Gumina, Charlie Ferrugia, and Kevin Starr. I am grateful for the graciousness of two men who shared vast North Beach knowledge: Don Casper and Al Baccari, two fine historians who practice other trades. Also to Mrs. Dede Baccari, Mrs. Giuseppa Corona, and Mrs. Frances Tarantino. Also, I am grateful for the help of Mayor Joe Alioto, Linda Arbunich, Wally Baldwin, Sam Basin, Louis Batemale, Sam Beler, Dante Benedetti, Nello Bianco, John Brucato and Frank Brucato, Ron Casteel, Yolan Chan, Mrs. Lily Cuneo, Caroline Drewes, Bernie Esser, Jerry Flamm, Mr. and Mrs.

Gus Gelardi, Dave Hansell, Gordy Jacobson, Quentin Kopp, Toinie Koski LaRocca, Walter Lister, Larry Lorenzoni, Hank Luisetti, Ralph Maher, Larry Mana, John Manaidas, Dr. Joseph Maniscalco, Justice John Molinari, Judge Charlie Peery, Faye Perlas, Lou Poletti, Father David Purdy, Joe Riccio, Rollie Rollovich, Guido Rossini, John Russo, Dr. Joseph and Iris Sabella, Dante and Tony Santora, Maria Geraldi Seefeldt, Rick Smith, Lou Spadia, Frank Strazzulo, Billy Walter, and Phyllis Wuerth. In Martinez, I thank Catherine Collins and Charlene Perry at the Historical Society, and Earl Dunivan. I will ever be grateful to Joe's oldest pals in San Francisco: Carlo "Hungry" Geraldi, Frank "Ciccio" LaRocca, Dario "Dempsey" Lodigiani, Vince "Niggy" Marino, Salvatore "Shabby" Minafo, and Frank Venezia. They were great friends to Joe, and to me. On that subject, another special thanks to Ben Langella, who generously shared his memories and became my friend as well. And I cannot leave San Francisco without saying thanks to two of my oldest friends—to Neil Fitelson, to Jon Rubin (and his wife, Diane Kefauver)—who helped me and hosted me and listened so patiently through five years of talk about Joe.

On the wider world of Joe D., I was fortunate to have the help and friendship of two men, Barry Halper and Jerry Romolt, whose knowledge of Joe was both long-standing and acute. I am also grateful for the help of Joe's friends Woody Allen, Dick and Kathy Burke, Jean Doumanian, Mario Faustini, Gianni Garavelli, Bernie Kamber, Henry Kissinger, Lola Mason, Dr. Rock Positano, Nat Recine, and Frank Scott. I send thanks to the eminent chairman of William Morris Agency, Norman Brokaw, whose friendship with Joe went back fifty years (since the days when Brokaw was trying to find work for a fetching young actress named Marilyn Monroe). I was also aided by information from Harry Bryant, Marsha Davidson, Joyce Hadley, Lillian Hershey, Steve Hissler, George Milman, John Palumbo, Ralph Peck, Bill Rodman, Ruth Roman, Nat Rosasco, and Dan Shedrick. On Joe's New York, I extend thanks to Frank Giuffreda, Sonny Grosso, Xavier Recigno, Pat Terzano, Judge Edwin Torres, Claire Trimble, and Myles Wilson. I owe special gratitude to Bob Solotaire for the beauty of his recollections and his photographs. On Toots Shor's in particular, I am grateful to Jerry Berns at 21, to Alice Effrat, Bill Fugazi, Frank Gifford, Christy Jacobson, Harry Lavin, Irving Rudd, Terry Smith, and Bert Sugar. I also derived valuable information from two books: *Toots,* by Bob Considine, and *The Wonderful World of Toots Shor,* by John Bainbridge. On the topic of Joe's doings in Newark, I owe thanks to Leonard Ceres and Fanny DiDonna, to Michael Immerso (and his book, *Newark's Little Italy: The Vanished First Ward),* to Geta and Bina Spatola (and their wonderful scrapbook), to Mark A. Stuart (and his book *Gangster #2: Longy Zwillman, the Man Who Invented Organized Crime).* On Joe's life in Florida, I thank Thelma

Beck, Joe Camilleri, Bob Cantrell, Sid Luckman, Joe Nacchio, Richard Rosenberg, Murray Sharan, Dave Sweeney, Al Tordella, Pauline Winick, and Dr. Lloyd Wruble. Within Joe's nationwide network, I gratefully acknowledge Milt Beaver, Bob Boffa, Sr., Sam Brody, Harry Hall, Eddie Liberatore, David Monette, Nick Nicolosi, George Randazzo, and Manny Rossen.

On the subject of the Seals and the PCL, I thank Steve Barath, Joe Buzas, Art Dikas, Tony Gomez, Eddie Joost, Bill Lillard, Larry "Lefty" Powell, Bill Raimondi, Gussie Suhr. Also, I am indebted to the historians Richard Beverage, Dick Dobbins, Alan Lubke; to Richard Leutzinger and his book, *Lefty O'Doul: The Legend That Baseball Nearly Forgot;* to Bill Swank and his book, *Memories of Lane Field.* I also found valuable information in *Runs, Hits and an Era* by Paul J. Zingg and Mark Madeiros.

On the topic of the Yankees, I was aided by Marty Appel, Rick Cerrone, Nick Priori, Arthur Richman, and last but never least, George Steinbrenner. I was also fortunate to have the help of two distinguished batboys: Thad Mumford and Bert Padell (both of whom, in later life, made good in other rackets). I'm also grateful for the help of a Hall of Fame broadcast team, Curt Gowdy and Mel Allen (who spent his last Sunday on earth with me). I also benefited from the work of Milton Gross in *Yankee Doodles,* and Harvey Frommer, who wrote *The Yankee Encyclopedia.* In addition, I would like to thank for their kindness to me: Rugger Ardizoia, Hank Bauer, Yogi Berra, Frenchy and Vicki Bordagaray, Bobby Brown, Tommy Byrne, Jerry Coleman, Charlie Devens, Mr. and Mrs. Tom Ferrick, Whitey Ford, Randy Gumpert, Buddy Hassett, Ralph Houk, Reggie Jackson, Mrs. Martha Keller, Clarence Marshall, Gil McDougald, Duane Pillette, Phil Rizzuto, Marius Russo, Art Schallock, Frank "Spec" Shea, Charlie Silvera, Moose Skowron, Enos "Country" Slaughter, Ed Stewart, Jim Turner, Butch Wensloff, Bill Wight, Hank Workman, and especially Tom and Eileen Henrich.

From the wider world of baseball, I am grateful to Johnny Babich, Eddie Bockman, Ralph Branca, Dolph Camilli, Pete Coscarart, Brandy Davis, Joe Foss, Joe Garagiola, Joey Goldstein, Dave Kaplan, Bob Lemon, Larry Lucchino, Ken Nigro, Dino Restelli, Broadway Charlie Wagner, and Al Zarilla. I got my first lessons on big-league life while I cowered at the knee of the great Ted Williams: for those lessons and for his example, I now send thanks to him. I learned a great deal from Kevin Kerrane's loving anatomy of the scouting life, *Dollar Sign on the Muscle.* I was guided on questions of major league fact by two stupendous volumes: *The Baseball Encyclopedia* from Macmillan, and *Total Baseball.* I also went to school on Leo Durocher's *Nice Guys Finish Last;* on Robert E. Hood's *The Gashouse Gang;* on Ray Robinson's *The Iron Horse;* on Curt Smith's *Voices of the Game;* on G. Edward White's *Creating the National Pastime;* and on three fine books by Robert W. Creamer—*Babe: The Legend Comes to Life, Stengel: His Life and Times,* and *Baseball in '41.* I was informed and inspired by pieces and collections from Roger Angell; by several compendia: *The Fireside Book(s) of Baseball, The Armchair Book of Baseball;* and by oral histories: *The Glory of Their Times, We Played the Game.* In that genre, one book was a recurring source of delight: Jerome Holtzman's *No Cheering in the Press Box.* I would also salute *The Long Season* and *Pennant Race,* by Jim Brosnan, the first author who spoke to me in the voice of the game. Within the commissioner's office, I owe special thanks to Rich and Susan Levin, to Frank Slocum, and to the ex-commish Faye Vincent. I owe great thanks to the curators and librarians at the Hall of Fame in Cooperstown, New York. And while I'm in town, I also send thanks to Joan and Ed Badgely and their distinguished son-in-law, Craig Timberg.

I was helped, propelled, bawled out, and encouraged by dozens of journalists on sports and lesser topics. In San Francisco, I salute the late Herb Caen, who popularized Joe's local nickname, "Fishhooks" (because he must have hooks in his pocket—that's why he'd never put his hand in there). I was lucky to be taken around town by Harry Jupiter of the *Examiner,* and I am grateful for the help of his colleagues on that paper, Bucky Walters, Dwight Chapin, Paul Wilner, and Judy Canter. I am also thankful for the help of Art and Jack Rosenbaum, Bob Stevens, and Ron Fimrite. In New York, I was aided by a group of eminent practitioners: Marty Glickman, Bill Mazer, Allan Barra, Art Rust, Dick Schaap at ABC Sports, Bob Faw at NBC News, and Charlie Rose from PBS, who graciously spoke up for me with sources who could be of help. The columnist Jack Newfield generously helped me on the topic of Jimmy Cannon. Jimmy Breslin was of help on every topic that came to mind. From the *Times,* I thank Blaine Harden, Ira Berkow, and Buster Olney. At the *Daily News,* I was fortunate to have help from Bill Gallo, from Michael Daly, Vic Ziegel, Joanna Molloy, and from my partners in crime, Bill Madden and Luke Cyphers. At the *Norfolk Virginian-Pilot,* Mack Daniels and Glenn Scott were generous with me, as was the kind and able head of that paper's library, Ann Johnson. I owe thanks to Ellen Warren at the *Chicago Tribune,* to Tom Fiedler and Edwin Pope at the *Miami Herald,* to Gordon Edes, who was (at the time) with the *Sun-Sentinel* of Fort Lauderdale. And in Washington, I was kindly helped by Ben Bradlee, Carl Cannon, Richard Cohen, and Bob Woodward. In addition, I was aided by information from several distinguished senior sportswriters: John M. Ross in Connecticut, Bill Heinz in Vermont, Leonard Koppett in California, and Shirley Povich in Washington. I was grateful also for encouragement from the dean of my local sporting press, John Steadman. And atop my list of *prominenti,* one man stands alone: Harold Rosenthal, the graceful writer for the *Herald Tribune,* was so kind to me, so helpful, and so full of fun, that my great regret at the close of this book is not having him at the party.

Apart from libraries at the Hall of Fame, and the *Norfolk Virginian-Pilot,* I also extend thanks to the New York Public Library; to Faye Thompson at the American Academy of Motion Picture Arts and Sciences; to Margaret Goosetray and Howard B. Gotlieb at the Department of Special Collections of the Boston University Libraries. Also, to the libraries at the *Baltimore Sun,* the *Philadelphia Inquirer,* and the *Los Angeles Times.* Lisa Davis was kind enough to share with me the fruits of her own research on the life of Joe DiMaggio. In addition, I received great research help from Heesoo Coue, from Anya Richards, and my comrade in arms Noah Gordon. The story herein was vastly enriched by the work of Laura McKellar, who was associate producer on the PBS documentary that was based on this book, and who towed into port rafts of information that I greedily plundered. I am also grateful for transcription help from Elizabeth Janega, and for the fine work of Shelly Coleman, who helped me make sense of the material I brought home.

I knew this book had run too long when the ladies of my small town started showing up with dishes of food (as they would for any illness in the house)—but they are emblematic of the friends and supporters who aided this project in every way. So, for advice and information, for kindness, encouragement, for free drinks, dinners, or guest beds, I thank Virginia and Peter Allen, Louise Avidon, Rachel and Stu Axelrod, Ben and Minnie Balter, Tony Barbieri, Joe Bargmann, Mike Blackman, Nicki Britton, President and Mrs. William Brody of the Johns Hopkins University, Dan and Marge Brook, Martha Bunn, George W. Bush, Jeb Bush, Chris Calhoun, Nancy Cardozo, Lee and John Carroll, Bob Coleman, Dennis Coleman, Judy Cramer, Lina Cramer, Marguerite Del Giudice, Paul Downey, Walter Dubler, Nate and Richard Durning, Bill Eddins, Don Eliason, Edgar and Faith Feingold, Earl and Eli Fendelman, Gene Foreman, David Carr Frank, Steve Friedman, Gary Hart, Lee Hendrickson, Tom Hendrickson, David Hirshey, Gerri Hirshey, Courtney Hodell, Jody Hotchkiss, Margo Howard, John Irvin, Mark Jacobson, Rob Janega, Professor Christopher Janney, Mary Janney, Beverly and Jonathan Jones, Susan Kamil, Connie Kaplan, Dave Kaplan, Dave Keating, Dan Kelson, Kristin Kimball, Ed Kosner, Tom Kunkel, Buddy and Elfrieda Lackritz, Terrell Lamb, Simon and June Li, Ron Liebman, Tom Lockner, Woody and Shirley Loller, Sterling Lord, David and Linda Maraniss, Michael Maren, Peter Matson, Bill McAuliffe, Jim McBride, Terry McDonnell, Jean McGarry, Joe McGovern, Emily McKellar, Jim Naughton, Dr. Helen and Ken Noble, Mark Obenhaus, Peter Osnos, Michael Pakenham, Emma Pearce, Bill Powers, Carol and Rachel Powers, and the late Chuck Powers, whom I miss every day; also, the very much alive Joan Reibman, Scott Richardson, Walt Riker, Gene Roberts, Alice Rosenthal, Gus Russo, Buzz and Mary Saner, Stu Seidel, Steve Seplow, Charlotte Sheedy, Leslie Sherrill, Martha Sherrill, Bill Shore, Debby Shore, Anna Deveare Smith, Nell Spence, Susan Squire, Deborah Stewart, Doran Twer, Jennifer Webb, Andrea Weinstein, Nadine and William I. White, Jr., William I. White III, Amanda Wilkins, James Williams, and Zoë Wolff. Special thanks to both Sarah Leen and Bill Marr: Sarah made the author's photograph; she and Bill lent their jewelers' eyes to selection and layout of other photos; and both were friends in our house in time of need. And on the subject of All-Star friends, I will ever be grateful to John C. Ryan, who kept this book and my family afloat when there was no money to go on—not because it would avail him in any way, nor even with a plausible prospect that his generosity could be repaid—but simply for the love in his heart.

WGBH in Boston helped to fuel this effort by commissioning a documentary based on research for this book. I am thankful for the support of Margaret Drain and Mark Samels at *The American Experience,* along with Nancy Farrell, Helen Russell, Christine Larson, and especially Susan Mottau. Special thanks also to Peter McGhee, head of national programming, and a great supporter of this DiMaggio story. I am, as always, grateful to Tommy Lennon, who taught me anything I know about TV.

Newsweek did me aid and honor by excerpting this book in the magazine and by commissioning a cover story obit at the time of Joe's death. I am especially grateful to Mark Whitaker, the editor-in-chief, who has shown such faith in this story, to my gentle editor, Cathleen McGuigan, and to the late Maynard Parker, who first made the match between the magazine and this book.

This book was first commissioned at Random House, and I thank the proprietor, Si Newhouse, and his editor-in-chief, Harry Evans, for reposing trust in me. Within that house, I also owe thanks for aid, encouragement, and support to Jason Epstein, Julia Hine, Jon Karp, and Adam Rothberg. I am also grateful for the support of Wanda Chappell, who is much mourned in that company and elsewhere.

At Simon & Schuster, where I happily landed, I am grateful for aid and support from Melissa Milsten, Michael Korda, Alice E. Mayhew, and the chief, Carolyn Reidy. I have benefited also from the exemplary work of the art director Jackie Seow, managing editor Irene Yohay, production editor Steve Messina, chief counsel Elisa Rivlin, director of marketing Michael Selleck, and publicity director Victoria Meyer. Alexandra Truitt saved the day with her brilliant photo research. I was saved from a thousand sins by the copy editing of Fred Chase. And most of all, I was saved from my own clumsiness by the deft work of my editor, Ruth Fecych.

No author, no book, could have a better shepherd

than Flip Brophy, my agent, advisor, and friend. She has helped, as always, every day and in all ways. As they used to say at Toots Shor's—but only about the best of the best—she is a champion with class.

In that august category, I also name Mark Zwonitzer, who produced the documentary for WGBH, and more or less in his spare time made this book twice as good as it was. Having Mark on a project is almost unfair. It's like trading in your car for a bulldozer—all of sudden nothing much stands in your way.

Through all the years of this book I have had the help and inspiration of Ruby Cramer, who is a good listener to her Dad's stories and who was kind enough, by her tenth year, to sit through a whole chapter at a time—and to laugh in all the right places. I thank her.

Finally, and most of all, I thank and give thanks for Carolyn White, who has caught every word I've pitched for fifteen years. As they say about the best in the backstop business, she calls a great game. She is a woman of many gifts—not least, patience—who bore with me through all the years of Joe, and who did the most to shape this book. As always, every word was written for her.

Richard Ben Cramer
July 28, 2000

INDEX

✦

Page numbers in *italics* refer to illustrations.

PICTURE CREDITS

✦

Page 124 (top): *Time*/TimePix

Page 124 (middle): California Historical Society, Dick Dobbins Collection, FN-32203

Pages 163 (top), 386 (bottom), 812: National Baseball Hall of Fame Library, Cooperstown, New York

Page 200 (top): Wallace Kirkland, *Life*/TimePix

Pages 200 (bottom), 613 (top): *New York Daily News*

Page 327 (bottom): National Archives

Page 387: Robert Solotaire

Page 409 (top): Courtesy of George Kauffer

Page 409 (bottom left): Archive Photos

Page 475: George Torrie, *New York Daily News*

Pages 548, 613 (bottom): Photofest

Page 774 (middle and bottom): © Christie's Images, Ltd.

Page 775: © 1989 David M. Spindel

Page 813: Sonia Moskowitz

Page 847 (bottom): Courtesy of B & J Collectibles

Page 886: Dan Farrell, *New York Daily News*

ABOUT THE AUTHOR

✦

Richard Ben Cramer won the Pulitzer Prize in 1979, for his work at the *Philadelphia Inquirer.* His magazine articles have appeared in *Rolling Stone, Esquire,* the *New York Times Magazine, Time,* and *Newsweek,* and have been anthologized in *The Best American Essays* and *The Best American Sports Writing of the Century.* He is also the author of *What It Takes: The Way to the White House,* and *Ted Williams: The Seasons of the Kid.* He lives with his wife and daughter on Maryland's Eastern Shore.